The Lady of the Hare

This work is the first document, relating to the practice of Jungian psychology, which records in detail the analyst's own past in the practice of analysis as well as the patients. John Layard sought to bring to psychology the illuminating study of all the humanities. This is an extraordinary and fundamental book.

JOHN LAYARD was a pioneering anthropologist and author of *Stone Men of Malekula*.

www.keganpaul.com

THE KEGAN PAUL LIBRARY OF ARCANA

AN ETHIOPIAN BOOK OF THE DEAD
E. A. Wallis Budge

THE BOOK OF MEDICINES
E. A. Wallis Budge

AMULETS AND MAGIC
E. A. Wallis Budge

THE QUEEN OF SHEBA AND HER SON MENYELEK
E. A. Wallis Budge

THE DIVINE ORIGIN OF THE CRAFT OF THE HERBALIST
E. A. Wallis Budge

THE ROMANCE OF SORCERY
Sax Rohmer

POSSESSION
T. K. Oesterreich

THE LADY OF THE HARE
John Layard

POISON DAMSELS
N. M. Penzer

OSIRIS
E. A. Wallis Budge

ELIXIRS OF LIFE
Mrs. C. F. Leyel

ETRUSCAN ROMAN REMAINS
Charles Godfrey Leland

EGYPTIAN MAGIC
E. A. Wallis Budge

THE
LADY OF THE HARE

being
a study in the healing power
of dreams

by

JOHN LAYARD

KEGAN PAUL
London • New York • Bahrain

First published in 2002 by
Kegan Paul Limited
UK: P.O. Box 256, London WC1B 3SW, England
Tel: 020 7580 5511 Fax: 020 7436 0899
E-Mail: books@keganpaul.com
Internet: http://www.keganpaul.com
USA: 61 West 62nd Street, New York, NY 10023
Tel: (212) 459 0600 Fax: (212) 459 36780
Internet: http://www.columbia.edu/cu/cup
BAHRAIN: bahrain@keganpaul.com

Distributed by:
Turpin Distribution
Blackhorse Road
Letchworth, Herts. SG6 1HN
England
Tel: (01462) 672555 Fax: 01462) 480947
Email: books@turpinltd.com

Columbia University Press
61 West 62nd Street, New York, NY 10023
Tel: (212) 459 0600 Fax: (212) 459 36780
Internet: http://www.columbia.edu/cu/cup

Printed in the USA, IBT Global

ISBN: 0-7103-0716-0

British Library Cataloguing in Publication Data
Layard, J. (John)
The Lady of the hare : being a study of the healing power
Of dreams.- (The Kegan Paul library of arcane)1.Psychoanalysis 2. Dreams
I.Title
154.6′3

ISBN 0710307160

Library of Congress Cataloging-in-Publication Data
Applied for.

CONTENTS

Detailed Summary
including brief description of Dreams

PART ONE

THE DREAM ANALYSIS

CONTENTS

CONTENTS

CONTENTS

CONTENTS

CONTENTS

THE HARE IN CLASSICAL ANTIQUITY

CONCLUSION

CONTENTS

PART THREE

MORE DREAMS ABOUT HARES AND RABBITS

ILLUSTRATIONS

PART I

PART II

ACKNOWLEDGEMENTS

The author's gratitude is due in the first place to the Lady of the Hare, appearing in this work under the pseudonym of 'Mrs. Wright', who has kindly allowed it to be published and from whom the author learnt quite as much as she learnt from him; and in the second place to the members of the Psychological Study Group in Oxford to whom Part I, dealing with the Dream Analysis, was first communicated, and who by their encouragement, criticism, and support have materially assisted him. In accordance with his view that Psychology should not restrict itself to the narrow field of curative medicine, but should illuminate and be illuminated by all the Humanities, this study group has as its foundation members a Professor of Logic, a Professor of the Philosophy of the Christian Religion, a College Tutor, a College Chaplain, a Priest, an Anthropologist, a Psychologist, and a Psychiatrist, whose initials with their consent appear here as a mark of his grateful esteem.

H.H.P.	H.P.K.	G.A.
L.W.G.	V.W.	R.G.M.
N.H.K.A.C.	M.F.	

The author is further indebted to the following friends who kindly read and criticized all or parts of the manuscript during its preparation for the press: Canon L. W. Grensted, Nevill Coghill, Esq., Dr. H. G. Baynes, Dr. Gerhard Adler, the Rev. Father Victor White, O.P., Dr. William Cohn, Dr. H. Meinhard, and Mrs. E. Martin-Clarke.

He also wishes to tender thanks to the firm that has undertaken to break new ground by the publication of this narrative, and in particular to the two partners most directly concerned: T. S. Eliot and Richard de la Mare.

JOHN LAYARD

1 *Northmoor Road,*
Oxford

INTRODUCTION

Many books have been written setting out the theory and practice of psychology, but few give full accounts of case histories. This is partly because the subject-matter is often too intimate to publish, and in any case is apt to be very lengthy, and partly also because of the difficulty experienced by the analyst in giving what is equally essential to a critical understanding of the analytical process, namely, an accurate account of his own role in the human drama.

So far as I know this is the first document relating to the practice of Analytical Psychology (which is the branch of psychological practice founded by Jung) in which any serious attempt has been made to record in any detail the analyst's own part in the process as well as the patient's.

In mentioning Jung in this context I do not mean to throw any of the blame for whatever mistakes may be detected in the handling of this case on to his method. Indeed, no method is more than a guide or framework within which each individual practitioner deals with a problem to the best of his personal ability, adding a little bit here and taking away there. Rather do I deliberately risk censure for the sake of giving the public some insight into a minute corner of that vast field of psychic experience concerned with the integration of personality through the activation of the redemptive process imminent but so often unrecognized within us all, both inside and outside religious communities, which it is the task of psychology as well as of religion to further.

Psychology is at once a new science and a very old one. It is old in that it seeks to unite the two opposing forces in human nature by means of a third factor, which is that of acceptance by the conscious mind of those primitive contents that form part of our psychic heritage, which, if not admitted, operate as negative autonomous complexes, but, when accepted, prove to be the keystone supporting the bridge. It is new in so far as it provides a new technique by means of which this unity may be approached and that which has hitherto been most feared or despised may be thereby transformed into spiritual strength.

This process is by no means antagonistic to religion, and is based on the rediscovery of what I believe to be the universal redemptive process underlying all religions, embracing body as well as spirit in its healing power. We all have in us the constituent elements of salvation. The trouble is that many of us don't know it. The aim of Analytical Psychology is to make conscious this salvation process, latent within us all but inoperative till we become receptive enough to perceive it and give it that honour which alone will release it from its prison in the deep caverns of the soul.

One of the channels through which this process expresses itself is that of dreams. All primitive peoples recognize this, and accordingly pay great attention to them, and it is thought by some that all mythology and all knowledge of the other side of life came to mankind through this channel, later canalized into dogma which is its static representation, true but lacking in redemptive efficacy so long as it is divorced from its organic source.

Though God spoke to the prophets in dreams and visions the Church is now apt to frown on them, considering them either to be vain fancies, a view that has now percolated to the common man, or else, if they are clearly important, to be, except in rare instances, of the Devil. The truth is that they may be taken as being of God in the sense that they still, as of old, contain messages that, if we know how to read them, point the way to spiritual growth, but equally as being of the Devil if we fail to see below their manifest content which so often darkens and distorts the spiritual meaning that lies beneath. For among the many levels on which any given dream may be interpreted there are always two diametrically opposite methods of approach. One of these sees in every image a purely personal content and thus often produces very negative results. The other is concerned with the impersonal forces behind the personal content, and seeks to activate the latent power which they possess to heal the ills which the former method does little more than disclose. A case in point is that of a dreamer who dreamt that he was raging at his mother, saying, 'You never listen to what I say!' This was, he said, quite literally true. Taken in this concrete sense the dream only intensified the opposition and provided no solution at all. Taken more deeply, however, the mother, who in her personal aspect appeared such a negative figure, nevertheless represented in the inner recesses of his psyche the pregnant qualities in his own nature which he, owing to his inability to understand, was thus opposing and helping to destroy. The positive message of the dream was that, in wasting his substance complaining that his actual mother would not listen to him, he was thereby violating his own soul in the form of the Eternal Mother lying hidden under the imperfections of his own mother-image, and would do better to ask her what she wanted of him. If he would only listen to her instead of trying to force her to listen to him, his own pregnant nature would respond and come to his help, and he would be one step on the way to becoming redeemed, and incidentally towards improving his relations with the actual mother.[1]

It is on this point as to which of these two methods of approach it is most expedient to stress, namely, that in which personal issues predominate or that in which the impersonal forces within are activated to perform their healing function in their own way, that Jung differs from other psychological teachers. Freud and his psychoanalytical followers, who think that religion with its insistence on supra-personal forces is an escape, tend to see the personal aspect only. The Analytical Psychologist, on the other hand, tries to see both, and of the two lays the main emphasis on the creative interpretation that treats personal issues as being only surface phenomena, knowing that the deeper forces have only to be made relatively conscious for them to purge the dross of personal conflicts with their healing power.

For this reason the barrier to publication of case histories by psychologists who place the main emphasis of their analysis

[1] The eternal mother here referred to is an aspect of the *anima* to which reference is made on p. 87.

on personal issues, and rightly hesitate to make public all the intimate details which it reveals, is by no means insuperable in the case of a Jungian analysis which does not concentrate on such details to any comparable extent but tends to resolve them in the crucible of more fundamental factors that express themselves less in terms of logical formulations than through symbols, which, as will be seen in the following account, have a dynamic power of their own.

Analysis conducted on these lines tends the deeper it goes to recognize symbols of an ever less personal nature, reaching down layer by layer through the stages of cultural evolution to early Christian times and beyond to the primitive beliefs out of which Christianity developed, and then returning upward again to make a synthesis of the varied experiences it has evoked. Some persons draw the bulk of their unconscious symbolism from one source, some from others out of the inexhaustible well, and, contrary to the general supposition, the deeper the analysis the quicker the cure. The case history here given has been selected for an initial publication on account of its direct use of Christian symbolism of a type known to all, though the forcefulness of it may surprise some who have regarded such symbols as mere fanciful imagery and not, as they are, the actual mirror of nature in the pregnant unconscious.

I deliberately refrain in this introduction from giving any psychological theory, because I wish to present the case as nearly as possible from the point of view of the patient happily ignorant of all such theories. Being a hard-working country woman helping her husband to earn his living from the soil, she was not overburdened with the secondhand substitutes for life doled out by modern city conditions, and lived in a small cottage devoid of any modern convenience in as direct contact with nature as is possible in these islands to-day. For this reason, the simplest approach had to be made, and was richly rewarded. Nor were any technical terms used throughout the analysis, though certain concepts were of course at the back of the analyst's mind, a brief note about some of these being inserted in the Theoretical Discussion beginning on p. 86.

This already disposes of the idea that education with a capital E is a necessary prerequisite to being analysed. Education in its commonly used sense of book-education may help, but is more usually a hindrance, and is of use only if it has been so conducted as not to be opposed to, but as fulfilling the natural law.

One brief word is needed to explain the relation between analyst and patient. This explanation is necessary only on account of the confusion introduced by psychologists themselves with regard to the phenomenon called transference. Transference is the shifting of emotions primarily directed towards the parents on to the analyst. Such emotions are always ambivalent. The parents are the life-givers and also the prime agents by whom instinct is inhibited in order to transform it into social behaviour. In the latter role they frequently figure as oppressors, and it is this, together with the possessive aspect of the parental relationship, that is the main object of inquiry among psychoanalysts of the school founded by Freud. Emphasis on personal reactions of this kind leads inevitably to the projection of love or hate on to the analyst, and, to protect themselves against this, Freudian analysts have evolved a complicated technique by means of which they believe themselves to be acting with complete impersonality. The frequent result is, however, an intense personal dependence of the patient upon the analyst, a dependence never satisfied on account of the artificiality of the technical barriers that are erected and which then have to be resolved by a yet more complicated technique which sometimes works but sometimes does not, and which in any case is apt to take a very long time.

The Analytical Psychologist of the Jungian school does not have to defend himself in anything like the same measure, because he does not seek to represent the personal parents but on the contrary concentrates as much as possible on the impersonal factors that lie beneath personal relationships. He has in mind the redemptive process which, once activated in the patient, tends to resolve personal complexes as farmyard manure is resolved and rendered innocuous in running water.

For this reason the personal loves and hates, because unhesitatingly accepted, become absorbed into the healing process. Therefore he does not need the paraphernalia of defence put up by the Freudian, but faces his patient as one human being faces another in ordinary human converse. The result is a deep mutual respect flowing between the two in their joint endeavour.

The process is quicker and surer than any purely reductive analysis conducted on personal lines, and is more fundamental. In other words, to put it briefly, 'Freud employs a reductive method, Jung a *prospective* one. Freud treats the material analytically, resolving the present into the past, Jung *synthetically*, building up out of the actual situation towards the future.'[1]

The analysis described in this book was unusually quick because the patient had never lost contact with the power of faith, either in persons or in essential religious truths. It took place in twelve interviews at intervals of a week or occasionally a fortnight. It did not pretend to have solved all the patient's problems, but it did revolutionize the dreamer's attitude to life, and laid the foundation for further progress which will be described in a later volume. Even before these later developments, however, the patient herself was so impressed with the new light it shed on so many aspects of the redemptive process, which she recognized as being applicable not only to herself but to mankind in general, that she readily gave permission for it to be published under the sole necessary disguise of altering all names.

NOTE ON THE MYTHOLOGY OF THE HARE

The above remarks refer exclusively to the first part of this book dealing with the actual analytical situation. This left, however, one large question-mark with regard to the interpretation of what was perhaps her most crucial dream in which she sacrificed a hare, from which the book takes its name. This dream (No. 9 in the series), which led to an intense experience

[1] *The Psychology of C. G. Jung*, by Jolan Jacobi (London, 1942), pp. 66, 67.

that largely altered the dreamer's life, was during the analysis interpreted along lines applicable to any form of animal sacrifice as symbolizing the transformation of instinct into spiritual power, but the reason why the hare should have been selected by the dreamer's unconscious in preference to any other animal remained obscure till chance brought to my notice the widespread mythological beliefs regarding the hare in many parts of the world, both ancient and modern. These proved so remarkably consistent throughout the world, and in addition corresponded to and illuminated so many details of this dream and of those immediately following it, that it became evident that the hare was to be numbered among what Jung calls the 'Archetypes', by which is meant symbolic images pregnant with power that have had great influence in the past and which live on in the deeper levels of the unconscious of Modern Man, unknown to and therefore inoperative in most, but ready to spring forth into effective action once the internal redemptive process is activated and begins to work. To complete this analytical account I have therefore included a Second Part dealing with *The Mythology of the Hare* which will be found to explain more fully than appeared in the analysis itself why this dream had such a notable effect.

NOTE ON THE ILLUSTRATIONS TO PART I

One criticism that may be levelled against this book is that, with the exception of the patient's own drawing of the angel on p. 33, the illustrations to Part I dealing with the actual dream material are only approximate reproductions of her own sketchy indications. This is due to the fact that such indications as she did make were all made on odd scraps of paper and so faintly and tentatively drawn that, even if they could have been reproduced, which is doubtful, they would have necessitated a great deal of explanation and consequent unnecessary waste of wartime paper. As they were all, however, in the nature of diagrams and not pictures, I therefore submitted them, together with the necessary explanations, to my friend Mr. Rupert Shephard, who has kindly traced some and redrawn others in pen and ink, introducing just enough perspective to indicate the relative positions of the various characters appearing in the dreams. They have all been submitted to the patient, and several were subsequently altered in accordance with her suggestions. She now passes them all as being good approximations to the visual impressions she wished to convey.

PERSONS APPEARING IN THE DREAMS

(all names are fictitious)

MRS. WRIGHT

MR. WRIGHT, her husband, a skilled cowman

MARGARET, their daughter

BERTHA, Mrs. Wright's unmarried sister

KATE, Mr. Wright's sister, a nurse

EILEEN, one of Mr. Wright's other sisters

THE VICAR

THE REV. MAC X, Presbyterian Minister

MISS HARDACRE

ABRAHAMS, the butcher

MRS. SMART, a neighbour

MRS. R., a neighbour

Part One
THE DREAM ANALYSIS

INTRODUCTORY

During the summer of 1940 the Vicar of a small village with whom I was acquainted told me of an extremely backward girl of 16,[1] and asked whether anything could be done to help her. She was the only daughter of a superior labourer named Wright who had migrated from Northern Ireland to England in order to take up a situation as cowman for a neighbouring farmer. They were, he said, god-fearing people and he would point them out to me in church. At first sight, apart from a habit of holding her head down as if slightly shrunk into her shoulders, the girl appeared outwardly normal, on the plump side and with ruddy cheeks. If there was anything specially noticeable about her it was perhaps a rather extreme quietness and circumspection, though this was in itself not necessarily out of keeping with the till recently feudal character of the village. The Vicar said, however, that it was indeed but the outward and visible symptom of a nature so retiring that she would speak to no-one but her mother and consequently had no real friends in the village, spending her time doing nothing but odd jobs in and about her parents' cottage and everlastingly reading any books she could lay hands on.

I said I had no idea whether I could do anything for her, but would, if the Vicar liked, see her mother.

After some time Mrs. Wright came to see me,[2] and we had a short talk during which I formed a very good opinion of the simplicity and sincerity of the mother but could gather little

[1] When subsequently exempted from wartime National Service she was classed as a High Grade Mental Defective.

[2] Mrs. Wright was 54 at the time of this interview.

information about her daughter Margaret apart from the fact that, when about three years old, she had suffered from convulsions, the origin of which was obscure, that she had left school before her time as she was considered too stupid to learn, and that the only folk she had any interest in outside the immediate family circle were old people, for whom she liked doing small services. Otherwise the only additions I could get to the Vicar's account were that she was a 'good girl' though utterly lacking in initiative, combined with his yet further emphasis on her voracious reading. I told Mrs. Wright, as I had told the Vicar, that I had no idea whether anything could be done, but that if the girl liked, and only if she did so, I would see her. Mrs. Wright said that, owing to some obscure physical ailment she had recently taken her daughter as an outpatient to a hospital in the neighbouring big town, but that the doctor had been so rude to her because she would not speak that it had upset her very much and she had retired to bed with a high temperature. I said that, as making contact would in any case be a delicate matter and depended very much on the girl acting from her own free will, I would not arrange to see her till she had recovered from this shock and from the resistance it must have caused to anything she could conceivably regard as 'treatment', and that it would be better to wait till she was up and about again before any suggestion was made that she should see me.

Next day I happened to see both parents at a village gathering, but as they said nothing about the girl, I did not either. I then had to go away on business for a week, and when I came back the Vicar told me that the parents had on the morning before the village meeting taken her to another hospital where she had been detained 'for observation' and kept in bed while her temperature continued to rise and fall. There she stayed for some time not greatly affected one way or another, apart from not liking the strange food—so different from what her mother cooked—while the doctors failed to make any diagnosis whatever.

INTERVIEW WITH THE DAUGHTER, 31ST JULY 1940

Meanwhile I had myself moved into the neighbouring city, whither Mrs. Wright one day brought her daughter, who had now left the hospital, to see me. I had provided tea and coffee and chocolate biscuits so as to produce as homely an atmosphere as possible and, with these as my assistants, asked the mother to leave the daughter alone with me. For an hour I tried every device to amuse or interest the daughter, but failed to produce anything more than a monosyllabic 'Yes' or 'No', except on a single occasion when, asked what kinds of book she liked reading, she managed to whisper the words 'Edgar Wallace'. When I inquired what any of the stories were about, dumbness once more enveloped her. She would look back with expressionless eyes, obviously harbouring terror behind an appearance of calm serenity which was the defence she had built up against any approach. Even attempts to make her more comfortable were fruitless. As an example of this, when I suggested that it might be more convenient for her if she put the half-filled cup she had been balancing for the past ten minutes on her immaculately clean dress down on to the small table by her side, she indeed put it down, though not to please herself but rather as a gesture of obedience to an imagined authority. Naturally, all this time, all her muscles were tense, but a whole hour failed to relax them. Worst of all, she was not even, on the face of it, confused, so that there was no possibility of putting her at her ease. Nor yet did she once smile, but throughout the whole interview sat like a statue, and even a wide range of pictures of various kinds failed to arouse so much as a twitter of response, either of approval or the reverse. At the end of an hour it was I who was beaten. Nothing seemed to have touched her, and in despair I went out to confess my utter failure to her mother.

FIRST INTERVIEW WITH THE MOTHER

31*st July* 1940 (*continued*)

As it was a beautiful summer's day, warm and radiant, I had asked the mother to wait outside in the garden. I told her what had happened, saying that I had failed to get anything out of her daughter, and she said, 'No, Margaret hardly ever speaks to anyone but me'. I was, however, struck by Mrs. Wright's calmness and laçk of any of those dominating qualities that one would normally have presumed in the mother of such a girl. I told her I was sorry I had not been able to achieve anything, saying that if I had a children's clinic I might set her daughter down in it and try to observe her in that way, but that, not having one, I failed to see what I could do. I did mention, however, that her daughter was evidently in a state of constant terror, and that her automatic and senseless obedience to any suggestion must cover a resentment that might very well lie at the root of her trouble. Seeking to find out the cause of her terror, I then asked Mrs. Wright whether she knew of anything that had happened during her daughter's childhood that might have given rise to such a deep and all-pervading inhibition.

This did not at first lead to any response, nor yet did my inquiries as to whether her daughter had ever had any sexual difficulties. Mrs. Wright said her daughter's periods were quite regular, and that, except for a little constipation she knew of no physical trouble of that kind.

This did, however, finally stir memories, for, after a long pause, she said, 'I have never told you about my sister.' The mother then told me that she was herself formerly a nurse specializing in midwifery, necessitating frequent absences from home, for which reason her elder sister Bertha had had a large share in the baby's upbringing, and for a considerable period had had the child in her sole charge. Mrs. Wright did not think that Bertha had been cruel to Margaret in any way, but said it was true that her sister was a very disappointed woman, never having married and having thrown over the only suitor she ever had owing to what Mrs. Wright described as 'false pride' over some peccadillo he had committed or was said to have committed. This had soured her sister for life, so much so that now, in her old age, none of her relatives would put up with her except Mrs. Wright herself, with whom she was now living, and had lived for many years. Mrs. Wright then described how very difficult she was, ending up by saying, 'Margaret cannot abide her. She never speaks when she is there, and always goes out of any room her aunt comes into.' I pointed out that this could not be very good for Margaret, and she then said, 'No, perhaps it's not', and went on to describe the loathing and contempt her sister Bertha had for her daughter, and how she never ceased criticizing her, saying her mother spoilt her and trying to make her do this and that, which made the family atmosphere far from pleasant. Asked how her husband liked it, Mrs. Wright said, 'He doesn't, but Bertha has no other home, and he agrees with me in saying we cannot possibly turn her out.' When I again pointed out that her sister's influence on Margaret might be very much worse than Mrs. Wright realized, she said, 'Perhaps that is so, but nothing will make me turn her out. I am the only sister who can put up with her, and if I turned her out her death would be on my hands and I could not bear it. Besides, she is my sister, and I couldn't do that, whatever happened.' I saw that, however bad the presence of the aunt might be for Margaret, there was a quality of loyalty and positive staunchness about Mrs. Wright that would be so damaged if she could ever have been persuaded to violate it—which was in itself very doubtful—that it would also injure her attitude towards her own daughter and so defeat its object. Moreover, anyone failing to perceive this would lose her confidence and forfeit the expression of a similar loyalty towards himself. So, in the interest of the very daughter to whose well-being the presence of the aunt was most harmful, it was quite clear that the aunt must stay. For this reason, after making quite clear to Mrs. Wright the probable effect on her daughter and after assuring myself that she was rather more fully aware than before of this aspect of the problem, I wholeheartedly acquiesced, contenting myself only with suggesting that, even allowing for her feelings of staunch loyalty towards her sister, there must be something that we did not at the moment quite understand about Mrs. Wright's own psychology that caused her to allow her good nature to be trespassed on so much to the detriment of her daughter.

Mrs. Wright, whose intelligence had become more and more apparent during this conversation, quite readily agreed, saying she could not herself make out why, having a husband she loved and having all her days striven to do her best, life should have proved so difficult for her. I said that, if we could find out why this was, we might be able to get at Margaret's problem through hers, and that, so far as I could see, this was the only way we could. She said, 'I'd do anything for Margaret. But what can I do?" I told her there was one way, and that was by somehow getting at the unconscious factors that seemed to nullify her own attempts at success. I said that dreams often showed us things about ourselves we did not consciously know, and asked whether she ever dreamt. She said, 'No, I never dream. Except, of course, when I was pregnant, as all women do.' I asked her whether she remembered any of the dreams she had had then, and she said, 'Yes, I once dreamt that my husband had died. It was a terrible dream. How can a woman have a dream like that about a man she loves?' I asked her whether she would like to have a talk about that some time. She said she would, and it was arranged that she should come next time without Margaret.

SECOND INTERVIEW

3rd August

There had been an unfortunate misunderstanding about the date of the interview, with the result that when Mrs. Wright arrived, I had only half an hour to spare. I was afraid that a first interview under such inauspicious circumstances might be abortive and spoil the whole analysis. As it turned out, however, that half-hour laid the foundation for very rapid progress.

Mrs. Wright lost no time beating about the bush, and opened the conversation directly by telling me that she had once had a vision of an angel. She had told it to her sisters at the time, but they laughed at it so much that she had never mentioned it to anyone again until now. This incident occurred while on a visit to America to look after her brother, during or after which she had first learned the elements of professional nursing. I understood her to say at the time that the incident occurred when she was 14 years old, though in a later interview[1] she said she must have been 19.

1. VISION (*The Warning Angel*)

'The vision occurred when I was wide awake one evening at dusk, when there appeared to me an angel. The angel looked lovely, the most beautiful thing I had ever seen, and stood with right arm raised above her head, with her forefinger pointing upwards. Her raiment was of dazzling white linen. Her face seemed to be made of light. Her eyes were dark. Behind her head there was a shining golden light.'

Mrs. Wright knew somehow that the vision was a portent of evil. She thought it meant that some loved one had died, and for some time expected to receive letters from home to that effect. No such letters, however, arrived, but shortly after-

[1] Fourth interview, on 14th August.

wards she herself was almost killed by being run over by a tram, though by God's grace she escaped unhurt.

I made no comment on this narrow escape, because the meaning of the warning was at that time by no means clear, though it became so later. When she had assured herself that I was taking her vision seriously and was not laughing at it as everyone else had done, she said:

2. VISION (*Warning Yellow Lights*)

'I quite often have Lights.' Asked what she meant, she said that a yellowish light sometimes appeared to her, also usually at dusk, and always at some spot where no material light could possibly be, and was always a warning of somebody's death. It was a dull yellow light, such as might be given out by an old stable lamp (though no lamp, of course, was visible) and quite different from the shining golden light she had seen behind the angel's head. The warnings indicated by these lights had often come true, and usually, if not always, referred to the death of one of her patients. The indication was so precise that the lights always appeared in the direction in which her patients lived.

I made no comment on this either, other than the silent comment of my extreme interest, remarking only to myself that yellow is the colour of intuition,[1] and dullness as opposed to brilliance indicates the quality of death.

She then told me the first of what she had previously described as her two 'pregnancy dreams'.

3. DREAM (*Death of husband while ploughing*)

She said: 'I dreamt that my husband was killed. He had gone out ploughing, and had been cut in half by the plough. I saw the horses careering about. When I woke up, I touched my husband in bed to make sure that he was alive.'

Quite naturally the Freudian explanation that this was a wish fulfilment dream leapt to my mind, but it was difficult to

[1] I later found that there are two intuition colours, yellow and blue, yellow being the extraverted and blue the introverted. (See footnotes on pp. 44 and 82.)

Fig. 1. VISION OF THE WARNING ANGEL

An exact reproduction of Mrs. Wright's own drawing, which she pleads as being quite inadequate to express the radiant beauty of the face looking down upon her, of the perfect symmetry of the right arm and hand, and of the golden light shining behind the angel's head.

reconcile this with the fact that I knew the husband to be a very decent and unusually balanced man, whom she truly loved. Instinctively this simple and cynical interpretation, though it might have some element of truth, revolted the sense of reverence I had already conceived towards the dreamer's problem. I also found it difficult to visualize just how a man *could* be cut in half by a plough, so I asked her if she could describe the dream to me in greater detail, pointing out that a man usually walked *behind* and not in front of his plough. How was it then that he seems to have been in front of it? And also at what part of his body had he been cut in half? In answer to the first question she said that that was just the puzzle. She had no idea why he had got in front. In answer to the second she said that he had not actually been cut in half, but that the coulter of the plough had pierced his abdomen, and that she had been horrified to see the red blood gushing out.

Though there was here an obvious reference to the wound in Christ's side from which flowed the redeeming blood, I made no further comment about this dream, as she was keen to go on to tell me the other.

4. DREAM (*Deep Water*)

She started straight off by saying, 'I was by deep water'. I could not refrain from remarking on the beauty of the English language and its foundation in dream imagery, and said: 'You really were in deep water, weren't you?' She smiled, and said, 'I had never thought of it in that way, but it's true.' Then she went on, 'In the dream it seemed that I was by the side of a lake. The lake was very deep and the water was muddy. Dreams of deep muddy water always mean trouble for me. On the far side of the lake was a beautiful green pasture. On my side there was a steep mountain. I wanted to get to the green pasture, but for some reason I cannot understand, I thought I had to climb the mountain to get there. I started climbing, but the surface of the mountain was made of loose stones and earth, and I kept on slipping down.'

There was no need for me to say anything further about the

meaning of muddy water. Had Mrs. Wright been a so-called 'educated' woman, it might have taken a whole hour to explain what this meant, but her simple Irish intuition knew all about it already. Nor was there any need to point out the biblical allusion to the green pastures as her rightful goal. The question I put to her was why, instead of swimming or taking a boat across the lake or going round it, to get to the green pasture, she had to take the 'stony path' up the mountain, which in fact would never have led there at all. She said, 'Life has always been difficult for me. I don't know why it should be, as I have always tried to do my best.' I said, 'Perhaps what you have thought the best was not. If you had managed to get up the mountain, you would have found yourself in a very much worse situation than the one in which you actually were. But God was kind to you, and put the stones and loose earth there so as to make you fall down. Now we know what the angel was warning you about. Her finger was pointing upwards.' She said, 'Yes, and the finger was the central point of the vision.' I pointed out that the angel was, in fact, warning her not to go up the hill. I then asked her what she actually thought the angel in her vision had been pointing towards. She said, 'It was pointing to heaven.' Mrs. Wright was a very religious woman, so this was a delicate point. I said, 'But the green pasture was heaven, and the dream says that going uphill is the wrong way.' She said, 'I was always taught that heaven was up above.' I said that perhaps God's angel was telling her that it was not. This part of the conversation ended on the query: Where then is heaven? Is it up the mountain to the right, or is it on the other side of the lake, where the green pasture is, to the left?

I asked her whether she saw any connection between this dream and the dream about her husband's death. She said, 'There seems to be something wrong about them both.' But she did not know what. I pointed out that in each case things were the wrong way round. Just as in the second dream she was going the wrong way to go to the green pasture, so in the first dream her husband was at the wrong end of the plough. If he had not been in front he would not have been killed, nor would the horses have shied. Her wrong assumption that she must climb the mountain in order to get to heaven was a repetition of the same motive of putting the husband in front of the plough. It was like 'putting the cart before the horse'.

This was as much as I thought necessary to say at this early stage. The words 'animus' or 'shadow'[1] did not cross my lips during the whole analysis, though the concepts of them were vital to it. The husband was not mentioned again, till at a later stage it became clear that the fatal wound in his side represented an incident in the crucifixion of her own well-meant but mistaken ideals.[2]

The whole interview had lasted just half an hour, but it had been enough.

[1] See page 87.

[2] Mrs. Wright's true willing sacrifice took place later in Dream 9, in which she sacrificed the Hare, thus reliving the experience of Dream 3 on a deeper level. This, when explained, proved to be the central point in her analysis (see p. 51).

THIRD INTERVIEW

8th August

Mrs. Wright opened the interview by telling me a dream.

5. Dream

'I was in an unknown place. It was the evening, and I was trying to get home. It was in a big unknown city, with lots of people around. I went to find out what time the bus left to go home. The bus driver said it left at 10.99.

'As I had some time to wait, I went to see my sister-in-law.[1] This woman is in real life a nurse, like myself, but she was always jealous of me because I got all the jobs and she didn't. The reason for this was that, while I did not mind doing small jobs about the house as well as nursing, she stood on her dignity and would not do anything beside what she was paid for, and insisted on being waited on and having meals in a room by herself.

'In the dream I knocked at her door, but all she would answer was "*m*", as if to say, "Oh drat, this woman coming to bother me again". However, she opened the door, but instead of letting me in, pulled up a chair and sat on it in the doorway.

'While she was sitting there, with me standing outside, I heard a man's voice inside mumbling something, but I could not hear what. I had the impression she was hiding him (and her relationship with him) from me.

'I saw her sister Eileen[2] there too.

'After that I lost them in the throng. I finally found myself in the bus, thankful I had not missed it and should get home all right.'

[1] Her husband's unmarried sister Kate, whose character is described later in the comment on this dream.

[2] Her husband's youngest sister, not discussed at the time, but who, as I learnt later, was inclined to be hysterical like Bertha. She also is unmarried.

The dreamer's intuition was such as to make it unnecessary for me to labour the point that catching the bus was a very positive sign, and that going 'home' meant finding her real self, as a child returning to the security of its parents or, in adult phraseology, to God. The evening also represented the time of casting off daytime attitudes, and of communing with God as he revealed himself in dreams.

She said that in the dream '10.99' seemed quite a natural time, which seemed peculiar only when she woke up. She had tried to translate it into actual time, but realizing that it came only to the meaningless hour of 11.39, had come to the conclusion that what it really meant was 'nearly 11', referring to the 'eleventh hour', implying that the situation, though urgent, was not yet too out of hand to mend.

The scene was neither in Ireland nor any other place that she knew, and therefore represented a purely psychological situation of which she was as yet unaware. It was, of course, clear to the analyst that the husband's sister was her *Shadow*, and the unknown man whom the *Shadow* was preventing her from seeing was her *animus*.[1] I did not, however, use any such technical terms to her, but pointed out quite simply that the door at which she was knocking was the door into her soul. I then went on to point out that, though in actual life she was herself the better nurse, who got the jobs precisely because she was human and humble enough not to stand on her dignity, nevertheless the sister-in-law in the dream represented an unconscious, rigidly obstructive element in herself, preventing full contact with her soul (and also probably with her husband), and that this part of herself was withholding some essential knowledge, represented by the 'lover' whose voice she could hear but could not understand.

Using her own religious experience as a basis on which to build, I compared the door through which her sister-in-law prevented her from going with the screen separating the nave of the church from the chancel, and suggested the 'lover' inside might well represent the priest who himself represented our Lord, the 'lover' of mankind. Alternatively his voice might

[1] See page 87.

represent the 'still small voice' of conscience. I reminded her that God 'moves in a mysterious way', and suggested that perhaps the reason why she could not understand what he said was because it might disagree with a ready-made conception of God, that might possibly not tally with the truth. She said she must try to find out what this nasty thing in her was. I told her that it was not so much a matter of finding out the nasty thing as of *seeing through* the nasty thing, to find out the healing truth which it masked.

So much for the collective symbolism of the dream. Hoping to find out possibly some more particular implication, and knowing the importance of doors as symbols, I asked her whether she could describe her sister-in-law's door more fully. She looked round the room in which we were sitting, which happened to be a College room with inner door leading to the bedroom, and said, 'It was a cream painted door, rather like that'. This could, of course, have been interpreted as an unconscious sexual projection on to the analyst, identifying the analyst with the unknown lover inside. Had this been pointed out, it would have produced either a positive sexual transference, which is the last thing an Analytical Psychologist wants, or else (which would have been more probable in this case) a justified revulsion leading to hopeless resistance, or even more probably to a breaking off of the analysis. No such suggestion was, of course, made, with the desired result that no such transference occurred throughout the whole analysis, which was on the other hand characterized by a deep respect of the analyst towards the patient, as well as of her to him.

All that I did point out, was the confirmation which this afforded of the symbolism of the inner and outer chamber, repeating on the one hand the motive of the nave and chancel of a church, and on the other hand that of her own conscious and unconscious processes. I closed the interview by suggesting that she might try to draw or paint her vision of the angel. She modestly protested her inability to draw, but I showed her published drawings of other patients, which convinced her that skill in draughtsmanship was by no means necessary in the analytical process.

FOURTH INTERVIEW

14th August

Mrs. Wright to-day brought her drawing of the angel reproduced in Fig. 1.

She said she was feeling much better since the last interview. She had, before reaching the end of the road outside my house come to the conclusion that she had made a great mistake in thinking that she could ever alter her sister's attitude. She heartily agreed with the comment 'Am I my brother's keeper?' She then said that, after coming to the end of the road, she had turned down into the main street of the town, where she had seen in a shop window some verses called 'Wit's End Corner', which went right home to her as they described the position she had been in for years. She had written them down on the back of her drawing of the angel. They were:

WIT'S END CORNER

Are you standing at 'Wit's End Corner'?
Yearning for those you love,
Longing and praying and watching
Pleading their cause above?
Trying to lead them to Jesus
Wondering if you had been true,
He whispers at 'Wit's End Corner'
'I'll win them as I won you'.

Are you standing at 'Wit's End Corner'?
Then you are just at the spot
To learn of the wondrous resources
Of Him who faileth not.
No doubt to a brighter pathway
Your footsteps will soon be led,
But only at 'Wit's End Corner'
Is the God who is able proved.

Though to the sophisticated mind these verses may sound somewhat banal, the psychological situation they portray often turns out to be the corner-stone of salvation. They imply, not only that a person will not as a rule think of submitting to analysis unless he is indeed at his wit's end, but also that it is in the inferior function that salvation is invariably found.

She then said that she had a dream which justified the interpretation put on the one which she had brought last week.

6. Dream

'I was going to a wedding, but before I got there I met my niece, who is now actually 19 years old but who in the dream appeared to be still only 14. This girl, though too young to be married, was dressed as a bride, and with her was an unknown boy of about 13, with beautiful face and flaxen hair. I kissed my niece. Then I bent down to kiss the boy. [When she said this she covered her face with her hands and silently wept. When she had recovered she went on]: But he turned his face away and would not kiss me.'

I asked why she wept. She said because he would not kiss her. While I was wondering what this meant, she added gently as if comforting herself, 'But he had a smile on his face, it was not a bad smile but a shy one. He was really too shy to let me kiss him.'

I then asked, 'Was he the bridegroom?' and she said, 'I do not know, he was dressed more like a page, and had a velvet suit on. I had expected to find the real bride and bridegroom in the church. But I never got there, but met these two on the way instead. I do not know whether he was the bridegroom or not. He *may* have been.'

I pointed out that the niece's real age, 19, was the same as her own when she had had the vision of the angel, so that in this respect the niece resembled herself (now beautified through her acceptance of the 'nasty' side of herself, represented by her sister-in-law in the previous dream) but that the scene really referred to the time when Mrs. Wright was herself 14, which was the niece's age in the dream. This age of puberty represented the parting of the ways, and I reminded her that she had first told me that she was 14 when she had the vision. I called attention to the fact that, though she had thought she was going to witness a marriage of fully sexed adults, what she had actually witnessed, was the union of a non-nubile girl with a non-nubile boy. That is to say that the marriage in question represented not a sexual union but a spiritual one, in the same way that the birth of Christ from an untouched virgin represented the spiritual rebirth of mankind. Thus, the marriage was more in the nature of the marriage of Christ with his Church, and also of the union of the conscious self with the soul. The boy represented her soul, beautiful but as yet shy. Being young, he represented growth, embracing all the potentialities of the adult. I pointed out also that just as the niece was an improved and beautified version of that side of herself which had been represented by her sister-in-law in the last dream, improved and beautified owing to the dreamer's acceptance of her own inferior function, so also the boy represented the unseen 'lover' in the previous dream, then hidden because unconscious, but now, for the same reason, come out into the open for her to view. As she was not very well acquainted with her soul, however, he was represented as being shy and not yet quite ready to embrace her. The improved relations between herself and this important component of her psyche were, however, very marked, and she would doubtless have further opportunities of getting on better terms with it. I told her that the problem was not only her own individual problem, but one which the whole modern world shared. For Christianity had got 'old' and was now having to be reborn out of our dreams, as it had previously been revealed in the Revelation of Saint John, in which dream processes were recognized as containing the highest spiritual values.

She said, 'Everything seems topsy-turvy now.' I said, 'Yes, things are quite literally topsy-turvy, so that it may well be that the heaven you are seeking is not overhead any longer, but by the inscrutable wisdom and bounty of God has changed its position, and is now to be found within instead of above.'

FIFTH INTERVIEW

20th August

Mrs. Wright opened the interview by saying in her quiet inward way that things had during the past week immensely improved at home. She no longer minded little things that used to worry her. The relationship with her sister was much better, and for the first time for years things were 'just as they used to be' before her mother died and they were all a happy family at home.

She then told me a dream.

7. Dream

Scene I

'I was walking up a gently rising path, when a man looked over my left shoulder. He was tall and lean, and had a pointed beard which was reddish brown with light glistening from it. As he looked over my left shoulder I was afraid, and recoiled with a shiver of fear, saying: "Please, don't touch me." He did not touch me, but passed by, and as he did so the words of Our Lord came into my head, "*Fear not*". And I ceased fearing. He passed by, and I noticed he was wearing a blue suit. It came into my mind that his face was like Christ's. He went straight on, and then disappeared.

Scene II

'Then I found myself approaching a place where there was a kind of circus going on. But I felt "This is not the place for me". It did not seem to be wholesome, and also one had to pay to get in.

Scene III

'So I retraced my steps, and then found myself going into a room in which there were a gentleman and two ladies. Also Margaret was there, in a brown dress she often wears. This is the first time Margaret has come into my dreams for a long time. She didn't look up at me at all as she usually does, as if to say, "Help me; tell me what to do", but just sat there calmly happy.

'The two ladies were sitting at a table, each studying an open book with patterns of embroidery on it. The patterns were like patchwork, made up of two colours: orange (later spoken of as yellow or gold) and blue (or, as she said, rather purple).[1] It might have been embroidery for church purposes.

'The man was the opposite type from the one who had passed by me at the beginning of the dream. He was stout, short, and clean shaven with a pale face, and dressed in a black suit, more fashionably than the other (who was poor). He was more like the owner of a shop, possibly a tailor (quite nice-looking), and was showing them how to make folds in a piece of black velvet that was draped over a chair. The way he did this was to gather in one of the strands near the selvedge (at the *bottom* of the cloth) so as to make folds as if for a curtain. It seemed as if he was showing this to the two ladies, but as a matter of fact they were bending over their books with their backs to him. The only person who was watching was Margaret, who sat near to where he was working. The thread he pulled out was black like the rest of the velvet.'

The keynote of the dream is of course 'Fear not', which she realized so fully that there was no need to discuss it. I said, 'If the first man was Christ, who was the other?' She said, 'Could it have been the Devil?' I said, 'He's wearing black, so might be, but didn't you think Christ was the Devil when he first looked over your shoulder with that pointed beard of his?' She said, 'Yes.' So I said, 'They seem to be rather mixed up, don't they? So perhaps, if this tailor is the Devil, he may also be Christ.' She laughed, and I said, 'Christ Himself has a dual

[1] She only saw one corner of the book as she looked over the left-hand lady's shoulder. She later associated the orange and blue with the coloured representation of Christ's robe seen in a picture (p. 77). Though I did not know this at the time, I now know that the two intermingled colours, yellow and blue, represent respectively extraverted and introverted intuition or spiritual perception (see footnote on p. 32 and p. 82, note 1).

Fig. 2. To illustrate Dream 7

Mrs. Wright enters a room, in which a gentleman-tailor in a black suit is showing Margaret (dressed in brown) a piece of black velvet draped over a chair, gathering in one of the strands of the selvedge so as to make folds as if for a curtain. Two ladies seated at a table are studying embroidery books.

character, hasn't he? He is both Son of God and Son of Man.' Then I pointed out all the dualities in the dream.

(1) Feeling of fear, then 'Fear not'.
(2) Two ways.
(3) Two men.
(4) Two women.
(5) Two books.
(6) Each book has two pages open.

We talked about the duality of everything: heaven and hell—light and darkness—day and night—good and evil—each pair composed of opposites necessary and complementary to one another. 'What would you do if it was *always* day? You would work yourself silly and never get any rest.' She said, 'Yes, that's what I've done.' I said, 'And what would you do if it was *always* night?' She said, 'You would get nothing done at all.'

So we discussed all sorts of opposites. I pointed out, and she finally agreed, that evil was necessary (i.e. inevitable) as well as good, so that anyone who tries to do good all the time *must* fail, because the other side has not been allowed for.

Then we talked about the tailor's *black* suit, contrasted with the *blue* (heavenly) suit of the man she realized was Christ. Black represents hell (what we don't know) which is as important as what we do. Christ Himself had to 'descend into hell' before He 'rose again into heaven', and also had to meet the Devil face to face before He entered on His mission. If He had not been to hell He would never have got to heaven, for the way to heaven is and must be *through hell*. This was not only her own problem, but has been mine, and is everyone's, and is a universal law.

At this she expressed huge relief. I said, 'And the black curtain is hell too, meaning what we don't know. And it is in front of Margaret. She is enveloped in it, and so are you with regard to her. But in the dream, because you were not afraid, the tailor (who is the dark side of God) is now showing her how to draw the curtain back so as to let in the light. You know what happens if you go wandering about in the dark. The same things are there as are there in the daytime, only you can't see them, and you go knocking up against them and bark your shins.' She laughed, and I said, 'So what you do is to put on a torch or light a candle, so that you can see. That's what the tailor is doing. He is showing her (and you) how to let *in* the light.'

We talked round and about this subject. Then she said, 'What are my lights [referring to the yellow "lights" she spoke of in our second interview] that warn me of deaths?' and told me of one such 'light' she had had last March, one evening when she was going out to feed her chickens. She saw a long yellow light streak down from the sky and then disappear behind a tree. No death that she knew of had come *from that direction*, so she had wondered whether this was a warning of her own approaching death, so that she might get herself ready. I said, 'It might be, but it might also be that only part of you had to die, as was the case with Saint Paul, so as to make ready the way for a new kind of life'. She said, 'I think it was to tell me of you, that God would send you to me. You are a minister of God.' I said, 'We all are', and she laughed.[1]

She then told me of her very rigid upbringing. She was brought up as a Presbyterian, and her husband was in the Church of England. He had always looked on things differently from her, saying she should take things more easily, but she had not believed him. Now she did, because I had showed her the way. I said, 'Not I, but your dreams.' She said, 'I never knew before that dreams meant anything, but now I know.' I said, 'That is the trouble with us all. I didn't either at one time. It's not only our individual problem, but one affecting our times.' We ended by discussing the decay of the Church and the prospect of its revitalization through contact with the life-giving knowledge vouchsafed through our dreams.

[1] For the importance of disclaiming the Saviour archetype, see p. 82.

SIXTH INTERVIEW

30th August

On arriving, Mrs. Wright said she had four dreams to tell.

8. Dream-vision

Dream-Vision of a woman clothed in a veil-like garment so thin that her form could be distinctly seen. The colour of the veil was a brownish fawn.

Mrs. Wright is a modest woman in the best sense of the word. A superficially more educated woman might have reacted differently, but by her this vision was taken for what it really was—a revelation of herself. When asked what she thought it meant, she said, 'I thought of what Saint Paul said about "seeing through a glass darkly". I could see her form underneath the veil.' She understood so clearly the significance of the vision as symbolizing a meeting with her own spiritual and so psychologically knowledgeable side that I said I had no more comment to make. She then told me the next dream.

9. Dream (*Sacrifice of the Hare*)

'The scene is near my home in Ireland, and I am walking with Margaret up to a square house belonging to a female cousin whom I know very well. The ground was covered with snow. Margaret was in a bit of a fuss wanting to hurry up and get the place dusted, but I told her not to be in such a hurry, as in any case, with the snow lying about, there wouldn't be much dust.

'There was a crowd of people close to the gates, but they didn't come in. As Margaret and I walked up the drive after going through the drive gates the owner of the house appeared, ordering Margaret in rather a bossy way to go into the house to fetch her a glass of lemonade. Margaret went in at the front door to do this, and I never saw her again.

'Then I went round alone into the kitchen at the back of the house. Inside there was a great light and everything was as white as it was outside, though how the snow got in there I cannot tell.

'There were people inside, too, and there, in a white bowl with a little water in it, was a live hare. Someone told me I had got to kill it. This seemed a terrible thing to do, but I had to do it. I picked up the knife (an ordinary kitchen knife) which seemed to have been placed ready for me and which was lying in the water inside the bowl beside the hare, and with a feeling of horror I started cutting into the fur and through to the skin beneath. I had to cut the hare straight down the middle of the back, and started to do this, but my hand trembled so much that, as I cut down, the knife slipped away from the straight line, and ended up by cutting obliquely into the hare's haunch.

'I felt awful doing this, but the hare never moved and did not seem to mind.[1]

'Though the ground outside was covered with snow we had left no footmarks on it.'

I said I would withhold comment on this dream till I had heard the other two.

10. Dream

'A man speaking over my shoulder said [and here Mrs. Wright wept for a moment and then pulled herself together and went on]: "Margaret and her mother may sleep together."'

Asked why she wept, Mrs. Wright said that, when Margaret was born and during her childhood, she had, in obedience to instructions issued to nurses, stifled her own motherly feelings and refused ever to have her baby in bed with her except when it was ill. She agreed now that this was foolish. I pointed out the wickedness of man with his puny conceit setting up his own rationalizations with regard to infant feeding against the instinctive knowledge implanted in both mothers and babies,

[1] She later (p. 63) told me of the look of extreme satisfaction and trust that had been in the hare's eyes as it looked back at her when she plunged the knife into its back.

which leads them to do the right thing by one another if only their instincts are allowed to operate in the way desired by both. I pointed out also the premium placed by this rationalized system on illness, as being the only method left open to a child of forcing its mother to give it that motherly attention which is its due, but of which this system has quite artificially deprived it.

What the dream meant was not necessarily that the mother should now take her 16-year-old daughter into her bed—though there was no reason why she should not do so even now—but its real meaning was a spiritual one, namely that as the mother improved, her own improvement would convey itself automatically to her daughter through the channel of the Collective Unconscious, and the daughter would herself get better.[1]

Mrs. Wright then told me her fourth dream in this week's series.

11. DREAM (*Dreamt the night before the interview*)

'Miss Hardacre was conducting an examination in Mathematics, but I could not do the sums.'

Miss Hardacre (a capable but not very sympathetic woman who has in the past been in a position to exert considerable influence over Mrs. Wright's life) here represents the strait-laced part of Mrs. Wright, previously seen in the figure of her sister-in-law in Dream 5. It was thus clear that Mrs. Wright was quite right not to be able to do such impersonal sums.

We now returned to a consideration of the dream about killing the hare.[2] Mrs. Wright had very little idea about the mean-

[1] This was in fact amply proved as the analysis proceeded, since, though during the period with which this volume deals I never saw the daughter again, she did in fact greatly improve. Some of the initial stages of her development are described later in these pages. Her subsequent development will be dealt with in a later volume, and is briefly referred to in the postscript at the end of this book.

[2] I report this conversation just as it occurred. I had at that time no knowledge of the widespread folk-tales and mythological beliefs from many parts of the world in which the hare figures as a self-sacrificing animal and symbol of spiritual insights. These, and in particular the association of the hare in folk-lore with Easter are dealt with in Part II of this book entitled *The Mythology of the Hare*, from which

ing of this dream, except that the snow in her opinion signified 'washing away sin'. I said, 'Surely the trouble is that you've not sinned enough—against your own mistaken ideals. You remember the mistake discovered in our second talk, indicated by the angel's warning against false idealism and the subsequent warning in Dream 4 against climbing the stony mountain. To-day's dream about the hare has another meaning.' Then I said I would like to make a guess, and asked whether there was any relation between the colour of the veil in Vision 8 with that of the hare. She said they were very similar. I said, 'So there's probably something beneath the hare's fur also that you should see. What would happen actually if you *had* killed the hare?' She said, 'I didn't want to kill it, but it seems I had to.' I said, 'It would have bled, wouldn't it?' She said, 'Yes.' I said, 'And the blood would have run into the bowl. I want to talk very carefully about this, because it is a mystery that no man can fully understand and can only be talked about with the greatest delicacy and reserve. You know about the blood of the Lamb which we now drink in the Communion Cup. The bowl is the cup. The whole dream is a preparation for the Communion Rite, in which Christ sheds His blood for the redemption of sin. *Your* sin has been being too "good" in a mistakenly idealistic way, so God sends his blood to correct the too great whiteness of the snow. That's why the hare didn't mind, because he is a willing sacrifice.'[1]

She said, 'It's wonderful that these mysteries still happen. I used to suppose it only happened once. That must be why we didn't leave any footsteps in the snow.'

it will be seen that many of the motives in Mrs. Wright's dream correspond in surprising detail with ancient symbolic wisdom of which neither she nor I had at the time any conscious knowledge at all.

As will be seen, therefore, in my ensuing conversations with Mrs. Wright no special emphasis was laid on the precise meaning of the hare, whose sacrifice was dealt with only in general terms as representing the transformation of blind instinct into spiritual power.

[1] The reader will not fail to notice the similarity between the willing sacrifice of the hare and that of the husband in Dream 3, now recapitulated on this deeper level.

I added, 'If the hare's blood *had* been shed into the bowl, it would have mixed with the water already *in* the bowl, like the mixing of wine and water in the Communion Cup, commemorating and carrying on the symbolism of the blood and water flowing from Christ's side.'

I then said, 'There's one more thing. I don't understand what your cousin has to do with it all. What was your relationship with her?' She said, 'She was one of my best friends. She was a very religious woman.' I said, 'You were a Presbyterian, weren't you? Was she too?' She said, 'Yes, but she was a little bit fierce.' I said, 'Oh, like Miss Hardacre?' She said, 'Yes.' I said, 'So she also may represent a rather restricting influence, like the one that stopped you from taking your child into your bed.' We then talked about the attitude of Presbyterians in Ireland towards the Communion Rite, which they perform (according to Mrs. Wright) only twice a year and which they regard not as a sacrifice but as something more closely resembling a commemorative meal.[1] I said, 'That's why your cousin only wanted lemonade, and why Margaret disappeared from the dream as soon as she obeyed the order to get this very bodiless drink, hardly a proper substitute for the body and blood of Christ. The reason why Margaret disappeared from the dream at that point was because she had been sent on a mistaken errand.'

Mrs. Wright was very silent for a time as the meaning of all this sank in. The analytical process is itself like the Mass, and like all true ritual as well as great works of dramatic art, in that it leads to peaks of emotion from which the participant has to be led back from scenes of glory very gently into the realms of everyday life, lest the sudden contrast damage the soul. For this reason the last five minutes of the interview were spent in talking of more mundane matters: and, instead of turning her out unprotected into the busy town, I was luckily able to leave her alone in my consulting-room for a time to gather herself together before leaving. How long she stayed there I do not know. When I came back after an hour she was gone.

[1] The doctrine of the Church of Scotland is much more Catholic.

SEVENTH INTERVIEW

4th September

Mrs. Wright told me to-day that, after leaving my room and going home, she had that night (30–31 August) had a 'wonderful experience'. She went to bed at the usual time, but woke up with a feeling of things rushing to and fro in her head, with the result that her head was 'like to burst'. This went on for a long time, with a feeling that something was sawing backwards and forwards in her brain, and every time it sawed a voice said, 'O Jesus, I have promised' (a quotation from the hymn continuing '—to serve thee to the end'). This had been the text of a sermon on the Holy Communion preached the previous Sunday by the Vicar who had had the insight to persuade her in the first instance to seek psychological treatment for her daughter. As she lay suffering in this way in her head, the voice repeated itself with even greater intensity, till she heard the clock striking twelve (a thing she rarely hears, as she sleeps soundly), when suddenly she herself started to repeat the words, altered into 'Jesus, I renew my promise'; and then with a feeling of intense relief fell off to sleep. Next morning she woke feeling body and spirit 'light as air', without the slightest sign of fatigue in spite of (really because of) what she had been through the previous night.

She told me also that, since this analysis began, she had found herself frequently remembering biblical texts which she had long forgotten, and had of late found herself inwardly praying as she worked.

There was no need to comment on the general meaning of the night's initiation experience, during which she accepted the pain leading to ultimate release; and I refrained from complicating matters by asking just what was meant by the promise made to Jesus, since its positive nature, whatever it might mean, was quite clear from the resulting feeling the following morning.

Fig. 3. To illustrate Dream 12

Mrs. Wright, 'taking shelter' from an air raid in a great square 'open to heaven' surrounded on three sides by buildings, prays in front of her fowl-house, while others who were there before her pray also. Later, she leaves the square and is now a schoolgirl taking leave, outside it, of an old schoolfriend wearing a square white object as of linen over her breast, who says, 'I am going away.' Mrs. Wright feels desolate, but is relieved when she says, 'I'm only going for three days.'

She then told me a dream she had had the following night (31 August–1 September).

12. Dream

Scene I

'I was in a wide open space (I don't know where) and suddenly noticed there was no-one about. I thought, "There must be an air raid." I felt afraid, and started looking for shelter. Then I saw through a gate some people kneeling down praying. I went in and found myself in a great square surrounded on three sides by buildings and on the fourth side by a wall separating it from the road in which I had been.

'Though the place was "open to heaven" and there was no roof, once inside I ceased being afraid. I did not, however, quite join the praying group, but went off by myself to where stood a caravan rather like one of my own fowl-houses which is on wheels, and there knelt down to pray. No bombs were dropped, and I began to wonder whether there had really been an air raid or not.

Scene II

'Then I came out of the square place, and there met a young girl with whom I used to be very friendly at school. I now seemed too to be a girl, and felt towards her the same warmth that we had felt all those years ago when we had been such close friends. I seemed to have a loose garment on me, which I put round her. She turned to me and said: "I am going away." I felt desolated and lonely, as I had done when we parted as girls, and said so to her, but she said: "Well, I'm only going for three days." There seemed to be a railway station near by, and it seemed she was going away by train, but when she said she was coming back, I felt happy again. I noticed her dress, which was black, with a square patch of dull white (as of linen) reaching from her neck almost to her waist.'

Asked what she thought about this dream, she said she had no idea what was meant by the air raid that never happened, though she quickly realized the relation between the square yard in this dream and the square house in which the incipient Communion Rite had been held in the previous dream about killing the hare.

When asked about the three days' absence of her friend, however, she said outright that it reminded her of the three days which Christ spent in hell before the resurrection, and that her feeling of despair and subsequent relief tallied well with what must have been the feeling of the disciples at that time.

I then pointed out the significance of the supposed air raid as indicating the powerful spirit of God descending out of the clear heavens upon man,[1] which can wreak destruction upon unbelievers—i.e. those outside the square yard—but which is the highest blessing to those gathered together within. Spirit is indeed powerful for evil as well as good, and the feeling of fear followed by one of safety on entering the holy place of prayer is typical of all religious experience once the power of the spirit is accepted. The same alternation of feeling took place when her friend said she was going away but then said she would come back in three days, and also when the man whom she took for the Devil looking over her shoulder in a previous dream[2] turned out to be Christ. I then pointed out that the plan of the yard resembled that of a church, with the fowl-house representing the altar and herself as the officiating priest. It was at first not quite clear why the altar should have been represented by a fowl-house, as she had not stated whether the fowls were reared for their meat or for their eggs. On being asked which, she said 'Eggs', whereon I suggested the parallel of Easter Eggs. She said, awestruck, 'Then it must all be about Good Friday and Easter.'[3]

I said, 'Yes, your girl friend whom you wrap round with your garment is your spiritual part whom you are now taking to yourself in the sense meant by a former voice saying that Margaret might henceforth sleep with her mother.[4] As you withdraw this projection into yourself the real Margaret will become free.' She said, 'She is becoming so already. Last week of her own will she kissed her aunty good night for the first time for years.'

I then pointed out that the square patch of white clothing on her friend's breast was like the square yard—a patch of consciousness surrounded by unconsciousness (the black dress), corresponding with the area of safety in the bosom of God *in-*

[1] This is a frequent motive in dreams, about which a whole volume could be written.

[2] See Dream 7.

[3] For the meaning of Easter Eggs and their connection with the hare sacrificed in Dream 9, see pp. 171 sqq.

[4] See Dream 10.

side the yard surrounded by the region of fear and danger outside. To my surprise this concept presented no difficulty.[1]

She then said, 'Why was I represented in the dream as being a child?' I said, 'Because it takes you back to a time when you still had a *childlike belief*. It means what Christ meant when He said, "You must become as a little child", believing the inner voice that so many adults have lost.'

I then asked whether the girl friend was at all like the veiled female figure in a former vision, and she said, 'Yes. She was taller than me, and would have grown into a woman like that one.'

She then said she thought she might have been remiss in not going to communion more often. I pointed out that the church in her dream was an open-air one, and square, unlike the church she goes to, and that the communion referred to was a communion inside herself, complementary to the external celebration which might complete and aid the inner process, but lacking which the inner process would still continue.

I did ask, however, what was the colour of the fowl-house in her dream, and she said, 'A reddish colour'. As she was showing signs of having had enough for one day, I refrained from pointing out the symbolic aspect of this as referring to the wine and to her husband's blood in the first dream, which is now clearly seen to refer on one level to the blood issuing from Christ's side when pierced on the Cross.

Nor did I point out that the number of worshippers she had indicated in the square yard was 8, which is the number signifying completion.[2]

[1] It may be noted that there is also an interesting parallel to the ephod, a piece of cloth worn apparently in this position by the Jewish high priest over his dress, and from which hung a pocket containing the oracle—the Urim and Thummim, by means of which the priest ascertained the divine will. Such symbols crop up in dreams, and the divine setting of this dream cannot be in doubt. As will be seen in the sequel, moreover, Mrs. Wright's dreams did indeed contain a markedly prophetic element.

[2] The number 8 is a reduplication of 4, representing the 4-square earth, the 4 cardinal points, the 4 psychological functions and innumerable other quaternities of psychological and religious import. In

As last week, the whole interview which I have described lasted less than three-quarters of an hour, and the remaining quarter of an hour was taken in again coming down to earth by her description of her career in America (where she had gone as a young woman to look after her brother) and of her subsequent experiences as midwife.

dreams it is often represented by 4 couples—4 men and 4 women. See C. G. Jung, *Psychological Types*, London, 1924, and John Layard, *Stone Men of Malekula*, London, 1942, pp. 643–8.

EIGHTH INTERVIEW

11th September

Last time there had been a symbolic representation of Easter and Good Friday, in this reverse order,[1] but no crucifixion, and in each case the human representatives had been female. To-day this lack was made good in a dream representing the sacrifice in which both victim and sacrificer were male.

Before this, however, there was one other matter that had to be cleared up, or 'way' that had to be opened. This was dealt with in the first two of the three dreams she now related as having taken place since the last interview.

13. Dream

The scene was in a small room at the back of the Wrights' cottage, near the kitchen, which was too damp to be used for a sitting-room and was therefore used as a store. The Rev. Mac X (Presbyterian Minister at the Wrights' former home in Ireland) was coming to tea, and the meal was to take place in this room. Bertha (Mrs. Wright's sister) was in a great state of mind because the floor was all over crumbs such as might have been swept carelessly off the table. She was working herself into a temper about these, and accusing Mrs. Wright of having caused the mess, and then suddenly collapsed into a swoon. (Mrs. Wright here explained that this is the time of year when

[1] It is characteristic of dreams in an early stage of analysis that certain archetypal situations such as a psychological death and resurrection are as it were broken up and experienced only in snatches, not always in their normal order, and sometimes missing out certain essential elements. This indicates that the patient is at the time not far enough advanced to appreciate their full meaning. In a successful analysis they are invariably lived through later on a deeper level involving a fuller awareness of their significance and having consequently a more integrating effect. This particular sequence of psychological events was in fact lived through at a later stage by Mrs. Wright in a manner that will be described in another volume.

Bertha in fact is in the habit of swooning, and that she [Mrs. Wright] has up till now always felt her sister might die and she might be to blame, and has therefore always been careful to lay her on her back and later get her up to bed where she has usually stayed for several days.) In the dream, however, she did not lay her down, but propped her up in a chair, where she left her leaning her head over the table. Mrs. Wright felt it was very unlike herself to do this and that it might be very wrong, but her husband said, 'Don't worry. Bertha will soon be all right'.

We first talked a bit about Bertha and these seasonal attacks always taking place in this month of the year. I said, 'This is what happens also in epilepsy. The fits are as a rule also preceded by something resembling anger, which is suppressed, so that the attacks are then turned against the subject.' I told her how these attacks were often seasonal in the same way as her sister's, and represented the re-enacting of the original drama causing the fit. I said I did not suggest that her sister was an epileptic, but did suggest that something of the same nature was taking place, and that it might very well be that this was the time of year at which the abortive love affair which had so soured Bertha had taken place. Mrs. Wright did not know whether this was the case, but said she would try and find out.

We then turned to the question of the crumbs, which were like those used in the Communion Rite as observed in the Presbyterian Church and regarded as being simply a commemorative meal. On the manifest level the event so commemorated would be Bertha's own personal trauma, but on the deeper level it was the Mass. The fact that the crumbs had been carelessly swept off the table signified on one level the disregard of the sacrificial nature of the rite as performed by the Presbyterians. On another level, it represented the crumbs falling from the master's table, through acceptance of which on the part of the Tyro-Phoenician woman in Matthew xv, 21–8 her daughter who had been vexed with a devil became healed. Her sister was too proud (one aspect of this pride had been the rejection of the lover and her consequent lifelong disappointment), and had to humble herself to the dust in order to lick up the fallen crumbs. That's why she swooned. The deep knowledge in Mrs. Wright's unconscious was therefore quite right in not treating the swooning as a disease, but in raising her to the communion-table to eat in company with all others who were sufficiently humble to partake.

The husband's voice saying 'Bertha will soon be all right' indicated on the one hand that Bertha *would* be all right if treated in this way (either in life through not having herself fussed over, or else in death which would be better than a living death ruled over by pride). On the other hand, Bertha represented the pride aspect of Mrs. Wright, in thinking that she was really her sister's keeper. More vitally still did the dream mean that, like the Tyro-Phoenician's daughter, Margaret would automatically recover in proportion to the extent to which Mrs. Wright herself could humbly accept the crumbs of revelation now being given to her in her dreams.

Mrs. Wright said that Margaret was already immeasurably better, and now kissed her aunt good night every night, so that she (Mrs. Wright) no longer had any hesitation in leaving them together after a lifetime spent in guarding them against contact lest something dreadful should befall.

She also said she now realized why the scene of the dream had been set in the store-room, since this represented the store of spiritual sustenance now coming into its own.

The next dream formed a bridge between this one and the next but one.

14. Dream-vision

This was more in the nature of a vision, in which she entered a square room which was a draper's store-room, where were displayed four bales of material, which she described as being respectively 'fawn, green, white, and flesh-pink'. They were arranged as in the illustration.

Asked what she thought of this, she said she thought it was a kind of ethereal counterpart of the store-room in the last dream, and gave her great comfort. What she particularly noticed was the lovely flesh-pink.

I did not at this point make any mention of the four functions,[1] nor of colour-symbolism in general, but I did note the contrast between the bright colours she now saw and the black cloth displayed to Margaret in Dream 7. The meaning of the flesh-pink became immediately apparent when we proceeded to a discussion of the following sacrificial dream, to which it clearly led up.

Fig. 4. To illustrate Dream Vision 14
Mrs. Wright enters a draper's square store-room displaying four bales of material of the colours indicated.

15. Dream

She first said that this dream was about a new butcher who had recently arrived at her village, and with whom she now dealt. His name was Abrahams, so he was presumably a Jew. He was good-looking and a fine figure of a man, quite young, and 'in the pride of his life'.

She dreamt that this butcher was there, and that an unknown doctor arrived and said, 'Well, he's a nice fellow', and

[1] See p. 57, note 2.

then said, 'This man must go through an operation'. The operating table was an ordinary kitchen table, on to which, to her astonishment, the patient got all by himself as if in the best of health, and fully clothed. There were no blankets, nor any of the paraphernalia ordinarily used for an operation. She herself had to prepare the bed into which he was to be placed after the operation, but quite forgot to ask the doctor what kind of antiseptic he used.

When asked, she said she had no idea whatever what the dream meant. The whole thing seemed so uncanny she could not make head or tail of it. So I began with the butcher, one who killed animals, as she herself in a previous dream had had to kill a hare.[1] This man, however, was both sacrificer (killer of animals, and I told her how in certain primitive religions the animal was always sacrificed before being eaten), and was himself at the same time the willing sacrifice, just as the hare had been. She then told me of the look of extreme satisfaction and trust that had been in the hare's eyes as it looked back at her when she plunged the knife into its back. This made her think of Christ, and we then realized the meaning of the butcher being a Jew. Still she could not understand why such an apparently fine healthy man should be sacrificed, and said, 'I have never fathomed why Christ, the perfect man, should have to suffer like that'.

We then talked about the nature of sacrifice, that it must be willing, and that it must be of something perfect or of the highest value. We talked of circumcision, the sacrifice of part of man's virile member, a sacrifice to God for the privilege of being redeemed of our animal nature. Beasts may be free to do what they like, but they are not human. Man in a primitive state may have been free to do what he liked, but had no knowledge of God. Being civilized had its advantages, but entailed the sacrifice of the exercise of untrammelled instinct. That's what is meant by sacrifice. By sacrifice we willingly give up part of our primitive natural satisfactions in return for all that is entailed by civilization and the spiritual benefits that true

[1] Dream 9.

civilization confers. Mrs. Wright then re-stated this all in terms of religion, substituting 'Church' for 'Civilization', and I agreed, so she added, 'The trouble is that the Church has not always accomplished its mission, and that's why we've got in such a muddle'. I said, 'Yes, that's why we have now to re-discover inside ourselves some of the truths the Church has still enshrined in its liturgy but has forgotten in its life.'

We then talked of the sacrifice of Isaac, which God commuted because Abraham had been willing to make it, so that the sacrifice of the spirit was now equivalent to the sacrifice of the flesh. That was what Bertha had had to do in the first dream,[1] and why Mrs. Wright was quite right in not treating her swoon as a disease but rather as a sign of redemption. In the last dream also Mrs. Wright was quite right in forgetting the antiseptic. Christ had no antiseptic on the wounds He suffered on the cross, nor had her hare, and if they had had, the sacrifice would have been worthless.

Once more she said, 'I had thought that it was only in olden times that men had had dreams to show them how to live. I never dreamt we had it in us now.'

At this point I saw that the high point of the day's analysis had been reached, and we then talked of more mundane and practical matters such as the greater prevalence of septicaemia in the West End of London than in the East End, because septicaemia was due to lack of spirituality quite as much as to lack of merely physical hygiene. She told me of one of the finest maternity doctors she had known in Ireland who rarely washed his hands and who had got into trouble with medical authorities because of the state of his doctor's bag, but who had never mishandled a case.

[1] Dream 13.

NINTH INTERVIEW

18th September

Today Mrs. Wright brought what she called 'three small dreams' which in fact turned out to be four.

16. Dream

'I was driving a black pony harnessed to a cart full of clover.[1] The pony was the one we used to have in Ireland. The clover was in flower—it was being taken to feed animals—and I noticed the threefold nature of the leaves. The countryside was one which I do not know, but I seem to have been there before. I was taking the pony to the blacksmith to be re-shod, though I remember now that I never even looked to see whether it needed it. Margaret was on the cart with me. After a time we met my sister Bertha by the side of the road, outside some house. A woman came out of the house and asked her if she would like some tea. She said yes, and asked Margaret if she would like to have some too. Margaret said she would, and got down off the cart. She asked me also if I would have some tea, but I said I would not, but must go on to get the pony shod. Margaret went into the house, and I did not see her again. I drove on through the lovely countryside, feeling again that it was a country I had been in before.'

17. Dream

'I was in a class, in a school. We were all sitting round in a circle, and the teacher (a man) was asking questions from left to right. He asked some girl, "What is a Church?" She answered, "*A Church is a place where we are sanctified and made holy by marriage to God.*" The teacher then skipped over the girls in between and pounced on me, saying, "*Who is higher*

[1] It is to be noted that this was the common purple-flowered clover, and not shamrock. Shamrock appeared later in Dream 37 (to be published in a future volume), which carries the symbolism of this dream a considerable stage further.

than God?" I said, "There is none higher than God." He said, "*Oh yes, there is one higher than God.*" I said, "I've never been taught that", whereon the teacher smiled knowingly, but said no more.'

Fig. 5. To illustrate Dream 17
The teacher in class asks 'Who is higher than God?'

18. Dream

'In the same class-room as the previous dream. Miss Hardacre was taking the class—it was a kind of religious exam—and asked some boy a question which he could not answer. She pressed him again, but he answered, "*I haven't time for lessons. I have to work so hard*". Miss Hardacre said harshly, "That's no excuse", and then turned to me asking a question which I also was unable to answer. The Vicar [who had recommended analysis to her] was there, and he said to me, "*But you do know.*" I said, "I don't know", and he again said, "But you do."'

19. Dream

'I was in a house with my husband's sister Kate, the one who is a nurse and who appeared in a previous dream.[1] The

[1] Dream 5.

house was a strange one. In real life Kate and I always disagree. Among other things I love flowers but she does not like them and despises me for growing them. But in the dream she was as friendly as anything, and said to me, "I have a lovely lot of flowers for you to see. Come and look at my lovely flowers." We were in a room, and in it was a miniature garden composed of two beautiful bowls. They were big shallow bowls with earth in them and beautifully tended grass like turf that covered the earth, and growing out of the grass were some lovely red dahlias, which I looked at with delight. I said, "They are beautiful", and was amazed at her liking the flowers and having planted them, and being so friendly.'

I asked her what she thought about the first dream, and about the unknown countryside seeming familiar. She had no answer, so I pointed out how this meant that the dream referred to a constantly recurring situation always reappearing under some new guise. This was clearly seen also in the fact that she was once more leaving Margaret with her sister, referring to the time when she had so disastrously left her there when a baby. She said, "Yes. I had thought of that, but this time I had no fear. I used to feel I must protect Margaret from her, but now I feel that Margaret is quite safe with her, and won't come to any harm.'

I then asked what she thought about the clover. She said, 'It's three leaves in one. That is the sign of the Trinity. I was very interested in those three leaves, and when I got up next morning I went out to have a look at some.'

I said, 'Then it looks as if this dream had something to do with the Trinity. What do you think it meant when the teacher asked, 'Who is higher than God?' She had no answer to this, any more than she had had in the dream. I then said, 'I want to be very careful about this, as we had to be careful about the dream about sacrificing the hare.[1] It's quite clear, isn't it, that the teacher knew what he was talking about?' She agreed, and I said, 'Yet he thinks there *is* someone higher than God. This sounds sacrilegious, yet the dream says it is so. What

[1] Dream 9.

he clearly means is higher than God as you conceive Him to be. What can it be that you have left out of account?' I asked her to name the persons of the Trinity, and then said, 'Are they the only power in the world?' She said, 'Well, no. There's Evil. There is the Devil. He is a bad power.' I asked her, 'What is evil?' She said, 'What is against God'. I said, 'What is it that is against God?' She said, 'It's not easy to say. I'd like you to tell me.' I said, 'Well, God is Light, isn't he? Then evil is dark, that means, what we don't know. We now speak of the Germans as evil, because we didn't know they were preparing to attack us. Or rather, we did know, but blinded ourselves to it. If we had admitted to ourselves what we in fact knew, and had prepared ourselves adequately against it, the evil would not have taken us unawares. Now that it has come, and that we are neither deluding ourselves as to its existence nor letting it overwhelm us we are recovering the strength that we had lost through our false sense of security, and it is now actually galvanizing our whole life. So there is a use in evil if we know it is there and don't pretend it is not. The trouble about Christianity in recent times is that it has become too falsely idealistic. We have come to think of God as giving us only those things which we regard as good, and have forgotten the Old Testament and that He can be also a God of Wrath. So Christianity has for many become a wishy-washy affair, and has lost the strength that comes from a recognition that God can be a Destroyer as well as a Creator;[1] for all things are possible to Him. He rules over the night as well as the day. But if we say He rules only over the day, what happens to the night? Now let's see what your dreams say about it. What dark object is there in them?'

She could not at first think of any, till she remembered the black pony. I pointed out that in that first dream of to-day's series the threefold symbol was repeated twice, first in the three-leaved clover, and then in the three persons, herself, Margaret, and Bertha, the figure who offered the tea being so shadowy that she hardly counted. I then talked about the symbolism of the cross, with its four arms, of which, on one sym-

[1] Compare, for example, Isaiah xlv, 7, and Hebrews x, 31; xii, 29.

bolic level, the three upper arms represent the Trinity and the fourth, plunged into the ground, represents the Devil who had been sent down to hell, and who for this reason had passed out of consciousness and been lost. Where then was the fourth sentient being in the dream? She said, 'The black pony. That means he is the Devil who is leading me astray.' I said, 'That may be what you have thought. It's certainly true that he is leading, as he is pulling the cart but are you sure he is leading you astray?' She said, 'Well, no. I was taking him to be shod.' I said, 'That means he is the unconscious power that you are preparing to use in your service by giving him the attention he needs. He is the hidden fourth power representing, like all animals, the instinctive reactions that we in our present civilization have tended to lose through our too great concentration on the light side of the godhead, thereby neglecting the dark. You know this already through the success of your dream-treatment of Bertha. It is precisely the instinctual knowledge that has to be resurrected, and that is symbolized here by the black pony. It is as fatal to neglect the powers of darkness as to neglect the powers of light. Both have to function together, for they are two sides of the same coin. That's what is meant by the marriage with God. What did the girl in the next dream (17) mean when she answered that "A Church is a place where we are sanctified and made holy by the marriage to God"? Is that a phrase used in your catechism?'

She said, 'No. I've never heard it before I heard her saying it in the dream.' I said, 'What does it mean?' She said, 'It seemed perfect when she said it, but, now you ask me, I can't say just what it does mean. You know. Will you tell me?' I said I didn't know anything, but could only act as a translator, as best I could, for the word of God revealed to her in her dream, and pressed her again to say what was meant by the word 'we'. How can 'we' be married to God? Who are '*we*'? She could not say, so I went on to point out that 'we' were evidently not sanctified until marriage with God. What things was it that had to be sanctified in us all? It was clearly our instincts. What then did it mean that our instincts had to be married to God? Clearly that they were of equal importance with the 'good' God she already knew, for only equals can be married. It meant that, while in the early days of Christianity an over-developed self-indulgence in the Roman world had to be countered by a move *against* instinctive or animal life, this process had gone too far, and must now be reversed till instinct was given its true place alongside that aspect of the godhead which represented conscious control, and that only when the two were properly balanced together could we live satisfactory lives. But only those things which were known could be controlled. Her instinct was represented by the pony, and it was to the pony that the Teacher referred as being 'the one higher than God', meaning not that he *was* higher than God, for, as we had seen, the two should be equal and married, but that he must for the moment be *represented* as 'higher', because our instincts had been too much neglected and therefore must for the time being be given most honour in order to make up for the dishonour they had of late suffered.[1]

Going on now to the last two dreams, it was clear that Miss Hardacre represented the too great conscious control over instinct, and it was for this reason that the unknown boy who stood for Mrs. Wright's soul was quite right in ignoring her questions, as he was fully occupied with the more important work in which she was engaged during analysis, just as the boy Christ had left his everyday occupation to go to the temple 'about his father's business'. She said, 'The boy in my dream was about twelve years old', which was Christ's age when this occurred. In the dream, Mrs. Wright was also quite right not to answer the irrelevant questions, just as she had not been able to do the sum required of her by Miss Hardacre in a previous dream.[2] But at the same time the Vicar, a representative of Christ, said, 'But you do know', meaning that her instinctive side did, though the true answer that this side of her would make would be quite unintelligible to Miss Hardacre, or to that side of herself which Miss Hardacre represented, and therefore remained unspoken, as the marriage with God referred to in

[1] Compare 1 Corinthians xii, 22, 23, 24; also the Augustinian phrase, 'God permits evil that good may come'.

[2] Dream 11.

the previous dream was there only adumbrated as a future possibility and was as yet by no means fully realized.

The last dream about Kate, her husband's sister, again represented the marriage under a different form, namely that with her own self-criticizing self, and was a comment on the dream about Miss Hardacre, whereby that part of herself became assimilated under the aegis of the sacrament represented by the two bowls, one for each side of herself, in which, growing in the green grass of simplicity, were the red flowers representing the blood of the hare she had been willing to sacrifice in a previous dream,[1] and of which the last dream represented the fruit.

[1] Dream 9.

TENTH INTERVIEW

2nd October

A fortnight had elapsed since the last interview, owing to my having been away.

20. Dream

'I was going with my husband along a lane towards my old home in Ireland. There was an air raid, though the curious thing was that the aeroplane I saw in the sky was not like an ordinary aeroplane, but had its wings in the middle. I was afraid, and started hurrying home to warn my own people. But my husband caught hold of my arm and said (as he often does in real life), "No need to worry". I obeyed him, and the aeroplane seemed to descend till it came down close to the gate leading up to the house, and stayed propped up against the low wall, just as one might prop up a bicycle. There it stood, with one wing touching the ground and the other sticking straight up into the air, with the fuselage parallel to the ground. Out of it came a German in a light blue suit, who seemed in no way to want to attack us, but just busied himself with repairing the middle part of the 'plane. I said to my husband, "This is a friendly German after all." I felt we had no need to fear. There was no need any more to warn my people, so we just went on walking together past the house.'

Mrs. Wright had already realized when waking that the supposed aeroplane was in fact an equal-armed cross, and that that was why her husband had told her there was no need to worry. We noted the now regular pattern of many of her dreams beginning with the motive of fear and ending with that of 'fear not'. She was, however, a little puzzled about the 'friendly' German till I pointed out to her that almost everyone was now having dreams about friendly Germans, this representing the esoteric complement to our overt defence against their attack.

The spirit called forth by their attack and our defence against it was regenerating an England that sorely needed regeneration, and in this sense the Germans, by attacking us, were indeed proving our best friends. I pointed out also the close parallel between the figure of the German in her drawing and that of Christ on the Cross. This meant that salvation came through our acceptance of the Shadow or 'other' hated or despised side

Fig. 6. To illustrate Dream 20

The raiding aeroplane in the form of a Cross descends, propping itself against a wall. The blue-suited pilot, instead of being hostile, quietly repairs the engine situated in the middle of the 'plane.

of ourselves, and that it was the acceptance of this Shadow and its resuscitation out of the unconscious that had caused the long lower limb of the Latin Cross to become shortened in her dream so as to make a balanced equal-sided union of complementary opposites, and that this in turn corresponded with the new balance she was finding in her life. The light blue colour of the German's suit, representing the sky or heavenly understanding, recalled the blue suit worn by the Christ-figure in Dream 7.

She said that, after having this dream, she woke up singing

> *Holy, Holy, Holy! Lord God Almighty!*
> *Early in the morning our song shall rise to thee.*

In singing this, she realized that, though for years she had not been able to sing, she was now singing like a lark. She said also that her whole health was better than it had been for years, that she no longer suffered from the acidity, rheumatism, and headaches that had constantly troubled her before this analysis began. The only physical disability now left to her was her eyesight. She still had to wear spectacles.

I asked her how Margaret was getting on. She said she was much better and more independent than she had ever been, that she was now able to stand up to her Aunt Bertha's bad tempers in a way she had never been able to do before, and that Mrs. Wright herself now felt the wells of friendship rising again towards her sister after all these years of trouble.

She then said that her second dream was about Bertha.

21. Dream

'The scene was in an unknown house. Bertha was preparing herself for marriage. I looked round, and was surprised to see nothing but women. I thought she must have someone to go to church with her to give her away. Then I thought, "Where is my father?", and went to look for him. I found him in some other room. He said, "I'm ready." I went back to tell them so, but found Bertha in a swoon. There she was, not even in her wedding-dress, but dressed in cream, with three other women round her, also dressed in cream instead of white, who should have been her bridesmaids, one on each side and one near her head. Unlike what I would have done in real life, I let her be.

'I then thought "Where is Margaret?" Someone said, "Margaret has gone to take a bath." I called out to her, and she called back, "Mother, I'm taking a bath." I called back, "All right, carry on."

'Then I went out into a corridor. There were two unknown ladies sewing. They were making a bed quilt, made by stitching together the tartans of all the Scottish clans. I said, "What a pretty covering for a sick bed", and the two ladies smiled.'

Mrs. Wright's first comment on this dream was, 'Does Bertha not being ready for the marriage, mean me?' We came to the conclusion, however, that, in view of the extremely posi-

FIG. 7. TO ILLUSTRATE DREAM 21

Bertha, too late for her wedding, lying in a swoon surrounded by the three women who should have been her bridesmaids, who stand looking at her prostrate body.

tive nature of the first dream it could not mean her, but quite literally referred to her sister Bertha, who indeed was not ready.[1] She told me that Bertha had not yet had her customary

[1] I have been criticized for not accepting Mrs. Wright's own suggestion that Bertha's unpreparedness for the marriage really referred to Mrs. Wright's own unwillingness to deal with her own shadow-problem (see p. 87) by still projecting it upon Bertha, unless, my critic adds, Bertha 'undergoes a remarkable but most improbable conversion'. There is indeed some theoretical validity in this, but the

autumn swooning fit which she usually had in September, but had been terribly bad-tempered—the kind of temper that usually led to the swooning fits but rather worse. I pointed out that the swooning could be taken from at least two angles. On the one hand it meant (as in the previous dream about the crumbs swept from the table)[1] that she must humble herself to the earth before any kind of salvation could come her way. On the manifest level, on the other hand, the swooning was a method of escape from her own tempers, by means of which she could temporarily forget her own annually recurring problem. I pointed out that, just as Mrs. Wright's own spiritual recovery was influencing her sister as well as Margaret, this was probably the cause of her sister no longer being able to find this illusive way out. I warned her, however, that for this reason her sister's tempers would for the time being almost certainly get worse, but that this was a necessary crucifixion that she would have to put up with, and that it would actually lead in the long run to an improvement, so long as Margaret, and Mrs. Wright herself, were not made to suffer too much on account of them. Mrs. Wright said that both she and Margaret were no longer seriously affected by them, and would put up with them cheerfully if it would do Bertha any good. I said there was no hope, in my opinion, of Bertha ever being ready for marriage, but that there was a distinct hope that she would become calmer and more tolerant as the general family situation improved.

Mrs. Wright herself remarked at this point that the position of the two women on either side of Bertha corresponded to the two wings of the aeroplane, and added that their dresses were almost the same colour as the wings, which were the colour of unbleached linen. Bertha thus represented the vertical bar of

whole subject of Bertha had to be handled with great tact and, as will be seen in a later volume, Mrs. Wright did accomplish her own spiritual union on a much deeper level than that seen in this dream, and Bertha's 'conversion' is at the time of publication far from being beyond the bounds of probability and in fact shows distinct signs of being realized.

[1] Dream 13.

the cross and the two 'bridesmaids' its arms. The symmetry was spoilt, however, by the third 'bridesmaid' standing near her head, thus indicating the seat of Bertha's trouble.

It had by this time become quite clear that the unpreparedness for the marriage was indeed Bertha's, and not Mrs. Wright's,[1] whereon the latter said, 'Then what does it mean about my father being ready when Bertha was not?' I pointed out that it was Mrs. Wright, and not Bertha, who had found out the father, and to whom he had said, 'I am ready', and that it was not only her earthly father, but also the Father in Heaven who thus told her that *he* was ready. There was no need to discuss what he was ready for (i.e. the marriage to God referred to in a previous dream[2]). The symbolism spoke for itself.

I then asked her why she thought Margaret had gone to take a bath. She said she did not know, but when I hinted at baptism she said, 'Yes, I had been thinking that myself. I used not to know what rebirth meant, but now I do.'

The only thing left to discuss was the tartan quilt made by the two unknown ladies. She first said, 'Does this mean the Scottish Church?'' But this suggestion had no content, and she then said, 'My family came originally from Scotland', whereon it became clear that, having made spiritual contact with her father and through him with the Father of all men, the joining of the tartans of all the Scottish clans symbolized the gathering together of all the innate forces which, arising from the branching family tree, had gone to build up her own individuality, the origins of which were thus traced back through an endless series of links to the dim distant past represented by the emergent godhead.

I said the two ladies reminded me of the two ladies looking at their books of embroidery patterns in Dream 7, and asked whether the tartans were of the same colours as those. She said, 'No, but I saw a picture the other day which showed me what those embroidery colours were. It was a picture of our Lord, and those colours were the colours of His robe.'

She said, 'Why should I think the tartan covering was for a

[1] But see footnote on p. 75. [2] Dream 17.

sick bed?' We came to the conclusion that this might partly refer to her profession as a nurse, but that it probably had a deeper meaning to the effect that all sickness was due to a break in the continuity of spiritual life which this gathering of the clans was designed to heal. Her last question was, 'Do I do wrong, then, to go on giving the village people the simple remedies they come to me for? Is this serving two masters?' I said, 'No. You can't advertise your own conversion like that. That is your own private matter. If it eventually affects them as it is already affecting Margaret and Bertha, well and good. But you won't do that by talking, and meanwhile, if these accustomed remedies give them comfort, there's no reason why they should not have them.'

She then told me she had had another snatch of a dream.

22. Dream

'I was surrounded in my own house by children, and the Vicar came in and asked if he could help. I said, "No", but he went on moving in and out among them.'[1]

As it so happened, I met the Vicar that afternoon, and he told me what an improvement he had noticed in Margaret, and that for the first time in her life she had actually answered some of his questions with something more than a plain 'Yes' or 'No', and had actually had a short conversation with him about the work she was doing.

[1] Mrs. Wright's rejection of the Vicar's help is in line with Bertha's rejection of marriage in the previous dream. (See footnote on p. 75.) The solution of this problem of the rejected *animus* as it occurred after the events here dealt with will be described in a later volume.

ELEVENTH INTERVIEW

9th October

Mrs. Wright started the interview by saying once more how immensely the whole family situation had improved. The whole village was remarking how much better Margaret was. She would now return the villagers' greetings out loud with a 'Good morning' or 'Good afternoon' instead of mumbling these to herself so that she could not be heard and was often thought to have made no reply at all. She had also started to knit quite well instead of dropping half her stitches as she had always done before, and had even begun to tend, mend, and iron her own clothes and for the first time in her life generally to take an interest in her personal appearance. She had also for the first time begun to say her prayers. When asked, 'What prayers?' Mrs. Wright said, 'The Lord's Prayer', and told how hitherto Margaret had been unable to struggle through it, but could now say it all through.

Then followed a brief discussion on the Lord's Prayer, including the fact that the words 'daily bread' have in this context an obvious spiritual meaning as well as a material one.

Mrs. Wright said also that she herself had never felt better in her life, that instead of the rheumatism and indigestion from which she had suffered for years and had accepted as inevitable, she now had 'neither ache, raik, nor pain'. For years all sorts of food had disagreed with her, but this week she had found she could eat anything—so much so that she had deliberately been eating all those things that had formerly upset her, and found she sustained no harm but on the contrary doubly enjoyed and profited from everything she touched.

The same, though in not quite so exuberant degree, was true of her sister Bertha, who not only had not swooned this autumn at all (though to compensate for this her tempers had at the time lasted a trifle longer), but was now far less bad-tempered than usual and was also enjoying food she had 'never had in years'. She then described a whole meal her sister Bertha had had of things that formerly she had refused to touch.

Even her husband, always good-tempered and placid, had become if possible yet more so than before.

After this panegyric, which was repeated at intervals throughout the session, Mrs. Wright said rather shyly that she had not done much dreaming, but had had one dream into which I and my wife came.

23. DREAM

'The dream was of a hospital, but there were no beds in it. It was a large building with many rooms, all filled with a bright light similar to the light in the kitchen in Dream 9 [in which she had sacrificed the hare]. You [the analyst] and your wife were both in it. There were lots of people there and you seemed to be entertaining. You walked about quietly among the guests, but what I most noticed was your wife, who moved more quickly among the people, as women do, and whose eyes shone like stars. She said to me, "I will show you your room". Then she took me into one of the rooms, in which there was a bed, and on it a night costume finely embroidered with lace. I said, "That costume is too fine for me. A plain one would do." But she said, "That is your costume." I began to undress, but had only taken off two garments when I awoke.

'Your little son was not there, but I noticed a little boy about five years old wearing a blue suit and a blue tam-o'-shanter.'

When asked what was the pattern embroidered on the lace, she made the drawing reproduced in Fig. 8, in which the squares represent the gathered-in lace and the curved lines the fronds of the palm leaf spreading on both sides of a central stem. Below this were a few tucks, whence downward the costume was plain.

Asked what she thought this meant, she said she had woken up repeating the words of a Rescue Mission hymn which ran,

Palms of victory, crowns of glory,
Palms of victory I shall wear.

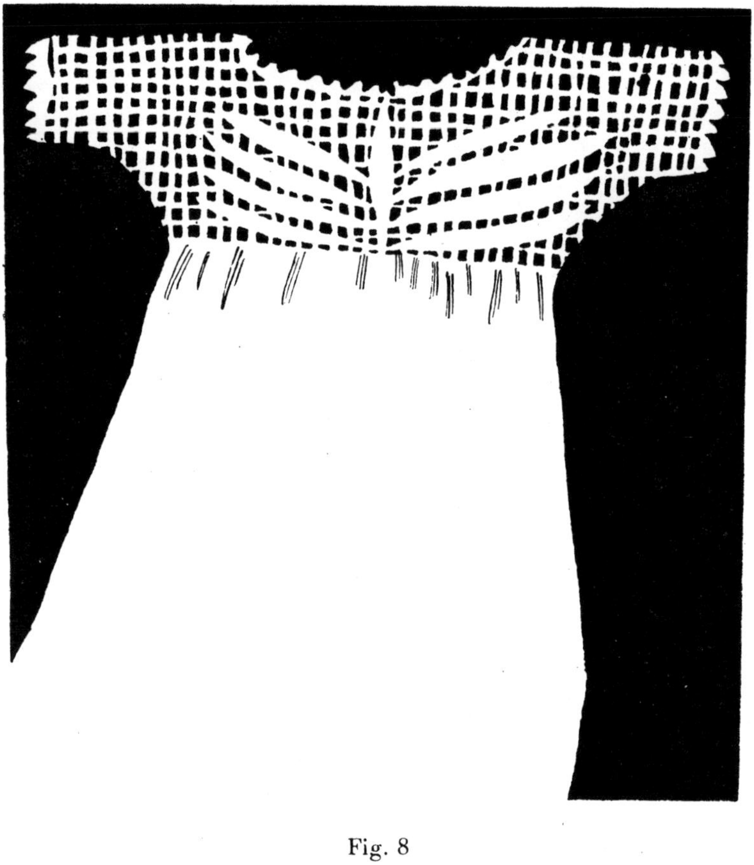

Fig. 8

The 'night costume' offered to Mrs. Wright in her dream by the analyst's wife.

These words were said with utter modesty indicating heartfelt acceptance devoid of any kind of inflated pride.

No word from me was needed to point out that the blue suit the boy was wearing was the same colour as that of the German airman in Dream 20 who turned out to be the crucified Christ, here reincarnated after the victory of Palm Sunday in the form of her own rejuvenated soul. I only added that 'blue' was the colour of heaven and meant understanding[1] —the understanding her dreams had brought her. Asked what was the exact shape of the boy's tam o'shanter, she said it was not worn, as some are, on one side, but was flat on his head, more like a child's sailor hat, had a central knob and resembled a halo.

I pointed out that the fact that the dream showed her this Christ-child and not my own son meant that what she took to be me and my wife were in fact not us but dream representations of the divine family. She agreed that no human eyes shone as did my wife's eyes in the dream. I had, however, taken great care throughout the analysis to deal with the danger of her transferring the Saviour archetype on to myself by disclaiming it on every occasion when it arose (cf. page 47), and took this opportunity of further emphasizing the obvious unsuitability of any such personal projection.

The brief survey of the dream then showed that it was in reality a visual representation of the opening phrases of that very Lord's Prayer she had been teaching her daughter, and which (now that, in terms of a previous dream,[2] 'Margaret and her mother may sleep together') her daughter was for the first time absorbing through the mediumship of her mother. Thus the bright light clearly set forth the setting of the opening phrase, 'Our Father which art in heaven', to which the blue of the Christ-child's suit and his halo also contributed. No direct allusion was found to 'Hallowed be thy name', unless it were the feeling of awe with which she regarded the dedicatory costume (in which the symbol of the spreading palm leaf as well as the shape of the garment itself closely resembled a

[1] In other words, introverted intuition (see footnotes on pp. 32, 44).

[2] Dream 10.

cross). 'Thy kingdom come' was, however, clearly represented by the hospital in which no beds were needed since the whole problem of everyday disease had now lost for her its material character and was seen as a result of her own analysis to depend on spiritual and not physical factors. Here she herself alluded to the phrase 'In my father's house are many mansions' as being represented by the great number of rooms the hospital contained. 'Thy will be done' was in turn represented by the now proven efficacy of believing in God's will as revealed in her own dreams. Perhaps most striking of all, however, was her reaction when I pointed out the significance of the phrase 'in earth as it is in heaven', whereon she said 'Yes, and the carpets were brown, the colour of the earth. They don't have carpets in real hospitals, do they?'

That ended the stage of the Lord's Prayer to which the dream took us, and we then wonderingly looked forward to how the second half would be dealt with in future dreams and what these would reveal.

The interview ended with her mentioning a neighbour, Mrs. R, a married woman having trouble with her husband (which, as Mrs. Wright put it, was her own fault) and who, attracted by Mrs. Wright's new-found stability, had confided in her, and asked her advice.

TWELFTH AND LAST INTERVIEW

16th October

Mrs. Wright came to-day saying that she had had a dream clearly referring to Mrs. R., but possibly also to herself.

24. Dream

'I was walking along the village street and met a woman covered from head to foot with a thick shroud of brown stuff darker than the brown tissue covering the lightly veiled form seen in a former dream.[1] This figure I felt to be that of Mrs. R. She was seeking the way into a field, but, being shrouded, stumbled and could not find her way because she could not see. One of the village women, Mrs. Smart, who had a sharp tongue and a sarcastic nature, jeered at her for stumbling, and made no offer of help. But I took her by the arm and led her towards the field. There was a green hedge (possibly a privet) higher than a man's head surrounding the field, and in it a gate, through which I saw the sun shining. I led her through the gate, and just inside it there was a man, who took her from me. I looked into the field, and saw a man ploughing. He was using an old-fashioned plough, not a tractor, and was getting the field ready for sowing. It was springtime (not autumn as it is now), for he had his coat off as if the weather was warm. He was probably going to sow spring oats'.

This dream just related occurred during the night. Next morning she had a brief vision.

25. Vision

It was the same field, in which green blades of corn were now showing above the earth. She woke up thinking to herself 'A sower went forth to sow', and as soon as she had time re-read the parable of the sower in Matthew xiii.

[1] Dream-Vision 8.

There was little comment to make on this dream, except to ask whether the ploughman was in any way like the figure of her husband in Dream 3. She said it was not, and that both the ploughman and the man into whose hands she delivered the shrouded figure were quite impersonal figures.

This dream clearly marked the end of a phase. Mrs. Wright said she felt this was the case, and that for the next few weeks she must get busy with her garden, pulling the weeds and getting it ready for the winter. So we parted for the time being, wondering what the next phase, especially in Margaret's development, would be.[1]

[1] The subsequent development, both of Mrs. Wright and her daughter, are summarized in the Note on p. 96, and will be dealt with in a later volume.

BRIEF THEORETICAL DISCUSSION

and summary of the dream-process

The reader may wonder what was the nature of the process by which the results here outlined were achieved. Was it by consciously readjusting her outlook that Mrs. Wright managed so to improve both her own condition and that of those immediately depending on her or was it by some other means unknown to the ordinary man?

The answer, so far as it can be given in logical terms, is that the conscious part of the process consists not so much in an effort of will as in a redirection of attention towards psychic factors of great power with which men and women nowadays are apt to lose contact owing to a lack of understanding of the problems involved.

Certain concepts are useful as tools by means of which these powers may be assimilated into the conscious mind and so made available for the conduct of life. Analytical Psychology does not think of that vast psychic field so glibly called the 'unconscious' as being in any way homogeneous, but conceives of it as being composed of two main parts not divided by any rigid line but which are nevertheless sufficiently distinct to merit separate names. Nearest the surface is what is termed the *personal unconscious,* which differs in each individual and contains those personal contents of the psyche that were once conscious but have been repressed out of consciousness for one reason or another, together with those personal potentialities which, thwarted by misconceptions, have become turned in on themselves and so, by failing to find expression, have taken on a negative character. The chief element in this personal unconscious is what is technically called the *Shadow,* which is the mirror image of our conscious evaluation of ourselves and is commonly represented in dreams by persons of the *same sex* as the dreamer.[1] This is the personal aspect, beneath which lies

[1] In a later stage in the integration process the Shadow often appears as a guide, either to warn or help.

the deep well of what is called the *impersonal* or *collective unconscious* which contains, on the other hand, all those driving forces of which the individual can never be fully aware, including those non-personal aspirations which in religious terminology have to do with the soul. These, belonging as they do to the 'other side' of life, appear, so far as the dream symbolizes them in human form, commonly as persons of the *opposite sex*. The technical term used for this soul phenomenon thus symbolized in men's dreams by women is the Latin word *anima* meaning 'soul' or 'breath',[1] while in the case of a woman, for whom it appears as something male, it is called the *animus*. In the present dream-series, therefore, in which the dreamer is a woman, various aspects of the *Shadow* (the repressed personal side of her character) are represented by women, and those of the soul or *animus* by men.

These are the main characters in the drama dealt with in the foregoing account, a brief summary of which will help to epitomize the analytical process so far as it has progressed at this stage of Mrs. Wright's development, showing to what extent personal misconceptions which had obscured the essential pattern of the psyche were removed and its harmony thereby restored.

The series starts off with a clear adumbration of opposites by the Angel's paradoxical warning against seeking heaven in the sky where the dreamer has been brought up to seek it. This play of opposites is carried a step further in highly dramatic fashion in the first two 'pregnancy' dreams.

In the first of these (Dream 3) her soul or *animus*, here projected on to the figure of her husband, is seen lacerated, owing, as the angel had indicated by its gesture, to her putting 'the cart before the horse', in other words the husband in front of instead of behind the plough. This would be equivalent to regarding God as a vague ideal to strive towards, rather than as the cause from which all life sprang and whom it is necessary to seek first in the past—this was the meaning of the ancestral tartan representing the roots of her being. The first need in tending a plant is to see that its roots are properly cared for and

[1] Compare p. 166.

watered, since without this all care lavished on its superstructure will be without avail. In the same way, a small child must first have its body and emotions nourished before any attempt is made by transforming them to develop its soul.

In the second pregnancy dream (Dream 4) the opposites are stated more clearly still in the contrast between, on the one hand, her mistakenly idealistic striving upwards towards the mountain crest on the right (or conscious) side, and on the other hand, the real starting place represented by the green pasture to the left which must be returned to before conscious effort can build anything other than castles in the air.

Her first task was to accept the 'shadow', in her case the falsely idealistic side of herself represented in the first place by the other nurse in Dream 5, indicating the sin of personal pride which always stands in the way of real communion with the soul or *animus* here represented by the concealed lover. Being a wise woman, she did accept, and as a reward her positive *animus* then appeared to her in the form of the young bridegroom in Dream 6.

But the soul is a very terrifying thing, partaking of the numinous ambivalent quality of God. Hence the inevitable conflict introduced by the concept of fear. What was it that Mrs. Wright had 'not to fear'? She certainly did fear. We all do, for fear is a part of nature, seen at its lowest in panic, and at its highest in the fear of the Lord. What she, like all of us, needed was to learn not to be afraid of fear. It was precisely this fear of fear that she overcame in Dream 7 when the man overtook her, and fear in the physical sense became transmuted into the numinous feeling of awe, or in psychological terms the *negative* (because unconscious) *animus* became transformed into a potent *positive animus* through the conscious performance of an act of faith. This act of faith overcoming fear was repeated in Dream 9 when she sacrificed the hare and in her subsequent experience the following night; in Dream 12 in which she overcame the lonely terror of the air raid by translating it into communal worship and awe; and finally in Dream 13 in the conquest of the self-righteous conceit that she was her sister's keeper.

All this time the 'shadow' had been becoming more and more absorbed, this process reaching its peak when in Dream 8 she saw the veiled form of her naked self, and during the same week (in Dream 10) accepted the identity of her own problem with that of her daughter Margaret, expressed by the voice saying, 'Margaret and her mother may sleep together', whereby she acquired a sense of oneness with fate, while at the same time refusing in Dream 18 the false intellectual knowledge which the reverse side of her 'shadow' represented by Miss Hardacre attempted to impose.

It will be noted that the culmination of her experience—her real conversion—was represented in purely symbolical terms in the dream sequence (Dreams 9, 12, 13, 14, and 15) following the sacrifice of the hare. A point not discussed in the analysis was just why the sacrificial animal appearing in Mrs. Wright's dream should have been a hare. At that time I was not aware of the mass of extremely relevant mythology from many parts of the world dealing with the hare as a self-sacrificing animal and as a symbol of spiritual insight, which I have since summarized in Part II on *The Mythology of the Hare.* I was then aware only of the hare as one of the animals into which witches were often said to transform themselves, and as a well-known witch's 'familiar', but since the significance of this was at the moment far from clear I refrained from calling attention to it, thinking it safer to concentrate purely on the more general significance of animal sacrifice as representing the transformation of unredeemed instinct into spiritual value.

What was, at any rate, quite clear was that this sacrifice represented the conquest over some pre-Christian and therefore deeply unconscious element that joined Mrs. Wright in that kind of unconscious tangle with destructive primitive forces that is technically called negative *participation mystique*, and which invariably leads to the projection of negative psychological contents on to some object. It was equally clear that the object upon which these negative contents were fixed was Margaret, since the very next dream (Dream 10) brought the welcome announcement that 'Margaret and her mother may sleep together'. This meant that the negative contents that Mrs. Wright had previously projected upon her daughter were now withdrawn, and that she could now do her daughter nothing but good. In other words the era of negative *participation* was at an end and a new era of positive *participation mystique* had dawned. It was this message that brought the relieving bitter-sweet tears to Mrs. Wright's eyes, and it was from this moment that Margaret began to improve.

A point worth the attention of theologians is the evidence that the dream process affords with regard to the relative values of ritual symbolism and dogma. It will be noted that it was not till after the symbolic sacrifice of the hare in Dream 9, subsequently repeated by that of the Jewish butcher in Dream 15, that the intellectual question as to the nature of God arose in Dream 17. In the same way the intellectual concept of the sacred marriage between God and Man followed the much earlier emotional experience expressed in purely human terms in the union of the non-nubile bride and bridegroom in Dream 6. This precedence in time and depth sequence of feeling over thought is of fundamental importance to the whole theory and teaching of religion. The fact that feeling precedes and *underlies* and provides the dynamic force for thought is of fundamental importance to all spiritual progress. Just as the body of the unborn babe miraculously developing within its mother's womb in nine months recapitulates all the stages of biological evolution, so also does it recapitulate all psychic evolution from the amoeba to man, including man's history up to the moment when the child breaks away from the maternal matrix and first sees the light of day. This is the basis of the whole concept of the collective unconscious. The child's first act of emancipation from the matrix is birth, when it achieves individuality in the body. Its second act of emancipation is when it becomes re-born by returning to the mother in a spiritual sense through full participation in Mother Church, the mystical *body* of Christ. During the interval between birth and rebirth it once more recapitulates, this time as an individual, the psychic development of the race, and *must* follow that development planned by God for each individual as well as for the race as a whole. Short cuts to heaven do not exist, but are offered at almost every turn by religious teaching that ignores this inevitable process and thus, instead of providing a short cut to heaven, furnishes all too easy a one in the opposite direction. Premature intellectualizations provide this very nicely! The world to-day is full of theory and of a vicious kind of pseudo-spirituality that kills life because it is not founded *on* life.

The world to-day does not believe in miracles because it forestalls them with an attempted miracle that is impossible, namely, the attempt to make a child into a man or woman before he or she has been a child. How can we as adults 'become as little children' if we have never *been* children, and thus have never known what it is to be a child? To be as little children we must live through the ordinary emotions of childhood. Margaret had not done this in the fullest sense, owing to circumstances that Mrs. Wright now bitterly regrets. But there is no human life, however mistakenly begun, that cannot be retrieved. So Christ taught, and so the Church professes to believe, though through pride due to its own impatience it does not always act up to this profession. There is a maxim that says 'More haste less speed'. Those who want to make children into good Christians before they are ripe and without going through the necessary preliminary stages cut off the very spirituality they hope to impose. Spirituality cannot be imposed. It can only grow. It has, moreover, its own laws of growth, which are divine laws not depending on the logic of men.

The same laws apply moreover to the individual as apply to the race. The race did not begin by formulating dogma. Dogma was, doubtless, latent from the beginning, as the adult is latent in the child. It is the aim (and perhaps even the prime cause) but it is not the Way. Christ was the Way, but was not unduly concerned with dogma. What he did say which is relevant here is that he came not to destroy the law, but to fulfil it. He certainly therefore had the concept of growth. The law, in so far as he conceived it in human terms, was the law of the Old Testament, which had to be absorbed and transformed, which is the opposite of being destroyed, since what is destroyed cannot be either absorbed or transformed. There are two parts of the Bible, the gradual Growth from early beginnings, and the Fulfilment which was Himself Who in His own person, incarnate through the medium of the Holy Ghost, joined the two opposites God and Man.

Now both the Old Testament and anthropology show that man's early development was far from being regulated by dogma, but proceeded by a system of trial and error, always guided in the long run towards higher things, but groping its way by means of symbolic beliefs of all kinds and by ritual practices expressing and gradually crystallizing these beliefs. Nor can anyone who has lived with primitive peoples, as the writer has, have any doubt as to the vivid nature of these beliefs and practices or of their immense value as indispensable vehicles of the nascent comprehension by mankind of the truths later expressed by dogma.

Nor has any psychologist who recognizes the significance of the 'other side' of things, nor any person having true spiritual insight, any doubt that each individual has to re-live in his own psychic development the same process. The Tree of Life is strong to save, but woe betide him who plucks the fruit of the Knowledge of Good and Evil before the time is ripe. We adults have a social duty towards the child. We have plucked of the Tree of the Knowledge of Good and Evil. That is our thorn, and the thorn is the thorn of consciousness which is at once our burden and our salvation, though being the latter only if we have the wit to unite it with the Tree of Life.

Childhood is the time of the Tree of Life, and we should tamper with it only if we have a very clear idea of what we are doing. Primitive peoples know this so well that they often deny that the child has a soul before Initiation. This means that they honour the child by not attempting to tamper with its spiritual development till the time when it is finally taken from its mother and is then introduced with tribulation into the tribe's concept of Good and Evil, at which period it is deemed to have become a man. This is the real meaning of Confirmation, 'When I was a child, I spake as a child, I understood as a child, I thought as a child, but when I became a man,

I put away childish things.'[1] Saint Paul knew that a child's thought was not a man's thought, and Christ says 'Suffer little children to come unto me, for of these is the kingdom of heaven.' The kingdom of heaven is at the beginning and at the end, but it must begin at the beginning. As we grow up we overlay the kingdom with worldly cares and misconceptions. These form the upper layers of consciousness. The child lies buried ever deeper in the unconscious levels. The child has unerring instinct and thinks in symbols. The profound efficacy of play therapy proves the immense curative value wrought by the release of this symbolic activity when it has been repressed by the false superimposition on it of adult thought. I have myself known a child's life altered overnight by an adult simply listening to its dreams without even commenting on them, and so joining the child's symbolic dream material with its conscious life. So long as the dream symbolism had been repressed owing to adult misconceptions about the child's spiritual life, it was engaged in actively destroying that life, but the admission of this dream material into consciousness turned the child from a morose, self-centred, and anti-social creature into a co-operative and happy human being.

The application of this to dogma is that dogma is true as an intellectual expression of what has been previously experienced through a combination of all the four functions of sensation, feeling, thinking and intuition by the most advanced adults of our race in closest contact with God. It is the flower of all these, and it may also be—and probably is—the root. It is a static truth which, on account of its very rigidity, may in practice actually stultify growth unless handled with the utmost care and with due and reverent regard for the growing organism which, in so far as the dogma fulfils and amplifies the stage of development to which that organism has attained, expands and enriches it. But in so far as the teaching of dogma jumps too far ahead or seeks to lead by intellectual argument into formulations which the living organism is not yet sufficiently evolved to follow, it deadens or retards the very development it seeks to foster.

[1] 1 Corinthians xiii, 11.

Thus Mrs. Wright's difficulties had all been due to such an imposition of quite proper ideals too early in life before the emotional background of experience had been lived through, and the success of the analysis rested on the precise re-living by means of symbols of the experience which a too early teaching of dogma had partly killed.

The key to this aspect of her analysis lay in the phrase attributed in Dream 18 to the Vicar as representative of God saying '*You* know'. 'You' here refers to the inner knowledge of the dreamer as brought to the threshold of consciousness, not by dogma, but by the experience of her own childlike inner nature.

The rest follows automatically. In the next dream (19), to resume psychological terminology, the negative 'shadow' representing the superimposed attitudes, hostile only because they *were* superimposed, becomes reconciled to beauty, that is to say to the creative urge of Mrs. Wright's own nature; and in the next dream (20), fortified by the *animus* represented by her husband, the dreamer sees the cross descend from heaven to earth, signifying among other things the descent of truth out of the clouds to a level at which Mrs. Wright can understand it in terms of her own life-process. From here onward the dream series is mainly occupied with consolidating the gains already won.

This answers, I think, in so far as we can answer it at present, the question posed at the beginning. The first part of the analytical process is to show what we are. The issue depends on whether we can accept this new knowledge or not. The great hindrance is pride, a pride based on the belief that men know better than nature. Pride is a necessary thing, but it has to be kept in its proper place. We may well pride ourselves on our material or moral achievement, but if this pride is not balanced by true humility it will have a fall. Like true religion, analysis shows us our faults as hindrances to the attainment of our heart's desire, the Tree of Life. It is up to us whether we accept the revelation or not. Freedom is the acceptance of truth, however that truth may hurt our pride. Acceptance brings wisdom. Wisdom brings power over ourselves, and opens the way for the operation of forces that no self-will can touch. It is this kind of will power that psychological analysis aims to reinforce, the will to submit one's personal will to the pattern of life which is the will of God, whose service is perfect freedom, freedom to act, live and love without the trammels of misconception based on false ideals. God has two aspects. On the one hand he includes all the forces of nature striving for life against every obstacle. On the other hand he is the Moral Law of which the purpose is to control nature. To serve God is to serve Him, not by opposing nature, but by transforming it in obedience to its own hidden laws which it is the purpose of psychology as the handmaiden of religion to reveal. Religion means a joining of these two principles. There is nothing that man cannot achieve within the limits of human frailty, will he but recognize that every material or moral advance opens beneath his feet a chasm of outraged nature which, if he ignore it, will drag him down; but which, if he give it due honour, will, transformed by this act of faith, prove an inexhaustible well of inner knowledge (the wisdom of the serpent) capable of fortifying him against all dangers, by enabling both sides of him to attain equal balance for the successful conduct of life.

Nor is this a selfish quest for purely individual salvation, for just as the branches of forest trees intermingle, so also do their roots. The psyche, which in the conscious is self-contained, also has roots that interpenetrate with those of others, whether we will it or not, and, nature seeking always a balance, increase of poise anywhere affects the whole circle in which we live, witness the family circle of Mrs. Wright.

Everything depends, not on the amount of will power available, but on its direction. Will power is fettered only when occupied with the manifest content. Free will is that which results from a recognition of the opposite or mirror-image of the manifest cast up out of the unconscious depths, and, recognizing it, obeys. The difficulty is, of course, to see it, and where formal religion may fail to reveal the inner light through lack of recognition of the individual way by which each one of us must find his own salvation within the framework of the universal redemptive process, there Analytical Psychology may help, always hoping that one day religion may once more be broadened and deepened, as in the early days of Christianity, to embrace the wayward path traced by the prodigal who reached the goal no less surely than his less wayward brother.

Perhaps a word may be put in here for science, for while modern Christianity tends to teach faith as a duty, Analytical Psychology has arrived at a similar faith through that same process of inductive reasoning by which the best scientists work, the main difference between this and the other sciences being that it applies methods hitherto used exclusively for the examination of material nature, to the nature of spirit. Analytical Psychology thus claims to have a foot in both camps, for while on the one hand it works in the same field of collective symbolism as does religion, on the other it does so with a sense of inquiry into these mysteries that emboldens its followers to think of it as the first modest attempt at a Science of Introversion, by means of which they hope that one day medicine, philosophy and religion may once more, as of old, find common ground for the pursuit of common aims.

SUBSEQUENT DEVELOPMENT OF MARGARET

The reader may well wonder, what, in the three years' interval since the analysis ended, has become of Mrs. Wright and her daughter, and of the aunt to whom so much of Margaret's apparent trouble was due. I say *apparent* trouble, because the sequel has been yet one more demonstration of the truth that God sends evil that good may come, though good does not come unless we know how to find it. This doctrine of the 'positive purpose of evil' has been amply vindicated in Margaret's case, no less than in her mother's.

After the last interview described in this book, which took place on the 16th of October 1940, I saw nothing of the Wright family for almost a year apart from a few fleeting calls at their village, in the course of other duties, to inquire how things were going on. Mrs. Wright showed every sign of continued well-being, and Margaret slowly continued to improve. After the lapse of just under a year, that is to say on the 8th October 1941, Mrs. Wright came to see me to report progress, and told me three outstanding dreams that had somewhat puzzled her but which she felt were important. These dreams, which will be published in a later volume, were of quite a different character from those hitherto recounted, and all pointed to the continued operation of the redemptive process on a considerably deeper level than she had hitherto plumbed. As was the case with her former dream about the hare, one of these dreams raised issues of a historico-mythological nature that at the time I was quite unable to fathom, but which I have since investigated and which I hope to discuss in a third volume completing this series.

Nevertheless, though conscious understanding lagged behind, the dreams had their effect in maintaining her contact with the healing forces welling up out of the collective unconscious and so helping her on her way.

After this brief interlude, I had no further contact with the family till, in April of the following year (1942) the manuscript for this book was accepted for publication and the publishers asked me to write a postscript describing the state of affairs in the Wright family, at an interval of what was then a year and a half after the formal analysis had ended. This proved a notable date, for from this renewed contact sprang a new phase in the development of the whole situation remarkable enough in itself and with possibilities still unforeseen.

Mrs. Wright then said that her dream-life had settled down into a rhythmical pattern consisting of alternating periods of intense dreaming, which, far from interfering with the normal activities of everyday life, enriched and intensified them, and were then followed by fallow periods in which the insight gained from her most recent dream-series was assimilated and made available for practical use.

I spent several days with long intervals between them (owing to wartime difficulties of transport) analysing the contents of the latest of such dream-series, and in August left for my brief annual holiday in Cornwall. While there, I had a letter from her saying that Margaret was about to be called up for National Service, and asking me, as Margaret was still quite unable to fend for herself, what she should do. A medical colleague who is a psychiatric expert kindly took the matter in hand and, after examining her, obtained exemption for her on the grounds that she was a High Grade Mental Defective. Mrs. Wright, in writing to thank me for having arranged the interview and expressing her gratitude for the sympathetic and understanding way in which the psychiatrist had handled the matter, added, 'I am sure you will be delighted to know that Margaret is doing very well and is very bright and happy, and not the Margaret that we used to know'.

I little suspected all that was behind these words, for, though I had every confidence that Margaret would improve greatly, I had not expected the degree of improvement which, on my return, I actually found. The above-mentioned letter reached me on the 8th of August. It was not till I had returned home and till Mrs. Wright had found time to come and see me that I learnt, on the 8th of September 1942, almost two years since the mother's formal analysis ended, the real extent of what had happened.

She told me that during the past month Margaret had completely altered. The first indication of this was when Margaret had started having daylight visions which were in effect the continuation and extension in a still deeper sense of Mrs. Wright's own night-time dreams. These visions quickly developed into what can only be termed 'second sight' combined with knowledge of certain aspects of her mother's past history obtained through visionary and auditory contact with her mother's father, who had died when Margaret herself was only three years old. This visionary perception of her maternal grandfather soon became merged with the traditional figure of Bonnie Prince Charlie who for the loyal Northern Irish Wright family with its Scottish descent was a legendary hero, and this concept in turn merged into or was replaced by a higher concept still, that of the Heavenly Father, under whose direct guidance she now believes herself to be.

A further development is that, without prompting of any

kind, Margaret has now taken to interpreting her mother's dreams, and even knows quite often what her mother has dreamt before she is told. She has, alongside this, acquired what her mother regards as a nascent power for spiritual healing, which it is too early yet to comment on, apart from the brief statement that the barrier of so-called mental deficiency that has cut her off from so many of the good things of this world, has had also as its positive purpose that of protecting her from many of its illusions, and especially from one of the subtlest illusions of all, namely, the belief that disease of the body is anything other than a disguised disease of the soul.

A detailed account of the mother's dream-process leading up to this result and of Margaret's own development will be described in the later volume to which reference has already been made, and into which, on account of the large quantity of new material, the postscript originally asked for by the publisher has now been expanded.

Part Two

THE MYTHOLOGY OF THE HARE

INTRODUCTORY

In any analysis there are certain key dreams which mark conspicuous turning-points in the dreamer's development. One such key dream dreamt by Mrs. Wright was, as we have already seen, Dream 9 in which she sacrificed the Hare. It will be remembered, however, that the form which the analysis of this dream took was one applicable to any kind of animal sacrifice, as representing the transformation of untutored instinct, through sacrifice, into spiritual value. Mrs. Wright being a devout Christian, I used the simile of the sacrifice of the Lamb to bring home its essential meaning. This treatment of the dream was efficacious beyond expectation, but left out of account the whole question of just why the animal chosen by her dream-mind to sacrifice was not a lamb but a hare.

This was because I was myself at that time completely ignorant of the immense role the hare has in fact played as a symbol in the complex mythological systems of many nations, including that of our own ancestors.

It was in fact not till more than two years later, and after the remarkable further development both of Mrs. Wright and of her daughter Margaret, referred to on page 96 and to be described fully in a later volume, that I became aware of the peculiar significance of the hare in the world's mythological systems, and of the reason why just that animal and no other offered itself for sacrifice at this juncture in Mrs. Wright's dream-life. The evidence, culled from religious records of some of the world's most ancient civilizations and from the folk-lore of some of the less advanced, is so striking, not only as an explanation in general terms of why Mrs. Wright's unconscious should have chosen precisely this symbol, but also on account of the light it sheds on certain details of the dream that had so far been only tentatively interpreted, that I feel no hesitation in setting the facts before the reader, partly in order to elucidate the dream material still further, and partly as one example among many of how the dream-mind is in fact a storehouse of ancient symbolic wisdom unsuspected by the most learned scholars of our time, and also, incidentally, quite unknown consciously to the dreamer.

THE HARE AS ARCHETYPE

In other words, the Hare is an Archetype in the sense used by Jung, who, after describing the personal unconscious as the repository of those purely personal experiences that have been repressed, says: 'Yet this personal unconscious appears to rest upon a deeper layer that does not derive from personal experience and achievement but is inborn. This deeper layer I call the *collective unconscious*. I have chosen the term 'collective' because this part of the unconscious is not individual, but universal; in contrast to the personal psyche, it has contents and modes of behaviour that are more or less the same everywhere and in all individuals. The collective unconscious, so far as we know, is self-identical in all Western men and thus constitutes a psychic foundation, superpersonal in its nature, that is present in every one of us. . . . The contents of the personal unconscious constitute the personal and private side of psychic life. They are chiefly the so-called *feeling-toned complexes*. The contents of the collective unconscious, on the other hand, are the so-called *archetypes*.

The term 'archetype' derives from Saint Augustine, and deals with 'ancient or, better yet, with primordial types—that is to say, with images impressed upon the mind since of old. . . . Primitive tribal lore treats of archetypes that are modified in a particular way . . . , changed into conscious formulas [*sic*] that are taught according to tradition, generally in the form of esoteric teaching. . . .

'Another well-known expression of the archetype is myth and fable. But here also we are dealing with conscious and specifically moulded forms that have been handed on relatively unchanged through long periods of time.'[1]

An archetype 'designates the psychic content that has as yet been subjected to no conscious treatment and so represents an immediate, psychic actuality'.[2] Thus, 'myths are related to psychic happening',[3] and, as such, continue to present themselves actively in dreams to express and actually bring about what the conscious mind alone is incapable either of understanding or of achieving.

Those who have read the foregoing narrative will have recognized already a number of such archetypes, which are familiar to them through their common heritage of Christian symbolism. Such were the Angel of Vision 1, the deep water and green pastures of Dream 4, the 'opener of the way' symbolized by the Vicar in several dreams, the various Christ symbols occurring throughout the dream-series, the sacrificial motives adumbrating the crucifixion in Dreams 9 and 15, the number 3 representing the initiation process in Dream 12, the bread-crumbs representing the Host in Dream 13, the Cross represented by the descending aeroplane in Dream 20, the palms of victory in Dream 23, the ploughing of the field in Dream 24, and the appearance of the growing corn in Vision 25, and many others.

The most efficacious archetype of all, however, and of greatest import perhaps for the very reason that archetypes have their strongest effect when not watered down by vain repetition, was one that is not recognized as a symbol at all by official Christendom, namely the Hare. And since this archetype has not, so far as I know, yet been taken note of by psychologists, I propose now to trace its history in such measure as is possble from available sources.

Since this inquiry covers four continents and includes mythological beliefs current in India, China, Ancient Egypt, and in

[1] C. G. Jung, *The Integration of the Personality*, London, 1940, pp. 52, 53.

[2] ibid., p. 54. [3] ibid., p. 55.

the classical periods of Greece and Rome, some of which are still held while others are recoverable only from ancient texts, and in North America where beliefs strikingly similar in essentials were held till the advent of the white man by the Algonkin and by the Aztecs of Mexico, as well as modern folk-tales from many parts of Africa and a mass of medieval and modern folk-lore from Europe, it has not been possible except in certain cases to establish anything like a historical sequence, and the aim has been rather to chronicle the various beliefs regarding the hare wherever they occur, and to attempt tentatively to interpret them in a psychologico-religious sense.

This task has been the easier in that, as the mass of evidence unfolded itself, the beliefs accompanying the use of the hare as a mythological symbol showed such remarkable similarity throughout the world as to leave no doubt whatever about its fundamental meaning. It would be anticipating the evidence to describe here just what the various gradations of meaning are, which are to be found summarized on pages 222–9. The full flavour of the psychologico-religious process cannot, however, be communicated by means of conclusions only, since psychology does not consist in cut-and-dried and pigeon-holed conclusions, but in a living growth, which, as in the case of the foregoing analysis of Mrs. Wright, can be appreciated only by following the facts in the order in which they present themselves.

The value of a knowledge of archetypes is well illustrated by the fact that, since this study of the Mythology of the Hare was completed, I have in daily practice come across many occurrences of the hare-symbol in the dreams of other patients, the significance of which I should otherwise largely have missed, all showing similar features, through the resulting understanding of which the patients have greatly benefited and their comprehension of the forces involved in the individuation process has been correspondingly deepened. It would be out of place to give these here, and I have therefore recorded a selection of them in Part III, and will begin this inquiry into the mythology by reminding the reader of the relevant features of Mrs.

Wright's Dream 9 of sacrificing the Hare from which it started, and from which it will be seen, after the inquiry has been concluded, that the Hare is indeed a living archetype still wielding its old power in the deeper levels of the psyche of Modern Man.

EXTRACT FROM MRS. WRIGHT'S DREAM OF SACRIFICING THE HARE

It will be remembered how, after approaching, in company with her daughter Margaret, a square house near her former home in Ireland, over ground covered with snow, and how Margaret then went in at the front door, the dream in Mrs. Wright's words went on:

'Then I went round alone into the kitchen at the back of the house. Inside there was a great light and everything was as white as it was outside, though how the snow got in there I cannot tell.

'There were people inside too, and there, in a white bowl with a little water in it, was a live hare. Someone told me I had got to kill it. This seemed a terrible thing to do, but I had to do it. I picked up the knife (an ordinary kitchen knife) which seemed to have been placed ready for me and which was lying in the water inside the bowl beside the hare, and with a feeling of horror I started cutting into the fur and through to the skin beneath. I had to cut the hare straight down the middle of the back, and started to do this, but my hand trembled so much that, as I cut down, the knife slipped away from the straight line, and ended up by cutting obliquely into the hare's haunch.

'I felt awful doing this, but the hare never moved and did not seem to mind.

'Though the ground outside was covered with snow, we had left no footmarks on it.'

It will be remembered also that Mrs. Wright later (p. 63) 'told me of the look of extreme satisfaction and trust that had been in the hare's eyes as it looked back at her when she plunged the knife into its back', and that this made her think of the willing sacrifice of Christ.

INTRODUCTORY

THE HARE AS SACRIFICIAL ANIMAL
THE GROWTH OF SYMBOLS

Since Mrs. Wright draws her immediate cultural heritage from the British Isles, and lives in an epoch in which for almost twenty centuries all symbolic wisdom has been suspect other than that sanctioned by a Church who regards herself as the exclusive channel of divine revelation and is therefore highly suspicious if not actually jealous of unmediated religious experience, it is not surprising that such symbolic wisdom should often present itself under the guise of pure superstition. I will therefore reverse the proverbial order and proceed from the apparently ridiculous to the sublime, by first quoting the well-known memorandum of Dr. White Kenneth. Bearing in mind the willing sacrifice of the hare in Mrs. Wright's dream, this memorandum is of no little interest in that it asserts that 'when one keeps a hare alive, and feedeth him till he have occasion to eat him, if he telles before he killes him that he will doe so, the hare will thereupon be found dead, having killed himself'.[1]

This apparently fantastic statement would at first sight appear to bear no possible relation to fact until we begin to compare it with other legends from more than one part of the world in which the hare figures as sacrificing itself, always in a very peculiar way. That is to say, that the special way in which it sacrifices itself is invariably, so far as I know, by leaping into a fire. Such an act recalls that of the phoenix, the mythical bird that burnt itself, whereon a new and rejuvenated bird sprang from the ashes. This motive of rejuvenation is so applicable to Mrs. Wright's case that it is worth while considering in the first place how such a story about the hare voluntarily leaping into the fire can ever have been invented, and in the second place the meaning of some of the legends that have grown up around this theme.

Now it is a truism that no symbol has ever been invented; that is to say that no one has ever successfully 'thought out' a symbol and used it to express a truth. Such artificial efforts

[1] Aubrey's *Remains of Gentilisme*, pp. 101–2, quoted by W. C. Black, *The Folk-lore Journal*, vol. i, p. 86.

are doomed to failure, and never succeed in drawing to themselves the power of real symbols, since they are no more than similes based on a mental process that never touches the depths of human personality. Such are the 'didactic' similes we know so well and react against so wisely. True symbols, on the other hand, are those that leap to mind without conscious effort. Symbols of this kind vary immensely as to their applicability, some being of purely individual significance, while others have a far deeper meaning. Those that go to build up mythology and folk-lore are those that leap simultaneously to many minds, or, being first expressed by one find ready soil in others, so that they become a common language. Some symbols are universal, such as the four elements, earth, water, fire, air. Others are more restricted, such as the particular symbols of the various world religions, like the cross or crescent, the Mithraic bull or the Jewish and Christian lamb. No one invented them. They grew out of the life of the people, and drew their symbolic value from what men thought to be their chief characteristics, the bull from its procreative power and the lamb from its gentle innocence. In this way the Egyptian scarab drew its symbolic value from its prolificness, and its habit of rolling its eggs in dung pellets that resembled the sun, the hawk from its swift soaring flight symbolizing power ascending upwards towards the sky, and its successor the dove from its soft sweetness symbolizing the power of love descending from heaven to earth. Other characteristics doubtless joined to these to produce other symbolic attributes, for no symbol is a simple thing.

The Hare also has more than one attribute, as we shall see, but one attribute well known to all farmers is its habit, when scrub is being burnt, of not running like a rabbit does before the fire comes too close, but of clinging till the last moment to its hiding-place until the flames close in on it, and then wildly rushing out with fur blazing so that it burns to death.[1]

[1] Compare among other references the account given by R. R. Clarke, *In Breckland Wilds*, Cambridge, 1937, p. 16, of a heath fire, in which he writes of 'a hare which remained in its form so long that when it at length fled its fur was ablaze. Maddened by the pain it tore off at tremendous speed, doubtless to die a lingering death somewhere among the bracken.'

This, doubtless, is the material or physical fact that gave rise to the notion of the hare as a willing victim leaping into the fire. The symbolic meaning of this is another matter, which will be discussed after we have briefly noted some of the legends in which it occurs.

THE HARE IN INDIA

THE BUDDHA, IN ONE OF HIS REBIRTHS, TAKES THE FORM OF A HARE AND IN A FERVOUR OF RENUNCIATION LEAPS INTO A FIRE. THE HARE IS UNSCATHED AND ITS IMAGE IS TRANSLATED INTO THE MOON

The best-known of such legends is probably that according to which the Buddha himself, in one of his rebirths before attaining full Buddhahood, took the form of a hare. The following account is an abridged translation, by the present writer, of this tale as rendered into German by Elsie Lüders[1] with certain modifications taken from the English translation of the same tale as edited by Professor E. B. Cowell.[2] It is one of the so-called Jātaka stories forming part of the lore of Southern (Hinayana) Buddhism, which are said to have been told by Buddha himself of his own earlier existences while still a Bodhisattva[3] (that is to say, a being that is destined to develop, in a future existence, into a Buddha), and contains one of the numerous references to the belief held in many parts of the world of the connection with the hare and the moon, a connection which will be explained later.

The tale relates how the Bodhisattva was in one of his incarnations reborn as a hare, and had three friends, a monkey, a jackal, and an otter. This 'wise hare' was in the habit of instructing his three friends in the teaching that 'a man should give alms, obey the law, and observe the regulations regarding the keeping of holy day'. One day the Bodhisattva looked at the moon, and seeing from this that the following day was a holy day,[4] said to the other three, 'To-morrow is a holy

[1] *Buddhistische Märchen*, translated by Elsie Lüders, Jena, 1921.

[2] *The Jātaka*, or stories of the Buddha's former births. Translated from the Pāli by various hands, under the editorship of Professor E. B. Cowell, Cambridge, 1895–1907, vol. iii, no. 316.

[3] This is the Sanskrit form of the word which in Pāli is spelt Bodhisatta. Its literal meaning is 'one who is on the way to the attainment of perfect knowledge'.

[4] Buddhism observes the new moon and full moon as holy days.

day. Observe it in that you make an oath to obey the law. . . . If therefore a beggar comes to you, give him of your food and do not think of eating till he has fed.' Each of the three animals then managed by trickery to steal from some human being its appropriate foodstuff, the otter some fish, the jackal two meat puddings, a newt, and a bottle of sour milk, and the monkey a bunch of mangoes. But the Bodhisattva (in the shape of the hare) thought to himself, "I will not bother to get any food for myself till the time comes. . . . If a beggar comes to me, I will give him the flesh of my own body.' Through the power of his renunciation, however, the stone seat covered with a white woollen blanket, on which the god Sakka[1] habitually sits in his heaven, began to grow very hot. On turning over in his mind the reason for this heat, Sakka at last perceived its cause, and decided to put the king of the hares to the test. After appearing in the form of a Brahman to the other three animals in turn, and being offered food by them but having refused it, he went to the hare, who asked, 'Why do you stand here?' The Brahman answered, as he had done to the others, 'Wise one, if I could get something to eat I would observe the holy day and so be able to fulfil my priestly duties'. The Bodhisattva, delighted at his words, answered: 'Brahman, thou hast done well to come to me for food. Now I will make you a gift such as I have never given before. But, following the law, you must destroy no life. Go, friend, fetch wood and make a fire, and tell me when it is ready. I will offer myself by leaping into the fire. But when my flesh is roasted, you must eat it, so that you can then go and fulfil your priestly duties.'

Then with his supernatural power Sakka created a fire of burning logs, and told the Bodhisattva. Then arose the hare

[1] Sakka is the king of the gods. *Sakka* is the Pāli form of the Sanskrit *Sakra*, 'strong', 'powerful', the usual epithet of Indra. Early Buddhism did not believe in gods, but reckoned with the fact that simple people could not do without them. The stone seat on which Sakka sits always grows hot by magic whenever an earthly being, through the power of its penance, or renunciation, or virtue, endangers Sakka's position as the king of the gods. Sakka feels the heat through the blanket and descends in disguise to put some temptation in the way of the pious being in order to save his own position.

from its form of *kusa* grass,[1] and said, 'If any small insects are in my hair they should not be destroyed', saying which he shook himself three times (so as to let them escape) and, offering his whole body as a free gift, leapt up, and, like a royal swan alighting on a lotus bed, threw himself in an ecstasy of joy into the burning fire. But the fire was powerless to heat so much as the pores of a hair on his body. It was as if he had leapt into snow. Then he turned to Sakka, and said, 'Brahman, the fire which thou hast made is too cold. . . . What is the meaning of this?' The other said, 'Wise one, I am no Brahman, I am Sakka, who came to put thy virtue to the test.' The Bodhisattva then bellowed like a lion,[2] 'though not only thee but the whole world should test my generosity, it would not find me unwilling'. Sakka replied, 'Wise one, thy virtue shall be known for a whole aeon.' Then he squeezed the mountain, and with the essence thus extracted he painted the hare's image on the moon's disk. Then Sakka returned to his heavenly seat. The four wise ones continued to live in amity, fulfilling the law, observing the holy days, and each fared according to his merits.

The Hare-Moon as symbol of Intuition, signifying the transformation of unredeemed instinct into spiritual power

This legend is one of a large number found in many parts of the world, in which the hare is connected with the moon, and in particular it is identified with the markings on the face of the moon, and becomes the 'Hare in the Moon', corresponding to our own 'Man in the Moon'.

It may be wondered what the connection between the hare and the moon can be. The answer lies, in my opinion, in the character common to both of apparent 'surprise' or 'fickleness'. The moon is traditionally 'fickle' in that it never appears two

[1] The word 'form' is of course the technical term for a hare's bed. *Kusa* grass is the sacred grass (*Poa cynosuroides*) of Brahmanic ritual since Vedic times.

[2] The 'lion's roar' is a conventional expression sometimes used in Buddhist literature for recital of the Buddhist doctrine. For this and other footnotes to this tale I am indebted to the kindness of Dr. H. Meinhard.

nights running in the same place or even in the same shape, and the same characteristics of surprise and variability are traditionally and actually associated with the hare, which pops up here and there among the shrubby undergrowth of woodland country or from the tall grass in which it has made its form, to be gone next moment, fleetly running till it appears again unexpectedly in some quite different direction. This is of course the reason why, in Europe and elsewhere, the hare is so closely associated with witches, who are popularly believed to have a similar habit of appearing from nowhere, and of riding on broomsticks at great speed from one place to another. This association of hares with witches will be discussed later in greater detail,[1] and is mentioned here only because, whatever witches may really be like, they are undoubtedly accredited in popular fancy (which is what myths are made of) with a strong negative intuition of a kind that knows just when, where, and how to carry out their devilish mission. This is of course a thoroughly negative aspect of intuition, due to the repression of witchcraft and its consequently being driven to practise only in secret, owing to which, though there are white witches as well as black, witchcraft came to be regarded as wholly bad.

Now the moon also is *par excellence* a symbol of intuition,[2] that is to say of the 'light in the darkness' which guides the

[1] See pp. 194 sqq.

[2] The word 'intuition' is here and throughout this work used in Jung's sense to designate a definite psychological function, which he deals with at some length on pp. 461–8, 505–10, and 567–9 of his *Psychological Types* (translated by H. Godwin Baynes), London, 1924.

In his general definition on pp. 567–8 he describes it as 'that psychological function which transmits perceptions *in an unconscious way*. Everything, whether outer or inner objects or their associations, can be the object of this perception. Intuition has this peculiar quality: it is neither sensation, nor feeling, nor intellectual conclusion, although it may appear in any of these forms. Through intuition any one content is presented as a complete whole, without our being able to explain or discover in what way this content has been arrived at. Intuition is a kind of instinctive apprehension, irrespective of the nature of its contents. Like sensation it is an *irrational* perceptive

traveller through the limitless spaces of that uncharted country which, for want of a better word, psychologists refer to as the Unconscious. Like all psychological functions, intuition may be used either for good or evil. It always appears as it were, 'out of the blue' in the form of complete certainty, a certainty that may bear the mark of highest spiritual knowledge, or on the other hand of machiavellian destructiveness.

There is no doubt which of the two is implied in the tale of the Buddha just quoted, which deals with precisely the same problem as was implicit in Mrs. Wright's dream, namely the transformation of untamed instinct into spiritual value. In Mrs. Wright's dream the hare representing instinct was a willing victim. The Buddhist story also demonstrates the deep truth, with which psychological findings agree, that instinct *wants* to transform itself into spirit, and will do so (as it has in fact done in the history of the human race) if not hampered by false ideology. This is of course the prime lesson to be drawn from Mrs. Wright's history, namely that when the artificial

function. Its contents, like those of sensation, have the character of being given, in contrast to the 'derived' or 'deduced' character of feeling and thinking contents. Intuitive cognition, therefore, possesses an intrinsic character of certainty and conviction which enabled Spinoza to uphold the *scientia intuitiva* as the highest form of cognition. Intuition has this quality in common with sensation, whose physical foundation is the ground and origin of its certitude. In the same way, the certainty of intuition depends upon a definite psychic matter of fact, of whose origin and state of readiness, however, the subject was quite unconscious.'

'In contrast to sensation, which deals with things as they are, [p. 463], intuition tries to encompass the greatest *possibilities*, since only through the awareness of possibilities is *intuition* fully satisfied. Intuition seeks to discover possibilities in the objective situation; hence as a mere tributary function (viz., when not in a position of priority) it is also the instrument which, in the presence of a hopelessly blocked situation, works automatically towards the issue, which no other function could discover.'

Intuition may be extraverted or introverted. Extraverted intuition is (p. 464) 'orientated by the object', but (p. 505) 'intuition, in the introverted attitude, is directed upon the inner object, a term we might justly apply to the elements of the unconscious. For the relation of inner objects to consciousness is entirely analogous to that of outer

clutter of mistaken thinking is removed, this process follows as automatically as the sun rises at dawn, the flowers bloom in the spring, or death follows life, and as death itself is followed by new life.

Fire the transforming medium

In all cases, however, some transforming influence has to be at work. In the case of the sun rising it is the movement of the earth, in the case of the flower it is the spring. In the case of the hare in this story, it is the fire. In this tale there are two kinds of fire, the internal fire of faith leading to the renunciation which so heated the stone seat that it activated the god, and the external fire of burning logs which the god made, into which the hare leapt.

Fire is, of course, one of the prime transformers. It transforms cold into heat, it transforms raw food into digestible meat, it breaks down compounds into their respective parts, and above all in spiritual language it is the fire that burns but does not

objects, although theirs is a psychological and not a physical reality. Inner objects appear to the intuitive perception as subjective images of things, which, though not met with in external experience, really determine the contents of the unconscious.'

In this way (p. 506) 'introverted intuition perceives all the background processes of consciousness with almost the same distinctness as extraverted sensation senses outer objects. For intuition, therefore, the unconscious images attain to the dignity of things or objects.'

Since it is with this introverted intuition that the mythological images dealt with in this book are concerned, one further quotation will give perhaps a pointer to what is to follow. As Jung says on pp. 507–8, 'Introverted intuition apprehends the images which arise from the *a priori*, i.e. the inherited foundations of the unconscious mind. These archetypes, whose innermost nature is inaccessible to experience, represent the precipitate of psychic functioning of the whole ancestral line, i.e. the heaped-up, or pooled, experiences of organic existence in general, a million times repeated, and condensed into types. Hence, in these archetypes all experiences are represented which since primeval time have happened on this planet. Their archetypal distinctness is the more marked, the more frequently and intensely they have been experienced. The archetype would be—to borrow from Kant—the noumenon of the image which intuition perceives and, in perceiving, creates.'

consume. So God appeared to Moses in the burning bush, and so Shadrach, Meshach, and Abednego passed unscathed through the fiery furnace prepared for them by Nebuchadnezzar, a fire so hot that it consumed those who cast them into it, but, as for those three, the king saw them come out 'upon whose bodies the fire had no power, nor was an hair of their head singed'.[1] So also with the Buddha in the form of a hare, 'the fire was powerless to heat so much as the pores of a hair on his body'. This means that the material body had been transformed into a spiritual one capable of resisting all evil or disintegration.

But fire has one more characteristic feature. It produces smoke, and smoke ascends to heaven. This is the meaning of burnt sacrifice, namely, that the smell and spiritual essence thereof ascend to heaven. Burnt sacrifice during the daytime therefore ascends to the sun, the sun ruling the social order and conscious life. But this is not Buddha's intention. Buddha desires Nirvana, that pregnant nothingness that is of the spirit only. So he sacrifices himself to the moon.

Sakka is one of the names given to Indra, who as a sky-god of lightning, thunder, and rain, and also as war-god, could be compared with the German Wotan or the Norse Thor, and with the more terrible aspects of Jove such as Jupiter Fulgur or Jupiter Tonans. Indra is moreover one of the eight guardians of the world whose place is in the East, which will be found to be of interest when we come to examine the connection of the hare with Easter.[2] It is presumably in his capacity of god of lightning that he spontaneously kindles the fire in which the Hare-Buddha sacrifices himself. It is thus the violent Sakka to whom the hare offers its body to eat, while he translated its spiritualized aspect associated with the self-sacrificing Buddha into the moon.

Further tales regarding the Hare-Buddha and the Moon

In this story, it is true, the hare's image is only painted on the moon, but in another version the hare is itself put in the moon. There is a tale told in Ceylon of how Buddha was wandering through a wood and met a hare, whom he told, in

[1] Daniel ix. 27. [2] See pp. 170 sqq.

answer to his question, that he was poor and hungry. 'Art thou hungry?' said the hare; 'make a fire then; then kill, cook, and eat me.' Buddha made a fire, and the hare leapt into it. Then Buddha exercised his skill as a god, rescued the benevolent hare from the flames, and placed it in the moon.[1] Here it is not the Buddha who changes himself into a hare, but it is for him that the hare sacrifices itself. The roles are reversed again in the statement that 'it was into a hare that the highest lord of heaven, according to the Mongolian belief, changed himself to feed a hungry traveller, and does not therefore the hare sit in the moon?' In all these versions it is clear that the hare represents the material part, or unredeemed instinct, of the Buddha, Bodhisattva, or god which is transformed into spirit by being translated to the moon, whence it shines down to earth in the form of divine intuition.

Steiner quotes yet another version, this time in the form of a Kalmuck legend to the effect that 'in the moon there lives a hare; it came there because the Buddha sacrificed himself and the spirit of the earth himself painted the picture of the hare upon the moon. The great truth is here expressed of the Bodhisattva who became Buddha and sacrificed himself, bestowing upon humanity, for its nourishment, the content of his own being, so that it now rays forth from the hearts of men into the world.'[2]

FOLK-TALES ILLUSTRATING THE HARE'S INTUITIVE FACULTY

The theme is taken up in innumerable folk-tales, in which the hare's intuitive faculty is shown in his ready wit and power of triumphing over the sheer weight of material might.

One of these clearly indicates the victory of intuition, as represented by the hare in conjunction with the moon, over

[1] W. G. Black, 'The Hare in Folk-lore,' *Folk-lore Journal*, vol. i, p. 88.

[2] *The Gospel of Saint Luke*, by Rudolf Steiner, translated by G. Metaxa, London, 1935, pp. 71–2. I am indebted to Mrs. Marcia A. B. Dodwell for calling my attention to this.

brute strength and the power of earth as represented by the elephant, or, in other words, of spirit over matter. It runs:

Tale of the Elephants and the Hares

'There is a great lake abounding in water, called Chandrasaras [which means Moon Lake], and on its bank there lived a king of the hares, named Śilīmukha. Now, once on a time, a leader of a herd of elephants, named Chaturdanta, came there to drink water, because all the other reservoirs of water were dried up in the drought that prevailed. Then many of the hares, who were subjects of that king, were trampled to death by Chaturdanta's herd, while entering the lake. When that monarch of the herd had departed, the hare-king, Śilīmukha, being grieved, said to a hare named Vijaya in the presence of others: "Now that the lord of elephants has tasted the water of this lake, he will come here again and again, and utterly destroy us all, so think of some expedient in this case. Go to him, and see if you have any artifice which will suit the purpose or not. For you know business and expedients, and are an ingenious orator. And in all cases in which you have been engaged the result has been fortunate."

'When dispatched with these words, the hare was pleased, and went slowly on his way. And following up the track of the herd he overtook that elephant-king and saw him, and being determined somehow or other to have an interview with the mighty beast, the wise hare climbed up to the top of a rock, and said to the elephant: "I am the ambassador of the moon, and this is what the god says to you by my mouth: 'I dwell in a cool lake named Chandrasaras; there dwell hares whose king I am, and I love them well, and thence I am known to men as the cool-rayed and the hare-marked; now thou hast defiled that lake and slain those hares of mine. If thou doest that again, thou shalt receive thy due recompense from me.' "

'When the king of the elephants heard this speech of the crafty hare he said in his terror: "I will never do so again: I must show respect to the awful moon-god." The hare said: "So come, my friend, I pray, and we will show him to you." After saying this, the hare led the king of elephants to the lake and showed him the reflection of the moon in the water. When the lord of the herd saw that, he bowed before it timidly at a distance, oppressed with awe, and never came there again. And Śilīmukha, the king of the hares, was present, and witnessed the whole transaction, and after honouring that hare, who went as an ambassador, he lived there in security.'[1]

This tale represents the elephant (earth) as bowing awe-struck before the reflection of the moon which symbolizes intuition. The elephant was wise in that it recognized a superior power.

The Lion and the Hare

The lion, in another story, was not so wise, but, as the following account shows, instead of seeing and honouring the moon, saw only his own reflection and was, in psychological jargon, therefore devoured by his Shadow.

[1] 'The Elephants and the Hares', in *The Ocean of Story*, London, 1924, translated by C. H. Tawney, vol. i, 121 BB. Dr. Meinhard has kindly called my attention to the fact that this story in which the elephants are represented as oppressed with numinous awe of the moon, is quoted by A. W. von Schlegel in *Indische Bibliothek*, vol. i (Bonn, 1820), pp. 216 sq. He mentions that the same motive—elephants worshipping the moon—is also related by the elder Pliny, *Historia naturalis*, liber viii, cap. i: 'In the wooded hill country of Mauretania, at the appearance of the new moon, the herds of elephants come down to a certain river, called Aurilo; they cleanse themselves by solemnly splashing themselves with water; and after having thus saluted the celestial luminary, they return to their forests.'

Another tale connecting hares with water and also faintly echoing the hare's efforts at self-sacrifice, though from a very different angle, is Aesop's tale of 'The Hares and the Frogs', according to which 'the Hares, oppressed with a sense of their own exceeding timidity, and weary of the perpetual alarm to which they were exposed, with one accord determined to put an end to themselves and their troubles by jumping from a lofty precipice into a deep lake below. As they scampered off in a very numerous body to carry out their resolve, the Frogs lying on the banks of the lake heard the noise of their feet, and rushed helter-skelter to the deep water for safety. On seeing the rapid disappearance of the Frogs, one of the Hares cried out to his companions: "Stay, my friends, do not do as you intended; for you now see that other creatures who yet live are more timorous than ourselves.'"

'There was in a certain forest a lion, who was invincible, and sole champion of it, and whatever creatures he saw in it he killed. Then all the animals, deer and all, met and deliberated together, and they made the following petition to that king of beasts: "Why by killing us all at once do you ruin your own interests? We will send you one animal every day for your dinner." When the lion heard this, he consented to their proposal, and as he was in the habit of eating one animal every day, it happened that it was one day the lot of a hare to present himself to be eaten. The hare was sent off by the united animals, but on the way the wise creature reflected, "He is truly brave who does not become bewildered even in the time of calamity, so, now that death stares me in the face, I will devise an expedient".

'Thus reflecting, the hare presented himself before the lion late. And when he arrived after his time, the lion said to him: "Hola! how is this that you have neglected to arrive at my dinner-hour, or what worse penalty than death, can I inflict on you, scoundrel?" When the lion said this, the hare bowed before him, and said: "It is not my fault, your Highness; I have not been my own master to-day, for another lion detained me on the road, and only let me go after a long interval. When the lion heard that, he lashed his tail, and his eyes became red with anger, and he said: "Who is that second lion? Show him me." The hare said: "Let your Majesty come and see him". The lion consented and followed him. Thereupon the hare took him away to a distant well. "Here he lives, behold him," said the hare, and when thus addressed by the hare, the lion looked into the well, roaring all the while with anger. And seeing his own reflection in the clear water, and hearing the echo of his own roar, thinking that there was a rival lion there roaring louder than himself, he threw himself in a rage into the well, in order to kill him, and there the fool was drowned. And the hare, having himself escaped death by his wisdom, and having delivered all the animals from it, went and delighted them by telling his adventure.'[1]

[1] 'The Lion and the Hare', *The Ocean of Story*, translated by C. H. Tawney, vol. v, 84 D.

This tale, like that of the hares and the elephants, shows the hare using a crafty wisdom that is of the nature of intuition in that it works in unseen ways, unseen that is to the lion but clearly seen by the hare. But the lion, far from seeking wisdom and finding it as the elephant did, sees instead only the projection of his own Shadow, which he attacks and so gets drowned in the water of his own unconscious. In other words, the lion leapt to a wrong conclusion and so met disaster.

Psychologically speaking, this disaster would mean madness, since madness consists in mistaking the symbol (the image) for reality and so being overwhelmed by the unconscious.

The Buddha (Ghatapandita) reproves his brother by crying for the Hare-Moon

One Indian tale about the Hare-Moon shows this quite clearly. This is the tale of a great king named Vāsudeva, whose son died and who, 'half dead with grief, neglected everything, and lay lamenting, and clutching the frame of his bed. Then Ghatapandita[1] thought to himself, "Except me, no one else is able to soothe my brother's grief; I will find some means of soothing his grief for him." So assuming the appearance of madness, he paced through the whole city, gazing up at the sky, and crying out, "Give me a hare! Give me a hare!" All the city was excited: "Ghatapandita has gone mad!" they said.

'Having been told of this, the king rose and, proceeding to

[1] Ghatapandita is another name for Buddha. The passage quoted is but the end of a long and involved story dealing with ten brothers, the eldest of whom is Vāsudeva and the youngest but one Ghatapandita. They conquer Dvārakā, the holy city of Krishna (on the west coast of the Kathiāwār peninsula), of which Vāsudeva becomes king.

The word Ghatapandita may mean 'learned (*pandita*) in water-jars (*gheta*)' or, since Indian compounds can sometimes be split up in different ways, perhaps 'the wise one with the water-jar'. The question is also complicated by the fact that this name appears in a Pāli, not in a Sanskrit text, and in Pāli *ghata* has a double meaning: (1) water-jar (as in Sanskrit), (2) clarified (or boiled) butter (corresponding to Sanskrit *ghrita*).

Ghatapandita, he got fast hold of him, and speaking to him uttered this stanza:

' "*In maniac fashion, why do you pace Dvārakā*[1] *all through,*
And cry, 'Hare, hare!' Say, who is there has taken a hare from you?"

'To these words of the king he only answered by repeating the same cry over and over again.'

To the king's offer, however, to make a hare, be it of gold, jewels, brass, silver, shell, stone, or coral, Ghatapandita replied:

' "*I crave no hare of earthly kind, but that within the moon.*" . . .

' "Undoubtedly my brother has gone mad," thought the king when he heard this. In great grief he said:

' "*In sooth, my brother, you will die, if you make such a prayer,*
And ask for what no man may pray, the moon's celestial hare."

Ghatapandita, on hearing the king's answer, stood stock still, and said: "My brother, you know that if a man prays for the hare in the moon, and cannot get it, he will die; then why do you mourn for your dead son?" '

This was, of course, a gentle hint that the king, in immoderately lamenting his dead son, was what we also should call 'crying for the moon'. Ghatapandita went on:

' "I, brother, pray only for what exists, but you are mourning for what does not exist." Then he instructed him by repeating two more stanzas:

' "*My son is born, let him not die!*" *Nor man nor deity*
Can have that boon; then wherefore pray for what can never be?

"*Nor mystic charm, nor magic roots, nor herbs, nor money spent,*
Can bring to life again that ghost whom, Kanha, you lament."

[1] The holy city of Krishna. See footnote above.

'The king, on hearing this, answered, "Your intent was good, dear one. You did it to take away my trouble." Then in praise of Ghatapandita he repeated four stanzas:

' "*Men had I wise and excellent to give me good advice:*
But now hath Ghatapandita opened this day mine eyes.

"*Blazing was I, as when a man pours oil upon a fire;*
Thou didst bring water, and didst quench the pain of my desire.

"*Grief for my son, a cruel shaft was lodged within my heart;*
Thou hast consoled me for my grief, and taken out the dart.

"*That dart extracted, free from pain, tranquil and calm I keep;*
Hearing, O youth, thy words of truth, no more I grieve nor weep."

'And, lastly:

' "*Thus do the merciful, and thus they who are wise indeed:*
They free from pain, as Ghata here his eldest brother freed."

'This is the stanza of Perfect Wisdom.'[1]

The moral of this story is clear, but Ghatapandita's utterance, 'I crave no hare of earthly kind, but that within the moon', also enshrines the truth, already expressed in the story of Buddha's self-sacrifice as a hare which then became translated into the moon, that the symbol taken literally is purely negative, but that taken symbolically it is of the highest spiritual value. It has been said that lunatics and saints both see similar visions, and that the world of difference between the two lies in the fact that when, for example, a lunatic or one suffering from delirium tremens has a vision of a snake he thinks it to be real and is correspondingly terrified, while the saint having the same vision would understand that it was a

[1] *The Jātaka*, or Stories of the Buddha's former births, translated by Rowse, under the editorship of Professor E. B. Cowell, Cambridge, 1895–1907, vol. iv, pp. 54–5.

symbol and would derive from it the wisdom for which this reptile is famous.

Returning to the story of the king's son, the supposed connection of the moon with lunacy is widespread, as witnessed by the word 'lunacy' itself, which is derived from the Latin *luna*, meaning 'the moon'. This is not surprising, for the moon, being the night luminary, represents the 'other side' or unseen aspect of things as opposed to the sun which represents the more conscious. The moon is thus a powerful symbol for the deep unconscious which, if honoured, is the source of all spiritual wisdom, but if dishonoured overpowers the subject and leads to madness.

Thus, though in mythological personification the various races of mankind differ remarkably in the sex which they attribute respectively to the sun and moon (the Latin peoples, for instance, regarding the moon as female and the sun as male, while the modern Germans regard the sun as female and the moon as male), the moon nevertheless in dreams almost always represents the contrasexual aspect of things, so that for a male the moon represents the mother (or wife) and the sun the father.

Dream of a modern child of the Moon as a negative mother-symbol

An instance of this occurred quite recently in my practice. I had in my house a small boy of about eight whose mother was one of the worst types of devouring woman. One night I heard him shouting, 'Don't, don't'. I went in to him and said, 'Have you been having a bad dream?' He said, 'No.' I said, 'But you've been shouting.' He said, 'I know, but I was awake.' I asked, 'Then what's been frightening you?' The moon was shining in at the window as he replied, 'I thought Mummy was with me, but she got smaller and smaller and went right up to the moon. Then the moon started getting bigger and bigger, and bigger and bigger, and came right at me, as if it were going to swallow me up.' This was the first dream-vision he had told me. I did not tell him what it meant, but the very fact of his reciting it released something in him that, along with the narration of many subsequent dreams of the most vivid character, changed him from being a frightened doormat to becoming an open-hearted and happy child.

Though we do not ourselves speak of the hare in the moon, the hare is for us nevertheless on occasion a symbol of madness as in the expression 'March hare', derived from the wild careering of hares during the mating season.

Philological connection between Sanskrit and Teutonic words for the Moon

Nor is the cultural distance between the British Isles and India so great when we reflect that, as Max Müller points out, our very word 'hare' (Anglo-Saxon, *hara*) is directly related, through the medium of the modern German *Hase* and the Old High German *haso* (all of which belong to the comparatively small group of words including relationship nouns, names of domestic animals, etc., which have cognate forms throughout all Indo-European languages), to the Sanskrit *śaśa* used for the same animal.[1] This word is also used in at least a dozen Sanskrit words for the moon, such as *Śaśin*, literally 'having the hare', and *Śaśānka*, 'having the marks of a hare'. Other Sanskrit compounds used to designate the moon which

[1] Max Müller, *Biographies of Words, and the Home of the Aryas*, London, 1880, p. 145, and cf. p. 164. Compare Anglo-Saxon *hara*. Le Page Renouf (see below, p. 151) says that the Sanskrit *çaça* (*śaśa*), like the Ancient Egyptian *unnu*, the appellative of 'a hare', and the Greek λαγῶς, all mean 'a leaper'. Mayers, discussing the hare-moon in China, says, 'In Sanskrit the *çaças* means properly the leaping one, as well as the hare, the rabbit, and the spots on the moon (the *saltans*), which suggest the figure of a hare'. (Mayers, *The Chinese Reader's Manual*, p. 235, quoting de Gubernatis, *Zoological Mythology*, ii, 76.)

N.B. It will be observed that in this brief philological discussion three different transliterations, *ś*, ç, and *sh*, are used for the same Sanskrit sibilant, according to the different authors quoted. The same sibilant *ś* is variously recorded by yet other authors as *ṡ* or *ś*, but it should be noted that they all represent the same Sanskrit sound, which differs from that of the *sh* in Vishnu, which may be written *ṣ*. In Pāli the three sibilants, *ś*, *ṣ*, and *s*, fall together, so that Sanskrit *Śakra* becomes Pāli *Sakka* and Sanskrit *śaśa* becomes Pāli *sasa*.

my friend Hari Prasad Shastri has told me of, and which are of interest to us here, are *Himkar*, which he translates 'the Creator of Snow' (but which may be otherwise rendered as *himakara*, 'causing or producing cold'), and *Shītānshu*, literally cool-rayed,[1] which he translates 'Essence of Coldness'.

The Hare-Man makes the best sexual partner

Finally, in the systematized *Kāmaśāstra*, or science of sexual love (*kāma*), men are divided into four types named after animals, of which the best, described as being mild and easy to live with, is the Hare-man (*śaśa*, the hare), and the other three are associated respectively with the horse (*aśva*), the antelope (*mṛiga*), and the bull (*vrishan*).

[1] See p. 116.

THE HARE IN CHINA[1]

The Hare-Moon is found also in China. Whether this is through direct influence from India cannot at present be stated with any certainty, although the possibility cannot be ruled out. It is, however, believed by more than one authority that Indian influence reached China as early as the fourth century B.C., owing to the close similarities found between the teachings of Taoism which arose in that century in China, and those of Buddhism which arose during the previous century in India.

Vision of the Han Emperor regarding the introduction of Buddhism

Buddhism did not receive official sanction in China, however, until the time of the Han Emperor called Ming Ti,[2] who reigned from A.D. 58 to A.D. 75, of whom it is said that he saw in a dream a tall male figure having a bright light on the summit of his head. He asked his ministers to interpret the dream, and one of them said, 'There lives in the west a god called Fo [the Chinese name for Buddha]. He is sixteen feet tall and he is the colour of yellow gold.' The Emperor then sent a mission to India to procure, so the legend runs, the image of the god he had seen in his dream. The mission took six years, from A.D. 61 to A.D. 67, over its task, and returned bearing sutras and images of the Buddha on a white horse. The missionaries were suitably lodged, and settled down to translate Buddhist texts into Chinese. After their death the place was consecrated as a Buddhist monastery, and after many vicissitudes Mahayana Buddhism became one of the recognized religions of China.

Whether the Hare-Moon symbolism in China is due to early Buddhist influence or not is uncertain. What is certain, how-

[1] This not being a learned treatise on China, Chinese names are throughout spelt according to the transcription of the authors quoted.

[2] Not to be confused with the Ming Dynasty.

ever, is that there are no known records of it before the fourth century B.C. (that is to say in the late Chou period) when Buddhist and other Indian influences were beginning to be felt. From this date onward there are frequent references to it, though, as might be expected, it developed in a way quite peculiarly Chinese.

The Hare derives its vital essence from the Moon where it compounds the Elixir of Life

Thus in China the mythical hare is not only seen in the moon's spots, but, according to Mayers,[1] from whose account much of the following information is taken, the hare (*lepus sinensis*) itself derives its origin from the vital essence of the moon, and is therefore at all times subject to its influence.[2] One Chinese authority actually asserts that the hare conceives by gazing at the moon, though earlier writers have alleged that the female hare becomes with young by licking the fur of the male.

In China, as in India, the hare is said also to inhabit the moon. I know of no legend of how it got there similar to the Indian legend of its self-immolation in fire and its subsequent translation by the god into the moon,[3] but the miraculous healing element in the Indian story is replaced in China by the belief that the hare lives in the moon eternally compounding

[1] William Frederick Mayers, *The Chinese Reader's Manual*, Shanghai, 1924, pp. 234–5.

[2] According to S. C. Nott (*Chinese Jade*, London, 1936, p. 86), this information is derived from the records of the Han dynasty, which flourished between 206 B.C. and A.D. 220.

[3] It is just possible that a faint recollection of its self-immolation is to be found in the Chinese proverbial phrase, 'sitting beside a stump on the watch for a hare', based on the legend narrated by Han Fei-tsze, to the effect that a husbandman of the state of Sung was ploughing one day when he saw a hare dash itself against a stump which stood in his field, and immediately fall dead. The foolish peasant, thereupon abandoning his plough, seated himself beside the stump to wait for another hare to come and do likewise.' (Mayers, *The Chinese Reader's Manual*, p. 235.) This may, however, have quite a different origin more closely connected with what we refer to as the 'March madness' of hares when they career wildly about during the mating season (referred to on page 123).

FIGURE 9. T'ang Mirror showing the Hare pounding the Herb of Immortality in the Moon

Left to right—Heng O [Ch'ang O] the Moon Queen; a Frog; the Lunar Tree; the Lunar Hare pounding the Drug of Immortality. From *Arts and Crafts of Ancient Annam; Discoveries at Lach-Truong*, by Professor O. Janse, *Illustrated London News*, 7 March 1936

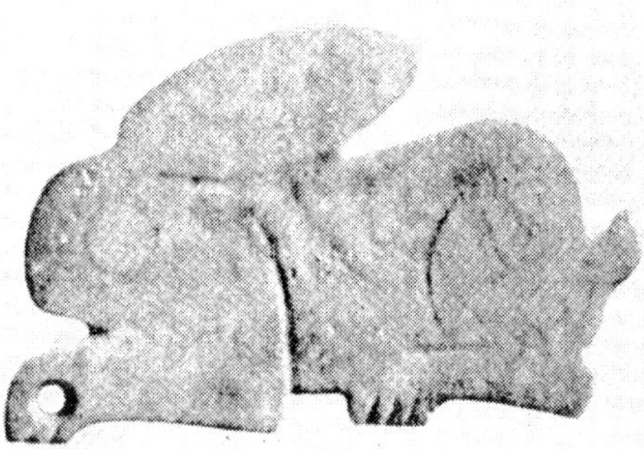

FIGURE 10. Jade Amulet in the form of a Hare

(late Chou period, 4th century B.C.) from *Chinese Jade*, by C. S. Nott, London, 1936, Pl. LXIX

the elixir of life. Thus Werner refers to the moon as symbolized by a hare on its hind-legs pounding rice in a mortar,[1] and Mayers refers to a later Taoist fable depicting the 'gemmeous' hare[2] as the servitor of the genii who employ it in pounding the drugs which compose the elixir of life.

Werner further refers to Chinese paintings depicting, associated together: (*a*) the moon-palace of Ch'ang O [the Moon Queen] who stole the pill of immortality and flew to the moon; (*b*) the fragrant tree which one of the genii, who are the Moon-Queen's servants, tried to cut down; and (*c*) a hare 'pestling medicine in a corner' (see Fig. 9). He says that these refer to a certain court functionary who, together with the then Emperor, went to a well-known holy mountain with the object of being initiated into the doctrine of immortality. The Emperor was instructed in the secrets of the doctrine by the spirit of this famous mountain who, when the Emperor was about to take his departure, begged him to allow the court official to remain with him. The new hermit (the court official) went out every day to gather the flowering plants which formed the only food of his master (the spirit of the mountain), and he took also to eating those flowers, so that his body gradually became spiritualized.[3]

The White Hare called 'bright eyes'

The Taoists claimed that the white hare was Ch'ang O's (the

[1] F. I. C. Werner, *Myths and Legends of China*, London, 1922, p. 176. He says the moon may be symbolized also by a three-legged toad.

[2] The word 'gemmeous', meaning 'relating to, having the nature of, or resembling gems', is interesting in this connection, since one of the most important dreams in Mrs. Wright's later dream-series (to be described in a later volume) centred round the representation of a bishop's mitre, and on examining the mitre of William of Wykeham, preserved in New College, Oxford, which he founded, I found to my surprise that among the jewels with which it is furnished are a number of small cameos representing hares in various postures.

[3] Werner, *Myths and Legends of China*, p. 179. These tales were written down in the late Chou period, but almost certainly go back to a much earlier time, the tales belonging to which were now first committed to writing.

Moon Queen's) servant. Mayers tells us that, like the fox, the hare lives a thousand years, and becomes white when half that period is completed. Another writer[1] on Chinese matters tells us that the white hare has from ancient times been thought of as divine, and is therefore always regarded as an auspicious omen, portending the reign of a beneficent and just ruler. Thus it is said that during the golden age of the Chou Dynasty white hares played in the streets of the capital city.

'The hare is also one of the animals sacrificed in the temple of the Imperial Ancestors. When so used it is known by the name *ming shih*, "bright eyes", because it is said that the hare's eyes, unlike those of any other animal, grow larger and brighter with age. The eyes of the hare were regarded by the Chinese as significant of the beginning of events and periods, and particularly of pubescence.'[2]

The whiteness of this hare and its bright eyes, together with the belief in their association with new life, is particularly interesting when we remember the snow covering the ground both outside and inside the kitchen in Mrs. Wright's dream, a snow in which no footprints were seen, as well as the accompanying white light, the whiteness of everything inside the room, and the white bowl in which the hare sat. It will be seen later how frequently in all parts of the world the mythical hare is represented as being white, and how often, as in the case of the Buddha legend, myths connected with the Hare include references to snow. All these symbols are undoubtedly connected with the white light of the moon, which represents direct intuitive knowledge.

The Red Hare

In China, however, not all the divine hares are white. The author mentioned above refers to ancient writings describing a red hare which, in company with the phoenix and the unicorn, appears as a harbinger of peace and prosperity. Mayers also refers to the red hare as 'a supernatural beast of auspicious

[1] S. C. Nott, *Chinese Jade*, pp. 86–7.

[2] Ibid. Note the Roman belief that the hare sleeps with its eyes open, cited on pp. 190 and 221 of the present work.

omen, which appears when virtuous rulers govern the Empire'.[1]

The Black Hare

One Chinese writer tells also of a black hare, saying, 'The black hare is more uncommon than the white hare. It comes from the North Pole bringing greetings from the moon goddess, and is auspicious of a successful reign. Now may the magic medicine be pounded with jade pestle and the divine nectar be prepared in a crystal cup.'[2]

Colours and Animal Deities of the Four Cardinal Points

All these references are rather obscure, but some light may be thrown on them by the fact that, in early Chinese beliefs found flourishing in the fourth century B.C. when the Hare-Moon makes its first recorded appearance on the Chinese historical scene, the Four Cardinal Points are represented by colours which are at the same time associated with four mythical animals and the four seasons, symbols representing the Deities of these four cardinal points. They are arranged as follows:

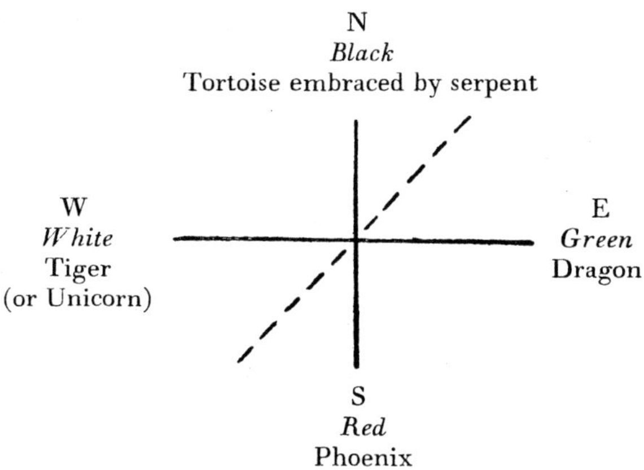

It will be noted that East and South are represented by the

[1] Mayers, *The Chinese Readers' Manual*, pp. 234–5.
[2] Quoted by S. C. Nott, *Chinese Jade*, p. 87.

complementary colours green and red, while North and West are represented by the complementary opposites black and white. This is a very interesting configuration, since it would appear that for the Chinese mind East (whence the sun rises) and South (which represents warmth and passion), through their association with colours, represent different aspects of Instinctual Life; while North (representing darkness) and West (the quarter of sundown and so signifying death), which have no colour at all, represent two aspects of Spirit.

This fits in with the concept of the moon as a white luminary shining in darkness, since it is precisely the moon that symbolizes the spiritual or 'other side' of life, the 'light in the darkness' as opposed to the sun that rules the conscious day. This is clearly the reason why the black hare comes from the North Pole with greetings from the moon-goddess.

The association of the red hare with the phoenix is equally clear, since the phoenix (which burns itself and rises rejuvenated from the ashes) belongs to the South, of which the colour is red. More obscure, however, is the association (cited above) of the red hare also with the Unicorn, which belongs to the West and of which the colour is white. I do not pretend to explain this.[1] But I would point out that the animal

[1] It is of interest to note that the unicorn is mentioned by Greek and Roman writers as a native of India (the earliest known reference is by Ctesias of Cnidas, physician to Artaxerxes II, Mnemon of Persia in about 400 B.C.), and that they describe its body as being white, its horn as being white at the base, black in the middle and tipped with red, while its head is red and its eyes blue. It is used frequently in medieval heraldry, and the sinister supporter of the insignia of the United Kingdom is a unicorn argent. The *Physiologus*, written in the first half of the second century A.D., describes the unicorn as being similar to a small white kid, so swift-footed that the huntsmen cannot catch it. It can only be caught by a trick. An untouched virgin is placed in its way, and as soon as the unicorn sees her, it runs straight towards her and throws itself into her lap, abandoning all fierceness. This is used as an allegory of the Immaculate Conception. Later the unicorn is conceived as a kind of white horse with a goat's beard, and as a symbol of chastity. The horn is said, already by Ctesias, to be a prophylactic against poison, and is used as a symbol of the cross. The Unicorn mentioned in various parts of the Old Testa-

symbol of the North is a tortoise coupled in sexual embrace with a serpent, from which embrace, that is to say out of the union of opposites (the tortoise being held to be female and the serpent male) in the black night of the soul, arose at a later date (in the Sung Dynasty, 960–1279) a deity in human form. Not one of the other three animal deities thus gave rise to a human god, and the god which thus arose out of the embrace was the Dark Emperor, who was the Supreme Lord of the Dark Heaven (i.e. of the soul). The revelation of this transformation came in a vision to the Emperor Hui Tsung, who was himself a great painter, and the Dark Emperor of his vision 'rose here to life at a time when animals as deities no longer had any meaning'.[1]

So also did Mrs. Wright's dream of sacrificing the hare lead directly to the darkest night of her life, when for three hours she suffered agony and was not only reborn herself, but also, through her acceptance of the revelation, released the bonds of her daughter Margaret, thus conferring rebirth on her also.

The Hare, as Resurrection Symbol, pounds the Herb of Immortality in the Moon

It is of interest further to note one final observation by Carl Hentze regarding the 'hare in the moon' as a resurrection symbol. Referring to the well-known Chinese mythical motive of 'Spittle flowing out of a vessel', he says: 'This is a widespread mythical motive, whose connection with the New Moon is

ment is frequently interpreted as an anticipatory symbol of Christ, whose resurrection at Easter, as symbol among other things of the rising sun, connects him with the East (see pp. 180–2). In China the hare is connected with the second lunar month corresponding to the Equinox, and is associated with Equality, and corresponds to the trigram ☲. There are eight such trigrams forming the basis of the system known as the Yi King, said to have been founded by Fu Hsi in 3322 B.C. The association with equality is interesting, since the main symbolism of this purely fabulous animal seems to rest on the concept of two horns joined into one, in other words of a union of opposites such as is the basis of all mystical phenomena.

[1] William Cohn, 'The Deities of the Four Cardinal Points in Chinese Art', *Transactions, Oriental Ceramic Society*, 1940–1, p. 72.

often quoted. . . . The connection of the vessel with the New Moon in China is due to the fact that the Chinese "Hare in the Moon" pounds the "Herb of Immortality" in a mortar. . . . Since the hare belongs to the moon, "immortality" can here only refer to the new rising (or resurrection) of the moon, so that the mortar is evidently the New Moon in which the "Herb of Immortality" is prepared, that is to say from which rejuvenation springs.'[1] (See Fig. 9.)

On this analogy, the white bowl in which Mrs. Wright's hare sat would represent the Full Moon with the Hare in it, preparing the 'Herb of Immortality'; 'immortality' here representing, of course, that new and deeper life that comes from renewed contact with the life-giving forces of the Impersonal Unconscious, which Mrs. Wright at this moment acquired and began to transmit to her daughter through the as yet unsevered spiritual umbilical cord still joining them, in the manner already seen in this volume and to be demonstrated more fully in its sequel.

The Hare Garden

While contemplating this humble mother and daughter in their joint search for spiritual truth, it is pleasant to think, at the other side of the world, in times gone by and at the other end of the social scale, in a society that still valued wisdom, of the 'Hare Garden' which was 'the name given by Prince Hiao of Liang to the pleasure grounds in which he sought recreation, surrounded by a retinue of scholars'.[2]

Moon Festival

In view further of the Easter associations of Mrs. Wright's dream, the following quotation from Billson may not be out of place. He says: 'There is a similarity also between the customs

[1] Author's translation from *Frühchinesische Bronzen und Kultdarstellungen*, by Carl Hentze, Antwerp, 1937, p. 100. He adds, 'This is why, in the Chinese myth of Yi Yin, it is again a "mortar" that rises out of the flood, . . . clearly that same "mortar" in which the hare prepares the "Herb of Immortality", that is to say the New Moon'.

[2] Mayers, *The Chinese Reader's Manual*, p. 235.

of the great Chinese Moon Festival and those which are still observed in England and Germany at the season of Easter. "This festival, known as the Yué-Ping (loaves of the moon), dates from the remotest antiquity. Its original purpose was to honour the moon. . . . On this solemn day all labour is suspended; the workmen receive from their employers a present of money; every person puts on his best clothes; and there is merry-making in every family. Relations and friends interchange cakes of various sizes, on which is stamped the image of the moon; that is to say, a hare couching amid a small group of trees." '[1]

The hare is also one of the Signs of the Zodiac in China, though I am not aware which constellation it represents.

PLASTIC REPRESENTATIONS OF THE HARE

I will close this brief summary of the beliefs connected with the Hare in China with a still briefer reference to some of its plastic representations. The most ancient of these known to me are the small jade carvings from the late Chou period (fourth century B.C.) figured in Berthold Laufer's fine book on *Archaic Chinese Jade.*[2] They range from about three or four inches in length and represent hares in all kinds of postures, all pierced as if for use as amulets. Laufer does not believe that they have any mythological significance, but my friend Dr. William Cohn (formerly Keeper of the Far Eastern Department of the Ethnological Museum in Berlin), who kindly called my attention to them as well as to other matters referred to in this section, thinks that they certainly had, as they are found so often in graves.

An outstanding example from the same period, called that of the Warring States lasting from 481 to 221 B.C., in the collec-

[1] C. J. Billson, 'The Easter Hare', *Folk-lore*, vol. iii, p. 460, quoting T. Harley, *Moonlore*, London, 1885, pp. 104–5.

[2] Berthold Laufer, *Archaic Chinese Jade, collected in China by A. W. Bahr, now in the Field Museum of Natural History, Chicago*, privately printed in New York, 1927. Plate xxiv and p. 38.

tion of the late Mr. Oscar Raphael, is figured by Nott[1] (see Fig. 10). This also is pierced, as if for use as an amulet.

There are also numerous Chinese representations of the Hare in the Moon depicted in pottery and on silk.

Buddhism also spread to Japan, and an outstanding example of painting on silk (based, like most Japanese Buddhist paintings, on a Chinese motive) is the Japanese Buddhist painting in Sung style executed by Takuma Shôga in A.D. 1191 as one of the screens depicting the Twelve Devas. It is of the Moon-goddess Gwatten holding in her hands a crescent moon, in the dark portion of which is seated a white hare.[2] (*See* Fig. 11.)

[1] *Chinese Jade*, plate lxix.

[2] H. Minamoto, *An Illustrated History of Japanese Art*, Kyoto, 1935. Illustration 110, p. 134.

FIGURE 11. The Moon-goddess Gwatten holding in her hands a crescent moon, in which is seated a White Hare

Part of a Japanese painting in Buddhist style executed by Takuma Shôga in 1191 A.D. as one of the screens depicting the Twelve Devas

THE HARE IN NORTH AMERICA

The Hare is a religious symbol not only in the Buddhism of Ceylon, India, China, and the surrounding lands, but was also worshipped as such on the other side of the Pacific by many of the pre-conquest inhabitants of North America. Not only so, but the myths of the New World correspond remarkably in main details with those of the Old.

Legend of the Déné Hareskins, who worship a Moon God, and of a white Hare's head thrown into a fire causing the Dawn

We have already met with the hare as a divine animal leaping with self-sacrificing ecstasy into the fire, and thence being translated into the moon. We have seen also the importance of the white hare in China. It is therefore of no little interest to read of a tradition among the Déné Hareskins, who worship a Moon-God who is a god of hunting, plenty, and also of death (death being, of course, a symbol of the 'other', that is to say the 'spiritual' life), to the effect that one of their number, who was beguiled into the underworld in which all paths were serpentine and where profound darkness reigned, effected his escape by throwing the head of a white hare into a fire, whereon it immediately became dawn.[1]

This points to a yet further extension of the idea already seen both in India and in China of the hare as a symbol of the 'light in the darkness'. Whereas the hare is there conceived of as being translated through sacrifice into the moon whence it casts its beams into the dark night of the soul, here it appears, through a similar sacrifice, to be the creator of dawning consciousness, whereby the soul's contents are brought into the light of day.

[1] Petitot, *Traditions Indiennes du Canada Nord-Ouest*, Paris, 1886, p. 173, quoted by Andrew Lang, *Myth, Ritual, and Religion* (first edition), London, 1887, vol. i, p. 184, note 2.

THE MYTHOLOGY OF THE HARE

THE GREAT HARE OF THE ALGONKIN

One of the great students of North American mythology is Dr. D. G. Brinton, who sums up the evidence regarding the beliefs centring round the Divine Hare as conceived by the Algonkin of North America in no uncertain terms. He begins by citing the more degraded late forms of belief, which only serve to throw into yet higher relief the vitality of the earlier and truly inspired myths. He says:

'From the remotest wilds of the north-west to the coast of the Atlantic, from the southern boundaries of Carolina to the cheerless swamps of Hudson's Bay, the Algonkins were never tired of gathering around the winter fire and repeating the story of Manibozho or Michabo, the Great Hare. With entire unanimity the various branches, the Pawhatans of Virginia, the Lenni Lenape of the Delaware, the warlike hordes of New England, the Ottawas of the far north, and the western tribes perhaps without exception, spoke of "this chimerical beast", as one of the old missionaries called it, as their common ancestor. The totem or clan which bore his name was looked up to with peculiar respect. In many of the tales which the whites have preserved of Michabo he seems half a wizard, half a simpleton. He is full of pranks and wiles, but often at a loss for a meal of victuals; ever itching to try his magic arts on great beasts and often meeting ludicrous failures therein; envious of the powers of others, and constantly striving to outdo them in what they do best; in short, little more than a malicious buffoon delighting in practical jokes, and abusing his superhuman powers for selfish and ignoble ends.

'But this is a low, modern, and corrupt version of the character of Michabo, bearing no more resemblance to his real and ancient one than the language and acts of our Saviour and the Apostles in the coarse Mystery Plays of the Middle Ages do to those recorded by the Evangelists.

'What he really was we must seek in the accounts of older travellers, in the invocations of the jossakeeds or prophets, and in the part assigned to him in the solemn mysteries of religion. In these we find him portrayed as the patron and founder of the meda worship,[1] the inventor of picture-writing, the father and guardian of their nation, the ruler of the winds, even the maker and preserver of the world and creator of the sun and moon. From a grain of sand brought from the bottom of the primeval ocean, he fashioned the habitable land and set it floating on the waters, till it grew to such a size that a strong young wolf, running constantly, died of old age ere he reached its limits. Under the name Michabo Ovisaketchak, the Great Hare who created the Earth, he was originally the highest deity recognized by them, "powerful and beneficent beyond all others, maker of the heavens and the world". He was founder of the medicine hunt in which after appropriate ceremonies and incantations the Indian sleeps, and Michabo appears to him in a dream, and tells him where he may readily kill game. He himself was a mighty hunter of old; one of his footsteps measured eight leagues, the Great Lakes were the beaver dams he built, and when the cataracts impeded his progress he tore them away with his hands. Attentively watching the spider spread its web to trap unwary flies, he devised the art of knitting nets to catch fish, and the signs and charms he tested and handed down to his descendants are of marvellous efficacy in the chase. In the autumn, in "the moon of the falling leaf", ere he composes himself to his winter's sleep, he fills his great pipe and takes a god-like smoke. The balmy clouds float over the hills and woodlands, filling the air with the haze of the "Indian summer".

'Sometimes he was said to dwell in the skies with his brother the snow, or, like many great spirits, to have built his wigwam in the far north on some floe of ice in the Arctic Ocean, while the Chipeways localized his birthplace and former home to the island Michilimakinac at the outlet of Lake Superior. But in the oldest accounts of the missionaries he was alleged to reside towards the east, and in the holy formulae of the meda craft, when the winds are invoked to the medicine

[1] The *meda* worship is the ordinary religious ritual of the Algonkin. A *jossakeed* is an inspired prophet who derives his power directly from the higher spirits, and not as the *medawin*, by instruction and practice.

lodge, the east is summoned in his name, the door opens in that direction, and there, at the edge of the earth, where the sun rises, on the shore of the infinite ocean that surrounds the land, he has his house and sends the luminaries forth on their daily journeys.'[1]

This account is so full of symbolic truth that it would take pages to discuss at all fully, so I will content myself with calling attention only to a few salient points.

Childlike aspect of Tales

In the first place, the tales of the hare as a kind of buffoon are partly degraded, but also the kind of tales children are told at a stage when they can enjoy humour but are not yet capable of consciously understanding the more esoteric knowledge of their elders; tales also repeated by adults in lighter vein much as a devoted Catholic may tell, from sheer familiarity, humorous stories about the saints which might shock his more puritanical brethren. At the same time they do indeed show the mischievous and often selfish aspect of intuitive behaviour when not balanced by common sense.

Inventor of Picture-writing

In the second place, the reference to the hare as the inventor of picture-writing is important, because this means that kind of symbolic wisdom which forms the whole subject-matter of this book. As will be seen later, the divine hare was closely connected with the Egyptian god Thoth, the Greek god Hermes, and the Roman Mercury, all of whom were supposed to have similarly invented writing which, in the case of the oldest of them, Thoth, was also picture-writing.[2]

Ruler of the Four Winds

Thirdly, as ruler of the four winds he shows himself to be the uniter of the four psychological functions, and as creator of the sun and moon rules also the zenith and nadir (the zenith

[1] D. G. Brinton, *The Myths of the New World*, New York, 1868, pp. 161–4.

[2] See p. 157.

below the earth), which represent the two spiritual elements added to the material fourfold creation, with himself the supreme seventh element uniting them all.

Grain of sand comparable to 'firmament'

Fourthly, the grain of sand brought up from the bottom of the primeval ocean, out of which habitable land is made, is a worldwide symbol of the establishment of conscious life amidst the chaos of surrounding unconscious forces. It is comparable to the creation of the firmament in the midst of the waters in the first chapter of Genesis, and, among innumerable other myths, to the dry land that the Polynesian god Mauwi fished up from the sea at the end of his fishing-rod. The 'growing' of the habitable land brought up by the Great Hare represents of course growing consciousness and the yeastlike quality of the Holy Spirit, which is itself so closely allied to balanced intuitive knowledge.

Medicine Hunt and appearance in Dreams

Fifthly, there is the medicine hunt, recalling the elixir of life mixed by the Hare in the Moon in China.

Sixthly, there is the reference to the Hare Michabo appearing in dreams telling the hunter where he may best kill his game.

Connection of the Hare with Snow and Whiteness

Seventhly, there is the remarkable reference to the hare's 'brother, the snow', recalling so vividly to mind the snow which in Mrs. Wright's dream not only surrounded the house but also penetrated into the kitchen in which she sacrificed her hare, and which was also filled with white light. White light symbolizes direct knowledge unadulterated by the intrusion of defiling elements, and it will be remembered how, in Mrs. Wright's dream, the divine nature of the snow was demonstrated by the fact that it showed no footprints. The connection of the hare with snow and whiteness in general is remarkably constant in all these accounts, from that of the white hare in China to many other references to snow throughout this narrative.

Connection with the East and Dawn

Eighthly and lastly, we are told that in the oldest accounts the hare was alleged to reside towards the east, that in the most sacred ritual the east is summoned in his name, that the door of the medicine lodge opens in that direction, since it is at the place where the sun rises, on the shore of the infinite ocean that surrounds the land, that the hare has his house. In dreams a door commonly represents a gateway leading to or from salvation. East is proverbially the white quarter,[1] and white is, moreover, the colour ordained to be worn by officiating priests at Easter, when the Son of Man rises in glory to rule men's hearts. The Dawn is met with again as one of the hare's attributes in Ancient Egypt, as will be seen below. Moreover, the hare is the sacred animal of Easter all over Europe, as will also appear later. Dawn also signifies the dawn of that superconsciousness which is commonly called rebirth, which is again what Mrs. Wright experienced as a result of her own hare-dream.

Andrew Lang further quotes Strachey as saying, '"The godly hare's house" is at the place of sun-rising; there the souls of good Indians "feed on delicious fruits with that great hare", who', Andrew Lang adds, 'is clearly the Virginian Osiris' whose attributes and whose connection with the Hare are discussed below in the section on 'The Hare in Ancient Egypt'.[2]

There is no need here to go into the long discussion by Andrew Lang of Brinton's arguments claiming philological affinity between the second element in the name given to the Great Hare, Michabou (*michi* 'great', *wabou* 'hare') and the Algonkin word *wab* meaning 'white'.[3] It is a long discussion

[1] An exception to this is the Chinese association of east with the emergent colour green.

[2] Strachey, *History of Travaile*, pp. 98–9, quoted by Andrew Lang, *Myth, Ritual, and Religion*, vol. ii, pp. 55–6, note 1.

[3] See Andrew Lang, 'Le Lièvre dans la Mythologie', *Mélusine*, vol. iii, cols. 265–6, and *Myth, Ritual, and Religion*, London, 1887, first edition, vol. ii, pp. 54–9, and second edition, 1901, vol. i, pp. xxvii–xxviii.

adding little to our knowledge, since the connection of the hare with 'snow', 'whiteness', 'the east', and 'dawn' is so clearly indicated in the actual mythological accounts. The argument is that on the philological evidence the connection was due simply to an unconscious pun, which Andrew Lang rightly rejects as being not only a quite unnecessary assumption but also irrelevant to the main issue, which is the incontrovertible fact that the hare is indeed accredited with these attributes not only among the Algonkin but also in other places as well, among which he cites Ancient Egypt, to which may now be added India, China, parts of Africa, and even medieval and modern Europe.[1]

The fact is that these common attributes have a deep psychological meaning quite independent of such superficial mechanism as puns, as has been demonstrated once more by Mrs. Wright, who never heard either of folk-lore or of comparative mythology but produced the same combination of symbols out of her own deep union with the collective psyche.

[1] Andrew Lang (*Mélusine*, iii, col. 265) states that the Hare-Moon was known also among the Aztecs, but gives no reference.

Not included in this section on North America, but mentioned later, is the myth of the 'grandmother in the moon' referred to in *Hiawatha* (see p. 171, note 1).

THE HARE IN ANCIENT EGYPT

THE HARE USED AS A HIEROGLYPH FOR THE AUXILIARY VERB 'TO BE'

The symbolic equation of the Great Hare with the Dawn is closely paralleled in Ancient Egypt, where the Hare-deity is connected with ideas of 'opening' and 'up-rising', in addition to its more universal connection with the moon. It is to the deep insight of Le Page Renouf into the workings of the human mind that we are indebted for this information, based on a psychological investigation into the reasons for the remarkable fact that an Ancient Egyptian hieroglyph used in writing for the auxiliary verb 'to be' is the hare.

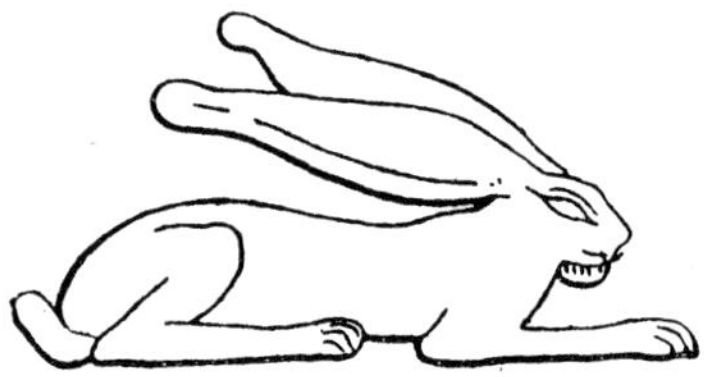

Fig. 12. Egyptian hieroglyph representing the Hare, used in writing for the auxiliary verb 'to be'

After N. de G. Davies, *The Mastaba of Ptahhetep and Akhethetep at Saqqareh,* Part I, Pl. VI, No. 62.

To understand the setting of his remarks it is necessary to remember that in Ancient Egyptian many hieroglyphs, whatever their origin in the representation of natural objects, have in the actual writing a purely phonetic value. It is as if our letter *a*, for instance, once stood for the name of some natural object but had later come to be used for every similar sound, in whatever word it occurred and quite irrespective of its original meaning, in such a way that this original meaning became eventually completely lost through its employment as a purely phonetic symbol.

In this way, the sign representing the hare is used in the hieroglyphic writing of Ancient Egypt for the sound rendered in our notation by Le Page Renouf as *un* and by modern scholars (since hieroglyphic writing does not include the transcription of vowels) as *wn*. As the authorities whom I shall quote in this section belong to the older school which used the transcription *un*, I shall, as this is not primarily a philological treatise, in order to avoid confusing the general reader, adopt this spelling rather than the more modern one though the latter is undoubtedly philologically the more correct.

This hieroglyph representing the hare, of which the phonetic value is *un*, is found throughout Ancient Egyptian writings, in combination with other hieroglyphs, all representing other sounds, in most cases in which the phonetic value of *un* occurs.

There is, however, one word in which this sign occurs alone, and that is the auxiliary verb 'to be', which is mostly written with the hieroglyph of the hare. The question arises as to why this should be the case, particularly as this hieroglyph with the value *un* nowhere in known Ancient Egypt writings *means* 'hare', which is in fact represented by quite a different word having the phonetic value transcribed by modern scholars as *sh't*.

This is the problem which Le Page Renouf set out to solve on the principle that philology alone can never find the solution of this and similar questions unless it enlarges its horizon by attempting to understand the more general workings of the human mind in its use of symbolic values. The obvious nature of this truth may be illustrated by an examination of numerous instances in our own language, of which I will mention one only, namely, our word 'understand', which means quite literally to 'stand under' a thing, in other words to get below the surface in order to gain knowledge of its 'underlying' causes. This happens to be an example of which the meaning is clear once it is pointed out, but numerous other words have become so condensed that the process of tracing them back to their original meaning is by no means so easy.

Some modern philologists have become so specialized that

this kind of symbolic thinking has become difficult for them or even impossible, and these deny outright that, in this case, the hare hieroglyph for *un* meaning 'to be' has any significance other than a purely accidental phonetic one. That such accidents occur in philology is of course patent to anyone who studies the numerous false folk-etymologies of which examples are familiar to all. This does not mean, however, that in innumerable cases the reverse process does not occur, and that original meanings do not get lost and that the use of language thereby does not become sadly impoverished. We have only to observe, for instance, that the Hebrew word translated in the Bible as 'firmament' means a 'hammered-out plate' and, in terms of human life, represents man's character forged out of a play of opposites which it on the one hand resists so that they do not break him, and on the other hand absorbs so that he includes (or should include) in his own person the power and wisdom of both, to realize how language arises out of direct images but loses in intensity as these images get lost and finally becomes an intellectual concept which even intellectuals now commonly fail to grasp.

It is to a similar problem with regard to the purely abstract concept contained in the verb *un*, 'to be' and to its symbolic origin indicated by the hieroglyph of the hare, that Le Page Renouf addresses himself. He says, 'A purely philological inquiry into the primitive meanings of the auxiliary verbs of the Egyptian language has led me to results which throw fresh light upon an interesting question of comparative mythology.'[1]

Referring then to Dr. Brinton's description of the Great Hare of the Algonkin as 'the impersonation of Light, a hero of Dawn' and to certain attempts by the more sophisticated type of philosopher to explain away such symbolism on falsely rationalistic grounds, he says: 'It is now universally acknowledged that the very best classical scholars were till lately utterly mistaken in their etymologies of the languages they knew best. . . .

'No attempt will be made here at a direct refutation of such

[1] P. Le Page Renouf, 'The Myth of Osiris Unnefer', in *Transactions of the Society of Biblical Archaeology*, vol. ix, 1893, p. 281.

explanations as I have alluded to. It will, however, be shown that the ancient Egyptians had myths very similar to that of the Michabo of the Algonkin, and that our knowledge of the Egyptian language enables us . . . to see clearly into the origin of these myths.'[1]

Osiris as 'opener and divider of the ways'

He then refers to Osiris, instancing among his many titles 'Prince of the Unseen World' and 'opener or divider of the ways' of light. Further, with reference to the connection existing in late Egyptian history between Osiris and the Sun-god Rā, he points out their complementary nature by saying "Osiris is the soul of Rā and Rā the soul of Osiris, according to Egyptian orthodoxy. As Rā was the most popular personification of the diurnal Sun, so was Osiris the most popular personification of the nocturnal Sun." Or, rather, as the ancient gloss on the text "I am Yesterday, and I know the Morrow", explains it, "Yesterday is Osiris (of which) the Morrow is Rā". And accordingly Osiris may be considered mythologically either as the father or the son of Rā; the son proceeding from the father, or the father proceeding from the son. The god has twin souls which meet at the heavenly Tattu[2] and are united into one personality.'

'The names of Rā and Osiris are united in prayers addressed to one divinity.'[3]

Osiris Unnefer

Le Page Renouf then refers for the first time to the title Osiris Unnefer, in which the phonetic value *un* represented by the hare occurs, quoting the phrases, '"Rā, Osiris Unnefer, the triumphant, the king of the gods, the mighty Disk whose rays give light". "He showers down light upon the earth at

[1] P. Le Page Renouf; 'The Myth of Osiris Unnefer', in *Transactions of the Society of Biblical Archaeology*, vol. ix, 1893, p. 282.

[2] Tattu (so spelt by Renouf) is the ancient city of Busiris in the Delta. Osiris is regularly called 'Lord of Tattu'.

[3] P. Le Page Renouf, 'The Myth of Osiris Unnefer', in *Transactions of the Society of Biblical Archaeology*, vol. ix, 1893, p. 283.

his rising",' and points out how 'In the Papyrus of Nebseni Horus comes to see his father Osiris, and "sees him Rā, as Unneferu the Lord of Tasert,"'[1] and how 'He is very fre-

Fig. 13. Osiris in the Moon-disk, with the sceptre in his hand and wearing the crown of Upper Egypt. Over him is written his kingly name Unnefer, beginning with the hieroglyph of the Hare

From Lepsius, *Denkmäler*, Section 4, Pl. 31a.

quently called "the king in heaven, the great one upon earth, the mighty sovereign in the nether world"'.[2]

Osiris Unnefer pictured as standing in the Moon's disk

He then goes on, however, to quote from the second chapter of the Book of the Dead the following text: '*Oh thou Only One! shining from the moon, grant that I may come forth at the*

[1] Tasert is a name for the cemetery, especially that of Abydos, and hence is used for the abode of the dead in general.

[2] P. Le Page Renouf, 'The Myth of Osiris Unnefer,' in *Transactions of the Society of Biblical Archaeology*, vol. ix, 1893, p. 283.

head of thy train', and says, 'The best illustration of this ancient text is the picture at Karnak of all the principal gods in adoration of Osiris, who is represented as standing in the moon-disk with the sceptre in his hand, and the royal crown upon his head. Over him is written his kingly name Unnefer.'[1]

Here, then, we find Osiris with his title Unnefer, beginning with the hieroglyphic sign *un* representing the hare, standing in the moon-disk precisely as does the mythical Hare in India, China, and North America (and as we shall see later, in parts of Africa).

Le Page Renouf does not here mention that, as will be seen below, Osiris was originally connected, not with the sun but with the moon, and that the concept of the Nocturnal Sun may well have originally referred to the Moon which in fact shines by night. He is here more concerned with the mythological evidence as throwing light on the original meaning of the syllable *un* as represented by the hieroglyph of the hare used by itself in Ancient Egypt to signify the verb 'to be', and on how and why the apparent transformation in meaning could have occurred.

Philological evidence of concrete images preceding abstract thought

He begins, 'It is a constant fact in the history of language that the name of an object is derived from *one* of its attributes, and the reason why this fact is not more generally recognized is that the languages which we speak have undergone many changes since the time when the names first came into use'.

He then instances many examples, such as 'redbreast' and 'lapwing' from our own language, and others from many other languages, and, referring to the other representations of Osiris under the symbol of a ram or ram-headed personage,

[1] P. Le Page Renouf, 'The Myth of Osiris Unnefer', in *Transactions of the Society of Biblical Archaeology*, vol. ix, 1893, p. 284. Compare the Malekulan myth, according to which Ta-ghar, the creator and god of light, is seen standing in the moon, on which he begets all human children who subsequently enter this world through the portal of their mothers' wombs. *See* John Layard, *Stone Men of Malekula*, London, 1942, pp. 212, 217.

goes on, 'No man, however well educated, can, at the present day, without special inquiry, tell the original meaning of the commonest words in the language which he speaks. It was not so at the time when the names were first adopted. When the Egyptian gave the name *šefit* to the ram, they thought of that powerful action exercised by his head, which has led more modern nations to give the name of *ram* to instruments of powerful energy. And it is an instructive fact that the proper name *Her-Šefït*, "Ram-faced", which is found in the later copies of the Book of the Dead, does not occur in the older copies; the ancient reading is *āa šefït*, "most powerful one".

'The explanation of the Ram-headed god will enable us more readily to understand the symbolism of another form of Osiris.'[1]

Hare-headed Divinity

'A Hare-headed divinity is seen in the temple of Dendera, seated upon an invisible throne, wrapped in mummy clothing, and with the two arms and hands in the position of holding the crook and flail, characteristic of Osiris.[2] The temple of Dendera itself is of recent date, but not so the Hare-headed divinity who appears in the usual vignettes of certain chapters[3] of the Book of the Dead, though here the throne is generally visible, and the hands hold knives.

Hare-headed Goddess

'There is also a Hare-headed goddess in the picture at Dendera, whose name is "*Unnut*,[4] the mistress of the city Unnut and of Dendera".[5] The city Unnut was the metropolis of the 15th nome of Upper Egypt, that of the Hare *Un*, called by the Greeks Hermopolites, on account of their worship of Thoth,

[1] P. Le Page Renouf, 'The Myth of Osiris Unnefer', in *Transactions of the Society of Biblical Archaeology*, vol. ix, 1893, p. 286.

[2] That is to say, with arms and hands crossed, which, without crook or flail would indicate an attitude of humility.

[3] Notably the 146th chapter.

[4] By modern scholars spelt *Wnt*.

[5] E. Lefébure corrects this to 'mistress of Unnu-t, regent of Dendera' (see below, p. 154).

but other chief divinities were worshipped here, especially Osiris. The male divinity would be called *Un* or *Unnu* even when the final vowel is omitted in writing.

'Such a divinity is mentioned at the opening of the 17th chapter of the Book of the Dead.

'"I am Tmu as *Unn*; I am One and only; I am Rā in his first risings."

'And in the glosses upon this opening passage it is spoken of "the sovereignty which Ra exercised as *Unn*" when as yet there was no firmament.'[1]

The name Unnefer or Unnu-neferu

After further discussion he continues: 'What, however, it may be asked, do we know of such a god? My answer is that Unnefer, or rather Unnu-neferu,[2] as a proper name, bears the same relation to Unnu, that Rā-neferu, Tmu-neferu, Horneferu, Ptah-neferu, Amon-neferu, Sebak-neferu, Amsu-neferu bear to Rā, Tmu, Horus, Ptah, Amon, Sebak, and Amsu. Unnu is the real name of which Unnu-neferu is a compound.

'The usual interpretation "the good being" of the name Unnefer, which has been current since the time of Champollion, is manifestly erroneous. There is no such noun in Egyptian as *Un* or *Unn* "a being". Mythology does not deal with such names as "good being". "Being" is much too metaphysical, and "good" much too ethical, a notion for names of this kind. A physical sense is the only one admissible. *Nefer*, primarily means *young*, *fair*, *beautiful*, and only secondarily *good*. It is used exactly like the Latin *juvencus*, *juvenca*, in the sense of a youth, a maiden, a foal, a young cow. . . . We also read of the *neferu* in the sense of a youthful troupe of men.

'The sense of beautiful is equally certain. *Nefer ḥra* is a well-known phrase for "of beautiful face". *Neferu* signifies "beautiful raiment, bravery". The wicked wife of the

[1] P. Le Page Renouf, 'The Myth of Osiris Unnefer', in *Transactions of the Society of Biblical Archaeology*, vol. ix, 1893, pp. 286–7.

[2] By modern scholars spelt *Wnn-nfrw*, transliterated as *Wenennofru*,'. The word was by the Greeks further compressed into *Onnophris*.

younger brother in the D'Orbiney Papyrus was *nefert em ḥāu-set*, "beautiful in all her limbs". *Neferu* is the usual Egyptian word expressing the graces, the beauty, the brightness, the glory of a god. It is said of a goddess in a text quoted by Champollion *meḥ pet ta em neferu-s*, "Heaven and earth are full of her glory"; and it would be easy to quote many expressions of the kind.

Hare-sign signifies 'leaping' or 'uprising', and hence 'being'

'Unnu-neferu signifies the "young, splendid, or glorious Hare". This at least is a signification which in the abstract admits of no contradiction.[1] The question is what is meant by Hare when applied to Osiris or the Sun,[2] and it is a question which can only be solved by an inquiry into the original sense of the Egyptian word signifying Hare.

'As the question has sometimes been raised, it is right to insist upon it that the sign 𓃹 has the value of *un*, and that it has no other value. . . . Now there is a variety of Egypt in words of which the syllable 𓃹 *un*, sometimes written 𓃹𓈖, is the essential part; and one and the same concept underlies the signification of them all, though one of them means a hare, another an *hour* (*unnut*), another a *calf* (*unnui*), another *open*, another *transgress*, *overleap* (*un*),[3] and the most frequent of all is the very colourless auxiliary verb which we translate "being".

'The fundamental notion is *up*, *rise*, *spring up*, *start up*. *Un ā*, "up with the hand", expresses the act of the hand rising suddenly, either in adoration of a god, or in the assault of an enemy.

'"Herbs and trees spring up (*her unun*) at thy presence," sings the Poet of the Disk-worshippers.'

After citing a large number of texts, too lengthy to repro-

[1] It must be admitted here that modern scholars do contradict it, but the rest of the evidence in this book culled from all parts of the world lends support to Le Page Renouf's thesis.

[2] For the earlier and more fundamental association of Osiris with the Moon, see below.

[3] There are, of course, many other such combinations having a great variety of meanings.

duce here, in which the word *un* is translated as meaning to 'spring up', 'rise up', etc., Le Page Renouf goes on, 'The connections between the notion of springing up and *un* "open", will be obvious to everyone who knows that our English word "open" is only the verbal form of "up", or who compares the German "auf" and "aufmachen". . . .

'Unnu, then, as the appellative of the "hare" signifies a "springer", "leaper", like the Sanskrit *çaça*, which has its origin in the root *çaç*, implying motion by springing, our own word *hare*, and the Anglo-Saxon *hara*. The Greek λαγώς, which is referred by Pott and other etymologists to the same root as the Sanskrit *laṅgh* "leap", has much the same meaning. *Unnut*, "an hour or moment", is identical with the word signifying "she-hare", and like it signifies "leaper". Our own poets speak of the fleeting hours—"hora agilis, praeceps, fugitiva". In Shelley's *Prometheus*, "The Hours were hounds, which chased the day like a wounded deer". . . .[1]

'But what shall we say of the auxiliary verb *un*? Is not Being a conception prior to all others? It may be so in some systems of Metaphysics, but it is certainly not so in the history of Language. The fact that 𓃹 is an auxiliary verb in the sense of "being" is the very reason why we should look out for the physical sense originally attached to it. All auxiliary verbs in Egyptian, as well as in other languages had originally a physical meaning. We know that *am*, *is*, *was*, *be*, *werden*, were originally verbs of breathing, dwelling, growing, and turning. . . . The case is quite the same in Egyptian. . . .'[2]

'The same kind of idiom is traceable in Hebrew and other Semitic languages. The word "rise" is perpetually used in the Old Testament without an intentional reference to the action of getting up: "rise and go down", "rise and cry", "rise and eat", "rise and sit".[3]

[1] P. Le Page Renouf, 'The Myth of Osiris Unnefer', in *Transactions of the Society of Biblical Archaeology*, vol. ix, 1893, pp. 288–90.

[2] ibid., pp. 291–2.

[3] With regard to the mythical and linguistic connection between the concepts of 'leaping' and 'creation', my friend, W. F. Jackson Knight, calls my attention to the fact that the Greek word θρώσκω, meaning

'And like the Egyptian *un* the Semitic very often acquires the derivative meanings of "being, existing, persisting".

'It is now, I trust, clear enough why *Unn* or *Unnu* should be an appropriate appellative of the rising Sun, who springs forth in glory and triumph.'[1]

Connection of the Hare-deity with Osiris the Moon-god

Le Page Renouf's article from which these quotations are made, though delivered in the form of a lecture in April 1886, was not published till 1893, but an earlier summary had appeared in *Academy* in May 1886 (p. 314) and parts of this summary were quoted by Andrew Lang in an article entitled 'Le Lièvre dans la Mythologie' appearing in the French jour-

'I leap', means also 'emit semen' and so 'beget'. Thus Aeschylus, in lines 658–61 of the *Eumenides*, written a year or two prior to 485 B.C., a play in which the relative roles of the father and mother are a cardinal issue, puts into Apollo's mouth the words, 'She who is called mother is not that one who gives life to the child. She is but one who nurses the swelling embryo. It is he who leaps [*θρῴσκον* 'the leaping one, i.e. the emitter of semen] who gives the life', that is to say that it is the father who is the true originator or creator of the child. In the same way θόρος is 'that which leaps', i.e. the semen. Similarly σπείρω means 'I sow seed' (i.e. cast it upon the ground), from which come σπόρος, a sowing, and σπερμα, the seed, that which is sown, whence our 'sperm', both these Greek words being used in connection with the human act of generation.

[1] P. Le Page Renouf, 'The Myth of Osiris Unnefer', in *Transactions of the Society of Biblical Archaeology*, vol. ix, 1893, pp. 292–3. Le. Page Renouf ends his article by calling attention to the large number of Egyptian porcelain figures in the British Museum representing the Hare, 'emblem of Osiris Onnophris' (the Greek spelling of Unnu-neferu), and to others in the Museum at Bulaq dating from the Saite period. He also quotes Maspero as saying, 'The hare was used frequently as an amulet, either to render the guardians of the other world favourable to the dead or else as representing the incarnation of Osiris'. Dr. Leemans also describes two of the monuments at Leyden as 'the Hare, one of the emblems of Osiris'. Modern scholars say there is no evidence as to what the precise purpose of the hare-amulets was, but it is interesting to compare their existence with that of the hare-amulets already noted from the late Chou period in China.

nal *Mélusine* of 1886–7[1] already referred to, in which he further discussed the evidence, though without apparently having Le Page Renouf's full text to refer to, with the result that he expressed himself unable to pronounce on the rival claims for the meaning of *un*, not seeing that there was in fact no contradiction between the two. Ten years later, in *Mélusine*, 1896–7 (vol. viii, cols. 25–9), Lefébure, having received a copy of the first edition of Lang's *Myth, Ritual, and Religion*, in an Appendix of which his previous article was reproduced under the title 'The Hare in Egypt',[2] took up the cudgels in favour of Le Page Renouf's interpretation, bringing a great deal of further evidence in support, particularly as regards the actuality of a Hare-deity in Egypt and its connection with Osiris in his aspect as Moon-god as being much more ancient than his equation with the Sun.[3]

Lefébure first points out that the apparent contradiction between the view expressed by certain savants following Plutarch and late Egyptian records that the title Unnefer given to Osiris means the 'Good Being' and Le Page Renouf's interpretation as meaning the 'Glorious Hare' is no contradiction at all if we regard the idea of the Hare as being the more primitive, and that of the 'Good Being' as being later, since, as Le Page Renouf intimates, this latter meaning is too metaphysical to be original.

He then proceeds, 'There were in Egypt two main figures capable of bearing the head or title of "hare"....

'One of these figures is the goddess *Un-t* or *Unnu-t* belonging to the city of that name, capital city of the fifteenth nome of Upper Egypt, which is also called *Un* or *Unnu*, that is to say,

[1] Andrew Lang, 'Le Lièvre dans la Mythologie', *Mélusine*, vol. iii, cols. 265–9. It is to be noted that in this article the title Unnefer is misprinted as 'Unneter'. This misspelling is corrected in the Appendix to his *Myth, Ritual, and Religion* referred to below.

[2] Andrew Lang, *Myth, Ritual, and Religion*, first edition, London, 1887, vol. ii, pp. 350–5. This appendix was omitted in the second edition published in 1901.

[3] E. Lefébure, 'Le Lièvre dans la Mythologie', *Mélusine*, vol. viii, cols. 25–9. All quotations from Lefébure are translated by the present writer from the original French.

according to several Egyptologists, the Nome of the Hare. The inhabitants of this nome adored a feminine deity called sometimes *Un-t*, sometimes Nehemauai, "she who averts evil", and sometimes Sefekh, "She who inverts the horns (the moon?)"; at Dendera the goddess Hathor was identified with this triple local form, here called also Shepes, "noble". As, from Pyramid times onward, this same city *Unnu* of the South had its parallel in the Northern *Unnu* of Lower Egypt, this goddess became doubled into an *Un-t* of the South and an *Un-t* of the North, which appear together on a monument of the Saite period. Of these the most important was she of the South, who existed in the IVth Dynasty as shown in a fire-lighting formula found in the temple of Unnu-t, the mistress of Unnu.[1] This goddess was, in the Ptolemaic period, represented as having the head of a hare, and was called Unnu-t, mistress of Unnu, regent of Dendera, and not mistress "of Unnu-t or Dendera" as Mr. Lang takes it to be in his discussion of M. le Page Renouf's memoir.[2] With her hare's head the figure of this goddess was used in the late periods [i.e. the Saite period onwards] as the hieroglyph representing the syllable *un*, as, for example, for the word for "hour", *un-t*, and for the word *un*, "to open".

'The other figure having, if not a hare's head, at least a similar name of which the hieroglyph represents a hare, was the god with whom we are concerned here, Osiris *Un-neferu*, whose name is written from New Empire times onward with the last word in the plural, *Un-nefer-u*. This more recent and rarer form of the title brings it into line with that found in the well-known proper names Ptah-nefer-u, Sebak-nefer-u, Ra-nefer-u, together with the honorific inversions Nefer-u-Ptah, and so on. It means therefore "the beauty" or the "splendour of Un". One even finds it in the form Nefer-Un.'[3]

[1] Book of the Dead, Spell 137A. In the rubric to this spell it is stated that 'these things shall be done secretly in the Underworld. They are mysteries of the Underworld.' (See E. A. Wallis Budge, *The Book of the Dead: The Chapters of the Coming Forth by Day*, London, 1898, p. 226.)

[2] See p. 148.

[3] E. Lefébure, 'Le Lièvre dans la Mythologie', *Mélusine*, vol. viii, cols. 25–6.

Lefébure goes on to give reasons for supposing that the name Unnefer may not have come into general use in Egypt till after the Old Kingdom,[1] but adds a warning that absence of evidence does not prove non-existence, since texts of this era are comparatively rare.

He then goes on to point out the further fact that 'Osiris is not exclusively, as M. le Page Renouf thinks, a solar god. [Indeed, the solar attribute of Osiris was a very late one.] The impression given by Egyptian texts indicates, on the contrary, that Osiris was fundamentally a being of the nether world, god of the dead, in other words a god of the underworld having the Nile as his efflux[2] and the moon for soul. The later equation of him with the sun was a secondary phenomenon, as it was with all the Egyptian gods.'[3]

He then cites a text recounting how Rameses IV himself inquired closely into the nature of Osiris according to the sacred books of Abydos, researches which he subsequently commemorated on a stela, and in which Osiris is nowhere confused with the sun. He also cites a royal protocol of Osiris which became popular from the XIIth Dynasty onwards, in which, 'in spite of the solar framework imposed by etiquette', Osiris Unnefer is described as 'the god who opens the womb (?) of the earth, the Nile, the bull of the abyss, a prince in Heliopolis (where he had a temple), the lord of the nether world, the heart's joy (a lunar title)[4] of the gods'.[5] He goes on, 'If Osiris was not the sun, it is apparent that he was often the moon, that is to say, the luminary of the dead, a type of symbolism of which the

[1] That is to say as a divine name, i.e. as an epithet of Osiris, which occurs first in the XIIth Dynasty. It was in use as a personal name already in the Old Kingdom.

[2] The Nile was thought to flow out of the mummified body of Osiris, an interesting parallel to the blood and water flowing from Christ's side and to the blood flowing from the wound of the Mithraic bull, thus causing the fertility of all things needful to man.

[3] E. Lefébure, 'Le Lièvre dans la Mythologie', *Mélusine*, vol. viii, col. 27.

[4] In fairness it must be pointed out that modern scholars deny the special lunar significance of this attribute.

[5] E. Lefébure, 'Le Lièvre dans la Mythologie', *Mélusine*, vol. viii, col. 28.

treatise on Isis and Osiris attributed to Plutarch bears the deepest imprint. There exist also representations and statuettes of Osiris the Moon, not of Osiris the Sun. Moreover, the city of Un belonging to the goddess Un-t was the Hermopolis of the Greeks, the city of the Egyptian Hermes, Thoth, who is the essential personification of the moon, and whose cult became joined with that of this goddess from the days of the Old Empire onward. Osiris himself, who was equated with Thoth had at Un a temple called *Nefer*, the place of his glories, *nefer-u*, probably a pun on the name Un-nefer, which through a further pun is translated "Beautiful Colours". Under these circumstances it is not surprising to find Osiris Unnefer figured inside the lunar disk, as is the case at Karnak,[1] and also the goddess of the Moon-city represented as, *par excellence*, having a hare's head.' He adds, very relevantly to the subject of this article, 'Do not almost all peoples of the earth take the marks on the moon to represent the image of a hare?'[2]

'The concept of a Lunar Hare can thus be traced back to a very remote antiquity in Egypt, since the hare, known on the banks of the Nile from earliest times, had already, in the historical period or at least by the XIIth Dynasty, lost its original name of *un*, which is not found either in Coptic, and which was retained only as a hieroglyphic sign representing the phonetic value of *un* in writing.'

Connection of the Hare-deity with Thoth, Hermes, and Mercury, and the association of all these with writing

After a brief summary, which does not concern us here, of its possible totemic nature, Lefébure ends his article with the words, 'We must not lose sight of the Osirian and Hermopolitan symbolism which has been referred to. . . . It would in fact be a very curious coincidence, that a hare-headed goddess should have been worshipped in the Moon City and that a Hare God called by the same name should have been placed in the moon if each of these was not the Hare-Moon.'[3]

The fact that the city of the hare-goddess Un was also the city

[1] See p. 147.

[2] E. Lefébure, 'Le Lièvre dans la Mythologie', *Mélusine*, vol. viii, cols. 28, 29. (Translated by the author.)

[3] ibid., col. 29.

of Thoth, who is himself the personification of the moon, and who in Greek times was identified with Hermes to such an extent that the city became called Hermopolis, is of special interest on account of what we actually know of Hermes and of his Roman counterpart the god Mercury. Though it is true that the metal we now call mercury was not so named till the thirteenth century A.D., the fact of its being named after the god, together with its adjective 'mercurial', alone gives a clue to what the god stood for. The metal mercury is unique in its versatility in that it is the only metal that is fluid at ordinary temperatures, that is to say that it is symbolically solid and fluid at once. It is thus the only metal that under ordinary circumstances *runs*. So the god Mercury, like his Greek counterpart Hermes, is regarded as the messenger of the gods, and bears wings on his head and feet to indicate his swiftness. The metal mercury is also moon-coloured, which brings it into line with the moon personified by Thoth. The gods Thoth, Hermes, and Mercury, of which the historically oldest is Thoth, are all regarded as personifying 'the external expression of thought, whether human or divine', of which, since he was a god, we may presume that the divine was earliest and therefore the most fundamental.

The chief symbol, both of Hermes and Mercury, was the caduceus or magic wand with twin serpents entwined round it, which is perhaps the world's most famous healing symbol. Hermes, Mercury, and Thoth were also said to be the inventors of writing. In the case of Thoth, this refers not only to written characters but also to literary composition and especially to the so-called 'sacred language'. Words are, of course, the chief messengers between man and man, and the attribution of the invention and patronage of writing to the god Thoth calls inevitably to mind the opening passages of Saint John's Gospel, saying, 'the Word was with God, and the word was God. . . . In him was life, and the life was the light of men. And the light shineth in darkness; and the darkness overpowered[1] it not.'

[1] The Authorized Version has 'comprehended', but 'overpowered' is a more accurate translation. James Moffatt translates the passage, 'Amid the darkness the Light shone, but the darkness did not master it'.

The light in the darkness is among early peoples commonly symbolized by the moon, which brings us back again to the moon-personality of Thoth, and to the fact that, as already seen, the Great Hare of the Algonkin is also credited with the invention of picture-writing, that is to say, of symbolic thought.

Finally, Hermes, under the form of Hermes Trismegistos, or Hermes the Thrice Greatest, came in medieval times to be regarded as the special depository of all magical knowledge. It is he who is said by some to have founded Hermopolis, the city of the hare-headed goddess. His alleged writings were famous throughout the Alexandrine period, and these 'hermetic' works formed the background of most European alchemy, that interesting mixture of early chemical experimentation and symbolic philosophy of which the main preoccupation was in its material aspect the transmutation of base metals into gold, in other words the spiritualization of matter, and in its spiritual aspect the transformation of base natures into divine, in other words the redemptive process of which Mrs. Wright's dream-sacrifice of the hare was a potent symbol.

THE HARE IN AFRICA

THE HARE AS TRICKSTER-HERO

Among the present-day inhabitants of the African continent the hare has no such deep mythical associations as we have seen it to have elsewhere. This does not mean that there are not numerous folk-tales associated with it. Frobenius indeed has constructed a map showing the distribution of folk-tales in which the hare figures as a kind of trickster-hero, a distribution covering the greater part of the Sudan stretching from Senegal on the west coast to the Red Sea on the east, and from thence spreading south to include many parts of East Africa, Rhodesia, whence it branches off into Angolia and also Portuguese East Africa and thence to Bechuanaland and the Transvaal.[1] In these areas the hare plays the role that other trickster animals play in other parts of the Continent. It has not been possible for me to examine all the tales recorded from these areas, but those published by Frobenius from among the Mande-speaking peoples inhabiting northern Liberia and the neighbouring districts, and also the Mossi to the north of the Gold Coast, while depicting the hare as a wise animal and trickster eluding his enemies through the exercise of his great ingenuity and, as such, being in the nature of humorous character-sketches, do not appear to have any mythological bearing which would warrant their inclusion in the present inquiry.[2]

[1] Leo Frobenius, *Erlebte Erdteile*, vol, vi, *Monumenta Africana*, Frankfurt, 1929, map 42, p. 420.

[2] Leo Frobenius, *Atlantis: Volksmärchen und Volksdichtungen Afrikas*, Jena, 1922, vol. viii, *Erzählungen aus dem Westsudan*, Tales 47–58 from the Mande-speaking peoples among whom the hare is called *Sani* or *Sonsanni*, and Tales 98 and 101–7 from the Mossi by whom the hare is called *Samba*.

For similar tales from among the Shilluk, see D. Westermann, *The Shilluk People, Their Language and Folk-lore*, Philadelphia, 1912; from Bari, Anuak, and Moru see *Folk Stories from the Sudan*,

It is nevertheless possible that, among the large number of these tales, some at least preserve in a disguised and humorous form a faint echo of mythological motives already encountered in other parts of the world. Instances of this are the following tales recorded by Madeleine Holland from among the Banyanja of Central Africa.

The Man tries to burn the Hare, but fails

The first, recalling the voluntary sacrifice of Buddha in the form of a Hare by leaping into a fire, relates how 'there was a Man who had often tried to get the Hare and kill him. One day he caught him and said, "Now, I have got you!" and tied him up to a tree and went to get some fire. He wanted to set all the grass round about alight and then the Hare would be burnt too. The Hare sat quiet until he saw a Jackal coming down the road; then he began to call out very loud. The Jackal said, "What is the matter?" The Hare said, "That man *will* go and get meat to feed me; and I don't know how to eat it." The Jackal said, "All right, if you don't like it, come away and tie *me* up where you are, because I am hungry for meat." He loosened the Hare and the Hare tied him up in his place. By and by a crowd came back with the Man shouting, "We'll burn you!" The Jackal says, "What are they shouting?" The Hare says, "They are saying they are bringing a great deal of meat." After the grass was burnt, the people found the body of the Jackal; but the Hare ran away.'[1]

Later, the Hare carried out a similar deception by means of which he caused the Man who tried to burn him in a hut to burn his children instead. The Man, not knowing that the Hare had decoyed his children into the hut and had itself escaped,

vol. iii. Further Anuak stories by E. E. Evans-Pritchard, together with some Moru stories contributed by T. H. B. Mynors, *Sudan Notes and Records*, 1941, vol. xxiv, pp. 69–84; from the Yao and Nyanja of Nyasaland, see Alice Werner, in *Folk-lore*, 1899, vol. x, pp. 282–93; from the Ronga, see H. A. Junod, *Les Chants et les contes des Ba-Ronga de la Baie de Delagoa*, Lausanne, 1897.

[1] Madeleine Holland, 'Folk-lore of the Banyanja', *Folk-lore*, 1916, p. 13.

set fire to the hut, whereon one of the children cried out, "I am not a hare, father; I am your child'; but the Man says, 'No, I know you are the Hare'. The child called out its own name, but the Man would not listen, and burnt them—and the Hare laughed.[1]

There is no indication here of any connection of the Hare with the Moon as in the Buddha story, but in another tale from the same collection there is at least a connection with the sky.

The Man proposes to the Hare that they should kill their mothers. The Hare puts his mother into the sky

'There was a Hare and he was the friend of a Man. One day the Hare said, "Let us kill our mothers, then we shall both be free". The Man thought it would be good, so he killed his mother. The Hare did not kill his mother; he only took his knife and stabbed at a plant with red juice till his knife was red, then he showed it to the Man and said, "With this knife I killed her". The Man thought she was dead, because he never saw her again; but the Hare had put her up in the sky. Every day he used to go by himself and she used to let down a rope and pull him up and give him food. The Man had no-one to feed him. He saw that the Hare was very fat and asked him who fed him. The Hare said, "No-one." Then the Man watched him and saw how he went to a certain place and said, "Cast down the rope", and a rope came down and he climbed up. So the next day the Man went and said, "Cast down the rope", but his voice was too loud. The Hare's mother knew it was not her child. So then the Hare came and the Man hid away and listened. He heard the Hare say softly, "Cast down the rope', and the rope came down and the Hare climbed up. Another day the man went and said very softly, "Cast down the rope", and the Hare's mother thought it was her son, so she let down the rope and the Man went up. He killed the Hare's mother and all the Hare's little ones; only one remained alive. Then he went away. When the Hare came he found the

[1] Madeleine Holland, 'Folk-lore of the Banyanja', *Folk-lore*, 1916, p. 13.

rope hanging: he went up and saw that his mother and all his little ones were dead except one small hare. He asked it, "Who has done this?" and it said, "Your friend the Man." The Hare went to his hut and wept. The Man came in and found him weeping and said, "What is the matter? why do you weep?" He said, "The sun is hurting my eyes." Next day he went and got red stones and heated them in a pot. He told the Man, "I have found a place where there is plenty of game. Lie in the road, open your mouth and shut your eyes and I will throw it in." The Man lay down in the road, opened his mouth and shut his eyes and the Hare threw the stones down his throat and killed him.'[1]

This tale, as well as establishing the hare's connection with the sky world, is deeply significant in view of the fact that of the two sexes the woman is the prime repository of instinct which the man representing society is in the habit of mistakenly wishing to destroy. The hare knows, on the other hand, as we have seen in the case of the Hare-Buddha, that instinct must not be destroyed but must on the contrary be transformed. In tricking the Man to kill his mother the hare thus demonstrates what mankind is always so prone to do to its instinctive life. The hare, on the contrary, transforms his, as symbolized by his putting his mother into the sky and remaining in communion with her there (the rope corresponding to Jacob's ladder which unites heaven and earth). The man, however, still bent on the same mischief, then also destroys the hare's, but suffers for it himself, though it will be noted that his destructive zeal does not entirely succeed, since one small hare still capable of growing up remains in the sky to maintain the hare's own connection with the spiritual world.

The Hare rides the Lion

One other tale is worth mentioning, called 'The Hare Rides the Lion': 'Once there was a Lion, who came to a town and said, "I want this man to be my brother and by and by I will take him to my house". The Man said, "Very well", so every

[1] Madeleine Holland, 'Folk-lore of the Banyanja', *Folk-lore*, 1916, pp. 25–6.

day the Lion came to visit him. By and by the Hare came in and saw this, so he went away and put on nice clothes and came back, saying, "I want this man to be my brother". The Men said, "No, he is the Lion's brother." He said, "The Lion is of no importance; he is my horse." The Man laughed but the Hare repeated it. He went home and the Men told the Lion what the Hare had said. The Lion was very angry and said he would go and get the Hare and make him tell them that he had spoken falsely. He went to the Hare and told him what the Men had said. The Hare denied it and said if he were not feeling so ill he would go and tell the Men themselves that they had said what was not true. The Lion wanted him to come and say so; but the Hare said he was too ill to walk. The Lion said, "Very well, I will carry you." The Hare said, "Very well, because I want to tell them it is a lie." So the Lion took him on his back. By and by the Hare says he is so weak that he will fall off unless the Lion will let him put a bridle in his mouth (a rope made of bark from a tree). The Lion submits and goes on with the rope in his mouth. By and by the Hare says the flies bother him so that he cannot hold on and asks the Lion to give him a little stick to drive them away. The Lion says, "Very well", and gives him a switch. Then they come near to the town and all the Men come out and see the Hare riding on the Lion's back and beating him with a switch. He says, "Hi! hi! didn't I say you were my horse?"'[1].

This, too, recalls the Indian tale quoted on page 117 in which the hare tricks the lion. In that tale the hare tricked the lion into destroying itself, but in this African version the lion (here representing brute force, or unredeemed instinct), is tamed by the hare, representing the power of mind over body, thus bringing it clearly into line, though on a humorous level, with concepts found in the previous tale and elsewhere of the hare as representing transformed instinct or spiritual power.

'The Hare's Skin in the Moon's Face'

While none of the tales from this central area which I have

[1] Madeleine Holland, 'Folk-lore of the Banyanja', *Folk-lore*, 1916, pp. 48–9.

read show the hare as being definitely connected with the moon, others from both north and south of the African continent quite definitely do. One such is a story told by the Abâbde Bedouin in the neighbourhood of the Hamâta mountains near the Red Sea due east of Aswân in Upper Egypt, of which the following is a free translation. It is entitled 'The Hare's Skin in the Moon's Face', and runs: 'Sun and Moon are two sisters. Formerly they were both cold. They walked side by side in the sky. Once they caught a hare, skinned it, and put it in the cooking-pot. While the hare was stewing, the two began to quarrel. They abused one another. In her rage the Sun picked up the hare's skin and flung it into the Moon's face. The Moon, on her part, grasped the cooking-pot and flung the boiling contents into the Sun's face. Since that time hare's skin is to be seen in the full Moon, and since that time the Sun is hot, and since that time they do not any more walk side by side in the sky.'[1]

THE ORIGIN OF DEATH

The other African area in which the hare is definitely connected with the moon is in the extreme south, where it appears in a Hottentot variant of the widespread South African myth dealing with the Origin of Death. The Bantu peoples all have similar myths, in which different animals are represented as taking the chief roles. In all these tales some animal is en-

[1] Hans Alexander Winkler, *Ägyptische Volkskunde*, Stuttgart, 1936, p. 332. Dr. Meinhard, who kindly called my attention to this tale, adds: 'It should be noted that the Fellaheen of the Nile Valley do not seem to have any such beliefs. From Upper Egypt to the Delta they see in the moon either a tree, or a human figure, or face, or a bowl containing flat cakes. The tree is usually a date-palm. The human figure in the moon is described sometimes as a 'man plaiting a basket', or as a 'basket-maker sitting under a date-palm', or else as 'the daughter of the wood-gatherer', or 'the wife of the wood-gatherer', sometimes also as 'the image of the Prophet', etc. See Winkler, ibid., pp. 238–9. The 'basket-maker' calls to mind the 'weaving' or 'spinning woman' in the moon of Indonesia and other parts of the world; in Polynesia, where there is no weaving, this concept is replaced by that of a 'plaiter in the Moon'.

trusted with a message to tell man of Immortality, but invariably gets the message wrong.

The Chameleon and the Lizard

Thus, among the Zulus, Unkulunkulu ('the old-old-one', the most ancient being) sends the chameleon, saying, '"Go, Chameleon, go and say, Let not men die." The chameleon set out; it went slowly; it loitered in the way; and, as it went, it ate of the fruit of a tree, which is called Ubukwebezane. At length Unkulunkulu sent a lizard after the chameleon, when it had already set out for some time. The lizard went; it ran and made great haste, for Unkulunkulu had said, "Lizard, when you have arrived, say, Let men die." So the lizard went, and said, "I tell you, It is said, Let men die." The lizard came back to Unkulunkulu, before the chameleon had reached his destination, the chameleon which was sent first, which was sent and told to go and say, "Let not men die."

'At length it arrived and shouted, saying, "It is said, Let not men die!" But men answered, "O! we have heard the word of the lizard; it has told us the word, 'It is said, Let men die.' We cannot hear your word. Through the word of the lizard men will die."'[1]

The Ronga tell the same story, also of chameleon and lizard.[2]

The use of the chameleon as the animal that really knows is interesting, since owing to its ability to change colour and to the fact that its eyes move independently of one another, it is a fitting symbol of extreme adaptability and of that 'seeing both ways' which is the essence of true spiritual life having one eye on the temporal affairs of men and the other eye simultaneously on the eternal affairs of God. Owing to its habit of living high up among the branches of trees and of inflating itself with air, it was in classical times accredited with the power of 'living on air', which is another symbol of spirit, derived

[1] H. Callaway, *The Religious System of the Amazula*, Natal, 1868, part I, pp. 3–4.

[2] H. A. Junod, *Les Chants et les contes des Ba-Ronga de la Baie de Delagoa*, Lausanne, 1897, p. 137.

from the Latin *spiritus*, meaning 'breath' or 'air'. The fact that its message of immortality was reversed by its biological cousin the lizard which has none of these qualities is a symbol that 'one way' thinking always does get its facts wrong because it is incapable of ever seeing the 'other side'.

The Moon sends the Hare to tell men of Immortality, but he gets the message wrong and the Moon slits his lip.

It must be admitted that in the Hottentot version of the myth the hare also is represented as the half-wit, though it is significant that in this version the hare is sent, not by an anthropomorphic 'old one' but by the Moon which itself every month dies and is reborn. Bleek quotes several forms of this Hottentot myth, one of which runs as follows:

'The Moon, it is said, sent once an Insect to Men, saying, "Go thou to Men, and tell them, 'As I die, and dying live, so ye shall also die, and dying live'".' The Insect started with the message, but whilst on his way was overtaken by the Hare, who asked, "On what errand art thou bound?" The Insect answered, "I am sent by the Moon to Men, to tell them that as she dies, and dying lives, they also shall die, and dying live." The Hare said, "As thou art an awkward runner, let me go" (to take the message). With these words he ran off, and when he reached Men, he said, "I am sent by the Moon to tell you, 'As I die, and dying perish, in the same manner ye shall also die and come wholly to an end'". Then the Hare returned to the Moon and told her what he had said to Men. The Moon reproached him angrily, saying, "Darest thou tell the people a thing which I have not said?" With these words she took up a piece of wood, and struck him on the nose. Since that day the Hare's nose is slit.'[1]

[1] W. H. I. Bleek, *Reynard the Fox in South Africa, or, Hottentot Fables and Tales.* London, 1864, pp. 69–72. According to another version: 'The Moon dies, and rises to life again. The Moon said to the Hare, "Go thou to Men, and tell them, 'Like as I die and rise to life again, so you also shall die and rise to life again'." The Hare went to the Men, and said, "Like as I die and do not rise to life again, so you shall also die, and not rise to life again". When he returned, the Moon asked him, "What hast thou said?" "I have told them,

We have already met in China with the hare pounding the Herb of Immortality in the moon. 'Immortality' is, by the way, like the 'eternity' of Christian belief, no mere hope for the future, but refers to that basic reality at the very centre of the psyche—the divine spark within—which *is* immortal and eternal, because it is universal, common in all ages to all life. It is the loss of this which, as in the Christian story of the Fall, all peoples on earth in their respective mythologies deplore, which in turn means, of course, that they have got out of touch with that ultimate reality which is eternal, and which all seek through their religions to regain.

The insistence on the splitting of the hare's lip is probably due also to its being used originally as a symbol for the split in men's lives that all these tales refer to, and which is commonly referred to as 'separation from God', that is to say, the separation of temporal values from their creative union with eternal truth.

The Hare kills a monster, but offends the Chief

Finally, W. G. Black quotes from Theal's *Kaffir Folk-lore*[1]

'Like as I die and do not rise to life again, so you shall also die and not rise to life again.'" "What," said the Moon, "hast thou said that?" And she took a stick and beat the Hare on his mouth, which was slit by the blow. The Hare fled, and is still fleeing. ['We are now angry with the Hare,' said the old Namaqua, 'because he brought such a bad message, and therefore we dislike to eat his flesh.']

In yet another version it was with a hatchet that the moon slit the hare's lip, whereon the hare 'raised his claws, and scratched the Moon's face; and the dark parts which we now see on the surface of the Moon are the scars which she received on that occasion'. With regard to a Bushman version of the Moon and Hare story called 'The Origin of Death', see W. H. I. Bleek and L. C. Lloyd, *Specimens of Bushmen Folk-lore*, London, 1911, pp. 56–65.

Dr. Meinhard, who called my attention to these stories, points out that the Tibetans tell similar tales regarding the hare as trickster, quoting Capt. W. F. O'Connor, *Folk Tales from Tibet*, London, 1906. The first tale ends with the hare being so amused by the mischief he had done 'that he leaned back on a handy stone, and laughed to such an extent that he actually split his upper lip. And it has remained split to this very day'.

[1] W. G. Black, *Folk-lore*, vol. iii, pp. 88–9.

to the effect that 'the animals . . . had made a kraal and appointed one after another the coney, the muishond, the duiker, and bluebuck, and the porcupine to keep watch over the fat stored therein, and to signal the approach of the inkalimeva (a fabulous animal). These all failed in the duty and were killed by the other animals. The sixth time that fat is put into the kraal the hare is selected as keeper of the gate, rather against his will. He skilfully makes an end of the dreaded inkalimeva, but as he eats the tail, which should have been reserved for the chief, he has to flee for his life.'

This tale beautifully illustrates both positive and negative aspects of the hare's intuitive power. Its ability to deal successfully with the mythical monster represents its deep knowledge of the world of inner reality, while its failure to satisfy convention provides just that apparent futility which justifies its widespread African reputation as a trickster.

The number 6 is a ritual number used among many peoples to indicate that spiritual knowledge which comes as a result of being able to reconcile 'both sides'. One of the best known symbols of this is the Jewish 'Shield of David', ✡ a six-pointed emblem formed of triangles (a double trinity), one pointing upwards towards the sky and the other downwards towards the earth, representing the union of external and internal realities.

FIGURE 14. Saxon 'Idol of the Moon' in the form of a goddess wearing a chapron representing the head and shoulders of a Hare, and holding a Moon-disk containing a human face

From R. Verstigan, *A Restitution of Decayed Intelligence*, Antwerp, 1605, Chapter 3

THE HARE IN EUROPE

SAXON GODDESS OF MONDAY WEARING A HARE-CHAPRON AND CARRYING A MOON-DISK

Having in a previous section dealt with the hare-headed goddess in Ancient Egypt and her connection with the moon, it may possibly come as less of a shock to the reader to find that our own Saxon ancestors worshipped a similar goddess also connected with the moon.

Thus, in a very interesting work published in 1605, we find a chapter headed 'Of the ancient manner of lyving of our Saxon ancestors. Of the Idolles they adored whyle they were pagans: and how they grew to be of greater name and habitation of any other people of Germany.' In this chapter, which deals with the deities connected with the several days of the week, we read:

'The next according to the cours of the dayes of the week, was the Idol of the Moon whereof wee yet retain the name of *Monday* instead of Mōōday, and it was made according to the picture heer following.

'The form of this Idol seemeth very strange and ridiculous, for beeing made for a woman shee hath a short cote lyke a man: but more strange it is to see her hood with such two long eares. The holding of a moon before her brest may seem to have bin to expresse what shee is, but the reason of her chapron with long eares, as also of her shorte cote and pyked shuwes, I do not fynd.'[1]

The accompanying illustration (Fig. 14), reproduced from this work, shows clearly that the 'chapron with long eares' is in fact a headdress representing the head and shoulders of a hare.

[1] R. Verstegan (pseudonym for Richard Rowlands), *A Restitution of Decayed Intelligence: In Antiquities. Concerning the most noble and renowned English nation*, Antwerp, 1605, chapter 3. I am indebted to Professor J. H. Hutton for calling my attention to this remarkable work.

It will be noted, morever, that the moon is held, not, as the writer suggests, before her breast but before her abdomen, thus indicating that the hare-goddess is in fact pregnant of the moon, and that in the moon's disk are delineated the features of what may be either an old woman, recalling the 'grandmother' in the moon of the Hiawathan story referred to on p. 171 (note 1), or else our own 'man in the moon' corresponding to the Malekulan belief referred to on p. 147 (note 1).

Pregnancy is another 'dawn' symbol, adumbrating 'new birth', and indicates almost more vividly than any previously cited myth the spiritually pregnant nature of the mythical hare so clearly seen in Mrs. Wright's dream.

REMNANTS OF WORSHIP OF A HARE-GODDESS IN MODERN EUROPE

THE EASTER HARE

CUSTOMS STILL EXTANT IN EASTERN EUROPE

It may be asked, 'Are there no remnants of this worship of the hare-goddess in modern Europe?' The answer is, of course, that there are. One such faint echo is the fact that children in Swabia may not make shadows on the wall to represent the sacred Moon Hare,[1] which recalls the Hare in the Moon of mythological belief elsewhere. More important than this, however, are the numerous European customs connected with the Hare that lays the Easter eggs. The Easter Hare and its accompanying coloured eggs have only recently been reintroduced into England, but represent a whole series of customs still living in many parts of Europe, where they are evidently a survival of what at one time must have been an organized ritual in honour of the hare-goddess.

Easter is itself of course the great Dawn Festival of Christianity, combining as it does the motive of the Resurrection with that of the springtime rebirth of nature. From the standpoint of nature-myth, it would be expected that it should be

[1] W. G. Black, 'The Hare in Folk-lore', *The Folk-lore Journal*, vol. i, p. 88, quoting Grimm.

most deep-rooted in Eastern Europe where the rebirth of nature after a snow-bound winter is so much more striking than in the more temperate climate of the West.

It was my good fortune, while writing this memoir, to meet an Austrian peasant woman who gave me in graphic terms the following account of what she says still happens in many parts of Austria, Czechoslovakia, Hungary, and other neighbouring lands.

First Easter Egg presented before Sunrise on Easter Day

'On Palm Sunday catkins (representing palms) are brought to church and are there consecrated, after which they are taken home and kept in the garden till Easter. On Easter Sunday a lovely rite commemorating the Resurrection is performed in each home, and takes the form of children rising *before sunrise* [note the dawn symbolism] to bring the catkins into the house. The first child to bring in such a catkin is immediately rewarded with the first Easter Egg.'

'Other eggs, hard-boiled and coloured, chiefly red and blue but also with other pigments, are hidden, in large quantities sometimes totalling several hundred, in "nests" all over the garden, and are searched for by the children when the family returns in the morning from High Mass.'

The Hare that lays the Easter Eggs mimed by child on visit to grandmother

'The hare that lays these eggs does not appear, however, until the afternoon, when the children all visit their grandmothers.[1] It does not seem to matter nowadays which grandmother it is, but it must be a grandmother or a grandmother

[1] This visiting of the grandmother is strangely reminiscent of the large number of cases in which the grandmother is connected with the moon, presumably as the archetype of the Old Woman. The reader will be reminded, among other instances, of the lines in Longfellow's *Hiawatha*:

Once a warrior, very angry,
Seized his grandmother, and threw her
Up into the sky at midnight;
Right against the moon he threw her;
'Tis her body that you see there.

substitute, such as an aunt if no actual grandmother is alive or near enough to receive the visit. Whoever the "grandmother" may be, however, the chief figure in the homely procession to her house (which may be miles away from the children's home) is a child dressed in a cape with head and ears representing a hare, who on his or her back carries a small water butt filled with coloured eggs.'

The reader will not fail in this account to recognize the 'hare-goddess' cited above. Nor will he fail to note that the eggs carried by the hare (albeit on the hare's back, since this is easier than in front) take the place of the moon 'carried' by the Saxon goddess, both being symbols of rebirth. The narrator proceeds:

'Meanwhile, "grandmother" has kneaded special Easter Cake made of fine dough puffed up with yeast and baked so as to give it a lovely golden brown colour. This cake is made in the shape of a platter, and is, too, filled with coloured eggs. Prayers are said, and then the afternoon feast consisting of all sorts of dainty foods is consumed. But the chief event, so far as the children are concerned, is the behaviour of the child dressed as a hare. The first eggs out of its butt are given to grandmother, then others to grandfather, and to the parents. It is now that the fun begins. The children all want eggs too. But the power is with the hare-child, who dodges here and there, in and out and round about the house and garden, chased by the rest, to whom it gives its eggs only at its own sweet will, at times stingily withholding, and at others showering its Easter gifts to favourites or others, who snatch and scramble till all the eggs are gone. Eggs from the Easter cake (which is in the form of a nest) are distributed more sedately, but this scramble is renewed when further nests full of coloured eggs are found and searched for all over the grandmother's garden, as in the morning at home.'

The same symbolism is found in the small coral islet of Vao, off the coast of Malekula in the Pacific Ocean, where the moon is called 'grandmother' and conceives children by the God of Light shining upon her, whence they descend to earth through the portal of their mothers' wombs (John Layard, *Stone Men of Malekula*, pp. 212–13).

Game of stabbing an Egg with a Silver Coin

Games also are played, at least one of which has ritual meaning. This consists in somebody holding a coloured egg, while a child, holding a silver coin of the approximate size of an English florin, has quickly to stab the egg with the coin. If the stabber aims well and manages to pierce the egg in the centre, piercing the shell so that the coin sinks right into the egg, both egg and coin are his.

The symbolism of this is clear. On the one hand, the egg of course represents potential life, but, as in real life, cannot come to fruition without fertilization from outside. The silver coin is clearly the fertilizing element. Silver traditionally represents the moon just as gold represents the sun. It is quite true that the egg itself was a few paragraphs back itself equated with the moon, but degraded symbolism, such as this, is apt to become a little mixed. Here, however, the egg clearly represents the dark matter that is penetrated by the light, just as the light of Christ penetrated the tomb, and so paved the way for the Resurrection. From another angle it also represents spirit penetrating matter, as the light of consciousness penetrates the dark night of the soul.

Sugar Eggs containing Religious Pictures. Live hares given as pets.

The same symbolism is seen in the making of sugar eggs, each hollow and with a little window in it, through which can be seen, inside the egg, a picture of Christ rising from the tomb, or of some other religious subject. The whole ritual calls inevitably to mind the Great Egg which is the central religious symbol in Easter Island, that lonely outpost in the Eastern Pacific with its huge megalithic monuments, where so much religious activity at one time took place.[1] Here in Eastern Europe, however, it is so intimately connected with the hare that not only is the hare supposed to lay the eggs, as symbolized by the hare-child bearing them on its back, but live hares are

[1] See Mrs. Scoresby Routledge, *The Mystery of Easter Island*, London, 1919, pp. 254 sqq.

actually given to children as pets and are let loose on Easter Day to play, so long as they do not altogether escape.

Symbolic play

All this information was given to me by my peasant Austrian friend with that mixture of robust humour and childlike delight that are the essence of such symbolic play, not only in Europe but also among primitive peoples, with some of whom the writer has lived and worked, and whose attitude towards that part of their ritual life is precisely similar.[1] She ended her account with sparkling eyes saying, 'But you know it isn't true. The hare doesn't really lay eggs', almost as if I really believed from her account that it did. This is a typically symbolic-intuitive remark, showing that with one part of herself she thought it was. Indeed, unless one part of the personality believed the make-believe, such play would not be possible. It is of course the spiritual part—that which the French call *esprit*—that in fact knows it to be true on a certain level. For the unconscious is the mirror opposite of the conscious. Thus, no material hare would be pleased to have its back slit open as happened in Mrs. Wright's dream, but in her dream it was, because the hare was in fact that unredeemed part of herself that wanted to be redeemed—i.e. transformed into, or united with, its opposite. Thus, in the spirit, the hare representing intuition does in fact lay the eggs of new life, because, of the four psychological functions, intuition alone is that which does actually bring about such transformations. This is of course akin to the famous saying *credo quia impossibile*, meaning that the apparently impossible *is* true, and only seems impossible if we confuse symbolic truth with its complementary opposite, namely the actual facts of a one-sidedly conceived purely materialistic world. I have no doubt whatever that such play stimulates and tends to actuate the inner knowledge of the incarnation of God in man, that is to say of the vitalizing effect of the re-entry of spirit into matter, far more effectively than many serious disquisitions heard from the pulpit or text books

[1] See John Layard, *Stone Men of Malekula*, London, 1942, part iii, on 'Ritual Life', particularly pp. 382 sqq., 511 sqq., 547.

on religious knowledge. Jung once said that the only divine thing he knew in mankind was humour, by which he meant that joyful sense of the incongruous that joins fact to fiction which is essentially the symbolic aspect of fact. This statement is itself a joke, and not to be taken either as blasphemous or as the final word, but is a symbolic way of indicating that union of opposites which warms the cockles of the heart, whether as secular joke or as the life-giving knowledge of the divine spark in man.

The date of Easter regulated by the Moon

Though there is little direct reference in this account to any connection between the Easter Hare and the Moon, it must be remembered that the date of Easter is itself in all Christian Churches regulated by the moon. Billson further points out that 'the moon's periodic death and revival suggest thoughts of Resurrection and Immortality, and recalls the South African myth already quoted in which the moon sends the hare to men, saying, "Like as I die and rise to life again, so you shall also die and rise to life again", which he refers to as an "Easter Gospel" '.[1]

In this connection it is of interest to note the curious mistake made by one writer[2] in taking the animal figured in Dürer's woodcut of the Last Supper (in his series known as 'The Smaller Passion') as the chief item in the meal to be a hare, whereas its tail bones show it quite clearly to be a lamb. The same writer refers to what he speaks of as a similar representation 'in the east window of the beautiful little chapel attached to the house in Gatton Park, described as being a fine specimen of Flemish or German medieval workmanship'. Mindful of the Mosaic law forbidding the Jews to eat the hare[3] and not having seen the east window in question, I can make no pronounce-

[1] See pp. 165 and C. J. Billson, 'The Easter Hare', *Folk-lore*, vol. iii, pp. 459–60, which gives a large number of references.

[2] T. H. Pattison, 'The Hare in representations of the Last Supper', *Notes and Queries*, 1856, 2nd series, vol. ii, p. 490, quoted by C. J. Billson, *Folk-lore*, vol. iii, p. 451, (note 1).

[3] Leviticus xi, 6.

ment on this, and merely mention the alleged anachronism in passing, in order to introduce the question as to whether the hare ever was a sacrificial animal in Europe.

THE HARE FORMERLY A SACRIFICIAL ANIMAL IN EUROPE

Billson, in a long and very interesting article on '*The Easter Hare*', answers this question in the affirmative by citing a considerable body of evidence, based partly on the European custom of eating the Easter Hare, best known in Pomerania, where hares are caught at Eastertide to provide a public meal,[1] and partly on customs still surviving until comparatively recently in England. One such refers to the custom of killing a hare on Good Friday, recorded in a Calendar of State Papers dated 1620.[2]

'*Hunting the Easter Hare*' *and the* '*Hallaton Hare-pie Scramble*'

The two most detailed accounts of such customs come from Leicestershire. A custom called 'Hunting the Easter Hare' survived late into the eighteenth century, and, as recorded in Throsby's *History of Leicester*, consisted of a mock hunting of the hare in the form of a dead cat[3] trailed before the hounds. The hunt ended at the Mayor's door, whither the dead cat had been trailed, loudly applauded by the populace, whereon the Mayor 'gave a handsome treat to his friends'.[4] This custom fell into disuse about the year 1767, though traces of it lingered in the form of an annual holiday or fair held on Easter Monday. Though Billson comments that from various other items of information 'the hunting was originally, as

[1] C. J. Billson, *Folk-lore*, vol. iii, p. 443, quoting Elton, *Origins of English History*, second edition., 1890, pp. 390.

[2] C. J. Billson, *Folk-lore*, vol. iii, p. 442.

[3] For the connection of hares with cats, see p. 197.

[4] C. J. Billson, *Folk-lore*, vol. iii, pp. 442–3, quoted from Throsby's *History of Leicester*, p. 166.

might be expected, that of a real hare', its sacrificial nature is not very apparent, but becomes more so when it is compared with another custom still in force in the year 1892 in another part of the same country, called the 'Hallaton Hare-pie Scramble and Bottle-kicking'. The word 'Hallaton' is said to mean 'Holy town', and here, 'at a remote period, a piece of land was bequeathed to the Rector conditionally that he and his successors *continued* annually 'two hare pies, a quantity of ale, and two dozen penny loaves, to be scrambled for on each succeeding Easter Monday at the rising ground called Hare Pie Bank''.'[1] This land, before the inclosure, was called 'Hare-crop-leys'. When possible, as in 1885, a hare, in sitting posture, was carried on top of a pole. The band, on the occasion recorded, struck up 'See the conquering hero comes', and the hare-pies were duly scrambled for by the spectators, who amused themselves by throwing the contents at one another.[2] Meanwhile, three men abreast have been carrying three wooden bottles, two full of ale, the third a dummy. After the pie-scramble and band playing, one of the large bottles was thrown into the circular hollow on the mound, giving rise to an organized contest for its possession. Next, the dummy was thrown and similarly fought for. Finally the third bottle was taken in triumph to the Market Cross, and its contents drunk with 'due honours'.[3]

Billson, summarizing the two customs, concludes: 'The leading motive of both processions is a hare. In the one case, the hare is followed to the Mayor's house, where a feast is eaten. Whether this feast originally comprised hare's flesh I have not been able to ascertain, though, from an entry in the Chamberlains' accounts, it appears that at one Easter Hunting a great many hares were caught, and these would presumably be used for the Mayor's banquet. At Hallaton the hare is carried in procession (sometimes in the shape of hare-pies, sometimes also mounted on a pole) from the parson's house to a

[1] C. J. Billson, *Folk-lore*, vol. iii, p. 444. [2] ibid., p. 445.

[3] Elsewhere on the Continent, the hare is sometime offered to the parish priest (*Hastings's Encyclopaedia*, p. 518b, quoting *Ann. Soc. Em. Flandre*, 5th series, i, 436).

sacred spot on the boundary of the parish, where the feast of hare-pie is eaten.

'At the Hallaton festival penny loaves are distributed to the people—a common form of survival in sacrificial customs.

'Both these rites take place on Easter Monday, at a season, that is, of special religious solemnity in the spring of the year.'[1]

From this and other evidence he concludes that these customs 'are relics of the religious procession and annual sacrifice of the god',[2] and later infers that 'one of the greatest festivals observed by our early Aryan, perhaps by our pre-Aryan ancestors, must have comprised a similar public and communal procession, in which a god was carried round the district, and afterwards slain and eaten, and this festival took place in the spring of the year'.[3]

The Anglo-Saxon Goddess Eostre and the Germanic Ostara

On the subject of the connection of the hare with Easter, Billson says: 'It has been suggested by Mr. Elton in his *Origins of English History*, that they are survivals of sacrificial rites connected with the worship of the Anglian goddess Eostre, who is mentioned by Bede as giving her name to the great Christian festival. But as to the very existence of this goddess, the opinions of mythologists are divided; for she is referred to only by Bede, and by him only in one passage, to explain the name 'Esturmonath', given to April by the early English.[4] Not a trace of her existence is left among other Teutonic peoples; but as the Germans also speak of "Ostermoneth", whereas all surrounding nations use the Biblical "Pascha", Jacob Grimm gives the goddess a German name also, "Ostara", and labels her, upon etymological grounds, "the divinity of the radiant dawn, of upspringing light, a spectacle that brings joy and blessing, and whose meaning could easily be adapted to the resurrection day of the Christian God".

'In Holtzmann's *German Mythology* she is also referred to as the goddess of Dawn. "The Easter Hare is unintelligible to

[1] C. J. Billson, *Folk-lore*, vol. iii, p. 463.
[2] ibid., p. 448.
[3] ibid., p. 463.
[4] See p. 180.

me!" he adds, "but probably the hare was the sacred animal of Ostara."'

He goes on: 'Oberle also concludes that the hare which laid the parti-coloured Easter eggs was sacred to the same goddess. Among other authorities who have no doubts as to her existence are W. Grimm, Wackernagel, Simrock, and Wolf. On the other hand, Weinhold rejects the idea on philological grounds, and so do Heinrich Leo and Hermann Oeser. Kuhn says, "The Anglo-Saxon Eostre looks like an invention of Bede", and Mannhardt also dismisses her as an etymological *dea ex machina.*

'The whole question turns, as Oberle says, upon Bede's credibility, with regard to which one is inclined to agree with Jacob Grimm, that it would be uncritical to saddle this eminent Father of the Church, who keeps Heathendom at arms' length and tells us less of it than he knows, with the invention of this goddess. Moreover, the Christianizing of England began at the end of the sixth century, and was completed about the end of the seventh, and as Bede was born in 672, he must have had opportunities of learning the names of heathen goddesses who were hardly extinct in his lifetime.

'But however this may be, whether there ever was a goddess named Eostre, or not, and whatever connection the hare may have had with the ritual of Saxon or British worship, there are good grounds for believing that the sacredness of this animal reaches back into an age still more remote, when it probably played a very important part at the great Spring Festival of the prehistoric inhabitants of this island.'[1]

Other Teutonic Hare-goddesses

The question of the existence or non-existence of a hare-goddess in Europe is, I think, amply answered in the affirmative by:

(*a*) Holtzmann's statement 'that the goddess Freyja was worshipped by the Swedes and Danes under the name "Astrild"—Austr-hildis; "so that Ostara might be Freyja herself

[1] C. J. Billson, *Folk-lore*, vol. iii, pp. 446–8.

or her daughter". It may be noted that Freyja "was attended by hares as her train-bearers and light-bearers".'[1] The mention of light-bearers once more recalls the motive of spiritual illumination so often met with in connection with the hare.

(*b*) The existence of the Saxon goddess holding the pregnant moon cited at the beginning of this section, who clearly, as there stated, goes back to pre-Christian times, but some of the practices and beliefs regarding whom, as seen in the various European customs I have cited, became incorporated into Christian tradition.

Philological evidence of the connection between Easter and the 'east' and 'dawn'

This raises once more the whole question of the meaning of the word 'Easter' itself. Since the Saxon Easter Goddess does seem to have been connected with the hare, and the hare so widely symbolizes 'dawn', and as dawn comes from the east, and Easter is the festival of the Resurrection symbolizing the birth of new life, it had occurred to me to wonder whether the actual word 'Easter' might have a very simple explanation indeed—so simple that philologists and churchmen alike had missed it—namely, that it was in fact cognate to the word 'east' as symbolizing the dawn from which new light came.

It further occurred to me that such a simple and obvious derivation should be susceptible of proof or disproof on plain philological grounds. I therefore inquired of my friend Mrs. Martin-Clarke to know what the derivation of the word actually was. She, like all authorities, pointed out that our only knowledge of the alleged goddess Eostre came from the passage in Bede's *De temporum Ratione,* chapter xv, dealing with the heathen English Calendar, in which April is said to be called Eostur-monath after the goddess Eostre, whose festival was celebrated in that month, which by Christians was called the

[1] See C. J. Billson, *Folk-lore,* vol. iii, p. 447, note 4 (quoting Henderson). Also W. G. Black, *Folk-lore Journal,* vol. i, p. 89. Krappe, *Folk-lore,* vol. iii, quoting Mannhardt, ascribes this note to the Teutonic goddess Holda.

Paschal month.[1] Now, *eo* and *ea* are interchangeable in the Northumbrian dialect that Bede spoke though he wrote in Latin, and in this context we may compare the Northumbrian word for Easter itself, which has the alternative forms *eastro* and *eostro*.

The question arises: Can the forms *Eostre*, *Eastro*, etc., in any way be connected with the adjective 'east', and so with 'dawn'? The Anglo-Saxon for the Christian festival is generally used in the plural, that is to say, *Eastron* (compare Old High German *Ōstarun*), though the two forms of the word beginning respectively with *eo* and *ea* are known, and the root of these is known to be cognate to the Anglo-Saxon adjective 'east' and with the Old Norse *austr*, with which may be compared the Lithuanian *auŝra* and the verb *auŝta* which means 'day is breaking', and all these are in turn cognate to the Sanskrit *usra* meaning 'dawn'. The insertion of the sound *t* between *s* and *r* is a well-known phonetic phenomenon arising from the difficulty of pronouncing *s* and *r* together without it.

Thus we get Sanskrit *usra* meaning 'dawn' becoming Old Norse *austr* meaning 'east', which has dropped the *r* in the common English pronunciation of our word 'east' when referring to the point of the compass, but has retained it in the name of the Easter festival.

Nor does the philological evidence end here, for allied to the Sanskrit *usra* is also the inferred Hellenic root ἀωσώς (*ausos*) giving rise on the one hand to the Aeolic ἄυως, Ionic ἠώς, Doric ἀως, and Attic ἕως, all meaning 'dawn', and on the other hand to the Old Latin form *Ausosa* which (since Indo-European *s* between vowels turns in classical Latin into *r*)[2] becomes the classical *Aurora*, that word for Dawn so dear to poets, and which, like the Anglo-Saxon *Eostre*, is personified in

[1] *The Complete Works of the Venerable Bede*, ed. J. A. Giles, London, 1843, vol. vi, p. 179. Compare also Jacob Grimm, *Teutonic Mythology*, trans. J. S. Stallybrass, London, 1882, vol. i, p. 289, in which the name is spelt Eostra.

[2] Compare, for example, Attic Greek γένος, genitive γένους, from γένεος, originally γένεσος, with Latin *genus*, *generis*.

the form of a goddess. From this it will be seen that our *east*, *Easter*, and the Latin *Aurora*, are cognate, all referring on the material plane to the 'dawn of day', and on the spiritual plane to the Resurrection.

HARE-CUSTOMS CONNECTED WITH THE AUTUMNAL EQUINOX

It will be noted that all the modern European customs hitherto cited have to do with Easter, that is to say, with the period of the vernal equinox, when winter dies and summer is born. Another set of European customs have to do, however, not with the vernal, but with the autumnal equinox when, at harvest, the fruits of summer are transformed into food for man, that is to say when, in the words of the folk-song, 'John Barleycorn must die' and his body become transmuted into human flesh. Here also the hare appears as an emergent symbol, and indeed takes its place among *The Spirits of the Corn and of the Wild* so brilliantly collected and described by Sir James Frazer in his two volumes called by this name.[1]

'Killing the Hare' and 'Cutting the Hare'

The setting in which these customs take place is at the end of harvest, when the area of standing corn is reduced by the reapers to ever smaller and smaller proportions. Every harvester knows the excitement which rises as, coincident with the joy of cutting the grain, the animals that have taken refuge in it make a dash for freedom, pursued with shouts by the reapers. First of the common animals to attempt escape are the rabbits, which from time to time dash for the surrounding hedge. But last of all, as in the case of the burning heath cited at the beginning of this account,[2] the hares cling to their shelter till the very last moment, and do not attempt to leave it till it is so reduced as to afford no further refuge. Then, as the last corn dies, the hare escapes. As Frazer points out: What can this be

[1] Sir James Frazer, *The Golden Bough*, Part V, 'Spirits of the Corn and of the Wild', London, 1933, vol. i, pp. 279–80.

[2] See p. 106.

but the embodied spirit of the corn itself? All round stand the reapers, ready with sticks or other implements to slay it. Thus arises the phrase 'killing the hare' used in many parts of Europe for the man who cuts the last corn, modified in Ayrshire and elsewhere in Scotland to 'cutting the hare', used for cutting the last sheaf which is itself called 'the hare'.[1]

'Hare's blood', the Spartan 'black broth', and the Irish 'Hares of Naas'

Similar customs are recorded from elsewhere in Europe, in all of which the cutting of the last corn appears at one and the same time as a practical and as a sacrificial act, perhaps the most striking of which is the Norwegian custom that the man who is thus said to 'kill the hare' must give 'hare's blood' in the form of brandy to his fellows to drink.[2]

This rite calls to mind the celebrated 'black broth' of the Spartans which was made of the blood and bowels of a hare, and also, very relevant to Mrs. Wright's Irish ancestry, the 'old and peculiar privilege of the Kings of Tara to be fed upon "the hares of Naas", a diet which, as Billson rightly remarks, probably owed its origin to religious ritual'.[3]

'Chasing the Callyach' in Ireland

One last piece of information regarding the hare as a corn spirit or something like it has just been sent to me by my friend the Irish poet Mr. W. R. Rodgers, who, referring to the Northern Irish custom known as 'chasing the callyach'[4] (callyach = a witch or a hare), writes 'In part of County Armagh almost every other farmer keeps a hound (of the beagle kind), and although occasionally I have heard jokes made about the "uselessness" of the hound (i.e. as a watchdog or for herding cattle) yet I have always noted that the hound is petted more

[1] Frazer, *The Golden Bough*, and *British Calendar Customs*, Scotland (London, 1937), vol. i, pp. 80 sqq.

[2] Frazer, *The Golden Bough*, Part V, 'Spirits of the Corn and of the Wild', p. 280.

[3] C. J. Billson, *Folk-lore*, vol. iii, p. 450.

[4] This is the Anglicized spelling. The Irish spelling is *caileach*.

than other dogs, and is looked after well. The hound is kept for the hunting of hares. The season for hunting the hare begins as soon as the harvest is gathered in. Then any farmer's son who wants a hunt takes the horn and goes out and blows it, and immediately all the hounds within earshot come running to where he is. Often too, a "meet" is held, and packs of hounds will be brought to it from considerable distances. It is always the younger farmers and farmers' sons who hunt. The older and more staid men never indulge in it. And "religious" (Protestant) people (and in particular "religious" women) openly condemn the sport, and not from "humane" motives. They condemn it, they say, because it is a "low" sport, and one in which only the riffraff take part. I suspect by riffraff they mean the Catholics and the indigenous people, though Protestants are just as fond of the sport. The men who follow the hunt do not follow it at close range, but move from hill to hill; indeed, any vantage point which allows them to overlook the hunt is used. Custom allows them access to all land, however private. The hare, they say, runs in a circle when hunted and will come back to the place she started from.'

'To attempt to intercept the hare by heading her off, i.e. cutting across the circle she is making in order to catch her in front, is looked on as a very wrong thing. She must be followed by scent. Nor must the hare be trapped in any kind of enclosure as of stone, brick, or (nowadays) wire-netting, but must have a clear run. In England, for example, gamekeepers will leave holes or gaps at the bottom of brick walls to let her through.'

On this interesting account I will make only two observations: first, that 'scent' and noses (particularly dogs' noses) are world-wide symbols for intuition, that is to say, psychological or spiritual knowledge, the kind of knowledge that works in unseen ways (compare Jung's definition of Intuition as 'that psychological function which transmits perceptions *in an unconscious way*',[1] or as 'perception of relations via the unconscious'[2]) as opposed to logical deduction which works by way of

[1] C. G. Jung, *Psychological Types*, London, 1924, pp. 567–8.

[2] C. G. Jung, *The Integration of Personality*, London, 1940, p. 14.

the conscious; and, secondly, that all spiritual knowledge 'goes in circles', that is to say that it has to do with rebirth which is itself a return to the beginning on a different psychic level, as opposed once more to logical deduction which works in a straight line from premise to consciously demonstrable conclusion, and in which 'arguing in a circle' is the greatest sin. If the hare is, in Northern Ireland, as elsewhere, a symbol of intuition, this ritually circular hunting of the hare is what might be expected.

I may here call attention to one further fact, namely, one well known to all hunters of hares and mentioned to Mr. Rodgers by an Irish farmer in connection with this rite, that when caught the hare 'cried like a child'. Since the object of rebirth is to 'become as a little child', its mention in this context may well represent a similar deeply unconscious intuitive motive.

The Hare 'enjoys being hunted'

Mr. Rodgers adds: 'A farmer of my acquaintance in County Armagh, assured me that the hare really enjoys being hunted. As proof of this he adduced the case of a hare which had reared her young close up against the back of a hounds' kennel on his farm. "It liked," he said, "to be near the hounds."'

What better symbolic image could be found of the basic truth enshrined in all 'willing sacrifice' that instinct *wants to be* transformed into spirit?

The ambivalence of the whole problem of spirit and instinct is well expressed in the following poem, written by Mr. Rodgers long before he was aware of the world-wide symbolic significance of this loved but at the same time hunted animal. It is entitled 'Beagles':[1]

Over rock and wrinkled ground
Ran the lingering nose of hound,
The little and elastic hare
Stretched herself nor stayed to stare.

[1] W. R. Rodgers, *Awake! and other Poems*, London, 1941, p. 9.

Stretched herself, and far away
Darted through the chinks of day,
Behind her, shouting out her name,
The whole blind world galloping came.

Over hills a running line
Curled like a whip-lash, fast and fine,
Past me sailed the sudden pack
Along the taut and tingling track.

From the far flat scene each shout
Like jig-saw piece came tumbling out,
I took and put them all together,
And then they turned into a tether.

A tether that held me to the hare
Here, there, and everywhere.

THE HARE MAKES THE ELIXIR OF LIFE

The recent reference to the Kings of Tara feeding upon 'the hares of Naas'[1] brings us back once more to the function of the sacrificial hare as the purveyor of the elixir of life. We have met with this already in China and North America. It will be noted that it is of course never the hare in its natural state that has this power, but only the hare when it has been sacrificed (as, for example, in India when it has reached the moon) that thus acquires this supernatural gift. This is of course the motive of all sacrifice. Thus, in the Mithraic Mysteries it is not till the bull is sacrificed that from its body spring forth all useful herbs, and from its spinal column the wheat that gives us bread, and from the blood flowing from its wounded side issues the vine that produces the sacred drink.[2] These things are of course to be considered symbolically, that is to say as spiritual

[1] See p. 183.

[2] Franz Cumont, *The Mysteries of Mithra* (translated by T. J. McCormick), Chicago, 1903, pp. 136–7.

fact as well as material fact. The supreme example is, of course, the blood and water flowing from the side of Christ, representing abundant life in body and spirit at once. This motive permeates sacrificial acts wherever they are performed and whatever they are. Among primitive peoples the sacrifice of any one species of food-animal is believed to lead to the increase of all food-animals of the same species, and what this really means is that the act when properly carried out, does in fact, by heightening his own instinctive knowledge and thus at the same time increasing his spiritual energy, put man in communion with the beasts and enable him to track them down and slay and eat them, and thus transmute their baser flesh into the more highly organized flesh and spirit of man. In higher religions the material aspect of prosperity tends to disappear and the spiritual to predominate over all others. Thus through the act of consecration in the Christian Mass, which is at the same time a sacrifice, base bread and wine are transformed into the body and blood of Christ, the effect of which is conceived to be primarily a spiritual one, but at the same time does in fact sustain the body through the power it gives to dispense with much unnecessary material food.

It is doubtless due to this spiritualizing effect of sacrifice that the hare is so frequently represented as being pregnant, as, for example, is the case of the Saxon goddess carrying the moon-image on her pregnant part, and of the child dressed up as a hare carrying the Easter eggs.[1]

Examples from European folk-lore

It is quite typical of the degradation of symbolic truth that, from being a spiritual fact, it gradually descends into the realm of superstition till it acquires a purely supposed material connotation and in the end becomes discredited and entirely disregarded. The process of decay is seen in many items of folklore. Billson thus quotes a belief current among the ancient Romans 'that eating hare's-flesh for seven days would make

[1] Compare also pp. 212 sqq. for the Greek view of the hare as a symbol of spiritual pregnancy.

anyone beautiful', a superstition enshrined in one of Martial's epigrams.[1]

Billson and Black both refer to Cogan's *Haven of Health*, written in 1605, in which he says, 'This much will I say as to the commendation of the hare, and of the defence of the hunter's toyle, that no one beast, be it never so great, is profitable to so many and so divers uses in Physicke as the hare and partes thereof', to which Black adds the quotation, 'The ankle-bone of the foote of an hare is good against the cramp'.[2] Black further cites another account to the effect that 'a Dorsetshire mother in the autumn of 1881 was somewhat troubled with the care of recently born twins. "On paying a visit to inquire after the mother, my wife was consulted as to the desirability of a dose of hare's brains (as a soporific). Mentioning the circumstances to my keeper in the hope of eliciting some information as to the prevalence of the belief, he told me that about a fortnight ago the wife of the keeper of the adjoining manor, who had been recently confined, called at his house and told his wife that she had been down to the squire's house to beg a hare's head from the cook in order to give the brains to her baby as a sedative."'[3] Similarly, Robert Burton, in his *Anatomy of Melancholy*,[4] mentions hare's ears applied to the feet among the many remedies against 'fearful dreams', and adds, 'It is good overnight to anoint the face with hare's blood, and in the morning to wash it with strawberry and cowslip water. . . .'

Billson further calls attention to such plant-names as 'harebell' and 'hare-parsley' as having some possible mythological meaning, though he inclines to think that these names are rather due to such facts as that 'harebell' is so called because it grows in places haunted by hares, and 'hare-parsley' because it is eaten by hares.[5]

[1] C. J. Billson, *Folk-lore*, vol. iii, pp. 456–7. See also p. 217 (note 1) of the present volume.

[2] W. G. Black, *The Folk-lore Journal*, vol. i, p. 86.

[3] ibid., p. 90.

[4] Part 2, sect. 5, member 1, subsection 6.

[5] C. J. Billson, *Folk-lore*, vol. iii, p. 457. Note the myrtle-groves to which the hare flees mentioned on p. 189.

HARES AS OMENS

The subject of folk-medicine leads on directly to a consideration of two further aspects of hare lore, namely the use of the hare as an omen and its more recent connection with witches.

Arnold and Boadicea

With regard to its use as an omen, Billson cites several classical instances. 'Thus, in Pausanias,[1] the priest of the moon-goddess [the Taurian Artemis referred to elsewhere[2]] instructs some exiles, who are searching for a propitious place to found a city, to build it in a myrtle grove into which they should see a hare flee for refuge. When Arnold and his German hordes besieged Rome a hare ran towards the walls, and, the Teutons pursuing, a panic seized the Romans, who looked on it as a fatal omen; they deserted the gates without striking a blow, and the barbarians entered.'[3]

Then he mentions the well-known case of Boadicea given by Dio in his *Roman History* [LXII, b] which I will quote here in full, to the effect that 'When the British Queen Boadicea had finished speaking to her people, she employed a species of divination, letting a hare escape from the fold of her dress; and since it ran on what they considered the auspicious side, the whole multitude shouted with pleasure, and Boadicea, raising her hand towards heaven, said, "I thank thee, Andraste . . . I supplicate and pray thee for victory. . . ."'[4]

Hare as fecundatrix

Not unlike this with respect to the part of the body from which the hare was loosed is the account given by de Gubernatis of how 'Philostratos narrates the case of a woman who had miscarried seven times in the act of child-birth, but who

[1] Pausanias, iii, 22. [2] See pp. 209, 220.

[3] C. J. Billson, *Folk-lore*, vol. iii, p. 453.

[4] Quoted by Ellen Ettlinger, 'Omens, and Celtic Warfare', *Man*, vol. xliii (Jan.-Feb. 1943), p. 13. See also Xiphiline, *Mon. Hist. Brit.*, lvii.

the eighth time brought forth a child, when her husband unexpectedly drew a hare out of his bosom. Although the moon is herself the timid and chaste goddess (or eunuch), she is, as pluvial, the *fecundatrix*, and famous as presiding over and predicting child-birth; this is why, when the hare-moon, or Lucina, assisted at parturition, it was sure to issue happily.' Parturition is, of course, another aspect of 'dawn', that is to say, that it also heralds the creation of new life.

Hare, like Moon, sleeps with eyes open. Blind Hare recovers sight by diving

De Gubernatis adds: 'The moon is the watcher of the sky, that is to say, she sleeps with her eyes open; so also does the hare, hence the *somnus leporinus* became a proverb.'[1] This is yet another way of referring to the moon as the 'light in the darkness' symbolizing inner knowledge.[2]

Black cites a cognate German example from more modern times referring to the hare's 'inner eye', saying, 'A blind hare it was, in the North German tale of "The Blue Riband", which ran before the princess, and by plunging in a brook, diving thrice under water, recovered its sight and scampered off, thus teaching her to lead Hans to the same water, with the satisfactory result that after he had plunged in it three times, he, like the hare, recovered his sight.'[3]

This last example is of great interest since it combines the use of the number 3 representing in ancient times the Initiation Process and since Christian times the Redemptive Process, as symbolized in Our Lord's 3-day passage through Death, with the true knowledge that it is only by trust in the healing power

[1] Angelo de Gubernatis, *Zoological Mythology*, London, 1872, vol. ii, pp. 80–1. A curious echo of the belief that the hare sleeps with its eyes open survives still in the modern medical term 'lagophthalmia', from the Greek λαγώφθαλμος, meaning 'hare-eyed'; used for a pathological condition associated with certain complaints such as meningitis and exophthalmia (goitre) in which, owing to the paralysis of the palpebral muscles, the patient is unable to close his or her eyelids.

[2] See also pp. 128 and 221.

[3] W. G. Black, *The Folk-lore Journal*, vol. i, p. 89.

of the deep Unconscious (here as so often, as in baptism, represented by water) that the spiritually blind can indeed receive their sight.

Omens paralleled by and possibly derived from dream symbolism

The use of omens in general appears to me to represent a kind of half-way house between real spiritual understanding and pure superstition, since on the one hand it recognizes the reality of the 'other side' of things in its use of a symbol, but on the other hand depends upon the chance whim of an actual animal (or whatever may be used as an omen) for the answer given. The whole process is exactly parallel to that kind of dream symbolism common to all peoples and no less to ourselves when we examine our dreams, in which the dreamer is, in his dream, actually led by some animal or another to discover the solution to his problem. One such modern dreamer once dreamt that he was asleep, and that a cat jumped on to his bed and brushed his face. In the dream he seemed to wake up, but, as he would do in real life, just turned over to go to sleep again. A second time the cat brushed his face, and this time he became slightly annoyed, being anxious to get all the sleep he could. However, the cat brushed his face yet a third time, this time so violently that he (still in his dream) could sleep no longer and had to sit up and take notice of what the cat wanted. It seemed it wanted to be let out. So, still in his dream, the dreamer opened his bedroom door, whereon the cat led him down the corridor of the modern house in which he actually was, till it arrived at a non-existent door at the end of the corridor, which it indicated it wanted to go through. The dreamer opened the door, and, lo and behold, in this modern house appeared an ancient spiral stone stairway, down which the cat led and he followed. Arrived at the bottom, another corridor revealed itself leading backwards directly beneath the first, which they both passed down till the dreamer found himself in a dream-room situated immediately below the bedroom in which he actually lay sleeping; and in this lower room representing his own Impersonal Unconscious was revealed to him the information which he needed for the solution of the problem which in fact actually beset him.

I believe this to be the kind of dream experience, which is in fact far from infrequent and still crops up constantly in psychological analysis, that gave rise among ancient peoples to the use of animals as omens. It is of course far superior in its efficacy to the observation of external omens, which may be quite fortuitous, because in a dream the dream symbols arise from the dreamer's own unconscious knowledge, or, shall we say, unconscious intuition of what his problem is, whereas external omens do not, unless we think that the human psyche does in fact influence actual animals in their behaviour, which is, of course, not impossible but for which I know of no proof. In any case, it is undoubtedly true that the more we trust to external objects instead of trusting to ourselves, that is to say, to the divine spark in us, the less likely we are to find any solution either for practical or for spiritual problems; and it is presumably for this reason that external omens have now lost all validity, and that we are now being forced once more to find truth in the depths of our own psyche, of which the ultimate centre is the divine spark that is the individual's mirror-image of the divine as approached through revealed religion.

Hare as bad omen

Omens are by no means only *directly* positive, as in the case cited above, but may also be *indirectly* so by pointing to some disaster which may be avoided. Thus, Billson refers to numerous examples from many parts of the world showing that 'to meet a hare is a very bad stroke of luck'. He goes on 'and many people, if they meet a hare when going to work, will return home, and not venture out again until the next meal has been eaten'.[1] The reference to eating is interesting, as in some obscure way referring to a sacrificial meal.

Running Hare portends fire. Impersonal Unconscious the mirror opposite of the Conscious

Gomme also refers to a belief found in south Northampton-

[1] C. J. Billson, *Folk-lore*, vol. iii, p. 454.

shire that 'the running of a hare along the street or mainway of a village portends fire to some house in the immediate vicinity'.[1] Billson refers to a similar belief recorded from Ely and also from Hungary, and says that in the Wheal Vor mine the appearance of a hare presages fatal accident.[2] The particular reference to fire cannot fail to call to mind the Buddhist legends of the hare sacrificing itself by leaping into a fire, and is a typical example of the complete reversal of values when symbolic understanding becomes lost, and is replaced by purely material concepts. For it is a psychological fact of universal application that the unconscious (that is to say, the collective, not the personal unconscious, in other words the spiritual world) is the mirror opposite of the conscious. The outstanding example is, of course, the symbolic interpretation of the death on Calvary as being the necessary precursor of the resurrection, and the Cross being the Tree of Life. The same principle permeates all spiritual understanding, and lies at the base of sacrifice. Fear is itself half of life. This is inevitable and unavoidable. What matters is our attitude towards fear. It will be remembered how 'fear' of the man coming up behind Mrs. Wright in Dream 7 was transmuted by Our Lord's words 'Fear not' into 'awe', whereon the feared stranger turned into a vision of Christ; how she had been horrified at the prospect of sacrificing the hare in Dream 9, but had nevertheless done it and received illumination; and how a similar conquest of fear took place yet again in Dreams 12 and 13; and how, on page 88, it was pointed out that fear is 'seen at its lowest in panic, and at its highest in fear of the Lord'. So, in the case of the Buddha as a hare leaping into the flames, fear was translated into divine knowledge. This was because the act was understood as a symbol, as was the Pentecostal fire descending upon the Apostles' heads, whereas the superstitions just cited, such as that of a hare portending disastrous fire, are due to precisely the same symbolic action conceived through ignorance as representing material fact. That a material outlook of this

[1] G. L. Gomme, 'Totemism in Britain', *Archaeological Review*, vol. iii (March–July 1889), p. 239.

[2] C. J. Billson, *Folk-lore*, vol. iii, p. 454.

kind does actually lead to disaster is seen in the innumerable floods, lightnings, plagues, wars, and other acts of destruction which the God of the Old Testament visited upon His Chosen People whenever they disobeyed Him, and the same fate has now overcome a Europe that has forgotten wisdom and still thinks in terms of economics or national pride of what are in fact the deeply spiritual problems that call for solution all over the world to-day. The individual problem facing Mrs. Wright in Dream 9 was, 'Is this a real hare, or is it a symbol of my own unredeemed nature?' She did not, of course, think in these terms, because it was a problem not of thinking but of intuitive knowledge brought out by the analytical process working in conjunction with a devout nature. But the choice was nevertheless there. Had Mrs. Wright thought in material terms, her gentle soul would have revolted from the sacrifice and her problems would have remained unsolved. But wisdom prevailed. She knew by this time that all things appearing in her dreams were symbols expressing spiritual truths. Trembling with numinous awe, she obeyed the voice which told her to commit what would in material fact have been a crime, but what in a spiritual setting was the highest act of self-sacrifice she could perform, and she had her reward. We in Europe shall not have our reward till we cease thinking in exclusively material terms, as the peasants referred to might think of a material fire caused by the running hare, and till we return to sanity by knowing that the real fire is the spiritual fire which burns but which does not consume, or alternatively that burns out the dross of illusory material values and leaves behind it the essence of truth, as does a wood fire that separates the transitory matter from the essential salts.

THE HARE AS WITCH'S FAMILIAR

Better known than the hare's use as an omen is its notorious role as one of the 'familiar' animals into which witches transform themselves when prosecuting their alleged nefarious designs.

'Participation mystique'

With regard to this kind of supposed transformation, Frazer quotes some relevant passages referring to similar beliefs among still living peoples. Thus, he says, 'The Malays believe that "the soul of a person may pass into another person or into an animal, or rather that such a mysterious relation can arise between the two that the fate of the one is wholly dependent on that of the other"'.[1] This he expands by further references, notably one taken from Codrington to the effect that the Mota word for soul is *atai*. 'The use of the word *atai* in Mota seems properly and originally to have been to signify something peculiarly and intimately connected with a person and sacred to him. . . . Whatever the thing might be the man believed it to be the reflection of his own personality; he and his *atai* flourished, suffered, lived, and died together. But the word must not be supposed to have been borrowed from this use and applied secondarily to describe the soul; the word carries a sense with it which is applicable alike to that second self, the visible object so mysteriously connected with the man, and to this invisible second self which we call the soul. There is another Mota word, *tamaniu*, which has almost if not quite the same meaning as *atai* has when it describes something animate or inanimate which a man has come to believe to have an existence intimately connected with his own. The word *tamaniu* may be taken to be properly '*likeness*', and the noun form of the adverb *tama*, as, "like". It was not everyone in Mota who had his *tamaniu*; only some men fancied that they had this relation to a lizard, a snake, or it might be a stone. . . . It was watched but not fed or worshipped; the natives believed that it came at call, and that the life of the man was bound up with the life of his *tamaniu*, if a living thing, or with its safety; should it die, or if not living get broken or be lost, the man would die.'[2]

This idea of 'sameness' or 'likeness' between a person and

[1] Frazer, *The Golden Bough*, Part VII, 'Balder the Beautiful', London, 1936, vol. ii, p. 197, quoting from Matthes.

[2] R. H. Codrington, *The Melanesians*, Oxford, 1891, pp. 250 sq.

his or her soul-image as externalized in a thing or animal is very relevant here, since it forces us to ask what quality in a witch would persuade her, or those observing her, to associate her soul or second self with a living hare. We must, I think, be careful to distinguish between these two kinds of observation, since there very definitely exists in certain cases a form of what is called *participation mystique* between men and animals, whereby they do indeed to some extent partake of one another's natures. Such a phenomenon exists in somewhat attenuated form among ourselves to-day in the relation between cats, or dogs, and their owners. People having close relation with cats are apt to develop somewhat feline characteristics, and even the cats themselves, those most independent of animals, develop a taste for human company. Much more so is this the case, of course, with dogs. We all know the doggy person with the brusque manner fostered by intimate company with this 'friend of man', and the community of fellowship existing between the real (not the superficial) rider to hounds and not only the hounds he leads but also the fox he hunts, together with the actual honour and admiration he accords to the objects of the chase. This is a fact, whatever we may think of the often artificial nature of fox-hunting to-day.

Nature of the connection between Hares and Witches

This kind of *participation mystique* might well account for the well-known relation existing between witches and cats—particularly black cats, which are, or are said to be, their frequent companions. It is doubtful, however, whether it can account for their association in the popular mind with hares, which appears to me to be due, not to the way in which witches regard themselves, but rather to the way in which *others* regard *them*.

This leads us to inquire just what a witch is. With regard to this question, there is little doubt that, in the first place, a witch is a woman with a highly developed intuitive faculty. There are, of course, white witches and black, that is to say, women who use their intuitive faculty or second-sight for good purposes or bad. In either case, intuition is to the onlooker always a surprising faculty, one that takes short cuts, leaps to conclusions (whether right or wrong), and generally behaves in what, to the less gifted in this way, appears to be an odd and somewhat mysterious manner. That is to say, that the intuitive faculty behaves not unlike a hare with regard to the hare's sudden appearances, its fleetness, its power of leaping so often met with in these pages, as well as its March madness when during the mating season it throws all other considerations to the winds in its pursuit of the desired object.

In the second place, witches, being introvert, usually compensate for their intense inner activity with an outwardly retiring nature giving the appearance of timidity or reserve, corresponding to the proverbial timidity of the hare, which gives rise to such expressions as 'he (or she) is timid as a hare' and to the refusal of certain peoples to eat the hare lest it would make the eater faint-hearted.

Coupled with these is the soft appearance of the hare, which (as in the case of the cat, another animal popularly associated with witches, especially when black) tends to make us think of it as a 'female' animal rather than as a male;[1] just as, in the opposite sense, dogs, whether in fact male or female, tend to be regarded as 'male'. Examples of the interchangeability of cats with hares in Europe are very frequent. Such are the contrasted statements that 'At Aurich, in East Friesland, the man who reaps the last corn "cuts the hare's tail off". In mowing down the last corner of a field French reapers sometimes call out, "We have the cat by the tail".'[2] And, with regard to witches, we have the numerous examples given by Frazer of the 'wounds inflicted on a witch-hare or witch-cat . . . seen on the witch herself'.[3]

Lastly, hares are hunted animals, and so, commonly, in Europe at least, was the witch.

[1] Hares are popularly referred to by huntsmen as 'puss', a term that appears to have originated in the seventeenth century, that is to say, in the age in which witch-hunting was so prevalent.

[2] J. G. Frazer, *The Golden Bough*, Part V, 'Spirits of the Corn and of the Wild', London, 1933, vol. i, p. 268.

[3] Frazer, *The Golden Bough*, Part VII, 'Balder the Beautiful', London, 1936, vol. i, pp. 316 sqq.

Witches transformed into Hares

Examples of witches being thought to turn themselves into hares are so numerous that only a few must be cited. Thus, Henderson tells us that 'The Hare is the most common disguise of the witch in all the northern countries of Europe'.[1] For example, 'Fishers of Fifeshire "look on all maukens (hares) to be devils and witches, and if they but see a sight of a dead mauken it sets them a trembling".'[2]

More familiar are such examples as those given by Frazer in his quotation of the sixteenth-century writer who states that the Irish 'account every woman who fetches fire on May-day a witch, nor will they give it to any but sick persons, and that with an imprecation, believing she will steal all the butter the next summer. On May-day they kill all the hares they find among their cattle, supposing them the old women who have designs on the butter. They imagine the butter so stolen may be recovered if they take some of the thatch hanging over the door and burn it.'[3]

Burning the Witch-Hare a purificatory measure

Not quite so familiar is the statement that in the Isle of Man, on May-day (Old Style) the break of day 'was the signal for setting the ling or gorse on fire, which was done for the sake of burning out the witches, who are wont to take the shape of hares'.[4]

This cannot fail to call to mind the catching alight of hares hiding in bracken cited near the beginning of this inquiry,[5] and its association with the spectacle of the self-sacrificing Buddha leaping into the flames in order to purify himself. The burning of witches, whether under the guise of hares or not, is also a purificatory sacrifice, but one of a very different kind,

[1] For this and other references see C. J. Billson, *Folk-lore*, vol. iii, p. 455. Witches also, apparently, had the power of changing men into hares, as was the case with the famous wizard, Sir Michael Scott, who was turned into a hare by the witch of Falsehope.

[2] W. G. Black, *The Folk-lore Journal*, vol. i, pp. 86–7.

[3] Frazer, *The Golden Bough*, Part I, 'The Magic Art and the Evolution of Kings', London, 1932, vol. ii, p. 53.

[4] ibid., p. 54. [5] See p. 106.

being indeed quite the other way round, since, instead of the corruptible body of the hare-Buddha sacrificing itself in order to transform itself for the good of the world into spirit, it is here the evil spirit of the witch which is supposedly destroyed in order to re-humanize the witch. Thus, in Frazer's view, which is most probably correct, 'the reason for burning a bewitched animal alive is a belief that the witch herself is in the animal, and that by burning it you either destroy the witch completely or at least unmask her and compel her to resume her proper human shape, in which she is naturally far less potent for mischief than when she is careering about the country in the likeness of a cat, a hare, a horse, or what not'.[1]

Nevertheless, it is more than possible that the belief concerning the self-sacrifice of Buddha and the practice of sacrificing the hare-witch, the first positive and the second negative, may have a common psychological origin, since Frazer regards the burning of witches and their supposed changelings as but a faint echo of the august rites of Beltane and Hallowe'en. Thus the burning of the hare-witch on the Isle of Man just cited occurred during the May Day rites attendant on what he refers to as '"the Druidical anniversary of Beil or Baal. . . . On the first of May, 1837, the Baal fires were, as usual on that day, so numerous as to give the island the appearance of a general conflagration." By May Day in Manx folk-lore is meant May Day, Old Style, or *Shenn Laa Boaldyn*, as it is called in Manx.'[2]

This burning he refers back to the practice, still mirrored in our present burning of Guy Fawkes on November 5th, of including the burnt sacrifice of men and animals at the ancient fire festivals of Beltane and Hallowe'en, and considers it to be due to a desire 'to break the power of witchcraft by burning or banning the witches and warlocks',[3] saying that 'the mode of

[1] Frazer, *The Golden Bough*, Part VII, 'Balder the Beautiful', London, 1936, vol. i, p. 321.

[2] ibid., p. 157.

[3] Frazer, *The Golden Bough*, Part VII, 'Balder the Beautiful', vol. ii, p. 41. He adds 'the victims most commonly burned in modern bonfires have been cats, and . . . cats are precisely the animals into which, with the possible exception of hares, witches were most usually supposed to transform themselves'.

execution by fire was chosen because . . . burning alive is deemed to be the surest mode of getting rid of these notorious and dangerous beings'. This seems to me to be a very negative way of looking at it (a view most certainly held by the actual burners of witches, and of the hares or other animals into which the witches may have been deemed to be transformed), but I submit that with regard to the human and animal sacrifices of the so-called Druids it would appear far more probable that this burnt-sacrifice was much more akin to the burnt-sacrifices of the Old Testament and many peoples in the pre-Christian era, and that these also were due to the same motive that inspired the Buddha when in the form of a hare he leapt into the flames in order to destroy his earthly body, not as a punishment but as a fulfilment whereby flesh was transformed into spirit for the benefit of all people.

The degradation of this positive sacrificial concept of purifying *oneself* into the negative one of getting rid of the evil in *others* is a typical misconception only too common in everyday life among all those who persist in seeing the 'mote' in their brother's eye but not the 'beam' in their own, and so project their own faults on others, as the good Christians of the witch-burning period projected their own negative psychological contents upon the unfortunate witches whom they thus destroyed instead of looking to the purging of their own sinful natures.

Degradation of a symbol. The Hare an 'uncanny animal'

With regard to this final stage of degradation in the mythological hare's progress throughout the centuries, all far-seeing writers on the subject agree that this is due to a total misconception of the unseen forces that rule human life—in fact to the intolerance of established and over-intellectualized dogmatists towards the older manifestations of spiritual activity that later forms have, for the time being at least, superseded. To quote from one only, W. G. Black, speaking of the lost 'high estate' of the hare, says, 'It did not at once acquire the repute of being either stupid or inspired by a witch. . . . The animal had been sacred, and the tradition perhaps shown in the use of the hare in augury perhaps [*sic*] was that the remembrance of this holiness long lingered. From primitive regard the descent is generally rapid, and we readily find an explanation for the hare's connection with witchcraft in the degradation of its character from the days of Buddha—a sacred animal becomes an uncanny animal, as heathen gods become devils when their worshippers change their faith. The process is a very common one.'[1]

Use of Silver Coins for shooting the Witch-Hare recalls Moon-symbolism

Nevertheless, even in the degraded era of witch-hunting, the connection between the moon and the hare still subsists, though under a disguised form. It is well known that, of the two precious metals known to the ancient world, gold represents the sun and the male element, and silver represents the moon and female. Thus we are all familiar with the superstition of turning over the silver in our pocket when seeing the new moon, in order to render the moon favourable to us, in the same way that we are all taught as children to utter the word 'hares' or 'rabbits' on the first day of each new month. It is, therefore, of interest to read Frazer's statement, supported by references to a very large number of authorities on folk-lore, that 'the only way to make sure of hitting a witch-animal is to put a silver sixpence or a silver button in your gun'.[2] Black also cites two cases of a similar nature.[3] It is sometimes stated that only a crooked sixpence will do. This is presumably an allusion to the 'crooked' nature of the witch's negative intuition, but the insistence on the round silver object representing the moon is quite clearly due to the kind of symbolism which speaks of 'paying a man out in his own coin', that is to say, that in order to counteract the intuitive moon-knowledge of the witch an equally powerful moon-symbol must be used. The value placed on this is indicated by the use else-

[1] W. G. Black, *The Folk-lore Journal,* vol. i, p. 89.

[2] Frazer, *The Golden Bough,* Part VII, 'Balder the Beautiful', vol. i, p. 316. Compare the account given on p. 173 of the game of thrusting a silver coin into the Easter egg.

[3] W. G. Black, *The Folk-lore Journal,* vol. i, p. 87.

where for the same purpose and in the same way of a consecrated wafer. Thus, 'Again, in the Vosges Mountains a great big hare used to come out every evening to take the air at the foot of the Mont des Fourches. All the sportsmen of the neighbourhood tried their hands on that hare for a month, but not one of them could hit it. At last one marksman, more knowing than the rest, loaded his gun with some pellets of a consecrated wafer in addition to the usual pellets of lead. That did the trick.'[1]

Degradation of attitude towards Witches and Ghosts

One of the most recent writers on the hare says, 'We are probably right in assuming that the lunar association of the hare made the shy animal "uncanny" in the eyes of primitive folk.'[2] This may be partly the case, but only, in my opinion, in so far as the feeling of awe is degraded through lack of real spiritual understanding into one of fright, as we now almost universally fear ghosts, whereas among truly primitive people ghosts are not considered as being hostile, but as being fundamentally friendly unless offended from one cause or another. Among most so-called (but not really) primitive peoples, love, reverence, and fear of ghosts alternate and intermingle according to circumstance, though among those Malekulans amongst whom I have lived the dominating feeling is one of love and reverence, unless the ghost has been injured in some way, either at the moment of death through being killed and so denied due burial, or else because after death it has not been duly honoured.[3] The problem with regard both to ghosts and to the hare, as to all other mythologically conceived phenomena, lies in the extent to which spiritual forces are honoured or not. It is a fact that if they are not honoured they become evil, and are responsible for the evil elements in the world, whereas if

[1] Frazer, *The Golden Bough*, Part VII, 'Balder the Beautiful', vol. i, p. 318. For further information on Hares and Witches, see article on the Hare in the *Handwörterbuch des deutschen Aberglaubens*.

[2] Alexandre H. Krappe, 'Old Celtic Taboos', *Folk-lore*, vol. liii, Dec. 1942, p. 201.

[3] See John Layard, *Stone Men of Malekula*, pp. 629 sqq.

they are honoured they become good, and yield up their power for the betterment of mankind, instead of this same power tending otherwise to its destruction. No primitive man, as no modern man who is not sunk in materialism, has any doubt that such powers exist, but if the heart that wields this power is evil, evil will ensue, and *vice versa*. But power it is, and cannot be destroyed, and if it is not allowed to work for good it will inevitably work for harm. As I envisage the problem, this has all along been the trouble with European witchcraft. For there have always and among all people been evil witches and good, that is to say, that there have always been women with strong intuitive powers, who have been forced to use these powers in an occult way, partly because society is in most places dominated by men, and partly because women are more closely in touch with earth-forces than men, who tend more towards social and less towards hidden modes of expressing their vital force.

This brings us back to the alleged 'fickleness' and 'unpredictable' nature of women (a reputation imposed on them naturally by men, because women's logic happens to be different from theirs) and to their consequent association with the vagaries of the moon, and, so far as the subject of this inquiry is concerned, with the elusive hare. There is little doubt that, logical thinking being predominantly a male function and intuition a female one, the persecution of witches in Europe was largely due to an over-systematized phase of man-dominated religion that led men to suspect all truly intuitive activities of women as bad and therefore as something to be eradicated at all cost—at the cost, as it has indeed turned out, of devitalizing men's own spiritual understanding, as is so evident to-day.

The uncanniness of the Hare as evidence of former sacredness

However this may be, the moon, having become the object of mere astronomical observation, has suffered a similar eclipse so complete that we use the word 'lunatic', derived from the Latin *luna*, the moon, exclusively as a synonym for 'insane'. The hare, too, once the symbol of radiant dawn and positive intuitive knowledge, has suffered a similar eclipse, and has come to be regarded, as Black puts it, as 'one of the most melancholy of animals in popular opinion'.[1] Thus, not unnaturally, 'Sir Thomas Browne tells us that in his time there were few above threescore years that were not perplexed when a hare crossed their path'.[2] He refers, of course, to a dying superstition, even in his day remembered only by the old. Even the hare itself seems to be conscious of its despised state, if we are to judge by the statement in Turberville's *Book on Hunting and Falconry* that 'the hare first taught us the use of the hearbe called Wyld Succory, which is very excellent for those who are disposed to be melancholicke: shee herselfe is one of the most melancholicke beasts that is, and to heale her own infirmitie she goeth commonly to sit under that hearbe'.[3]

Instances of the hare's uncanniness and of the consequent tendency to regard it as an unlucky omen could be multiplied, but space and patience will not allow, and I will content myself with one more quotation from Billson regarding his view of the reason. He says, 'The main evidence for the ancient sacredness of the hare rests upon its subsequent unpopularity, and the superstitions which cluster round it. It is of course a matter of common observation that the deities of one age become the devils of another; that, in the lapse of years, objects which were formerly worshipped and held in pious honour become, under a new dispensation, the most ill-omened and outcast. Thus we may often argue back from the present unpopularity of an animal to its former divinity.'[4]

With regard to those two factors most commonly associated with the hare, namely 'Moon' and 'Women', we have in a nutshell two of the most far-reaching transformations in history, from moon-worship to sun-worship, and from matriarchy to the almost exclusively patrilineal system that has ruled the

[1] W. G. Black, *The Folk-lore Journal*, vol. i, p. 85.

[2] ibid., p. 84.

[3] Quoted by W. G. Black, *The Folk-lore Journal*, vol. i, p. 85. Compare Prince Henry's question in Shakespeare's *King Henry IV*, Part I, Act 1, Scene 2, 'What sayest thou to a hare, or the melancholy of Moorditch?' to which Falstaff replies, 'Thou hast the most unsavoury similes.'

[4] C. J. Billson, *Folk-lore*, vol. iii, p. 453.

modern world and now only shows signs of being modified, or at least balanced by the rediscovery of the true role of women in our man-ridden world, a role that will not be one of rivalling men at men's jobs, but of reinstating the earth-value of the female element in life, to the neglect of which the instability of modern life is so largely due. Perhaps, when this is accomplished, we shall return to the view expressed in Russian and Chinese folk-tales, that the hare is associated with the Waters of Life,[1] or to the more moderate one expressed in many other tales of it as 'an exceptionally wise and crafty spirit, the guide of men, and the protector of other animals', as in China where the hare appears as 'the guardian of the wild beasts, and defends the lamb from the wolf',[2] though it is true that yet other folk-tales represent him as 'the crafty guardian and shifty schemer'.[3]

The Hare as symbol of the Repentant Sinner

I may perhaps quote here a phrase pregnant with meaning which I happen to have run across almost by chance in a Dictionary of Art to the effect that the hare is 'a symbol of the repentant sinner returning to God, as for example, in a representation carved in marble in the Catacombs of a hare running towards a dove which has an olive branch in its beak'. The entry closes, 'The hare later becomes a symbol of fear'.[4]

What better epitaph could there be on the death of spiritual love, and its substitution by all that is most negative under a superimposed feeling of the wrong kind of guilt?

HARE TOTEMS AND TABOOS

Many authors, including Andrew Lang, Black, Billson, and others, have discussed the claims of the hare to be a totem animal. There is no doubt that a number of non-European cases of hare-totemism occur. The definitions of totemism are

[1] C. J. Billson, *Folk-lore*, vol. iii, p. 461.

[2] ibid., p. 461, quoting De Gubernatis, ii, 79.

[3] ibid., quoting de Gubernalis, ii, 76–7.

[4] *Kunstlelexikon*, by Wilhelm Spemann, Berlin and Stuttgart, 1905, under the heading *Hase.*

so various, however, that I do not propose to go into this question here, but will simply refer to some of the supposed relics of hare-totemism in Europe.

The most frequently quoted of these is Julius Caesar's statement (*De Bello Gallico*, v, 12) regarding the Britons that 'they may not eat the hare, chicken, or goose, but kept these animals for pleasure'.[1] Krappe adds regarding the hare, 'There can be no doubt as to the correctness of Caesar's statement: as late as the nineteenth century the peasants of western Brittany could hardly endure to hear the name of the animal. In parts of Wales hares were not killed down to the reign of Queen Victoria; in the south-west parts of England the peasants, as late as the last century, would eat neither hare nor rabbit. The peasants of Kerry, Ireland, are even now said to abstain from hare, whatever the reason alleged.'[2] He further adds a long list of other countries or districts scattered throughout the world in which the hare is for religious reasons taboo.[3]

Taboo against pronouncing the names of the Hare or of Women at sea

There is also in the British Isles a widespread aversion to uttering the name of the hare, particularly at sea. Thus 'Mr. Gregor notes that to say to a fisherwoman of the north-east of Scotland that there is a hare's foot in her creel, or to say to a fisherman that there is a hare in his boat, arouses great ire, and calls forth strong words; the word "hare" is not pronounced at sea. In Cornwall a maiden who has been deceived and dies, haunts her deceiver in the guise of a white hare, sometimes saving his life, but in *the end* causing his death.'[4]

Billson also records that the prohibition against uttering the word 'hare' at sea is found amongst the fishermen of the west of Ireland.[5] The writer of this article is himself familiar with

[1] 'Leporem et gallinam et anserem gustare fas non putant; haec tamen alunt animi voluptatisque causa.'

[2] A. H. Krappe, *Folk-lore*, 1942, pp. 198–9.

[3] See also C. J. Billson, *Folk-lore*, vol. iii, p. 450, for an even longer list.

[4] W. C. Black, *The Folk-lore Journal*, vol. i, p. 87.

[5] C. J. Billson, *Folk-lore*, vol. iii, p. 452.

the fishermen of a Cornish village, among whom, even as late as twenty-five years ago when he himself went fishing with them, it was still absolutely forbidden to mention either a hare or women on board a fishing-boat. The taboo against mentioning women is commonly attributed to the fear of mutual jealousy among the crew, but no reason is given for not mentioning hares. The taboo against uttering the name of the hare may of course be a relic of totemism, itself a highly specialized and socialized form of the kind of *participation mystique* which I have spoken of above, but which, though it presumably had its origin in individuals, has in totemic societies been adopted and, so to speak, conventionalized by a whole community.

There is, indeed, with regard to the subject under discussion, at least one relevant attribute held in common between hares, women, and the sea which might give rise to the phenomenon known as 'linked totems', and this is the unpredictability to men of the way in which all three appear to behave. It will be remembered, however, that the sea is subject in the movement of tides to the moon, so that to this trio the moon must also be added, which seems to bring this superstition in line with the general configuration of hare associations now seen to be almost world-wide. Whether this be indeed a totemic configuration or not I am unable to say. The taboo against mentioning hares or women may, on the other hand, be a quite simple case of it being considered unwise to mention lightly, while under her sway, the goddess that rules the waves. Or, alternatively, it may be that formerly the hare-moon-goddess was necessarily invoked during sea voyages, and that this pre-Christian custom brought down on it the anathema of the Church according to the law by which many heathen customs become prohibited on the introduction of a new religion, but nevertheless live on under a negative guise.

THE HARE IN CLASSICAL ANTIQUITY

The connection of the hare with Easter, and through this with the Anglo-Saxon goddess Eostre, and in later times in Europe with witches, leads on to the last lap in this summary of the hare's mythical attributes, namely, to the beliefs held concerning this animal and to its symbolic use in classical times in Greece and Rome.[1]

THE HARE AS AN OMEN. AESCHYLUS'S ACCOUNT OF THE TWO EAGLES DEVOURING A PREGNANT HARE

A few references have already been made in passing to the use made by the Romans of the hare as an omen and in various other symbolic ways.[2]

Perhaps the best-known reference to the hare in classical Greek writing is, however, the famous passage in Aeschylus's *Agamemnon* (lines 104–39) in which the chorus reports an omen that appeared outside the palace as the army assembled under the leadership of Agamemnon and Menelaus before setting out for the siege of Troy. The chorus tells how two eagles, one black and one white, were seen feeding on a hare 'richly pregnant with young which had missed the last laps of its race' (see Fig. 15). Calchas interpreted the two eagles as representing the two princes Agamemnon and Menelaus, and declared

[1] It is worth mentioning that, though in late classical times the ancients sometimes confused the hare with the rabbit and the Greeks called the rabbit by a variety of names formed from diminutives of the word λαγώς meaning a hare, such as 'half-hare', 'little hare', etc., no such confusion can have occurred earlier than the first century B.C. before which rabbits were unknown in classical lands, having been introduced, probably from Spain, for the first time about this date. As all the most important references cited in this section date from before the time when the rabbit was introduced, there is no doubt whatever that the animal referred to in them is definitely a hare.

[2] See pp. 189, 190, 205.

FIGURE 15. Two Eagles feeding upon a Hare

(see Aeschylus's *Agamemnon*, lines 104-39) Silver tetradrachm of Akragas, in the British Museum. About 413-6 B.C. After Hill, *Select Greek Coins*, Pl. 58, 2

that the omen signified that the army would capture and pillage Troy. The passage ends with the assertion that Artemis, who was antagonistic to the expedition, was angry with the two eagles for eating and killing the hare.

In view of what the hare symbolizes in other parts of the world, it is clear that we have here a symbolic representation of these two princes imbibing intuitive knowledge of what would be necessary to the success of their quest. In terms of what they set out to achieve, the hare which they devoured presumably represented Troy, that city of so great mythological import symbolizing the womb pregnant with the stolen graces of Helen, who was herself a pre-Christian symbol of the Holy Grail abounding with all those spiritual gifts symbolized by physical beauty that men desire and for which the Greeks were willing to sacrifice so much life, treasure, and time.[1] On yet another level of interpretation, it is clear that the hare having 'missed the last laps of its race' indicated the sacrifices that yet had to be made, or possibly the time that must elapse, before the end was achieved and the full pregnancy of satisfaction could be attained. It will be remembered that the moment of victory came when the Greeks sprang fully armed from out the belly of the horse (Aeschylus elsewhere refers to them as the horse's nestlings—in Norse mythology the horse gave birth to all the world), and it would be quite typical of the dream mind from which mythology is made to use this as a symbol for the birth of the hare's young representing the spiritual power that had been incubating inside the bodies of the Greek leaders until the final release of these powers resulting in the capture of Troy and the redemption of the lost treasure in the form of Helen.

The obvious connection, in this account, of the hare with

[1] Compare Oliver St. J. Gogarty in *Others to Adorn*, London, 1938, pp. 39 and 82, on the cock about to mount the hen, 'your body all a Troy to house desire', and 'I give more praise to Troy's redoubt, For love kept in, than was kept out'. For these and some other references in this section I am indebted to my friend Mr. W. F. Jackson Knight, who has a very great perception for the symbolism underlying much classical literature.

love and pregnancy, leads on to an examination of two aspects of Greek culture with regard to this animal that are so different from anything hitherto mentioned as to be almost in a category by themselves. The first has to do with beliefs about the actual animal's own supposed peculiar reproductive ability, and the other with what is clearly connected with this, namely, the symbolic use to which this reproductive ability is put in the employment of the hare in Greek art and literature as a love-symbol and aphrodisiac.

BIOLOGICAL BELIEFS REGARDING THE HARE'S FERTILITY

For Greek beliefs regarding the abnormal fertility and peculiar reproductive ability of the hare I am indebted to the account given in Pauly-Wissowa's great Classical Encyclopaedia,[1] from which the following quotation taken from the article on the Hare, and translated into English, is made. The part of the article cited itself consists entirely of summaries of and quotations from classical authors. It says:

'Hares mate at very frequent intervals, that is to say, every month during the whole summer, and females conceive even while still pregnant. They produce milk even before the young are born. Nor do they bring forth their young all at one time, but at irregular intervals whenever they wish, and the young are born blind.[2] It is said further that during pregnancy the uterus contains nipples within itself (for the unborn young to suck from).[3] Herodotus certainly exaggerates when he asserts that, while the female is still carrying her young, some of whom are already befurred, while others are not, and a third part are only beginning to take shape, she conceives yet again. It is, however, pertinent to note that the Father of History [Herodotus] remarks that God bestowed particular fertility on

[1] Pauly's *Real-Encyclopädie der Classischen Altertumswissenschaft*, neue Bearbeitung von Georg Wissowa, Stuttgart, 1894.

[2] Aristotle, *Historia Animalium*, vi, 33, p. 579b, 30.

[3] ibid., iii, 1, p. 511a, 29.

all creatures that are at the same time timid and edible.[1] Aelian[2] relates a remarkable tale which I will here give in his own words: "A huntsman of my acquaintance, an honest fellow incapable of lying, told me this queer story. He affirmed that male hares not only beget, but bear young and suffer the pains of labour, and rear as many as two or three. This seemed to me at first to be quite unbelievable, but the following incident confirmed it. He assured me that he had himself found a male hare half-dead, whose belly was swollen. He cut it open, and in fact found within it a uterus containing three young. When he took them out, they lay as still as a lump of meat; but as soon as the sun warmed them they came to life. One of them stirred, then opened its eyes, put out its tongue, and opened its mouth for hunger. He naturally gave the little ones milk to drink and successfully reared them, which seems to me proof of their miraculous birth. I cannot bring myself to doubt this story, since, as I have said already, the man was neither a liar nor a boaster." Female hares are said also to bear young without having a male to impregnate them.[3] According to Aristotle, the great fertility of the hare is caused by the possession of a womb divided into several parts,[4] shown outwardly by the unusual thickness of the fur.[5] All animals have an evil smell during their mating season,[6] so that the hare has it almost the whole year[7] though it is true that young hares have it also.'[8]

Apart from noting that the ancients had, of course, many erroneous notions regarding natural history, it is not necessary

[1] Aristotle, *Historia Animalium*, iii, 108; cf. Pliny, *Historia Naturalis*, viii, 219, x, 179, 182; Xenophon, *Cynegeticus*, v, 12; Aristotle, *Historia Animalium*, v, 9, p. 542, 6, 31; *Physics*, ed. Ideler, i, 178; Plutarch, *Moralia*, 829b.

[2] Aelian, *Historia Animalium*, xiii, 12. (It should be noted that Aelian is a humorous Roman writer who wrote in Greek but is said never to have been in Greece.)

[3] Archelaus, quoted by Pliny, *Historia Naturalis*, viii, 218.

[4] Aristotle, *Problemata*, x, 14, p. 892b, 1.

[5] ibid., *de Generatione Animalium*, iv, 5, p. 774a, 31.

[6] Theophrastus, *de Odoribus*, 61.

[7] ibid., *Historia Plantarum*, vi, 20, 4.

[8] Xenophon, *Cynegeticus*, v, 13.

to comment on these very interesting beliefs except to point out the obvious connection between the attribution of miraculous fertility, here attached to the hare as an actual animal, and the attribution of divine reproductive power akin to 'grace' attached by other peoples to the hare as a symbol. It may well be asked which of the two attributions, the symbolic or the material, came first. Folk-lorists of the materialistic school will doubtless favour the latter, but I incline to think that while the hare may indeed be prolific (and it must not be forgotten that hares and rabbits were in late classical times often confused) this would not by itself be enough to account for the above reports, and that the widespread ideas about the supernatural attributes of the hare may also have played their part in producing these 'miraculous' stories.

THE HARE AS A LOVE-SYMBOL

Very different from the crude biological beliefs cited above are the conceits mentioned in Greek literature and above all depicted in Greek works of art regarding the hare as a love-gage, and in particular its close association with Aphrodite and Cupids and the Bacchic mythical and ritual cycle.

When the Greek gods were gathered together by man's ingenuity upon Olympus and had become the objects of speculation and the pegs on which the mingled intellectual and artistically imaginative fantasies of this gifted people could be hung, among other things the hare had its place in this cosmogony. How far the love-gage was conceived as actual—for it is depicted also as taking place between mortals—and how far it symbolized a more spiritual union I leave the reader to judge from the evidence cited below, culled mainly from an article on vase-paintings published as long ago as 1862 in the *Compte-rendu* of the Russian Imperial Archaeological Commission,[1] relevant passages from which I here render in English.

[1] Ludolf Stephani, *Erklärung einiger Vasengemälde der Kaiserlichen Ermitage, Compte-Rendu de la Commission Impériale Archéologique pour l'année* 1862, St. Petersburg, 1863. The pages quoted are pp. 62 to 73. I am indebted to Dr. H. Meinhard for calling my attention to this work. I here give only some of the numerous refer-

Fig. 16. A SATYR PLAYING WITH A HARE

From a clay calyx-krater in the Jatta collection at Ruvo. Attic work of the early fourth century B.C. After *Monumenti dell' Instituto,* 2 Pl. 59.

Satyrs, Maenads and the Bacchic ritual cycle

The author begins with a catalogue of the various appearances of the hare in connection with Satyrs without any too obvious mythological or symbolic import. On the first vase he mentions, a Satyr wearing a white band in his hair is seen trying to catch a hare which in its turn tries to escape. He goes on, 'Similarly on a coin of Messana, Pan is about to seize a hare,

ences to the Greek and Latin authors cited. Those interested in further study are referred for more detailed references to the work in question.

The subject is very briefly handled in the article 'Hase' in Otto Keller's *Die Antike Tierwelt,* Leipzig, 1909, p. 216, containing a few further items of information, as for instance that wedding-rings were often decorated with the image of a hare.

and on an incised gem the same god is seen in the act of disembowelling a game animal, apparently a hare, hung on a tree'.

'In a famous representation of the myth of Io, a Satyr[1] is seen playing with the same animal, holding out to it a string of beads (see Fig. 16). On a marble relief a Satyr is seen teasing a panther by dangling a hare before it, while another Satyr in the form of a Herm[2] offers the same animal to the young Dionysus himself to play with. A vase painting by Amasis shows two Maenads presenting a hare to the bearded Dionysus, and in another beautiful vase-painting a Maenad named Tragoedia does the same.[3] On an incised gem the cult image of Dionysus himself appears to be holding a hare in his hand.'

'One vase-painter portrays six Satyrs armed with clubs chasing a hare. On the base of a candelabrum in the Imperial Hermitage is depicted a Satyr bringing a captured hare for sacrifice, and on each of two incised gems is seen a Satyr triumphantly holding up his prey.'

'Another vase-painting shows a hare in a cave attending a meeting between Dionysus, a Maenad, and a Satyr, while in a third Dionysus joins the Satyrs and the Maenads in greeting Apollo who is seen approaching upon a swan (see Fig. 17). On a fourth vase-painting two Satyrs watch a pair of hares playing together, and on a Roman marble relief a hare puts in an appearance at a Bacchic sacrifice.'

'Lastly, with regard to a relief in the Villa Albani, the meaning of which is difficult to grasp, the presence of the *thyrsos*[4] and the mask can hardly leave any doubt of the fact

[1] The Satyrs and Cupids that figure so largely in the following account both have the common characteristic that they playfully do everything and anything they like, a fitting symbol of that carefree attitude to life that also informs the Graeco-Roman symbolic attitude towards the hare.

[2] A herm is a small pillar surmounted by a human head, with the human genitals carved on the pillar. It has been supposed that all Greek gods were originally represented in this way, but by the fourth century B.C. in Athens they were all held to represent Hermes, whence the word 'herm.'

[3] The Maenad in this painting holds the hare behind Dionysus's back.

[4] A sacred wand.

FIGURE 17. Apollo riding upon a swan, with Hare beneath

The other figures are of two women (Muses?) and a Satyr. Clay bell-krater in the British Museum. Attic work of the early fourth century B.C.

FIGURE 18. Luxuria, accompanied by a Hare

Drawing by Pisanello now in the Albertina in Vienna

J. Mathey, *Portraits and Studies of Women*, says (p. vii) that Luxuria is a symbol of sensual delight and carnal pleasures, and that the hare is assigned to her as the symbol of fertility

that here, too, the hare is present by virtue of his connection with the Bacchic mythical and ritual cycle. The same motive obviously lies at the root of Aeschylus's well-known phrase: "Bromios [Dionysus] haunts the place, I know it well, since the time when the god took command of the Maenads and contrived death for Pentheus like a hare."[1]

Aphrodite, Eros and the Cupids

'It was quite natural for the ancients to place the hare in this context on account of the marked analogy between the nature of the hare's being and of the ideas centring round the Bacchic myth and ritual. Such qualities possessed by the hare are swift-footedness, curiosity, fearfulness, and aphrodisian lasciviousness, qualities which are as conspicuous in the character of the Satyrs as in the hare. That it was particularly the last-mentioned of the hare's supposed characteristics on which the ancients laid most stress is clear from the fact that they connected the hare also so closely with Aphrodite and Eros.'

'The passage in Philostratus in which he gives the clearest indication of it is well known. It is the one in which he speaks of "the most acceptable sacrifice to Aphrodite: you know of course the legend of the hare, that it possesses the gift of Aphrodite [i.e. fertility] to a superlative degree".'[2]

'We thus find the hare regarded as an emblem (or attribute) of Aphrodite in two indisputable representations of her and may therefore, with more or less probability, be justified in thinking of her in connection with other female figures [painted on vases] accompanied by a similar emblem.'

'With regard also to the close relation existing between the hare and Eros we may recall to mind above all the information given us on this subject by Philostratus when he describes a painting that is said to have represented Cupids hunting hares, in which he says, "and let not yonder hare escape us, but let us

[1] Aeschylus, *Eumenides*, 24; referring to the fact that Pentheus had tried to suppress the worship of Dionysus.

[2] Philostratus, *Imagines*, i, 6. Compare Eustathius, *Commentaries on the Iliad*, A, p. 87, 37. The hare is an offering to Cupids. It should be noted that Philostratus wrote as late as the third century A.D.

join the Cupids in their hunting". This creature sits under the apple-trees and feeds on the fallen apples, but leaves many half-eaten. The Cupids hunt him up and down and rout him out, one with clapping of hands, another with a cry, a third waving his cloak. Some fly over him with shouts, others follow his trail on foot, and one starts him up as if he were going to hurl himself on him and the hare goes off on another course. Another schemes to catch the hare by the leg, but the hare slips away just when he thought he'd caught him. So they laugh and fall over, one on his side, the other on his face, and others on their backs, in every attitude of disappointment. Nevertheless, none of them shoots an arrow, but they try to catch him alive [as Aphrodite's favourite offering].'[1]

'In agreement with this we see on a vase, in a wall-painting and on a glass vessel representations of Cupids, with or without dogs, running in pursuit of a hare. Elsewhere they fly in pursuit. Thus, on one, a relief, are represented two Cupids, one of them armed with a club, trying to catch a hare in a trap; and on a cornelian, a Cupid rushing upon a hare emerging from a snail-shell.

'Other classical artists depict Cupids who have already caught their prey and are hurrying away with it either by flying or running, or resting with it when caught. In yet other ancient works of art we find, for example, Cupids watching two hares playing together or themselves playing with the beloved animal, kissing it or driving a chariot drawn by hares.[2] In yet other representations a hare may be seen quietly sitting at the foot of a Cupid-herm or near a Cupid completely formed.'

'Lastly, in a well-known marble relief representing a sumptuous banquet in a world populated only by Cupids and Psyches, one Cupid brings in a hare, while another plays with a second hare on the ground.'

The Hare as love-charm and customary love-gift

'It was on account of this emphasis by the ancients laid on

[1] Philostratus, *Imagines*, i, 6.

[2] It should be noted, however, that the hare is not the only animal that is depicted as being harnessed to the Cupids' chariot.

FIGURE 19. Eros with Hare

From a clay amphora of Panathenaic shape in Naples. Attic work of about 490-480 B.C. After Beazley *Der Berliner Maler*, Pl. 10.

Eros carries in his right hand a flute-case, to which is attached a box containing the mouth-piece. In his left hand he carries a lyre with its tortoise-shell sounding-box. Beneath crouches a hare

the hare's aphrodisian nature that they endowed it with the power of a love-charm,[1] so that it is not surprising to find, on a beautiful necklace recovered from a Crimean tomb, among other amulets one representing a hare, and also to meet with a representation of the same animal on a magic nail.'

'This fact explains also a great number of other works of art which otherwise would be unintelligible, in which hares are found closely associated with youths, men, and women, and obviously have the meaning of love-gages.'

'So we meet with youths in the act of presenting a hare, or having just given one, to a beautiful woman to win her love.'

'We see men handing the same animal as a gift to youths, or *vice versa*; youths having just received one from men who in the picture appear to be occupying themselves with the gift; or paintings in which hares are hung up between men and youths, thus clearly indicating the nature of their relationship.'

'Also in cases where individual men, or individual youths or boys, are in various ways brought together by means of a hare, or where hares are being exchanged as gifts between youths, there can no longer be any doubt that these gifts have the same meaning.'

'If, therefore, a hare is depicted in connection with the meeting of Poseidon and Amymone, or with the attack of Nessos on Deianeira;[2] if it is associated with Herakles reposing from his

[1] Thus, Philostratus, *Imagines*, i, 6: 'But perverted lovers recognize in the hare a certain power to produce love, and try to secure the objects of their affection by the compulsion of magic art'. It is to be noted that Philostratus wrote in the third century A.D. when magic had acquired a much greater importance in the classical world than hitherto.

So also Pliny, *Historia Naturalis*, xxviii, 79: 'The people think that if you eat a hare your body acquires sexual attractiveness for nine days, a vulgar superstition, which, however, must have some truth in it since the belief in it is so widespread.' [Pliny probably refers to Italian rather than Greek folk-lore.]

So also Martial in one of his tart epigrams (Martial, v, 29): 'Whenever you send me a hare, Gellia, you say to me, "You will be beautiful for seven days". If you are not making fun of me, my love, if you mean what you say, you, Gellia, have never had a hare to eat.'

[2] Poseidon and Amymone were lovers, and Nessos's attack on Deianeira was a sexual assault.

labours, who, as is well known is at such a juncture wont to apply himself to every kind of material pleasure with no less energy than ordinarily to heroic deeds; if a hare peeps at the

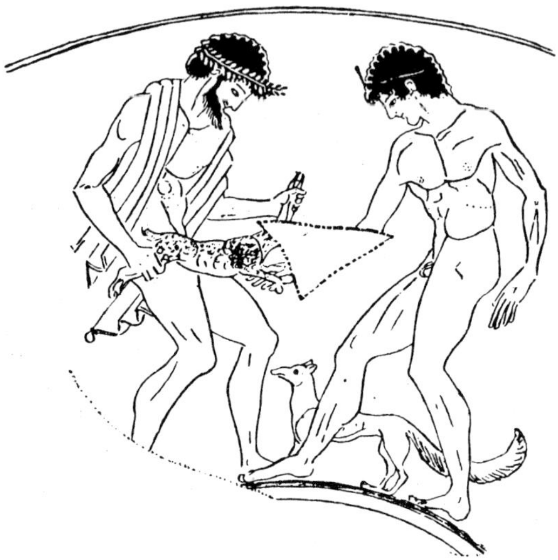

Fig. 20. MAN OFFERING A HARE TO A YOUTH

From a clay calyx in Boston. Attic work of about 500 B.C. After Hartwig, *Meisterschalen*, Pl. 26. The symbolism of this love-scene is an interesting study in the psychology of complementary opposites. The man pursues the youth, but inwardly he is pursued by his desire. Therefore the sought-after youth brings the dog (the hunter), and the man brings the hare (the hunted).

orgiastic dances indulged in by girls and youths, or if it is present during the quiet conversation between a man and a woman, no-one who has read the evidence given above, can remain ignorant as to the meaning the artists intended to convey.'[1]

[1] The author says in a note:

'It is as a symbol of aphrodisian delight and not as material food that, on a Roman sarcophagus (Garrucci, *Mus. Lateran. Tav*, 30), the hare is represented as being brought to a festive meal. For the hare is depicted as being alive, and is not brought like the foodstuffs upon a

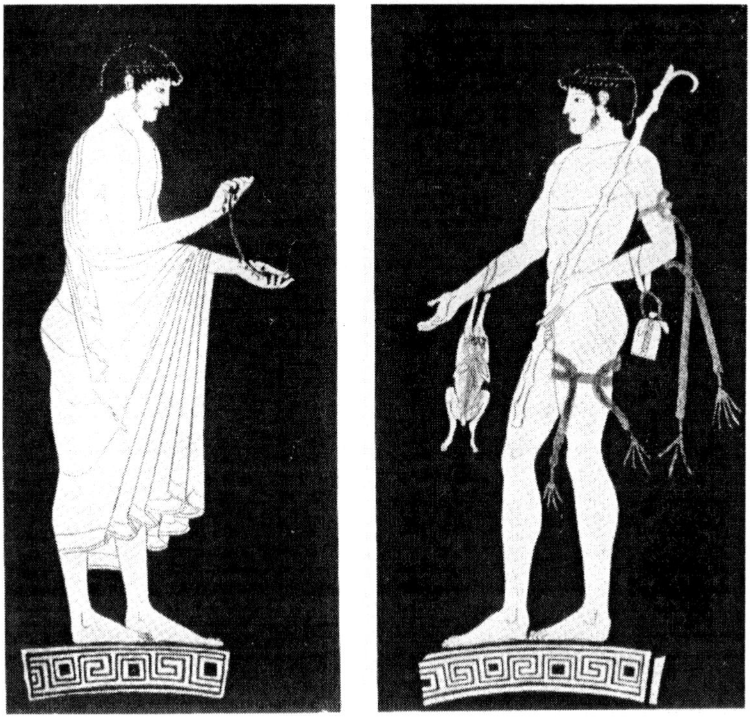

FIGURE 21. The Victorious Athlete receives tribute, including a dead Hare, from an admiring friend

Clay amphora of Panathenaic shape in Boston. Attic work of about 490 B.C. After Caskey and Beazley, *Attic Vase Paintings in the Museum of Fine Arts, Boston*, Pl. 5

The author then goes on to say that not all representations of the hare in Greek art are symbolically significant, since the hare is often used, as are so many other animals, with purely decorative intent or to fill in unwanted gaps in the design, such as the space between a horse's legs. He goes on, however, to say that 'if this happens in the Bacchic *thiasos*,[1] if the rider is a Satyr and the animal on which he rides is a panther, it cannot be doubted that the artist, in depicting a hare of all animals between the panther's feet, was led to choose this animal by virtue of its close connection with Bacchic concepts.

'If we notice the same animal beneath the horse of Oenomaus or that of Tertus, this probably hints at a love relation.[2]

'The hare is, however, depicted elsewhere in a similar position without our being able to presume any other reason for it than that which would apply to any other hunted animal.

'The hare as a quite ordinary object of the chase is in this way closely connected with gods and heroes, not only in legend but also in works of art.

dish. The same is true with regard to the African tombstone of a Roman soldier, on which his small son is represented as bringing a hare, while his daughter holds in her hands a dove and a bunch of grapes (*Revue archéol.*, 1863, pl. 8).' It appears doubtful, however, to the present writer whether this offering of a hare by a boy to his dead father is capable of an aphrodisian interpretation, unless it were an indication of carnal pleasure in the hereafter. Could not an alternative explanation be that it was an expression of filial love, as appear to be the dove and grapes brought by the daughter?

Elsewhere (on p. 64, note 5), however, the authors calls attention to the large number of hares represented on Roman tombs, where they are depicted usually as eating grapes.

I here put forward the suggestion that if, as in other parts of the world as we have seen, the hare is a symbol for intuition, this may possibly represent a union between divine intuition and the red blood of earth.

[1] *Thiasos* is a body of worshippers, here referring to the famous 'Bacchus and his rout'.

[2] It has been rightly pointed out that as the horse's chief attribute in this connection is fleetness, so also is the hare's. I suggest, however, that, if the horse symbolizes physical fleetness, the hare symbolizes a fleetness of spirit that is akin to the intuitive faculty that we have seen associated with it elsewhere.

'In the first place, Artemis herself is called λαγωβόλος[1] [shooter[2] of hares]; in a remarkable bronze object she is depicted as holding two hares in her hands, and is elsewhere often seen closely associated with them. In such scenes she is often accompanied by her brother Apollo, and by her companion Aura.

'Next to the fox, the hare is the game most frequently hunted by the Centaurs, such as Chiron, Pholos, and others.

'Adonis also, and Perseus and Orion hunt hares, and in a famous vase-painting Theseus, Actaeon, Tydeus, and Castor are seen hunting together.

'Elsewhere mortals, unidentifiable men and youths, are seen bent on the same form of amusement, or dogs without huntsmen alone chasing and catching hares. Zeus's eagle also pursues the sport, and the hare is also depicted in kitchen scenes.

'The hare thus also becomes, in later times, a regular attribute of the seasons, whether these latter appear in the form of women or of boys or Cupids.'

As a seasonal emblem[3] the hare in the late Graeco-Roman world appears to fall into line with its use as a zodiacal sign in China and among the Aztecs, but in all other respects the Greek view of the hare, both in its supposed biologically miraculous fertility and in its use as a love-gage, is unique. It seems to me to mirror not only the extraordinary ingenuity of the Greek mind but also what might be called its whimsically agnostic and materialistic outlook, an outlook that placed it for a few centuries in the very forefront of the world's cultural development but lacked that second sight or sense of complementary opposites without which stability and durability cannot exist.

As I have said above, just how far the aphrodisian attribute

[1] Thus Nonnus, *Dionysiaca*, xxxiii, p. 126, depicts Eros as saying, 'But if the Archeress [Artemis], the huntress of hares, moves her [Aphrodite] to anger, I will draw the fiery Olympian sword of Orion to harry Artemis, and I shall drive her out of heaven'.

[2] i.e. with bow and arrow.

[3] It seems to have represented winter, possibly on account of the alpine hare's coat turning white in winter in order to approximate its colour to the snow.

of the hare was materially conceived and how far it may have been thought of also as symbolic of spiritual truth I cannot say, and can only leave it to the reader to decide.[1] It does seem at first sight, however, as if we are here dealing with the degradation of a symbol. If we may judge from all that has been said about hare symbolism in other parts of the world it would appear that the hare was venerated in the first place on grounds quite other than purely sexual ones as symbolizing the transformation of instinct into spirit, and that its use for symbolizing simple untransformed sex is purely secondary.

The Hare sleeps with its eyes open

Finally, there is the widespread belief already mentioned,[2] which is of no little interest, that the hare sleeps with its eyes open. Thus, Xenophon[3] says, 'When he is awake he shuts his eyes, but when he sleeps his eyelids remain open though his eyes do not move'. Various attempts have been made to explain this curious statement on physiological lines, but to the psychologist it is clear that this is a symbolic way of saying that the hare 'sees with the inward or spiritual eye', which has been misconstrued by the material-minded in classical times to refer to physical fact.

Later on in the same work this author remarks, 'When going quietly it springs; no-one ever saw or will ever see a hare walking',[4] which brings to mind the symbolism of the hare as a 'leaper' so often met with in these pages and giving rise to its use as a symbol of dawn and of the faculty of intuition.

[1] Those interested in following the trail of the hare as a love-symbol in modern European folk-lore will find much material to hand in the article on the hare in the *Handwörterbuch des deutschen Aberglaubens*.

[2] See pp. 128 and 190.

[3] Xenophon, *Cynegeticus*, v, 11, quoted by Otto Keller, *Die antike Tierwelt*, Leipzig, 1909, p. 217.

[4] Xenophon, *Cynegeticus*, v, 31.

CONCLUSION

This survey, which makes no claim to completeness (since literature is inexhaustible, and in any case this is no academic treatise), has at least touched, however briefly, on most recorded aspects of the subject of which I am aware, and, for lack of both time and space, I propose now to draw it to a close in the hope that it may nevertheless have added something to our knowledge of a small corner of archetypal research.

We have ranged over a fair area of the world's surface, as well as a stretch of some six thousand years of time, and have witnessed on the one hand a remarkable uniformity in the fundamental symbolic notions connected with the hare by mankind throughout the ages, and on the other hand a great variety of detail.

Let us now turn back and gather the threads, so far as is possible, of the various mythological concepts we have met with.

The Hare as (often a Willing) Sacrifice

Beginning with the central motive of Mrs. Wright's dream, which is that of sacrifice, we have seen this in highly developed form in the case of the Buddha as a hare sacrificing himself by leaping into the fire and so transmuting his fleshly instinct into spirit and its immediate connection with the moon, that 'light in the darkness' which illuminates the inner life of man.

The motive of sacrifice we have seen reflected in the Déné Hareskin legend about throwing the head of a white hare into the fire whereon it immediately became dawn, and more faintly in Europe in Dr. White Kenneth's quaint report about the hare that 'kills itself', in the 'black broth' of Sparta made of the blood and bowels of a hare, in the feeding of the Kings of Tara upon 'the hares of Naas', in the widespread harvest custom of 'killing the hare' and drinking of the 'hare's blood', in the Pomeranian custom of eating the Easter Hare, in the English custom of killing a hare on Good Friday, in the

Leicestershire rite of 'Hunting the Hare' on Easter Monday, and the subsequent eating of 'hare-pies'.

Hare Deities

Various taboos on eating the hare at ordinary seasons and on mentioning its name probably indicate its sacred nature. As god of the nether world the hare is found associated with Osiris as moon-god of the dead, and with the goddess Unnu-t. Among the Algonkin of North America the Great Hare is the creator, and in Europe we find the hare-headed goddess, tutelary deity of the Moon-day we now call Monday probably associated with the Anglo-Saxon Eostre, whose name is equivalent to our Easter. The Teutonic goddess Frejya is also said to have been attended by hares.

Association with the Moon

The association of the hare with the moon is almost world-wide, being found in India, China, North America, Ancient Egypt, among the Hottentots, and, by virtue of the connection of the hare in Europe with Easter, among ourselves also, since Easter is the great moon-festival which also ushers in the spring.

Symbol of Dawn, Easter and the 'east'

This festival follows, and is entirely dependent on, being the result of, the supreme sacrifice of Good Friday, which is the darkness which ushers in the dawn. It is therefore significant to what an extent the hare itself figures as a dawn-symbol. It does so, in fact, almost universally. We may begin with Ancient Egypt, where, in Le Page Renouf's view, the very word for hare means 'leaper' and is connected with such concepts as 'uprising', 'opening', 'becoming' (hence the use of the hare hieroglyph for 'to be', and also 'to be created'), so that the word *Unnu* itself becomes 'an appropriate appellative of the rising sun, who springs forth in glory and triumph'.

The sun rises in the east, so also the Indian god Sakka who translated the image of the hare into the moon has his place in the east, and the Algonkin medicine-lodge has its door opening to the east and summons the east in the name of the Great Hare, the creator-deity. In Europe the hare is also connected with Easter, the name of which feast has been shown to be derived from Sanskrit roots meaning 'the east' and 'dawn', from which also are derived through different channels the Greek ἕως and the Latin *Aurora*. Mention has also been made of the Easter Egg, laid by the Easter Hare, and of the eastern European custom of making sugar images of it with little windows looking into them, through which are seen pictures of religious subjects such as Christ rising from the tomb.

Association with Whiteness and Snow

Closely connected with the east is the colour white (if that which has no colour, or includes all colours, may be so called). Mythological allusions to the hare and its accompanying phenomena are throughout the world extraordinarily insistent on white and whiteness, which is itself equated with the brightest possible light. Beginning with Mrs. Wright's dream, it will be remembered that, though her hare was brown (fawn-coloured), outside the house the ground was covered with a miraculous snow on which no footprints were left, and inside the kitchen in which the sacrifice took place 'there was a great light and everything was as white as it was outside'. Also the bowl in which the hare sat was white. If we now turn to the mythology of the hare throughout the world, we notice, first, that the stone seat on which the god Sakka sat, and which through the power of the Hare-Buddha's renunciation became so warm, was covered with a white woollen blanket. Then, when the hare leapt into the fire but was unharmed, it is said that it was as if he had leapt into snow. This might at first sight be taken to be a simple figure of speech to express its coldness, but it means also the pure light of intuition as opposed to the earthly light of the fire.[1] It is therefore interesting in this connection to

[1] Compare the descriptions of Our Lord at His transfiguration, when He first spoke of His coming sacrifice, that 'His face did shine as the sun and His raiment was white as the light' (Matt. xvii, 2). Mark (ix. 29) says of His raiment that it was 'white as snow', and Luke (ix, 29) that it was 'white and glistering'. The same language is used of the appearance of the angel who rolled back the stone from the tomb, whose raiment was 'white as snow' (Matt. xxviii, 3; see also Mark xvi, 5).

note the reference among the Algonkin to the Great Hare's 'brother, the snow'. Brinton points out also that the syllable *wab* occurring in the Great Hare's name also means 'white'. In China also, though red and black hares are mentioned, the most prominent hare in mythology is the white hare, which lives a thousand years and becomes white when half that period is completed. There is here doubtless a reference to the arctic hare, which in fact turns white in winter, but what is significant is the choice of this white hare as the chief mythological symbol. It is said also in China that the white hare is the Moon Queen's servant. It will be remembered also that it was the head of a white hare that in the Déné Hareskin story was thrown into the fire and produced the dawn. Whiteness—usually described as 'silveriness'—is also commonly connected with the moon. For this reason we turn the silver in our pockets on sight of the New Moon, and it will be remembered that in the Austrian game of piercing the Easter-egg laid by the hare the object that pierces it must be a silver coin. Silver is also useful in the hunting of the witch-hare in Europe. Thus, as has been stated, 'the only way to make sure of hitting a witch-animal is to put a silver sixpence or a silver button in your gun'. Sometimes it must be a 'crooked sixpence', but a still more efficacious method is to use for the same purpose a consecrated wafer—also a round white object—mixed with the shot.

Symbol of Intuition

Mention of the moon and silver, both symbols of intuition, brings us once more to the subject of the hare as representing pre-eminently this psychological function. Too much has been said about this throughout this survey to need stressing it any further, so that all I will do now is to bring together a few of the possibly subtler forms of expressing it. Intuition is a peculiar function—possibly the most fundamental—which enables a man to receive instantaneous perceptions about things, which are correct though not based on logical deduction but rather on direct subliminal knowledge. Children have it, of course, and animals, but we are apt to lose it as we grow up. Spiritual understanding of the 'other side' of things depends on its recovery, that is to say on its 'redemption' or 'salvation' from the dark recesses of the soul into which it has been thrust as into a kind of cold-storage. This is particularly the case to-day when purely intellectual processes are so overestimated that we are apt to distrust and so be afraid of our 'intuitions', which, since we do not honour them, are indeed apt to revenge themselves on us by coming up in a negative or unreliable form. This, however, is only the case in so far as we dishonour them by not joining them to our other, more generally considered to be 'respectable', functions of thinking, feeling, and sensation, because they need precisely the check which these other functions can provide. Coming, as they do, directly and without any apparent intermediary into consciousness, they do in fact bear messages from the 'other' world of non-conscious values. Therefore, it is not surprising to find the hare (itself a fleet-footed animal appearing in surprising places) saying, in the Indian story, 'I am the ambassador of the moon, and this is what the gods say to you by my mouth'; or, in the Hottentot story, being charged by the moon to bring a message to man to tell man of his immortality (though it is true he forgot the message by the way); or that the hare-moon in Egypt should be equated with Thoth, himself equated with the Greek Hermes and the Roman Mercury, who are themselves messengers of the gods as shown by the wings they bear on head and feet.

The Hare as Omen

Different from these but possibly to be classed under this heading is the use of the hare as an omen according to the direction in which it runs, as described by Pausanias, and in the case of Boadicea, and of the running of a hare portending fire.

Association with Picture-writing

It is a characteristic of intuitive knowledge that it often makes itself felt in the form of pictures, seen in dreams or visions which present themselves in pictorial form. It is therefore not surprising that the Great Hare of the Algonkin should be accredited with the invention of picture-writing, and Thoth with the invention of hieroglyphs, of which the hare-sign itself is one.

The Hare makes the Elixir of Life

Another magical attribute of the hare is the widespread view of it as the maker and purveyor of the elixir of life. This is the case in China, where the hare mixes the Herb of Immortality on the moon; in North America where the Great Hare is the founder of the medicine hunt and in whose house at the place of sun-rising the souls of good Indians feed on delicious fruits; in its connection through association with Thoth and Hermes who, as Hermes Trismegistos, became later the patron of alchemy; and in a degraded literal sense in medieval Europe where parts of the hare's body were said to have many healing properties. All but the last of these are connected, of course, with the gift of, or search for, immortality, with which the hare-amulets of Ancient Egypt, China, and Greece are also doubtless connected. It is with a message of immortality that the moon sends the hare to mankind among the Hottentots, and in the South African myth the moon sends the hare with the message, 'Like as I die and rise to life again, so you shall die and rise to life again'. Doctrines of immortality are, of course, implicit also in the worship of the Great Hare of the Algonkin, as in our own Easter festival and in the Easter eggs laid by the hare at this season, and if a hare lays eggs she must be previously pregnant, as is the Anglo-Saxon hare-goddess who clasps the moon to her belly. Artemis also sees eagles feasting on a pregnant hare, and the hare-moon, Lucina, assists at parturition. In Ancient Greece this motive is translated into pure superstition regarding the biological productivity of hares, and the hare becomes, as we have seen, a symbol of love.

The Hare as Witch-animal

Finally, in a totally negative way, hares, from being goddesses, are in medieval and modern Europe reduced to the status of witch-animals, using their intuitive-productive capacity for negative purposes.

Influence of the Hare Dream on Mrs. Wright

In Mrs. Wright's own dream-history the sacrifice of the hare in Dream 9, surrounded by bright light and with its snow-white setting, did indeed bring about a transformation of instinct, and thereby of her whole personality, in the direction of intuitive knowledge and of a spiritual pregnancy benefiting not only herself but her daughter Margaret to an extreme degree. It will be remembered that her next dream (Dream 10) contained the direct message that 'Margaret and her mother may sleep together', meaning that the mother-love that had been cloyed was now purged of inhibiting misconceptions and could now flow directly into her daughter. This was followed by Dream 11 confirming the last by emphasizing Mrs. Wright's release from the authoritarian influence of a falsely intellectual external world. Then, when the analysis had made her conscious (which she had not been before) of the full meaning of these dreams, came Dream 12 marking the descent of spirit from on high (symbolized by the supposed air-raid), together with the prayer before the fowl-house containing the unseen Easter eggs, symbols of new life, followed by the Good Friday scene of parting from her school friend for three days. Then came Dream 13 referring to the Last Supper and the adumbrated recovery of Bertha, and after that Dream 14 introducing the motive of human flesh seen in the flesh-pink material, leading up to the sacrifice (dreamt of as an 'operation') of the young well-set-up Jewish butcher symbolizing Christ. This in turn was followed by Dream 16 introducing the dark aspect of God in the form of the black pony, and Dream 17 referring to sanctification and 'marriage to God'. And so the analysis proceeded.

She was, of course, as totally ignorant as I was of the world-wide mythology of the hare that has just been summarized. Nevertheless, some of the chief motives in it, namely, the sacrifice, the whiteness symbolized by the snow, the bright light symbolizing the dawn and direct intuition (a light which occurred again with much more defined meaning later in her career, as will be described in a subsequent volume), the association with Good Friday and Easter and Easter eggs, and the realization of divine love, all came into her dream-series, showing the deep connection existing in the inner world of the psyche of individual modern men and women with the whole mythological history of mankind. The fact that the dream of sacrificing the hare had no effect on her till enough of its meaning was explained, and that it then produced this great effect, demonstrates clearly—and it is only one of innumerable examples—not only the power of the archetype but also the part it plays in the redemptive process that lies latent within us all, though it remains comparatively inoperative till joined to consciousness, but becomes so potent a force for good when activated by being recognized and honoured.

Part Three
MORE DREAMS ABOUT HARES AND RABBITS

SHOWING THE MYTHOLOGICAL MOTIVES ON WHICH THEY ARE BASED AND THEIR RELATION TO EVERYDAY LIFE

Since making the foregoing investigation into the Mythology of the Hare, I have taken particular note of the occurrence of dreams about hares and rabbits in the analysis of other patients, both past and present, and have been so impressed by the references they all contain to different aspects of the mythological hare cycle that I have thought them of sufficient interest to include some of them here. I take this opportunity of thanking the respective dreamers for kindly allowing me to do so.

It is the nature of archetypes, as they appear in dreams, that, while preserving their archetypal characteristics, the details and context of their appearances have always a special bearing on the dreamer's own problem. Just as different localities emphasize different aspects of any one myth, thereby presumably indicating the state of inner development of the particular communities in which they are found, so in the case of individuals a similar selective process is seen to be at work. Thus in dreams, which deal fundamentally with universal problems, we get an infinite number of variations, all of which nevertheless centre round one feature or other of the archetypal pattern.

As will be seen from the dreams about to be cited, just as no one mythological cycle includes all the mythological attributes associated with the hare, so also no single dream embraces them all, but each dream includes a definite reference to one or other of them, elaborated in terms of the dreamer's own personal problem. It would make an interesting theoretical study to determine what characteristic of a particular dreamer causes the correspondence with a given variation of the mythological pattern associated with a particular locality or perhaps era in the world's history. But such speculation is outside the scope of this book, and would demand a far greater body of evidence than I am here able to present. I will therefore content myself merely with citing such dreams as have recently come to my notice, and it is important to note that in all these cases the dreamer had no conscious knowledge whatever, any more than had Mrs. Wright, that the hare was of any importance as a mythological figure, and much less of any of the beliefs held concerning it that have been described in this book, except possibly a vague memory of the connection of the hare with witches in Europe, a motive that incidentally does not enter into a single one of these dreams.

Association of Hares with Rabbits

It may surprise some readers that, among hare dreams, I include also dreams about rabbits. Though rabbits differ from hares in many essential ways, notably in their methods of self-defence, which for the hare is running and for the rabbit burrowing, and in the loneliness of the hare as opposed to the gregarious habits of the rabbit, they belong to the same genus and have so much in common that town-dwellers to-day often fail to distinguish between the two. As pointed out on p. 208, note 1, they were sometimes confused also by the ancients, the Greeks calling the rabbit by diminutives of the common word for the hare, such as 'half-hare', 'little hare', etc. It is also to be noted that before the first century B.C. there were no rabbits in classical lands, rabbits having been introduced thither from Spain for the first time about this date. Spain is also said to be the land whence they were introduced into Britain, having originally been brought to Europe from North Africa, as they were later introduced with disastrous consequences from Europe into Australia. Hares and rabbits are also so closely allied that instances (though rare ones) are on record of their interbreeding, and the grey rabbit of North America is a kind of intermediate species which normally does not burrow, though when hard pressed it may escape into any accessible hole.

H. Kunike goes so far as to write a whole article on 'The Rabbit in the Moon'. He speaks of the Great Rabbit of the Prairie Indians in the same way as we speak of the Great Hare of the Algonkin, and adds that they sometimes refer to the moon as 'Rabbit's Eye'. He also perceived the truth which I have emphasized in this book regarding the archetypal nature of this mythological cycle, which he associates with the rabbit and which others associate with the hare. Thus Siecke in reviewing his article says: 'The remarkable agreement [regarding this cycle] found in the beliefs of different peoples of the earth who otherwise have no connection with one another forces us, as Dr. Kunike rightly shows, to the conclusion "that they must be due to some common underlying natural cause".'[1]

We have only to think of the White Rabbit in *Alice in Wonderland* to realize the obvious connection between this visionary character in the Lewis Carroll mythological cycle and the association both of hares with whiteness, and of the hare as the 'opener of the way' or 'of the womb'[2] (which is what the White Rabbit is in the Alice saga, by showing her the way into the rabbit hole which is the gateway into the inner world), to realize the universality of the symbolic imagery connected with both hares and rabbits in the collective psyche. The child-mind is well aware of it, as seen in the nursery custom of say-

[1] H. Kunike, 'Das Kaninchen im Monde, insbesondere in der Mythologie der Nordamerikanischen Indianer', in the journal *Die Sterne*, Potsdam, 1925, pp. 267–75. Dr. H. Meinhard kindly called my attention to this after my Part II on *The Mythology of the Hare* was already in print. I have been unable to find a copy of the original article, and the above quotation is from a review of it by E. Siecke, in the *Ethnologischer Anzeiger*, Stuttgart, vol. i, 1928, Abteilung B, p. 31.

H. Kunike has also written another article on the Toad in the Moon ('Die Kröte im Monde') among the American Indians in *Die Sterne*, 1924, pp. 79–83, to which also I have been unable to gain access, but which should prove of interest in connection with the Frog accompanying the Hare in the Moon in the Chinese T'ang mirror illustrated in Fig. 9.

[2] See pp. 151–2, 155, 223.

ing 'hares' last thing at night on the last day of the old month and 'rabbits' (sometimes 'white rabbits') first thing on the first morning of the new, a quite obvious symbol of 'dawn' and 'new life' fittingly connected with the moon despite the calendrical convention that the month no longer coincides with the moon's phases though it originally did. This is supposed to be a 'lucky' act just as the white hare was regarded as an auspicious omen in China (see p. 128). Sometimes in nursery custom the roles of hare and rabbit are reversed, and 'rabbits' is said at the end of the old month and 'hares' at the beginning of the new. But the association between the two animals and their symbolic meaning is clear.

If any doubt is still entertained as to the propriety of associating hare-dreams with rabbit-dreams I think the way in which the dreams dealing with rabbits fit in with the archetypal pattern of the hare will prove sufficient answer.

Dream of a doe-rabbit having to transfer her habitation underground or else be burnt.

The first dream I propose to cite, though it is about rabbits, recalls so definitely the self-sacrifice of the Hare-Buddha by leaping into the fire that I have no hesitation in including it. In case the similarity of this dream-motive to the mythological material might be ascribed by the critical reader to some kind of unconscious suggestion or telepathic influence passing from analyst to patient, I should like to point out that, like Mrs. Wright's dream, this one occurred and was recorded more than a year *before* the analyst himself had any knowledge that such world-wide mythology existed.

The dreamer was a married woman of highly over-extraverted nature, who dreamt that she saw two conical earth-mounds. The right-hand mound was intact, but the left-hand mound was partly demolished, showing it to be the hutlike dwelling-place of a doe-rabbit who was sitting inside, and that its earth-covering had an internal lining of straw. A buck-rabbit was standing outside, between the two mounds, and was engaged in setting fire to the doe-rabbit's hut with a lighted stick. The doe-rabbit inside the hut complained to the buck, 'Please, *Monsieur Lapin*, do not set fire to the thatch of my house!' The buck-rabbit, with which the dreamer identified herself, replied, 'If you are idiotic enough to build such an erection on the surface of the ground instead of burrowing deeply where you belong, I must'. The dream was very vivid and had all the impact of a vision.

Fig. 22

The buck rabbit burns down the doe-rabbit's hut to 'send her underground.'

This dream is a very deep one. The maleness of the buck-rabbit is emphasized by the phallic emblem he wields in the shape of the lighted stick representing the external or male fire, and the doe-rabbit's female nature is emphasized by the fact that, with her, the fire is an internal one represented by the lighted thatch *inside* the roof of her hut. In Freudian terms the action of the dream would represent an attempted sexual union refused by the woman. But the union desired by the male and refused by the female is not one of sex but of the spirit, and the buck-rabbit states quite clearly what is the obstruction, namely, in terms of the dream, that the female has made her dwelling above ground and not below 'where she belongs'. That is to say that the female has rivalled the male instead of supporting him from below by developing the truly female and earthy part of her own nature. Though not stated in so many words in the dream, it is clear that the right-hand mound is also a hut and belongs to the male who represents not only the husband but also, if the dream is taken on the purely subjective level, the dreamer's own properly extraverted side. But a balanced psyche needs equal weight on both sides of the dividing line, namely a strong inner life to balance the outer. The dreamer in fact lived so much on the surface (as shown by both huts being above ground) that at the time this dream was dreamt she could achieve real creative union neither with her husband nor with her own internal *animus*.

Since, like the hare, the rabbit stands for intuition, the two rabbits together with their two huts may be interpreted as representing the two aspects of intuition, the male on the right hand representing extraverted intuition and the female on the left hand the complementary function of introverted intuition. It is an axiom of psychology that no element of the psyche is in itself wrong, but that any wrongness there is arises from the misplacement of any given element, whereon what would be positive when in the right place becomes negative when in the wrong. The two conical huts may be likened to the two triangles in the Shield of David mentioned on p. 168, of which the triangle pointing upward represents external reality and the triangle pointing downward represents internal reality. In that symbol the two are creatively united, each being the mirror opposite of the other. But in this dream they are not so united, and the female triangle corresponding to the doe-rabbit's hut is in its wrong place, that is to say above ground and pointing upward, causing the dreamer at that time in actual life to project her own unrecognized internal contents externally on to others in a negative way, giving rise to difficulties in her relationship with just those who possessed the feminine qualities which she lacked through not recognizing them in herself, difficulties which she was either unable to account for or else found rationalized excuses to explain.

With regard to external and material things the dreamer was thoroughly well equipped, having her feet well on the ground, so that in the dream the right-hand (extravert) hut is solid and in its right place and is in no need of being changed. But she could not make proper contact either with her husband or with society as a whole (except with people very similar to herself) because she was always invading their spheres and trying to dominate them. It is to remedy this state of affairs that the buck-rabbit in the dream proposes the burning, that is to say the transformation, of the left-hand hut which should have been the positively introverted one but was, instead, negatively extraverted with the above-mentioned results. Two sames cannot unite, and so, in order to bring about their creative union, the left-hand dwelling had to be transferred underground, involving the dreamer's withdrawal of negative projections and their transformation into positive self-knowledge of her own inner nature.

The transforming medium is the fire, wielded objectively by her husband and subjectively by her own *animus*. But here again the same conflict is seen, since she identifies herself with the *animus* as represented by the buck-rabbit and not with the female rabbit, which means that intellectually she has the desire but emotionally she still rebels. Still, the desire is there, and when the feminine side of herself agrees the transformation will doubtless take place, and it is a fact that the dream occurred at a moment when she was beginning to realize the need for some such fundamental revision of habitual attitude. At the same time, the use of the French language by the doe-rabbit when she addressed the buck-rabbit as '*Monsieur Lapin*' showed how very much of a foreign language to her the world of the spirit still was.

The existence of two fires, the external fire of the buck-rabbit and the internal fire of the doe, is a particularly interesting feature. This juxtaposition refers to a symbolic truth that I have observed in dreams, namely that whereas the Pentecostal fire descends upon men from above, as on the Apostles' heads, for women it arises out of the earth, as seen in women's dreams in which their shoes catch fire (as this woman actually dreamt some time later) or the floor or wainscoting of a room (as opposed to the roof) gets set alight. This represents the internal fire which the buck-rabbit was driving the doe to accept through sacrifice of her negative externalization (in other words, unconscious pride) as symbolized by the burning of the externally usurping hut and the transferring of the doe-rabbit's dwelling to below the ground. This corresponds to the self-sacrifice of the Hare-Buddha in the fire and the transference of his image into the moon which is the 'light in the darkness' that rules the night, symbolizing the inner world. Everyone is, like this doe, afraid of sacrifice, but it should be noted that, just as the Hare-Buddha, because a willing sacrifice, did not himself get burnt, for 'the fire was powerless to heat so much as the pores of a hair on his body . . . it was as if he had leapt into snow' (p. 110), so also the doe-rabbit will not get burnt if she obeys, but will if she does not. This means that the woman *will* get psychologically and spiritually burnt up if she continues her double externalization (symbolized by *both* huts being above ground), but will find self-realization both within herself and in relation to her husband and to society as a whole if she becomes humbly receptive enough to the command of her *animus* to internalize that half of her nature which belongs inside, that is to say, become really acquainted with herself.

Dream of cooking the white meat of a Rabbit which turns into a child

Another rabbit dream is that of a young woman who dreamt: 'I am in a kitchen cooking, standing over a stove, and with a spoon in my hand am stirring some white meat in a saucepan. The meat is the size and shape of a rabbit. As I turn it over it becomes whiter till it seems almost luminous, and a girl friend standing beside me shows me that what I am cooking is no longer a rabbit but is a child. In the dream this mysterious business seemed quite natural, but when I woke up I felt utterly horrified at what I had done.'

This dreamer had been forced through highly unsatisfactory home conditions into living an unnaturally extravert life, underneath which was a nameless cavern of unoccupied because unrecognized spiritual power, of which she felt terrified as of a vortex into which she might some day be suddenly dragged, and of which for this reason she had become mortally afraid. She was, at the time of dreaming, on the point of opening up the deeper levels of her psyche, but the life she found there was all so strange to her that its various manifestations often appeared both frightening and, to her, quite incomprehensible.

This dream has in it the luminous whiteness so frequently associated with the hare (see pp. 224–5), which in the deep psyche represents direct intuitive knowledge and at this level always carries with it a mysterious and ghostly feeling somewhat akin to awe. Only when, as in this case, the inner meaning is not recognized does this feeling of awe turn into dismay or horror, which it will be noted did not occur within the dream itself since to the dream mind the process that was taking place was a perfectly natural one, but which was felt acutely on waking.

The dream actually represented a very positive advance. As in real life cooking means the transformation of raw food into something that can be more easily digested, so cooking in dreams also means transformation but in a spiritual sense, that is to say the making of some difficult truth digestible in order that it may be swallowed and, as in the previous dream, internalized. Ezekiel swallowing the roll of the Law (in order to 'inwardly digest' it) is a case in point. Such food might to the conscious mind not seem very appetizing, yet when he had eaten it he found it 'as honey for sweetness'.[1] What actually happened in this dream was that by means of a spoon, which is a receptive instrument symbolizing female or introvertly intuitive thinking, the dreamer was 'turning over' her problem, that is to say, was seeking what lay beneath the external appearance, and so was confronted with the 'illumination', which she herself took simply to be the white meat of a rabbit. It needed the greater knowledge possessed by her girl friend, a real person who had herself been successfully analysed and thus

[1] Ezekiel ii, 8 to iii, 4.

represented the dreamer's own 'positive shadow', to show her what was indeed the fact, namely that her hitherto unrecognized intuitive knowledge as represented by the rabbit was capable of being made conscious, as symbolized by its transformation into a human child. This was, of course, the 'holy child' trailing with it the 'clouds of glory' of which Wordsworth speaks, that is to say, her own divinely childlike nature, that had been so damagingly obscured by fear and by a superimposed religious education that had proved worse than useless by turning her against religious symbolism in all its forms and thus yet further divorcing her from the reality of her own inner life. This mysterious dream was then, when understood, far from being a horrid act, but, on the contrary, was pregnant with all the possibilities of new life. It is, incidentally, of interest to note that the cooking took place in a saucepan, which is a round vessel corresponding in this respect to the round white bowl in which Mrs. Wright sacrificed her hare, and to the round full moon in which the transformed image of the Hare-Buddha was displayed. This brief dream thus includes four motives of the Buddha story: the sacrifice, that is to say the transformation, represented by the cooking, the luminous whiteness, the round container, and the rebirth.

The analytical process was proving that the apparently frightening symbols were in fact pregnant with healing virtue, and that the mystery, far from being an insult to the dreamer's intelligence (which so many at first take anything mysterious to be), was on the contrary the revelation of a profundity in her own psyche before which her conscious ego could only prostrate itself in grateful acceptance and do its best to understand. This dream was one of many, all dealing on different levels with the acceptance of the childlike intuitive faculty in herself, whereby the power of emotion within herself could be transformed, from being a merely negative force inevitably dragging her down into an abyss of nameless fears, into a positive guide illuminating the deep recesses of her soul and so leading to creative life.

Dream of sacrificing a Rabbit by hitting the right side of its head with a white stone

Another rabbit dream also represents the rabbit as a sacrificial animal—as, in fact, all hare and rabbit dreams that have come to my notice do. This dreamer was a woman in middle life, who dreamt:

'I am standing at a desk in a square room (the desk resembles partly my own and partly the analyst's), trying to kill a small animal with a lovely brown fur coat. I am trying to do this by grasping its body in my left hand and rapping the left side of its head on the desk, and have been trying to do so for twenty-four hours.

'While I am absorbed in this job of killing, an unknown man who clearly has every right to be there comes in through the door behind me and to the left, and crosses over to the window on my right and stands with his back to it, watching what I am doing. I say to him, "I have been trying to kill it this twenty-four hours", as if I am acting on some preconceived and unconsidered notion that I must kill, but do not question why, or whether I want to or not. But it won't die, but on the contrary looks uncomplainingly at me with its bright eyes set in a remarkably broad face. It makes no attempt to defend itself or to escape, nor does it display any kind of animosity, but playfully bites me with mouse-like teeth. I wonder whether I shall be infected by the bite, but do not feel pain or fear, in fact have no feeling sensation or emotion at all.

'Up till now I have been trying to kill it by grasping its body in my left hand and striking the left side of its head against the desk. But now, still keeping it in my left hand, I try to kill it by hitting the right side of its head with some object which I had in my right hand and which I think was a white stone.

'At last I think that I have killed it, and see the result, which is the *left half* of a bleached rabbit's skull such as one may find anywhere on the downs. The right half of the skull was not there, but what was particularly remarkable was that the left half which I now saw had, to my surprise, the dead white brain still in it. It did not seem possible that this was the animal that I had just killed, but there it was.'

Though the dreamer had no knowledge whatever of the mythology described in this book, the dream nevertheless includes four of the hare's most widely attested attributes: (*a*) its sacrificial nature, (*b*) that it is a willing sacrifice, (*c*) its bright eyes (also attested by Mrs. Wright), and (*d*) the whiteness so often associated with the hare, represented (though the animal itself was brown) by the bleached skull, the white brain within the skull, and the white stone with which it was killed.

It would take a long time to analyse the dream fully, and there is space here to refer only to certain salient points.

In the first place the room is square, a shape so often symbolizing the inner psyche, witness the square house in which Mrs. Wright sacrificed her hare (see p. 48), and the desk quite clearly represents the sacrificial altar, as did the operating table in Mrs. Wright's Dream 15.

'This twenty-four hours' meant to the dreamer at first simply 'all night and all day', but later she thought that it referred to that period twenty-four years ago when she was battling with certain peculiarly severe problems of adolescence. Later still, following the suggestion that it might also mean 'all my life', it dawned on her that twenty-four signified her own age reversed, which was forty-two, so that on this level the number symbolized a return to the beginning, in other words rebirth.

The animal's bright eyes set in a broad face reminded her of a mentally deficient girl she had once dealt with, and indicate, in my opinion, the intuitive knowledge[1] of all mental defectives that lies deep hidden behind an appearance of inability, the unexpressed wisdom of the newly born child as yet uncontaminated by the illusions of a materially minded and disbelieving world, a deep wisdom of which the so-called mental defective is the unconscious carrier precisely because the conscious does not supervene, and from whom this pearl of great

[1] Compare the Prairie Indians' reference to the Moon as 'Rabbit's Eye' (see p. 232).

price can be dug out through right handling based on an unreserved belief in human instinctive knowledge as mirroring the divine will. There is no space here to expand this thesis, which will form one of the main themes of a future volume. All I wish to point out here is that the 'bright eyes' thus also indicate a rebirth motive, that of regaining the inborn wisdom of the child.

This also explains why the effort to kill the rabbit by crushing the *left* side of its head was not allowed by the dream-mind, but on the contrary the successful sacrifice consisted in striking it on the *right* side of its head with the white stone held in the right hand, thus, as it turned out, demolishing the right side altogether but leaving the left side of the ancient bleached skull intact. This is because 'left' represents instinctive (and therefore potentially spiritual) life symbolizing the wisdom of the ages, while 'right' signifies external control. Thus we speak of the 'right arm of the law' (meaning man-made law), and not the left. It was the wrong kind of control over the instinctive-spiritual process exercised by the 'right' or conscious side due to fear and disbelief that had to be sacrificed, and not, as she had been doing all her life (symbolized by 'these twenty-four hours') the 'left' or unconscious side from which these processes spring.

As seen throughout *The Mythology of the Hare* and summarized on pp. 224–5, luminous whiteness represents direct intuitive knowledge corresponding to Wordsworth's 'clouds of glory' trailed by the child at birth, and this accounts in the dream for the bleached appearance of the ancient skull representing the wisdom of the past containing the apparently dead white brain, which, however, cannot really have been dead, else it would have long since disappeared. The whiteness of the skull and of the brain, which impressed itself particularly on her mind, as well as the whiteness of the stone with which the sacrifice was eventually performed, corresponds very closely with the luminous whiteness of the rabbit's flesh that was being cooked in the previous dream and that in fact turned into a child. The bleached ancient and now apparently lifeless skull corresponds to the lack of emotion and feeling sensation in the dream, and might superficially seem negative, but becomes positive if taken as representing deep buried and ancient wisdom which may be difficult to get at, but is, when found, more positive than anything the merely rationalizing ego can ever know.

Important was the feeling that the dreamer was acting on some preconceived and unconsidered notion unknown to herself. This is exactly what Mrs. Wright did on sacrificing her hare, and is also seen in the apparent meaninglessness (until interpreted) of the action of the two other dreams that I have just cited. It is characteristic of the internal redemptive process that it acts *for* and *in spite of* one's conscious self in accordance with laws which the conscious ego has so largely forgotten but which have to be obeyed and, in so far as possible, understood. The internal redemptive process is, however, inoperative unless it has conscious support, and the change-over from the mistaken attempt to destroy the left side of the skull representing instinct to the successful sacrifice of the right side representing her former mistaken conscious attitudes, and the use for this purpose of the white stone in the right hand representing the dreamer's newly recovered belief in the correctness of her intuitive faculty, indicates that she is on the point of realizing this and of taking action accordingly.

The question once more is: What did the rabbit which she was sacrificing represent? That it wanted to be sacrificed is clear from its lack of any kind of resistance, from the trusting look in its bright eyes, and from its playful biting of her with its needle-like teeth. Biting in dreams (even when it looks like attack, and may look very frightening) is always a love-act symbolized by the merging or entry of each protagonist into the other, the teeth of the 'attacker' (the male, active, intrusive element or 'lover') entering into the 'attacked', and the flesh (the female, passive element) of the 'attacked' one simultaneously entering into the mouth of the so-called 'attacker'. It is only the one-track thinker who ignores this symbolic meaning of 'attack' by failing to understand the mirror-opposite nature of the deeper levels in the unconscious, and that love is only mistaken for assault when it is refused. This is the meaning of the dreamer's fear of 'infection'. Infection in dreams means 'impregnation', and, the dream always being an effort at integration, infection here means impregnation by the primaeval instinct which is at one with spirit and signifies the acquirement of spiritual power.

On a more personal level the rabbit represents (with its bright childlike eyes and mouselike teeth) the 'mousily' diffident and unassuming side of the dreamer's nature that has to be transformed by more self-assertive action.[1] Indeed, her perfectly natural instincts had, both forty-two years ago when she was born and again twenty-four years ago at adolescence, all seemed to her to have been 'knocked on the head' (as in the dream she first knocked the left side of the rabbit's head), and it was now time that she put things right again by knocking on the head, in other words sacrificing, the right-hand side representing the consciously resulting 'mousy' feeling that the unmerited rebuffs of her childhood had caused in her and that had proved only a false refuge, and that she now took matters into her own hands by recovering her belief in her own instinctive reactions. The unknown man (her positive *animus*) silently watching her quite clearly approved of what she was doing, and himself represented what, if she succeeded, would be her reward through union with him, internally in the form of instinctive-spiritual power, and externally, if matters took that course, in the form of union with a real man.

It is of interest that, after realizing the various implications of this rabbit-dream, she recalled another dream that she had had a little earlier of all the animals in the Zoo coming out of their cage. Like the three objects in her rabbit-dream, all the animals were white, representing externally things unaccustomed to the light, such as her wrongly repressed instincts, but internally the white light of self-knowledge. Her immediate reaction on having this dream had been 'The lion shall lie down with the lamb', meaning that now the union of opposites was at hand, and that, after all, instinct was right

[1] It is worth noting that the dreamer is not, as are so many women, in real life afraid of mice, but likes them, and thinks of them kindly as 'wee timorous beasties'.

and could go hand-in-hand with spirit and with right social behaviour, since, however opposed they might appear to be, they were ultimately one.

Dream of shooting a Hare which flies up into the sky and then returns

The last dream I propose to cite is a real hare-dream, dreamt by a young priest well versed in psychological thinking, but, like the other dreamers, having no knowledge of the mythology of the Hare and being quite astonished when he heard of it and of how his dream fitted into the archetypal pattern.

'I am out shooting (formerly a favourite occupation of mine) in a very green countryside, with long grass and luxuriant hedges. I put up a hare from close by my feet. My gun is at the ready, and I put it to my shoulder and snap the left-hand barrel at the hare, which is just entering the hedge. I know that I have hit the hare, but fear it will escape. It goes through a hole in the hedge, beside which, on my side of the hedge and to the right, is standing an unknown older man with longish white hair and wearing a white shirt and dark trousers. Scared apparently by him, the hare when it reaches the field on the other side of the hedge turns to the left. It runs some distance, and then flies up into the air, turns on its back and dies as it turns over, and falls to earth dead. I set out to retrieve the hare. It is of the golden-brown, tawny colour I associate in particular with the hares found in my home county.'

By Freud the gun would be regarded as a phallic emblem, as indeed it is if it is realized that a phallic emblem is not a sexual organ, but, on the contrary, a symbol representing the transformation of sex into spiritual power. Shooting with the left-hand barrel means conscious use of the internal intuitive faculty always associated with the 'left', indicating that the dream has to do with spiritual values as opposed to direct sexual ones, which would have required the right-hand barrel. This much would have been deducible from the bare symbolism of the dream without the aid of any personal associations. It turned out to be indeed the case, since it later transpired that the dream was the culminating one of a series dealing with what the dreamer had thereby discovered to be a totally unresolved attitude towards celibacy, which was the goal that he had set himself.

The dreamer was practised in that particular form of self-analysis which consists in holding written conversations with his own *anima*, who had by now become his constant inner guide. As an example of such conversations, I here give, with his consent, that part of the subsequent day's discussion with her that touched on this dream:

'*She:* Hence you can sacrifice the hare; and you know all about hares!

'*He:* Do they fly through the air? I must ask my psychologist.

'*She:* Never mind about him for the moment. This one did. What's flying?

'*He:* Taking wings? Becoming spiritualized?

'*She:* Yes. Compare the wind in yesterday's dream. In the air the hare dies. It can then return to earth, the sacrifice accomplished. The blood of the sacrifice is always poured on the ground, or on some sacred object.

'*He:* And the unknown man?

'*She:* He is the old, pre-sacrifice man who didn't accept the female. The hare goes past, that is beyond him; breaking through the hedge, which is the restraining limit set by the man, into the *open* ("he brought me forth . . . into a large place", Psalm xviii, 19), where it can fly up, and die.'

The female referred to here as being something that the pre-sacrifice man did not accept is, of course, on the one hand the *anima* herself who represents the contrasexual or spiritual aspect of the man, but is, in a more general sense, also the whole 'other side' of life represented by the other side of the hedge, in other words the world either of sex (if untransformed) or, if transformed, of spirit. The death or 'sacrifice' of the hare symbolizes precisely this transformation. Though the psychologist himself could have said all this (in fact had said it before he heard the *anima's* comment), she quite rightly overrides him, and thereby proves the efficacy of the analytical treatment, since for a man the main goal of such treatment is the establishment of effective contact with the *anima* and so freeing the patient from the analyst, just as for a woman the chief aim is the re-establishment of contact with her *animus*, as was the case with Mrs. Wright.

The whiteness so frequently associated with the hare is seen in this dream in the unknown older man's white hair and shirt, though in this case it takes on a special meaning owing to its association with the darkness of his trousers. The upper parts of the body as contrasted with the lower are symbolically in the same relation to one another as is the conscious in its relation to the unconscious, or as the mind in its relation both to sex and to spirit (which is transformed sex). In his case the illumination does not extend below the belt, meaning that his sex has not been transformed, and it is for this reason that the *anima* refers to him as the 'pre-sacrifice man', in other words the Old Adam representing the dreamer's unresolved 'shadow'. The same dichotomy that is seen in the upper and lower parts of the man is seen also in the two sides of the hedge. The dreamer, being illuminated in his mind, consciously shoots the hare on the near (conscious) side, but the transformation takes place on the other side, that is to say, that the illumination has to become more internalized. The hare, representing the sex desirous of being transformed,[1] is naturally averse to the unresolved 'shadow', and so runs to the left in order to avoid it, and thereby leads the dreamer's attention still more deeply into the spiritual world. It is in this doubly deep level (represented both by the 'other side' and by the 'left') that it flies up into the air, as the image of the Hare-Buddha was elevated into the moon, both being resurrection symbols. Then it turns on its back, again symbolizing the turning or transformation of sex or extraverted intuition into spirit or introverted intuition. As it does this, it dies, indicating a certain finality in the process, or, as the *anima* says, that 'the sacrifice is accomplished'.

The *anima* does not, however, say just what sacrifice, or rather what extent of sacrifice. If the dreamer had been the

[1] See pp. 112, 185.

consummated Buddha, the hare doubtless would not have returned to earth at all, but would have soared ever upward. But even the Buddha had to undergo successive rebirths before attaining full Buddhahood. And so the hare still has to return to earth, that is to say, in one sense to be reincarnated, or in a more everyday sense to bring the dreamer to earth to attend to his still unsolved problems.

With this, I will take leave of the reader, with the promise that in the not far distant future the story of Mrs. Wright's development and that of her daughter Margaret will be resumed, not in the simple narrative form adopted in Part I of this book, but in the form of a somewhat deeper analysis of Mrs. Wright's dream process as it continued later quite independently of the analyst, and of the role her daughter played in it.

INDEX

In the absence so far of any adequate Dictionary of Symbols (supposing such a complex undertaking to be possible) this Index has been made with a view to furnishing future compilers of such a work, as well as the reader, with some sort of a key to the meaning of the dream symbolism and its associated mythology that have been outlined in this book.

For expert assistance in this attempt I have to thank Mrs. Alice Meinhard, who also compiled the index to the ritual and mythological material in my *Stone Men of Malekula*.

INDEX

INDEX

Industrial Safety Series, 7

Critical Temperatures for the Thermal Explosion of Chemicals

Takashi Kotoyori

National Institute of Industrial Safety
1-4-6 Umezone, Kiyose, Tokyo 204-0024, Japan

Elsevier
Amsterdam – Boston – Heidelberg – London – New York – Oxford
Paris – San Diego – San Francisco – Singapore – Sydney – Tokyo

ELSEVIER B.V.
Radarweg 29
P.O. Box 211, 1000 AE
Amsterdam, The Netherlands

ELSEVIER Inc.
525 B Street
Suite 1900, San Diego
CA 92101-4495, USA

ELSEVIER Ltd.
The Boulevard
Langford Lane, Kidlington,
Oxford OX5 1GB, UK

ELSEVIER Ltd.
84 Theobalds Road
London WC1X 8RR
UK

First edition 2005

Library of Congress Cataloging in Publication Data
A catalog record is available from the Library of Congress.

British Library Cataloguing in Publication Data
A catalogue record is available from the British Library.

ISBN-13: 978-0-444-52119-4
ISBN-10: 0-444-52119-4

♾ The paper used in this publication meets the requirements of ANSI/NISO Z39.48-1992 (Permanence of Paper).
Printed in The Netherlands.

Preface

Knowledge regarding the two characteristic temperatures, the T_c and the SADT,* which are used to express the thermal instability of a chemical of the TD type and that of a chemical of the AC type,** having each an arbitrary shape and an arbitrary size, placed each in the atmosphere under isothermal conditions,*** respectively, is indispensable in temperature control to prevent such a chemical from exploding thermally.

In this connection, when charged in the open-cup cell, or confined in the closed cell, in accordance with the self-heating property of the chemical, and subjected to the adiabatic self-heating test started from a T_s, if 2 cm^3 of a chemical continues to self-heat over the T_s at a rate depending on the value of T_s in accordance with the Arrhenius equation, after its having been warmed up to the T_s, the self-heating behavior of the chemical is said to be of the TD type. In this sense, the oxidatively-heating behavior of 2 cm^3 of a gas-permeable oxidatively-heating substance, such as sawdust, coal dust or oil-soaked lagging, charged in the draft cell, into which an arbitrary oxidizing gas is supplied, and subjected to the adiabatic oxidatively-heating test started from a T_s, is also of the TD type. It is, therefore, possible to calculate the critical temperature for the spontaneous ignition or T_c for a gas-permeable oxidatively-heating substance, having an arbitrary shape and an arbitrary size, placed in the atmosphere under isothermal conditions, in the same manner as applied to the calculation of the T_c for a chemical of the TD type.

In order to determine the T_c for a chemical of the TD type, including every gas-permeable oxidatively-heating substance, and the SADT for a chemical of the AC type, including every powdery chemical of the quasi-AC type, having each an arbitrary shape and an arbitrary size, placed each in the atmosphere under isothermal conditions, it has been required so far to follow, by experimental measurements, the whole self-heating process of the chemical up to the actual thermal explosion, or up to the actual spontaneous ignition. The actual explosion, or ignition, experiment, however, requires much effort, time, space and material and, therefore, is dangerous and expensive. Very few values of T_c or SADT are thus available at present.

On the other hand, there have certainly been some cases so far, in each of which the value of T_c for a chemical of the TD type was attempted to calculate

---

* For the individual definitions of the T_c and the SADT, refer to **Notation**.

** A classification of self-heating chemicals is introduced in **Chapter 3**.

*** The adjective, isothermal, or, non-adiabatic, is used to express such a state that the temperature of the atmosphere which surrounds a self-heating chemical is maintained at a definite value throughout the self-heating process of the chemical, with the result that the heat generated by the exothermic decomposition reaction of the chemical is allowed to transfer from the chemical to the atmosphere. The same is true of the oxidatively-heating process of a gas-permeable oxidatively-heating substance.

by substituting the physical quantities, such as λ, c, ρ, U and S, and the chemical quantities, such as E, A_0 and ΔH, all of which require to be measured separately by specific experimental methods, respectively, of the chemical into either of the two equations constituting the thermal explosion theory, *i.e.*, the Semenov equation and the Frank-Kamenetskii or F-K equation.

Such calculations have, however, been haunted by the uncertainty of measured values, especially, of the chemical quantities, E, A_0 and ΔH, which specify as a whole the rate of heat generation per unit volume per unit time in the early stages of the self-heating process of a chemical of the TD type, including every gas-permeable oxidatively-heating substance, because these chemical quantities are very difficult to measure precisely by means of conventional experimental techniques. The values of E and A_0 of a chemical may be determined by thermal analysis, or by measuring the rate of the exothermic decomposition reaction, of a small quantity of the chemical at temperatures far higher than room temperature, respectively. Such circumstances are, however, not necessarily the same as those which lead to the actual thermal explosion, or to the actual spontaneous ignition, of the chemical. That is, the experimental conditions of the forced external heating for the chemical followed by a rapid rate of increase in temperature of the chemical are clearly different from the actual conditions of the spontaneous heating of the chemical itself followed by a slow rate of increase in temperature of the chemical. Besides, although the value of ΔH of an ordinary substance in general is measured based on the complete combustion reaction, there is always a possibility that the value of ΔH which a chemical of the TD type, including every gas-permeable oxidatively-heating substance, generates in the early stages of the self-heating process, or of the oxidatively-heating process, is that of an incomplete exothermic decomposition reaction, or of an incomplete oxidative decomposition reaction, accompanied with the formation of some transient and unstable intermediate.

Now, are introduced herein entirely new and simple procedures to calculate the T_c for a chemical of the TD type, including every gas-permeable oxidatively-heating substance, having an arbitrary shape and an arbitrary size, placed in the atmosphere under isothermal conditions, and, the SADT for a chemical of the AC type, including every powdery chemical of the quasi-AC type, having an arbitrary shape and an arbitrary size, confined in an arbitrary closed container of the corresponding shape and size, and placed in the atmosphere under isothermal conditions.

The procedure to calculate the T_c for a chemical of the TD type, including every gas-permeable oxidatively-heating substance, having an arbitrary shape and an arbitrary size, placed in the atmosphere under isothermal conditions, is, in particular, based on the basic concept of the thermal explosion theory that whether the thermal explosion or the spontaneous ignition of a chemical of the TD type, including every gas-permeable oxidatively-heating substance, having an arbitrary shape and an arbitrary size, placed in the atmosphere under isothermal conditions, occurs or not is decided, based on the balance between the rate of heat generation in the chemical and the rate of heat transfer from the chemical to the atmosphere at the critical state for the thermal explosion which exists at the end of the early stages of the self-heating process. According to this procedure, we require neither to follow by experimental measurements the whole self-heating process of the chemical of the TD type up to the actual thermal explosion, or up to the actual spontaneous ignition, to determine the T_c, nor to measure the values of the chemical quantities, E, A_0 and ΔH, respectively, to calculate the T_c.

For the purpose of calculating the T_c for a chemical of the TD type, including every gas-permeable oxidatively-heating substance, having an arbitrary shape and an arbitrary size, placed in the atmosphere under isothermal conditions, we have only to perform, on the one hand, several adiabatic self-heating tests, or several adiabatic oxidatively-heating tests, which are started from each T_s with mutual intervals of 1~2 K, in order to calculate the heat generation data of the chemical, for 2 cm^3 each of several samples of the chemical charged, or confined, each in some one of the open-cup, the draft or the closed cell, in accordance with the self-heating property of the chemical, for the time required for the temperature of each sample of the chemical to increase by 1.25 K from the corresponding T_s in the adiabatic self-heating test, or from the corresponding standard temperature in the adiabatic oxidatively-heating test, respectively, and, we have only to measure, on the other hand, the heat transfer data of the chemical, having an arbitrary shape and an arbitrary size, placed in the atmosphere under isothermal conditions, in temperature differences of 1.25 K between the inside of the chemical and the atmosphere, under conditions of no air circulation.

In **Chapter 1**, after both the Semenov and the F-K equation were derived, it is confirmed that both equations express the balance between the rate of heat generation in a chemical of the TD type, including every gas-permeable oxidatively-heating substance, having an arbitrary shape and an arbitrary size, placed in the atmosphere under isothermal conditions, and, the rate of heat transfer from the chemical to the atmosphere at the critical state for the thermal explosion which exists at the end of the early stages of the self-heating process, respectively. It is then concluded that the Semenov equation is appropriate for the calculation of the T_c for a liquid chemical of the TD type and the F-K equation is appropriate for the calculation of that for a solid chemical of the TD type, including every gas-permeable oxidatively-heating substance.

In **Chapter 2**, is derived the adiabatic temperature increase equation, which holds between the rate of heat generation per unit volume per unit time in the early stages of the self-heating process of a small-scale chemical of the TD type, including every small-scale gas-permeable oxidatively-heating substance, having the spatially uniform distribution of internal temperature, subjected to either of the two kinds of adiabatic tests, and, the rate of increase in temperature of the chemical, assuming the effect of the concentration of the chemical on the rate of the exothermic decomposition reaction in the early stages of the self-heating process to be of the zeroth order.

In **Chapter 3**, a classification of self-heating chemicals, except gas-permeable oxidatively-heating substances, is introduced. Treatments of gas-permeable oxidatively-heating substances are made in **Chapters** 7 and **8**. Self-heating chemicals are divided into two large groups, *i.e.*, the thermal decomposition or TD type and the autocatalytic reaction or AC type. The TD type is subdivided into liquid chemicals, for each of which the Semenov equation is applied to calculate the T_c, and, solid (powdery, in reality) chemicals, for each of which the F-K equation is applied to calculate the T_c. On the other hand, the AC type is subdivided into high explosives of the true AC type and powdery chemicals of the quasi-AC type.

When confined in the closed cell and subjected to the adiabatic self-heating test started from a T_s, or to the isothermal storage test performed at a T_t, 2 cm^3 of a chemical of the AC type, including every powdery chemical of the quasi-AC type, does not continue to self-heat over the T_s or the T_t, after its having been warmed up to the T_s or the T_t; rather, it starts to self-heat after the lapse of the induction period of the autocatalytic reaction, or of the quasi-autocatalytic reaction, of the chemical in both tests. That is, the self-heating behavior of a chemical of the AC type is not of the TD type, so that it is impossible to apply either of the two equations of the thermal explosion theory to the calculation of the T_c for the chemical. Instead, it is possible to calculate the SADT for a chemical of the AC type, including every powdery chemical of the quasi-AC type, having an arbitrary shape and an arbitrary size, confined in an arbitrary closed container of the corresponding shape and size, and placed in the atmosphere under isothermal conditions, by applying an empirical formula holding for the induction period of the autocatalytic reaction, or of the quasi-autocatalytic reaction, of 2 cm^3 of the chemical subjected to the isothermal storage test.

The T_c for a chemical of the TD type, including every gas-permeable oxidatively-heating substance, depends on its shape and size. On the other hand, the SADT for a chemical of the AC type, including every powdery chemical of the quasi-AC type, does not depend, in principle, on its size or quantity. The difference between the concept of the T_c and that of the SADT is discussed at the end of this chapter.

In **Chapter 4**, an adiabatic self-heating process recorder is explained in detail. This recorder is used to perform the adiabatic self-heating test, or the adiabatic oxidatively-heating test, which is started from a T_s, in order to calculate ultimately the heat generation data of a chemical of the TD type, including every gas-permeable oxidatively-heating substance, for 2 cm^3 of the chemical charged, or confined, in some one of the open-cup, the draft or the closed cell, in accordance with the self-heating property of the chemical, for the time required for the temperature of the chemical to increase by 1.25 K from the T_s in the adiabatic self-heating test, or from the corresponding standard temperature in the adiabatic oxidatively-heating test.

Is then explained in detail the procedure to calculate the values of the two coefficients, *a* and *b*, of an empirical formula. This formula is obtained directly from the adiabatic temperature increase equation derived in **Chapter 2** and holds for the self-heating process, or for the oxidatively-heating process, in the early stages, of 2 cm^3 of a chemical of the TD type, including every gas-permeable oxidatively-heating substance, charged, or confined, in some one of the open-cup, the draft or the closed cell, in accordance with the self-heating property of the chemical, and subjected to either of the two kinds of adiabatic tests. The values of the two coefficients, *a* and *b*, thus calculated, of the empirical formula are then used as the heat generation data of the chemical, together with the heat transfer data, to calculate the T_c for the chemical, having an arbitrary shape and an arbitrary size, placed in the atmosphere under isothermal conditions, by applying the reduced form of the Semenov equation or that of the F-K equation.

Although any other existent adiabatic self-heating process recorders are also useful for the calculation of the heat generation data of a chemical of the TD type, including every gas-permeable oxidatively-heating substance, the recorder used in a series of adiabatic self-heating tests, or in a series of adiabatic oxidatively-heating tests, described herein is introduced in this chapter. It is, however, hoped that any new and simple apparatus functioning better than the recorder will be devised in the future on referring to the present author's experience gained in using the recorder, because the recorder used herein has clearly some defects.

In **Chapter 5**, is first explained the reason why the Semenov equation is applicable to the calculation of the T_c for an arbitrary volume of a liquid charged in an arbitrary container and placed in the atmosphere under isothermal conditions without stirring the liquid or without circulating air around the container.

In this connection, the self-heating behavior of every self-heating liquid chemical, with the exception of liquid high explosives, such as nitroglycerin, of the true AC type, is of the TD type. A self-heating liquid chemical of the TD type or self-heating liquid chemicals of the TD type are, therefore, described herein simply as a liquid or liquids.

The procedure to calculate, by applying the reduced form of the Semenov equation, the T_c for an arbitrary volume of a liquid charged in an arbitrary container and placed in the atmosphere under isothermal conditions is then introduced by taking the procedure to calculate the value of the BAM test for 400 cm^3 of 99 % *tert*-butyl peroxybenzoate (TBPB), assuming that it is charged in a 500 cm^3 Dewar flask used in the BAM (Bundesanstalt für Materialforschung und -prüfung, Berlin) heat-accumulation storage test and is placed in the atmosphere under isothermal conditions, as an example. Results obtained for ten organic liquid peroxides, including TBPB, are successively presented.

In **Chapter 6**, the procedure to calculate, by applying the reduced form of the F-K equation, the T_c for a powdery chemical of the TD type, having some one of several specific shapes as well as an arbitrary size, confined in an arbitrary closed container of the corresponding shape and size and placed in the atmosphere under isothermal conditions, is introduced by taking the procedure to calculate the T_c for 98 % α, β-azobis(isobutyronitrile) (AIBN), assuming that it is confined in a fiber drum, 39.5 cm in inside diameter, 59.2 cm in inside length, and is placed in the atmosphere under isothermal conditions, as an example. Results obtained for ten powdery chemicals of the TD type, including AIBN, are successively presented.

In **Chapter 7**, is explained in detail the procedure to perform several adiabatic oxidatively-heating tests, which are started from each T_s with mutual intervals of 1~2 K, in order to calculate the heat generation data of a gas-permeable oxidatively-heating substance, for 2 cm^3 each of several samples of the substance charged each in the draft cell, into which an arbitrary oxidizing gas is supplied, for the time, Δt, required for the temperature of each sample of the substance to increase by 1.25 K from the corresponding standard temperature, respectively.

In this connection, as stated already, the oxidatively-heating behavior of a gas-permeable oxidatively-heating substance, such as sawdust, coal dust or oil-soaked lagging, is also of the TD type. A gas-permeable oxidatively-heating substance of the TD type or gas-permeable oxidatively-heating substances of the TD type are, therefore, described herein simply as a gas-permeable oxidatively-heating substance or gas-permeable oxidatively-heating substances.

Besides, whenever the adiabatic oxidatively-heating test is performed for an oxidatively-heating liquid, such as unsaturated fatty acid, the liquid is tested, in principle, in the form of oil-soaked adsorbent cotton at relatively low temperatures, or in the form of oil-soaked glass wool at relatively high temperatures. And, the T_c for a heap of the oil-soaked adsorbent cotton, or the T_c for that of the oil-soaked glass wool, having some one of the several specific shapes as well as an arbitrary size, placed in the atmosphere under isothermal conditions, is also calculated in the same manner as applied to the calculation of the T_c for a heap of a gas-permeable oxidatively-heating substance.

For the above reasons, both gas-permeable oxidatively-heating substances and oxidatively-heating liquids are dealt with as gas-permeable oxidatively-heating substances all together herein.

In **Chapter 8**, the sawdust of every wood species is dealt with as a representative of gas-permeable oxidatively-heating substances. The individual oxidatively-heating properties of the sawdusts of fifteen wood species, which are measured, on the one hand, by TG-DTA performed in air, and, on the other hand, by the adiabatic oxidatively-heating test performed in air, respectively, are first described.

The procedure to calculate, by applying the reduced form of the F-K equation, the T_c for a sawdust heap, having some one of the several specific shapes as well as an arbitrary size, placed in the atmosphere under isothermal conditions, is then introduced by taking the procedure to calculate the T_c for a sawdust heap of Port Orford cedar, assuming that it is formed into an infinite slab, 60.96 cm in thickness, and is placed in the atmosphere under isothermal conditions, as an example. Results obtained for the sawdust heaps of fifteen wood species, including Port Orford cedar, are successively presented.

In **Chapter 9**, is introduced the procedure to calculate the SADT for a high explosive of the true AC type, having an arbitrary shape and an arbitrary size, confined in an arbitrary closed container of the corresponding shape and size, and placed in the atmosphere under isothermal conditions, by applying the empirical formula holding for the induction period of the autocatalytic reaction of 2 cm^3 of the high explosive confined in the closed cell and subjected to the isothermal storage test, by taking the procedure to calculate the SADT for collodion cotton (12.19 % N) as an example. Results obtained for eight high explosives of the true AC type, including collodion cotton, are successively presented.

Although any other existent isothermal storage testing devices are also useful for the calculation of the SADT for a chemical of the AC type, including every powdery chemical of the quasi-AC type, the device used to perform a series of isothermal storage tests described herein is introduced in this chapter.

Finally in **Chapter 10**, is introduced the procedure to calculate, in the same manner as applied to the calculation of the SADT for a high explosive of the true AC type, the SADT for a powdery chemical of the quasi-AC type, having an arbitrary shape and an arbitrary size, confined in an arbitrary closed container of the corresponding shape and size, and placed in the atmosphere under isothermal conditions, by applying the empirical formula holding for the induction period of the quasi-autocatalytic reaction of 2 cm^3 of the chemical confined in the closed cell and subjected to the isothermal storage test, by taking the procedure to calculate the SADT for 97 % lauroyl peroxide as an example. Results obtained for five powdery chemicals of the quasi-AC type, including lauroyl peroxide, are successively presented.

In conclusion, the following three points are added.

First, every chemical becomes liable to self-heat after a long-term storage; in the meantime, very fresh products of chemicals in general are also more liable to self-heat than the normal ones, irrespective of whether they are of the TD type or of the AC type. It is, therefore, possible that the true value of T_c, or that of SADT, is fairly lower than that calculated herein. Measures for this are to assign a due safety margin to each value of T_c or SADT calculated herein. It is for the above reasons that a temperature 30 K lower than the value of the BAM test, or that of SADT, calculated for each of organic liquid peroxides, powdery chemicals of the TD type, high explosives of the true AC type and powdery chemicals of the quasi-AC type, is proposed herein as the upper limit temperature for the safe handling of the chemical.*

Secondly, there is also a possibility that the value of T_c, or that of SADT, for a chemical including some impurity, which may promote or catalyze the exothermic decomposition reaction, or the autocatalytic reaction, of the chemical, is considerably lower than that for the pure chemical. For instance, some cases are known, in each of which a chemical reacts with the material of the cell in which the chemical is charged, or confined, in thermal analysis or in some thermal instability test. It is, however, of course possible to calculate the value of T_c, or that of SADT, for an arbitrary self-heating mixture by applying some one of several kinds of procedures presented herein.

Thirdly, it is hoped that some apparatus, by means of which the value of T_c, or that of SADT, for an arbitrary self-heating chemical, having an arbitrary shape and an arbitrary size, placed in the atmosphere under isothermal conditions, is calculated automatically based on some one of several kinds of procedures presented herein, is developed in the future.

---

* Theoretically speaking, it is not very appropriate to specify the upper limit temperature for the safe handling for a chemical of the TD type, including every gas-permeable oxidatively-heating substance, because the T_c for a chemical of the TD type is not a temperature value specific to the chemical; rather, it depends on its shape and size. Nevertheless, it is also certain that the size of a chemical of the TD type corresponding to a value of T_c 30 K lower than that calculated herein for the chemical is a tremendous one. At all events, however, it is certain that the best way for us is to avoid accumulating any self-heating chemical in bulk at all times. A subject relevant to this point is argued in **Subsection 6.7.2**.

Table of contents

Notation

A_0	Frequency factor in the rate constant of the exothermic decomposition reaction, of the zeroth order, of a chemical of the TD type, including every gas-permeable oxidatively-heating substance; or, frequency factor in the rate constant of the decomposition reaction, of the zeroth order, of a high explosive of the true AC type to generate the autocatalyst [mol/(cm^3·min)].
AC type	Autocatalytic reaction type.
A_n	Frequency factor in the rate constant of the exothermic decomposition reaction, of the n-th order, of a chemical of the TD type, including every gas-permeable oxidatively-heating substance; or, frequency factor in the rate constant of the decomposition reaction, of the n-th order, of a high explosive of the true AC type to generate the autocatalyst [(mol)$^{1-n}$/(cm^3)$^{1-n}$·(min)].
a	Numerical coefficient defined by Equation (44) or Equation (59).
b	Numerical coefficient defined by Equation (44) or Equation (59).
b	Point of time when 2 [cm^3] of a chemical of the AC type, including every powdery chemical of the quasi-AC type, confined in the closed cell and subjected to the isothermal storage test performed at a T_t starts the autocatalytic reaction or the quasi-autocatalytic reaction.
C	Molar heat capacity [cal/(mol·K)].
$[C]$	Molar concentration of a chemical [mol/cm^3].
c	Specific heat capacity [cal/(g·K)].
$c\rho$	Heat capacity per unit volume [cal/(cm^3·K)].
d	Day.
div	Divergence operator.
E	Activation energy in the rate constant of the exothermic decomposition reaction of a chemical of the TD type, including every gas-permeable oxidatively-heating substance; or, activation energy in the rate constant of the decomposition reaction of a high explosive of the true AC type to generate the autocatalyst [cal/mol].
e	Base of natural logarithm.

EOT	Exothermic onset temperature.
grad	Gradient operator.
h	Hour.
h	Film coefficient of heat transfer [cal/(cm^2·min·K)].
J_0	Zeroth order Bessel function.
J_1	First order Bessel function.
K	Equilibrium constant.
k_0	Rate constant of the exothermic decomposition reaction, of the zeroth order, of a chemical of the TD type, including every gas-permeable oxidatively-heating substance; or, rate constant of the decomposition reaction, of the zeroth order, of a high explosive of the true AC type to generate the autocatalyst [mol/(cm^3·min)].
k_n	Rate constant of the exothermic decomposition reaction, of the n-th order, of a chemical of the TD type, including every gas-permeable oxidatively-heating substance; or, rate constant of the decomposition reaction, of the n-th order, of a high explosive of the true AC type to generate the autocatalyst [(mol)$^{1-n}$/(cm^3)$^{1-n}$·(min)].
L	Liter.
l	Wall thickness of a liquid container [cm].
ln	Natural logarithm.
m	meter.
m	Mass [g].
n	natural number.
Q	Electric heat generated per unit time in a resister-thermocouple composite set in a draft cell in order to simulate the self-heating process of a chemical of the TD type, including every gas-permeable oxidatively-heating substance [cal/min].
q_1	Quantity of heat generated per unit time in the whole volume of a fluid filled in the container and placed in the atmosphere maintained at a T_a [cal/min]
q_2	Quantity of heat transferred per unit time from a fluid filled in the container and placed in the atmosphere maintained at a T_a, through the whole fluid surface, across the container walls, to the atmosphere [cal/min].
R	Gas constant [cal/(mol·K)].

r	Radius [cm].
S	Whole fluid surface [cm^2].
SADT	Temperature at which the self-accelerating decomposition reaction, or the autocatalytic reaction, or the quasi-autocatalytic reaction, that may lead to the ultimate thermal explosion of a chemical of the AC type, including every powdery chemical of the quasi-AC type, having an arbitrary shape and an arbitrary size, confined in an arbitrary closed container of the corresponding shape and size, and placed in the atmosphere under isothermal conditions, starts just 7 d after the placement of the container in the atmosphere maintained at the temperature [K]. {To put it concretely, the SADT of a chemical of the AC type, including every powdery chemical of the quasi-AC type, is a value of T_t corresponding to a value of Δt of 10,080 min, *i.e.*, 7 d, in Equation (59), ln $\Delta t = a/T_t + b$, holding for the induction period of the autocatalytic reaction, or of the quasi-autocatalytic reaction, of 2 cm^3 of the chemical confined in the closed cell and subjected to the isothermal storage test. As a matter of fact, however, the SADT may be regarded as the critical (or the lowest) temperature below which the thermal explosion of a chemical of the AC type, including every powdery chemical of the quasi-AC type, cannot occur.}
Se	Semenov number [dimensionless] (Se = 1/e = 0.367879 · · ·).
s	Second.
s	Point of time when the adiabatic control for 2 cm^3 of a chemical of the TD type, including every gas-permeable oxidatively-heating substance, charged, or confined, in some one of the open-cup, the draft or the closed cell, in accordance with the self-heating property of the chemical, and subjected to either of the two kinds of adiabatic tests started each from a T_s, and, the record of the self-heating process of the chemical, are started, respectively.
T	Temperature of a chemical, or, that of a substance [K].
T_a	Temperature of the atmosphere, *i.e.*, air at atmospheric pressure, in which a chemical of the TD type, including every

	gas-permeable oxidatively-heating substance, having an arbitrary shape and an arbitrary size, is placed under isothermal conditions [K]. (When a container, in which a liquid is charged, is placed in a set-up in order to measure the main heat transfer data of the liquid, the T_a is expressed as the $T_{set\text{-}up}$.)
T_{atm}	Temperature of the atmosphere around 2 cm^3 of a chemical of the TD type, including every gas-permeable oxidatively-heating substance, charged, or confined, in some one of the open-cup, the draft or the closed cell, in accordance with the self-heating property of the chemical, and subjected to either of the two kinds of adiabatic tests started each from a T_s [K]. (After the start of the adiabatic control, the T_{atm} is raised automatically by the adiabatic control in order that the condition, $\Delta T_{diff} = T - T_{atm} = 0$, may always hold.)
T_c	Critical (or the lowest) temperature below which the thermal explosion of a chemical of the TD type, including every gas-permeable oxidatively-heating substance, having an arbitrary shape and an arbitrary size, placed in the atmosphere under isothermal conditions, cannot occur [K].
TD type	Thermal decomposition type.
T_s	Starting temperature in the adiabatic self-heating test, or in the adiabatic oxidatively-heating test, performed for 2 cm^3 of a chemical of the TD type, including every gas-permeable oxidatively-heating substance, charged, or confined, in some one of the open-cup, the draft or the closed cell, in accordance with the self-heating property of the chemical [K].
$T_{set\text{-}up}$	Temperature of the atmosphere in a set-up, in which the main heat transfer data of a liquid charged in the container is measured [K].
T_t	Testing temperature in the isothermal storage test performed for 2 cm^3 of a chemical of the AC type, including every powdery chemical of the quasi-AC type, confined in the closed cell [K].
t	Time [min].
U	Mean overall coefficient of heat transfer from a fluid filled in the container and placed in the atmosphere under isothermal

	conditions, through the whole fluid surface, across the container walls, to the atmosphere [cal/(cm^2·min·K)].
V	Volume [cm^3].
x	Spatial coordinates [cm].

Greek Symbols

α	Thermal diffusivity [cm^2/min].
α_e	Effective thermal diffusivity of a powdery chemical of the TD type, including every gas-permeable oxidatively-heating substance [cm^2/min].
β_{n}	Positive roots of $J_0(r_{cylinder}\beta_{\mathrm{n}}) = 0$.
Δ	Laplacian operator.
Δ_{ξ}	Dimensionless Laplacian operator.
ΔH	Molar heat of reaction [cal/mol].
ΔT	Difference between the temperature of a chemical and the T_s in the adiabatic self-heating test, or in the adiabatic oxidatively-heating test [K]. (The adiabatic self-heating test, or the adiabatic oxidatively-heating test, which is started from a T_s, performed for 2 cm^3 of a chemical of the TD type, including every gas-permeable oxidatively-heating substance, charged, or confined, in some one of the open-cup, the draft or the closed cell, in accordance with the self-heating property of the chemical, is interrupted as soon as the temperature of the chemical increases by the definite value of ΔT of 1.25 K from the T_s.)
ΔT_{diff}	Temperature difference, in the adiabatic self-heating test, or in the adiabatic oxidatively-heating test, between the T_{ref} and the T_{atm}, or between the temperature of a chemical and the T_{atm} K.
ΔT_{rad}	Radial temperature difference effected in the non-steady state between the periphery and the axial center of the specimen of a powdery chemical of the TD type, including every gas-permeable oxidatively-heating substance, charged in a cylindrical cell heated at a very slow rate, ϕ, [K].
Δt	Time required for the temperature of 2 cm^3 of a chemical of the TD type, including every gas-permeable

oxidatively-heating substance, charged, or confined, in some one of the open-cup, the draft or the closed cell, in accordance with the self-heating property of the chemical, and subjected to either of the two kinds of adiabatic tests started each from a T_s, to increase by the definite temperature difference, ΔT, of 1.25 K from the T_s [min].

δ Frank-Kamenetskii's δ [dimensionless].
δ_c Frank-Kamenetskii number [dimensionless].
θ Dimensionless temperature.
κ Heat transfer factor used by N. N. Semenov.
λ Thermal conductivity [cal/(cm·min·K)].
ξ Dimensionless coordinates.
π Ratio of the circumference to the diameter.
ρ Specific gravity, or density [g/cm^3].
τ Dimensionless time.
τ_{ad} Frank-Kamenetskii's adiabatic induction period.
ϕ Rate of increase in temperature, or, heating rate [K/min].

Subscripts

a of the atmosphere around a chemical of the TD type, including every gas-permeable oxidatively-heating substance, having an arbitrary shape and an arbitrary size, placed under isothermal conditions.
atm of the atmosphere around 2 cm^3 of a chemical charged, or confined, in some one of the four types of cells, *i.e.*, the open-cup, the draft, the touch-flow or the closed cell, in accordance with the self-heating property of the chemical, and subjected to either of the two kinds of adiabatic tests.
autocatalyst of an autocatalyst.
c critical.
cylinder of an infinite cylinder.
diff difference.
e effective.
elec electric.
f fluid.
h high.

inner	inner.
l	low.
liq	liquid.
lim	limiting.
n	of the n-th order.
rad	radial.
r-cylinder	at the periphery of an infinite cylinder.
ref	of the reference material.
r-inner	at an arbitrary inner radius.
s	starting.
set-up	of a set-up.
solid	solid
t	testing.
threshold	at the threshold.
0	of the zeroth order; or, at the axial center of an infinite cylinder.

Chapter 1 An approach to the thermal explosion theory

1.1 The basic concept of the thermal explosion theory

As stated in **Preface**, the basic concept of the thermal explosion theory is that whether the thermal explosion or the spontaneous ignition of a chemical of the TD type, including every gas-permeable oxidatively-heating substance, having an arbitrary shape and an arbitrary size, placed in the atmosphere under isothermal conditions, occurs or not is decided, based on the balance between the rate of heat generation in the chemical and the rate of heat transfer from the chemical to the atmosphere at the critical state for the thermal explosion which exists at the end of the early stages of the self-heating process.*

In other words, when the chemical is placed in the atmosphere maintained at a T_a higher than the T_c, the chemical, which has been maintained at room temperature until the placement, continues to self-heat over the T_a in such a manner as shown in Fig. 1 even under isothermal conditions, with the result that the temperature of the chemical continues to increase acceleratedly to cause the ultimate thermal explosion of the chemical sooner or later.

That is, it is understood that it is the balance between the rate of heat generation in a chemical of the TD type, including every gas-permeable oxidatively-heating substance, having an arbitrary shape and an arbitrary size, placed in the atmosphere under isothermal conditions, and, the rate of heat transfer from the chemical to the atmosphere at the above-mentioned critical state for the thermal explosion, and not the balance throughout the whole self-heating process up to the thermal explosion that is the object of argumentation in the thermal explosion theory.

Incidentally, the effect of the concentration of a chemical of the TD type on the rate of the exothermic decomposition reaction, in the early stages of the self-heating process, of the chemical is assumed to be of the zeroth order in the thermal explosion theory [1]. In other words, it is assumed in the thermal explosion theory that the concentration of the chemical remains virtually constant while the self-heating process is in the early stages, because the consumption of the chemical caused by the reaction can be neglected while the self-heating process is in the early stages.

* The critical state for the thermal explosion is a state corresponding to the point of tangency which is shown in Fig. 2 presented in **Section 1.2**. And, the self-heating process of a chemical of the TD type from a temperature, *e.g.*, the $T_{a,c}$, which is also shown in Fig. 2, situated below T_1 up to T_1 is referred to as the early stages of the process.

It thus follows that it is permitted to express the concentration term in the rate equation as $[C\ ]^0$, *i.e.*, as unity virtually, in the thermal explosion theory.* This approach is referred to as the zeroth-order assumption.

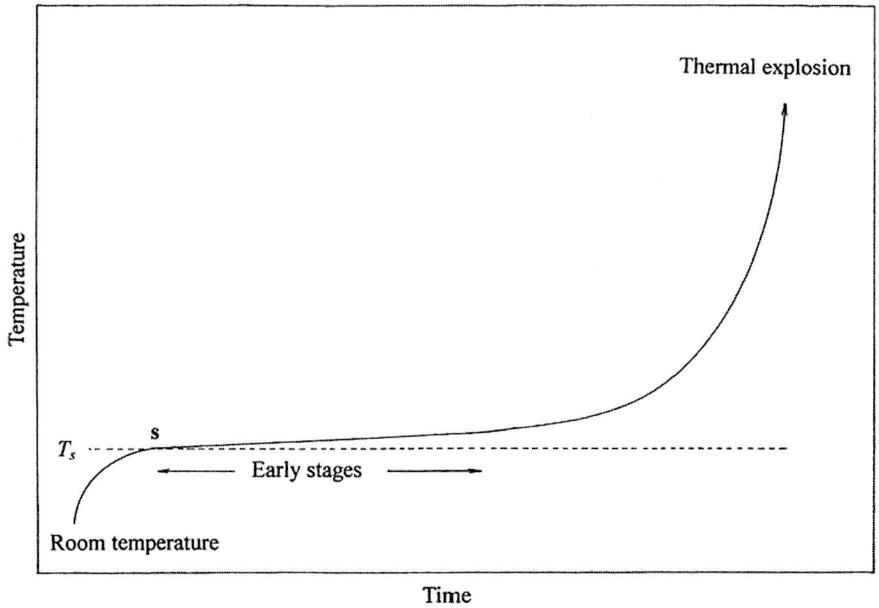

Figure 1. The whole self-heating process up to the thermal explosion of 2 cm^3 of a chemical of the TD type charged in the open-cup cell, or confined in the closed cell, in accordance with the self-heating property of the chemical, and subjected to the adiabatic self-heating test started from a T_s.

The rate equation in the thermal explosion theory is then expressed with the rate constant, $A_0 \exp[- E/RT]$, alone. In other words, the rate of the exothermic decomposition reaction, in the early stages of the self-heating process, of a chemical of the TD type, including every gas-permeable oxidatively-heating substance, is thought, in the theory, to depend only on one variable, T, *i.e.*, the temperature of the chemical, included in the rate constant. It is thus seen that the theory is in fact very simple by virtue of the zeroth-order assumption.

* In this regard, it is also possible to consider that the concentration term is absorbed, as a constant, into the frequency factor, A_0, in the rate equation, because the concentration of the chemical remains virtually constant while the self-heating process is in the early stages. At all events, the concentration term is absent on account of the zeroth-order assumption in both the Semenov and the F-K equation.

The larger the molar heat of reaction, ΔH, which is one of the chemical quantities specifying the rate of heat generation per unit volume per unit time, in the early stages of the self-heating process, of a chemical of the TD type, including every gas-permeable oxidatively-heating substance, the better holds the zeroth-order assumption. In this regard, there is also a comment that, when the so-called adiabatic self-heat, $\Delta H/C$ [K], of a chemical of the TD type takes a value of the order of $10^2 \sim 10^3$, the zeroth-order assumption is applicable to the rate of the exothermic decomposition reaction, in the early stages of the self-heating process, of the chemical [2].

1.2 Derivation of the Semenov equation*

Let us suppose that a closed container, in which a self-heating fluid** is filled, is placed in the atmosphere maintained at a T_a.

The spatial distribution of temperature in the fluid is assumed to be uniform while the self-heating process is in the early stages.

Assuming the temperature of the fluid to be T_f, the quantity of heat generated per unit time in the whole volume, V, of the fluid, q_1, is expressed as

$$q_1 = V \cdot \Delta H \cdot A_0 \exp\left[-\frac{E}{RT_f}\right], \tag{1}$$

where the zeroth-order assumption is, needless to say, made.

On the other hand, assuming the cooling mode of the fluid to be Newtonian, the quantity of heat transferred per unit time from the fluid, through the whole fluid surface, across the container walls, to the atmosphere, q_2, is expressed as

$$q_2 = US(T_f - T_a). \tag{2}$$

When T_a is varied in the range, $T_{a,l} < T_{a,c} < T_{a,h}$, we get the response shown in Fig. 2,*** where are drawn one q_1 curve with regard to the heat generation and three q_2 lines, with regard to the heat transfer, corresponding each to the three values of T_a, respectively.

When the curve is above a line for a given value of T_a, the heating of the fluid takes place, and when it is below a line, the cooling does. The two intersections

---

* This derivation is performed anew herein on referring to the original formulation performed by Semenov [3].

** The fluid was assumed to be a self-heating gas in the formulation performed by Semenov.

*** Fig. 2 is sometimes referred to as the Semenov diagram.

of the straight line of heat transfer with the heat generation curve degenerate at the limit to the point of tangency. In other words, the temperature of the fluid maintained at first at $T_{a,c}$ increases spontaneously up to T_1, at which q_1 comes into contact with q_2(Ⅱ). In brief, for $T_{a,l} \leqq T_a < T_{a,c}$ we get no thermal explosion, while for $T_{a,c} < T_a \leqq T_{a,h}$ we do; and, the $T_{a,c}$ is the lowest temperature required for the fluid to explode thermally. The $T_{a,c}$ is thus expressed anew as the critical temperature for the thermal explosion, T_c, of the fluid. In this connection, ΔT_c ($= T_1 - T_c$) is called the pre-explosion rise.

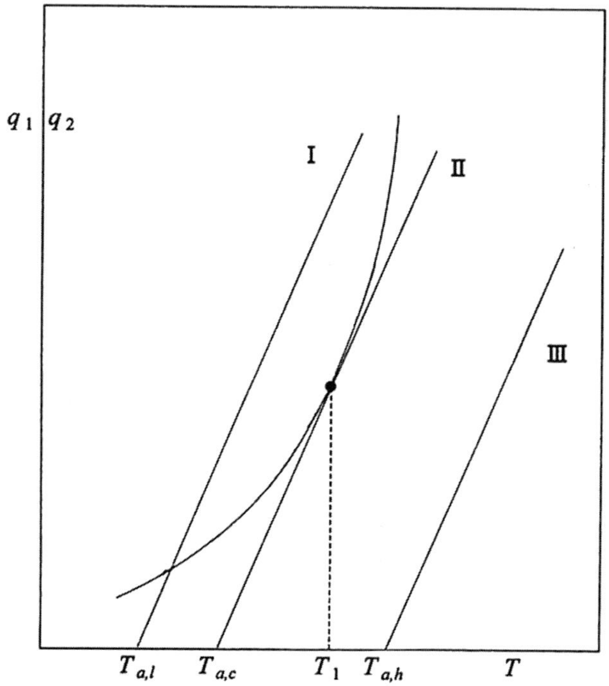

Figure 2. The temperature dependence of q_1 and q_2.

From Eqs. (1) and (2), the following two equations are derived at the point of tangency.

First, from one condition, $[q_1]_{T(f)=T(1)} = [q_2(\text{II})]_{T(f)=T(1)}$,

$$\Delta H \cdot A_0 V \exp\left[-\frac{E}{RT_1}\right] = US(T_1 - T_c). \tag{3}$$

Secondly, from the other condition, $[dq_1/dT_f]_{T(f)=T(1)} = [dq_2(\text{II})/dT_f]_{T(f)=T(1)}$,

$$\frac{\Delta H \cdot A_0 EV}{RT_1^2}\exp\left[-\frac{E}{RT_1}\right] = US. \tag{4}$$

Substituting Eq. (3) into Eq. (4), to eliminate the *US* term, we get a quadratic equation with respect to T_1, *i.e.*,

$$\frac{RT_1^2}{E} - T_1 + T_c = 0. \tag{5}$$

Hence, the root of Eq. (5) is expressed as

$$T_1 = \frac{1 \pm \sqrt{1 - 4\frac{R}{E}T_c}}{2\frac{R}{E}}. \tag{6}$$

In Eq. (6), the term, $4RT_c/E$, in general takes a value far less than unity. This is confirmed by a fact that, when a representative value of T_c of 350 K (*ca.* 77 ℃) and a similarly representative value of *E* of 40 kcal/mol are substituted tentatively into the term, $4RT_c/E$, it takes a value of about 0.07.

Under such circumstances, on having adopted the following roughest approximation in Eq. (6),

$$\left(1 - 4\frac{R}{E}T_c\right)^{1/2} \cong 1 - 2\frac{R}{E}T_c, \tag{7}$$

if we adopt further the plus sign in Eq. (6), we get

$$T_1 = \frac{E}{2R}\left[1 + \left(1 - 4\frac{R}{E}T_c\right)^{1/2}\right] \cong \frac{E}{2R}\left(2 - 2\frac{R}{E}T_c\right) = \frac{E}{R} - T_c. \tag{8}$$

However, when the representative values of T_c and *E*, which were just substituted above into the term, $4RT_c/E$, are again substituted into Eq. (8), we find T_1 to take an unrealistic value of about 20,000 K.

On the other hand, if we adopt the minus sign as well as the roughest approximation above referred to in Eq. (6), we get the following realistic relation between T_1 and T_c, *i.e.*,

$$T_1 = \frac{E}{2R}\left[1-\left(1-4\frac{R}{E}\right)^{1/2}\right] \cong \frac{E}{2R}\times\frac{R}{E}T_c = T_c. \tag{9}$$

Such being the case, expanding the square root in Eq. (6) as a series, on adopting the minus sign, we obtain

$$\begin{aligned} T_1 &= \frac{E}{2R}\left[1-\left(1-4\frac{R}{E}T_c\right)^{1/2}\right] \\ &= \frac{E}{2R}\left[2\left(\frac{RT_c}{E}\right)+2\left(\frac{RT_c}{E}\right)^2+4\left(\frac{RT_c}{E}\right)^3+\cdots\right]. \end{aligned} \tag{10}$$

Taking up to the second term in the series thereby obtained, Eq. (10) is reduced to

$$T_1 \cong T_c + \frac{RT_c^2}{E}. \tag{11}$$

It thus follows that the pre-explosion rise, ΔT_c, is expressed as

$$\Delta T_c = T_1 - T_c = \frac{RT_c^2}{E}. \tag{12}$$

Dividing both sides of Eq. (12) by T_c, we get

$$\frac{\Delta T_c}{T_c} = \frac{T_1}{T_c} - 1 = \frac{RT_c}{E}, \tag{13}$$

where $\Delta T_c/T_c$, which is equal to RT_c/E, necessarily takes a value far less than unity,* because the value of the term, T_1/T_c, is close to unity, as shown in Eq. (9).

On the other hand, it is also possible to rearrange Eq. (12) as follows:

---

* The term, $\Delta T_c/T_c$, in general takes a value of 0.01∼0.02.

$$\frac{1}{T_1} = \frac{1}{T_c + \Delta T_c} = \frac{1}{T_c\left(1 + \frac{\Delta T_c}{T_c}\right)}. \tag{14}$$

However, $\Delta T_c / T_c$ takes, as stated above, a value far less than unity, so that it will be permitted to rearrange Eq. (14) further as

$$\frac{1}{T_1} \cong \frac{1}{T_c}\left(1 - \frac{\Delta T_c}{T_c}\right). \tag{15}$$

Substituting Eqs. (12), (13) and (15) into Eq. (3), to eliminate T_1,* we obtain

$$\frac{\Delta H \cdot A_0 EV}{USRT_c^2} \exp\left[1 - \frac{E}{RT_c}\right] = 1. \tag{16}$$

Besides, it is also possible to rearrange Eq. (16) in the following manner,

$$\mathrm{Se} = \frac{1}{\mathrm{e}} = \frac{\Delta H \cdot A_0 EV}{USRT_c^2} \exp[-\frac{E}{RT_c}] \cong 0.36788. \tag{17}$$

Eq. (17) is usually referred to as the Semenov equation.

1.2.1 Comment on the wall temperature, T_0, in Semenov's formulation

In Semenov's book, it reads as follows [4]:

「

If a gas reaction is proceeding at a rate, *w*, measured as the number of product molecules appearing per second, the amount of heat produced per second in the entire volume, *V*, will be

$q_1 = VQ'w$

---

* This substitution is performed in order to express T_c as a function of the physical and chemical quantities only.

> where Q is the heat per elementary act of reaction, being Q/N, where Q is the heat of reaction (per g-mole) and N is Avogadro's number (6×10^{23}). Initially, when the consumption of the reactants can be neglected, the reaction rate will be given as a function of the absolute temperature, T, and number of reactant molecules, a, by $k_1 a \exp(-E/RT)$ for unimolecular process and by $k_2 a^2 \exp(-E/RT)$ for bimolecular. Hence
>
> $$Nq_1 = VQka^n \exp(-E/RT) \qquad (1)$$
>
> where n = 1 for unimolecular reactions and 2 for bimolecular. The heat transferred to the walls from the reaction volume will be
>
> $$q_2 = \kappa(T - T_0)S \qquad (2)$$
>
> where κ is a heat transfer factor, T the gas temperature, T_0 the wall temperature and S the wall surface.

It appears in Semenov's formulation that the wall temperature, T_0, is supposed to be given and to be constant throughout the whole self-heating process of a gas filled in a container, irrespective of cooling conditions.

If, however, T_0 is the temperature of the container wall, it can not remain at its initial value throughout the whole self-heating process at all, because the reaction heat flows into the wall from the gas all the time. Therefore, after T_0 has reached the temperature of the gas, a perfect adiabatic condition will be established for the gas, with the result that the heat transfer from the gas to the wall ceases.

Or, would it be supposed in Semenov's formulation that the walls of the container were of infinite thickness, of infinite heat content or of infinite thermal conductivity, so that T_0 was kept constant over a long time? Such a situation will not be realistic. Besides, it seems that such a supposition that the container wall has a large overall coefficient of heat transfer is inconsistent with the Semenov model* that the rate of heat transfer from a self-heating fluid filled in a container and placed in the atmosphere under isothermal conditions, through the whole fluid surface, across the container walls, to the atmosphere is far less than the rate of thermal conduction in the fluid.

Thus, T_0 should, in fact, be interpreted as a constant atmospheric temperature, T_a; in other words, it is the T_a that is thought in Semenov's formulation to be maintained at a constant value. Besides, Semenov's formulation should be

---

* For the term, the Semenov model, refer to **Section 1.4**.

thought to have been performed on the assumption that the container has a comparatively thin wall, and, the heat is transferred by the thermal conduction from the self-heating fluid, through the whole fluid surface, across the container walls, to the atmosphere maintained at a T_a, as discussed in **Subsection 5.3.1**.

If T_0 is in fact T_a, and, if T_a is maintained at a constant value, a description on page 2 of Semenov's book [5], *i.e.*,

「

If now, while keeping P constant, we vary T_0 in the range $T_{0,l} < T_0 < T_{0,h}$, we get the response shown in Figure 73,* where there is one q_1 curve and three q_2 lines, for three values of T_0. We can show that for $T_{0,l} < T_0$ we get no self-ignition, while for $T_{0,h} > T_0$ we do.

」

should be read as follows:

「

If a closed container, in which a self-heating fluid has been filled at room temperature, is set in the atmosphere, the temperature of which, T_a, is kept constant, the temperature of the fluid in the container increases slowly until it reaches T_a. Then, for $T_{a,l} \leqq T_a < T_{a,c}$, where $T_{a,c}$ corresponds to the T_c for the fluid defined herein, we get no thermal explosion, while for $T_{a,c} < T_a \leqq T_{a,h}$ we do.

」

1.3 Derivation of the Frank-Kamenetskii equation

An equation holding between the rate of heat transfer per unit volume per unit time by the thermal conduction in a stationary medium, *i.e.*, in a solid, in reality, and, the rate of increase in temperature of the solid is given in the following form,

$$c\rho\frac{\partial T}{\partial t} = div\lambda gradT. \tag{18}$$

This is referred to as the Fourier equation regarding the thermal conduction.

* Figure 73 in Semenov's book corresponds to Fig. 2 in **Section 1.2**.

Following the example of Eq. (18), an equation holding among the rate of heat generation per unit volume per unit time in a solid chemical of the TD type, having an arbitrary shape and an arbitrary size, placed in the atmosphere maintained at a T_a, the rate of heat transfer per unit volume per unit time by the thermal conduction in the solid chemical, and, the rate of increase in temperature of the solid chemical in the early stages of the self-heating process is expressed as

$$c\rho\frac{\partial T}{\partial t} = div\lambda grad T + \Delta H \cdot A_0 \exp\left[-\frac{E}{RT}\right], \tag{19}$$

where the zeroth-order assumption is, of course, made [6].

If the dependence of the thermal conductivity on the temperature is neglected, Eq. (19) is reduced to Eq. (20).

$$c\rho\frac{\partial T}{\partial t} = \lambda \cdot \Delta T + \Delta H \cdot A_0 \exp\left[-\frac{E}{RT}\right], \tag{20}$$

where Δ, div·grad, is the Laplacian operator.

In this connection, when the shape of the solid chemical takes the one-dimensional axial symmetry, the term, ΔT, is expressed as

$$\Delta T \equiv \left(\frac{\partial^2}{\partial x^2} + \frac{j}{x}\frac{\partial}{\partial x}\right)T, \tag{21}$$

where j is a dimensionless number denoting the shape of the solid chemical; for instance, the value of j of 0, 1 and 2 denotes an infinite slab, an infinite cylinder and a sphere, respectively.

Now, when a solid chemical of the TD type is placed in the atmosphere maintained at a temperature below T_1, which is shown in Fig. 2 in **Section 1.2**, a spatially gradient distribution of temperature is effected in the solid chemical. However, the temperature as a whole does not vary with time; in other words, the spatially gradient distribution of temperature effected in the self-heating solid chemical placed in the atmosphere maintained at a temperature below T_1 is stationary. The stationary equation of the thermal explosion theory, Eq. (22), is thus obtained by considering the value of the derivative with regard to the time to be zero in Eq. (20). This approach is called the stationary theory of the thermal explosion [7].*

---

* For the argument made in this paragraph, refer to **Section 2.3** as well.

$$\Delta T = -\frac{\Delta H \cdot A_0}{\lambda} \exp\left[-\frac{E}{RT}\right]. \tag{22}$$

In order to express Eq. (22) as one containing only the dimensionless quantities, a dimensionless coordinates, ξ, is first expressed as

$$\xi \equiv \frac{x}{r}, \tag{23}$$

where x expresses the spatial coordinates.
The dimensionless Laplacian operator is then expressed as

$$\Delta_\xi = r^2 \cdot \Delta. \tag{24}$$

Secondly, when the temperature, T, of a solid chemical of the TD type, having an arbitrary shape and an arbitrary size, placed in the atmosphere maintained at a T_a, is immediately above the T_a, if two conditions, *i.e.*, $(T - T_a) << T_a$ and $RT_a << E$, hold simultaneously, it is possible to apply the so-called Frank-Kamenetskii's method of expanding the exponent, *i.e.*, Eqs. (25) and (26), to the exponential term in Eq. (22) [8].*

$$\exp\left[-\frac{E}{RT}\right] \cong \exp\left[-\frac{E}{RT_a}\right] \cdot \exp[\theta], \tag{25}$$

where

$$\theta \equiv \frac{E(T - T_a)}{RT_a^2}. \tag{26}$$

Eq. (22) is then rewritten in the following dimensionless expression,

* The F-K's method of expanding the exponent is applied to make the exponential term integrable. Another example is presented with regard to Eqs. (25)~(39) in **Section 2.4**. For this method, refer to a footnote in **Section 2.7** as well.

$$\Delta_\xi \theta = \Delta T \cdot r^2 \cdot \frac{\Delta \theta}{\Delta T} = -\frac{\Delta H \cdot A_0 E r^2}{\lambda R T_a^2} \exp\left[-\frac{E}{RT_a}\right] \cdot \exp[\theta]$$
$$= -\delta \cdot \exp[\theta], \tag{27}$$

where

$$\delta \equiv \frac{\Delta H \cdot A_0 E r^2}{\lambda R T_a^2} \exp\left[-\frac{E}{RT_a}\right]. \tag{28}$$

δ is also a dimensionless number and is sometimes called the Frank-Kamenetskii's δ.

We see from Eq. (28) that, once the size of a solid chemical of the TD type, placed in the atmosphere under isothermal conditions, is specified; in other words, once the values of ΔH, A_0 and E of the exothermic decomposition reaction, in the early stages of the self-heating process, of the solid chemical as well as the values of λ and r of the solid chemical are fixed, respectively, the value of δ increases with increasing the atmospheric temperature, T_a. There is, however, the upper limit value, or the critical value, of δ, *i.e.*, δ_c, which δ is able to take for a shape of the solid chemical, because there is also the upper limit atmospheric temperature, or the critical temperature, T_c, above which the stationary gradient distribution of temperature in the self-heating solid chemical ceases to be possible, with the result that the temperature of the solid chemical continues to increase acceleratedly to cause the ultimate thermal explosion of the solid chemical.

The following equation, therefore, holds for every shape which a solid chemical of the TD type takes.

$$\delta_c = \frac{\Delta H \cdot A_0 E r^2}{\lambda R T_c^2} \exp[-\frac{E}{RT_c}]. \tag{29}$$

Eq. (29) is referred to as the Frank-Kamenetskii equation [9].

As explained above, the value of δ_c depends only on the value of j, the dimensionless number denoting the shape of a solid chemical, irrespective of the size or the quantity of the solid chemical.

Now, if we apply, in addition to Eqs. (21), (23) and (25), further one dimensionless quantity, τ, which is expressed as Eq. (30), to Eq. (20) [10],

$$\tau \equiv \frac{\alpha t}{r^2} = \frac{\lambda t}{c \rho r^2}, \tag{30}$$

Eq. (20) is rewritten, in the dimensionless form, in the following manner.

$$\frac{\partial \theta}{\partial \tau} = \frac{\partial^2 \theta}{\partial \xi^2} + \frac{j}{\xi}\frac{\partial \theta}{\partial \xi} + \delta \cdot \exp[\theta]. \qquad (31)$$

Assuming the shape of a solid chemical to be an infinite slab, that is, assuming the value of *j* to be 0 in Eq. (31); besides, noting that the value of the term, $\partial \theta / \partial \tau$, in Eq. (31) is zero, in accordance with the stationary theory of the thermal explosion, Eq. (32) is obtained.

$$\frac{d^2 \theta}{d\xi^2} = -\delta \cdot \exp[\theta]. \qquad (32)$$

Frank-Kamenetskii calculated the value of δ_c for an infinite slab at 0.878 by integrating Eq. (32). Successively, he calculated the value of δ_c for an infinite cylinder and that for a sphere at 2.00 and 3.32, respectively [11].

Long afterward, T. Boddington *et al.* calculated the values of δ_c for several specific shapes including the three above referred to, respectively. The values of δ_c calculated by them are listed in Table 13 in **Section 6.5**.

1.4 The balance, which is contained in both the Semenov and the F-K equation, between the rate of heat generation and the rate of heat transfer

Both the Semenov and the F-K equation are in fact the same in the sense that each of them describes the balance between the rate of heat generation per unit volume per unit time in a liquid chemical, or a solid chemical, of the TD type, having an arbitrary shape and an arbitrary size, placed in the atmosphere under isothermal conditions, and, the rate of heat transfer per unit volume per unit time from the chemical to the atmosphere at the critical state for the thermal explosion which exists at the end of the early stages of the self-heating process.

Let us confirm that the balance above referred to is actually contained in both equations.

The Semenov equation, *i.e.*, Eq. (17),

$$\text{Se} = \frac{1}{\text{e}} = \frac{\Delta H \cdot A_0 EV}{USRT_c^2} \exp[-\frac{E}{RT_c}] \cong 0.36788. \qquad (17)$$

can be rearranged in the following manner,

$$\mathrm{Se} = \frac{\Delta H \cdot A_0 \exp[-\dfrac{E}{RT_c}]}{\dfrac{US}{V} \cdot \dfrac{RT_c^2}{E}}. \tag{17'}$$

The numerator of Eq. (17') is the molar heat of reaction multiplied by the rate equation, although the concentration term is absent in the rate equation on account of the zeroth-order assumption. The units are thus cal/(cm$^3 \cdot$min), expressing the rate of heat generation per unit volume per unit time in an arbitrary volume of a self-heating fluid filled in an arbitrary container and placed in the atmosphere under isothermal conditions. On the other hand, the units of the denominator as a whole are also cal/(cm$^3\cdot$min), but the denominator may be thought to express the rate of heat transfer per unit volume per unit time from the fluid, through the whole fluid surface, across the container walls, to the atmosphere, because U is included in it.* It thus follows that Se is a dimensionless number. However, the essential importance of Eq. (17') lies in the fact that, as shown in **Section 1.2**, the Semenov number, Se, expresses originally the balance between the rate of heat generation in an arbitrary volume of a self-heating fluid filled in an arbitrary container and placed in the atmosphere under isothermal conditions, and, the rate of heat transfer from the fluid to the atmosphere at the critical state for the thermal explosion which exists at the end of the early stages of the self-heating process.

A similar relation is seen to hold in the F-K equation as well.

The F-K equation, *i.e.*, Eq. (29),

$$\delta_c = \frac{\Delta H \cdot A_0 E r^2}{\lambda R T_c^2} \exp[-\frac{E}{RT_c}], \tag{29}$$

can be rearranged in the following manner,

$$\delta_c = \frac{\Delta H \cdot A_0 \exp[-\dfrac{E}{RT_c}]}{\dfrac{\lambda}{r^2} \cdot \dfrac{RT_c^2}{E}}. \tag{29'}$$

* In this connection, note that the term, RT_c^2/E, in the denominator is equivalent to the pre-explosion rise, ΔT_c, in the Semenov's scheme. This relation is expressed as Eq. (12) in **Section 1.2**. Note that the same term is included in the rearranged F-K equation as well.

The numerator in this case also expresses, of course, the rate of heat generation per unit volume per unit time in a solid chemical of the TD type, having an arbitrary shape and an arbitrary size, placed in the atmosphere under isothermal conditions. On the other hand, the denominator as a whole has also the same units as the numerator, but it may be thought to express the rate of thermal conduction per unit volume per unit time in the solid chemical, because λ is included in it.

Incidentally, the SI unit is not necessarily used in the thermal explosion theory. First, if joule is used instead of thermochemical calorie, the calculation of the T_c becomes somewhat troublesome.* Secondly, the thermal explosion is a phenomenon close to the human life; in this regard, cubic centimeter is suitable for the case, while cubic meter is too big as a volume unit. And thirdly, the thermal explosion is a very slow phenomenon; in this regard, minute is suitable for the case, while second is too short and too quick as a time unit.

1.5 The relationship holding among Se, δ_c and the Biot number

In view of Eqs. (17') and (29'), it is evident that both equations contain differences only in the terms expressing the rate of heat transfer per unit volume per unit time per K, *i.e.*, US/V in Eq. (17') and λ/r^2 in Eq. (29').

In other words, we see that we have only to replace US/V with λ/r^2 in order to exchange Se and δ_c for each other.

Further, we notice that the ratio of δ_c to Se provides the Biot number. That is,

$$\text{The Biot number} = \frac{Ur}{\lambda} \rightarrow \delta_c / \text{Se} = \left(\frac{US}{V}\right) / \left(\frac{\lambda}{r^2}\right), \qquad (33)$$

where S/V, the ratio of surface area to volume of a body, provides a numerical coefficient including $1/r$, *e.g.*, $1/r$ for an infinite slab, $2/r$ for an infinite circular cylinder and $3/r$ for a sphere.

Now, the characteristic of the Semenov model, which is illustrated by the diagram of the left-hand side in Fig. 3, is the spatially uniform distribution of internal temperature. It seems most natural to think that this mode of temperature distribution arises from the heat transfer mode that the heat generated by the exothermic decomposition reaction occurring in a very slowly self-heating fluid filled in a container and placed in the atmosphere under isothermal conditions is transmitted uniformly throughout the fluid on account of its own fluidity.

---

* To cite one instance, although a description that the specific heat capacity of water is just 1 cal/(g·K) is simple, another description that the specific heat capacity of water is 4.184 J/(g·K) is somewhat complicated.

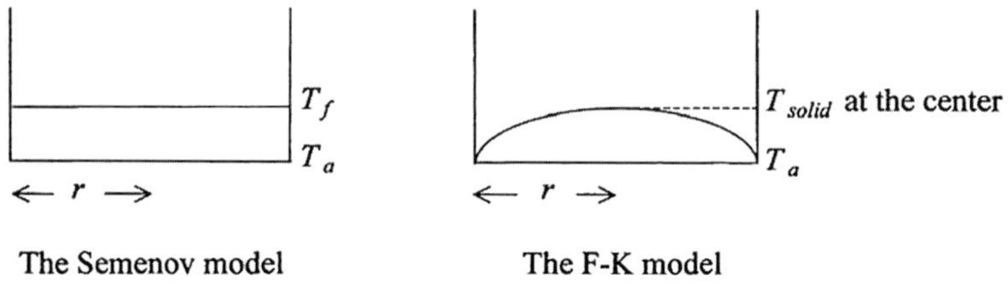

Figure 3. The Semenov model and the F-K model.

In the thermal conduction theory, such a distribution in general is thought to be caused on condition that the rate of heat transfer from the self-heating fluid filled in a container and placed in the atmosphere under isothermal conditions, through the whole fluid surface, across the container walls, to the atmosphere is far less than the rate of thermal conduction in the fluid. In other words, this condition is expressed as $U << \lambda$, which is equivalent to that the Biot number takes a small value.

The above condition is the formal definition of the Semenov model. The Semenov equation becomes effective under the condition above referred to and defines the T_c for an arbitrary volume of a self-heating fluid (a self-heating liquid chemical, in general) of the TD type charged, or confined, in an arbitrary container and placed in the atmosphere under isothermal conditions. The Semenov equation is thus appropriate for the calculation of the T_c for every liquid chemical of the TD type.*

In this connection, there are cases where the very ultimate of the Semenov model, in which the condition, $Ur/\lambda = 0$, holds, is referred to as the Semenov's boundary conditions or the Semenov extreme [12].

On the other hand, the characteristic of the F-K model, which is illustrated by the diagram of the right-hand side in Fig. 3, is the spatially gradient distribution

* As commented in **Preface**, the self-heating behavior of every self-heating liquid chemical, with the exception of liquid high explosives, such as nitroglycerin, of the true AC type, is of the TD type, so that a self-heating liquid chemical of the TD type or self-heating liquid chemicals of the TD type are described hereafter simply as a liquid or liquids.

of internal temperature. It seems most natural to think that this mode of temperature distribution arises from the heat transfer mode that the heat generated by the exothermic decomposition reaction occurring in a very slowly self-heating solid chemical placed in the atmosphere under isothermal conditions is transmitted from the inside of the solid chemical to the whole surface by the thermal conduction in the absence of the fluidity of the solid chemical itself and then the heat is transferred through the whole surface to the atmosphere. In this connection, the F-K model holds on the assumption that the whole surface is kept at the atmospheric temperature.

In the thermal conduction theory, such a distribution in general is thought to be caused on condition that the rate of thermal conduction in the self-heating solid chemical placed in the atmosphere under isothermal conditions is far less than the rate of heat transfer from the solid chemical through the whole surface to the atmosphere. In other words, this condition is expressed as $U >> \lambda$, which is equivalent to that the Biot number takes a large value.

The above condition is the formal definition of the F-K model. The F-K equation becomes effective under the condition above referred to and defines the T_c for a solid chemical of the TD type, having an arbitrary shape and an arbitrary size, placed in the atmosphere under isothermal conditions. The F-K equation is thus appropriate for the calculation of the T_c for every solid chemical of the TD type.*

In this connection, there are cases where the very ultimate of the F-K model, in which the condition, $Ur/\lambda = \infty$, holds, is referred to as the Frank-Kamenetskii's boundary conditions or the Frank-Kamenetskii limit [12].

At all events, both N. N. Semenov and D. A. Frank-Kamenetskii formulated originally each individual equation in order to define the T_c for a chemical of the TD type, including every gas-permeable oxidatively-heating substance, having an arbitrary shape and an arbitrary size, placed in the atmosphere under isothermal conditions.

It is, therefore, supposed in both the Semenov and the F-K model that there exists necessarily a certain temperature difference between the inside of a chemical of the TD type, having an arbitrary shape and an arbitrary size, placed in the atmosphere under isothermal conditions, and, the atmosphere, as illustrated in Fig. 3.

Some heat loss, therefore, necessarily occurs from a chemical of the TD type, irrespective of liquid and powdery, having an arbitrary shape and an arbitrary size, placed in the atmosphere under isothermal conditions, to the atmosphere.

---

* Each individual solid chemical of the TD type exists, in reality, in the form of a powder, or of an aggregation of coarse particles. Nevertheless, however, the F-K equation is applicable to the calculation of the T_c for a powdery chemical of the TD type, including every gas-permeable oxidatively- heating substance, as well. Individual procedures to calculate the values of T_c for these substances are explained in **Chapters 6**, **7** and **8**, respectively.

It is thus said that whether the thermal explosion of a chemical of the TD type, including every gas-permeable oxidatively-heating substance, having an arbitrary shape and an arbitrary size, placed in the atmosphere under isothermal conditions, ultimately occurs or not, or simply the T_c for the chemical, is decided, based on the balance between the rate of heat generation in the chemical and the rate of heat transfer from the chemical to the atmosphere at the critical state for the thermal explosion which exists at the end of the early stages of the self-heating process.

Now, the original purpose of a series of studies described herein was to determine the value of T_c for a chemical of the TD type, including every gas-permeable oxidatively-heating substance, having an arbitrary shape and an arbitrary size, placed in the atmosphere under isothermal conditions, by calculation based on the Semenov equation, or on the F-K equation, not by any direct (experimental) measurements.

All we have to do to accomplish this purpose is to know the rate of heat generation in the chemical, in concrete terms, the heat generation data of the chemical, and, the rate of heat transfer from the chemical, having an arbitrary shape and an arbitrary size, placed in the atmosphere under isothermal conditions, to the atmosphere, in concrete terms, the heat transfer data of the chemical, in the early stages of the self-heating process, respectively.

The heat generation data of a chemical of the TD type, including every gas-permeable oxidatively-heating substance,* are calculated ultimately by performing several adiabatic self-heating tests, or several adiabatic oxidatively-heating tests, which are started from each T_s with mutual intervals of $1 \sim 2$ K, for 2 cm^3 each of several samples of the chemical charged, or confined, each in some one of the open-cup, the draft or the closed cell, in accordance with the self-heating property of the chemical, for the time required for the temperature of each sample of the chemical to increase by 1.25 K from the corresponding T_s in the adiabatic self-heating test, or from the corresponding standard temperature in the adiabatic oxidatively-heating test, respectively. On the other hand, the heat transfer data of the chemical, having an arbitrary shape and an arbitrary size, placed in the atmosphere under isothermal conditions,** are required to be measured by experimental methods, in temperature differences of 1.25 K between the inside of the chemical and the atmosphere, under conditions of no air circulation.

---

* For the heat generation data of a chemical of the TD type, irrespective of liquid and powdery, including every gas-permeable oxidatively-heating substance, refer to **Sections 2.4**.

** For the heat transfer data of an arbitrary volume of a liquid charged in an arbitrary container and placed in the atmosphere under isothermal conditions, refer to **Subsection 5.3.2**. For the heat transfer data of a powdery chemical of the TD type, including every gas-permeable oxidatively-heating substance, having an arbitrary shape and an arbitrary size, placed in the atmosphere under isothermal conditions, refer to **Section 6.2**.

The above approach, *i.e.*, the heat generation data by the adiabatic self-heating test, or by the adiabatic oxidatively-heating test, and, the heat transfer data by experimental measurements, has been adopted throughout a series of studies described herein in order to calculate the T_c for a chemical of the TD type, including every gas-permeable oxidatively-heating substance, having an arbitrary shape and an arbitrary size, placed in the atmosphere under isothermal conditions.

1.6 A brief history of the thermal explosion research

It is said that it was J. H. van't Hoff that for the first time presented the idea that whether the thermal explosion of a self-heating substance occurs or not is decided, based on the balance between the rate of heat generation in the substance and the rate of heat transfer from the substance, having an arbitrary shape and an arbitrary size, placed in the atmosphere under isothermal conditions, to the atmosphere [13]. In the meantime, he is well-known in that he presented in 1884 the van't Hoff equation, Eq. (34), expressing the variation of the equilibrium constant with temperature.*

$$\frac{d \ln K}{dT} = \frac{\Delta H}{RT^2}. \tag{34}$$

The equilibrium constant, *K*, is needless to say the ratio of the rate constant of the forward reaction, k_n, to that of the reverse reaction, k_n', as expressed in Eq. (35).

$$K = \frac{k_n}{k_n'}. \tag{35}$$

Immediately after the presentation of the van't Hoff equation, S. A. Arrhenius presented in 1889, on the analogy of the van't Hoff equation, Eq. (36), expressing the variation of the rate constant with temperature. He thus established simultaneously the concept of the activation energy as well.

$$\frac{d \ln k_n}{dT} = \frac{E}{RT^2}. \tag{36}$$

The integrated form of Eq. (36), *i.e.*, Eq. (37), is referred to as the Arrhenius equation at the present time. The mathematical expression for the rate of

* There exists the magnificent system of thermodynamics behind him.

chemical reaction, in fact, for the rate of heat generation of an arbitrary self-heating substance, has thus become possible ever since.

$$k_n = A_n \exp[-\frac{E}{RT}]. \tag{37}$$

As seen hereafter, it is possible to comment on the Arrhenius equation in the following manner; on the one hand, in order to calculate the T_c for a chemical of the TD type, including every gas-permeable oxidatively-heating substance, having an arbitrary shape and an arbitrary size, placed in the atmosphere under isothermal conditions, all we have to do is, in the result, to make the Arrhenius plot with regard to the self-heating process, or with regard to the oxidatively-heating process, in the early stages, of 2 cm^3 of the chemical, charged, or confined, in some one of the open-cup, the draft or the closed cell, in accordance with the self-heating property of the chemical, and subjected to either of the two kinds of adiabatic tests; on the other hand, in order to calculate the SADT for a chemical of the AC type, including every powdery chemical of the quasi-AC type, having an arbitrary shape and an arbitrary size, confined in an arbitrary closed container of the corresponding shape and size, and placed in the atmosphere under isothermal conditions, all we have to do is, in the result, to make the Arrhenius plot with regard to the induction period of the autocatalytic reaction, or of the quasi-autocatalytic reaction, of 2 cm^3 of the chemical confined in the closed cell and subjected to the isothermal storage test. The problem of calculating the T_c, or the SADT, for a self-heating chemical, having an arbitrary shape and an arbitrary size, placed in the atmosphere under isothermal conditions, thus reduces itself to one of making the Arrhenius plot with regard to the self-heating process, in the early stages, of 2 cm^3 of the chemical subjected to either of the two kinds of adiabatic tests, or subjected to the isothermal storage test.

Based on these precursors' achievements, Semenov established the thermal explosion theory by formulating the Semenov equation with regard to the T_c for a fluid in 1934 [14].

In this connection, Frank-Kamenetskii was also certainly so great as to formulate the F-K equation with regard to the T_c for a solid in 1939 [15]. On the other hand, however, it may be permitted to say that he exerted a harmful influence on the thermal explosion research by asserting in his book, "Diffusion and Heat Transfer in Chemical Kinetics", that it is indispensable, in the thermal explosion research of liquids, to stir liquid samples or to circulate air around the containers [16]. As explained in detail in **Section 5.2**, however, it is useless, or rather, as discussed in detail in **Section 5.8**, it is harmful, in the thermal explosion research of liquids, to stir liquid samples or to circulate air around the containers. In this regard, few doubtful assertions are included in Semenov's book, "Some Problems of Chemical Kinetics and Reactivity".

After world war Ⅱ, the thermal explosion theory was transferred to the western world, and it was studied predominantly and earnestly in the United Kingdom. Achievements performed by P. H. Thomas, T. Boddington and P. C. Bowes are in particular known. Their main interest was, however, focused on the T_c for a solid, because they considered the calculation of the T_c for a liquid to be very difficult on account of the harmful influence exerted by Frank-Kamenetskii. Nevertheless, however, they were not able to establish the calculation method of the T_c for a solid to the last. Their work ended by proposing a procedure to determine the T_c for a relatively large-scale solid by extrapolating the actually measured values of T_c for several small-scale samples of the solid on the graph.*

Since the 1980's, people called the chemicals safety circles appeared and attempted to calculate the so-called SADT for each individual self-heating chemical. They, however, attempted to do so by applying a few equations, which appear in the initial stages of the derivation process of the Semenov equation, to every self-heating chemical, irrespective of whether it is of the TD type or of the AC type, or, irrespective of whether it is liquid or solid. We have, therefore, no choice but to say that, theoretically speaking, their approach to the subject was almost meaningless.

But now, as presented herein, the thermal explosion theory has become practically usable and accessible to everyone, so far as our purpose is to calculate the T_c, or the SADT, for an arbitrary self-heating chemical, having an arbitrary shape and an arbitrary size, placed in the atmosphere under isothermal conditions.

---

* For further details of their proposition, refer to **Subsection 7.1.1**.

References to Chapter 1

[1] D. A. Frank-Kamenetskii, Diffusion and Heat Transfer in Chemical Kinetics, 2nd Ed., Translated from Russian by J. P. Appleton, Plenum Press, New York-London, 375 (1969).
[2] Edited by C.F.H. Tipper, Oxidation and Combustion Reviews, **2**, Elsevier Publishing Co., Amsterdam, 130 (1967).
[3] N. N. Semenov, Some Problems of Chemical Kinetics and Reactivity, **2**, Translated from Russian by J. E. S. Bradley, Pergamon Press, London, 1-4 (1959).
[4] N. N. Semenov, *ibid.*, 1.
[5] N. N. Semenov, *ibid.*, 2.
[6] D. A. Frank-Kamenetskii, *ibid.*, 333.
[7] D. A. Frank-Kamenetskii, *ibid.*, 342-345.
[8] D. A. Frank-Kamenetskii, *ibid.*, 338-341.
[9] D. A. Frank-Kamenetskii, *ibid.*, 413.
[10] P. H. Thomas, Some Approximations in the Theory of Self-Heating and Thermal Explosion, Trans. Faraday Soc., **56**, 833-839 (1960).
[11] D. A. Frank-Kamenetskii, *ibid.*, 379-384.
[12] P. H. Thomas, On the Thermal Conduction Equation for Self-Heating Materials with Surface Cooling, Trans. Faraday Soc., **54**, 60-65 (1958).
[13] J. H. van't Hoff, Lectures on Theoretical and Physical Chemistry, English Translation by R. A. Lehfeld, Arnold, London, (1898-99).
[14] N. N. Semenov, Chain Reactions (in Russian), ONTI, Leningrad, 110 (1934); Chemical Kinetics and Chain Reactions (in English), Clarendon Press, Oxford, (1935).
[15] D. A. Frank-Kamenetskii, Zh. Fiz. Khim., **13**, 738 (1939).
[16] D. A. Frank-Kamenetskii, Diffusion and Heat Transfer in Chemical Kinetics, 2nd Ed., Translated from Russian by J. P. Appleton, Plenum Press, New York-London, 347, 348, 374, *etc.* (1969).

Chapter 2 The adiabatic temperature increase equation

2.1 Introduction

As a matter of fact, it is very difficult to calculate the T_c for a chemical of the TD type, including every gas-permeable oxidatively-heating substance, having an arbitrary shape and an arbitrary size, placed in the atmosphere under isothermal conditions, by applying the Semenov or the F-K equation only, because, as stated in **Preface**, the chemical quantities, E, A_0 and ΔH, which specify as a whole the rate of heat generation per unit volume per unit time in the early stages of the self-heating process of the chemical and are included in both the Semenov and the F-K equation, are very difficult to measure precisely by means of conventional experimental techniques.

It, however, becomes very easy to calculate the T_c, if both the Semenov and the F-K equation are reduced to the simpler forms by substituting the two coefficients, a and b, of an empirical formula, $\ln \Delta t = a/T_s + b$, *i.e.*, Eq. (44), which is derived in **Section 2.4**, into each equation, respectively.

Eq. (44) holds between a T_s and the time, Δt, required for the temperature of a definite quantity* of a chemical of the TD type, including every gas-permeable oxidatively-heating substance, charged, or confined, in some one of the open-cup, the draft or the closed cell, in accordance with the self-heating property of the chemical, and subjected to the adiabatic self-heating test, or to the adiabatic oxidatively-heating test, which is started from the T_s, to increase by a definite temperature difference, ΔT, from the T_s.

Eq. (44) is obtained directly from Eq. (43), *i.e.*, an equation called the adiabatic temperature increase equation.

Eq. (43) is in fact the integrated form of Eq. (38) given in **Section 2.2** and is derived, prior to Eq. (44), in **Section 2.4**. A few derivation processes of Eq. (43) from Eq. (38) are introduced in the present chapter.

---

* As a matter of fact, 2 cm^3 has been used herein as the standard sample volume in the adiabatic self-heating test, or in the adiabatic oxidatively-heating test, performed for a chemical of the TD type, including every oxidatively-heating substance.

2.2 An equation holding between the rate of heat generation per unit volume per unit time in the early stages of the self-heating process of a small-scale chemical of the TD type, including every small-scale gas-permeable oxidatively-heating substance, having the spatially uniform distribution of internal temperature, subjected to either of the two kinds of adiabatic tests, and, the rate of increase in temperature of the chemical

When a small-scale chemical of the TD type, irrespective of liquid and solid, including every small-scale gas-permeable oxidatively-heating substance, the diameter of which is of the order of, say, 10 mm, is charged, or confined, in some one of the open-cup, the draft or the closed cell, in accordance with the self-heating property of the chemical, and subjected to either of the above-mentioned two kinds of adiabatic tests, the spatially uniform distribution of temperature is effected necessarily in the chemical; so it is done, while the self-heating process is, in particular, in the early stages.

An equation, Eq. (38), then holds between the rate of heat generation per unit volume per unit time in the early stages of the self-heating process of a small-scale chemical of the TD type, including every small-scale gas-permeable oxidatively-heating substance, having the spatially uniform distribution of internal temperature, subjected to either of the two kinds of adiabatic tests, and, the rate of increase in temperature of the chemical, assuming the effect of the concentration of the chemical on the rate of the exothermic decomposition reaction in the early stages of the self-heating process to be of the zeroth order.

$$c\rho\frac{dT}{dt} = \varDelta H \cdot A_0 \exp\left[-\frac{E}{RT}\right]. \tag{38}$$

As regards the validity of Eq. (38), it is also possible to consider in the following manner.

That is, that the spatial distribution of temperature is uniform in a small-scale chemical of the TD type subjected to either of the two kinds of adiabatic tests is equivalent to that the term, ΔT, in Eq. (20) presented in **Section 1.3** takes the value of zero in the chemical. Eq. (20) is re-presented below for convenience' sake.

$$c\rho\frac{\partial T}{\partial t} = \lambda \cdot \Delta T + \varDelta H \cdot A_0 \exp\left[-\frac{E}{RT}\right]. \tag{20}$$

2.3 Validity of the substitution of the two coefficients, *a* and *b*, of Eq. (44) into the F-K equation as well as the Semenov equation

It will be permitted to say that the leading concept in **Section 2.2** is in accordance with the nonstationary theory of the thermal explosion in the F-K's scheme [17]. It is assumed in this theory that the temperature of a chemical of the TD type, placed in the atmosphere maintained at a temperature situated below the critical state for the thermal explosion which exists at the end of the early stages of the self-heating process, varies with time, but it is uniform throughout the chemical (see the Semenov model in Fig. 3 in **Section 1.5**).

Now, the Semenov equation is certainly based on the nonstationary theory of the thermal explosion, because this equation holds on the assumption that the spatial distribution of temperature in a fluid filled in the container and placed in the atmosphere maintained at a temperature situated below the critical state for the thermal explosion, is uniform (refer to **Section 1.2**). In this regard, it has been ascertained in a series of studies, which are described in **Subsections 5.5.3** and **5.7.2**, as well that the spatial distribution of temperature in an arbitrary volume of a liquid charged in an arbitrary container and placed in the atmosphere under isothermal conditions is perfectly uniform in the early stages of the self-heating process, except the thin upper surface layer, even if it is not stirred mechanically [18].

Besides, it is self-evident, as stated in the preceding section, that the spatial distribution of temperature, in particular, in the early stages of the self-heating process, or of the oxidatively-heating process, in a small-scale chemical of the TD type, including every small-scale gas-permeable oxidatively-heating substance, subjected to either of the two kinds of adiabatic tests, is the very ultimate of the Semenov model, because the condition, the Biot number = $Ur/\lambda = 0$, holds strictly in such a chemical.

On the other hand, it is assumed in the stationary theory of the thermal explosion, on which the F-K equation is based, that the term, $\partial T/\partial t$, in Eq. (20) takes the value of zero, but the term, ΔT, takes a definite value. In other words, as stated in **Section 1.3**, it is assumed in the latter theory that the temperature of a solid (powdery, in reality) chemical of the TD type, including every gas-permeable oxidatively-heating substance, having an arbitrary shape and an arbitrary size, placed in the atmosphere maintained at a temperature situated below the critical state for the thermal explosion, does not vary with time as a whole, but there is a spatially gradient distribution of temperature in the chemical (see the F-K model in Fig. 3 in **Section 1.5**). It must, thus, be admitted that the spatial distribution of temperature in a powdery chemical of the TD type, placed in the atmosphere under isothermal conditions, is a gradient one even in the early stages of the self-heating process.

Nevertheless, however, it is certain that the three equations, *i.e.*, the Semenov equation, the F-K equation and Eq. (38), refer to the identical slow rate of heat generation per unit volume per unit time in the early stages of the self-heating process, or of the oxidatively-heating process, of a chemical of the TD type, including every gas-permeable oxidatively-heating substance, so far as the rate of heat generation is concerned. It is thus inferred that the variables, E, A_0 and ΔH, included in the above three equations express the identical chemical quantities specifying as a whole the rate of heat generation per unit volume per unit time in the early stages of the self-heating process, or of the oxidatively-heating process, of a chemical of the TD type, respectively.

It is thought, therefore, that the variables which characterize the reduced form of the F-K equation are not the heat generation data of a powdery chemical of the TD type but the heat transfer data of the chemical, *i.e.*, the effective thermal diffusivity, α_e, the shape factor, δ_c, and the radius, r.*

For the above reasons, as will be explained in detail in **Section 2.4**, it is presupposed herein that it is valid to substitute the two coefficients, a and b, of Eq. (44) into the F-K equation as well as the Semenov equation, in order to reduce them to the simpler forms, respectively.

2.4 Derivation of the adiabatic temperature increase equation

When the temperature, T, of 2 cm^3 of a chemical of the TD type, irrespective of liquid and powdery, including every gas-permeable oxidatively-heating substance, charged, or confined, in some one of the open-cup, the draft or the closed cell, in accordance with the self-heating property of the chemical, and subjected to either of the two kinds of adiabatic tests started each from a T_s, is immediately above the T_s, if two conditions, *i.e.*, $(T - T_s) \ll T_s$ and $RT_s \ll E$, hold simultaneously, it is possible to apply, in the same manner as applied to Eqs. (22)~(27) in **Section 1.3**, the Frank-Kamenetskii's method of expanding the exponent, *i.e.*, Eqs. (25) and (26) presented in **Section 1.3**,

$$\exp\left[-\frac{E}{RT}\right] \cong \exp\left[-\frac{E}{RT_s}\right] \cdot \exp[\theta], \tag{25}$$

and

$$\theta \equiv \frac{E(T - T_s)}{RT_s^2}, \tag{26}$$

* For the reduced form of the F-K equation, and, for the heat transfer data of a powdery chemical of the TD type, including every gas-permeable oxidatively-heating substance, having an arbitrary shape and an arbitrary size, placed in the atmosphere under isothermal conditions, refer to **Section 6.2**.

to the exponential term in Eq. (38), in order to make it integrable [8].
Besides, if Eqs. (28) and (30) presented in **Section 1.3**,

$$\delta \equiv \frac{\Delta H \cdot A_0 E r^2}{\lambda R T_s^2} \exp\left[-\frac{E}{RT_s}\right] \tag{28}$$

and

$$\tau \equiv \frac{\alpha t}{r^2} = \frac{\lambda t}{c\rho r^2}, \tag{30}$$

are also applied, together with Eqs. (25) and (26), to Eq. (38), Eq. (38) is expressed in the dimensionless form in the following manner.

$$\begin{aligned} \frac{d\theta}{d\tau} &= \frac{d\theta}{dT} \cdot \frac{dT}{d\tau} = \frac{d\theta}{dT} \cdot \frac{dT}{dt} \cdot \frac{dt}{d\tau} = \frac{d\theta}{dT} \cdot \frac{dT}{dt} \cdot \left[\frac{1}{\left(\frac{d\tau}{dt}\right)}\right] \\ &= \frac{E}{RT_s^2} \cdot \frac{\Delta H \cdot A_0}{c\rho} \exp\left[-\frac{R}{RT_s}\right] \cdot \exp[\theta] \cdot \frac{r^2 \cdot c\rho}{\lambda} \\ &= \frac{\Delta H \cdot A_0 E r^2}{\lambda R T_s^2} \exp\left[-\frac{E}{RT_s}\right] \cdot \exp[\theta] = \delta \cdot \exp[\theta]. \end{aligned} \tag{39}$$

On integrating Eq. (39) from zero to θ and from zero to τ, Eq. (40) is obtained.

$$\tau = \frac{1 - \exp[-\theta]}{\delta}. \tag{40}$$

On expressing Eq. (40) again in the dimensional form by substituting ($\lambda \cdot \Delta t$)/($c\rho r^2$) for τ and ($E \cdot \Delta T$)/RT_s^2 for θ into it, Eq. (41) is derived.

$$\Delta t = \frac{c\rho R T_s^2}{\Delta H \cdot A_0 E}\left(1 - \exp\left[-\frac{\Delta T \cdot E}{RT_s^2}\right]\right) \exp\left[\frac{E}{RT_s}\right], \tag{41}$$

where Δt is the time required for the temperature of 2 cm^3 of a chemical of the TD type, including every gas-permeable oxidatively-heating substance, subjected to either of the two kinds of adiabatic tests started each from a T_s to increase by a definite temperature difference, ΔT, from the T_s.

Expanding the second term in parentheses, and taking up to the second term in the series thereby obtained, Eq. (41) is reduced to Eq. (42).

$$\Delta t = \frac{\Delta T \cdot c\rho}{\Delta H \cdot A_0} \exp\left[\frac{E}{RT_s}\right]. \tag{42}$$

Taking the natural logarithms on both sides of Eq. (42) and rearranging them, we get the integrated form of Eq. (38) as shown below.

$$\ln \Delta t = \frac{E}{RT_s} + \ln\left[\frac{\Delta T \cdot c\rho}{\Delta H \cdot A_0}\right]. \tag{43}$$

The gradient, a, and the intercept, b, of, an empirical formula, *i.e.*, Eq. (44),

$$\ln \Delta t = \frac{a}{T_s} + b, \tag{44}$$

are then expressed as

$$a = \frac{E}{R} \tag{45}$$

and

$$b = \ln \frac{\Delta T \cdot c\rho}{\Delta H \cdot A_0}. \tag{46}$$

In fact, when charged, or confined, in some one of the open-cup, the draft or the closed cell, in accordance with the self-heating property of the chemical, and subjected to either of the two kinds of adiabatic tests started each from a T_s, 2 cm^3 of a chemical of the TD type, including every gas-permeable oxidatively-heating substance, warms up to the T_s within tens of minutes; thereafter, it continues to self-heat, or to heat oxidatively, over the T_s at a very slow, but virtually constant, rate depending on the value of T_s in accordance with the Arrhenius equation; and under such circumstances, Eq. (44), $\ln \Delta t = a/T_s + b$, holds between a T_s K and the time, Δt min, required for the temperature of the chemical to increase by a definite value of ΔT from the T_s in the adiabatic self-heating test, or from the corresponding standard temperature in the adiabatic oxidatively-heating test (refer to Fig. 15 in **Section 3.3**).*

In this connection, it is also possible to say that 2 cm^3 of a chemical of the TD type, including every gas-permeable oxidatively-heating substance, subjected to either of the two kinds of adiabatic tests has its own Eq. (44), $\ln \Delta t = a/T_s + b$, to the effect that the equation has the two coefficients, *a* and *b*, specific to the self-heating process, or to the oxidatively-heating process, in the early stages, of 2 cm^3 of the chemical subjected to either of the two kinds of adiabatic tests, so that the equation holds only for the self-heating process, or for the oxidatively-heating process, in the early stages, of 2 cm^3 of the chemical subjected to either of the two kinds of adiabatic tests.

The values of the two coefficients, *a* and *b*, of Eq. (44), $\ln \Delta t = a/T_s + b$, are calculated by applying the regression analysis to several combinations of the value of $\ln \Delta t$ with that of $1/T_s$, which are determined, based on several digital records obtained each from several adiabatic self-heating tests, or from several adiabatic oxidatively-heating tests, which are started from each T_s with mutual intervals of 1~2 K, performed each, for 2 cm^3 each of several samples of the chemical charged, or confined, each in some one of the open-cup, the draft or the closed cell, in accordance with the self-heating property of the chemical, for the time, Δt, required for the temperature of each sample of the chemical to increase by a definite value of ΔT of 1.25 K from the corresponding T_s in the adiabatic self-heating test, or from the corresponding standard temperature in the adiabatic oxidatively-heating test. For concrete examples of such calculations, refer to **Subsection 6.3.6** or **(6)** of **Subsection 8.4.1** as well as **Section 4.7**.

Now, it is seen in Eq. (44), $\ln \Delta t = a/T_s + b$, that, although the coefficient, *b*, is a function of the specific gravity, in fact, the loading density, ρ, of the chemical in the cell, as the individual units indicate, both coefficients, *a* and *b*, do not depend on the size, or on the quantity, of the chemical, respectively.**, ***

In the meantime, it is also possible to consider that, after all, we have replaced, in the above derivation process, the variables, *E*, A_0 and ΔH, which are included in Eqs. (38) and (43) as the chemical quantities specifying as a whole the rate of heat generation per unit volume per unit time in the early stages of

* For the standard temperature in the adiabatic oxidatively-heating test, refer to **(2)** of **Subsection 8.3.1**.

** For the constant, ΔT, refer to the discussion given below.

*** In this connection, it is evident that *E* is evaluated from *a*, and, A_0 from *b*, if the values of ΔH and $c\rho$ are known.

the self-heating process, or in the early stages of the oxidatively-heating process, of a chemical of the TD type, including every gas-permeable oxidatively-heating substance, but which are very difficult to measure precisely by means of conventional experimental techniques, with, the two numerical values, *a* and *b*, which are the two coefficients of the empirical formula, Eq. (44), $\ln \Delta t = a/T_s + b$, and which are very easy to calculate by applying the regression analysis to several digital records obtained each from several adiabatic self-heating tests, or from several adiabatic oxidatively-heating tests, performed each for 2 cm^3 each of several samples of the chemical.

Synthesizing our understanding above referred to and the inference, made in **Section 2.3**, that the variables, E, A_0 and ΔH, included in the three equations, that is, the Semenov equation, the F-K equation and Eq. (38), express the identical chemical quantities specifying as a whole the rate of heat generation per unit volume per unit time in the early stages of the self-heating process, or in the early stages of the oxidatively-heating process, of a chemical of the TD type, including every gas-permeable oxidatively-heating substance, respectively, an important and useful proposition is obtained that it is possible to replace the chemical quantities, E, A_0 and ΔH, included in the Semenov equation, or in the F-K equation, with, the two coefficients, *a* and *b*, of the empirical formula, Eq. (44), holding for the self-heating process, or for the oxidatively-heating process, in the early stages, of 2 cm^3 of a chemical of the TD type, including every gas-permeable oxidatively-heating substance, charged, or confined, in some one of the open-cup, the draft or the closed cell, in accordance with the self-heating property of the chemical, and subjected to either of the two kinds of adiabatic tests.

In fact, apart from the constant, ΔT, we may regard the values of the two coefficients, *a* and *b*, as the simplified chemical quantities specifying as a whole the rate of heat generation per unit volume per unit time in the early stages of the self-heating process, or in the early stages of the oxidatively-heating process, of a chemical of the TD type, including every gas-permeable oxidatively-heating substance, and therefore these are called hereafter the heat generation data of a chemical of the TD type, including every gas-permeable oxidatively-heating substance.

The unit of E/R is K; on the other hand, that of the term, $(\Delta T \cdot c\rho)/(\Delta H \cdot A_0)$, is min. It is, however, thought that it is not the common practice to append any unit to the logarithm of a variable or a term, so that *a* and *b* are treated herein as a mere numerical coefficient, respectively.

The heat generation data are used, together with the heat transfer data, to calculate the T_c for a chemical of the TD type, including every gas-permeable oxidatively-heating substance, having an arbitrary shape and an arbitrary size, placed in the atmosphere under isothermal conditions, by applying the reduced form of the Semenov equation, or that of the F-K equation, expressed in terms of the heat generation data and the heat transfer data.*

Incidentally, once one particular chemical of the TD type, including every gas-permeable oxidatively-heating substance, is specified, the values of ΔH and A_0 of the exothermic decomposition reaction in the early stages of the self-heating process, or of the oxidative decomposition reaction in the early stages of the oxidatively-heating process, of the chemical as well as the values of c and ρ of the chemical itself are automatically fixed, even if each of these values is not measured actually, in the sense stated under Eq. (28) in **Section 1.3**, respectively; on the other hand, as to the value of ΔT, it is possible to choose it arbitrarily in the two kinds of adiabatic tests.

It has been ascertained, as to the value of ΔT, that, when the value of $\ln \Delta t$ is plotted against that of $1/T_s$, on several values of ΔT, with reference to a self-heating process, in the early stages, of 2 cm^3 of a certain chemical of the TD type subjected to the adiabatic self-heating test started from a T_s, several straight lines, which are almost parallel with one another, are obtained.**

However, it has been made an established rule in the two kinds of adiabatic tests, which are started each from a T_s, performed for 2 cm^3 of a chemical of the TD type, including every oxidatively-heating substance, to interrupt each test, as soon as the temperature of the chemical in the cell increases by the definite value of ΔT of 1.25 K from the T_s in the adiabatic self-heating test, or from the corresponding standard temperature in the adiabatic oxidatively-heating test. Some reasons why a value of ΔT of 1.25 K was chosen as the definite value of ΔT in the two kinds of adiabatic tests are explained in **Subsection 4.5.8**. In this regard, in order to make Eq. (44) valid, it is thought to be desirable to make the plot on a value of ΔT as small as possible, from the standpoint of the Frank-Kamenetskii's method of expanding the exponent as well.

In this connection, let us suppose that the following relation exists in Eq. (46).

$$\Delta T_2 = \mathrm{n} \cdot \Delta T_1 . \tag{47}$$

where n is a natural number.

It is then possible to express Eq. (46) in the following two forms, *i.e.*,

$$b_1 = \ln \frac{\Delta T_1 \cdot c\rho}{\Delta H \cdot A_0} \tag{48}$$

and

---

* For the derivation of the reduced form of the Semenov equation, refer to **Subsection 5.3.2**.

** The plot of $\ln \Delta t$ versus $1/T_s$ made in accordance with Eq. (44) is a sort of the so-called Arrhenius plot.

$$b_2 = \ln \frac{\Delta T_2 \cdot c\rho}{\Delta H \cdot A_0} = \ln \mathrm{n} + b_1. \tag{49}$$

It thus follows that it has been confirmed that n in ΔT_2 and ln n in b_2 cancel in Eq. (72), which is the reduced form of the Semenov equation, and, in Eq. (79), which is the reduced form of the F-K equation; in other words, it has been verified that the value of T_c calculated by applying Eq. (72), or Eq. (79), does not depend on the value of ΔT.

On the other hand, the T_s of each run in the two kinds of adiabatic tests performed for a chemical of the TD type, irrespective of liquid and powdery, including every gas-permeable oxidatively-heating substance, is selected on the basis of the self-heating property, or of the oxidatively-heating property, of the chemical tested to give estimated rates of increase in temperature of 1.25 K/h. Under such experimental conditions, the weight-loss of the chemical in the cell is negligible and even the color change of the chemical is scarcely seen after every run.

Incidentally, a fact should also be noted down here that the temperature dependence of the individual values of c and ρ of 99 % di-*tert*-butyl peroxide (DTBP) vary inversely as each other (Table 1).

Table 1

The temperature dependence of the individual values of c and ρ of DTBP.

Temperature ℃	10	20	30	40	50
c cal/(g·K)	0.477	0.482	0.486	0.491	
ρ g/cm^3	0.806	0.796	0.786		

In other words, it is thought to be shown in Table 1 that the value of the product, $c\rho$, for DTBP is substantially invariable in the range of room temperature to several tens degrees C.

2.5 An alternative method to derive the adiabatic temperature increase equation

The derivation method of the adiabatic temperature increase equation, which is introduced in the preceding section, is very difficult to understand. First of all, we cannot understand very well the reason why dimensionless numbers, such as θ, δ and τ, are needed to derive the equation. Fortunately, however, we have an alternative method to derive, though qualitatively, the equation in a far simpler manner.

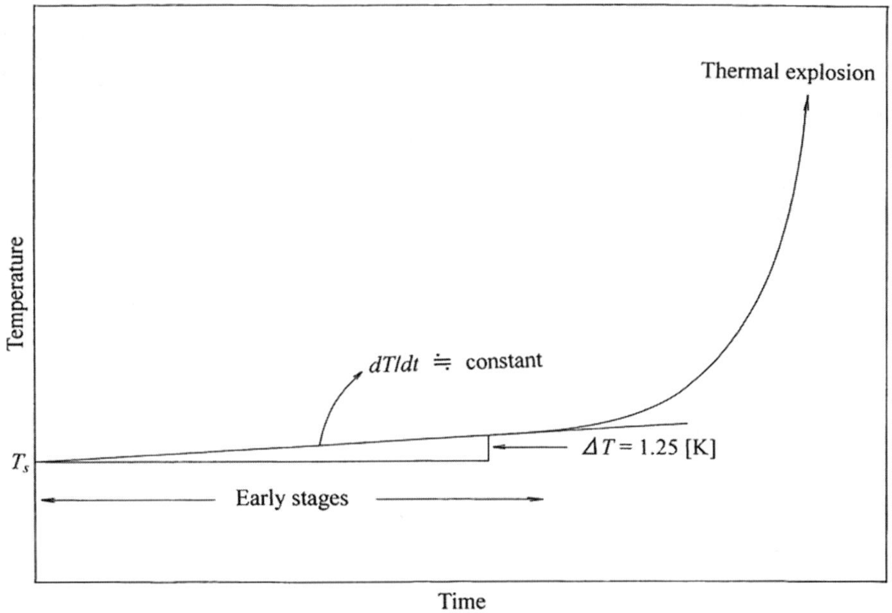

Figure 4. The linear approximation of the self-heating process or curve, in the early stages, of 2 cm^3 of a chemical of the TD type charged in the open-cup cell, or confined in the closed cell, in accordance with the self-heating property of the chemical, and subjected to the adiabatic self-heating test started from a T_s.

When charged in the open-cup cell, or confined in the closed cell, in accordance with the self-heating property of the chemical, and subjected to the adiabatic self-heating test started from a T_s,* 2 cm^3 of a chemical of the TD type warms up to the T_s within tens of minutes; thereafter, it continues to self-heat over the T_s at a very slow, but virtually constant, rate depending on the value of

* The argument made in the present section holds, in principle, in the adiabatic oxidatively-heating test, performed for every gas-permeable oxidatively-heating substance, as well.

T_s in accordance with the Arrhenius equation. That is, a condition that the value of dT/dt remains virtually constant holds within a narrow range of temperature immediately above the T_s, *i.e.*, in the early stages of the self-heating process of 2 cm^3 of a chemical of the TD type subjected to the adiabatic self-heating test started from a T_s (Fig. 4).*

The above phenomenon is as a matter of course a direct consequence of a fact that the effect of the concentration of a chemical of the TD type on the rate of the exothermic decomposition reaction, in the early stages of the self-heating process, of the chemical is virtually of the zeroth order.

If the value of dT/dt of 2 cm^3 of a chemical of the TD type charged in the open-cup cell, or confined in the closed cell, in accordance with the self-heating property of the chemical, and subjected to the adiabatic self-heating test started from a T_s remains virtually constant within a narrow range of temperature immediately above the T_s, the right-hand side of Eq. (50), which is derived at once from Eq. (38), must also take a constant value, C.

$$\frac{dT}{dt} = \frac{\Delta H \cdot A_0}{c\rho} \exp\left[-\frac{E}{RT_s}\right] = \mathrm{C}. \qquad (50)$$

The following definite integral then becomes possible,

$$\int_{t_1}^{t_2} dt = \left(\frac{1}{\mathrm{C}}\right) \int_{T_1}^{T_2} dT. \qquad (51)$$

The result is,

$$\Delta t = \frac{\Delta T}{\mathrm{C}} = \frac{\Delta T \cdot c\rho}{\Delta H \cdot A_0} \exp\left[\frac{E}{RT_s}\right]. \qquad (52)$$

Eq. (52) is nothing else but Eq. (42).

2.6 Frank-Kamenetskii's adiabatic induction period, τ_{ad}

Frank-Kamenetskii also tried to express his adiabatic induction period, τ_{ad} [19]. It is expressed as

---

* For the validity of the linear approximation of the self-heating process or curve, in the early stages, of 2 cm^3 of a chemical of the TD type subjected to the adiabatic self-heating test started from a T_s, an argument is made in **Section 2.7**.

$$\tau_{ad} = \left(\frac{c\rho}{\Delta H \cdot A_0} \right) \int_{T_s}^{T_m} \exp\left[\frac{E}{RT} \right] dT, \tag{53}$$

where T_m expresses a sufficiently high temperature in the F-K's scheme.

After having been converted into an integrable form by applying the method of expanding the exponent, *i.e.*, Eqs. (25) and (26) presented in **Section 1.3** [8], Eq. (53) is integrated to yield Eq. (54).

$$\begin{aligned}
\tau_{ad} &= \left(\frac{c\rho}{\Delta H \cdot A_0} \right) \exp\left[\frac{E}{RT_s} \right] \int_{T_s}^{T_m} \exp\left[-\left(\frac{E}{RT_s^2} \right) (T - T_s) \right] dT \\
&= \left(\frac{c\rho}{\Delta H \cdot A_0} \right) \exp\left[2\frac{E}{RT_s} \right] \int_{T_s}^{T_m} \exp\left[-\frac{ET}{RT_s^2} \right] dT \\
&= \left(\frac{c\rho}{\Delta H \cdot A_0} \right) \left(-\frac{RT_s^2}{E} \right) \exp\left[2\frac{E}{RT_s} \right] \left\{ \exp\left[-\frac{ET}{RT_s^2} \right] \right\}_{T_s}^{T_m} \\
&= \left(\frac{c\rho}{\Delta H \cdot A_0} \right) \left(-\frac{RT_s^2}{E} \right) \exp\left[2\frac{E}{RT_s} \right] \left\{ 0 - \exp\left[-\frac{E}{RT_s} \right] \right\} \\
&= \left(\frac{c\rho}{\Delta H \cdot A_0} \right) \left(\frac{RT_s^2}{E} \right) \exp\left[\frac{E}{RT_s} \right].
\end{aligned} \tag{54}$$

If the following equation, Eq. (55),* which expresses the maximum increase in temperature, ΔT, up to the explosion limit in the F-K's scheme [20], is substituted into Eq. (54),

$$\Delta T \cong \frac{RT_s^2}{E}, \tag{55}$$

Eq. (54) is seen to take the same structure as Eq. (42).

In this connection, the explosion limit, a term used in the F-K's scheme, corresponds to the critical state for the thermal explosion in the Semenov's scheme.

---

* Note that Eq. (55) is the same, in structure, as Eq. (12) in **Section 1.2.**

In the derivation process introduced above, the symbol T_* used by F-K has been replaced herein with T_s.

2.7 Validity of the linear approximation of the self-heating process or curve, in the early stages, of 2 [cm^3] of a chemical of the TD type charged in the open-cup cell, or confined in the closed cell, in accordance with the self-heating property of the chemical, and subjected to the adiabatic self-heating test started from a T_s

The differential equations, in which one of the unknown variables, *e.g.*, temperature, enters in a nonlinear manner, *i.e.*, as an exponential function, while its derivative enters in a linear form, are often dealt with in the thermal explosion theory. Such an equation is called quasilinear in mathematics [21]. For instance, we have assumed in Eq. (50) presented in **Section 2.5** that the value of dT/dt remains virtually constant while the self-heating process of 2 cm^3 of a chemical of the TD type, subjected to the adiabatic self-heating test, is in the early stages.*

It will, thus, be necessary here for us to confirm *a posteriori*, with reference to some concrete example, the validity of the linear approximation of the self-heating process or curve, in the early stages, of 2 cm^3 of a chemical of the TD type charged in the open-cup cell, or confined in the closed cell, in accordance with the self-heating property of the chemical, and subjected to the adiabatic self-heating test started from a T_s.** The confirmation illustrated below is performed with reference to the experimental data which are determined for the ten organic liquid peroxides and are listed in Table 8 in **Subsection 5.7.1**.

First, let us return to Eq. (38) or (50).

$$\frac{dT}{dt} = \frac{\Delta H \cdot A_0}{c\rho}\exp\left[-\frac{E}{RT}\right]. \qquad (38) \text{ or } (50)$$

In Eq. (38) or (50), the term, $(\Delta H \cdot A_0)/(c\rho)$ K/min, as a whole may be regarded as a proportionality constant, or as a conversion factor. All we have to do, in considering the temperature dependence of the value of dT/dt in the early stages of the self-heating process of 2 cm^3 of a chemical of the TD type subjected to the adiabatic self-heating test, is then to know the temperature dependence of the value of the term, exp[- E/RT].

---

* In this regard, it may be permitted to say that the Frank-Kamenetskii's method of expanding the exponent, which has been applied in **Sections 1.3** and **2.4**, is, in the result, nothing else but the linear approximation of the exponential function.

** The argument made in the present section holds, in principle, in the adiabatic oxidatively-heating test, performed for every gas-permeable oxidatively-heating substance, as well.

Secondly, let us assume the mean value of T_s to be 60 ℃ in the adiabatic self-heating tests performed each for the ten organic liquid peroxides charged each in the open-cup cell, because the value of T_s ranges from 26 ℃ for 69.5 % *tert*-hexyl peroxyneodecanoate in isoparaffin (THPN) to 100 ℃ for 99 % di-*tert*-butyl peroxide (DTBP), as stated in **Subsection 5.4.1**.

Thirdly, let us assume that the coefficient, *a*, *i.e.*, *E*/*R* K, of Eq. (44) holding for the individual self-heating processes, in the early stages, of 2 cm^3 each of the ten organic liquid peroxides charged each in the open-cup cell and subjected each to the adiabatic self-heating test, takes a mean and constant value of 14,000 K, on comparing the values of '*a*' presented Table 8 in **Subsection 5.7.1**.

The temperature dependence, from 60 ℃ up to 61.25 ℃, of the value of the term, exp[- *E*/*RT*], is then calculated as shown in Table 2.

Table 2
The temperature dependence, from 60 ℃ up to 61.25 ℃, of the value of the term, exp[- *E*/*RT*], on the assumption that the coefficient, *E*/*R*, takes a constant value of 14,000 K.

Temperature		Value of exp[- *E*/*RT*]	Increment
℃	K	$\times 10^{-19}$	$\times 10^{-19}$
60.0	333.15	5.618159145	
		)	0.179852784
60.25	333.4	5.798011929	
		)	0.185327817
60.5	333.65	5.983339746	
		)	0.19096073
60.75	333.9	6.174300476	
		)	0.196755817
61.0	334.15	6.371056293	
		)	0.202717458
61.25	334.4	6.573773751	

17.01 % up, in total, {from 5.618 · · · (at 60 ℃) to 6.573 · · · (at 61.25 ℃)}

And lastly, let us assume that, at the time when the adiabatic self-heating test was started from a T_s of 60 ℃ for 2 cm^3 of an organic liquid peroxide charged in the open-cup cell,* the gradient of the self-heating process or curve, *i.e.*, the rate of increase in temperature, of the peroxide was 1.15 K/h.

Then, according to the result of the calculation given in Table 2, at the time when the adiabatic self-heating test started from the T_s is interrupted, *i.e.*, at the time when the temperature of the peroxide has increased by 1.25 K from the T_s, the rate of increase in temperature of the peroxide will be about 1.346 (= 1.15 × 1.1701) K/h.

Now, as stated in **Section 2.4**, the T_s of each run in the two kinds of adiabatic tests performed for a chemical of the TD type, including every gas-permeable oxidatively-heating substance, is selected on the basis of the self-heating property of the chemical tested to give estimated rates of increase in temperature of 1.25 K/h.

When the rate of increase in temperature of 2 cm^3 of the chemical subjected to the adiabatic self-heating test started from a T_s has varied or has accelerated from 1.15 up to 1.346 K/h after the lapse of one hour, we may assume that the rate has remained, in fact, at a mean, and almost constant, value of 1.25 $\{\fallingdotseq (1.15 + 1.346)/2\}$ K/h during this one hour.

The linearity, of this order, of the self-heating process or curve, of 2 cm^3 of a chemical of the TD type subjected to the adiabatic self-heating test started from a T_s, recorded for the time, Δt, required for the temperature of the chemical to increase by the definite value of ΔT of 1.25 K from the T_s, is exemplified by a digital record of the self-heating process, which is presented in Table 5 in **Section 4.7**, of 2 cm^3 of 99 % *tert*-butyl peroxybenzoate (TBPB) charged in the open-cup cell and subjected to the adiabatic self-heating test started from a nominal T_s of 76 ℃, for the time, Δt, required for the temperature of TBPB to increase by the definite value of ΔT of 1.25 K from the nominal T_s.

* For details of the experimental procedure performed for each of the ten organic liquid peroxides, refer to **Section 5.4**.

References to Chapter 2

[8] D. A. Frank-Kamenetskii, Diffusion and Heat Transfer in Chemical Kinetics, 2nd Ed., Translated from Russian by J. P. Appleton, Plenum Press, New York-London, 338-341 (1969).
[17] D. A. Frank-Kamenetskii, *ibid.*, 349.
[18] T. Kotoyori, Critical Temperatures for the Thermal Explosion of Liquids, Combust. & Flame, **95**, 307-312 (1993).
[19] D. A. Frank-Kamenetskii, *ibid.*, 352.
[20] D. A. Frank-Kamenetskii, *ibid.*, 346.
[21] D. A. Frank-Kamenetskii, *ibid.*, 331.

Chapter 3 A classification of self-heating chemicals

A classification of self-heating chemicals is introduced in the present chapter. Treatments of gas-permeable oxidatively-heating substances are made in **Chapters** 7 and **8**.

3.1 A broad classification of self-heating chemicals into the two large groups, *i.e.*, the TD type and the AC type

As stated in **Preface**, each individual self-heating chemical, including every gas-permeable oxidatively-heating substance, is classified into either of the two large groups, *i.e.*, the thermal decomposition or TD type and the autocatalytic reaction or AC type.

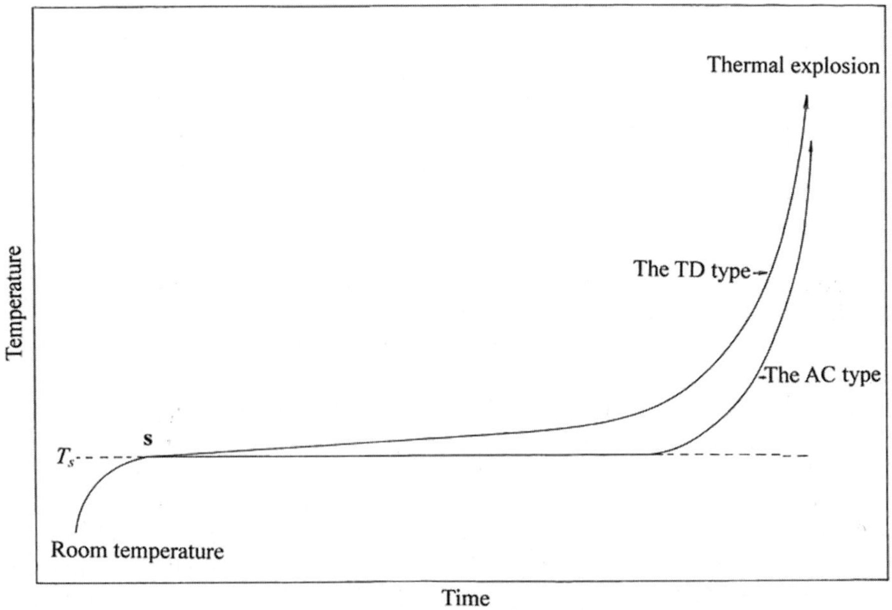

Figure 5. The whole self-heating process up to the thermal explosion of 2 cm^3 of a chemical of the TD type charged in the open-cup cell, or confined in the closed cell, in accordance with the self-heating property of the chemical, and subjected to the adiabatic self-heating test started from a T_s, and, the whole self-heating process up to the thermal explosion of 2 cm^3 of a high explosive of the true AC type confined in the closed cell and subjected to the adiabatic self-heating test started from a T_s on the low temperature side.

In Fig. 5 are shown the whole self-heating process up to the thermal explosion of 2 cm^3 of a chemical of the TD type charged in the open-cup cell, or confined in the closed cell, in accordance with the self-heating property of the chemical, and subjected to the adiabatic self-heating test started from a T_s, and, the whole self-heating process up to the thermal explosion of 2 cm^3 of a high explosive of the true AC type confined in the closed cell and subjected to the adiabatic self-heating test started from a T_s.

The whole self-heating process up to the thermal explosion of 2 cm^3 of a chemical of the TD type charged in the open-cup cell, or confined in the closed cell, in accordance with the self-heating property of the chemical, and subjected to the adiabatic self-heating test started from a T_s is of course the same as that shown in Fig. 1 in **Section 1.1** or that shown in Fig. 4 in **Section 2.5**. Thus, as explained in **Section 1.1**, when a chemical of the TD type, including every gas-permeable oxidatively-heating substance, having an arbitrary shape and an arbitrary size, is placed in the atmosphere maintained at a T_a higher than the T_c of the chemical, it continues to self-heat over the T_a even under isothermal conditions in such a manner as shown in Fig. 5, because the rate of heat generation in the chemical exceeds the rate of heat transfer from the chemical to the atmosphere throughout the whole self-heating process up to the thermal explosion, with the result that the temperature of the chemical continues to increase acceleratedly to cause the ultimate thermal explosion of the chemical sooner or later.

On the other hand, when confined in the closed cell and subjected to the adiabatic self-heating test started from a T_s on the low temperature side, 2 cm^3 of a high explosive of the true AC type warms up to the T_s within tens of minutes, but it does not continue to self-heat over the T_s, although it is placed under adiabatic conditions. In fact, the temperature remains at the T_s over a long time; in the meantime, the decomposition reaction of the high explosive to generate an autocatalyst, such as NO_2 radical, proceeds very slowly all through this time, *i.e.*, during the induction period of the autocatalytic reaction of the high explosive, at a rate depending on the value of T_s in accordance with the Arrhenius equation. Once, however, the concentration of the autocatalyst in the high explosive attains to a definite threshold value in the course of time, the decomposition reaction to generate only the autocatalyst ceases; instead, an (active and exothermic) autocatalytic reaction, the aspect of which is entirely different from the decomposition reaction to generate the autocatalyst, of the high explosive itself starts; thereafter, the autocatalytic reaction accelerates gradually.

It is well-known that such a self-heating behavior as described above is observed really in the spontaneous ignition process of a nitrate ester, such as collodion cotton (Fig. 6). Chemicals of the true AC type thus form a group intrinsically different, in the decomposition reaction mechanism, from chemicals of the TD type.

It is impossible to apply either of the two equations of the thermal explosion theory to the calculation of the T_c for a high explosive of the true AC type, or for a powdery chemical of the quasi-AC type,* because the two equations are formulated on the assumption that, when a chemical, having an arbitrary shape and an arbitrary size, is placed in the atmosphere maintained at a T_s under adiabatic conditions, it continues to self-heat over the T_s at a rate depending only on the temperature of the chemical, based on the zeroth-order assumption, in accordance with the Arrhenius equation, respectively (refer to **Section 1.1**).

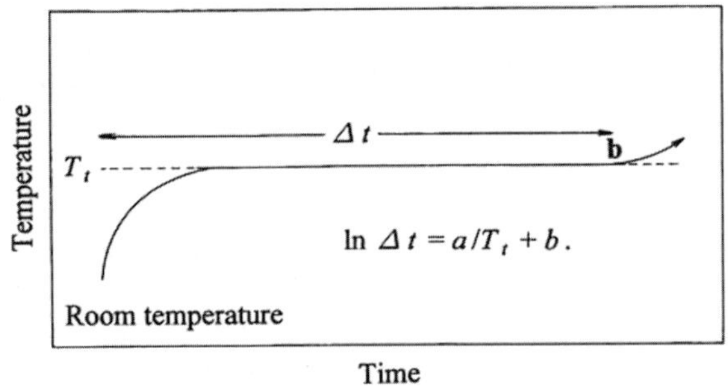

Figure 6. The induction period, of the autocatalytic reaction, of 2 cm^3 of a high explosive of the true AC type confined in the closed cell and subjected to the isothermal storage test performed at a T_t on the low temperature side, recorded for the time, Δt, from the insertion of the cell into the isothermal storage testing device till the start of the autocatalytic reaction of the high explosive at the T_t.

Fortunately, however, by applying an empirical formula, $\ln \Delta t = a/T_t + b$, *i.e.*, Eq. (59), which is derived in the following section and holds for the induction period of the autocatalytic reaction, or of the quasi-autocatalytic reaction, of 2 cm^3 of a chemical of the AC type, including every powdery chemical of the quasi-AC type, confined in the closed cell and subjected to the isothermal storage test, it is possible to calculate the SADT for the chemical, having an arbitrary shape and an arbitrary size, confined in an arbitrary closed container, including the closed cell used in the isothermal storage testing device, of the corresponding shape and size, and placed in the atmosphere under isothermal conditions.** Eq. (59) is presented in Figs. 6, 7 and 16 as well.

In any event, it is clear that it is the self-heating process, in the early stages, of a chemical of the TD type, having an arbitrary shape and an arbitrary size, placed in the atmosphere under isothermal conditions, and not the induction

---

* As will be explained hereafter in the present chapter, the self-heating behavior of a powdery chemical of the quasi-AC type is also of the AC type.

** For the definition of the SADT, refer to **Notation**.

period of the autocatalytic reaction of a high explosive of the true AC type, having an arbitrary shape and an arbitrary size, confined in an arbitrary closed container of the corresponding shape and size, and placed in the atmosphere under isothermal conditions, that is the object of argumentation in the thermal explosion theory.*

3.2 Derivation of an empirical formula, ln $\Delta t = a/T_t + b$, *i.e.*, Eq. (59), which is used to calculate the SADT for a chemical of the AC type, including every powdery chemical of the quasi-AC type, having an arbitrary shape and an arbitrary size, confined in an arbitrary closed container of the corresponding shape and size, and placed in the atmosphere under isothermal conditions

As stated in the preceding section, the condition for the (active and exothermic) autocatalytic reaction of a high explosive of the true AC type itself to start is that the concentration of the autocatalyst in the high explosive attains to the definite threshold value, irrespective of whether the temperature of the high explosive is high or low. The higher the temperature, the faster becomes the rate of the decomposition reaction of the high explosive to generate the autocatalyst, and *vice versa*; in other words, the higher the temperature, the shorter becomes the induction period, and *vice versa*.

If, thus, the induction period of the autocatalytic reaction, the threshold molar concentration of the autocatalyst, the rate of the decomposition reaction of the high explosive to generate the autocatalyst, the rate constant of the decomposition reaction, of the n-th order, of the high explosive to generate the autocatalyst, the molar concentration of the high explosive, the order of the decomposition reaction of the high explosive to generate the autocatalyst, the frequency factor in the rate constant of the decomposition reaction, of the n-th order, of the high explosive to generate the autocatalyst and the temperature of the high explosive maintained at a constant value are each expressed as Δt, $[C_{autocatalyst\text{-}threshold}]$, $d[C_{autocatalyst}]/dt$, k_{n}, $[C]$, n, A_{n} and T_t, the equation holding among them is expressed in the following form.

$$\Delta t = \frac{\left[C_{autocatalyst-threshold}\right]}{d\left[C_{autocatalyst}\right]/dt} = \frac{\left[C_{autocatalyst-threshold}\right]}{k_{\mathrm{n}}[C]^{\mathrm{n}}} = \frac{\left[C_{autocatalyst-threshold}\right]}{A_{\mathrm{n}}[C]^{\mathrm{n}}}\exp\left[\frac{E}{RT_t}\right]. \qquad (56)$$

* For the other object of argumentation in the thermal explosion theory, refer to **Section 1.1**.

As a matter of fact, however, Eq. (56) is reduced to the following form, because the effect of the concentration of a high explosive of the true AC type on the rate of the decomposition reaction of the high explosive to generate the autocatalyst in the induction period is assumed to be of the zeroth order.

$$\Delta t = \frac{\lfloor C_{autocatalyst-threshold} \rfloor}{d\lfloor C_{autocatalyst} \rfloor / dt} = \frac{\lfloor C_{autocatalyst-threshold} \rfloor}{k_0} = \frac{\lfloor C_{autocatalyst-threshold} \rfloor}{A_0} \exp\left[\frac{E}{RT_t}\right]. \quad (57)$$

Taking the natural logarithms on both sides of Eq. (57), and then rearranging them, we get

$$\ln \Delta t = \frac{E}{RT_t} + \ln \frac{\lfloor C_{autocatalyst-threshold} \rfloor}{A_0}. \quad (58)$$

The gradient, a, and the intercept, b, of an empirical formula, *i.e.*, Eq. (59),[*]

$$\ln \Delta t = \frac{a}{T_t} + b, \quad (59)$$

are then expressed as

$$a = \frac{E}{R} \quad (60)$$

and

$$b = \ln \frac{\lfloor C_{autocatalyst-threshold} \rfloor}{A_0}. \quad (61)$$

In fact, when confined in the closed cell and subjected to the isothermal storage test performed at a T_t, 2 cm^3 of a high explosive of the true AC type warms up to the T_t within tens of minutes, but the temperature remains at the T_t

[*] It is clear that Eq. (59) is the same in form, which is of the Arrhenius type, as Eq. (44).

over a long time; in the meantime, the decomposition reaction of the high explosive to generate an autocatalyst, such as NO_2 radical, proceeds very slowly all through this time, at a rate depending on the value of T_t in accordance with the Arrhenius equation. Once, however, the concentration of the autocatalyst in the high explosive attains to a definite threshold value in the course of time, an (active and exothermic) autocatalytic reaction of the high explosive itself starts; and under such circumstances, Eq. (59), $\ln \Delta t = a/T_t + b$, holds between a T_t K and the time, Δt min, from the insertion of the closed cell into the isothermal storage testing device till the start of the autocatalytic reaction of the high explosive at the T_t, *i.e.*, the induction period of the autocatalytic reaction of the high explosive at the T_t (Fig. 6). The same is true, to all appearances, of the induction period of the quasi-autocatalytic reaction of every powdery chemical of the quasi-AC type as well.

In this connection, it is also possible to say that 2 cm^3 of a chemical of the AC type, including every powdery chemical of the quasi-AC type, confined in the closed cell and subjected to the isothermal storage test has its own Eq. (59), $\ln \Delta t = a/T_t + b$, to the effect that the equation has the two coefficients, *a* and *b*, specific to the induction period of the autocatalytic reaction, or of the quasi-autocatalytic reaction, of 2 cm^3 of the chemical confined in the closed cell and subjected to the isothermal storage test, so that the equation holds only for the induction period of the autocatalytic reaction, or of the quasi-autocatalytic reaction, of 2 cm^3 of the chemical confined in the closed cell and subjected to the isothermal storage test, in a similar manner as 2 cm^3 of a chemical of the TD type, including every gas-permeable oxidatively-heating substance, charged, or confined, in some one of the open-cup, the draft or the closed cell, in accordance with the self-heating property of the chemical, and subjected to either of the two kinds of adiabatic tests has its own Eq. (44), $\ln \Delta t = a/T_s + b$.

The values of the two coefficients, *a* and *b*, of Eq. (59), $\ln \Delta t = a/T_t + b$, are calculated by applying the regression analysis to several combinations of the value of $\ln \Delta t$ with that of $1/T_t$, which are determined, based on several analog/digital records obtained each from several isothermal storage tests performed each at each T_t with mutual intervals of 1～2 K, for 2 cm^3 each of several samples of the chemical confined each in the closed cell, for the time, Δt, from the insertion of each cell into the isothermal storage testing device till the start of the autocatalytic reaction, or of the quasi-autocatalytic reaction, of the chemical at the corresponding T_t. For concrete examples of such calculations, refer to **Subsections 9.3.6** and **10.2.6**.

Now, it is seen in Eq. (59), $\ln \Delta t = a/T_t + b$, that the variable, T_t, including the SADT, is a function of the variable, Δt, only; in the meantime, as the individual units indicate, both coefficients, *a* and *b*, do not depend on the size, or on the quantity, of the chemical, respectively. It thus follows that the SADT, including an arbitrary value of T_t, for a chemical of the AC type, including every powdery chemical of the quasi-AC type, having an arbitrary shape and an arbitrary size, confined in an arbitrary closed container of the corresponding shape and size, and placed in the atmosphere under isothermal conditions, does not depend, in principle,* on its size or quantity.

The physical or chemical meaning of the above indication is considered in the following manner:

The SADT for a high explosive of the true AC type depends on the induction period of the autocatalytic reaction; however, the autocatalytic reaction does not depend, in principle, on the quantity of the high explosive. On the other hand, as will be explained hereafter in the present chapter, the SADT for a powdery chemical of the quasi-AC type depends on the phase transition, the melting; however, it does also not depend, in principle, on the quantity of the chemical.

Based on our understanding above referred to, an important and useful proposition** is obtained that it is possible, in principle, to regard the SADT calculated in accordance with Eq. (59) holding for the induction period of the autocatalytic reaction, or of the quasi-autocatalytic reaction, of 2 cm^3 of a chemical of the AC type, including every powdery chemical of the quasi-AC type, confined in the closed cell and subjected to the isothermal storage test, as the SADT for the chemical, having an arbitrary shape and an arbitrary size, confined in an arbitrary closed container of the corresponding shape and size, and placed in the atmosphere under isothermal conditions.

In other words, the SADT for a chemical of the AC type, including every powdery chemical of the quasi-AC type, having an arbitrary shape and an arbitrary size, confined in an arbitrary closed container of the corresponding shape and size, and placed in the atmosphere under isothermal conditions, is calculated, in accordance with the definition of the SADT, at a value of T_t corresponding to a value of Δt of 7 d, *i.e.*, 10,080 min, in Eq. (59), $\ln \Delta t = a/T_t + b$, holding for the induction period of the autocatalytic reaction, or of the quasi-autocatalytic reaction, of 2 cm^3 of the chemical confined in the closed cell and subjected to the isothermal storage test. For concrete examples of such calculations, refer to **Sections 9.4** and **10.3**.

---

* When a chemical of the AC type, including every powdery chemical of the quasi-AC type, having an arbitrary shape and an arbitrary size, confined in an arbitrary closed container of the corresponding shape and size, is placed in the atmosphere maintained at a T_t, the larger the size of the chemical, the temperature of which has been maintained at room temperature until the placement, the longer becomes naturally the time required for the temperature of the chemical as a whole to increase from room temperature up to the T_t.

** The other important and useful proposition is obtained in **Section 2.4** with regard to the replacement of the chemical quantities, E, A_0 and ΔH, included in the Semenov or the F-K equation, with, the two coefficients, a and b, of the empirical formula, Eq. (44), holding for the self-heating process, or for the oxidatively-heating process, in the early stages, of 2 cm^3 of a chemical of the TD type, including every gas-permeable oxidatively-heating substance, charged, or confined, in some one of the open-cup, the draft or the closed cell, in accordance with the self-heating property of the chemical, and subjected to either of the two kinds of adiabatic tests.

3.3 Powdery chemicals of the quasi-AC type

In addition to chemicals of the TD type and those of the true AC type, there exist chemicals referred to as powdery chemicals of the quasi-AC type.

When confined in the closed cell and subjected to the isothermal storage test performed at a T_t, 2 cm^3 of a powdery chemical of the quasi-AC type warms slowly up to the T_t, but the temperature remains near the T_t over a long time, because a phase transition, the endothermic melting, of the chemical occurs almost simultaneously with the exothermic decomposition reaction all through this time. Once, however, the chemical finishes melting in the course of time, an apparently sudden quasi-autocatalytic reaction of the resultant liquefied chemical starts.

Once a molecule of a powdery chemical of the quasi-AC type is released from the 'cage' composed of the surrounding crystal lattice by melting, it probably starts to decompose exothermically. The reason why they are qualified as of the quasi-AC type is that, although they do not decompose in accordance with the autocatalytic reaction mechanism, the self-heating behavior of 2 cm^3 of a powdery chemical of the quasi-AC type confined in the closed cell and subjected to the isothermal storage test performed at a T_t resembles apparently that of 2 cm^3 of a high explosive of the true AC type placed under the same conditions as the former (Figs. 6 and 7). Powdery chemicals of the quasi-AC type exist in considerable numbers (refer to **Subsection 10.4.2**).

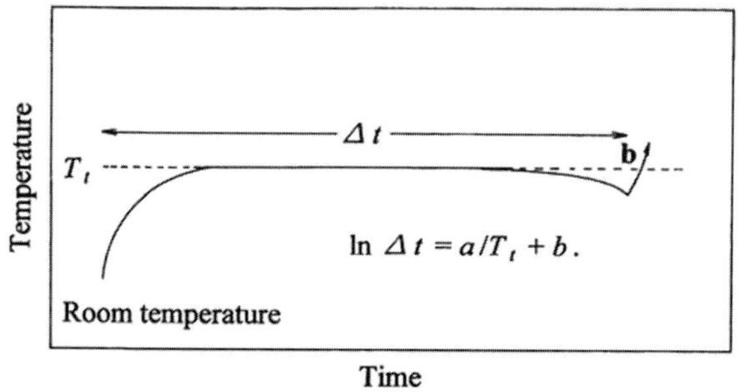

Figure 7. The induction period, of the quasi-autocatalytic reaction, of 2 cm^3 of a powdery chemical of the quasi-AC type confined in the closed cell and subjected to the isothermal storage test performed at a T_t on the high temperature side, recorded for the time, Δt, from the insertion of the cell into the isothermal storage testing device till the start of the quasi-autocatalytic reaction occurring simultaneously with the finish of melting of the chemical at the T_t.

2 cm^3 of a chemical of the AC type, including every powdery chemical of the quasi-AC type, confined in the closed cell and subjected to the isothermal

storage test performed at a T_t starts the autocatalytic reaction, or the quasi-autocatalytic reaction, at the point of time "**b**" in Figs. 6, 7 and 16. As stated in **Section 3.2**, the higher the T_t, the smaller becomes the value of Δt, and *vice versa*; in other words, the higher the T_t, the shorter becomes the induction period of the autocatalytic reaction, or of the quasi-autocatalytic reaction, and *vice versa*.

3.4 Correlation among the pattern of the TG-DTA curve of a self-heating powdery chemical, the two types of self-heating behaviors, *i.e.*, the TD type and the quasi-AC type, and the two equations of the thermal explosion theory

The type of the self-heating behavior of a self-heating powdery chemical is closely related to the pattern of the thermogravimetry-differential thermal analysis (TG-DTA) curve which the chemical affords. In other words, it is possible, in principle, to infer the self-heating behavior of a self-heating powdery chemical to be either of the TD type or of the quasi-AC type by glancing over the TG-DTA curve of the chemical, so that it is also possible to infer the equation of the thermal explosion theory applied to calculate the T_c of the chemical to be either the Semenov equation, *i.e.*, Eq. (17) presented in **Section 1.2**, or the F-K equation, *i.e.*, Eq. (29) presented in **Section 1.3**, or neither equation.

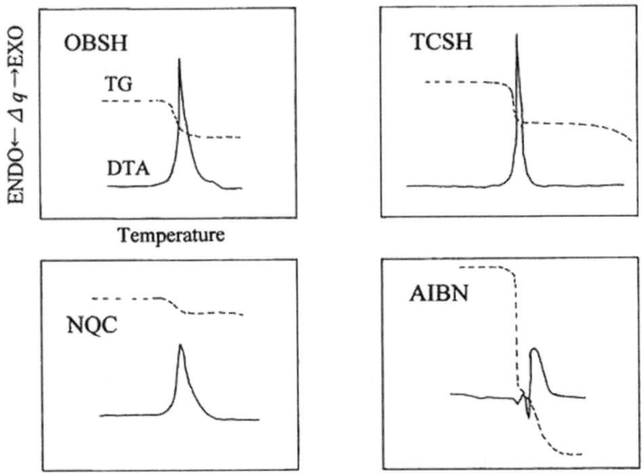

Figure 8. Individual TG-DTA curves of the four powdery chemicals of the TD type.

Individual TG-DTA curves, which are each recorded with a glass open-cup cell, 5 mm in diameter, 2.5 mm in depth, at a value of ϕ of 2.5 K/min in air at atmospheric pressure, of four of the ten powdery chemicals of the TD type, which are listed in Table 14 in **Subsection 6.7.1**, are presented in Fig. 8.

It is obvious that the absence of the melting point is characteristic of the DTA curve of a powdery chemical of the TD type. That is, a powdery chemical of this type decomposes prior to melting. The self-heating behavior of a powdery chemical, such as 98 % α, α'-azobis(isobutyronitrile) (AIBN), which decomposes explosively prior to any remarkable exothermic decomposition reaction, is also of the TD type, so that the F-K equation is applied to calculate its T_c. When confined in the closed cell and subjected to the adiabatic self-heating test started from a T_s in the range of 65 to 74 ℃, 2 cm^3 of AIBN shows such a self-heating behavior, which is typical of liquid, or powdery, chemicals of the TD type, as exemplified in Fig. 15.

On the other hand, individual TG-DTA curves, which are also each recorded with the glass open-cup cell, 5 mm in diameter, 2.5 mm in depth, at the same value of ϕ of 2.5 K/min in air at atmospheric pressure, of four of the five powdery chemicals of the quasi-AC type, which are listed in Table 26 in **Subsection 10.4.1**, are presented in Fig. 9.

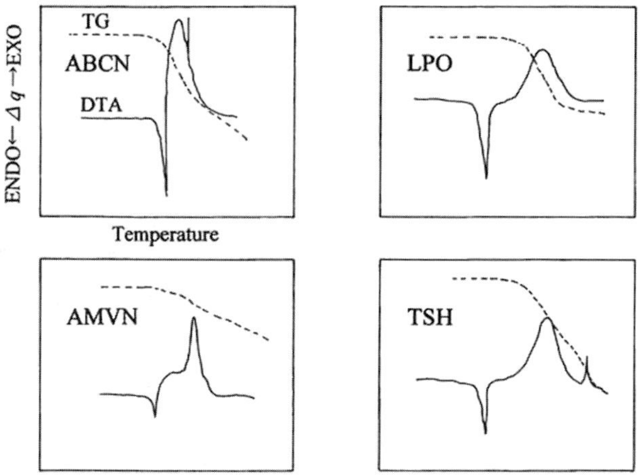

Figure 9. Individual TG-DTA curves of the four powdery chemicals of the quasi-AC type.

It is obvious in Fig. 9 that one characteristic of the DTA curve of a powdery chemical of the quasi-AC type is the presence of the melting point [22]. Another characteristic of the DTA curve of a powdery chemical of this type is that the curve shifts successively from the endothermic peak caused by melting to the exothermic peak caused by the exothermic decomposition reaction.* TG curves of powdery chemicals of the quasi-AC type tell that they decompose slowly in most cases.

The property of each individual powdery chemical of the quasi-AC type varies in a continuous fashion with the interval between the endothermic peak and the exothermic peak in the DTA curve which the chemical affords. Both peaks are in particular close together in the case of ABCN or AMVN, as shown in Fig. 9. The pattern of the DTA curve of a typical powdery chemical of the quasi-AC type, such as ABCN or AMVN, is thought to reflect the fact that, when heated, a phase transition, the endothermic melting, takes place in parallel with a chemical reaction, the exothermic decomposition reaction, in it, as shown diagrammatically in Fig. 10.

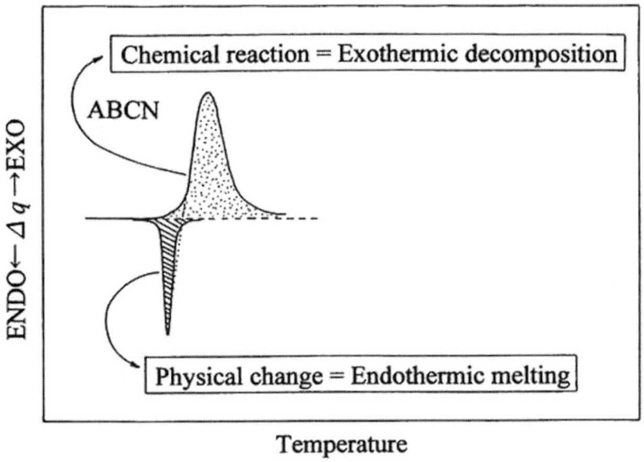

Figure 10. Simultaneous occurrence of a phase transition, the endothermic melting, and a chemical reaction, the exothermic decomposition reaction, in ABCN as a representative of powdery chemicals of the quasi-AC type.

When confined in the closed cell and subjected to the isothermal storage test performed at a T_t, 2 cm^3 of a powdery chemical of the quasi-AC type starts the exothermic decomposition reaction in the liquid phase while the liquid and the solid phases coexist, and the heat flux from the exothermically decomposing liquid is utilized for the endothermic melting of the powdery chemical, so that the system is maintained under quasi-isothermal conditions until the chemical finishes melting. In this connection, when powdery chemicals of the quasi-AC type, such as ABCN and AMVN, are subjected to the isothermal storage test,

* This characterization or definition is subject to some exceptions. For further details, refer to explanations given about Figs. 13 and 14.

they start to self-heat suddenly and rapidly in a state similar, in appearance, to the half-melted shaved ice.

The above phenomenon that the endothermic melting takes place in parallel with the exothermic decomposition reaction is thought to occur in every powdery chemical of the quasi-AC type, although this fact is not necessarily revealed explicitly in the DTA curve.

In the last analysis, the relative position of the exothermic onset temperature or EOT and the melting point of a self-heating powdery chemical become the key for the correlation referred to in the headline of the present section, as diagrammed in Fig. 11.

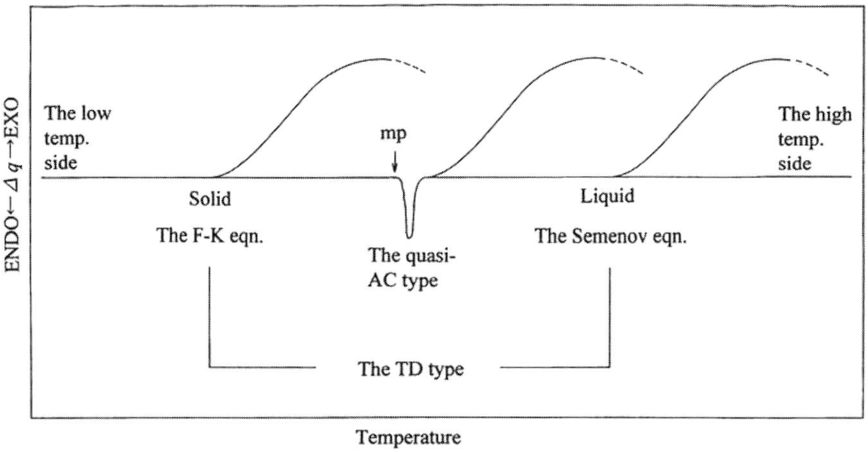

Figure 11. Correlation among the pattern of the TG-DTA curve of a self-heating powdery chemical, the two types of self-heating behaviors, *i.e.*, the TD type and the quasi-AC type, and the two equations of the thermal explosion theory.

The T_c for a chemical, such as 98 % *N*-methyl-*N*-nitroso-*p*-toluenesulfonamide (MNTS, Diazald®), which is powdery at room temperature but decomposes exothermically as a liquid at temperatures higher than its melting point, is calculated by applying the Semenov equation (Fig. 12).

In addition to liquid chemicals of the TD type of the kind above referred to, once either a powdery chemical of the TD type or that of the quasi-AC type is dissolved in some solvent at room temperature, it also becomes a liquid to which the Semenov equation is applied to calculate the T_c. In this connection, it is a matter of course that a chemical which is liquid at room temperature has its freezing point at a temperature far lower than room temperature.

As stated already, the T_c for a chemical, which is powdery at room temperature and decomposes exothermically as a powder at temperatures lower than its melting point, is calculated by applying the F-K equation.

However, a powdery chemical, such as 98 % 1-nitroso-2-naphthol (1N2N), which affords an endothermic peak far smaller than the subsequent exothermic peak in the DTA curve (see Fig. 13), also self-heats as a powdery chemical of the TD type at temperatures lower than its melting point, although the DTA curve as a whole is similar, in pattern, to that of a powdery chemical of the quasi-AC type.

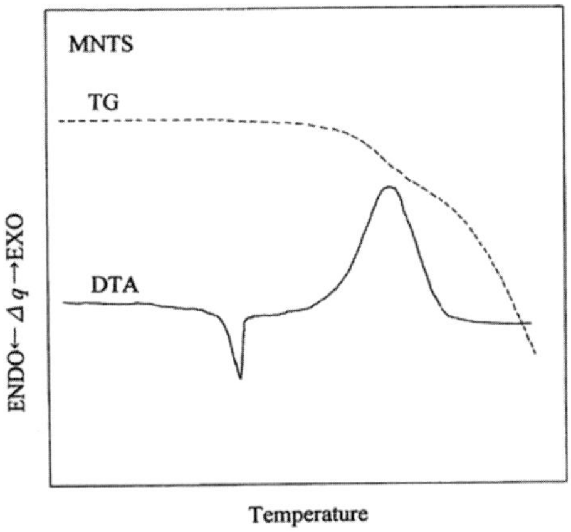

Figure 12. The TG-DTA curve of 98 % *N*-methyl-*N*-nitroso-*p*-toluenesulfonamide (MNTS, Diazald®).

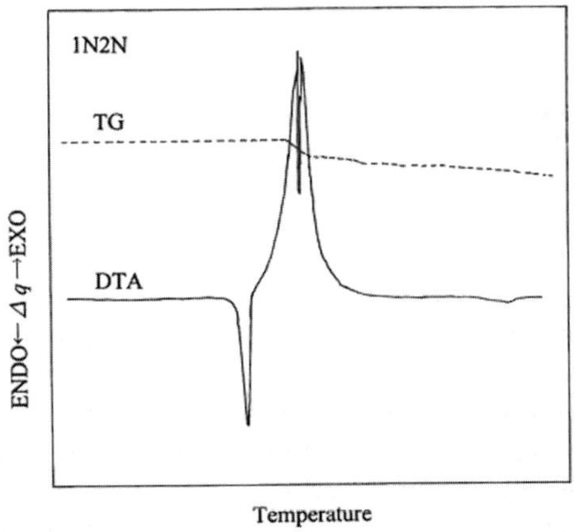

Figure 13. The TG-DTA curve of 98 % 1-nitroso-2-naphthol (1N2N).

Besides powdery chemicals of the kind above referred to, a powdery chemical, such as 97 % benzenesulfohydroxamic acid (BSHA), which affords an endothermic peak and the subsequent exothermic peak in the DTA curve but decomposes explosively almost simultaneously with the finish of melting, also self-heats as a powdery chemical of the TD type at temperatures lower than its melting point (Fig. 14).

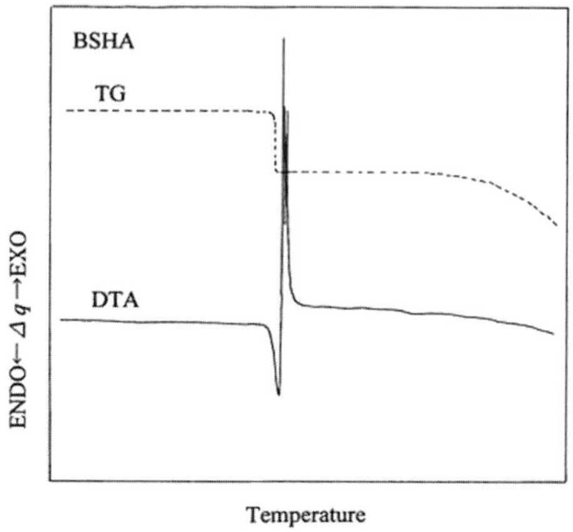

Figure 14. The TG-DTA curve of 97 % benzenesulfohydroxamic acid (BSHA).

After all, it follows that, when the behavior of a powdery chemical which is shown in the TG-DTA curve is some one of the following three, *i.e.*,

(1) if the powdery chemical self-heats without melting; or,

(2) if the powdery chemical affords an endothermic peak far smaller than the subsequent exothermic peak in the DTA curve; or,

(3) if the powdery chemical decomposes explosively, irrespective of whether it affords an endothermic peak caused by melting and the subsequent exothermic peak caused by the exothermic decomposition reaction in the DTA curve or not;

it is possible to say that the self-heating behavior of the chemical is of the TD type.

If a powdery chemical decomposes explosively without melting in thermal analysis, it may be called a typical or perfect powdery chemical of the TD type, because the chemical shows simultaneously two of the three behaviors some one of which is required for the chemical to be of the TD type.

Each molecule of liquid chemicals of the TD type decomposes as a free one in the liquid phase. On the other hand, each molecule of powdery chemicals of the TD type decomposes while it remains fixed within the 'cage' composed of the surrounding crystal lattice in the solid phase. Therefore, once innumerable molecules decompose almost simultaneously throughout each individual crystal, it appears that the whole sample collapses in a moment to form fine particles or gaseous products, with the result that this phenomenon is recorded as an explosively decomposing process of the sample in thermogravimetry, as shown in Fig. 8.

Both liquid and powdery chemicals of the TD type are, however, the same to the effect that their exothermic decomposition reactions are accompanied with no phase transition. Therefore, when charged in the open-cup cell, or confined in the closed cell, in accordance with the self-heating property of the chemical, and subjected to the adiabatic self-heating test started from a T_s, 2 cm^3 each of a liquid chemical, or a powdery chemical, of the TD type continues to self-heat over the T_s at a very slow, but virtually constant, rate depending on the value of T_s in accordance with the Arrhenius equation, after its having been warmed up to the T_s.

This is the reason why either the Semenov equation or the F-K equation is applied to calculate the T_c of a chemical of the TD type.

In the last analysis, self-heating chemicals are classified into the two large groups, the TD and the AC type, but in fact they are subdivided into the following four groups in all, in accordance with the difference in the self-heating process which, when subjected to the adiabatic self-heating test started from a T_s, 2 cm^3 each of them each show, or, in accordance with the difference in the characteristic temperature, *i.e.*, the T_c or the SADT, to express each individual thermal instability, as presented in Table 3.

Apart from powdery high explosives of the true AC type, chemicals which are powdery at room temperature are classified into the following three groups in accordance with the difference in the self-heating process, in the early stages, which, when subjected to the adiabatic self-heating test started from a T_s, 2 cm^3 each of them each show.

Group Ⅰ. Powdery chemicals to each of which the Semenov equation is applied to calculate the T_c. When charged in the open-cup cell, or confined in the closed cell, in accordance with the self-heating property of the chemical, and subjected to the adiabatic self-heating test started from a T_s, 2 cm^3 of a powdery chemical of this group melts at once, when the T_s is above the melting point of the chemical. The resultant liquefied chemical warms up to the T_s within tens of minutes; thereafter, it continues to self-heat over the T_s at a very slow, but virtually constant, rate depending on the value of T_s in accordance with the Arrhenius equation (Fig. 15) [23].

Group Ⅱ. Powdery chemicals to each of which the F-K equation is applied to calculate the T_c. When charged in the open-cup cell, or confined in the closed cell, in accordance with the self-heating property of the chemical, and subjected to the adiabatic self-heating test started from a T_s, 2 cm^3 of a powdery chemical of this group warms up to the T_s within tens of minutes; thereafter, it continues to self-heat over the T_s as a powder at a very slow, but virtually constant, rate depending on the value of T_s in accordance with the Arrhenius equation (Fig. 15) [24].

Table 3
A classification of self-heating chemicals.

Class	Type	*A chemical which is powdery at room temperature*		The characteristic temperature to express the thermal instability (The T_c or the SADT)
Self-heating chemicals	The TD type	self-heats as a liquid after melting.	*A chemica which is liquid or dissolved at room temperature*	The T_c is calculated by applying the Semenov equation.
		self-heats as a powdery chemical.		The T_c is calculated by applying the F-K equation.
	The AC type	*A powdery chemical of the quasi-AC type*		The SADT is calculated by performing the isothermal storage test.
		A liquid, gelatinous, powdery or solid high explosive of the true AC type		The SADT is calculated by performing the isothermal storage test.

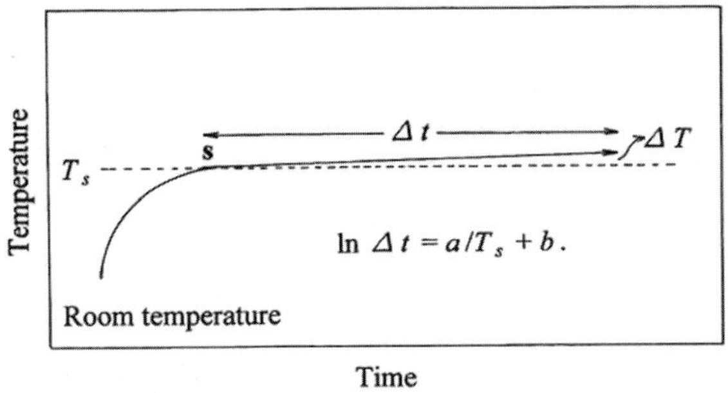

Figure 15. The self-heating process, of 2 cm^3 of a chemical of the TD type charged in the open-cup cell, or confined in the closed cell, in accordance with the self-heating property of the chemical, and subjected to the adiabatic self-heating test started from a T_s, recorded for the time, Δt, required for the temperature of the chemical to increase by the definite value of ΔT of 1.25 K from the T_s.

Group Ⅲ. Powdery chemicals to each of which neither of the two equations of the thermal explosion theory can be applied to calculate the T_c. When confined in the closed cell and subjected to the adiabatic self-heating test started from a T_s, 2 cm^3 of a powdery chemical of this group warms slowly up to the T_s, but the temperature remains near the T_s until the chemical has finished melting. Once, however, the chemical finishes melting in the course of time, an apparently sudden quasi-autocatalytic reaction of the resultant liquefied chemical starts [25].

As explained already, with the exception of powdery high explosives of the true AC type, powdery chemicals of Group Ⅰ, powdery chemicals of Group Ⅱ and chemicals which are liquid themselves or dissolved in any solvents at room temperature are said to be of the TD type, and, powdery chemicals of Group Ⅲ are said to be of the quasi-AC type.

In this connection, the classification, above referred to, of self-heating chemicals into the TD type and the AC type may be compared with the classification, performed by Frank-Kamenetskii, of the combustion into the thermal combustion and the autocatalytic combustion [26].

The self-heating process, of 2 cm^3 of a chemical of the TD type charged in the open-cup cell, or confined in the closed cell, in accordance with the self-heating property of the chemical, and subjected to the adiabatic self-heating test started from a T_s, recorded for the time, Δt, required for the temperature of the chemical to increase by the definite value of ΔT of 1.25 K from the T_s, is shown in Fig. 15. The adiabatic control and the record of the self-heating process, in the early stages, of 2 cm^3 of the chemical are started at the point of time "**s**" in Fig. 15, respectively. The higher the T_s, the shorter becomes the time required for the temperature of the chemical to increase by the definite value of ΔT K from the T_s, and *vice versa*.

Under such circumstances, an empirical formula, *i.e.*, Eq. (44) derived in **Section 2.4**, holds between the T_s K and the time, Δt min, as presented in Fig. 15. Eq. (44) is re-presented below for convenience' sake.

$$\ln \Delta t = \frac{a}{T_s} + b, \tag{44}$$

where a and b are a coefficient, respectively. The original structure of Eq. (44) is derived as the adiabatic temperature increase equation, *i.e.*, Eq. (43), in **Section 2.4**.

As stated in **Preface** and in **Section 2.4**, the values of the two coefficients, a and b, of Eq. (44) holding for the self-heating process, or for the oxidatively-heating process, in the early stages, of 2 cm^3 of a chemical of the TD type, including every gas-permeable oxidatively-heating substance, charged, or confined, in some one of the open-cup, the draft or the closed cell, in accordance with the self-heating property of the chemical, and subjected to either of the two kinds of adiabatic tests, are used as the heat generation data of the chemical, together with the heat transfer data, to calculate the T_c for the chemical, having an arbitrary shape and an arbitrary size, placed in the atmosphere under isothermal conditions, by applying the reduced form of the Semenov equation, or that of the F-K equation, expressed in terms of both the heat generation data and the heat transfer data [23, 24 and 27]. Adiabatic conditions are required to make Eq. (44) valid. It thus follows that it is an adiabatic self-heating process recorder, and not an isothermal storage testing device that is indispensable in order to calculate the T_c for a chemical of the TD type, including every gas-permeable oxidatively-heating substance, having an arbitrary shape and an arbitrary size, placed in the atmosphere under isothermal conditions.

In this connection, the linear approximation of the self-heating process or curve, in the early stages, of 2 cm^3 of a chemical of the TD type charged in the open-cup cell, or confined in the closed cell, in accordance with the self-heating property of the chemical, and subjected to the adiabatic self-heating test started from a T_s, which is shown in Fig. 4 presented in **Section 2.5**, applies to the self-heating process or curve recorded immediately after the point of time "**s**" in Fig. 15.

The self-heating process of a powdery chemical of the quasi-AC type confined in the closed cell and subjected to the isothermal storage test performed at a T_t on the high temperature side, which is presented in Fig. 7, is in fact somewhat exaggerated. It is observed, in general, that the rate of drop in temperature caused by melting of a powdery chemical of the quasi-AC type increases as the melting proceeds. Such a melting process of a powdery chemical of the quasi-AC type as described above suggests evidently that the melting proceeds apparently in accordance with the heterogeneous reaction kinetics. That is, the melting proceeds at the surface of separation between the liquid and the solid phases, and, the rate of melting increases in proportion to the surface area, which in turn increases as the melting progresses.

In any event, when confined in the closed cell and subjected to the isothermal storage test performed at a T_t on the high temperature side, such an induction period of the quasi-autocatalytic reaction as shown in Fig. 7 is recorded for 2 cm^3 of a powdery chemical of the quasi-AC type. In the meantime, the start of the quasi-autocatalytic reaction of the chemical is so evident that it is easy to locate the exothermic onset point, *i.e.*, the position of the point of time "**b**", on the chart of the strip-chart recorder.

On the other hand, when confined in the closed cell and subjected to the isothermal storage test performed at a T_t on the low temperature side, the time interval up to the start of the quasi-autocatalytic reaction occurring simultaneously with the finish of melting of 2 cm^3 of a powdery chemical of the quasi-AC type becomes naturally far longer, and the temperature decrement caused by melting also becomes of the order of 0.1 ~ 0.2 K only. In the meantime, the rate of increase in temperature of the chemical after the start of the quasi-autocatalytic reaction also becomes so slow, as shown in Fig. 16, that it becomes somewhat uncertain to locate the point of time "**b**" on the chart of the strip-chart recorder (see Fig. 143 in **Subsection 10.2.5**, as an example). The same is true of the induction period of the autocatalytic reaction of a high explosive of the true AC type (see Fig. 125 in **Subsection 9.3.5**, as an example).

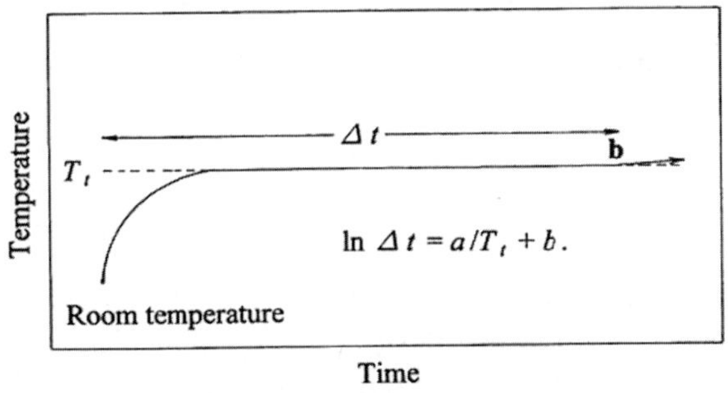

Figure 16. The induction period, of the quasi-autocatalytic reaction, of 2 cm^3 of a powdery chemical of the quasi-AC type confined in the closed cell and subjected to the isothermal storage test performed at a T_t on the low temperature side, recorded for the time, Δt, from the insertion of the cell into the isothermal storage testing device till the start of the quasi-autocatalytic reaction occurring simultaneously with the finish of melting of the chemical at the T_t.

3.5 The difference between the concept of the T_c and that of the SADT

The concept of the T_c and that of the SADT are not necessarily distinguished clearly from each other at the present time.

The concept of the T_c fits only the self-heating process or behavior, in the early stages, of a chemical of the TD type, including every gas-permeable oxidatively-heating substance, having an arbitrary shape and an arbitrary size, placed in the atmosphere under isothermal conditions. The T_c, in each of the two equations of the thermal explosion theory, defines such a temperature as, when a chemical of the TD type, including every gas-permeable oxidatively-heating substance, having an arbitrary shape and an arbitrary size, is placed in the atmosphere maintained at the T_c, the chemical, the temperature of which has been maintained at room temperature until the placement, continues to self-heat over the T_c, and, when the chemical as a whole has self-heated up to a temperature* at the critical state for the thermal explosion which exists at the end of the early stages of the self-heating process, the rate of heat generation in the chemical becomes equal to the rate of heat transfer from the chemical to the atmosphere. When the chemical is placed in the atmosphere maintained at a T_a higher than the T_c, the rate of heat generation in the chemical exceeds the rate of heat transfer from the chemical to the atmosphere throughout the whole self-heating process up to the thermal explosion, with the result that the temperature of the chemical continues to increase acceleratedly to cause the ultimate thermal explosion of the chemical sooner or later.

Both the Semenov and the F-K equation include the variables with regard to space, such as r, δ_c, S or V. In other words, the T_c for a chemical of the TD type, including every gas-permeable oxidatively-heating substance, depends on its shape and size, because the heat-accumulation condition in the chemical or the rate of heat transfer from the chemical to the atmosphere depends on the ratio of surface area to volume. Both equations, however, include no variable with regard to time. For instance, although it is possible to calculate a value of T_c for 400 cm^3 of an organic liquid peroxide, which is charged in a 500 cm^3 Dewar flask used in the BAM (Bundesanstalt für Materialforschung und -prüfung, Berlin) heat-accumulation storage test** and is placed in the atmosphere under isothermal conditions, by applying the Semenov equation [23],*** no information regarding the time, from the placement of the Dewar flask in the BAM heat-accumulation storage testing device maintained at the T_c till the thermal explosion of the peroxide, accompanies the T_c.

On the other hand, the time, Δt, including that corresponding to the SADT, *i.e.*, 10,080 min, from the placement of an arbitrary closed container, in which a

---

* This is a temperature corresponding to T_1 in Fig. 2 in **Section 1.2**.

** For further details of the BAM heat-accumulation storage test, refer to **Subsection 5.5.2**.

*** A value of T_c, for a chemical of the TD type, measured by the BAM heat-accumulation storage test is referred to as the value of the BAM test for the chemical herein.

chemical having the corresponding shape and size is confined, in the atmosphere maintained at a T_t till the start of the autocatalytic reaction, or of the quasi-autocatalytic reaction, of the chemical can be calculated only for a chemical of the AC type, including every powdery chemical of the quasi-AC type, as the function of T_t in accordance with Eq. (59) holding for the induction period of the autocatalytic reaction, or of the quasi-autocatalytic reaction, of 2 cm^3 of the chemical confined in the closed cell and subjected to the isothermal storage test.

In other words, the concept of the SADT is in harmony only with the induction period of the autocatalytic reaction, or of the quasi-autocatalytic reaction, of 2 cm^3 of a chemical of the AC type, including every powdery chemical of the quasi-AC type, confined in the closed cell and subjected to the isothermal storage test.

The similarity between the T_c and the SADT is, however, as follows: according to the experience of a company, where a series of the BAM tests were each performed actually for some dozens of organic peroxides [23], the time required for each peroxide to explode thermally at its value of the BAM test was 1~2 d in most cases, or 3 d at the longest; however, no matter how long the test was allowed to continue for each peroxide at temperatures below its value of the BAM test, no peroxide exploded thermally; on the other hand, it has been ascertained throughout a series of isothermal storage tests, which were each performed for powdery chemicals of the quasi-AC type, and, details of which are described in **Chapter 10**, that, when confined in the closed cell and subjected to the isothermal storage test performed at a T_t, on the high temperature side, corresponding to a value of Δt of 1~2 d in Eq. (59) holding for the induction period of the quasi-autocatalytic reaction of 2 cm^3 of a powdery chemical of the quasi-AC type confined in the closed cell and subjected to the isothermal storage test, 2 cm^3 of the chemical starts the quasi-autocatalytic reaction so rapidly and forcefully as to explode with certainty; in the meantime, when confined in the closed cell and subjected to the isothermal storage test performed at a T_t, on the low temperature side, corresponding to a value of Δt of 5~7 d in Eq. (59), 2 cm^3 of the chemical starts the quasi-autocatalytic reaction so slowly and faintly as to explode hardly.

References to Chapter 3

[22] D. I. Townsend, H. D. Ferguson and H. T. Kohlbrand, Application of ARC Thermokinetic Data to the Design of Safety Schemes for Industrial Reactions, Proceedings of the AIChE 28th Annual Loss Prevention Symposium, Atlanta, Georgia, 1994, AIChE, New York, Paper No. 9a, 4 (1994).
[23] T. Kotoyori, Critical Temperatures for the Thermal Explosion of Liquid Organic Peroxides, Process Safety Progress, **14**, 37-44 (1995).
[24] T. Kotoyori, Critical Ignition Temperatures of Chemical Substances, J. Loss Prevention in the Process Industries, **2**, 16-21 (1989).
[25] T. Kotoyori, The SADT of Solids of the Quasi-Autocatalytic Decomposition Type, J. Hazardous Materials, **A 64**, 1-19 (1999).
[26] D. A. Frank-Kamenetskii, Diffusion and Heat Transfer in Chemical Kinetics, 2nd Ed., Translated from Russian by J. P. Appleton, Plenum Press, New York-London, 301 (1969).
[27] T. Kotoyori, Critical Ignition Temperatures of Wood Sawdusts, Proceedings of the 1st International Symposium on Fire Safety Science, Gaithersburg, Maryland, 1985, Hemisphere Publishing Corporation, Washington D.C., 463-471 (1985).

Chapter 4 An adiabatic self-heating process recorder

4.1 Introduction

In order to calculate the T_c for a chemical of the TD type, including every gas-permeable oxidatively-heating substance, having an arbitrary shape and an arbitrary size, placed in the atmosphere under isothermal conditions, it is required to determine both the heat generation data and the heat transfer data of the chemical in the early stages of the self-heating process, respectively.

As explained in detail in **Section 2.4**, to determine the former data, *i.e.*, the heat generation data of a chemical of the TD type, is nothing else but to calculate the values of the two coefficients, *a* and *b*, of the empirical formula, ln $\Delta t = a/T_s + b$, *i.e.*, Eq. (44), holding for the self-heating process, or for the oxidatively-heating process, in the early stages, of 2 cm^3 of the chemical charged, or confined, in some one of the open-cup, the draft or the closed cell, in accordance with the self-heating property of the chemical, and subjected to the adiabatic self-heating test, or to the adiabatic oxidatively-heating test.

In the present chapter, an adiabatic self-heating process recorder is explained in detail. This recorder is used to perform the adiabatic self-heating test, or the adiabatic oxidatively-heating test, which is started from a T_s, for 2 cm^3 of a chemical of the TD type, charged, or confined, in some one of the four kinds of cells,* *i.e.*, the open-cup, the draft, the touch-flow or the closed cell, in accordance with the self-heating property of the chemical, for the time, Δt, required for the temperature of the chemical to increase by the definite value of ΔT of 1.25 K from the T_s in the adiabatic self-heating test, or from the corresponding standard temperature in the adiabatic oxidatively-heating test (Fig. 17) [28].

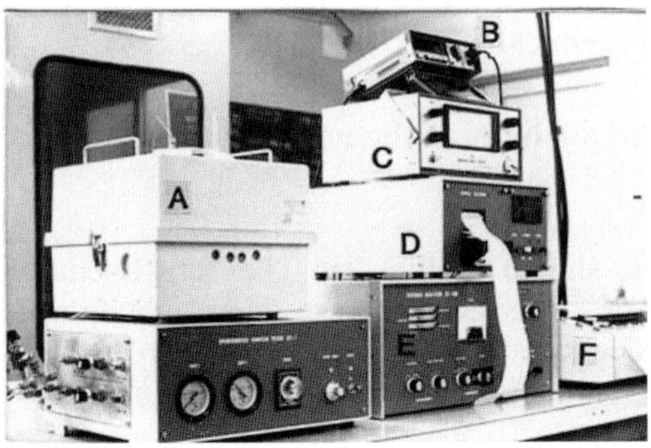

Figure 17. Overall view of an adiabatic self-heating process recorder.

A. Air bath; **B**. Digital D.C. microvoltmeter; **C**. Analog D.C. microvoltmeter used for the zero-suppression procedure; **D**. Digital D.C. millivolt recorder; **E**. Control unit; **F**. Two-pen strip-chart recorder.

* Not the three kinds of cells! For further details, refer to **Subsection 4.2.2**.

Is then explained in detail, in **Section 4.7** at the end of the present chapter, the procedure to calculate the heat generation data of a chemical of the TD type, including every gas-permeable oxidatively-heating substance, by applying the regression analysis to several combinations of the value of $\ln \Delta t$ with that of $1/T_s$, which each are determined, based on several digital records obtained each from several adiabatic self-heating tests, or from several adiabatic oxidatively-heating tests, which are started from each T_s with mutual intervals of 1∼2 K, performed each, for 2 cm^3 each of several samples of the chemical charged, or confined, each in some one of the open-cup, the draft or the closed cell, in accordance with the self-heating property of the chemical, for the time, Δt, required for the temperature of each sample of the chemical to increase by the definite value of ΔT of 1.25 K from the corresponding T_s in the adiabatic self-heating test, or from the corresponding standard temperature in the adiabatic oxidatively-heating test, by taking the procedure to calculate the heat generation data of 99 % *tert*-butyl peroxybenzoate (TBPB) as an example.

In brief, the adiabatic self-heating process recorder is exclusively used to perform the adiabatic self-heating test, or the adiabatic oxidatively-heating test, in order to calculate ultimately the heat generation data of a chemical of the TD type, including every gas-permeable oxidatively-heating substance, although it is also possible to perform the adiabatic self-heating test for 2 cm^3 of a chemical of the AC type, including every powdery chemical of the quasi-AC type, confined in the closed cell by means of the recorder.*

On the other hand, as mentioned in **Preface**, and as detailed in **Chapters 9** and **10**, an isothermal storage testing device is exclusively used to perform the isothermal storage test at a T_t, in order to calculate ultimately the SADT for a chemical of the AC type, including every powdery chemical of the quasi-AC type, having an arbitrary shape and an arbitrary size, confined in an arbitrary closed container of the corresponding shape and size, and placed in the atmosphere under isothermal conditions, for 2 cm^3 of the chemical confined in the closed cell, for the time, Δt, from the insertion of the cell into the isothermal storage testing device till the start of the autocatalytic reaction, or of the quasi-autocatalytic reaction, of the chemical at the T_t.

4.2 Structure and performance of the air bath of the adiabatic self-heating process recorder

The cross section of the air bath is shown in Fig. 18. The cell assembly including a draft cell is drawn in this cross section, because this was drawn in the early stages of a series of studies described herein, when a series of studies concerning gas-permeable oxidatively-heating substances were predominantly

---

* A mention relevant to this possibility is made in **Subsection 9.2.2**.

performed by means of the draft cell in the adiabatic oxidatively-heating test (refer to **Section 7.2** as well as **Subsection 4.2.2**).

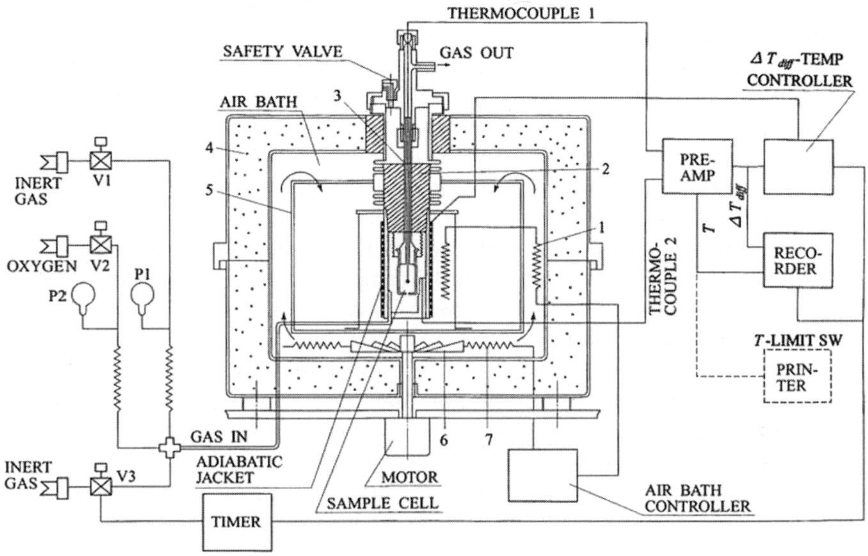

Figure 18. Cross section of the air bath of the adiabatic self-heating process recorder. **1**. Resistance thermometer; **2**. Glass wool; **3**. Glass vent tube; **4**. Glass wool; **5**. Wind guide plate; **6**. Fan; **7**. Heater.

4.2.1 Design philosophy

(1) The PID-SCR temperature control technique* is adopted for the adiabatic control. Besides, other devices are also adopted to attain as complete an adiabatic control as possible. To cite an instance, a pre-amplifier is incorporated before the PID controller to amplify the ΔT_{diff}, *i.e.*, the temperature difference between the temperature of 2 cm^3 of a chemical of the TD type, including every gas-permeable oxidatively-heating substance, and the T_{atm}. A zero suppression circuit is composed of this amplifier to cancel the slight stray-, or pseudo-, thermoelectromotive force of the differential thermocouple. Such a pseudo-thermoelectromotive force of a differential thermocouple may still appear even if the temperature of 2 cm^3 of the chemical and the T_{atm} are physically the same, and even if the two thermocouples to make up the differential thermocouple are

* A temperature control technique utilizing the SCR (silicone-controlled rectifier) which operates by means of the P (proportional), I (integral) and D (differential) control circuits..

so selected that their thermoelectromotive forces may be almost the same as each other in the range of room temperature to 200 ℃. Further, a cold junction utilizing the thermoelectric refrigeration in order to maintain the refrigerant at 0 ℃ is adopted in place of the room temperature-compensating circuit. Ultimately an adiabatic control of the order of ±0.2 μV in the case of the Type K, CA (chromel-alumel), thermocouple, which corresponds to ±0.005 K, has been achieved in the early stages of the self-heating process of a chemical of the TD type, including every gas-permeable oxidatively-heating substance. The minimum detectable rate of increase in temperature of a chemical of the TD type, including every gas-permeable oxidatively-heating substance, by means of the recorder is less than 1 μV/h, *i.e.*, less than about 0.025 K/h.*

(2) The adiabatic control is performed between the temperature of 2 cm^3 of the chemical and the T_{atm}, not between the temperature of 2 cm^3 of the chemical and that of the inside wall of the adiabatic jacket, in order to hold the chemical under true adiabatic conditions.

(3) An air bath is adopted instead of a liquid bath, considering that the heat capacity of the former is much smaller than that of the latter. That the heat capacity of the bath is small means that it is possible to heat the atmosphere in the adiabatic jacket, which is set in the air bath, at a rate high enough to follow a rapid increase in temperature of 2 cm^3 of a chemical of the TD type, including every gas-permeable oxidatively-heating substance, in the two kinds of adiabatic tests.

4.2.2 The cell assembly and the adiabatic jacket

Three kinds of Pyrex glass open cells, *i.e.*, the open-cup cell, the draft cell and the touch-flow cell, as well as one kind of Pyrex glass closed cell, which each have a capacity of about 2 cm^3, are available for the adiabatic self-heating process recorder. The three kinds of glass open cells are shown in Fig. 19.

In the open-cup cell, air is not allowed to flow through a chemical charged in the cell; this cell is, therefore, not used in the adiabatic oxidatively-heating test, but used only in the adiabatic self-heating test performed for a non-volatile liquid or powdery chemical of the TD type at atmospheric pressure. In the draft cell, a gas is allowed to flow through a chemical charged in the cell from a hole at the center of the base of the cell to the glass vent tube; this cell is, therefore, appropriate for the adiabatic oxidatively-heating test performed for gas-permeable oxidatively-heating substances, such as relatively coarse powders or oil-soaked fibers. In the touch-flow cell, a gas is allowed to flow from a hole in the side wall of the cell to the glass vent tube, sweeping over the surface of a

---

* An increment in thermoelectromotive force of 1 μV corresponds to temperature increments of 0.025 K in the case of the CA thermocouple. A footnote relevant to this thermoelectromotive force is given in **Subsection 4.5.8** as well.

chemical charged in the cell; this cell is, therefore, appropriate for the adiabatic oxidatively-heating test performed for gastight oxidatively-heating substances, such as very fine powders* or viscous substances. The touch-flow cell is, however, not fit to measure the heat generation data required to calculate the T_c for a gastight oxidatively-heating substance, because it is not necessarily ensured to cause the homogeneous oxidatively-heating reaction to take place in such a substance, as specified above, charged in the touch-flow cell. The touch-flow cell is, therefore, used only to examine approximately the oxidatively-heating property of such a substance as specified above. In the three kinds of open cells, the space in each cell leads through the glass vent tube to the atmosphere outside the air bath. That is, a chemical charged in each of the open cells is held at atmospheric pressure while tested.

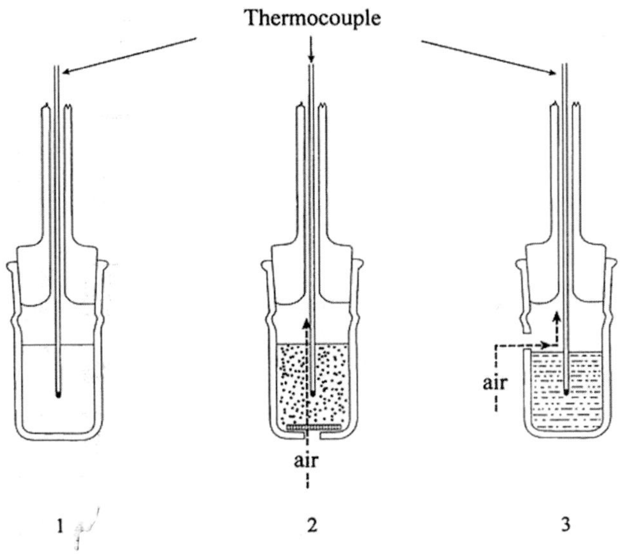

Figure 19. The three kinds of glass open cells.
1. Open-cup cell; **2**. Draft cell; **3**. Touch-flow cell.

On the other hand, the glass closed cell is indispensable in the adiabatic self-heating test performed for a chemical of the TD type that is volatile or decomposes to evolve corrosive and/or toxic gases while tested (Fig. 20).

* A matter concerning this is described in a footnote in **Subsection 8.2.1**.

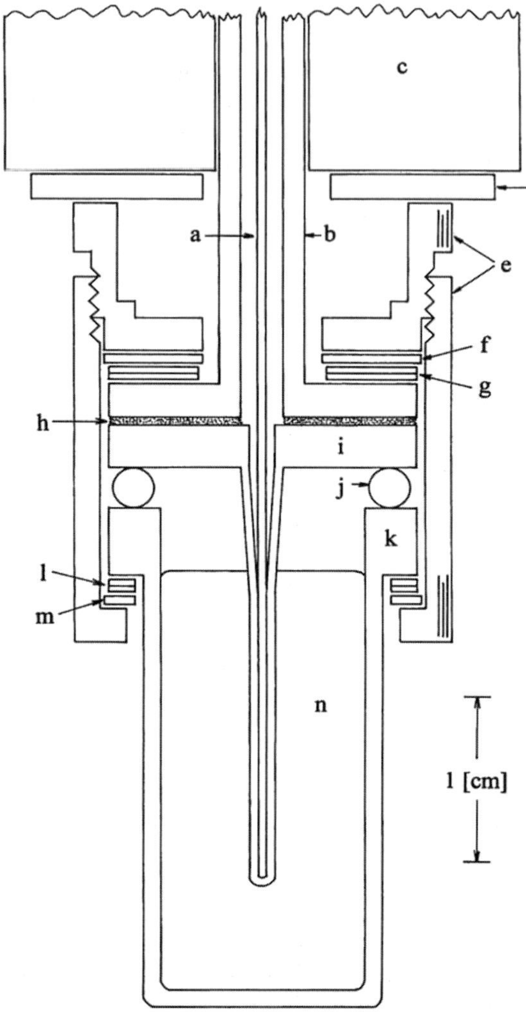

Figure 20. The cell assembly including the glass closed cell.

a. Stainless steel-sheathed CA thermocouple, 0.5 mm in outside diameter; **b**. Glass flange tube; **c**. Glass wool; **d**. Aluminium round plate; **e**. Cap nut; **f**. Stainless steel washer, 1 mm in thickness; **g**. Two PTFE washers, 0.3 mm each in thickness; **h**. Inorganic adhesive agent; **i**. Glass capillary flange containing the thermocouple to measure the T_{ref} or the temperature of a self-heating chemical; **j**. O-ring; **k**. Closed cell; **l**. Two PTFE washers, 0.3 mm each in thickness; **m**. Stainless steel washer, 1 mm in thickness; **n**. Reference material or self-heating chemical.

The closed cell itself and the cell assembly including the closed cell are explained exclusively in the present chapter. The structure and the characteristics of the closed cell are described in **Section 4.4**. The experimental procedure by means of the closed cell is described in **Section 4.5**.

At all events, the cell assembly including some one of the open-cup, the draft, the touch-flow or the closed cell, in which 2 cm^3 of a chemical of the TD type, including every gas-permeable oxidatively-heating substance, is charged, or confined, in accordance with the self-heating property of the chemical, is inserted ultimately into the adiabatic jacket, which in turn is set in the air bath of the adiabatic self-heating process recorder, in order to perform the adiabatic self-heating test, or the adiabatic oxidatively-heating test, for the chemical.

The structure of the adiabatic jacket is shown in Fig. 74 in **Section 7.2**, in particular, in connection with the performance of the adiabatic oxidatively-heating test.

The jacket is a nickel cylinder with a horizontal base plate. The outside surface of the jacket is coated with thin ceramics for insulation. The coated cylinder is wound with the Kanthal[*] wire, 0.6 mm in diameter, 4.5 m in length, which is then covered and fixed with the beryllia cement[**]. The rated output of the heater is 300 W. The heater is able to heat the atmosphere in the jacket at the maximum heating rate of 20 K/min in order that the condition, $\Delta T_{diff} = T - T_{atm} = 0$, may always hold,[***] while the adiabatic control is performed for the self-heating process, or for the oxidatively-heating process, in the early stages, of a chemical of the TD type, including every gas-permeable oxidatively-heating substance. The space between the inside wall of the jacket and the glass flange tube, or the glass vent tube, is filled with glass wool to shut off the heat loss from the space around the sample cell. It is ascertained that the temperature distribution in the space within 2 cm above and below the cell is less than $\pm$ 0.05 K while the adiabatic control is performed.

4.2.3 Gas supplying system

This system is originally equipped in order to perform the adiabatic oxidatively-heating test. That is, this system is used to examine the effect of an oxidizing gas, such as air or oxygen gas, at atmospheric pressure on the oxidatively-heating process, in the early stages, of 2 cm^3 of a chemical of the TD type, including every oxidatively-heating substance, charged in the draft cell, or in the touch-flow cell, in the adiabatic oxidatively-heating test. On the other hand, the adiabatic self-heating test is performed for a chemical of the TD

---

[*] The trade name of the material for the heating wire manufactured by Kanthal Corporation in Sweden. This material is in particular excellent in heat resistance..

[**] It is known that beryllia has a value of λ larger than any other metal oxide..

[***] For this condition, refer to **Subsections 4.5.4** and **4.5.7**.

type charged in the open-cup cell, or confined in the closed cell. Details of the gas supplying system are thus given in **Subsection 7.2.1**.

4.2.4 Temperature measuring system

One thermocouple, which, as shown in Fig. 20, is contained in the glass capillary tube projecting downward from the under surface of the glass capillary flange, is inserted axially to the longitudinal center of 2 cm^3 of a reference material, or of 2 cm^3 of a chemical of the TD type, confined in the closed cell to measure the T_{ref} or the temperature of the chemical. The other thermocouple to measure the T_{atm} is inserted from the base plate of the adiabatic jacket into a thin nickel tube, which in turn penetrates vertically the base plate. The nickel tube is fixed about 1 mm apart from the inside wall of the adiabatic jacket in order that the thermocouple may detect the true T_{atm} around the reference cell, or around the sample cell, as stated in **(2)** of **Subsection 4.2.1**. The points of the two thermocouples are held on the same horizontal plane. A differential thermocouple is then composed of the two. The thermocouples used are Philips stainless steel-sheathed CA thermocouples, 0.5 mm in outside diameter each, and are so selected that their thermoelectromotive forces may be almost the same as each other in the range of room temperature to 200 ℃ in order that they may be appropriate for the adiabatic control, as stated in **(1)** of **Subsection 4.2.1**.

4.2.5 Performance of the adiabatic control

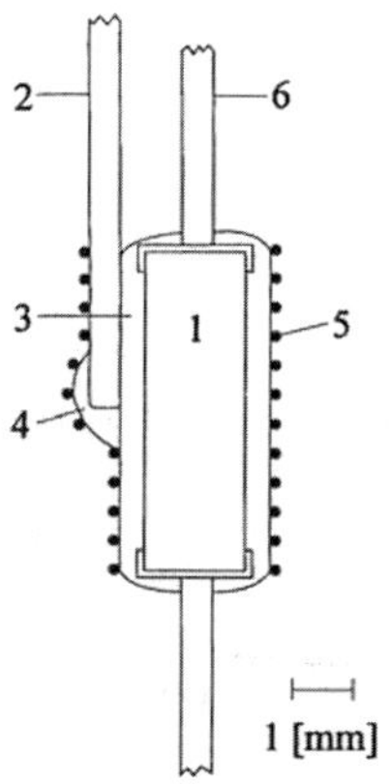

Figure 21. The resistor-thermocouple composite, in place of 2 cm^3 of a chemical of the TD type, set in the glass draft cell and subjected to the adiabatic self-heating test started from a T_s near 60 ℃ under static conditions.

1. Heating wire; **2**. Stainless steel-sheathed CA thermocouple, 0.5 mm in outside diameter; **3**. Epoxide resin; **4**. Adhesive agent; 5. Sewing cotton; **6**. Leading-in wire.

Several self-heating processes, in the early stages, of 2 cm^3 of a chemical of the TD type, including every oxidatively-heating substance, have been simulated by generating the electric heat at several rates, by means of a constant voltage D.C. power source, in a resistor-thermocouple composite, in place of 2 cm^3 of the chemical, set in the glass draft cell and subjected to the adiabatic self-heating test started from a T_s near 60 ℃ under static conditions, *i.e.*, under conditions of no gas flowing through the cell (Figs. 21 and 22). The rated value and the size of the resistor are 10 Ω, 2.5 mm in diameter, 6 mm in length, respectively.

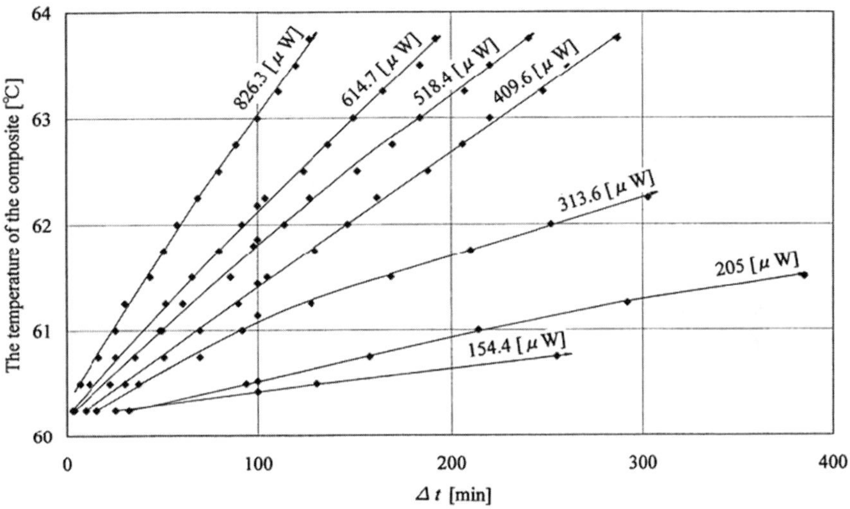

Figure 22. Dependence of the rate of increase in temperature of the resistor-thermocouple composite set in the draft cell and subjected to the adiabatic self-heating test started from a T_s near 60 ℃ under static conditions on the rate of electric heat generation, Q_{elec} μW.

It has been ascertained, in result, that, as the temperature rises away from the T_s at each rate of electric heat generation, the rate of increase in temperature of the composite decreases gradually; and, although the electric heat is generated under adiabatic conditions, the temperature comes to cease to increase midway at the rates of electric heat generation less than 150 μW (Fig. 22). It has also been observed, besides, that the time from the start of the power supply to the resistor till the detection, by means of the thermocouple, of the actual heating of the resistor-thermocouple composite becomes gradually longer with decreasing the value of Q_{elec}. The latter phenomenon is probably effected by the heat capacity of the composite.

It has also been ascertained, however, that the temperature increases almost linearly with time during about 100 min after the actual heating of the composite has been detected by means of the thermocouple at each rate of electric heat generation. Therefore, the increment in temperature, ΔT K, by which the temperature of the composite increases from the T_s 100 min after the actual heating of the composite has been detected by means of the thermocouple at each rate of electric heat generation, has been plotted against the rate of electric heat generation, Q_{elec} μW (Fig. 23).

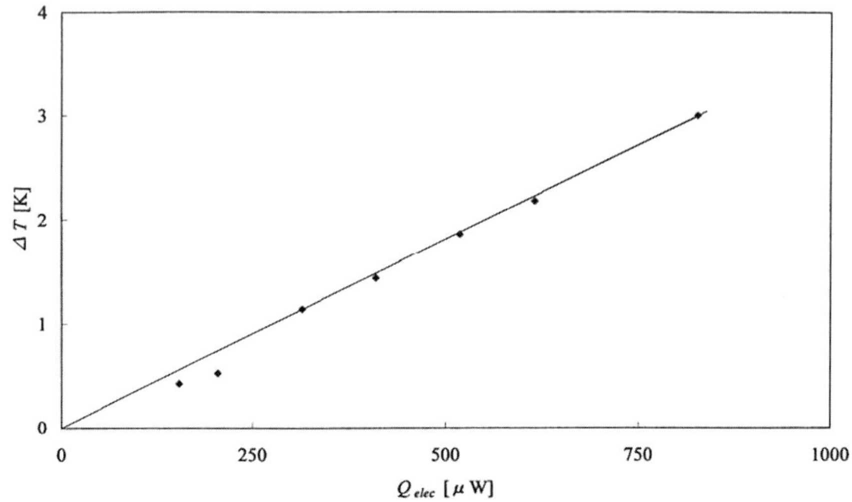

Figure 23. The plot of the increment in temperature, ΔT K, by which the temperature of the composite increases from the T_s 100 min after the actual heating of the composite has been detected by means of the thermocouple at each rate of electric heat generation, versus, the rate of electric heat generation, Q_{elec} μW. Data used are in common with those plotted in Fig. 22.

A good proportionality is seen to hold between ΔT and Q_{elec} in Fig. 23. The plot passes through the origin. It is inferred, therefore, that the self-heating process, or the oxidatively-heating process, in temperature ranges of 2～3 K immediately above a T_s, of 2 cm^3 of a chemical of the TD type, including every gas-permeable oxidatively-heating substance, charged, or confined, in some one of the open-cup, the draft or the closed cell, in accordance with the self-heating property of the chemical, and subjected to either of the two kinds of adiabatic tests started each from the T_s in the adiabatic self-heating process recorder is recorded under almost perfectly adiabatic conditions.

On the other hand, it is apparent to us in Fig. 22 that, as the temperature of the composite rises away from the T_s at each rate of electric heat generation, the adiabatic control becomes gradually broken. As stated in **Subsection 4.4.6**, the glass closed cell used in the recorder is not perfectly explosion-proof besides. Therefore, the adiabatic self-heating process recorder is not appropriate for the record of the whole self-heating process up to the thermal explosion of 2 cm^3 of a chemical of the TD type, including every gas-permeable oxidatively-heating substance, placed under adiabatic conditions.

The two points above referred to are considered to be the characteristics of the recorder.

In this connection, it is impossible to record precisely, with the two-pen strip-chart recorder only, the very slowly self-heating process, or the very slowly oxidatively-heating process, in temperature ranges of 2～3 K immediately above a T_s, of 2 cm^3 of a chemical of the TD type, including every gas-permeable oxidatively-heating substance, subjected to either of the two kinds of adiabatic tests. It becomes possible to record it, however, only when the digital D.C. microvoltmeter, the digital output of which is read to 1 μV, and the digital D.C. millivolt recorder, the digital output of which is recorded to 10 μV, are used together.

As stated in **Preface**, for the purpose of calculating the T_c for a chemical of the TD type, including every gas-permeable oxidatively-heating substance, having an arbitrary shape and an arbitrary size, placed in the atmosphere under isothermal conditions, we have only to perform, apart from the measurement of the heat transfer data of the chemical, several adiabatic self-heating tests, or several adiabatic oxidatively-heating tests, which are started from each T_s with mutual intervals of 1～2 K, in order to calculate the heat generation data of the chemical, for 2 cm^3 each of several samples of the chemical charged, or confined, each in some one of the open-cup, the draft or the closed cell, in accordance with the self-heating property of the chemical, for the time, Δt, required for the temperature of each sample of the chemical to increase by the definite value of ΔT of 1.25 K from the corresponding T_s in the adiabatic self-heating test, or from the corresponding standard temperature in the adiabatic oxidatively-heating test, respectively.

The adiabatic self-heating process recorder, by means of which it is possible to calculate easily, simply and with certainty the heat generation data of a chemical of the TD type, including every gas-permeable oxidatively-heating substance, is, therefore, sufficiently useful, so far as our purpose is to calculate the T_c for a chemical of the TD type, including every gas-permeable oxidatively-heating substance, having an arbitrary shape and an arbitrary size, placed in the atmosphere under isothermal conditions.

It is, however, evident that this recorder requires still considerable improvements, in particular, regarding the performance of the adiabatic control.

Incidentally, plots shown in Figs. 22 or 23 may give us a clue to determine, by experimental measurements, the value of ΔH which a chemical of the TD type, including every gas-permeable oxidatively-heating substance, generates in the early stages of the self-heating process, or of the oxidatively-heating process, accompanied with the formation of some transient and unstable intermediate.

4.3 Development of the glass closed cell

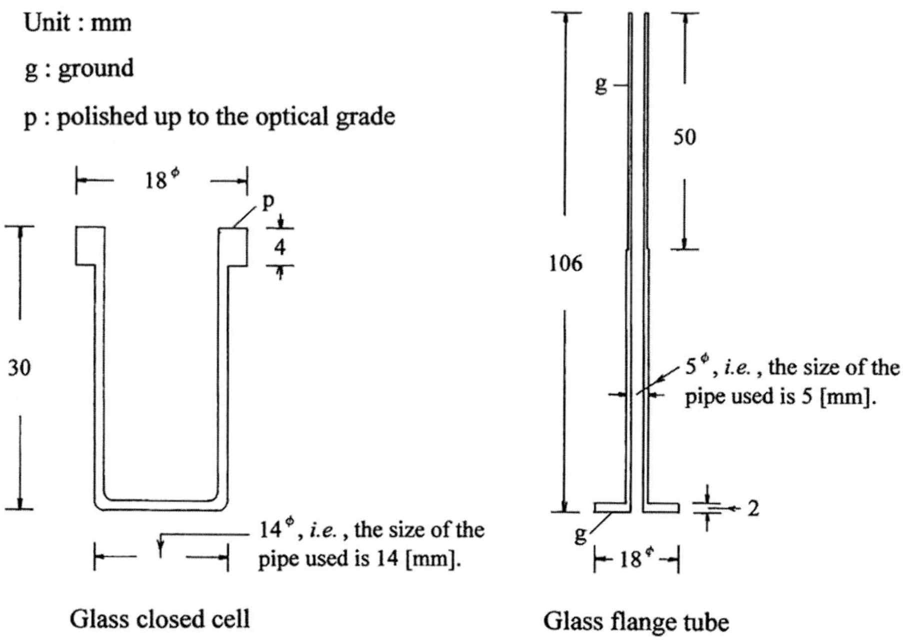

Figure 24. The glass closed cell and the glass flange tube.

When placed in the atmosphere maintained at a T_a a little higher than room temperature, self-heating chemicals, irrespective of whether they are of the TD type or of the AC type, have the common property to self-heat even under confined conditions, *i.e.*, even in the absence of oxygen, respectively. They each are usually stored or transported under confined conditions, *e.g.*, being confined in a polyethylene bag, which in turn is packaged in a container, such as fiber drum. It is, therefore, advisable, from a practical point of view as well, to examine the self-heating process or behavior of a chemical under confined conditions. In the meantime, when heated in the adiabatic self-heating test, or in the isothermal storage test, most self-heating chemicals tend to vaporize or decompose to evolve gases which are often corrosive and/or toxic. The vaporization of a chemical during a thermal instability test makes the test itself impossible; besides, the endothermic effect caused by the vaporization of the chemical during the test covers the self-heating process of the chemical tested. For the above reasons, it has always been one of the indispensable experimental requirements to examine the self-heating process of a chemical confined in a certain closed cell in the thermal instability test.

A glass closed cell having an inside volume of about 2 cm^3 has thus been devised and used in a series of studies, described herein, as well (Fig. 24).

4.4 Characteristics of the glass closed cell

4.4.1 Requisites for the material of the closed cell used in the thermal instability testing apparatus

Pyrex glass has been chosen as the material of the closed cell. Glass is liable to break, so that it is always under the necessity of being handled with care. Glass is, therefore, not necessarily appropriate for the industrial material in general use. On the other hand, however, it has several advantageous properties, such as small heat capacity per unit volume, $c\rho$,* low thermal conductivity,** excellent corrosion resistance, easy processibility by glass blowing as well as transparency. That the value of $c\rho$ of a cell material is small means that the value of the thermal inertia*** of the cell is small; and, that the value of λ is low means that the heat loss from the cell is minimized. It is possible by glass blowing to make a thermally sensitive thin capillary tube into which the thermocouple is fitted closely. Besides, it is also possible because of the transparency to observe visually the self-heating, decomposing or melting state of a chemical confined in the glass closed cell during the thermal instability test. For the above reasons, glass is considered to be most appropriate for the material of the cell used in the thermal instability testing apparatus which operates under adiabatic conditions, or under isothermal conditions.

On the contrary, metals are of course far tougher than glass. It is, however, clear that every metal is not appropriate for the material of the cell used to record the very slow or faint self-heating process, in the early stages, of a chemical in the thermal instability test, on account of the large values of ρ and λ. Besides, most metals each are vulnerable to corrosion by specific chemicals. To cite one instance, chemicals that decompose to evolve HCl while tested corrode stainless steel easily. That most metals each are vulnerable to corrosion by specific chemicals means in another aspect that there is also a possibility that a specific metal promotes the decomposition reaction of a chemical including a specific atom or group. Moreover, it is also of course impossible to observe visually the state of a chemical confined in a metallic closed cell during the test. For the above reasons, not every metal is necessarily appropriate for the material of the cell used in the thermal instability testing apparatus.

---

* The values of c and ρ of Pyrex glass are 0.17 cal/(g·K) and 2.5 g/cm^3 at 25 ℃, respectively.

** The value of λ of Pyrex glass is 0.0026 cal/(cm·s·K) at 25 ℃.

*** For the term, the thermal inertia, refer to a reference [29].

4.4.2 Merits of a cell of small size

That the cell used in the two kinds of adiabatic tests is of small size means that the test requires little effort, time, space, sample quantity, *etc.*; and therefore, it is safe and inexpensive.

4.4.3 Separable cell structure

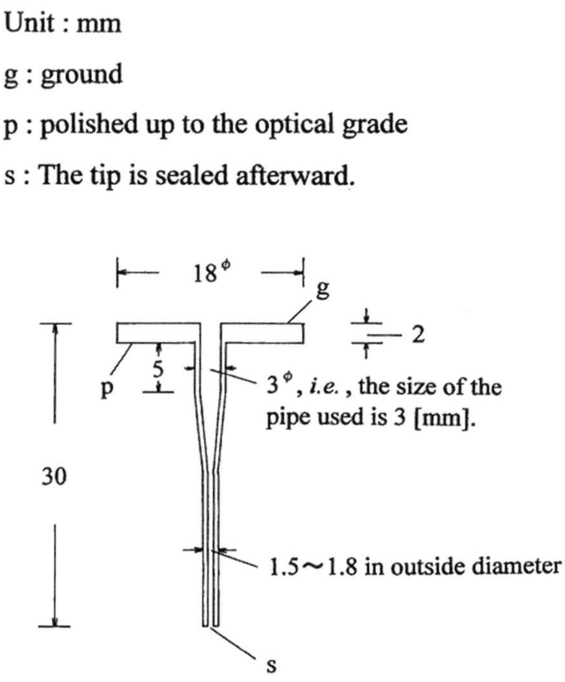

Figure 25. The glass capillary flange.

The cell assembly except the cell is called the stem (refer to Fig. 20 in **Subsection 4.2.2** and Fig. 74 in **Section 7.2**). The stem used in the cell assembly including the closed cell is made by sticking, with an inorganic adhesive agent, the glass flange tube (Fig. 24) on the glass capillary flange (Fig. 25), into both of which a thermocouple to measure the T_{ref}, or the temperature of a self-heating chemical, is inserted and fixed beforehand. As to the cell assembly including the closed cell, the stem serves us **(1)** as the suspender for the closed cell, and, **(2)** as the conduit pipe for the thermocouple to measure the T_{ref}, or the temperature of the chemical, in the adiabatic self-heating test. As stated in **Section 4.1**, the adiabatic self-heating process recorder has fundamentally the function to perform the adiabatic self-heating test, or the adiabatic oxidatively-heating test, for 2 cm^3 of a chemical of the TD type, including every gas-permeable oxidatively-heating substance, charged, or confined, in some one of the open-cup, the draft, the touch-flow or the closed cell, in accordance with the self-heating property of the chemical, for the time, Δt, required for the temperature of the chemical to increase by the definite value of ΔT of 1.25 K from a T_s in the range of room temperature to 200 ℃. There exists, however, no organic adhesive capable of withstanding temperatures in excess of 100 ℃ for a long time. The main component and the coefficient of linear expansion (after curing) of the inorganic adhesive agent, which is used for the stem composed of the glass flange tube and the glass capillary flange, are zirconia (ZrO_2) and 5×10^{-6} K^{-1}, respectively; in the meantime, the coefficient of linear expansion of Pyrex glass is 3.3×10^{-6} K^{-1}, with the result that an adhesive strength of 100 kgf/cm^2 is obtained between the adhesive agent and Pyrex glass. It is possible to constitute the stem composed of the glass flange tube and the glass capillary flange without exposing the thermocouple to any hot working, such as welding or glass blowing, by applying the preparing method above referred to.

The closed cell is always under the necessity of being demounted from the stem for carrying about, washing, drying, recharging with samples, *etc*. In this regard, when the protective tube, into which the thermocouple is inserted and fixed beforehand, is fixed in the cell or is clamped directly on the outside surface of the cell, such experimental operabilities, of the cell, as enumerated above are lost. The cell assembly has thus been designed in order that the closed cell and the stem, into which the thermocouple to measure the T_{ref} or the temperature of the chemical is inserted and fixed beforehand, may be separable from each other in order to facilitate the experimental operations.

4.4.4 Gastightness by means of the Viton O-ring

After a Viton O-ring has been sandwiched between the under surface of the stem and the upper flange of the closed cell, the stem is finally recombined with the closed cell by tightening the cap nut in order to construct the cell assembly (Fig. 20). The Viton O-ring withstands a condition of 230 ℃ × 24 h. Viton is a common name for the copolymer of hexafluoropropylene and vinylidene difluoride. The material designation given by the ASTM to this copolymer is FKM. The quality standard of the O-ring used for the closed cell is JIS (the Japanese Industrial Standard) B 2401-4D-p-12.5. The under surface of the stem and the upper flange of the closed cell are polished up to the optical grade in order to make the contacts among the O-ring and the glass surfaces above and below the ring as close as possible.

4.4.5 To be useful not only for the calculation of the T_c for a chemical of the TD type, having an arbitrary shape and an arbitrary size, confined in an arbitrary closed container of the corresponding shape and size, and placed in the atmosphere under isothermal conditions, but also for the calculation of the SADT for a chemical of the AC type, including every powdery chemical of the quasi-AC type, having an arbitrary shape and an arbitrary size, confined in an arbitrary closed container of the corresponding shape and size, and placed in the atmosphere under isothermal conditions

At all events, the glass closed cell is not perfectly pressure-proof. As stated repeatedly above, however, for the purpose of calculating the T_c for a chemical of the TD type, having an arbitrary shape and an arbitrary size, confined in an arbitrary closed container of the corresponding shape and size, and placed in the atmosphere under isothermal conditions, we have only to perform, apart from the measurement of the heat transfer data of the chemical, several adiabatic self-heating tests, which are started from each T_s with mutual intervals of 1～2 K, in order to calculate the heat generation data of the chemical, for 2 cm^3 each of several samples of the chemical confined each in the closed cell, for the time, Δt, required for the temperature of each sample of the chemical to increase by the definite value of ΔT of 1.25 K from the corresponding T_s, respectively. When the temperature of 2 cm^3 of the chemical subjected to the adiabatic self-heating test increases by 1.25 K from the T_s, however, the pressure built up in the closed cell is only a limited one.

Therefore, the adiabatic self-heating test by means of the glass closed cell introduced herein is considered to be substantially sound from another standpoint as well as one considered in **Subsection 4.2.5**, so far as our purpose is to calculate the T_c of a chemical of the TD type, having an arbitrary shape and an arbitrary size, confined in an arbitrary closed container of the corresponding shape and size, and placed in the atmosphere under isothermal conditions.

On the other hand, as shown in Fig. 124 in **(14)** of **Subsection 9.3.2**, the glass closed cell of the same kind is used in an isothermal storage testing device as well. For the purpose of calculating the SADT for a chemical of the AC type, including every powdery chemical of the quasi-AC type, having an arbitrary shape and an arbitrary size, confined in an arbitrary closed container of the corresponding shape and size, and placed in the atmosphere under isothermal conditions, we have only to perform several isothermal storage tests at each T_t with mutual intervals of 1～2 K, in order to calculate the values of the two coefficients, a and b, of Eq. (59) holding for the induction period of the autocatalytic reaction, or of the quasi-autocatalytic reaction, of 2 cm^3 of the chemical confined in the closed cell and subjected to the isothermal storage test, for 2 cm^3 each of several samples of the chemical confined each in the closed cell, for the time, Δt, from the insertion of each cell into the isothermal storage testing device till the start of the autocatalytic reaction, or of the quasi-autocatalytic reaction, of the chemical at the corresponding T_t, *i.e.*, during the induction period of the autocatalytic reaction, or of the quasi-autocatalytic reaction, of the chemical at the corresponding T_t, respectively. Once the temperature of the chemical of the AC type increases by 0.3 K (by 0.2 K as to nitroglycerin) from each T_t, the isothermal storage test is automatically interrupted. When the temperature of 2 cm^3 of the chemical subjected to the isothermal storage test increases by 0.2 ~ 0.3 K from the T_t, however, the pressure built up in the closed cell will not be so high as that effected in the adiabatic self-heating test.

It thus follows that the glass closed cell devised herein is useful not only for the calculation of the T_c for a chemical of the TD type, having an arbitrary shape and an arbitrary size, confined in an arbitrary closed container of the corresponding shape and size, and placed in the atmosphere under isothermal conditions, but also for the calculation of the SADT for a chemical of the AC type, including every powdery chemical of the quasi-AC type, having an arbitrary shape and an arbitrary size, confined in an arbitrary closed container of the corresponding shape and size, and placed in the atmosphere under isothermal conditions.

Incidentally, the thermal sensitivity of the thermocouple to measure the T_{ref}, or the temperature of the chemical, increases naturally with decreasing the wall thickness of the glass capillary tube of the glass capillary flange; in the meantime, the pressure resistance of the tube decreases naturally with decreasing the wall thickness. Therefore, it is required to achieve a proper balance between the thermal sensitivity of the thermocouple and the pressure resistance of the tube. The glass capillary tube, which has a very small radius of curvature, is, however, able to bear far higher external pressures than may be expected.

4.5 Detailed procedure to perform the adiabatic self-heating test, which is started from a T_s, for 2 cm^3 of a chemical of the TD type confined in the closed cell, for the time, Δt, required for the temperature of the chemical to increase by the definite value of ΔT of 1.25 K from the T_s

As a matter of fact, however, the experimental procedure explained in the present section is, in principle, in common with **(1)** the procedure for 2 cm^3 of a non-volatile liquid or powdery chemical of the TD type charged in the open-cup cell, which is explained in **Section 5.4**, and **(2)** the procedure for 2 cm^3 of a gas-permeable oxidatively-heating substance charged in the draft cell, which is explained in **Section 7.4** and in **Subsection 8.4.1**, as well as **(3)** the procedure for 2 cm^3 of a chemical of the TD type confined in the closed cell, which is explained in **Section 6.3**.*

The procedure to prepare the cell assembly including the closed cell, which is explained in **Subsection 4.5.2**, is, therefore, in principle, in common with the procedure to prepare the cell assembly including some one of the three types of open cells, which is explained in **Section 7.3**.

4.5.1 Preheating of the air bath of the adiabatic self-heating process recorder and the choice of a nominal T_s in the adiabatic self-heating test, which is started from the nominal T_s, performed for 2 cm^3 of a chemical of the TD type confined in the closed cell

The temperature of the air bath, *i.e.*, the nominal T_s of the run, is set at a proper value by means of the temperature dial on the air bath on the basis of the self-heating property of the chemical tested to give estimated rates of increase in temperature of 1.25 K/h in the adiabatic self-heating test.

To begin with, the main power supply connected to the adiabatic self-heating process recorder is switched on.

The power supplies connected to the cold junction, the air bath, the digital D.C. microvoltmeter, the digital D.C. millivolt recorder and the two-pen strip chart recorder are then switched on, respectively. The ΔT_{diff} pen of the two-pen strip chart recorder is, however, left on the "short" position until the thermal equilibrium state is attained nearly around the reference material confined in the closed cell and inserted into the adiabatic jacket maintained at the nominal T_s of the run. For the term, the ΔT_{diff} pen, refer to **Subsection 4.5.4**.

4.5.2 Procedure to prepare the reference cell assembly including the closed cell

It is always indispensable for almost all self-heating chemicals, irrespective of whether they are of the TD type or of the AC type, to determine the T_s or the T_t of each run by inserting the reference cell assembly into the adiabatic jacket in the adiabatic self-heating process recorder, or into the aluminium block bath in the isothermal storage testing device, prior to the insertion of the sample cell

* The whole procedure to perform the adiabatic self-heating test by means of the closed cell is explained in detail in **Chapter 6**, in connection with the procedure to calculate the T_c for a powdery chemical of the TD type, having some one of several specific shapes including the class A geometries as well as an arbitrary size, confined in a fiber drum, and placed in the atmosphere under isothermal conditions.

assembly into the jacket, although this procedure is not required for most adiabatic oxidatively-heating tests.*

The procedure to prepare the reference cell assembly including the closed cell is exhibited below by means of a series of photographs. In this connection, the closed cell used to prepare the reference cell assembly is needless to say of the same type and size as that used to prepare the sample cell assembly.

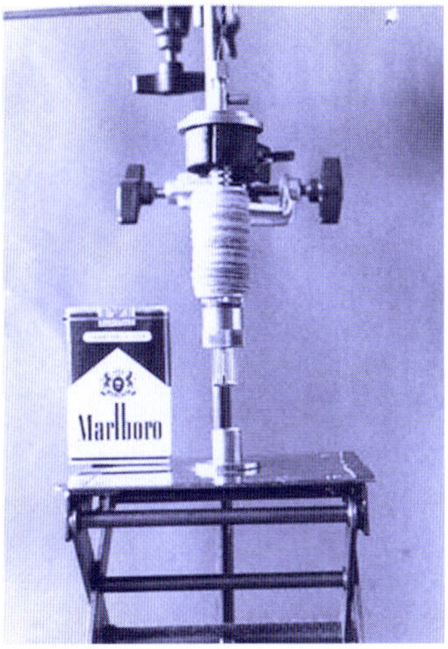

Figure 26. This photograph shows a general view of the reference cell assembly including the glass flange tube combined with the empty closed cell by means of the cap nut. The assembly is held in the vertical position by means of a clamp of a stand. It is possible to slide the stand horizontally on the laboratory desk. On the other hand, a laboratory jack, at the center of the upper plate of which a pedestal is stuck, is fixed on the desk. The position of the stand is then adjusted horizontally in order that the assembly may be aligned vertically with the pedestal. A pack of cigarettes is put on the laboratory jack, and by the side of the assembly, to show the relative size of the closed cell. The cell measures 1.4 cm in outside diameter and about 3 cm in length; in other words, it is about half the size of a thumb.

* For further details, refer to the final paragraph at the beginning of **Section 7.3**.

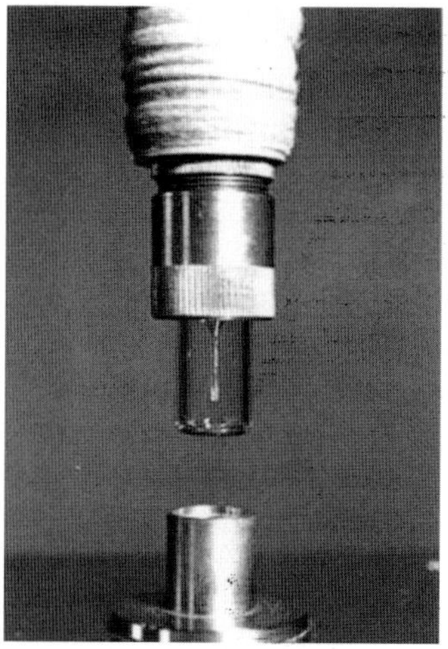

Figure 27. This is an enlarged view of the reference cell assembly including the empty closed cell and the pedestal.

Figure 28. The empty reference cell assembly is set on the pedestal by raising the laboratory jack.

Figure 29. The empty reference cell assembly, which is set on the pedestal, is dismantled by loosening the cap nut. An O-ring is seen to be sandwiched between the under surface of the stem, *i.e.*, the under surface of the glass capillary flange, and the upper surface of the flange of the glass closed cell.

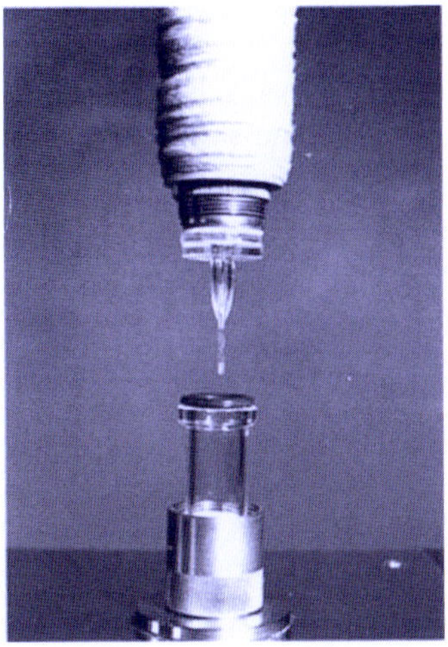

Figure 30. The empty closed cell is separated from the glass capillary flange by lowering the laboratory jack. It may be observed that the thermocouple is inserted into the glass capillary tube projecting downward from the under surface of the glass capillary flange.

Figure 31. 2.2 g of silica powder, the volume of which is about 2 cm^3, is charged in a closed cell, *i.e.*, the cell with which the reference cell is prepared. In this photograph, however, the cell is filled with milk in place of silica powder for the convenience of photography. It has been made a rule in the adiabatic self-heating test performed for every chemical, irrespective of liquid and powdery, of the TD type to use silica powder as the reference material. In this connection, silica powder is used as the reference material in the isothermal storage test as well.

Figure 32. The reference cell, on the flange of which an O-ring is put concentrically, thus prepared is then pressed concentrically and softly up to the under surface of the glass capillary flange by raising again the laboratory jack to construct the reference cell assembly; in the meantime, the CA thermocouple, which is inserted into the glass capillary tube projecting downward from the under surface of the glass capillary flange, to measure the T_{ref}, or the temperature of a chemical of the TD type, is inserted automatically and axially to the longitudinal center of silica powder charged in the cell.

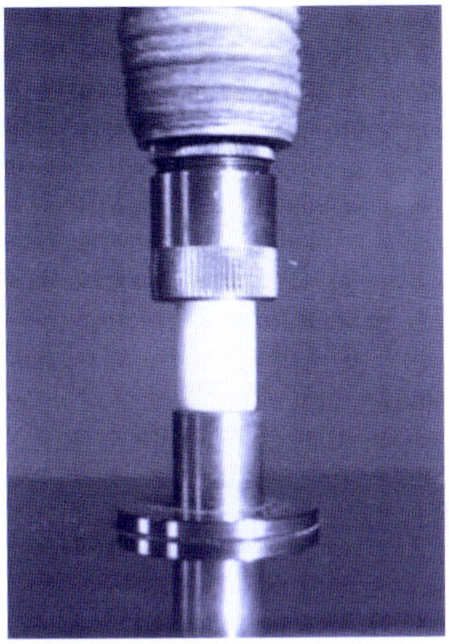

Figure 33. The reference cell assembly is finally completed by tightening the cap nut.

Figure 34. After having lowered again the laboratory jack a little, a fairly small vibrator is applied to the base of the closed cell in order that silica powder confined in the cell may come closely in contact with the glass capillary tube. The reference cell assembly is now ready for the adiabatic self-heating test.

4.5.3 Insertion of the reference cell assembly into the adiabatic jacket set in the preheated air bath

Figure 35. The reference cell assembly has, in fact, been prepared at the rear side of the adiabatic self-heating process recorder.

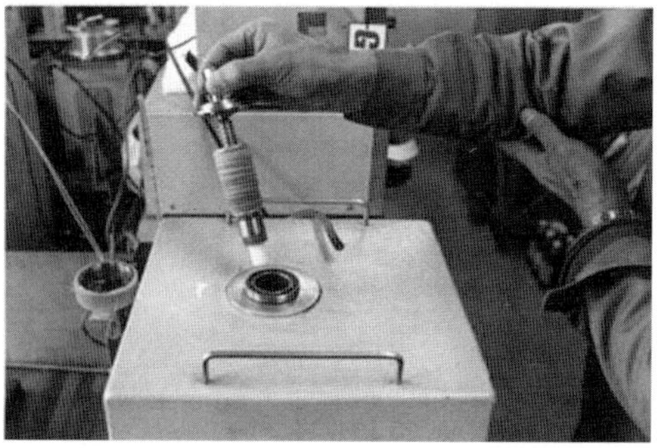

Figure 36. The reference cell assembly thus prepared is inserted into the adiabatic jacket set in the preheated air bath of the recorder.

Figure 37. Insertion of the reference cell assembly into the adiabatic jacket has now been finished.

4.5.4 Curves drawn by the *T* pen and the ΔT_{diff} pen on the strip chart of the two-pen strip chart recorder

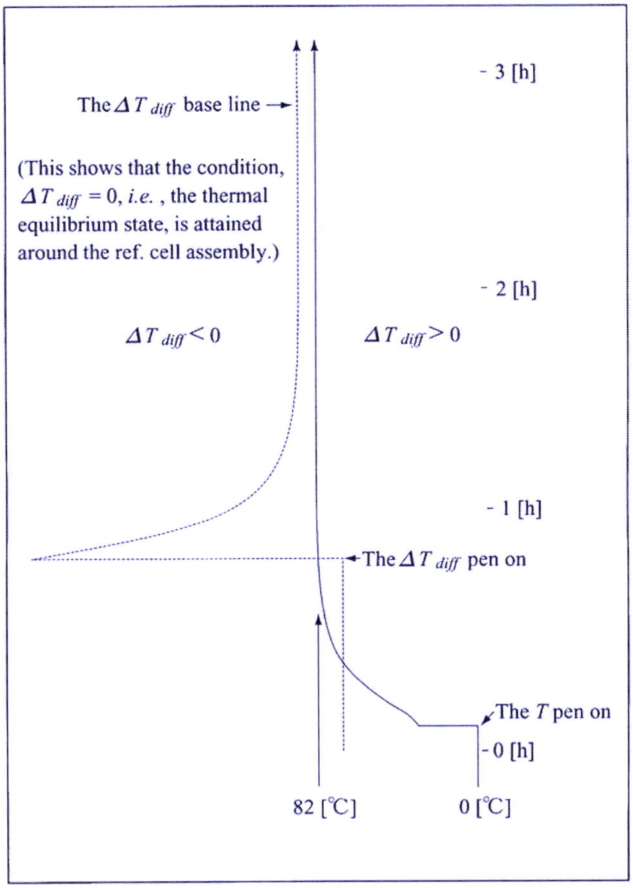

Figure 38. An instance of two curves drawn by the *T* pen and the ΔT_{diff} pen on the strip chart of the two-pen strip chart recorder by the time that the thermal equilibrium state has been attained around the reference material confined in the closed cell and inserted into the adiabatic jacket maintained at a nominal T_s of 82 ℃.

The two pens of the two-pen strip chart recorder are composed of the temperature or *T* pen and the temperature difference or ΔT_{diff} pen. After the reference cell assembly has been inserted into the adiabatic jacket set in the air bath, which is now being heated up to the temperature, T_s, the *T* pen records the variation of the T_{ref} with time on the strip chart; in the meantime, the ΔT_{diff} pen records the variation of the temperature difference, ΔT_{diff}, between the T_{ref} and the T_{atm} with time on the strip chart.

The thermal equilibrium state is attained around the reference material confined in the closed cell and inserted into the adiabatic jacket maintained at the nominal T_s of the run 2～3 h after the insertion of the reference cell assembly into the jacket. After the thermal equilibrium state has nearly been attained around the reference material, the power supply to the analog D.C. microvoltmeter is switched on; in the meantime, the ΔT_{diff} pen of the two-pen strip chart recorder is also switched over from "short" to "on". It is then observed that the indicator of the analog D.C. microvoltmeter enters on to the scale span of the meter from the minus side where the condition, $\Delta T_{diff} = (T_{ref} - T_{atm}) < 0$, holds, and, it comes to stay near the graduation line of zero at the center of the scale span of the meter; in the meantime, the ΔT_{diff} pen of the two-pen strip chart recorder also enters on to the strip chart of the two-pen strip chart recorder from the minus side. For the term, the minus side, refer to the paragraph after the following.

In the course of time, both the T pen and the ΔT_{diff} pen come to run parallel with the time axis on the strip chart (see Fig. 38). In this thermal equilibrium state, the position of the T pen on the temperature axis perpendicular to the time axis indicates the T_s of the run. However, the exact value of the T_s is noted down separately as the digital output of the thermoelectromotive force of the CA thermocouple to measure the T_{ref} in the following subsection.

In the meantime, the linear locus drawn by the ΔT_{diff} pen on the strip chart in this state is called the ΔT_{diff} baseline. When the thermal equilibrium state is attained among the T_{ref}, the T_s and the T_{atm}, the ΔT_{diff} takes a constant value of zero. That is, the condition, $\Delta T_{diff} = T_{ref} - T_s = T_{ref} - T_{atm} = 0$, holds at this state. Therefore, when, after the reference cell assembly was removed from the adiabatic jacket, the sample cell assembly including 2 cm^3 of a chemical of the TD type has been inserted into the jacket maintained at the identical T_s, if the ΔT_{diff} pen gets into the region on the right side of the ΔT_{diff} base line, facing the two-pen strip chart recorder, we may judge that the chemical has already begun to self-heat in the cell, because the conditions, $\Delta T_{diff} = (T - T_s) > 0$ and $\Delta T_{diff} = (T - T_s) < 0$, hold in the region on the right-hand side of the line and in the region on the left-hand side of the line, respectively. The region on the right-hand side of the line is thus usually referred to as the plus side, and the region on the left-hand side of the line is as the minus side.

4.5.5 Determination of the exact value of T_s of the run

The digital output of the thermoelectromotive force, which is indicated as a number of four figures in μV unit on the digital D.C. microvoltmeter, of the CA thermocouple to measure the T_{ref} is first noted down as the exact value of T_s of the run, after the thermal equilibrium state has been attained around the reference material confined in the closed cell and inserted into the adiabatic jacket maintained at the nominal T_s of the run. Fluctuations of the value of the T_s in the thermal equilibrium state are within $\pm 0.5\ \mu V$.

Secondly, the zero-suppression procedure* is performed.

4.5.6 Insertion of the sample cell assembly into the adiabatic jacket maintained at the T_s of the run and the start of the adiabatic self-heating test for 2 cm^3 of a chemical of the TD type confined in the closed cell

The power supply to the analog D.C. microvoltmeter is then switched off for a while; in the meantime, the ΔT_{diff} pen of the two-pen strip chart recorder is also switched over from "on" to "short" for a while.

The reference cell assembly is successively taken out of the jacket, and the sample cell assembly including a closed cell, in which a definite quantity of a chemical of the TD type, the volume of which is also about 2 cm^3, has been confined in the same manner as performed to prepare the reference cell assembly in **Subsection 4.5.2**, is inserted into the adiabatic jacket. The quantity of a chemical of the TD type tested depends naturally on the specific gravity.

Although the temperature of the chemical begins to increase from a temperature near room temperature after the insertion of the sample cell assembly, the thermal equilibrium state comes again to be attained around the chemical confined in the closed cell and inserted into the adiabatic jacket maintained at the T_s of the run in the course of tens of minutes. After the thermal equilibrium state has nearly been attained around the chemical, the power supply to the analog D.C. microvoltmeter is again switched on; in the meantime, the ΔT_{diff} pen of the two-pen strip chart recorder is also switched over again from "short" to "on". It is then observed that the indicator of the analog D.C. microvoltmeter enters again on to the scale span of the meter from the minus side; in the meantime, the ΔT_{diff} pen of the two-pen strip chart recorder also enters again on to the strip chart of the two-pen strip chart recorder from the minus side.

Once the indicator of the analog D.C. microvoltmeter reaches the graduation line of zero at the center of the scale span of the meter, the adiabatic control by means of the adiabatic self-heating process recorder and the record of the self-heating process, in the early stages, of 2 cm^3 of the chemical confined in the

* A procedure to cancel electrically the slight pseudo-thermoelectromotive force of the differential thermocouple, which is composed of the thermocouple to measure the temperature of the reference material, or the temperature of the chemical tested, and that to measure the T_{atm}, by operating the zero-suppression circuit. The concrete procedure is to set the indicator of the analog D.C. microvoltmeter to the graduation line of zero at the center of the scale span of the meter.

closed cell by means of the digital D.C. millivolt recorder are started, respectively. This point of time corresponds to the point "**s**" in Fig. 15 presented in **Section 3.4**.

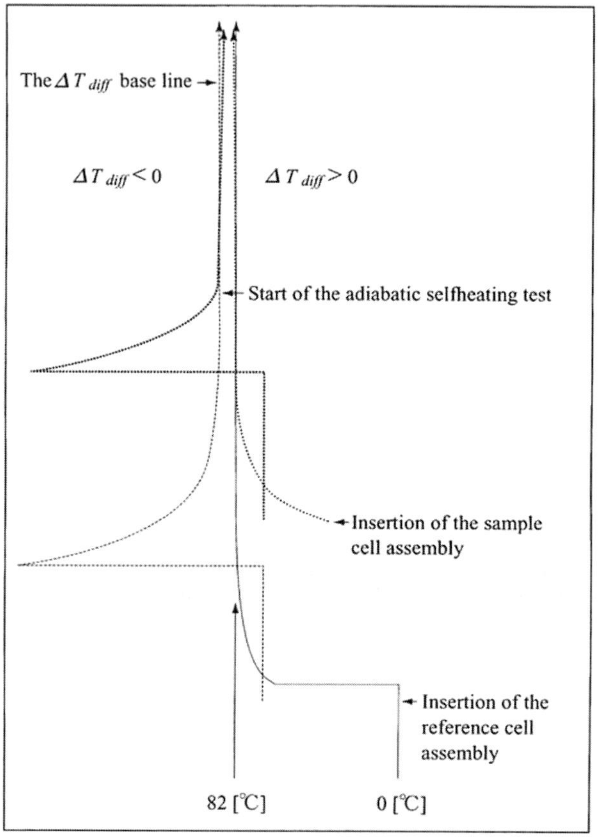

Figure 39. An instance of two curves drawn by the T pen and the ΔT_{diff} pen on the strip chart of the two-pen strip chart recorder before and after the start of the adiabatic self-heating test performed for 2 cm^3 of a chemical of the TD type confined in the closed cell and inserted into the adiabatic jacket maintained at the nominal T_s of 82 ℃.

At this time, the ΔT_{diff} pen also gets to the ΔT_{diff} base line on the strip chart of the two-pen strip chart recorder (Fig. 39). However, the temperature of the chemical of the TD type tested, which is indicated by the digital D.C. microvoltmeter, in general takes a value slightly lower than that of the T_s at this time, because, while the T_{atm}, the temperature of the atmosphere around the chemical, is still slightly lower than the T_s, the chemical begins to self-heat in the cell, so that the temperature of the chemical catches the T_{atm} up.

4.5.7 Record of the self-heating process, in the early stages, of 2 cm^3 of a chemical of the TD type confined in the closed cell and inserted into the adiabatic jacket kept always at the very slowly increasing temperature of the chemical itself by the adiabatic control

After the start of the adiabatic control, the T_{atm} is raised automatically by the adiabatic control in order that the condition, $\Delta T_{diff} = T - T_{atm} = 0$, may always hold, with the result that the heat generated in the self-heating chemical is all accumulated in it, and, it continues to self-heat at a very slow, but virtually constant, rate depending on the value of T_s; in the meantime, the temperature of the space in the air bath, except that in the adiabatic jacket, is maintained at the T_s of the run throughout every run.

The self-heating process, in the early stages, of 2 cm^3 of the chemical confined in the closed cell and inserted into the adiabatic jacket kept always at the very slowly increasing temperature of the chemical itself by the adiabatic control is recorded in the digital representation as the variation of the value, with time, of the thermoelectromotive force of the thermocouple to measure the temperature of the chemical; to put it concretely, the numerical value of the thermoelectromotive force of the thermocouple is printed out every minute by means of the digital D.C. millivolt recorder, in such a manner as exemplified in Table 5 presented in **Section 4.7**, in order to utilize the record for the calculation of the values of the two coefficients, a and b, of Eq. (44) holding for the self-heating process, in the early stages, of 2 cm^3 of the chemical confined in the closed cell and subjected to the adiabatic self-heating test.

On the other hand, however, the self-heating process, in the early stages, of 2 cm^3 of the chemical confined in the closed cell and subjected to the adiabatic self-heating test is recorded, as an analog signal as well, with the T pen on the strip chart of the two-pen strip chart recorder to look about the process as a whole.

In the meantime, the ΔT_{diff} pen runs almost parallel with the time axis on the strip chart of the two-pen strip-chart recorder after the start of the adiabatic control. This denotes that the state, $\Delta T_{diff} = T - T_{atm} = 0$, is realized in and around 2 cm^3 of the chemical confined in the closed cell and subjected to the adiabatic self-heating test. The ΔT_{diff} pen, however, comes to drift toward the plus side on the strip chart in the course of time. This denotes that the state, $T > T_{atm}$, comes to occur in and around 2 cm^3 of the chemical confined in the closed cell, in spite of the adiabatic control, because the rate of increase in temperature, *i.e.*, the rate of the exothermic decomposition reaction, of 2 cm^3 of the chemical confined in the closed cell and subjected to the adiabatic self-heating test accelerates gradually.[*] This fact is useful for catching the temperature range in which the condition, $\Delta T_{diff} = T - T_{atm} = 0$, holds exactly. The ΔT_{diff} pen is useful, besides, for judging whether or not the thermal equilibrium is attained around 2 cm^3 of the chemical charged, or confined, in some one of the open-cup, the draft or the closed cell, in accordance with the self-heating property of the chemical, and inserted into the adiabatic jacket maintained at a T_s, immediately before the start of the adiabatic self-heating test, or of the adiabatic oxidatively-heating test.

Once the temperature of the chemical in the cell reaches a temperature preset on the two-pen strip chart recorder, the limit switch works in order that the main power supply to the adiabatic self-heating process recorder may be cut automatically. However, It has been made an established rule in the two kinds of adiabatic tests, which are started each from a T_s, performed for 2 cm^3 of a chemical of the TD type, including every gas-permeable oxidatively-heating substance, to interrupt each test, as soon as the temperature of the chemical in the cell increases by the definite value of ΔT of 1.25 K from the T_s in the adiabatic self-heating test, or from the corresponding standard temperature in the adiabatic oxidatively-heating test. Some reasons why a value of ΔT of 1.25 K was chosen as the definite value of ΔT in the two kinds of adiabatic tests are explained in the following subsection.

4.5.8 Some reasons why a value of ΔT of 1.25 K was chosen as the definite value of ΔT in the two kinds of adiabatic tests performed each for 2 cm^3 of a chemical of the TD type, including every gas-permeable oxidatively-heating substance

The first reason is that, as inferred in **Subsection 4.2.5**, the self-heating process, or the oxidatively-heating process, in temperature ranges of 2~3 K immediately above a T_s, of 2 cm^3 of a chemical of the TD type, including every gas-permeable oxidatively-heating substance, subjected to either of the two kinds of adiabatic tests started each from the T_s by means of the adiabatic self-heating process recorder is recorded under almost perfectly adiabatic conditions.

The second reason is that it is observed usually in the adiabatic self-heating test performed for 2 cm^3 of a chemical of the TD type that the temperature of the chemical continues to increase at a virtually constant rate, while it increases by 50 μV, in the case of the CA thermocouple, from a T_s as shown diagrammatically in Fig. 4 in **Section 2.5**, and as shown by a digital record of the digital D.C. millivolt recorder presented in Table 5 in **Section 4.7**. That is, so long as the increment in temperature of 2 cm^3 of a chemical of the TD type subjected to the adiabatic self-heating test started from a T_s are within 50 μV

[*] The same phenomenon is observed of course in the adiabatic oxidatively-heating test, performed for a gas-permeable oxidatively-heating substance by means of the cell assembly including the draft cell, as well.

immediately above the T_s, the linear approximation of the self-heating process or curve that the value of dT/dt remains virtually constant usually holds. And this approximation is fundamental to the qualitative derivation of the adiabatic temperature increase equation, as explained in **Section 2.5**.

Fig. 4 in **Section 2.5** is re-presented here as Fig. 4' for convenience' sake.

A temperature higher than a T_s by 50 μV, in the case of the CA thermocouple, is shown by (Region B) in Figure 4'. At a temperature, such as shown by (Region C), however, the rate of increase in temperature of 2 cm^3 of a chemical of the TD type subjected to the adiabatic self-heating test is seen to come to accelerate gradually. On the other hand, a temperature, which is shown by (Region A), higher than the T_s by 10~20 μV, *i.e.*, by 0.3~0.5 K, is too low upon which to rely.

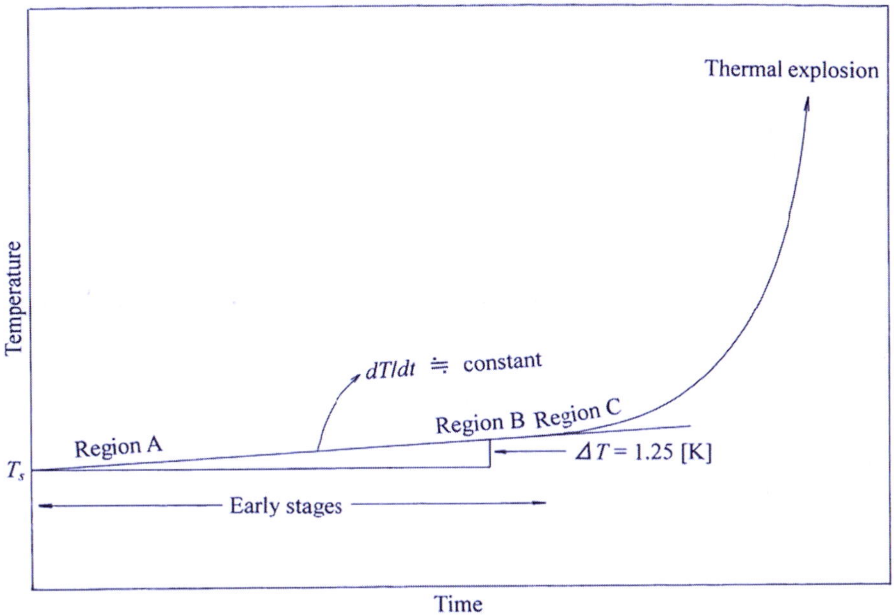

Figure 4'. The linear approximation of the self-heating process or curve, in the early stages, of 2 cm^3 of a chemical of the TD type charged in the open-cup cell, or confined in the closed cell, in accordance with the self-heating property of the chemical, and subjected to the adiabatic self-heating test started from a T_s.

In this connection, (Region B) may, in fact, be regarded as a temperature near the critical state for the thermal explosion which exists at the end of the early stages of the self-heating process of a chemical of the TD type, including every gas-permeable oxidatively-heating substance, in the Semenov scheme, although the critical state for the thermal explosion is a concept holding under isothermal conditions and (Region B) is that holding under adiabatic conditions.

The third reason is that, although the temperature of 2 cm^3 of a chemical of the TD type, including every gas-permeable oxidatively-heating substance, subjected to either of the two kinds of adiabatic tests started each from a T_s is printed out every minute by means of the digital recorder as the numerical value of the thermoelectromotive force, the digital output of which is read to 10 μV, of the CA thermocouple to measure the temperature of the chemical, as stated in **Subsections 4.2.5** and **4.5.7**, and as shown by the digital record of the digital D.C. millivolt recorder presented in Table 5 in **Section 4.7**, it was preferred in the early stages of a series of studies described herein to interrupt the record of the self-heating process of the chemical subjected to either of the two kinds of adiabatic tests started each from a T_s, when the temperature of the chemical had increased by a definite increment, in the thermoelectromotive force, of a round number, such as 50, 100, 200 or 500 μV, from the T_s.

In the last analysis, it was concluded, in view of all the factors above referred to, that an increment in thermoelectromotive force of 50 μV was most appropriate as the value of ΔT. The unit of ΔT is, however, K, so that a value of ΔT of 1.25 K, which is not always equal to the increment in thermoelectromotive force of 50 μV in the case of the CA thermocouple,* was chosen ultimately as the definite value of ΔT in the two kinds of adiabatic tests performed each for 2 cm^3 of a chemical of the TD type, including every gas-permeable oxidatively-heating substance.

4.6 Some problems accompanied with the adiabatic self-heating test performed by means of the adiabatic self-heating process recorder

4.6.1 Effect of the range of the pre-amplifier on the precision of the adiabatic control

The precision of the adiabatic control by means of the adiabatic self-heating process recorder depends exclusively on the range of the pre-amplifier to amplify the value of ΔT_{diff}. That is, as the pre-amplifier of the recorder is set at successively wider ranges, the detection limit to amplify the value of ΔT_{diff} extends gradually, so that the adiabatic control becomes gradually more insufficient, with the result that the rate of increase in temperature of 2 cm^3 of a chemical of the TD type, including every gas-permeable oxidatively-heating substance, subjected to either of the two kinds of adiabatic tests performed each by means of the recorder becomes gradually less than what should be realized

* This is effected by a fact that an increment in temperature of 1 K from a T_s does not always correspond to an increment in thermoelectromotive force of 40 μV in the case of the CA thermocouple. A case relevant to this fact is exemplified in **Section 4.7**.

properly, on account of the heat loss from the chemical. Therefore, it has been tried to determine the range of the pre-amplifier at which the adiabatic control for the self-heating process of 2 cm^3 of a chemical of the TD type, including every gas-permeable oxidatively-heating substance, subjected to either of the two kinds of adiabatic tests is performed substantially without heat loss from the chemical, by examining the effect of the range of the pre-amplifier on the rate of increase in temperature of a mixture of 50 μL of linolic acid and 50 mg of cotton wool charged in the draft cell, into which oxygen gas is supplied at a flow rate of 2 cm^3/min at atmospheric pressure, and subjected to the adiabatic oxidatively-heating test started from a T_s near 60 ℃, keeping the other conditions constant.

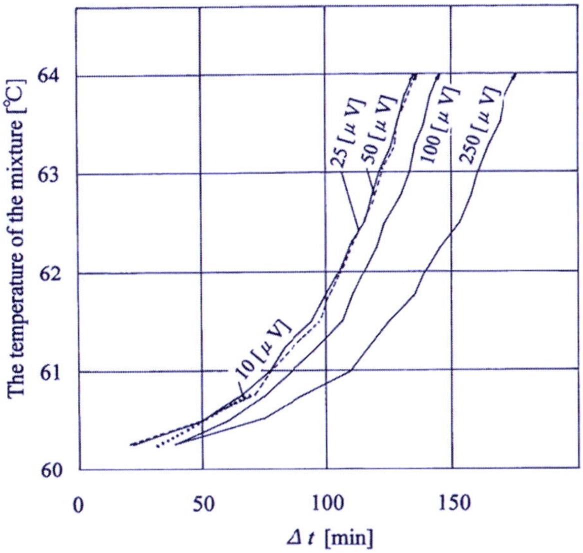

Figure 40. Effect of the range of the pre-amplifier on the rate of increase in temperature, of a mixture of 50 μL of linolic acid and 50 mg of cotton wool charged in the draft cell, into which oxygen gas is supplied at a flow rate of 2 cm^3/min at atmospheric pressure, and subjected to the adiabatic oxidatively-heating test started from a T_s near 60 ℃, keeping the other conditions constant.

It has been ascertained, in result, that the rate of increase in temperature of the mixture decreases gradually at ranges above ±100 μV, but the rate is kept almost constant at ranges below ±50 μV (Fig. 40). Therefore, ±50 μV has been chosen as the standard range of the pre-amplifier of the recorder in the two kinds of adiabatic tests, considering the stability of the adiabatic control as well.

4.6.2 Comparison of the rate of increase in temperature of 2 cm^3 of 98 % benzoyl peroxide (BPO)* charged in the metallic cell and subjected to the adiabatic self-heating test with that of 2 cm^3 of BPO charged in the glass cell and placed under the same conditions as the former

The self-heating processes of 2 cm^3 each of three samples of BPO charged each in the three kinds of open-cup cells and subjected each to the adiabatic self-heating test started from each T_s near 82 ℃ were recorded.

It has been ascertained, in result, that the rate of increase in temperature of BPO charged in the stainless steel open-cup cell and that of BPO charged in the aluminium open-cup cell are both much less than that of BPO charged in the glass open-cup cell, keeping the other conditions constant (Fig. 41).

That is, it is clear that a part of the heat of the exothermic decomposition reaction of BPO charged in each of the two kinds of metallic open-cup cells is used to heat up the cell as well as BPO itself. In other words, it follows that it is most advisable to use the glass cell having a small heat capacity in every thermal instability testing apparatus including the isothermal storage testing device.

---

* A sort of of powdery chemical of the TD type.

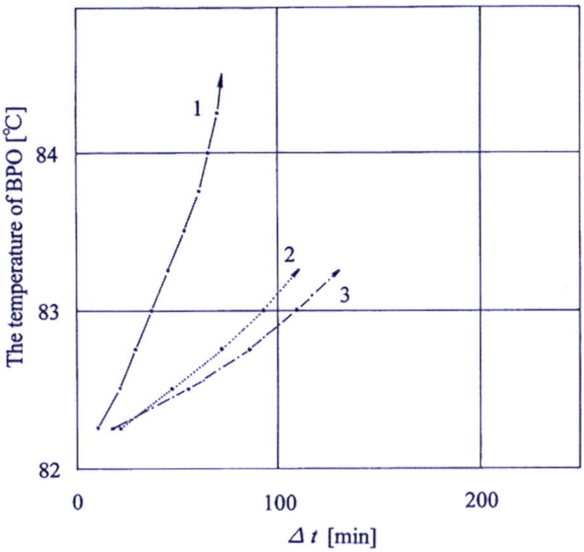

Figure 41. The self-heating processes, of 2 cm^3 each of three samples of BPO charged each in the three kinds of open-cup cells and subjected each to the adiabatic self-heating test started from each T_s near 82 ℃, recorded each in temperature increments of 2~3 [K] from the corresponding T_s.

1. The self-heating process, of 2 cm^3 of BPO charged in the glass open-cup cell and subjected to the adiabatic self-heating test started from a T_s near 82 ℃, recorded in temperature increments of 3 K from the T_s.

2. The self-heating process, of 2 cm^3 of BPO charged in a stainless steel open-cup cell and subjected to the adiabatic self-heating test started from a T_s near 82 ℃, recorded in temperature increments of 2 K from the T_s.

3. The self-heating process, of 2 cm^3 of BPO charged in an aluminium open-cup cell and subjected to the adiabatic self-heating test started from a T_s near 82 ℃, recorded in temperature increments of 2 K from the T_s.

4.6.3 Comparison of the rate of increase in temperature of 2 cm^3 of BPO confined in the glass closed cell and subjected to the adiabatic self-heating test with that of 2 cm^3 of BPO charged in the glass open-cup cell and placed under the same conditions as the former

The rate of increase in temperature of 2 cm^3 of BPO confined in the glass closed cell and subjected to the adiabatic self-heating test started from a T_s near

81 ℃ in general is less than that of 2 cm^3 of BPO charged in the glass open-cup cell and placed under the same conditions as the former (Fig. 42).

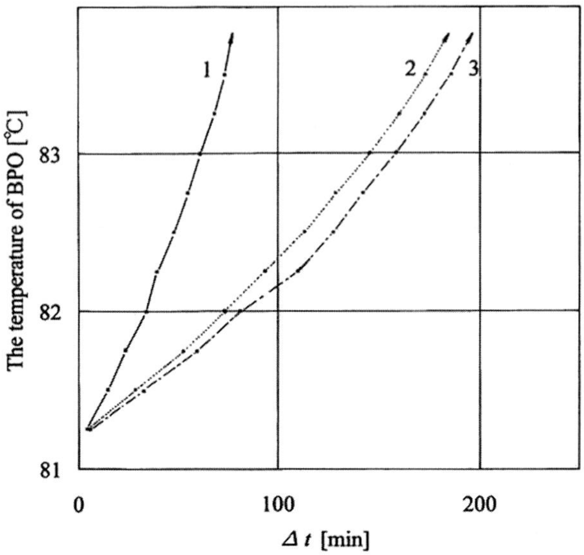

Figure 42. The self-heating processes, of 2 cm^3 each of three samples of BPO charged, or confined, each in the three kinds of cells and subjected each to the adiabatic self-heating test started from each T_s near 81 ℃, recorded each in temperature increments of 3 K from the corresponding T_s.

1. The self-heating process, of 2 cm^3 of BPO charged in the glass open-cup cell and subjected to the adiabatic self-heating test started from a T_s near 81 ℃, recorded in temperature increments of 3 K from the T_s.

2. The self-heating process, of 2 cm^3 of BPO confined in the glass closed cell, covered with the glass capillary flange containing the thermocouple to measure the temperature of BPO, and subjected to the adiabatic self-heating test started from a T_s near 81 ℃, recorded in temperature increments of 3 K from the T_s.

3. The self-heating process, of 2 cm^3 of BPO confined in the glass closed cell, covered with a tantalum small tube flange containing the thermocouple to measure the temperature of BPO, and subjected to the adiabatic self-heating test started from a T_s near 81 ℃, recorded in temperature increments of 3 K from the T_s.

On account of this effect, the value of T_c calculated by substituting the heat generation data, which are calculated based on the experimental data obtained with the glass closed cell in the adiabatic self-heating test, into Eq. (72) derived in **Subsection 5.3.2**, or into Eq. (79) derived in **Section 6.2**, is necessarily higher than that calculated by substituting the heat generation data, which are calculated based on the experimental data obtained with the glass open-cup cell in the test, into each equation, keeping the values of the other variables in both equations constant.

Three values of the BAM test for BPO calculated each by substituting the three pairs of heat generation data, which are each calculated based on the experimental data obtained each with the three kinds of cells, which are referred to in Fig. 42, in the test, into Eq. (72) are presented in Table 4, assuming that 400 cm^3 each of three samples of BPO are each charged in the 500 cm^3 Dewar flask used in the BAM heat-accumulation storage test and are each placed in the atmosphere under isothermal conditions, keeping the other conditions constant.

Table 4

Confinement dependence of the value of the BAM test for BPO.

Value of the BAM test	Kind of the sample cell
℃	
74.6	The glass open-cup cell, into which the thermocouple, which is covered with a glass capillary tube, to measure the temperature of BPO is inserted.
77.6	The glass closed cell covered with the glass capillary flange, in which the thermocouple to measure the temperature of BPO is contained.
78.9	The glass closed cell covered with the tantalum small tube flange, in which the thermocouple to measure the temperature of BPO is contained.

It is shown in Table 4 that the difference between the value of the BAM test for BPO calculated by substituting the heat generation data, which are calculated based on the experimental data obtained with the glass closed cell covered with the tantalum small tube flange containing the thermocouple to measure the temperature of BPO in the test, into Eq. (72), and, the value calculated by substituting the heat generation data, which are calculated based on the experimental data obtained with the glass closed cell covered with the glass capillary flange containing the thermocouple to measure the temperature of BPO in the test, into the same equation is of the order of 1 K, in spite of the evident difference, in the heat capacity, between the two kinds of glass closed cells. This difference is markedly small compared with the difference of 3∼4 K between the value of the BAM test for BPO calculated by substituting either of the two pairs of heat generation data, which are each calculated based on the experimental data obtained each with the two kinds of glass closed cells in the test, into Eq. (72), and, the value of the BAM test for BPO calculated by substituting the heat generation data, which are calculated based on the experimental data obtained with the glass open-cup cell in the test, into the same equation.

That is, the fact that the heat capacities of the two kinds of glass closed cells are larger than that of the glass open-cup cell is thought to contribute partly to the fact that the rates of increase in temperature of 2 cm^3 each of two samples of BPO confined each in the two kinds of glass closed cells are less than that of 2 cm^3 of BPO charged in the glass open-cup cell, so that the two values of the BAM test for BPO calculated each by substituting the two pairs of heat generation data, which are each calculated based on the experimental data obtained each with the two kinds of glass closed cells in the test, into Eq. (72) is necessarily higher than the value calculated by substituting the heat generation data, which are calculated based on the experimental data obtained with the glass open-cup cell in the test, into the same equation. We may, however, ascribe the dominant reason which effects the above differences among the three values of the BAM test for BPO to the fact that the exothermic decomposition reaction of BPO, which is accompanied with gas evolution, is suppressed under confined conditions in accordance with the Le Chatelier principle*.

For the above reasons, it is not advisable to use the closed cell in the adiabatic self-heating test from a point of view that we should always endeavor to get a T_c on the low temperature side, or on the safety side, for every chemical of the TD type. We have, nevertheless, no choice but to use some closed cell in the adiabatic self-heating test performed for a chemical of the TD type which is volatile or decomposes to evolve corrosive and/or toxic gases while tested. Conversely speaking, it follows that it is always advisable to use the thermally sensitive glass open-cup cell in the adiabatic self-heating test, unless the chemical tested is volatile or decomposes to evolve corrosive and/or toxic gases while tested.

* This principle may be stated in the following form. If a change occurs in one of the factors, such as temperature or pressure, under which a system is in equilibrium, the system will tend to adjust itself so as to annul, as far as possible, the effect of that change.

4.7 Procedure to calculate the values of the two coefficients, *a* and *b*, of Eq. (44), ln $\Delta t = a/T_s + b$, holding for the self-heating process, or for the oxidatively-heating process, in the early stages, of 2 cm^3 of a chemical of the TD type, including every gas-permeable oxidatively-heating substance, charged, or confined, in some one of the open-cup, the draft or the closed cell, in accordance with the self-heating property of the chemical, and subjected to either of the two kinds of adiabatic tests

Is explained, first of all, in detail the procedure to determine the time, Δt, required for the temperature of 2 cm^3 of a chemical of the TD type, including every gas-permeable oxidatively-heating substance, charged, or confined, in some one of the open-cup, the draft or the closed cell, in accordance with the self-heating property of the chemical, and subjected to either of the two kinds of adiabatic tests started each from a T_s, to increase by the definite value of ΔT of 1.25 K from the T_s in the adiabatic self-heating test, or from the corresponding standard temperature in the adiabatic oxidatively-heating test, by taking the procedure to determine the time, based on the two kinds of digital records obtained each from the adiabatic self-heating test, which is started from a nominal T_s of 76 ℃, performed, for 2 cm^3 of 99 % *tert*-butyl peroxybenzoate (TBPB) charged in the open-cup cell, for the time, Δt, required for the temperature of TBPB to increase by the definite value of ΔT of 1.25 K from the nominal T_s, as an example (Table 5).

In the case of the digital record of the self-heating process exemplified in Table 5, the digital D.C. microvoltmeter indicates that the exact value of the T_s of this run is 3111.5 μV. This value of T_s is determined, based on the fact that the indication of the digital D.C. microvoltmeter has fluctuated constantly between 3111 and 3112 μV for 1 to 2 h after the thermal equilibrium state has been attained around the reference material charged in the open-cup cell and inserted into the adiabatic jacket maintained at the nominal T_s of 76 ℃ in the adiabatic self-heating process recorder.

This value of D.C. microvoltage corresponds to 76.2805 ℃, *i.e.*, 349.4305 K, according to the thermoelectromotive force table for the Type K, *i.e.*, CA, thermocouples. A value of $1/T_s$ of 2.8618×10^{-3} K^{-1} is, hence, immediately calculated.

The value of (T_s + 1.25 K), *i.e.*, 350.6805 K, is next expressed as 3163.281 μV again according to the thermoelectromotive force table for the CA thermocouples.

The value of ΔT of 1.25 K expressed in μV unit, therefore, amounts to 51.781 (= 3163.281 - 3111.5) μV in this run. That is, the value of ΔT in each run is not always equal to the increment in thermoelectromotive force of 50 μV in the case of the CA thermocouple, as stated in **Subsection 4.5.8**.

Table 5. A digital record of the self-heating process, of 2 cm^3 of TBPB charged in the open-cup cell and subjected to the adiabatic self-heating test started from a nominal T_s of 76 ℃, for the time, Δt, required for the temperature of TBPB to increase by the definite value of ΔT of 1.25 K from the nominal T_s.

	min	mV	
3.17 mV → 3168 µN at 45 min	045	3.17	
	044	3.16	
	043	3.16	8 min
	042	3.16	
Here is T_s + 1.25 K. →	041	3.16	→ Δt = 41.2248 min.
	040	3.16	
	039	3.16	∴ ln Δt = 3.71904.
	038	3.16	
3.16 mV → 3158 µN at 37 min	037	3.16	
	036	3.15	
	035	3.15	
	034	3.15	
	033	3.15	
	032	3.15	8 min
	031	3.15	
	030	3.15	
	029	3.15	
	028	3.14	
	027	3.14	
	026	3.14	
	025	3.14	
	024	3.14	8 min
	023	3.14	
	022	3.14	
	021	3.14	
	020	3.13	
	019	3.13	
	018	3.13	
	017	3.13	
	016	3.13	9 min
	015	3.13	
	014	3.13	
	013	3.13	
	012	3.13	
	011	3.12	
	010	3.12	
	009	3.12	
	008	3.12	8 min
	007	3.12	
	006	3.12	
	005	3.12	
	004	3.12	
	003	3.11	
	002	3.11	4 min
	001	3.11	
	000	3.11	

T_s = 3111.5 µN →
- → T_s = 349.4305 K
- → $1/T_s = 2.8618 \times 10^{-3}\ K^{-1}$
- → T_s + 1.25 K = 3163.281 µN

Now, one temperature value, of 2 cm^3 of TBPB charged in the open-cup cell, of 3158 μV was indicated by the digital D.C. microvoltmeter 37 min after the start of the adiabatic self-heating test for TBPB, and the other temperature value, of 2 cm^3 of TBPB in the cell, of 3168 μV was indicated by the microvoltmeter 45 min after, so that the time, Δt, required for the temperature of 2 cm^3 of TBPB in the cell to increase by the definite value of ΔT of 1.25 K from the T_s must exist between 37 and 45 min.

This time, Δt, is calculated at 41.2248 min by the proportional allotment. This proportional allotment may be allowable, because an almost constant rate of increase in temperature of 2 cm^3 of TBPB charged in the open-cup cell and subjected to the adiabatic self-heating test has been realized all through this run. A value of $\ln \Delta t$ of 3.71904 is, hence, calculated immediately.

The other combinations of the value of $\ln \Delta t$ with that of $1/T_s$, which are required to make the plot of $\ln \Delta t$ versus $1/T_s$ with regard to several self-heating processes, of 2 cm^3 each of several samples of TBPB charged each in the open-cup cell and subjected each to the adiabatic self-heating test started from each T_s with mutual intervals of 1～2 K, recorded each for the time, Δt, required for the temperature of each sample of TBPB to increase by the definite value of ΔT of 1.25 K from the corresponding T_s, besides, which are required for the regression analysis to calculate the values of the two coefficients, *a* and *b*, of Eq. (44), $\ln \Delta t = a/T_s + b$, holding for the self-heating process, in the early stages, of 2 cm^3 of TBPB charged in the open-cup cell and subjected to the adiabatic self-heating test, are also determined in the same manner as explained above (see also Figures 45 and 46 in **Subsection 5.4.5**).

The result of the regression analysis to calculate the heat generation data of TBPB, *i.e.*, the values of the two coefficients, *a* and *b*, of Eq. (44), $\ln \Delta t = a/T_s + b$, holding for the self-heating process, in the early stages, of 2 cm^3 of TBPB charged in the open-cup cell and subjected to the adiabatic self-heating test, is presented in Table 6.

Table 6

The result of the regression analysis applied, in order to calculate the heat generation data of TBPB, to five combinations of the value of ln Δt with that of $1/T_s$, which are each determined, based on five digital records obtained each from five adiabatic self-heating tests, which are started from each T_s in the range of 73.18 to 79.62 ℃ with mutual intervals of 1～2 K, performed each, for 2 cm^3 each of five samples of TBPB charged each in the open-cup cell, for the time, Δt, required for the temperature of each sample of TBPB to increase by the definite value of ΔT of 1.25 K from the corresponding T_s. Data used are in common with those presented in Fig. 45 and plotted in Fig. 46.

MATERIAL ... TBPB

DATA NUMBER	X	Y	A*X+B
1	2.88739	4.31422	4.298766
2	2.87242	3.97191	3.969480
3	2.86180	3.71904	3.735878
4	2.85323	3.52308	3.547369
5	2.83472	3.16346	3.140216

COEFFICIENT OF Y = A * TT + B A = 21.99638
COEFFICIENT OF Y = A * TT + B B = -59.2134

DISTRIBUTION = 0.000553 STANDARD DEVIATION = 0.023512

Values of ln Δt and $1/T_s$ used in the regression analysis are in common with those presented in Fig. 45 and plotted in Fig. 46 in **Subsection 5.4.5**. The values of Δt and T_s presented in Figs. 45 and 46 are, however, all rounded. For further details, compare Tables 5 and 6 in the present section with Figs. 45 and 46 in **Subsection 5.4.5**.

Each value of X in Table 6 has been obtained by multiplying the corresponding value of $1/T_s$ by 1,000; in the meantime, each value of Y is nothing else but the corresponding value of ln Δt. The value of a for TBPB is, therefore, calculated by multiplying the value of A, which is presented in Table 6, by 1,000.

The values of the two coefficients, a and b, thus calculated, of Eq. (44), $\ln \Delta t = a/T_s + b$, holding for the self-heating process, in the early stages, of 2 cm^3 of TBPB charged in the open-cup cell and subjected to the adiabatic self-heating test, 21996.38 and -59.2134, *i.e.*, the heat generation data of TBPB, are presented as such in Table 8 in **Subsection 5.7.1**.

References to Chapter 4

[28] T. Kotoyori and M. Maruta, An Adiabatic Self-Ignition Testing Apparatus, Thermochimica Acta, **67**, 35-44 (1983).
[29] D.I. Townsend and J.C. Tou, Thermal Hazard Evaluation by an Accelerating Rate Calorimeter, Thermochimica Acta, **37**, 12 (1980).

Chapter 5 Procedure to calculate the T_c for an arbitrary volume of a liquid charged in an arbitrary container and placed in the atmosphere under isothermal conditions

5.1 Introduction

It is possible to calculate the T_c for an arbitrary volume of a liquid charged in an arbitrary container and placed in the atmosphere under isothermal conditions by applying the reduced form of the Semenov equation.*

That is, for the purpose of calculating the T_c for an arbitrary volume of a liquid charged in an arbitrary container and placed in the atmosphere under isothermal conditions, we have only to perform, on the one hand, several adiabatic self-heating tests, which are started from each T_s with mutual intervals of 1～2 K, in order to calculate the heat generation data of the liquid, for 2 cm^3 each of several samples of the liquid charged each in the open-cup cell, for the time, Δt, required for the temperature of each sample of the liquid to increase by the definite value of ΔT of 1.25 K from the corresponding T_s, respectively, and, we have only to measure, on the other hand, apart from the measurements of the individual values of c and ρ of the liquid, the main heat transfer data**, *i.e.*, the individual values of q_2 and (T_{liq} - $T_{set\text{-}up}$), of an arbitrary volume of the liquid charged in an arbitrary container and placed in the atmosphere maintained at a $T_{set\text{-}up}$, in temperature differences of 1.25 K between the T_{liq} and the $T_{set\text{-}up}$, under conditions of no air circulation.

Thus, the procedure to calculate the T_c for an arbitrary volume of a liquid charged in an arbitrary container and placed in the atmosphere under isothermal conditions by applying the reduced form of the Semenov equation is introduced in the present chapter by taking the procedure to calculate the value of the BAM

* It is also of course possible to calculate the T_c for an arbitrary volume of a liquid confined in an arbitrary closed container and placed in the atmosphere under isothermal conditions by applying the reduced form of the Semenov equation. It is, however, required in such a case to obtain both the heat generation data and the heat transfer data of the liquid under confined conditions. In this connection, the adiabatic self-heating tests were performed, in the present chapter, at atmospheric pressure for nine organic liquid peroxides, other than DTBP, respectively, because these nine peroxides are not very volatile or do not decompose to evolve corrosive and/or toxic gases while tested, respectively.

** The two data, q_2 and (T_{liq} - $T_{set\text{-}up}$), in the five heat transfer data, *i.e.*, q_2, (T_{liq} - $T_{set\text{-}up}$), c, ρ and V, of an arbitrary volume of a liquid charged in an arbitrary container and placed in the atmosphere under isothermal conditions are called the main heat transfer data of the liquid, because c, ρ and V are a relatively easily measurable physical quantity, respectively. In particular, the volume, V, of a liquid charged in an arbitrary container is a physical quantity easily measurable without performing any specific experiment.

test for 400 cm^3 of TBPB,* assuming that it is charged in the 500 cm^3 Dewar flask used in the BAM (Bundesanstalt für Materialforschung und -prüfung, Berlin) heat-accumulation storage test and is placed in the atmosphere under isothermal conditions, as an example.

The values of the BAM test thus calculated each for ten organic liquid peroxides, including TBPB, ranged from 22.7 ℃ for THPN to 92.4 ℃ for DTBP.

These values of the BAM test calculated herein in general are in fair agreement with the corresponding values measured each actually by a series of BAM heat-accumulation storage tests performed at a peroxide manufacturing company, respectively.

5.2 The reason why the Semenov equation is applicable to the calculation of the T_c for an arbitrary volume of a liquid charged in an arbitrary container and placed in the atmosphere under isothermal conditions without stirring the liquid or circulating air around the container

It has already been confirmed well that it is possible, in principle, to calculate the T_c for a powdery chemical of the TD type, including every gas-permeable oxidatively-heating substance, having an arbitrary shape and an arbitrary size, placed in the atmosphere under isothermal conditions, by applying the F-K equation, *i.e.*, Eq. (29) derived in **Section 1.3**. On the other hand, the method to calculate the T_c for an arbitrary volume of a liquid charged in an arbitrary container and placed in the atmosphere under isothermal conditions has so far been left unresolved.

The Semenov equation, Eq. (17) derived in **Section 1.2**, *i.e.*, one of the two equations constituting the thermal explosion theory,

$$\frac{\varDelta H \cdot A_0 EVe}{USRT_c^2}\exp\left[-\frac{E}{RT_c}\right] = 1, \tag{17}$$

originally describes, as explained in **Section 1.2**, that the T_c for a self-heating fluid, which was actually assumed to be a self-heating gas in the original formulation performed by Semenov, filled in an arbitrary container and placed in the atmosphere under isothermal conditions is decided, based on the balance between the rate of heat generation in the fluid and the rate of heat transfer from the fluid to the atmosphere at the critical state for the thermal explosion which exists at the end of the early stages of the self-heating process. In this

* For the abbreviations of organic liquid peroxides tested herein, refer to Table 7 in **Subsection 5.7.1**.

connection, the spatial distribution of temperature in the fluid was assumed to be uniform by Semenov.

Now, every liquid may also have the uniform distribution of internal temperature as a kind of fluid. In other words, as stated in **Section 1.5**, it will be permitted to say that a condition, $U << \lambda$, holds at all times, on account of its own fluidity, in an arbitrary volume of every liquid charged in an arbitrary container and placed in the atmosphere under isothermal conditions. The problem in considering the critical condition for the thermal explosion of a liquid is, thus, not the heat transfer by the convection in the mass of the liquid, but the heat transfer or the heat loss by the conduction from the liquid charged in an arbitrary container and placed in the atmosphere under isothermal conditions, through the whole liquid surface, across the container walls, to the atmosphere.

Researchers, who each participated in the past in the study of the thermal explosion of any liquid, nevertheless, used to consider that it was improper and impossible to apply the Semenov equation to the calculation of the T_c for an arbitrary volume of a liquid charged in an arbitrary container and placed in the atmosphere under isothermal conditions, because they considered that the Semenov's prerequisite that the spatial distribution of temperature in and around the fluid be uniform did not hold on account of the convection or the buoyancy to occur in the self-heating liquid.*

It has thus been made a common sense hitherto to stir a liquid or to circulate air around the container in order to make sure of the Semenov's prerequisite, whenever it is attempted to measure the T_c for the liquid. Even if a liquid charged in the container is stirred, however, the fact that the value of U of the liquid charged in the container is not uniform all over the liquid surface still remains as an inevitable reality, as discussed in **Subsection 5.3.2**.

On the other hand, as Verhoeff described in his book [30], and as even we can foresee readily, the vigorous convection or even the bubbling comes to occur in a self-heating liquid, as the liquid temperature increases acceleratedly over the critical state for the thermal explosion. These phenomena are, however, to occur in the stages immediately before the thermal explosion. In such stages, the prerequisite that the spatial distribution of internal temperature of the liquid be uniform may or may not break. In either case, such phenomena or stages have no concern with the Semenov equation, because such phenomena do not occur at all while the self-heating process is in the early stages.

Our logic thus finds its way to a proposition that the Semenov equation is applicable to the calculation of the T_c for an arbitrary volume of a liquid charged in an arbitrary container and placed in the atmosphere under isothermal conditions, provided the spatial distribution of temperature in the mass of the liquid is as uniform as that in a normal gas while the self-heating process of the liquid is in the early stages.

---

* It is thought that this consideration originated from the Frank-Kamenetskii's assertion [16].

In this regard, it has been ascertained in a series of experiments to measure the individual main heat transfer data of several volumes of kerosene charged each in the corresponding containers and placed each in the atmosphere maintained at each $T_{set\text{-}up}$ near 50 ℃ that the scattering of the spatial distribution of temperature in the mass of kerosene, which is not mechanically stirred and is maintained at temperatures 0.9~1.3 K higher than the $T_{set\text{-}up}$, is less than $\pm 1\ \mu V$ in the case of the CA thermocouple, *i.e.*, less than ± 0.025 K in every case, except the thin upper surface layer, which is less than 5 mm in thickness, and in which the temperature is about 0.025 K higher than that in the mass of kerosene (refer to **Subsections 5.5.3** and **5.7.2**).* In these experiments, it was made a rule to limit the value of (T_{liq} - $T_{set\text{-}up}$) to 0.9~1.3 K,** as an experimental technique to make the spatial distribution of temperature in the mass of kerosene as uniform as possible. It was thought that the above rule had good reasons for simulating the early stages of the self-heating process of a liquid.

Based on the above ascertainment, the spatial distribution of temperature in the mass of a liquid in the early stages of the self-heating process has been assumed to be as uniform as that in a normal gas throughout a series of studies, with regard to the values of T_c for liquids, described in the present chapter, even if the liquid is not mechanically stirred.

It thus follows that it is possible to apply the Semenov equation to the calculation of the T_c for an arbitrary volume of a liquid charged in an arbitrary container and placed in the atmosphere under isothermal conditions without stirring the liquid or without circulating air around the container, provided the heat generation data of the liquid are calculated based on the experimental data obtained while the self-heating process is in the early stages, and, provided the main heat transfer data of the liquid charged in the container are also measured while the self-heating process is in the early stages.

And actually, it has been substantiated that it is possible to calculate the T_c for an arbitrary volume of a liquid charged in an arbitrary container and placed in the atmosphere under isothermal conditions, by substituting both the heat generation data of the liquid, which are calculated based on the experimental data obtained in temperature differences of 1.25 K between the T_{liq} and the T_s, and, the main heat transfer data of the liquid, which are measured in temperature differences of 1.25 K between the T_{liq} and the $T_{set\text{-}up}$, under conditions of no air circulation, as well as the individual values of c and ρ of the liquid, into the reduced form of the Semenov equation, *i.e.*, Eq. (72) derived in **Subsection 5.3.2**.

---

* In these experiments, the thermocouple to measure the T_{liq} of kerosene was movable in the vertical direction.

** For the values of (T_{liq} - $T_{set\text{-}up}$) of 0.9~1.3 K, refer to **Subsections 5.5.3** and **5.7.2**.

5.3 Derivation of equations

5.3.1 Mean overall coefficient of heat transfer, *U*, of a fluid filled in the container and placed in the atmosphere under isothermal conditions

According to Semenov and Frank-Kamenetskii, the mode of heat transfer from a fluid filled in a container and placed in the atmosphere under isothermal conditions, through the whole fluid surface, across the container walls, to the atmosphere is almost entirely conductive. In Semenov's book, it reads as follows [31].

「

> We now consider the heat transfer from gas to vessel wall in more detail.
> Putting $q_2 = \kappa(T - T_0)S$, we suppose the transfer convective; it is then very difficult to calculate κ. However, it has been shown that if $P<1$ [atm] and the vessel is small, as is usual in self-ignition experiments, and ΔT_s is also small*, the transfer is almost entirely conductive. Frank-Kamenetskii first noted this, and replaced convective heat transfer by conductive in self-ignition theory.

」

On the other hand, it is established in chemical engineering that the laminar flow, not the convective flow, occurs within the fluid film**, so that the heat transfer from the fluid, through the fluid film, to the solid wall is performed by the conduction.

The existence and the property of the fluid film were confirmed and studied by A. A. Noyes and W. R. Whitney [33], W. Nernst [34] and L. Prandtl [35] early in the 20th century.

A temperature distribution effected at the time when the heat transfer is performed from a fluid to a solid wall is exemplified in Fig. 43. To cite one instance, such a temperature distribution was confirmed by I. Langmuir similarly early in the 20th century [36].

---

* ΔT_s, in the Semenov's scheme, expresses the same concept as ΔT_c, the so-called pre-explosion rise, in Eq. (12) in **Section 1.2**, or, ΔT in Eq. (55) in **Section 2.6**.

** The thin fluid layer in the immediate neighborhood of the solid surface is called the fluid film [32]. In this connection, there are instances where the fluid film is referred to as the laminar film, the boundary layer or the viscous sublayer.

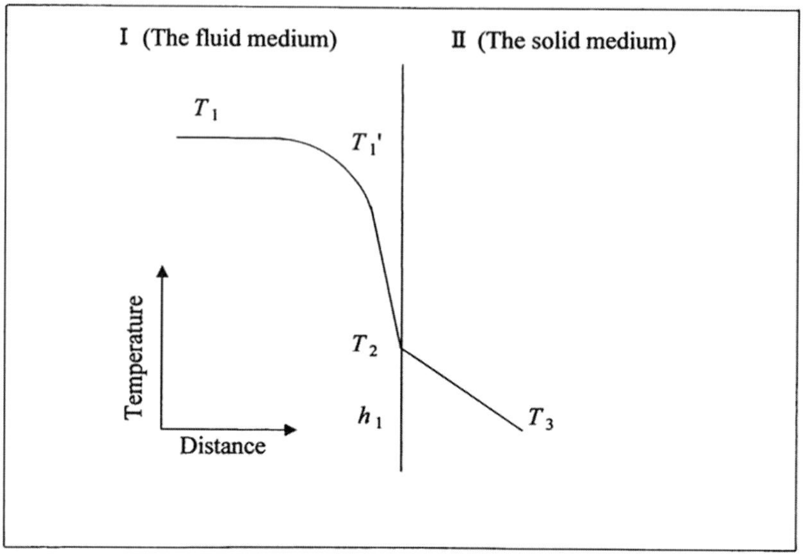

Figure 43. A temperature distribution in the heat transfer between a fluid and a solid.

As a matter of fact, the fluid film in which the convective flow does not occur and the region in which the temperature gradient can be recognized are not the same; rather, the thickness of the latter region is far wider than that of the former film. Besides, the boundary between the fluid film and the mass of fluid in which the convective flow occurs is not well-defined, so that the position of a temperature such as T_1' in Fig. 43 can not be determined exactly. Therefore, one makes it a rule to express the heat transfer in this occasion with the following equation, expressing the temperature difference between the two mediums concerned as (T_1 - T_2),

$$q_2 = hS(T_1 - T_2), \tag{62}$$

where h is called the film coefficient of heat transfer. The coefficient, h, has units of cal/(cm^2·min·K), and these units correspond, expressing dimensionally, to those of λ/length.

Installations, in each of which the heat transfer is carried out between two kinds of fluids including air across a metal wall, are often used in the chemical industry.

The temperature distribution in such an occasion is shown by means of T_1, T_1', T_2, T_3, T_4' and T_4, because two kinds of fluid films exist on both sides of the solid wall (Fig. 44).

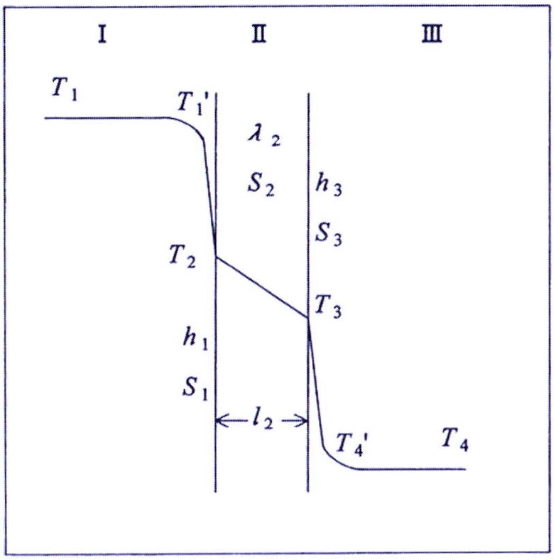

Figure 44. A temperature distribution in the heat transfer between two fluids across a solid wall.

The following equations then hold for the fluid medium I, for the solid medium II and for the other fluid medium III, respectively.

For the fluid medium I : $$q_2 = h_1 S_1 \left(T_{liq} - T_2\right) = \frac{T_{liq} - T_2}{\dfrac{1}{h_1 S_1}}. \qquad (63)$$

For the solid medium II : $$q_2 = \frac{\lambda_2 S_2 \left(T_2 - T_3\right)}{l_2} = \frac{T_2 - T_1}{\dfrac{l_2}{\lambda_2 S_2}}. \qquad (64)$$

For the fluid medium III : $$q_2 = h_3 S_3 \left(T_3 - T_a\right) = \frac{T_3 - T_a}{\dfrac{1}{h_3 S_3}}. \qquad (65)$$

In Eqs. (63) and (65), T_1 and T_4 are assumed to be T_{liq} and T_a, respectively. Thus,

$$\left(T_{liq} - T_2\right) + \left(T_2 - T_3\right) + \left(T_3 - T_a\right) = q_2\left(\frac{1}{h_1 S_1} + \frac{l_2}{\lambda_2 S_2} + \frac{1}{h_3 S_3}\right). \tag{66}$$

So we obtain,

$$q_2 = \frac{T_{liq} - T_a}{\dfrac{1}{h_1 S_1} + \dfrac{l_2}{\lambda_2 S_2} + \dfrac{1}{h_3 S_3}}. \tag{67}$$

However, the following equation may also hold in a simplified expression, because the rate of heat transfer, q_2, is proportional as a whole to both the temperature difference between the two fluids I and III, (T_{liq} -T_a), and the whole fluid surface, S,

$$q_2 = US\left(T_{liq} - T_a\right). \tag{68}$$

Comparison of Eqs. (67) and (68) immediately leads to the result,

$$US = \frac{1}{\dfrac{1}{h_1 S_1} + \dfrac{l_2}{\lambda_2 S_2} + \dfrac{1}{h_3 S_3}}. \tag{69}$$

U is called the mean overall coefficient of heat transfer, because it is the coefficient of heat transfer extending over the two kinds of fluid films sandwiching a solid wall in between them. The units of U are cal/(cm^2·min·K), which are of course the same as those of h.

5.3.2 Derivation of the reduced form of the Semenov equation

A proposition is obtained in **Section 2.4** to the effect that it is possible to replace the chemical quantities, E, A_0 and ΔH, included in the Semenov equation,

$$\frac{\Delta H \cdot A_0 E V e}{U S R T_c^2} \exp\left[-\frac{E}{R T_c}\right] = 1, \tag{17}$$

with the two coefficients, *a* and *b*, of Eq. (44),

$$\ln \Delta t = \frac{a}{T_s} + b, \tag{44}$$

holding for the self-heating process, or for the oxidatively-heating process, in the early stages, of 2 cm^3 of a chemical of the TD type, including every gas-permeable oxidatively-heating substance, charged, or confined, in some one of the open-cup, the draft or the closed cell, in accordance with the self-heating property of the chemical, and subjected to either of the two kinds of adiabatic tests.

Taking the natural logarithms on both sides of Eq. (17), and then rearranging them, we get

$$2 \ln T_c + \frac{(E / R)}{T_c} = \ln\left[\frac{(\Delta H \cdot A_0)(E / R) V e}{U S}\right]. \tag{70}$$

Substituting Eqs. (45) and (46) presented in **Section 2.4**, *i.e.*,

$$a = \frac{E}{R} \tag{45}$$

and

$$b = \ln[\Delta T \cdot c\rho] - \ln[\Delta H \cdot A_0], \tag{46}$$

for (E / R) and $\ln(\Delta H \cdot A_0)$ in Eq. (70), respectively, we obtain

$$2 \ln T_c + \frac{a}{T_c} = \ln\left[\frac{a c \rho V e \cdot \Delta T}{U S}\right] - b. \tag{71}$$

In considering the application of Eq. (71)[*] to the calculation of the T_c for an arbitrary volume of a liquid charged in an arbitrary container and placed in the atmosphere under isothermal conditions, two physical quantities, U and S, present some seeming difficulties. First, the value of U of a liquid charged in the container and placed in the atmosphere under isothermal conditions is not uniform all over the liquid surface; to put it concretely, the upper surface of the liquid is directly in contact with air in the container, which in turn is in contact with a shelf or a floor at its base, while the other surfaces of the liquid are indirectly in contact with the atmosphere outside the container across the walls. Secondly, it is somewhat troublesome to measure precisely the value of S of a liquid charged in the container. Thirdly, although the temperature of the mass of a liquid is almost uniform on account of the convection, the upper thin surface layer tends to take a value of temperature slightly higher than that of the mass for the same reason or on account of the buoyancy.

The only practical way these difficulties can be solved well is to measure simultaneously both the value of U (as the mean value over the whole surface of a liquid) and the value of S of a liquid charged in the container in the form of their product, US. The term, US, is defined by the following equation[**], *i.e.*,

$$q_2 = US\left(T_{liq} - T_{set-up}\right). \tag{68'}$$

It is possible to calculate, based on Eq. (68'), the value of US of an arbitrary volume of a liquid charged in an arbitrary container and placed in the atmosphere under isothermal conditions, by measuring the temperature difference, (T_{liq} - $T_{set\text{-}up}$), which is effected at a steady state under static conditions, *i.e.*, under conditions of no air circulation, between the inside of the liquid and the atmosphere, at the time when a definite electrical heat flow, q_2, is generated in a nonconducting liquid, such as kerosene, charged in the container in place of the (self-heating) liquid. For further details of the experimental method to measure the values of q_2 and (T_{liq} - $T_{set\text{-}up}$) of an arbitrary volume of a liquid charged in an arbitrary container and placed in the atmosphere under isothermal conditions, refer to **Subsections 5.5.3** and **5.7.2**. The volume of the nonconducting liquid must, of course, be equal to that of a liquid to be charged in the container of the same type and size.

Substituting Eq. (68') into Eq. (71), to eliminate the term, US, we obtain

$$2\ln T_c + \frac{a}{T_c} = \ln\left[\frac{ac\rho V\mathrm{e}\cdot \Delta T\left(T_{liq} - T_{set-up}\right)}{q_2}\right] - b. \tag{72}$$

---

[*] It is apparent to us that a relation, $\rho V = m$, holds in Eqs. (71) and (72).

[**] As commented in **Notation**, when a container, in which a liquid is charged, is placed in a set-up in order to measure the main heat transfer data of the liquid, the T_a is expressed as the $T_{set\text{-}up}$.

We see from Eq. (72) that, so far as our purpose is to calculate the T_c for an arbitrary volume of a liquid charged in an arbitrary container and placed in the atmosphere under isothermal conditions, we may dispense with the direct knowledge of the values of E, A_0, ΔH, U and S of the liquid. This is what is pointed out in **Section 2.4**.

The values of the five variables, q_2, $(T_{liq} - T_{set\text{-}up})$, c, ρ and V, included in Eq. (72) are called hereafter the heat transfer data of an arbitrary volume of a liquid charged in an arbitrary container and placed in the atmosphere under isothermal conditions, by contrast with the heat generation data of a chemical of the TD type, *i.e.*, the values of the two coefficients, a and b, of Eq. (44).

It is considered in Eq. (72) that the values of q_2, $(T_{liq} - T_{set\text{-}up})$ are both the shape factor and the size factor, or the quantity factor, of a liquid charged in the container and placed in the atmosphere under isothermal conditions, and, the value of V is only the size factor, or the quantity factor, of the liquid.

In this connection, the individual values of c and ρ, as well as the heat generation data, a and b, of a liquid depend on the kind of the liquid, but these values do not depend on its shape and size.

In any event, the T_c for an arbitrary volume of a liquid charged in an arbitrary container and placed in the atmosphere under isothermal conditions is calculated by substituting the five heat transfer data above referred to and the heat generation data, a and b, as well as the base of natural logarithm, e, and the definite value of ΔT of 1.25 K, into Eq. (72), *i.e.*, the reduced form of the Semenov equation.

The procedure to perform several adiabatic self-heating tests, which are started from each T_s with mutual intervals of 1∼2 K, in order to calculate the heat generation data of a liquid, for 2 cm^3 each of several samples of the liquid charged each in the open-cup cell, for the time, Δt, required for the temperature of each sample of the liquid to increase by the definite value of ΔT of 1.25 K from the corresponding T_s, respectively, is explained in detail **Section 5.4** by taking the procedure performed for 2 cm^3 of TBPB charged in the open-cup cell as an example.

The experimental method to measure the main heat transfer data of an arbitrary volume of a liquid charged in an arbitrary container and placed in the atmosphere maintained at a $T_{set\text{-}up}$, in temperature differences of 1.25 K between the T_{liq} and the $T_{set\text{-}up}$, under conditions of no air circulation, is explained in detail in **Subsections 5.5.3** and **5.7.2**.

The individual experimental methods to measure the values of c and ρ of a chemical are explained in **Subsection 5.5.4**.

The concrete procedure to calculate the T_c for an arbitrary volume of a liquid charged in an arbitrary container and placed in the atmosphere under isothermal conditions is illustrated in **Section 5.6** by taking the procedure to calculate the value of the BAM test for 400 cm^3 of TBPB, assuming that it is charged in a

500 cm^3 Dewar flask used in the BAM test and is placed in the atmosphere under isothermal conditions, as an example.

It is seen in Eq. (71) that, generally speaking, the value of T_c for an arbitrary volume of a liquid charged in an arbitrary container and placed in the atmosphere under isothermal conditions increases with increasing the value of US; on the other hand, the value of T_c decreases with increasing the individual values of c, ρ and V.

In this connection, it is apparent to us that it is also possible to calculate, in the same manner as performed for a liquid, the T_c for an arbitrary quantity of a self-heating gas filled, or confined, in an arbitrary container and placed in the atmosphere under isothermal conditions.

5.4 Procedure to perform several adiabatic self-heating tests, which are started from each T_s with mutual intervals of 1～2 K, in order to calculate the heat generation data of a liquid, for 2 cm^3 each of several samples of the liquid charged each in the open-cup cell, for the time, Δt, required for the temperature of each sample of the liquid to increase by the definite value of ΔT of 1.25 K from the corresponding T_s, respectively

The procedure described in the above heading is explained in the present section by taking the procedure performed for 2 cm^3 of TBPB charged in the open-cup cell as an example.

5.4.1 Preheating of the air bath of the adiabatic self-heating process recorder and the choice of a nominal T_s in the adiabatic self-heating test performed for 2 cm^3 of TBPB charged in the open-cup cell

The temperature of the air bath is set at a proper value, *i.e.*, the nominal T_s of the run, by means of the temperature dial on the air bath on the basis of the self-heating property of the liquid tested to give estimated rates of increase in temperature of 1.25 K/h in the adiabatic self-heating test. It is usually a temperature 20～30 K lower than the EOT, which is measured by thermal analysis, such as DTA or DSC, of each liquid in the case of liquids tested herein, with the result that the T_s ranged from 27.29 ℃ for THPN to 100.6 ℃ for DTBP. As to TBPB, the T_s ranged from 73.18 to 79.62 ℃.

To begin with, the main power supply connected to the adiabatic self-heating process recorder is switched on.

The power supplies connected to the cold junction, the air bath, the digital D.C. microvoltmeter, the digital D.C. millivolt recorder and the two-pen strip chart recorder are then switched on, respectively. The ΔT_{diff} pen of the two-pen strip chart recorder is, however, left on the "short" position until the thermal equilibrium state is nearly attained around the reference material charged in the open-cup cell and inserted into the adiabatic jacket maintained at the nominal T_s of the run. For the term, the ΔT_{diff} pen, refer to **Subsection 4.5.4**.

5.4.2 Procedure to prepare the reference cell assembly including the open-cup cell

2.2 g of silica powder, the volume of which is about 2 cm^3, is charged in an open-cup cell, *i.e.*, the cell with which the reference cell is prepared. The glass jig mentioned in a footnote in **Section 7.3** is used at this time to provide a thin vertical hole at the center of silica powder charged in the cell in order to facilitate the insertion of the thermocouple into silica powder.

The reference cell thus prepared is then set on the pedestal which is stuck at the center of the upper plate of the laboratory jack, which in turn is fixed on the laboratory desk. The position of the stand, by means of which the stem including the glass vent tube is held in the vertical position, is next adjusted by sliding the stand horizontally on the desk in order that the glass vent tube may be aligned vertically with the reference cell set on the pedestal.

The reference cell is then combined concentrically and softly with the ground glass joint of the glass vent tube by raising the laboratory jack to construct the reference cell assembly; in the meantime, the CA thermocouple, covered with a glass capillary tube, to measure the T_{ref} is inserted automatically and axially to the longitudinal center of silica powder charged in the cell. The reference cell combined with the ground glass joint of the glass vent tube is finally supported firmly with a thin aluminium washer and two springs. After having lowered the laboratory jack a little, a fairly small vibrator is applied to the base of the open-cup cell in order that silica powder charged in the cell may come closely in contact with the glass capillary tube.

For further details of the procedure to prepare the reference cell assembly including the open-cup cell, refer to **Section 7.3**.

5.4.3 Insertion of the reference cell assembly into the adiabatic jacket set in the preheated air bath and the determination of the exact value of T_s of the run

The reference cell assembly thus prepared is inserted into the adiabatic jacket set in the preheated air bath.

The thermal equilibrium state is attained around the reference material charged in the open-cup cell and inserted into the adiabatic jacket maintained at the nominal T_s of the run 2～3 h after the insertion of the reference cell assembly into the jacket. After the thermal equilibrium state has nearly been attained around the reference material, the power supply to the analog D.C.

microvoltmeter is switched on; in the meantime, the ΔT_{diff} pen of the two-pen strip chart recorder is also switched over from "short" to "on". It is then observed that the indicator of the analog D.C. microvoltmeter enters on to the scale span of the meter from the minus side, and, it comes to stay near the graduation line of zero at the center of the scale span of the meter; in the meantime, the ΔT_{diff} pen of the two-pen strip chart recorder also enters on to the strip chart of the two-pen strip chart recorder from the minus side. For the term, the minus side, refer to **Subsection 4.5.4**.

Curves drawn by the T pen and the ΔT_{diff} pen on the strip chart of the two-pen strip recorder, by the time that the thermal equilibrium state has been attained around the reference material charged in the open-cup cell and inserted into the adiabatic jacket maintained at the nominal T_s of the run, are similar to those illustrated in Fig. 38 in **Subsection 4.5.4**.

The digital output of the thermoelectromotive force of the CA thermocouple to measure the T_{ref} is then noted down as the exact value of T_s of the run, and the zero-suppression procedure is performed. For the term, the zero-suppression procedure, refer to a footnote in **Subsection 4.5.5**.

5.4.4 Insertion of the sample cell assembly into the adiabatic jacket maintained at the T_s of the run and the start of the adiabatic self-heating test for 2 cm^3 of TBPB charged in the open-cup cell

The power supply to the analog D.C. microvoltmeter is then switched off for a while; in the meantime, the ΔT_{diff} pen of the two-pen strip chart recorder is also switched over from "on" to "short" for a while.

The reference cell assembly is successively taken out of the jacket, and the sample cell assembly including an open-cup cell, in which 2 cm^3 of TBPB has been charged in the same manner as performed to prepare the reference cell assembly in **Subsection 5.4.2**, is inserted into the adiabatic jacket. 2 cm^3 was chosen herein as the standard sample volume in the adiabatic self-heating test performed for each liquid. The quantity of a liquid tested, however, depends naturally on the specific gravity, with the result that it ranged from about 1.6 g for DTBP to about 2.3 g for BPOD in the case of liquids tested herein.

Although the temperature of TBPB begins to increase from a temperature near room temperature after the insertion of the sample cell assembly, the thermal equilibrium state comes to be attained again around TBPB charged in the open-cup cell and inserted into the adiabatic jacket maintained at the T_s of the run in the course of tens of minutes. After the thermal equilibrium state has nearly been attained around TBPB, the power supply to the analog D.C. microvoltmeter is again switched on; in the meantime, the ΔT_{diff} pen of the two-pen strip chart recorder is also switched over again from "short" to "on". It is then observed that the indicator of the analog D.C. microvoltmeter enters again on to the scale span of the meter from the minus side; in the meantime, the ΔT_{diff} pen of the two-pen strip chart recorder also enters again on to the strip chart of the two-pen strip chart recorder from the minus side.

Once the indicator of the analog D.C. microvoltmeter reaches the graduation line of zero at the center of the scale span of the meter, the adiabatic control by means of the adiabatic self-heating process recorder and the record of the self-heating process, in the early stages, of 2 cm^3 of TBPB charged in the open-cup cell by means of the digital D.C. millivolt recorder are started, respectively. This point of time corresponds to the point "**s**" in Fig. 15 presented in **Section 3.4**.

At this time, the ΔT_{diff} pen also gets to the ΔT_{diff} base line on the strip chart of the two-pen strip chart recorder (see Fig. 39 in **Subsection 4.5.6**). However, the temperature of TBPB indicated by the digital D.C. microvoltmeter in general takes a value slightly lower than that of the T_s at this time, because, while the T_{atm}, the temperature of the atmosphere around TBPB, is still slightly lower than the T_s, TBPB begins to self-heat in the cell, so that the temperature of TBPB catches the T_{atm} up.

5.4.5 Record of the self-heating process, in the early stages, of 2 cm^3 of TBPB charged in the open-cup cell and inserted into the adiabatic jacket kept always at the very slowly increasing temperature of TBPB itself by the adiabatic control

After the start of the adiabatic control, the T_{atm} is raised automatically by the adiabatic control in order that the condition, $\Delta T_{diff} = T - T_{atm} = 0$, may always hold, with the result that the heat generated in the self-heating TBPB is all accumulated in it, and, it continues to self-heat at a very slow, but virtually constant, rate depending on the value of T_s; in the meantime, the temperature of the space in the air bath, except that in the adiabatic jacket, is maintained at the T_s of the run throughout every run.

The self-heating process, in the early stages, of 2 cm^3 of TBPB charged in the open-cup cell and inserted into the adiabatic jacket kept always at the very slowly increasing temperature of TBPB itself by the adiabatic control is recorded in the digital representation as the variation of the value, with time, of the thermoelectromotive force of the thermocouple to measure the temperature of TBPB; to put it concretely, the numerical value of the thermoelectromotive force of the thermocouple is printed out every minute by means of the digital D.C. millivolt recorder, in such a manner as exemplified in Table 5 presented in **Section 4.7**, in order to utilize the record for the calculation of the values of the two coefficients, a and b, of Eq. (44), $\ln \Delta t = a/T_s + b$, holding for the self-heating process, in the early stages, of 2 cm^3 of TBPB charged in the open-cup cell and subjected to the adiabatic self-heating test.

On the other hand, however, the self-heating process, in the early stages, of 2 cm^3 of TBPB charged in the open-cup cell and subjected to the adiabatic self-heating test is recorded, as an analog signal as well, with the T pen on the strip chart of the two-pen strip chart recorder to look about the process as a whole.

The test is interrupted as soon as the temperature of TBPB in the cell increases by the definite value of ΔT of 1.25 K from the T_s.

The other combinations of the value of $\ln \Delta t$ with that of $1/T_s$, which are required to make the plot of $\ln \Delta t$ versus $1/T_s$ with regard to several self-heating processes, of 2 cm^3 each of several samples of TBPB charged each in the open-cup cell and subjected each to the adiabatic self-heating test started from each T_s in the range of 73.18 to 79.62 ℃ with mutual intervals of 1～2 K, recorded each for the time, Δt, required for the temperature of each sample of TBPB to increase by the definite value of ΔT of 1.25 K from the corresponding T_s, besides, which are required for the regression analysis to calculate the values of the two coefficients, a and b, of Eq. (44), $\ln \Delta t = a/T_s + b$, holding for the self-heating process, in the early stages, of 2 cm^3 of TBPB charged in the open-cup cell and subjected to the adiabatic self-heating test, are also determined in the same manner as explained above.

Five self-heating processes, of 2 cm^3 each of five samples of TBPB charged each in the open-cup cell and subjected each to the adiabatic self-heating test started from each T_s in the range of 73.18 to 79.62 ℃ with mutual intervals of 1～2 K, recorded each for the time, Δt, required for the temperature of each sample of TBPB to increase by the definite value of ΔT of 1.25 K from the corresponding T_s, are presented in Fig. 45. The point marked with "**0**" on the time axis in Fig. 45 corresponds to the point of time "**s**" in Fig. 15 presented in **Section 3.4**.

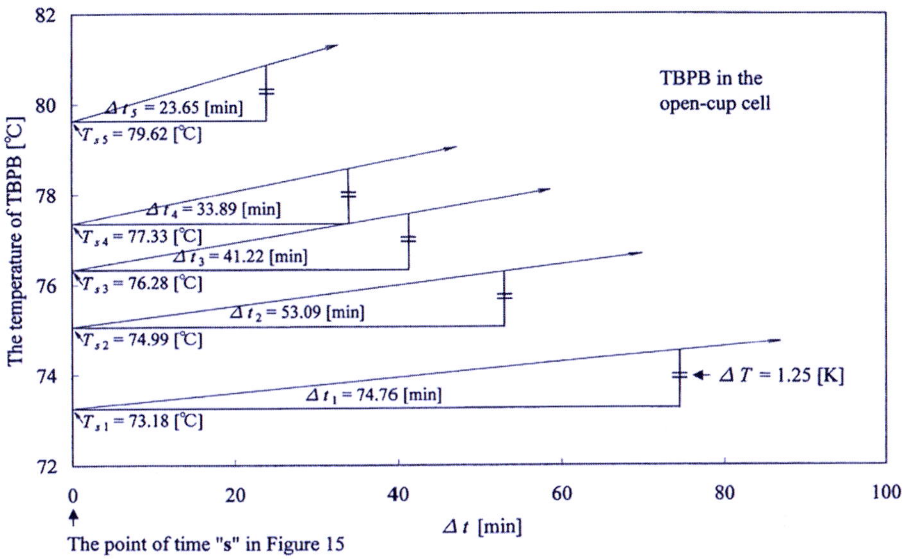

Figure 45. Five self-heating processes, of 2 cm^3 each of five samples of TBPB charged each in the open-cup cell and subjected each to the adiabatic self-heating test started from each T_s in the range of 73.18 to 79.62 ℃ with mutual intervals of 1～2 K, recorded each for the time, Δt, required for the temperature of each sample of TBPB to increase by the definite value of ΔT of 1.25 K from the corresponding T_s.

The plot of $\ln \Delta t$ versus $1/T_s$ made for 2 cm^3 each of five samples of TBPB is shown in Fig. 46.

It is obvious in Fig. 46 that the empirical formula, $\ln \Delta t = a/T_s + b$, *i.e.*, Eq. (44), presented in Fig. 15 in **Section 3.4** holds well between a T_s and the time, Δt, required for the temperature of 2 cm^3 of TBPB charged in the open-cup cell and subjected to the adiabatic self-heating test started from the T_s to increase by the definite value of ΔT of 1.25 K from the T_s.

For the value of a coefficient, 21996.38, of the equation, $\ln \Delta t = 21996.38/T_s$ - 59.2134, *i.e.*, Eq. (44) holding for the self-heating process, in the early stages, of 2 cm^3 of TBPB charged in the open-cup cell and subjected to the adiabatic self-heating test, refer to the explanation given under Table 6 in **Section 4.7**.

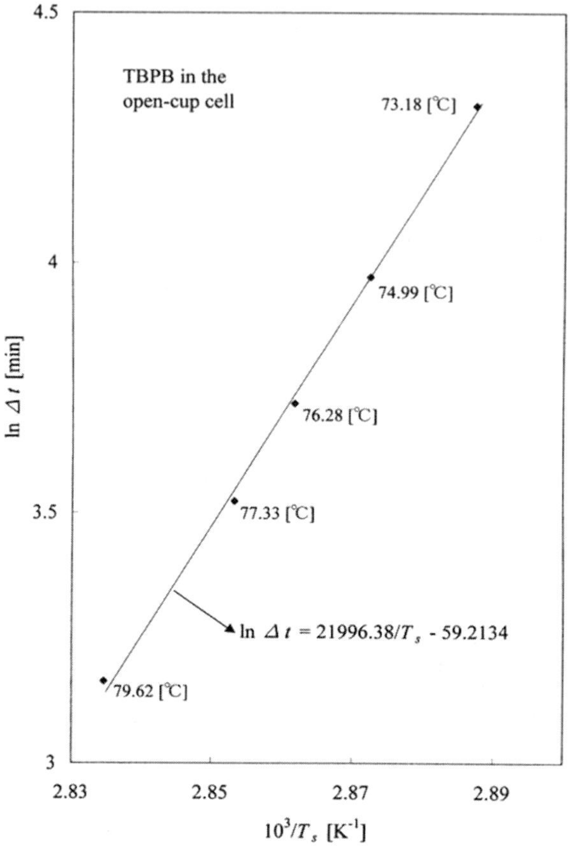

Figure 46. The plot of ln Δt versus $1/T_s$ made with five combinations of the value of ln Δt with that of $1/T_s$, which are each determined for five self-heating processes, of 2 cm^3 each of five samples of TBPB charged each in the open-cup cell and subjected each to the adiabatic self-heating test started from each T_s in the range of 73.18 to 79.62 ℃ with mutual intervals of 1∼2 K, recorded each for the time, Δt, required for the temperature of each sample of TBPB to increase by the definite value of ΔT of 1.25 K from the corresponding T_s.

Usually one working day is required to perform one run of the adiabatic self-heating test. About one week per one set of the adiabatic self-heating process recorder is, therefore, required to make the plot of ln Δt versus $1/T_s$ with several combinations of the value of ln Δt with that of $1/T_s$ for a chemical of the TD type. The same is true of every gas-permeable oxidatively-heating substance.

5.4.6 Calculation of the heat generation data of TBPB, *i.e.*, the values of the two coefficients, *a* and *b*, of Eq. (44), ln $\Delta t = a/T_s + b$, holding for the self-heating process, in the early stages, of 2 cm^3 of TBPB charged in the open-cup cell and subjected to the adiabatic self-heating test

The result of the regression analysis to calculate the heat generation data of TBPB is presented in Table 6 in **Section 4.7**.

5.5 Individual procedures to measure the four heat transfer data, *i.e.*, q_2, (T_{liq} - $T_{set\text{-}up}$), *c* and ρ, of an arbitrary volume of a liquid charged in an arbitrary container and placed in the atmosphere under isothermal conditions

The primary purpose of the study described in the present chapter was to calculate the values of the BAM test for the ten organic liquid peroxides*, assuming that 400 cm^3 each of the ten peroxides are each charged in the 500 cm^3 Dewar flask used in the BAM test and are each placed in the atmosphere under isothermal conditions, and then, to compare the values calculated herein with the corresponding values measured actually, respectively. Fortunately, the results of a series of BAM heat-accumulation storage tests performed each, at NOF Corporation, Taketoyo, Aichi, Japan, for some dozens of organic peroxides, including the ten organic liquid peroxides tested herein, were available.**

5.5.1 An assumption that every liquid, having each the same volume, charged each in the same container and placed each in the atmosphere under isothermal conditions, takes the same values of q_2 and (T_{liq} - $T_{set\text{-}up}$), irrespective of kind of liquid

When we measure the values of q_2 and (T_{liq} - $T_{set\text{-}up}$) of an arbitrary volume of a liquid charged in an arbitrary container and placed in the atmosphere under isothermal conditions, in temperature differences of 1.25 K between the T_{liq} and the $T_{set\text{-}up}$, all we have to expect of the liquid is that the liquid has the spatially uniform distribution of internal temperature in the early stages of the self-

---

* As commented in a footnote in **Section 3.5**, a value of T_c measured for a chemical of the TD type by the BAM heat-accumulation storage test is referred to as the value of the BAM test for the chemical herein.

** For the experience gained in NOF Corporation where a series of BAM tests were each performed actually for some dozens of organic peroxides, refer to **Section 3.5**.

heating process. In other words, the first requisite that a liquid should fulfill for the measurement of the values of q_2 and $(T_{liq} - T_{set\text{-}up})$ is that the condition, $U < < \lambda$, holds in the liquid in the early stages of the self-heating process. And, it is self-evident that this condition holds in almost every liquid.

Now, it is certain that the value of U of a liquid charged in the container depends somewhat on the kind of the liquid, because the factor, h_1, the film coefficient of heat transfer from the liquid to the container wall, is included in Eq. (69) presented in **Subsection 5.3.1**. Eq. (69) is re-presented below for convenience' sake.

$$US = \frac{1}{\dfrac{1}{h_1 S_1} + \dfrac{l_2}{\lambda_2 S_2} + \dfrac{1}{h_3 S_3}}. \tag{69}$$

Nevertheless, however, it is also quite certain that the value of U depends for the most part on the value of the term, l_2/λ_2, the ratio of the thickness to the thermal conductivity of the container wall, on the assumption that every liquid container is placed in the atmosphere, so that the factor, h_3, the film coefficient of heat transfer from the container wall to the atmosphere, takes always a constant value.

An assumption has thus been made herein that every liquid, having each the same volume, charged each in the same container and placed each in the atmosphere under isothermal conditions, takes the same values of q_2 and $(T_{liq} - T_{set\text{-}up})$, irrespective of kind of liquid.

It then follows that we may use almost every liquid for the measurement of this kind.

It is, however, not very advisable to generate any electric heat, q_2, in a self-heating liquid; besides, it is also undesirable to generate the electric heat in a liquid conductor of electricity, such as water, because a short circuit may be formed in it.

The final decision has thus been made herein that, in order to measure the main heat transfer data of an arbitrary volume of an organic liquid peroxide charged in an arbitrary container and placed in the atmosphere under isothermal conditions, kerosene, a sort of nonconducting liquid, is used in place of every organic liquid peroxide.

5.5.2 The BAM heat-accumulation storage test

400 cm^3 of a chemical is charged in a Dewar flask having an inside volume of 500 cm^3 in the BAM test. A thermocouple covered with a glass sheath is suspended from the lid of the flask in order that its soldered joint may be situated 6 cm above the bottom of the flask. The flask is set in a test chamber

maintained at a constant temperature (Fig. 47).* The storage test is repeated every time with a fresh sample at a series of values of $T_{set\text{-}up}$, until the value of the BAM test for the chemical is determined [37].

5.5.3 Experimental method to measure the values of q_2 and (T_{liq} - $T_{set\text{-}up}$) of 400 cm³ of kerosene charged in the Dewar flask, used in the BAM test and set in an aluminium box maintained at a $T_{set\text{-}up}$, under conditions of no air circulation, in temperature differences of 1.25 K between the T_{liq} and the $T_{set\text{-}up}$

The experimental method to measure the main heat transfer data of an arbitrary volume of a liquid charged in an arbitrary container and placed in the atmosphere under isothermal conditions is explained in detail in the present subsection by taking the procedure performed for 400 cm^3 of kerosene charged in a Dewar flask, which is used in the BAM test and is set under conditions of no air circulation in an aluminium box maintained at a $T_{set\text{-}up}$, in temperature differences of 1.25 K between the T_{liq} and the $T_{set\text{-}up}$, as an example.

A Dewar flask, in which 400 cm^3 of kerosene, one CA thermocouple to measure the T_{liq} and a Nichrome wire of about 1.7 Ω are contained, is set under conditions of no air circulation in an aluminium box settled in a fairly large thermostat, which in turn is placed in an air-conditioned room maintained at an almost constant (room) temperature. In this connection, the temperature of the thermostat is maintained at a constant temperature 2～3 K higher than the $T_{set\text{-}up}$. The other thermocouple to measure the $T_{set\text{-}up}$ is held outside the flask set in the aluminium box. The thermocouples used are calibrated in the range of 40 to 60 ℃ before the measurement (Figs. 48-53).

* This testing condition shows clearly that the BAM test is a sort of isothermal storage test, *i.e.*, a sort of non-adiabatic self-heating test, performed for 400 cm^3 of a chemical of the TD type placed in the atmosphere under isothermal conditions. The BAM test thus provides a value of T_c for 400 cm^3 of a chemical, of the TD type, placed in the atmosphere under the specified isothermal conditions of the BAM test.

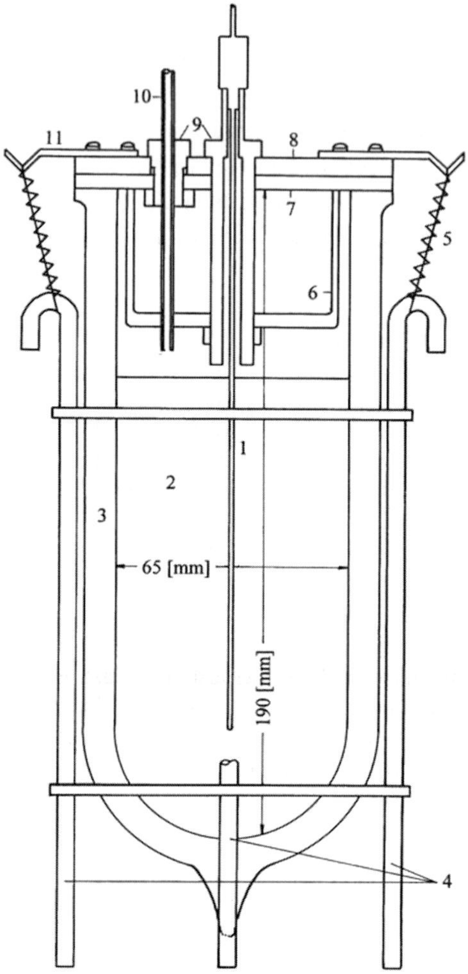

Figure 47. A Dewar flask having an inner capacity of 500 cm^3.

1. CA thermocouple; **2**. Liquid sample; **3**. Dewar flask; **4**. Retaining device; **5**. Spring; **6**. Glass cup; **7**. Glass lid; **8**. PTFE (polytetrafluoroethylene) lid; **9**. PTFE sealing; **10**. PTFE capillary tube; **11**. Stainless steel strip.

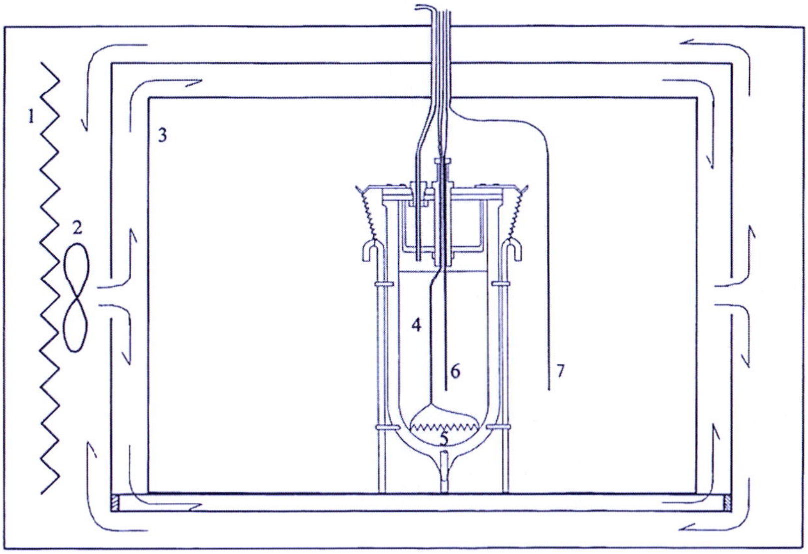

Figure 48. The set-up to measure the main heat transfer data of 400 cm^3 of kerosene charged in a Dewar flask used in the BAM test. The flask is set under conditions of no air circulation in an aluminium box settled in a fairly large thermostat.
1. Heater; **2**. Fan; **3**. Aluminium box with a 1 mm thick wall; **4**. 400 cm^3 of kerosene; **5**. Nichrome wire of about 1.7 Ω; **6**. CA thermocouple to measure the T_{liq}; **7**. CA thermocouple to measure the $T_{set\text{-}up}$.

Figure 49. The actual measuring state for the main heat transfer data of 400 cm^3 of kerosene charged in the Dewar flask. The flask is set under conditions of no air circulation in an aluminium box settled in a fairly large thermostat.

Figure 50. The Nichrome wire used to heat kerosene charged in the Dewar flask. The wire was prepared by cutting off a part of a Nichrome wire, 1 kW (at 100 V) in rated output.

Figure 51. The aluminium box is then closed with its front plate.

Figure 52. The thermostat is finally shut with its own door. The whole set-up is now ready for the measurement of the main heat transfer data of 400 cm^3 of kerosene charged in the Dewar flask.

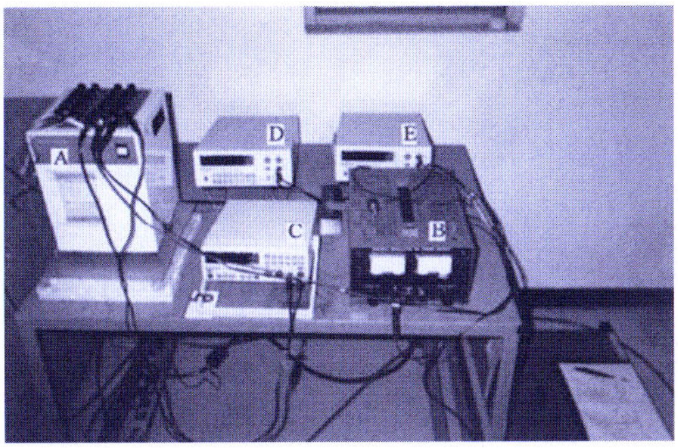

Figure 53. Measuring instruments placed next to the thermostat.
A. Cold junction utilizing the thermoelectric refrigeration in order to maintain the refrigerant at 0 ℃; **B**. Constant voltage D.C. powder source; **C**. Digital millivoltmeter used to measure the T_{liq} or the $T_{set\text{-}up}$; **D**. Digital millivoltmeter used to measure the D.C. potential difference between both ends of the Nichrome wire; **E**. Digital milliammeter used to measure the D.C. current flowing through the Nichrome wire.

In general, the thermal instability of chemicals, including organic liquid peroxides, becomes of interest in the range of room temperature to about 100 ℃. In this regard, a Dewar flask is made largely of glass, except some quantity of polytetrafluoroethylene and a small quantity of silver, so that a decision has been made herein that the experimental measurement regarding the main heat transfer data of an arbitrary volume of kerosene charged in an arbitrary container is performed in the aluminium box maintained at a $T_{set\text{-}up}$ near 50 ℃, because the thermal properties of these substances are not thought to vary to a great extent in the range of room temperature to 100 ℃, respectively.

For the above reasons, it has also been made a rule in the measurement of this kind to preheat the atmosphere in the aluminium box up to a $T_{set\text{-}up}$ near 50 ℃. In the meantime, a rapid electric heating of kerosene in the Dewar flask is first performed with a value of q_2 far larger than 0.04 W until the value of T_{liq} approaches 50 ℃; thereafter, a very slow heating of kerosene charged in the Dewar flask is continued at a value of q_2 of about 0.04 W* until the three physical quantities, q_2, T_{liq} and $T_{set\text{-}up}$, have taken steady values, respectively.

The steady state is usually established within 10 h of the start of the heating of kerosene.

Values at the steady state were as follows:

$$q_2 = 0.15029\ \text{A} \times 0.25987\ \text{V} = 0.039056\ \text{W} \fallingdotseq 0.560075\ \text{cal/min}.$$

* 0.04 W is only about 0.02 % of the rated output of the Nichrome wire used to heat kerosene charged in the Dewar flask, so that it is far from bringing the wire to a red heat..

$(T_{liq} - T_{set\text{-}up}) = 50.7024\ ℃ - 49.8171\ ℃ = 0.8853$ K;

It has been ascertained, by moving the thermocouple to measure the T_{liq} in the vertical direction in kerosene charged in the flask, that the scattering of the spatial distribution of temperature in the mass of kerosene, which is not mechanically stirred and is maintained at temperatures 0.9～1.3 K higher than the $T_{set\text{-}up}$, is less than ±1 μV in the case of the CA thermocouple, *i.e.*, less than ±0.025 K, except the thin upper surface layer, which is less than 5 mm in thickness, and in which the temperature is about 0.025 K higher than that of the mass of kerosene.

5.5.4 Individual procedures to measure the values of *c* and ρ of a chemical

The values of *c* of the ten organic liquid peroxides were measured by the adiabatic scanning calorimetry and are presented in Table 8 in **Subsection 5.7.1**, respectively. As noted down at the end of **Section 2.4**, the value of *c* of every chemical bears some temperature dependence. In this regard, the temperature at which the value of *c* of each individual organic liquid peroxide was measured is presented in parentheses after the corresponding value of *c* in Table 8.

The variation of the value of the BAM test for an organic liquid peroxide with the value of *c* differs naturally from one peroxide to another. Generally speaking, however, a decrease of 0.05 cal/(g·K) in the value of *c*, the magnitude of which is the maximum error conceivable in the measurement of the value of *c* and corresponds to about 10 % of the value of *c* of an average organic chemical, causes an increase of about 0.5 K in the value of the BAM test calculated by applying Eq. (72), keeping the values of the other variables in the equation constant. A fluctuation, of such an extent, of the value of the BAM test is, however, thought to be within the error range of the result of the BAM test performed for a liquid.

The values of ρ of the ten organic liquid peroxides were measured by means of a specific gravity meter and are presented in Table 8, respectively. As noted down at the end of **Section 2.4**, the value of ρ of every chemical also bears some temperature dependence. In this regard, the value of ρ, which is presented in Table 8, of every organic liquid peroxide is that at 20 ℃, because 400 cm^3 each of the ten peroxides were measured off at room temperature, respectively. The variation of the value of the BAM test for an organic liquid peroxide with the value of ρ is also of the same order of magnitude as that with the value of *c*. That is, a decrease of 0.05 g/cm^3 in the value of ρ, the magnitude of which is the maximum error conceivable in the measurement of the value of ρ and corresponds to about 5 % of the value of ρ of an average organic liquid, causes an increase of about 0.3 K in the value of the BAM test calculated by applying Eq. (72), keeping the values of the other variables in the equation constant.

5.6 Concrete procedure to calculate the value of the BAM test for 400 cm^3 of TBPB charged in the 500 cm^3 Dewar flask, used in the BAM test, and placed in the atmosphere under isothermal conditions

It is of course possible to calculate the T_c for an arbitrary volume of a liquid charged in an arbitrary container and placed in the atmosphere under isothermal conditions by applying the reduced form of the Semenov equation, *i.e.*, Eq. (72).

In order to compare the values of T_c calculated each for the ten organic liquid peroxides charged each in the container and placed each in the atmosphere under isothermal conditions with one another, however, it is required to calculate the individual values of T_c, assuming that these peroxides are each placed under the same conditions of shape and size. The same is true of powdery chemicals of the TD type and of gas-permeable oxidatively-heating substances.

A decision was thus made herein to calculate the individual values of the BAM test for the ten organic liquid peroxides by applying Eq. (72), assuming that 400 cm^3 each of these peroxides are each charged in the 500 cm^3 Dewar flask used in the BAM test and are each placed in the atmosphere under isothermal conditions.*

As an example, the concrete procedure to calculate the value of the BAM test for TBPB is illustrated in the present section.

The heat generation data, a and b, of TBPB were calculated in **Subsection 5.4.6** and are given in Table 8 in **Subsection 5.7.1**, respectively.

On the other hand, the values of q_2 and $(T_{liq}$ - $T_{set\text{-}up})$ of 400 cm^3 of a liquid charged in the 500 cm^3 Dewar flask, used in the BAM test, and placed in the atmosphere under isothermal conditions were measured in **Subsection 5.5.3**.

The values of c and ρ of TBPB were measured in **Subsection 5.5.4**, respectively.

The above four heat transfer data of TBPB charged in the Dewar flask, used in the BAM test, and placed in the atmosphere under isothermal conditions are also given in Table 8 in **Subsection 5.7.1**, respectively.

Further, the value of V of 400 cm^3 of TBPB is of course 400 cm^3.

And, the values of e and ΔT are 2.718281828 and 1.25 K, respectively.

The value of the right-hand side of Eq. (72), *i.e.*,

---

* The Semenov model holds for a chemical of the TD type, irrespective of liquid or powder, charged in the Dewar flask used in the BAM test. For further details, refer to **Section 6.8**.

$$2\ln T_c + \frac{a}{T_c} = \ln\left[\frac{ac\rho V\mathrm{e}\cdot \Delta T\left(T_{liq} - T_{set-up}\right)}{q_2}\right] - b, \tag{72}$$

for 400 cm^3 of TBPB above referred to is thus calculated in the following manner:

$$\ln\left[\frac{ac\rho V\mathrm{e}\cdot \Delta T\left(T_{liq} - T_{set-up}\right)}{q_2}\right] - b$$

$$= \ln\{[21996.38 \times 0.46 \times 1.043 \times 400 \times 2.718281828 \times 1.25 \times 0.8853]$$

$$\div 0.560075\} + 59.2134$$

$$= 16.93666953 + 59.2134$$

$$= 76.15006953.$$

On the other hand, if the value of the BAM test for TBPB is assumed to be 341.10483 K or 67.95483 ℃, the value of the left-hand side of Eq. (72) is calculated in the following manner:

$$2\ln T_c + \frac{a}{T_c} = 2\ln 341.10483 + 21996.38 \div 341.10483$$

$$= 11.6643797 + 64.48568905$$

$$= 76.15006875.$$

The difference between both sides is thus

$$76.15006953 - 76.15006875 \fallingdotseq 0.0000008.$$

The above whole calculation is performed actually by inputting the individual values of a, b, c, e, ΔT, V, ρ, q_2 and (T_{liq} - $T_{set\text{-}up}$) to a computer program used to calculate the T_c for a chemical of the TD type, including every gas-permeable oxidatively-heating substance.

The value of the BAM test thus calculated for TBPB, 67.95483 ℃, is finally rounded to 68.0 ℃ and is presented as such, together with the values of the BAM test calculated each for the nine organic liquid peroxides, other than TBPB, in the same manner as performed for TBPB, in Table 8 in **Subsection 5.7.1**.

5.6.1 Consideration of the above calculation from a different aspect

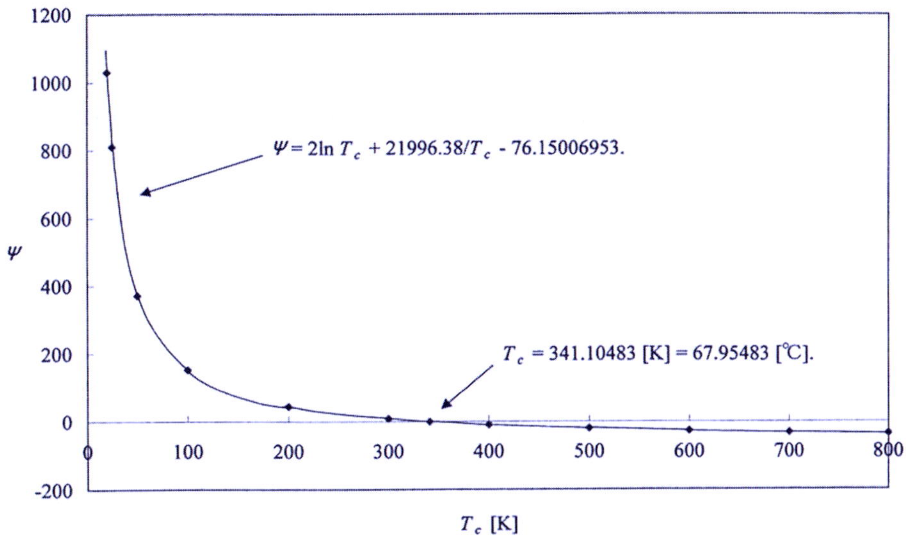

Figure 54. The plot of Ψ versus T_c for 400 cm^3 of TBPB charged in the Dewar flask and placed in the atmosphere under isothermal conditions.

Let us consider the calculation performed in the preceding subsection from a different aspect.

An equation, Ψ, is derived at once from Eq. (72). That is,

$$\Psi = 2\ln T_c + \frac{a}{T_c} - \left\{ \ln\left[\frac{ac\rho V\mathrm{e}\cdot \Delta T\left(T_{liq} - T_{set-up}\right)}{q_2} \right] - b \right\}. \quad (73)$$

As to 400 cm^3 of TBPB charged in the Dewar flask, used in the BAM test, and placed in the atmosphere under isothermal conditions, the values of the variables, a, b, c, ρ, V, $(T_{liq} - T_{set\text{-}up})$ and q_2, apart from the two constants, e and ΔT, in Eq. (72) are fixed at 21996.38, -59.2134, 0.46, 1.043, 400, 0.8853 and 0.560075, respectively, so that Ψ is rewritten as,

$$\Psi = 2\ln T_c + \frac{21996.38}{T_c} - 76.15006953. \tag{74}$$

The plot of Ψ versus T_c for 400 cm^3 of TBPB above referred to is given in Fig. 54. The function, $\Psi(T_c) = 0$, is seen, in the figure, to have only one root, 341.10484 K or 67.95484 ℃.

5.7 Results and discussion

5.7.1 The values of the BAM test calculated each for the ten organic liquid peroxides, including TBPB

Table 7
The ten organic liquid peroxides tested herein.

Abbr.	Trivial Name and Concentration
THPN	69.5 % *tert*-Hexyl peroxyneodecanoate in isoparaffin.
TBPD	51.0 % *tert*-Butyl peroxyneodecanoate in water, as an OW type emulsion.
BPOD	A mixture of 49.8 % benzoyl peroxide derivatives in dimethyl phthalate.
THPH	94.1 % *tert*-Hexyl peroxy-2-ethylhexanoate.
TPIC	88.8 % 1,1,3,3-Tetramethylbutyl peroxyisopropylcarbonate.
TBPC	97.0 % *tert*-Butyl peroxyisopropylcarbonate.
TBTH	90.5 % 1,1-bis(*tert*-Butyl peroxy)-3,3,5 -trimethylcyclohexane.
TBPI	75.0 % *tert*-Butyl peroxyisopropylcarbonate in isoparaffin.
TBPB	99.0 % *tert*-Butyl peroxybenzoate.
DTBP	99.0 % Di-*tert*-butyl peroxide.

The values of the BAM test were each calculated for the ten organic liquid peroxides, including TBPB, assuming that 400 cm^3 each of these peroxides are each charged in the Dewar flask, used in the BAM test, and are each placed in the atmosphere under isothermal conditions.

The list of the ten organic liquid peroxides tested herein is given in Table 7. These peroxides are all products of NOF Corporation, Taketoyo, Aichi, Japan, and were tested without further purification.

The adiabatic self-heating tests for the nine organic liquid peroxides, other than TBPB, were also performed in the same manner as done for TBPB, respectively.

The ten plots of $\ln \Delta t$ versus $1/T_s$ made each for the ten organic liquid peroxides, including TBPB, are presented in Fig. 55.

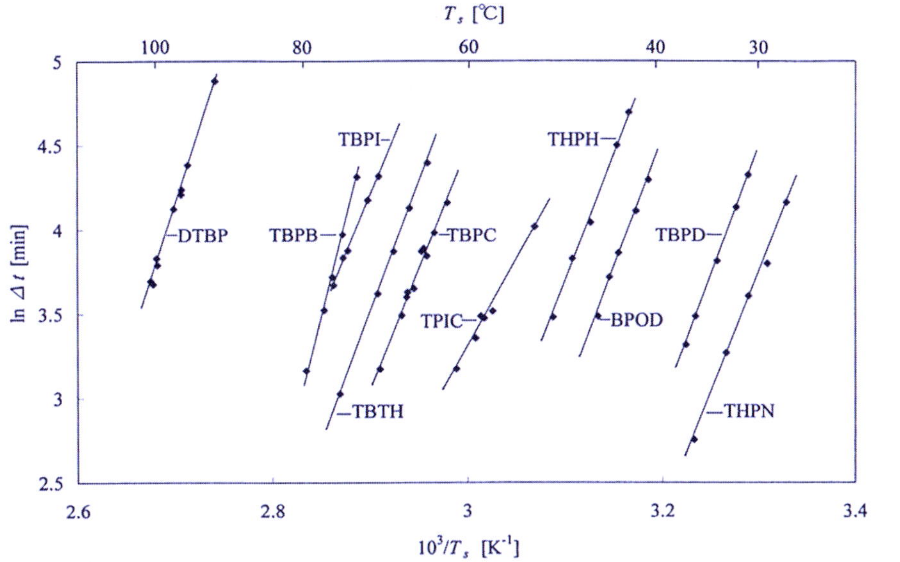

Figure 55. The ten plots of $\ln \Delta t$ versus $1/T_s$ made each for the ten organic liquid peroxides.

It is possible to see roughly from Fig. 55 the relative liability of these organic liquid peroxides to self-heating or ultimate thermal explosion. That is, we can tell that THPN and TBPD are relatively easy to explode thermally, but TBPB and DTBP are relatively hard to do so. In this regard, TPIC and TBPC are medium in the liability to thermal explosion.

The individual values of the two coefficients, a and b, of Eq. (44) holding for the individual self-heating processes, in the early stages, of 2 cm^3 each of the nine organic liquid peroxides, other than TBPB, charged each in the open-cup cell and subjected each to the adiabatic self-heating test were also calculated by applying the regression analysis to the individual combinations of the value of $\ln \Delta t$ with that of $1/T_s$ and are presented in Table 8.

Table 8
Experimental parameters of the ten organic liquid peroxides and comparison of the values of the BAM test calculated each for these peroxides, assuming that 400 cm^3 each of these peroxides are each charged in the 500 cm^3 Dewar flask, used in the BAM test, and are each placed in the atmosphere under isothermal conditions, with, the corresponding values measured each actually by a series of BAM heat-accumulation storage tests performed at NOF Corporation. Unless otherwise noted in the superscripts, the heat generation data of these peroxides were calculated based on the experimental data obtained with the open-cup cell, in principle, in the adiabatic self-heating test, respectively.

Organic Liquid Peroxide	Coefficients of Eq. (44) a	b	Specific heat capacity c cal/(g·K)	Specific gravity ρ g/cm^3	q_2[a] cal/min	$(T_{liq} - T_{set\text{-}up})$[a] K	The value of the BAM test calcd. herein ℃	The value of the BAM test measured [℃] Go	No Go
THPN	14358.45	-43.647	0.44(20℃)	0.856	0.560075	0.8853	22.7	25	20
TBPD	15577.53	-46.904	0.71(20℃)	0.927	0.560075	0.8853	24.0	30	25
BPOD	15313.49	-44.4702	0.43(30℃)	1.154	0.560075	0.8853	35.5	40	35
THPH	15314.99	-43.7903	0.47(40℃)	0.894	0.560075	0.8853	41.1	40	35
TPIC	10536.58	-28.3185	0.46(50℃)	0.932	0.560075	0.8853	47.4	50	45
TBPC	14349.84	-38.5735	0.47(60℃)	0.966	0.560075	0.8853	57.3[b]	55	50
TBTH	15306.39	-40.8952	0.46(60℃)	0.911	0.560075	0.8853	61.7	65	60
TBPI	13846.76	-35.9631	0.49(60℃)	0.910	0.560075	0.8853	67.0	70	65
TBPB	21996.38	-59.2134	0.46(70℃)	1.043	0.560075	0.8853	68.0[c]	65	60
DTBP	18179.73	-44.9614	0.51(90℃)[d]	0.796	0.560075	0.8853	92.4[c), f]	-	-

Superscripts:
[a] These are the main heat transfer data of 400 cm^3 of a chemical charged in the Dewar flask, used in the BAM test, and placed in the atmosphere under isothermal conditions.
[b] The value of the BAM test for TBPC calculated by substituting the heat generation data, calculated based on the experimental data obtained with the closed cell in the adiabatic self-heating test, into Eq. (72) was 60.4 ℃.

[c] The value of the BAM test for TBPB calculated by substituting the heat generation data, calculated based on the experimental data obtained with the closed cell in the adiabatic self-heating test, into Eq. (72) was 69.2 ℃.

[d] The value of *c* of 0.51 for DTBP was determined by extrapolating the values measured each at 20, 30, 40 and 50 ℃ to the one at 90 ℃.

[e] A value of T_c for DTBP, 92.4 ℃, was calculated by substituting the heat generation data, calculated based on the experimental data obtained with the closed cell in the adiabatic self-heating test, into Eq. (72), because DTBP are volatile while tested.

[f] According to a reference [38], the so-called 10-h $t_{1/2}$ value for DTBP in dodecane is 129 ℃.

The values of the BAM test calculated each for the ten organic liquid peroxides, including TBPB, are summarized in Table 8 in the order of increasing value of the BAM test, together with the corresponding values measured each actually by a series of BAM heat-accumulation storage tests performed at NOF Corporation, for comparison [23].

The values of the BAM test thus calculated each for the ten organic liquid peroxides ranged from 22.7 ℃ for THPN to 92.4 ℃ for DTBP.

These values of the BAM test calculated herein in general are in fair agreement with the corresponding values measured each actually by a series of BAM heat-accumulation storage tests performed at the peroxide manufacturing company, respectively.

For instance, when 400 cm^3 of THPN was subjected to the BAM test at 25 ℃, the result was "GO"; but, when subjected at 20 ℃, it didn't go. The exact value of the BAM test for THPN must, therefore, exist between 25 and 20 ℃. In the meantime, according to Table 8, the value of the BAM test for THPN has been calculated, herein, at 22.7 ℃. It thus follows that the agreement is reasonable in the case of THPN, and so forth.

At all events, however, it will be reasonable, in practice, to consider a temperature 30 K* lower than the value of the BAM test calculated herein for an organic liquid peroxide as the upper limit temperature for the safe handling of the peroxide. For instance, -10 ℃ will be the upper limit temperature for the safe handling of THPN, 10 ℃ for BPOD, 20 ℃ for TPIC, and so forth.

* For a matter relevant to this safety margin, refer to **Section 6.8**.

5.7.2 The values of T_c calculated each for the ten organic liquid peroxides, assuming that 5 or 10 L each of these peroxides are each charged in the corresponding 5 or 10 L polyethylene practical container and are each placed in the atmosphere under isothermal conditions

The main heat transfer data of 5 or 10 L of kerosene charged in the corresponding 5 or 10 L polyethylene practical container, which is set under conditions of no air circulation in an aluminium box maintained at a $T_{set\text{-}up}$ near 50 ℃ and settled in a fairly large thermostat, have been measured in temperature differences of 1.25 K between the T_{liq} and the $T_{set\text{-}up}$, in almost the same manner as performed for 400 mL of kerosene charged in the Dewar flask in **Subsection 5.5.3** (Fig. 57). These containers are used by NOF Corporation, Japan, to deliver 5 or 10 kg each of organic liquid peroxides to the users, respectively. The measurements of the 10 L polyethylene practical container with a 1.5 mm thick wall are shown in Fig. 56.

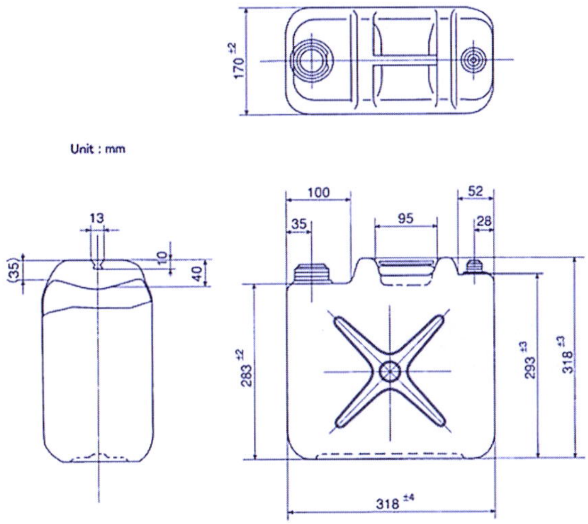

Figure 56. The measurements of the 10 L polyethylene practical container with a 1.5 mm thick wall.

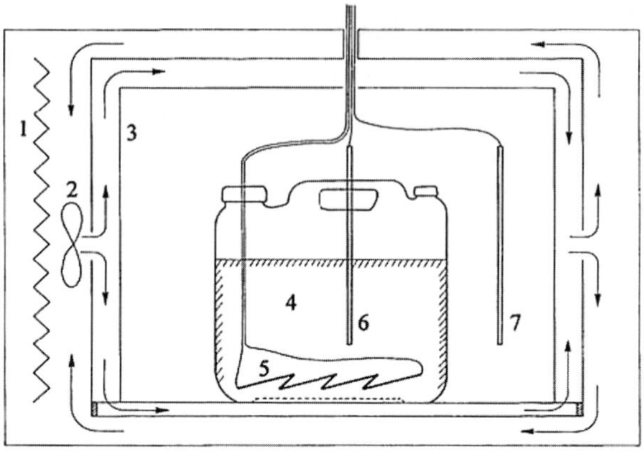

Figure 57. The set-up to measure the main heat transfer data of 5 or 10 L of kerosene charged in the corresponding 5 or 10 L polyethylene practical container. The container is set under conditions of no air circulation in an aluminium box settled in a fairly large thermostat.

1. Heater; **2**. Fan; **3**. Aluminium box with a 1 mm thick wall; **4**. 5 or 10 L of kerosene; **5**. Nichrome wire of about 9.5 Ω; **6**. CA thermocouple to measure the T_{liq}; **7**. CA thermocouple to measure the $T_{set\text{-}up}$.

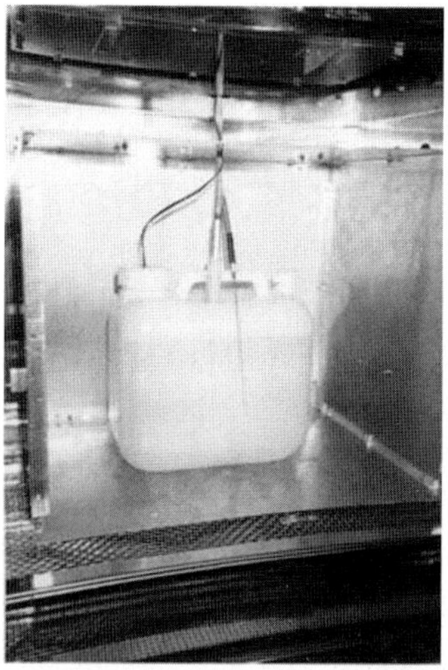

Figure 58. The actual measuring state for the main heat transfer data of 10 L of kerosene charged in the corresponding 10 L polyethylene practical container. The container is set under conditions of no air circulation in an aluminium box settled in a fairly large thermostat.

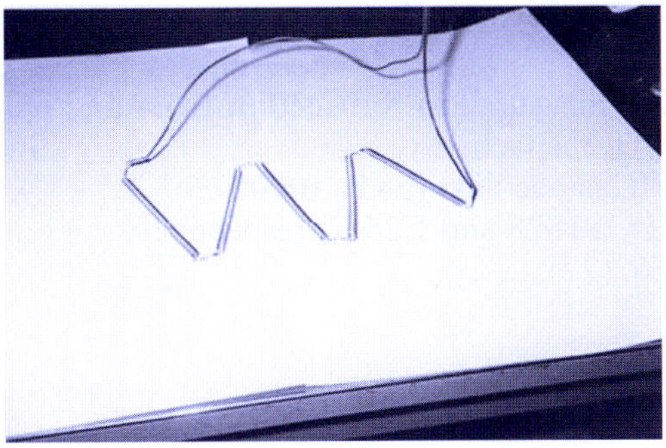

Figure 59. The Nichrome wire used to heat 5 or 10 L of kerosene charged in the corresponding 5 or 10 L polyethylene practical container. The wire was prepared by cutting off a part of a Nichrome wire, 1 kW (at 100 V) in rated output.

Values at the steady state were as follows:

For the 10 L polyethylene practical container;

$q_2 = 0.46004 \text{ A} \times 4.4241 \text{ V} = 2.03526 \text{ W} \fallingdotseq 29.18637 \text{ cal/min}.$

$T_{liq} - T_{set\text{-}up} = 50.8452\ ℃ - 49.5976\ ℃ = 1.2476 \text{ K}.$

For the 5 L polyethylene practical container;

$q_2 = 0.38084 \text{ A} \times 3.5975 \text{ V} = 1.37007 \text{ W} \fallingdotseq 19.6473 \text{ cal/min}.$

$T_{liq} - T_{set\text{-}up} = 51.0610\ ℃ - 49.7439\ ℃ = 1.3171 \text{ K}.$

The spatial distribution of temperature in the mass of 5 or 10 L of kerosene charged in the corresponding 5 or 10 L polyethylene practical container was found to be as uniform as that in the Dewar flask, except the thin upper surface layer, in either case.

The individual values of T_c were then calculated for the ten organic liquid peroxides by applying Eq. (72), assuming that 5 or 10 L each of these peroxides are each charged in the corresponding 5 or 10 L polyethylene practical container and are each placed in the atmosphere under isothermal conditions.

As an example, the concrete procedure to calculate the T_c for 10 L of TPIC charged in the corresponding 10 L polyethylene practical container and placed in the atmosphere under isothermal conditions is illustrated in the present subsection.

The heat generation data, a and b, of TPIC were calculated in **Subsection 5.7.1** and are given in Table 8, respectively.

On the other hand, the values of q_2 and (T_{liq} - $T_{set\text{-}up}$) of 10 L of a liquid charged in the 10 L polyethylene practical container and placed in the atmosphere under isothermal conditions are, as presented above, 29.18637 cal/min and 1.2476 K, respectively.

The values of c and ρ of TPIC were measured in **Subsection 5.5.4** and are also given in Table 8 in **Subsection 5.7.1**, respectively.

Further, the value of V of 10 L of TPIC is needless to say 10000 cm^3.

And, the values of e and ΔT are 2.718281828 and 1.25 K, respectively.

The value of the right-hand side of Eq. (72), *i.e.*,

$$2\ln T_c + \frac{a}{T_c} = \ln\left[\frac{ac\rho V\mathrm{e}\cdot\Delta T\left(T_{liq} - T_{set-up}\right)}{q_2}\right] - b, \tag{72}$$

for 10 L of TPIC above referred to is thus calculated in the following manner.

$$\ln\left[\frac{ac\rho V\mathrm{e}\cdot\Delta T\left(T_{liq} - T_{set-up}\right)}{q_2}\right] - b$$

$$= \ln\{[10536.58 \times 0.46 \times 0.932 \times 10000 \times 2.718281828 \times 1.25 \times 1.2476]$$

$$\div 29.18637\} + 28.3185$$

$$= 15.69666085 + 28.3185$$

$$= 44.01516085.$$

On the other hand, if the T_c for 10 L of TPIC above referred to is assumed to be 324.70899 K or 51.55899 ℃, the value of the left-hand side of Eq. (72) is calculated in the following manner.

$$2\ln T_c + \frac{a}{T_c} = 2\ln 324.70899 + 10536.58 \div 324.70899$$

$$= 11.56585873 + 32.44930176$$

$$= 44.01516049.$$

The difference between both sides is thus

44.01516085 - 44.01516049 ≑ 0.0000004.

The above whole calculation is performed actually by inputting the individual values of a, b, c, e, ΔT, V, ρ, q_2 and $(T_{liq} - T_{set\text{-}up})$ to a computer program used to calculate the T_c for a chemical of the TD type, including every gas-permeable oxidatively-heating substance.

The value of T_c thus calculated for 10 L of TPIC above referred to, 51.55899 ℃, is finally rounded to 51.6 ℃ and is presented as such, together with the values of T_c calculated each for the nine organic liquid peroxides, other than TPIC, in the same manner as performed for 10 L of TPIC, in Table 9.

Table 9
The values of T_c [℃] calculated each for the ten organic liquid peroxides, assuming that 5 or 10 L each of these peroxides are each charged in the corresponding 5 or 10 L polyethylene practical container and are each placed in the atmosphere under isothermal conditions. The heat generation data used to calculate the values of T_c are quoted from Table 8 in **Subsection 5.7.1**, respectively. The values of the BAM test calculated each for these peroxides are also quoted from Table 8, for comparison.

Container	THPN	TBPD	BPOD	THPH	TPIC	TBPC	TBTH	TBPI	TBPB	DTBP
The Dewar flask	22.7	24.0	35.5	41.1	47.4	57.3	61.7	67.0	68.0	92.4
The 10 L PE container	25.2	26.3	38.1	43.8	51.6	60.4	64.8	70.5	70.1	95.4
The 5 L PE container	26.8	27.8	39.7	45.4	54.2	62.4	66.7	72.7	71.5	97.3

In this connection, it is said that the BAM test provides a chemical with the thermal isolation corresponding to a commercial package of 30 L net volume [39].

At all events, an important and useful proposition obtained in the present subsection is that it is possible to calculate the T_c for an arbitrary volume of a liquid charged in an arbitrary container and placed in the atmosphere under isothermal conditions, provided a thermostatic space large enough for the size of the container is prepared.*

5.8 Comparison of the values of *U* calculated each for the three kinds of volumes of kerosene charged each in the corresponding containers used herein, with, the values of *U* measured each by other researchers for a few kinds of liquids charged each in the corresponding containers other than those used herein

It is, as a matter of fact, relatively easy to calculate approximately the value of *S* (the whole surface area) of an arbitrary volume of a liquid charged in an arbitrary container. Once the value of *S* of the liquid is fixed, it also becomes possible to calculate approximately the value of *U* of the liquid charged in the container and placed in the atmosphere under isothermal conditions from their product, *US*.

As an example, it will be permitted to assume the shape of kerosene charged in the Dewar flask used in the BAM test to be a composite of a cylinder and a hemisphere (see Fig. 47 in **Subsection 5.5.2**).

The value of *S* of 400 cm^3 of kerosene charged in the Dewar flask is thus calculated in the following manner.

First, the volume of the hemisphere, V_1, is calculated in the following manner.

$$V_1 = (4/3) \times \pi \times 3.25^3 \times (1/2) = 71.897 \text{ cm}^3.$$

Secondly, expressing the length of the cylinder as x cm, the following equation holds:

$$\pi \times 3.25^2 \times x + V_1 = \pi \times 3.25^2 \times x + 71.897 = 400.$$

* As the size of the thermostatic space is rendered larger, or, as the heat capacity of the thermostatic space is rendered larger, it becomes possible to measure more favorably the main heat transfer data of an arbitrary volume of a liquid charged in an arbitrary container and placed in the atmosphere under isothermal conditions. In other words, as the size of the thermostatic space is rendered larger, it becomes possible to keep the $T_{set\text{-}up}$ more invariable during the measurement of the main heat transfer data of the liquid.

$\therefore x = 9.8877$ cm.

The value of S is, therefore, calculated in the following manner.

$$S = \pi r^2 + 2\pi r \times 9.8877 + (1/2) \times 4\pi r^2$$

$$= \pi \times 3.25^2 + 2\pi \times 3.25 \times 9.8877 + (1/2) \times 4\pi \times (3.25)^2$$

$$= 33.183 + 201.91 + 66.366 = 301.46 \text{ cm}^2.$$

Substituting the value of S thus calculated, together with the value of (T_{liq} -T_{set-up}) of 0.8853 K and the value of q_2 of 0.039056 W (refer to **Subsection 5.5.3**), into Eq. (68') in **Subsection 5.3.2**, the value of U of kerosene charged in the Dewar flask and placed in the atmosphere under isothermal conditions is calculated in the following manner.

$$U = \frac{q_2}{S \times \left(T_{liq} - T_{set-up}\right)} = 0.039056 \div (4.184 \times 301.46 \times 0.8853)$$

$$= 3.4976 \times 10^{-5} \text{ cal/(cm}^2\text{·s·K)}.$$

Similarly, it will be permitted to assume the shape of kerosene charged in a PE (polyethylene) practical container to be a rectangular parallelepiped, neglecting some curved surfaces at corners.

The values of U thus calculated each for the three kinds of volumes of kerosene charged each in the corresponding containers used herein, and, the values of U measured each by other researchers for a few kinds of liquids charged each in the corresponding containers other than those used herein, are presented in Table 10.

Table 10
Comparison of the values of U calculated each for the three kinds of volumes of kerosene charged each in the corresponding containers used herein, with, the values of U measured each by other researchers for a few kinds of liquids charged each in the corresponding containers other than those used herein.

	S	q_2	Temp. diff.	U	Individual positions of the two thermocouples placed to measure the temperature difference in each work. These positions each correspond to some one of T_1, T_3 And T_4 in Figs. 44 and 60.
	cm^2	cal/s	K	$cal/(cm^2 \cdot s \cdot K)$	
Dewar flask	301.46	0.009335	0.8853	3.4978×10^{-5}	$(T_1 - T_4)$, in fact $(T_{liq,\,static} - T_{set\text{-}up,\,static})$
10 L container	3,082	0.4864	1.2476	1.2650×10^{-4}	$(T_1 - T_4)$, in fact $(T_{liq,\,static} - T_{set\text{-}up,\,static})$
5 L container	1,896	0.3275	1.3171	1.3115×10^{-4}	$(T_1 - T_4)$, in fact $(T_{liq,\,static} - T_{set\text{-}up,\,static})$
Bowes' work	54~100[a)]	3.9~8.0	2.6~8.0	$\sim 8.80 \times 10^{-4}$	$(T_3 - T_4)$, in fact $(T_{solid} - T_{air,\,stirred})$
Merzhanov's work	154~264[a)]	-[b)]	-	$\sim 9.50 \times 10^{-3}$	$(T_1 - T_4)$, in fact $(T_{liq,\,stirred} - T_{liq,\,flowing}$[c)]$)$

Superscripts:
a) These values of S were calculated herein, based on the diameters and the ratios of charge length to diameter which were described in both papers, respectively.
b) The mark "-" indicates that the corresponding data were not reported in the paper published by Merzhanov *et al.* [40].
c) The heat-exchanger, glycerol, was probably being flowed turbulently in Merzhanov *et al.*' work.

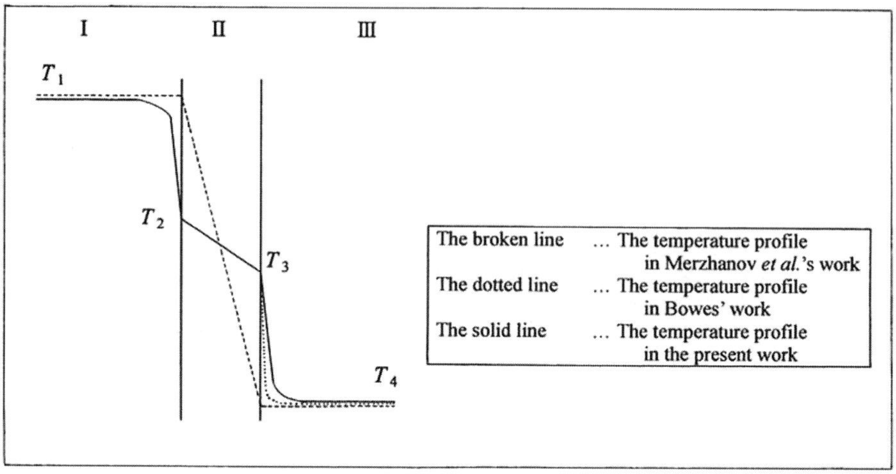

Figure 60. Individual temperature distribution patterns in the experiments performed each by three researchers to measure the values of U of a few kinds of liquids charged each in the corresponding containers.

Let us compare the values of U calculated each for the three kinds of volumes of kerosene charged each in the corresponding containers used herein, with, the values of U measured each by other researchers for a few kinds of liquids charged each in the corresponding containers other than those used herein.

The values of U reported each by Merzhanov *et al.* for the three kinds of volumes of tetryl charged each in the corresponding glass vessels are on the average about 73 times larger than the values of U calculated each for the two kinds of volumes of kerosene charged each in the corresponding polyethylene practical containers. And, the values of U measured each by Bowes are on the average about 7 times larger than those calculated each for the two kinds of volumes of kerosene charged each in the corresponding polyethylene practical containers.

Merzhanov *et al.* neither described in detail their experimental conditions to measure the coefficient of heat transfer, α, which corresponds to U in the notation adopted herein, nor reported the individual values of q_2 and $(T_{liq} - T_{set\text{-}up})$ in their paper [40].

In Merzhanov *et al.*'s paper, it reads as follows:

「

EXPERIMENTAL

The method described earlier[2] (Fig. 1)* was modified by the introduction of a stirring device. The charge was placed in a cylindrical glass vessel with double walls, between which was circulated the heat-exchanger (glycerol), heated in a thermostat to the temperature of the experiment. The temperature drop between the thermostat and glycerol in the vessel did not exceed 0.3 K. The temperature rise in the substance was measured by a copper-constantan thermocouple, one junction of which, in a thin glass capillary, was placed in the substance, and the other in the thermostat. The change of the temperature with time was recorded by means of a potentiometer. The internal diameter, *d*, of the vessel was measured by calipers: its variation did not exceed 2 %. The length, *l*, of the charge (or rather l/d) was known and the weight of the substance taken was determined from the given value of l/d and the density ρ

$$m = \rho \frac{\pi d^3}{4}\left(\frac{l}{d}\right);$$

The density was determined by means of a pyknometer.

The stirrers were made of stainless steel, since kinetic studies[5,8] showed that stainless steel does not affect the rate of thermal decomposition of the substances investigated. In order to choose the method of stirring, the viscosity and its temperature dependence were determined in an Ostwald viscometer for DINA (dinitroxydiethylnitramine) and for tetryl. The viscosity of DINA at the temperatures of the experiment is similar to that of water at room temperature. Therefore water was used as a model of DINA in the preliminary estimation of the efficiency of the stirring. A propeller stirrer was used for stirring DINA. In order to avoid the distortion of the surface of the stirred substance the axle of the stirrer was placed

---

* This figure is omitted in this quotation.

not in the centre of the vessel but at a distance equal to 1/3 of the diameter from the wall. The uniform temperature of the substance was achieved by a suitable rate of stirring and was checked by a differential thermocouple (one junction in the centre and the other near the wall of the vessel). The rate of temperature rise in the substance did not depend on the rate of stirring in the chosen range of stirrer speeds.

Since the viscosity of tetryl is nearly ten times greater than that of DINA, stirring by a propeller stirrer did not eliminate the temperature gradient near the walls of the reaction vessel. This was proved by experiments with externally heated model substances having similar viscosity (aqueous glycerol). Therefore a piston stirrer, moving along the axis of the vessel, was used for tetryl. This stirrer displaces the central layers of the substance towards the walls. It was possible to use this type of stirrer, because tetryl has a large condensed residue (77 % of its initial volume). Since the maximum rate of non-isothermal decomposition of tetryl under critical conditions corresponds to $\eta_{cr} \fallingdotseq 0.5$, the decrease in volume during the relevant time does not exceed 12 %. Therefore it is not necessary to change the rate of stirring during the experiment. The gap between the stirrer and the vessel wall was 2-3 mm; the frequency was 1-1.5 movements per second. Both types of stirrers efficiently stirred the substance and caused no apparent distortion in the models.

The determination of the coefficient of heat transfer through the reaction vessel wall was very important. Special calculations and determinations proved that with the rate of circulation of glycerol used the vessel wall was cooled fast enough to assume that the outer wall was kept at a constant temperature. The coefficient of heat transfer through the wall is equal to λ_{wall}/d_{wall}, where λ_{wall} is the thermal conductivity and d_{wall} the thickness of the wall.

Under our conditions, λ_{wall}/d_{wall} should coincide with the coefficient of heat transfer α from the inner surface of the wall to the surrounding medium. This was confirmed by experimental determinations of α for various vessels using an external heat source. A heating spiral on a glass support was placed in the stirred model of the explosive (water or a mixture of water and glycerol), the temperature of which was determined by a thermometer with the accuracy ± 0.1 K. The coefficient of heat transfer was determined as the ratio of the heat flux passing through a unit surface area of the vessel wall to the temperature difference causing the flux:

$$\alpha = \frac{P}{S \cdot \Delta T},$$

where P is the power of the heater in cal sec^{-1}, $S = \pi dl + (\pi d^2)/4$ the surface of contact of the substance with the vessel walls (the heat transfer to the air was neglected), and ΔT the temperature difference between the substance in the vessel and the heat exchanger. The values of α so obtained coincided within 10 % with the values of λ_{wall}/d_{wall}.

References

2. A. G. Merzhanov, V. G. Abramov and F. I. Dubovitskii, Dokl. Akad. Nauk SSSR, 128, 1238 (1959).
5. F. I. Dubovitskii, Yu. I. Rubtsov, V. V. Barzykin and G. B. Manelis, Izv. Akad. Nauk SSSR, Otd. Khim. Nauk, 1126 (1960).
8. F. I. Dubovitskii, Yu. I. Rubtsov and G. B. Manelis, Izv. Akad. Nauk SSSR, Otd. Khim. Nauk, 1763 (1960).

TABLE 2

Experimental and calculated data on the thermal explosion of tetryl.

Diameter of the charge	Heat-transfer coefficient of the vessel α,	Ratio of length to diameter	Weight of charge	T_{cr} calc.	T_{cr} expt.	Pre-explosion temp. rise calc.*	Pre-explosion temp. rise expt.
cm	cal/(cm^2·K·s)	l/d	g	℃	℃	K	K
4.90	9.5×10^{-3}	3	420	151	152	~10	9
4.50	9.5×10^{-3}	3	330	151	151	~10	24
3.75	8.5×10^{-3}	3	187	152	153	~10	15

* The critical pre-explosion temperature rise was calculated in accordance with the equation, $\Delta T_{cr} = (RT_0^2)/E$.

It is, however, certain that they attempted to measure the temperature difference between a stirred liquid and a (probably turbulently) flowing liquid used as the heat exchanger.

In the meantime, as clearly seen in Fig. 44 in **Subsection 5.3.1**, the temperature drop in the heat transfer between a solid and a fluid occurs for the most part in the fluid film concerned. That is, the fluid film constitutes the predominant resistance or barrier for the heat transfer between the solid and the fluid.*

The value of h in a fluid film, *i.e.*, that of h_1, is originally proportional to the value of λ of the fluid itself. As the value of the temperature gradient in a fluid film increases on account of the decrease in thickness of the film, however, the value of h_1 increases even in the identical fluid.** In other words, the value of h_1 of a liquid in which the forced convective flow is made is necessarily larger than that of the liquid in which the natural convective flow is allowed, because the thickness of the fluid film decreases with the increase in rate of the forced convective flow. Besides, it is also possible to point out a fact that the value of λ of an ordinary liquid in general are much larger than that of an ordinary gas.

Hence, their values of α must have been very large. This inference is verified by their values of α presented in Table 10 in the present section and in TABLE

* In this regard, Frank-Kamenetskii also describes that the main diffusion resistance is localized within the so-called viscous sublayer, *i.e.*, the fluid film [41].

** Remember that, expressing dimensionally, h or $U = \lambda$/length.

2 in their paper quoted. This result was brought about by reason that, as they commented consciously or unconsciously in their paper, a condition, $\alpha = \lambda_{wall}/d_{wall}$, was effected under their experimental conditions, by maximizing both the value of h_1 and that of h_3 in Eq. (69) in **Subsection 5.3.1**.

At all events, as pointed out in **Subsection 5.3.2**, it is apparent to us that, keeping the values of the other variables in Eq. (71) constant, the value of T_c for a liquid increases with increasing the value of U.*

On the other hand, Bowes measured the values of the so-called surface transfer coefficient, which is identical with the factor, h_3, the film coefficient of heat transfer from the container wall to the atmosphere, for solid aluminium cylinders in the stirred air, respectively. That is, the temperature differences he measured correspond to (T_3 - T_4) in Fig. 60 in the present subsection and that in Fig. 44 in **Subsection 5.3.1**.

In Bowes' book, it reads as follows [42]:

「

Measurement of heat-transfer coefficients

Aluminium cylinders in vented furnace The surface heat-transfer coefficients, *h*, for the aluminium containers in the stirred air of the working space in the vented furnace were estimated from measurements of the heat-transfer coefficients for solid aluminium cylinders of similar dimensions and surface finish. The cylinders were heated electrically at a known power input by small heaters in central cavities (0.6 cm diameter) and the steady-state temperature difference between the cylinder surface and the air in the working space was measured by means of a differential thermocouple. Measurements were made on two sizes of cylinder with a length to diameter ratio of 1.7, and heat-transfer coefficients for other sizes were estimated by fitting the following equation for heat and mass transfer from small spheres, due to Ranz and Marshall [1952], to the observations:

$$N_{Nu} = 2 + 0.6 N_{Pr}^{1/3} N_{Re}^{1/2} \qquad A(1)$$

* For a high value of T_c, for tetryl, of the order of 152 ℃, that Merzhanov *et al.* reported in their paper [40], refer to **Subsection 9.6.4**.

The results obtained are given in the following table:

Diameter	Energy Input	Temp diff	h	N_{Nu}	N_{Re}	Velocity
cm	cal/s	K	cal/(cm^2·s·K)			cm/s
3.8	3.48	2.6	8.1×10^{-4}			
				46*	6660	368
3.8	7.95	5.3	8.8×10^{-4}			
2.8	6.96	8.0	9.5×10^{-4}	38	4500	338

*Based on mean value of h for the two results.

References

W. E. Ranz and W. R. Marshall, Chemical Engineering Progress, **48**, 173 (1952).

⌋

The fluid film in his case would be probably thinner than that in static air, because T_4 in his case was the temperature of the stirred air, with the result that a value of h_3 in his case would be relatively larger than the one proper.

In any event, it is clear that it was the value of U, and not the value of h_3, of a liquid charged in the container and placed in the (static) atmosphere under isothermal conditions that he should have measured.

Incidentally, Bowes discussed in his book, "Self-Heating: Evaluating and Controlling the Hazards", some dimensionless numbers, such as the Grashof number, the Reynolds number and the Prandtl number, which are all used in order to discuss the convective flow in fluid mechanics.

As stated repeatedly herein, however, whether the thermal explosion of an arbitrary volume of a liquid charged in an arbitrary container and placed in the (static) atmosphere under isothermal conditions occurs or not is decided by the ratio of the rate of heat generation in the liquid to the rate of heat transfer from the liquid to the atmosphere at the critical state for the thermal explosion which exists at the end of the early stages of the self-heating process. This orthodox approach to the thermal explosion research of every liquid has thus no concern with any convective flow inliquids. In this regard, Semenov did not leave any comment, to the effect that stirring is indispensable in the thermal explosion research of every self-heating fluid, either [3].

References to Chapter 5

[3] N. N. Semenov, Some Problems of Chemical Kinetics and Reactivity, **2**, Translated from Russian by J. E. S. Bradley, Pergamon Press, London, 1-4 (1959).
[9] D. A. Frank-Kamenetskii, Diffusion and Heat Transfer in Chemical Kinetics, 2nd Ed., Translated from Russian by J. P. Appleton, Plenum Press, New York-London, 413 (1969).
[16] D. A. Frank-Kamenetskii, *ibid.*, 347, 348, 374, *etc.*
[23] T. Kotoyori, Critical Temperatures for the Thermal Explosion of Liquid Organic Peroxides, Process Safety Progress, **14**, 37-44 (1995).
[30] J. Verhoeff, Experimental Study of the Thermal Explosion of Liquids, Prins Maurits Laboratorium TNO, Rijswijk, The Netherlands, 67 (1983).
[31] N. N. Semenov, *ibid.*, 6.
[32] D. A. Frank-Kamenetskii, *ibid.*, 261.
[33] A. A. Noyes and W. R. Whitney, Zeits. Phys. Chem., **23**, 689 (1897).
[34] W. Nernst, Zeits. Phys. Chem., 47, 52 (1904).
[35] L. Prandtl, Verh. d.3., Intern. Math. Kongr., Heidelberg, (1904).
[36] I. Langmuir, Trans. Am. Electrochem. Soc., **23**, 299 (1913).
[37] Committee of Experts on the Transport of Dangerous Goods, United Nations, Recommendations on the Transport of Dangerous Goods, Tests and Criteria, 2nd ed., United Nations, New York, 205-209 (1990).
[38] The Kirk-Othmer Encyclopedia of Chemical Technology, 4th Ed., **14**, 445 (1995).
[39] A. C. Hordijk and J. J. de Groot, Experimental Data on the Thermal Kinetics of Organic Peroxides, Thermochim. Acta, **101**, 45-63 (1986).
[40] A. G. Merzhanov, V. V. Barzykin, V. G. Abramov and F. I. Dubovitskii, Thermal Explosion in the Liquid Phase with Heat Transfer by Convection only, Russian J. Phys. Chem., **35**, 1024-1027 (1961).
[41] D. A. Frank-Kamenetskii, *ibid.*, 274.
[42] P. C. Bowes, Self-Heating: Evaluating and Controlling the Hazards, Elsevier Science Publishers B. V., Amsterdam, 490 (1984).

Chapter 6 Procedure to calculate the T_c for a powdery chemical of the TD type, having some one of several specific shapes including the so-called class A geometries as well as an arbitrary size, confined in an arbitrary closed container of the corresponding shape and size, and placed in the atmosphere under isothermal conditions

6.1 Introduction

It is possible, in principle, to calculate the T_c for a powdery chemical of the TD type, having an arbitrary shape and an arbitrary size, confined in an arbitrary closed container of the corresponding shape and size, and placed in the atmosphere under isothermal conditions, by applying the reduced form of the F-K equation, provided the value of δ_c for the shape of the chemical is known.*

If, however, the powdery chemical of the TD type, placed in the atmosphere under isothermal conditions, has some one of several specific shapes including the so-called class A geometries** as well as an arbitrary size, the calculation of the T_c for the chemical becomes very simple, because the values of δ_c for these specific shapes have already been calculated by T. Boddington *et al.*, respectively [58], with the result that, as explained in **Section 6.2**, the heat transfer data required to calculate the T_c for such a chemical as specified above is only the value of the effective thermal diffusivity,*** α_e, of the chemical.

That is, for the purpose of calculating the T_c for a powdery chemical of the TD type, having some one of the several specific shapes above referred to as well as an arbitrary size, confined in an arbitrary closed container of the corresponding shape and size, and placed in the atmosphere under isothermal conditions, we have only to perform, on the one hand, several adiabatic self-heating tests, which are started from each T_s with mutual intervals of 1～2 K, in order to

---

* It is also of course possible to calculate the T_c for a powdery chemical of the TD type, having an arbitrary shape and an arbitrary size, charged in an arbitrary (open) container of the corresponding shape and size, and placed in the atmosphere under isothermal conditions, by applying the reduced form of the F-K equation, so long as the value of δ_c for the shape of the chemical is known. It is, however, required in such a case to obtain the heat generation data of the chemical under open conditions, *i.e.*, at atmospheric pressure. In this connection, the adiabatic self-heating tests were performed, in the present chapter, under confined conditions for eight powdery chemicals of the TD type, other than OBSH and DPT, respectively, because the eight chemicals are all volatile or decompose to evolve corrosive and/or toxic gases while tested. On the other hand, as to the main heat transfer data *i.e.*, the value of α_e, of every powdery chemical of the TD type, we have no choice, under the present situation, but to use only the value measured at atmospheric pressure by applying the constant-heating-rate method.

** For the term, the class A geometries, refer to **Section 6.5**.

*** For the term, the effective thermal diffusivity, α_e, refer to **Subsections 6.4.2** and **6.4.3**.

calculate the heat generation data of the chemical, for 2 cm^3 each of several samples of the chemical confined each in the closed cell, for the time, Δt, required for the temperature of each sample of the chemical to increase by the definite value of ΔT of 1.25 K from the corresponding T_s, respectively, and, we have only to measure, on the other hand, in order to calculate the value of α_e of the chemical, a heating rate, ϕ, and a limiting radial temperature difference, $(\Delta T_{rad})_{\lim}$, which is effected in the non-steady state in temperature differences of 1.25 K between the periphery and the axial center of a moderate-sized specimen of the chemical when the outside surface of a cylindrical cell containing the specimen is heated at the rate, ϕ.

Thus, the procedure to calculate the T_c for a powdery chemical of the TD type, having some one of the several specific shapes including the class A geometries as well as an arbitrary size, confined in an arbitrary closed container of the corresponding shape and size, and placed in the atmosphere under isothermal conditions, by applying the reduced form of the F-K equation is introduced in the present chapter by taking the procedure to calculate the T_c for powdery AIBN,* assuming that it is confined in a fiber drum, 39.5 cm in inside diameter, 59.2 cm in inside length, and is placed in the atmosphere under isothermal conditions, as an example.

The values of T_c thus calculated each for nine powdery chemicals of the TD type, including powdery AIBN, ranged from 51.3 ℃ for NQC to 80.8 ℃ for DPT.

These values of T_c calculated herein in general are in fair agreement with some corresponding temperature values measured each in different ways by other researchers for some of the powdery chemicals of the TD type tested herein, respectively.

The procedure to calculate the critical temperature for the spontaneous ignition or T_c for a gas-permeable oxidatively-heating substance, having some one of the several specific shapes above referred to as well as an arbitrary size, placed in the atmosphere under isothermal conditions, by applying the reduced form of the F-K equation, in the same manner as performed for a powdery chemical of the TD type, is introduced in **Chapters 7** and 8. Principles and experimental procedures which are common to both powdery chemicals of the TD type and gas-permeable oxidatively-heating substances are, however, explained in the present chapter.

6.2 Derivation of the reduced form of the F-K equation

A proposition is obtained in **Section 2.4** to the effect that it is possible to replace the chemical quantities, E, A_0 and ΔH, included in the F-K equation,

---

* For the abbreviations of powdery chemicals of the TD type tested herein, refer to Table 14 in **Subsection 6.7.1**.

$$\delta_c = \frac{\Delta H \cdot A_0 E r^2}{\lambda R T_c^2} \exp[-\frac{E}{RT_c}], \tag{29}$$

with the two coefficients, *a* and *b*, of Equation (44),

$$\ln \Delta t = \frac{a}{T_s} + b, \tag{44}$$

holding for the self-heating process, or for the oxidatively-heating process, in the early stages, of 2 cm^3 of a chemical of the TD type, including every gas-permeable oxidatively-heating substance, charged, or confined, in some one of the open-cup, the draft or the closed cell, in accordance with the self-heating property of the chemical, and subjected to either of the two kinds of adiabatic tests.

Taking the natural logarithms on both sides of Eq. (29), and then rearranging them, we get

$$2\ln T_c + \frac{(E/R)}{T_c} = \ln\left[\frac{(\Delta H \cdot A_0)(E/R) r^2}{\lambda \cdot \delta_c}\right]. \tag{75}$$

Substituting Eqs. (45) and (46) presented in **Section 2.4**, *i.e.*,

$$a = \frac{E}{R} \tag{45}$$

and

$$b = \ln[\Delta T \cdot c\rho] - \ln[\Delta H \cdot A_0], \tag{46}$$

for (E/R) and $\ln(\Delta H \cdot A_0)$ in Eq. (75), respectively, we obtain

$$2\ln T_c + \frac{a}{T_c} = \ln\left[\frac{ac\rho r^2 \cdot \Delta T}{\lambda \cdot \delta_c}\right] - b. \tag{76}$$

The thermal conductivity, λ, is expressed as the product of the thermal diffusivity, α, and the heat capacity per unit volume, $c\rho$, [43]*, *i.e.*,

$$\lambda = \alpha \cdot c\rho, \tag{77}$$

so that an equation,

$$2\ln T_c + \frac{a}{T_c} = \ln\left[\frac{ar^2 \cdot \Delta T}{\alpha \cdot \delta_c}\right] - b, \tag{78}$$

is finally obtained.

Eq. (78) is namely the reduced form of the F-K equation.

As commented in a footnote in **Section 1.5**, however, a solid chemical of the TD type exists, in reality, in the form of a powder or an aggregation of coarse particles. Eq. (78) should thus be expressed, to be exact, in the following form in the case of a powdery chemical of the TD type, including every gas-permeable oxidatively-heating substance.

$$2\ln T_c + \frac{a}{T_c} = \ln\left[\frac{ar^2 \cdot \Delta T}{\alpha_e \cdot \delta_c}\right] - b, \tag{79}$$

where the variable, α_e, denotes the effective thermal diffusivity of an imaginary solid as which the powder is regarded temporarily. For further details, refer to **Subsection 6.4.2**.

We see from Eq. (79) that, so far as our purpose is to calculate the T_c for a powdery chemical of the TD type, including every gas-permeable oxidatively-heating substance, having an arbitrary shape and an arbitrary size, placed in the atmosphere under isothermal conditions, we may dispense with the direct knowledge of the values of E, A_0 and ΔH of the powdery chemical. As stated in **Subsection 5.3.2** as well, this is what is pointed out in **Section 2.4**.

The values of the three variables, α_e, δ_c and r, included in Eq. (79) are called hereafter the heat transfer data of a powdery chemical of the TD type, including every gas-permeable oxidatively-heating substance, having an arbitrary shape and an arbitrary value of r, placed in the atmosphere under isothermal conditions, by contrast with the heat generation data of a chemical of the TD type, *i.e.*, the values of the two coefficients, a and b, of Eq. (44).

It is clear in Eq. (79) that the value of δ_c is the shape factor of a powdery chemical of the TD type, including every gas-permeable oxidatively-heating

---

* The thermal conductivity, λ, the thermal diffusivity, α, and the specific heat capacity, c, are called the three thermal constants or the three constants of heat.

substance, and, the value of r is the size factor, or the quantity factor, of the chemical.

In this connection, the value of α_e and the heat generation data, a and b, of a powdery chemical of the TD type, including every gas-permeable oxidatively-heating substance, depend on the kind of the chemical, but these values do not depend on its shape and size.

In any event, the T_c for a powdery chemical of the TD type, including every gas-permeable oxidatively-heating substance, having an arbitrary shape and an arbitrary value of r, placed in the atmosphere under isothermal conditions, is calculated, in principle, by substituting the three heat transfer data above referred to and the heat generation data, a and b, as well as the definite value of ΔT of 1.25 K, into Eq. (79), *i.e.*, the reduced form of the F-K equation.

However, the point to which attention should be called here is that, as stated in **Section 6.1**, when a powdery chemical of the TD type, including every gas-permeable oxidatively-heating substance, placed in the atmosphere under isothermal conditions, has some one of the several specific shapes including the class A geometries as well as an arbitrary value of r, the calculation of the T_c for the chemical becomes very simple, because the values of δ_c for these specific shapes have already been calculated by T. Boddington *et al.*, respectively [58], with the result that the heat transfer data required to calculate the T_c for such a chemical as specified above is only the value of α_e of the chemical. For the values of δ_c calculated by T. Boddington *et al.*, refer to Table 13 in **Section 6.5**. The value of α_e of a powdery chemical of the TD type, including every gas-permeable oxidatively-heating substance, is thus called the main heat transfer data of the powdery chemical, by contrast with the main heat transfer data of an arbitrary volume of liquid charged in an arbitrary container and placed in the atmosphere under isothermal conditions, *i.e.*, the values of q_2 and (T_{liq} - $T_{set\text{-}up}$).

The procedure to perform several adiabatic self-heating tests, which are started from each T_s with mutual intervals of 1∼2 K, in order to calculate the heat generation data of a powdery chemical of the TD type, for 2 cm^3 each of several samples of the chemical confined each in the closed cell,* for the time, Δt, required for the temperature of each sample of the chemical to increase by the definite value of ΔT of 1.25 K from the corresponding T_s, respectively, is explained in detail in **Section 6.3** by taking the procedure performed for 2 cm^3 of powdery AIBN confined in the closed cell as an example.

An equation and the procedure to calculate the value of α_e of a powdery chemical of the TD type, including every gas-permeable oxidatively-heating substance, by applying the constant-heating-rate method is explained in detail in **Section 6.4**.

The concrete procedure to calculate the T_c for a powdery chemical of the TD type, having some one of the several specific shapes as well as an arbitrary

---

* When a powdery chemical of the TD type is not very volatile or does not decompose to evolve corrosive and/or toxic gases while tested, the open-cup cell should be used.

value of r, confined in an arbitrary closed container of the corresponding shape and size, and placed in the atmosphere under isothermal conditions, is illustrated in **Subsection 6.6.1** by taking the procedure to calculate the T_c for powdery AIBN, assuming that it is confined in a fiber drum, 39.5 cm in inside diameter, 59.2 cm in inside length, and is placed in the atmosphere under isothermal conditions, as an example.

It is seen in Eq. (79) that, generally speaking, the value of T_c for a powdery chemical of the TD type, including every gas-permeable oxidatively-heating substance, having an arbitrary shape and an arbitrary value of r, placed in the atmosphere under isothermal conditions, increases with increasing the individual values of α_e and δ_c; on the other hand, the value of T_c decreases with increasing the value of r.

6.3 Procedure to perform several adiabatic self-heating tests, which are started from each T_s with mutual intervals of 1~2 K, in order to calculate the heat generation data of a powdery chemical of the TD type, for 2 cm^3 each of several samples of the chemical confined each in the closed cell, for the time, Δt, required for the temperature of each sample of the chemical to increase by the definite value of ΔT of 1.25 K from the corresponding T_s, respectively

The procedure described in the above heading is explained in the present section by taking the procedure performed for 1.2 g of powdery AIBN, the volume of which is about 2 cm^3, confined in the closed cell as an example.

6.3.1 Preheating of the air bath of the adiabatic self-heating process recorder and the choice of a nominal T_s in the adiabatic self-heating test performed for 1.2 g of AIBN confined in the closed cell

The temperature of the air bath is set at a proper value, *i.e.*, the nominal T_s of the run, by means of the temperature dial on the air bath on the basis of the self-heating property of the chemical tested to give estimated rates of increase in temperature of 1.25 K/h in the adiabatic self-heating test. It is usually a temperature 20~30 K lower than the EOT, which is measured by thermal analysis, such as DTA or DSC, of each chemical in the case of powdery chemicals of the TD type tested herein, with the result that the T_s ranged from 57.25 ℃ for MNTS (Diazald®) to 109.7 ℃ for DPT. As to AIBN, the T_s ranged from 66.83 to 74.0 ℃.

To begin with, the main power supply connected to the adiabatic self-heating process recorder is switched on.

The power supplies connected to the cold junction, the air bath, the digital D.C. microvoltmeter, the digital D.C. millivolt recorder and the two-pen strip chart recorder are then switched on, respectively. The ΔT_{diff} pen of the two-pen strip chart recorder is, however, left on the "short" position until the thermal equilibrium state is nearly attained around the reference material confined in the closed cell and inserted into the adiabatic jacket maintained at the nominal T_s of the run. For the term, the ΔT_{diff} pen, refer to **Subsection 4.5.4**.

6.3.2 Procedure to prepare the reference cell assembly including the closed cell

2.2 g of silica powder, the volume of which is about 2 cm^3, is charged in a closed cell, *i.e.*, the cell with which the reference cell is prepared.

The reference cell, on the flange of which an O-ring is put concentrically, thus prepared is then set on the pedestal which is stuck at the center of the upper plate of the laboratory jack, which in turn is fixed on the laboratory desk. The position of the stand, by means of which the stem including the glass capillary flange is held in the vertical position, is next adjusted by sliding the stand horizontally on the desk in order that the glass capillary flange may be aligned vertically with the reference cell set on the pedestal.

The reference cell is then pressed concentrically and softly up to the under surface of the glass capillary flange by raising the laboratory jack to construct the reference cell assembly; in the meantime, the CA thermocouple, which is inserted into the glass capillary tube projecting downward from the under surface of the glass capillary flange, to measure the T_{ref} is inserted automatically and axially to the longitudinal center of silica powder charged in the cell. The reference cell assembly is finally completed by tightening the cap nut. After having lowered the laboratory jack a little, a fairly small vibrator is applied to the base of the closed cell in order that silica powder confined in the cell may come closely in contact with the glass capillary tube.

For further details of the procedure to prepare the reference cell assembly including the closed cell, refer to **Subsection 4.5.2**.

6.3.3 Insertion of the reference cell assembly into the adiabatic jacket set in the preheated air bath and the determination of the exact value of T_s of the run

The reference cell assembly thus prepared is inserted into the adiabatic jacket set in the preheated air bath.

The thermal equilibrium state is attained around the reference material confined in the closed cell and inserted into the adiabatic jacket maintained at the nominal T_s of the run 2～3 h after the insertion of the reference cell assembly into the jacket. After the thermal equilibrium state has nearly been attained around the reference material, the power supply to the analog D.C. microvoltmeter is switched on; in the meantime, the ΔT_{diff} pen of the two-pen strip chart recorder is also switched over from "short" to "on". It is then observed that the indicator of the analog D.C. microvoltmeter enters on to the scale span of the meter from the minus side, and, it comes to stay near the graduation line of zero at the center of the scale span of the meter; in the meantime, the ΔT_{diff} pen of the two-pen strip chart recorder also enters on to the strip chart of the two-pen strip chart recorder from the minus side. For the term, the minus side, refer to **Subsection 4.5.4**.

Curves drawn by the T pen and the ΔT_{diff} pen on the strip chart of the two-pen strip chart recorder, by the time that the thermal equilibrium state has been attained around the reference material confined in the closed cell and inserted into the adiabatic jacket maintained at the nominal T_s of the run, are similar to those illustrated in Fig. 38 in **Subsection 4.5.4**.

The digital output of the thermoelectromotive force of the CA thermocouple to measure the T_{ref} is then noted down as the exact value of T_s of the run, and the zero-suppression procedure is performed. For the term, the zero-suppression procedure, refer to a footnote in **Subsection 4.5.5**.

6.3.4 Insertion of the sample cell assembly into the adiabatic jacket maintained at the T_s of the run and the start of the adiabatic self-heating test for 1.2 g of AIBN confined in the closed cell

The power supply to the analog D.C. microvoltmeter is then switched off for a while; in the meantime, the ΔT_{diff} pen of the two-pen strip chart recorder is also switched over from "on" to "short" for a while.

The reference cell assembly is successively taken out of the jacket, and the sample cell assembly including a closed cell, in which 1.2 g of AIBN has been confined in the same manner as performed to prepare the reference cell assembly in **Subsection 6.3.2**, is inserted into the adiabatic jacket. The quantity of a powdery chemical of the TD type tested depends naturally on the specific gravity, with the result that it ranged from 0.7 g for TCSH to 3 g for CHC in the case of powdery chemicals of the TD type tested herein.

Coarse crystals or particles should be tested after having been crushed in an agate mortar.

When occasions demand, there are cases in each of which a fairly small vibrator is applied to the base of the closed cell in order that the chemical confined in the cell may come closely in contact with the glass capillary tube.

Although the temperature of AIBN begins to increase from a temperature near room temperature after the insertion of the sample cell assembly, the thermal equilibrium state comes to be attained again around AIBN confined in the closed cell and inserted into the adiabatic jacket maintained at the T_s of the run in the course of tens of minutes. After the thermal equilibrium state has nearly been attained around AIBN, the power supply to the analog D.C. microvoltmeter is again switched on; in the meantime, the ΔT_{diff} pen of the two-pen strip chart recorder is also switched over again from "short" to "on". It is then observed that the indicator of the analog D.C. microvoltmeter enters again on to the scale span of the meter from the minus side; in the meantime, the ΔT_{diff} pen of the two-pen strip chart recorder also enters again on to the strip chart of the two-pen strip chart recorder from the minus side.

Once the indicator of the analog D.C. microvoltmeter reaches the graduation line of zero at the center of the scale span of the meter, the adiabatic control by means of the adiabatic self-heating process recorder and the record of the self-heating process, in the early stages, of 1.2 g of AIBN confined in the closed cell by means of the digital D.C. millivolt recorder are started, respectively. This point of time corresponds to the point "**s**" in Fig. 15 presented in **Section 3.4**.

At this time, the ΔT_{diff} pen also gets to the ΔT_{diff} base line on the strip chart of the two-pen strip chart recorder (see Fig. 39 in **Subsection 4.5.6**). However, the temperature of AIBN indicated by the digital D.C. microvoltmeter in general takes a value slightly lower than that of the T_s at this time, because, while the T_{atm}, the temperature of the atmosphere around AIBN, is still slightly lower than the T_s, AIBN begins to self-heat in the cell, so that the temperature of AIBN catches the T_{atm} up.

6.3.5 Record of the self-heating process, in the early stages, of 1.2 g of AIBN confined in the closed cell and inserted into the adiabatic jacket kept always at the very slowly increasing temperature of AIBN itself by the adiabatic control

After the start of the adiabatic control, the T_{atm} is raised automatically by the adiabatic control in order that the condition, $\Delta T_{diff} = T - T_{atm} = 0$, may always hold, with the result that the heat generated in the self-heating AIBN is all accumulated in it, and, it continues to self-heat at a very slow, but virtually constant, rate depending on the value of T_s; in the meantime, the temperature of the space in the air bath, except that in the adiabatic jacket, is maintained at the T_s of the run throughout every run.

The self-heating process, in the early stages, of 1.2 g of AIBN confined in the closed cell and inserted into the adiabatic jacket kept always at the very slowly increasing temperature of AIBN itself by the adiabatic control is recorded in the digital representation as the variation of the value, with time, of the thermoelectromotive force of the thermocouple to measure the temperature of AIBN; to put it concretely, the numerical value of the thermoelectromotive force of the thermocouple is printed out every minute by means of the digital D.C. millivolt recorder, in such a manner as exemplified in Table 5 presented in **Section 4.7**, in order to utilize the record for the calculation of the values of the two coefficients, a and b, of Eq. (44), $\ln \Delta t = a/T_s + b$, holding for the self-heating process, in the early stages, of 1.2 g of AIBN confined in the closed cell and subjected to the adiabatic self-heating test.

On the other hand, however, the self-heating process, in the early stages, of 1.2 g of AIBN confined in the closed cell and subjected to the adiabatic self-heating test is recorded, as an analog signal as well, with the T pen on the strip chart of the two-pen strip chart recorder to look about the process as a whole.

The test is interrupted as soon as the temperature of AIBN in the cell increases by the definite value of ΔT of 1.25 K from the T_s.

The other combinations of the value of $\ln \Delta t$ with that of $1/T_s$, which are required to make the plot of $\ln \Delta t$ versus $1/T_s$ with regard to several self-heating processes, of 1.2 g each of several samples of AIBN confined each in the closed cell and subjected each to the adiabatic self-heating test started from each T_s in the range of 66.83 to 74.0 ℃ with mutual intervals of 1.5～2 K, recorded each for the time, Δt, required for the temperature of each sample of AIBN to increase by the definite value of ΔT of 1.25 K from the corresponding T_s, besides, which are required for the regression analysis to calculate the values of the two coefficients, a and b, of Eq. (44), $\ln \Delta t = a/T_s + b$, holding for the self-heating process, in the early stages, of 1.2 g of AIBN confined in the closed cell and subjected to the adiabatic self-heating test, are also determined in the same manner as explained above.

Five self-heating processes, of 1.2 g each of five samples of AIBN confined each in the closed cell and subjected each to the adiabatic self-heating test started from each T_s in the range of 66.83 to 74.0 ℃ with mutual intervals of 1.5 ~2 K, recorded each for the time, Δt, required for the temperature of each sample of AIBN to increase by the definite value of ΔT of 1.25 K from the corresponding T_s, are presented in Fig. 61. The point marked with "**0**" on the time axis in Fig. 61 corresponds to the point of time "**s**" in Fig. 15 presented in **Section 3.4**.

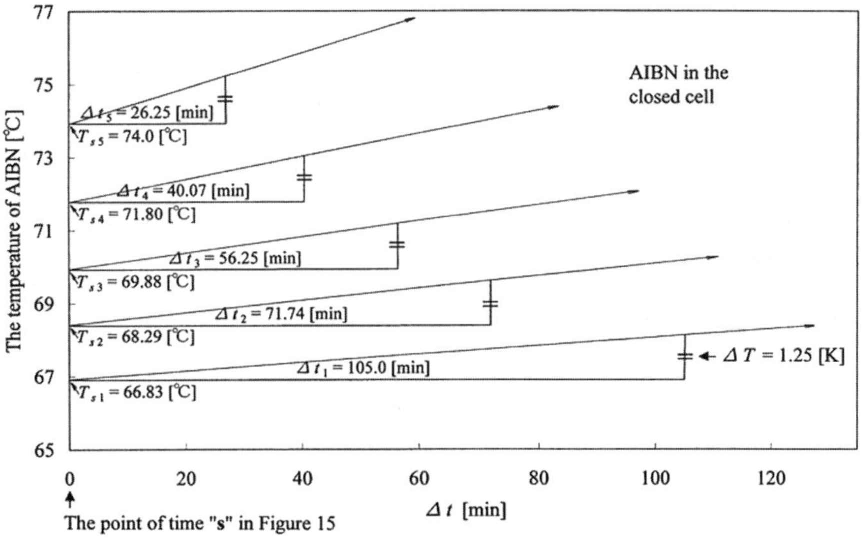

Figure 61. Five self-heating processes, of 1.2 g each of five samples of AIBN confined each in the closed cell and subjected each to the adiabatic self-heating test started from each T_s in the range of 66.83 to 74.0 ℃ with mutual intervals of 1.5~2 K, recorded each for the time, Δt, required for the temperature of each sample of AIBN to increase by the definite value of ΔT of 1.25 K from the corresponding T_s.

The plot of $\ln \Delta t$ versus $1/T_s$ made for 1.2 g each of eight samples of AIBN is shown in Fig. 62.

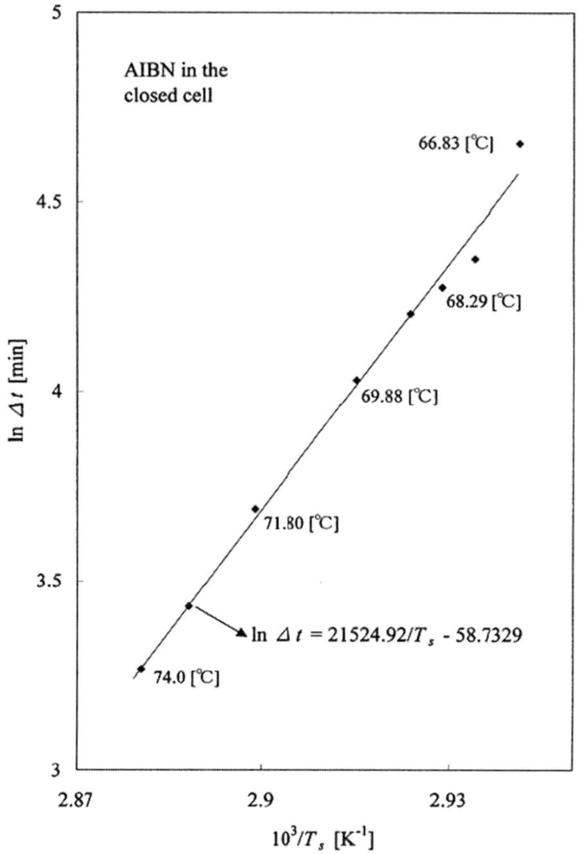

Figure 62. The plot of $\ln \Delta t$ versus $1/T_s$ made with eight combinations of the value of $\ln \Delta t$ with that of $1/T_s$, which are each determined for eight self-heating processes, five self-heating processes of which are presented in Fig. 61, of 1.2 g each of eight samples of AIBN confined each in the closed cell and subjected each to the adiabatic self-heating test started from each T_s in the range of 66.83 to 74.0 ℃ with mutual intervals of 0.6～2 K, recorded each for the time, Δt, required for the temperature of each sample of AIBN to increase by the definite value of ΔT of 1.25 K from the corresponding T_s.

It is obvious in Fig. 62 that the empirical formula, $\ln \Delta t = a/T_s + b$, *i.e.*, Eq. (44), presented in Fig. 15 in **Section 3.4** holds well between a T_s and the time, Δt, required for the temperature of 1.2 g of AIBN confined in the closed cell and subjected to the adiabatic self-heating test started from the T_s to increase by the definite value of ΔT of 1.25 K from the T_s.

For the value of a coefficient, 21524.92, of the equation, $\ln \Delta t = 21524.92/T_s - 58.7329$, *i.e.*, Eq. (44) holding for the self-heating process, in the early stages, of 1.2 g of AIBN confined in the closed cell and subjected to the adiabatic self-heating test, refer to the explanation given under Table 11 in the following subsection.

6.3.6 Calculation of the heat generation data of AIBN, *i.e.*, the values of the two coefficients, *a* and *b*, of Eq. (44), $\ln \Delta t = a/T_s + b$, holding for the self-heating process, in the early stages, of 1.2 g of AIBN confined in the closed cell and subjected to the adiabatic self-heating test

The result of the regression analysis to calculate the heat generation data of AIBN is presented in Table 11.

Values of $\ln \Delta t$ and $1/T_s$ used in the regression analysis are in common with those presented in part in Fig. 61 and plotted in Fig. 62. The values of Δt and T_s presented in Figs. 61 and 62 are, however, all rounded. For an instance similar to this, refer to Tables 5 and 6 in **Section 4.7** and Figs. 45 and 46 in **Subsection 5.4.5**.

Table 11

The result of the regression analysis applied, in order to calculate the heat generation data of AIBN, to eight combinations of the value of ln Δt with that of $1/T_s$, which are each determined, based on eight digital records obtained each from eight adiabatic self-heating tests, which are started from each T_s in the range of 66.83 to 74.0 ℃ with mutual intervals of 0.6~2 K, performed each, for 1.2 g each of eight samples of AIBN confined each in the closed cell, for the time, Δt, required for the temperature of each sample of AIBN to increase by the definite value of ΔT of 1.25 K from the corresponding T_s. Data used are in common with those presented in part in Fig. 61 and plotted in Fig. 62.

MATERIAL ... AIBN

DATA NUMBER	X	Y	A＊X+B
1	2.94131	4.65435	4.578565
2	2.93399	4.34736	4.421003
3	2.92875	4.27306	4.308212
4	2.92374	4.20395	4.200372
5	2.91521	4.02981	4.016765
6	2.89893	3.69075	3.666339
7	2.88824	3.43233	3.436237
8	2.88060	3.26767	3.271787

COEFFICIENT OF Y = A＊TT + B A = 21.52492
COEFFICIENT OF Y = A＊TT + B B = -58.7329

DISTRIBUTION = 0.002202 STANDARD DEVIATION = 0.046928

Based on the result, the value of a for AIBN is calculated by multiplying the value of A, which is presented in Table 11, by 1,000 in the same manner as performed for the value of A of TBPB in **Section 4.7**.

The values of the two coefficients, a and b, thus calculated, of Eq. (44), $\ln \Delta t = a/T_s + b$, holding for the self-heating process, in the early stages, of 1.2 g of AIBN confined in the closed cell and subjected to the adiabatic self-heating test, 21524.92 and -58.7329, *i.e.*, the heat generation data of AIBN, are presented as such in Table 15 in **Subsection 6.7.1**.

6.4 Equation and procedure to calculate the value of α_e of a powdery chemical of the TD type, including every gas-permeable oxidatively-heating substance, by applying the constant-heating-rate method

6.4.1 Equation to calculate the thermal diffusivity, α, of a solid

An equation, *i.e.*, Eq. (80), in which the thermal diffusivity, α, of a solid is included as one variable, is given in a book written by Jaeger *et al.* [44].

Let us suppose that an infinite* circular cylinder is placed in the space (Fig. 63).

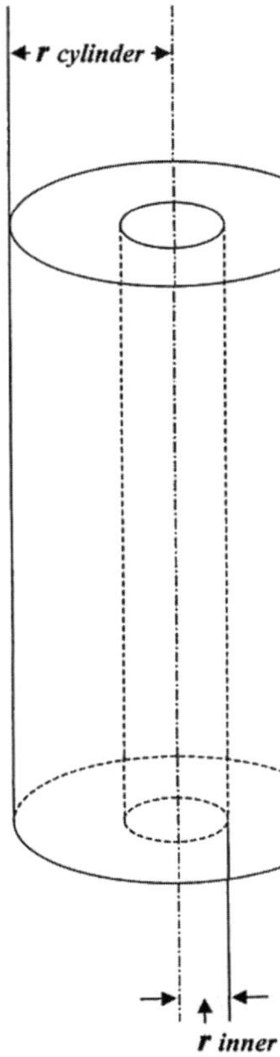

Figure 63. An infinite circular cylinder.

* The adjective "infinite" means that the heat loss at both ends of the cylinder is assumed to be negligible.

When the outside surface of the cylinder, the radius of which is expressed as $r_{cylinder}$ and the initial temperature of which is assumed to be zero, is heated radially and symmetrically at a very slow rate, ϕ, the variation of temperature, $T_{r\text{-}inner}$, at an arbitrary inner radius, r_{inner}, with time is expressed by Eq. (80).

$$T_{r-inner} = \phi\left(t - \frac{r_{cylinder}^2 - r_{inner}^2}{4\alpha}\right) + \frac{2\phi}{r_{cylinder}\cdot\alpha}\sum_{n=1}^{\infty}\exp\left[-\alpha\beta_n^2 t\right]\frac{J_0(r_{inner}\beta_n)}{\beta_n^3 J_1(r_{cylinder}\beta_n)}, \tag{80}$$

where $J_0(x)$, $J_1(x)$ and β_n are the zeroth order Bessel function, the first order Bessel function and the positive roots of $J_0(r_{cylinder}\beta_n) = 0$, respectively.

The best combination of the values of $r_{inner\ 1}$ and $r_{inner\ 2}$ seems to be $r_{inner\ 1} = 0$ and $r_{inner\ 2} = r_{cylinder}$; and therefore, both are taken as these values hereafter.

Expressing the temperatures at two radii, 0 and $r_{cylinder}$, as T_0 and $T_{r\text{-}cylinder}$, respectively; besides, noting that $J_0(0) = 1$ and $J_0(r_{cylinder}\beta_n) = 0$, we get

$$T_0 = \phi\left(t - \frac{r_{cylinder}^2}{4\alpha}\right) + \frac{2\phi}{r_{cylinder}\cdot\alpha}\sum_{n=1}^{\infty}\frac{\exp\left[-\alpha\beta_n^2 t\right]}{\beta_n^3 J_1(r_{cylinder}\beta_n)} \tag{81}$$

and

$$T_{r-cylinder} = \phi t. \tag{82}$$

The radial temperature difference between $T_{r\text{-}cylinder}$ and T_0, *i.e.*, ΔT_{rad}, is, therefore, expressed as

$$\begin{aligned}\Delta T_{rad} &= T_{r-cylinder} - T_0 \\ &= \frac{r_{cylinder}^2\cdot\phi}{4\alpha} - \frac{2\phi}{r_{cylinder}\cdot\alpha}\sum_{n=1}^{\infty}\frac{\exp\left[-\alpha\beta_n^2 t\right]}{\beta_n^3 J_1(r_{cylinder}\beta_n)}.\end{aligned} \tag{83}$$

According to a series of researches performed by Kosaka *et al.* [45～47], it is confirmed that the value of the second term of the right-hand side of Eq. (83) converges on zero within a few minutes of the start of heating. Eq. (84) thus holds in the non-steady state.

$$\alpha = \frac{r_{cylinder}^2 \cdot \phi}{4(\Delta T_{rad})_{\lim}}, \tag{84}$$

where the variable, $(\Delta T_{rad})_{\lim}$, denotes a nearly constant value which the variable, ΔT_{rad}, takes in the non-steady state after the value of the second term of the right-hand side of Eq. (83) has converged on zero.

Eqs. (81)~(84) were derived by Kosaka *et al.* [45]. The variable, $(\Delta T_{rad})_{\lim}$, in Eqs. (84) and (85) was, however, introduced newly herein.

As a mater of fact, before a series of papers were published by Kosaka *et al.*, a procedure to calculate the value of α of an arbitrary solid, which is based on a concept near that of Kosaka *et al.*, had been presented in a book edited by Tye as one of the so-called non-steady state methods to measure a few thermal constants [48]. Fig. 64 is quoted from page 186 of Tye's book. Two experiments [49, 50], in which the values of α of solid ZrO_2, Ta, ZrC and TiC were each calculated at considerably high temperatures, are also introduced in the same book.

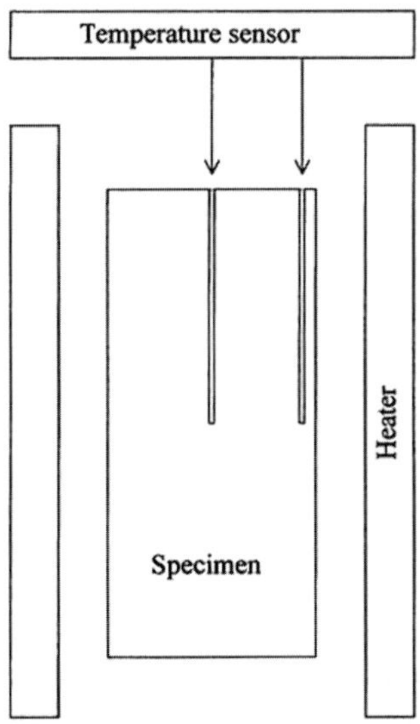

Figure 64. Cross-sectional view of an idealized cylindrical specimen used for determining the thermal diffusivity.

6.4.2 Equation to calculate the effective thermal diffusivity, α_e, of a powder

As commented in **Sections 1.5** and **6.2**, a solid chemical of the TD type, including every gas-permeable oxidatively-heating substance, exists, in reality, in the form of a powder or an aggregation of coarse particles. Nevertheless, however, Eq. (84) is applicable to the calculation of the T_c for a powder as well. Needless to say, however, the thermal diffusivity calculated by applying the constant-heating-rate method,* which is explained in the following subsection, to a powder is the effective thermal diffusivity, α_e, of an imaginary solid as which the powder is regarded temporarily. Therefore, Eq. (84) should, to be exact, be expressed in the following form in the case of a powder.

$$\alpha_e = \frac{r_{cylinder}^2 \cdot \phi}{4(\Delta T_{rad})_{\lim}}, \tag{85}$$

where $r_{cylinder}$ denotes, in fact, the distance between the points of the two thermocouples inserted each axially to the longitudinal center of a cylindrical powdery specimen at the axial center of the specimen and at a radius a little smaller than the true $r_{cylinder}$ (see Fig. 68).

The value of α_e of a powder is, of course, considerably different from the value of α of the original solid, the fine fragments of which constitute the powder. It is, however, known that a relation, $\alpha >> \alpha_e$, in general holds between the two values of thermal diffusivity regarding the same substance.

The value of α_e of a powder depends on many factors, such as particle size, particle shape, void ratio and kind of the gas existing among particles of the powder, as well as kind of the original solid.

To cite one instance, the finer the powder, the smaller is the value of α_e of the powder [47]. This effect may be ascribed to the fact that the finer the powder, the more increases the number of contacts among particles per unit volume; in other words, the finer the powder, the more increases the resistance against the thermal conduction between adjoining particles of the powder as a whole, with the result that the value of α_e of the powder decreases. Besides, it is ascertained that the larger the value of λ of the gas existing among particles of the powder, the larger is the value of α_e of the powder; and, the higher the pressure of the gas existing among particles of the powder, the larger is the value of α_e of the powder.

At all events, main conclusions obtained by a series of researches performed by Kosaka *et al.* regarding the individual values of α_e of some powders are that the value of α_e of a powder does not depend so much on the value of α of the

---

* The method to calculate the value of α or that of α_e by substituting the individual values of ϕ and $(\Delta T_{rad})_{\lim}$ into Eqs. (84) or (85) is referred to as the constant-heating-rate method herein.

original solid; and, the decisive factors controlling the value of α_e of a powder are the kind, in fact the thermal conductivity, and the pressure of the gas existing among particles of the powder as well as the thermal conduction at the points of contact among adjoining particles of the powder [47, 51~53].

A selection of the individual values of α_e of some powders are given in Table 12. As shown in the table, organic powdery chemicals, inorganic powdery chemicals, sawdusts and metallic powders take the values of α_e of 0.06~0.09, 0.10~0.25, 0.14~0.18 and 0.10~0.30 cm^2/min, respectively.

Table 12
A selection of the individual values of α_e of some powders.
These values of α_e, except the ones measured herein and the ones, to which reference numbers are each attached, were measured predominantly by Kosaka *et al.* by applying the constant-heating-rate method, respectively [47, 51~53].

Powder	α_e cm²/min
Organic powdery chemicals of the TD type	0.06~0.08 [a)]
Starch	0.08 [54]
Amorphous carbon	0.06~0.12 [55]
Carbon granule	0.33
Sawdust of each wood species	0.14~0.18 [b)]
LiF	0.07
Na_2CO_3	0.10
Na_2S	0.12
NaCl	0.23
Na_2SO_4	0.09
K_2CO_3	0.09
K_2SO_4	0.15
KCl	0.24
$MgSO_4$	0.12
CHC (calcium hypochlorite)	0.13 [a)]
$CaCO_3$	0.12 [c)]
Al_2O_3	0.15
Aluminium powder at 200 ℃	0.26 [d)]
Silica powder	0.15~0.20 [e)]
Silicon carbide powder	0.18
Diatomaceous earth	0.12
Soil	0.13~0.18 [56]
Fe_2O_3	0.18
Iron powder	0.12 [f)]
Stainless steel powder	0.13 [g)]
NiO	0.18
Zircon ($ZrSiO_4$) powder	0.17

(Continued on the following page)

Superscripts:

a) The values of α_e of the eight organic powdery chemicals of the TD type and that of CHC were measured herein by applying the constant-heating-rate method and are presented in Table 15 in **Subsection 6.7.1**, respectively.

b) The value of α_e of the sawdust of each wood species was measured herein by applying the constant-heating-rate method and is presented in Table 21 in **(1)** of **Subsection 8.4.4**.

c) The value of α of solid marble at room temperature is about 0.7 cm^2/min [45].

d) The value of α of solid aluminium at 100 ℃ is about 50 cm^2/min [47].

e) The value of α of crystalline silicon dioxide at 300 to 1,000 K is 0.4~1.2 cm^2/min [57].

f) The value of α of solid carbon steel (0.43 % C) at room temperature is about 6 cm^2/min [46].

g) The value of α of solid stainless steel, SUS 304, at room temperature is about 2 cm^2/min [45].

6.4.3 A radial temperature difference measuring apparatus made by applying the constant-heating-rate method

(1) Structure of the apparatus

The values of ϕ and $(\Delta T_{rad})_{\lim}$ of a moderate-sized specimen of a powdery chemical of the TD type, including every gas-permeable oxidatively-heating substance, were measured herein by means of a radial temperature difference measuring apparatus, which was originally designed by M. Kosaka by applying the constant-heating-rate method [47].

Figure 65. Overall view of a radial temperature difference measuring apparatus.
A. Control unit; **B**. Cylindrical furnace used to heat the cell containing a powdery specimen at a very slow rate; **C**. Holder for the cell containing a powdery specimen.

Figure 66. Cylindrical furnace in which the holder for the cell containing a powdery specimen is enclosed.

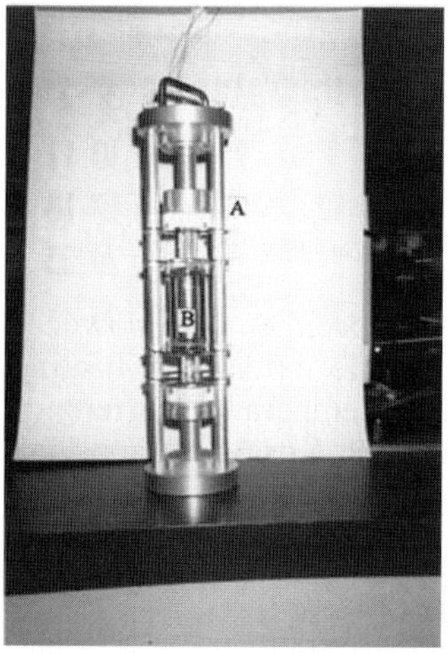

Figure 67. **A**. Holder for the cell containing a powdery specimen; **B**. Cell containing a powdery specimen.

A cross section of the cell containing a powdery specimen is shown in Fig. 68. The cell in turn is enclosed in the furnace; and, a set of radiation shields is placed above and below the cell in the furnace.

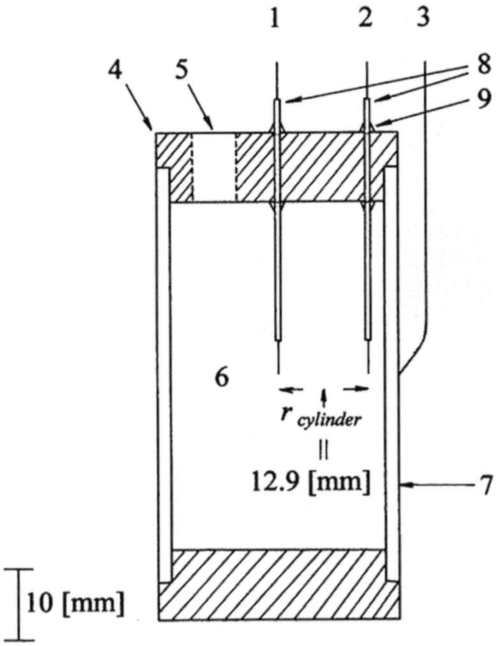

Figure 68. The cell containing a powdery specimen.

1, **2**, **3**, Stainless steel-sheathed CA thermocouple, 0.5 mm in outside diameter; **4**, Pyrophyllite [$Al_2Si_4O_{10}(OH)_2$] lid, 3.4 cm in diameter, 1 cm in thickness; **5**, Hole, 8 mm in diameter, used to charge the cell with a powdery specimen; **6**, Powdery specimen; **7**, Aluminium cylinder, 3.4 cm in outside diameter, 3 cm in inside diameter, 6 cm in length; **8**, Two alumina insulating sleeves, into which thermocouples 1 and 2 are each inserted, 1.2 mm each in outside diameter; **9**, Inorganic adhesive agent.

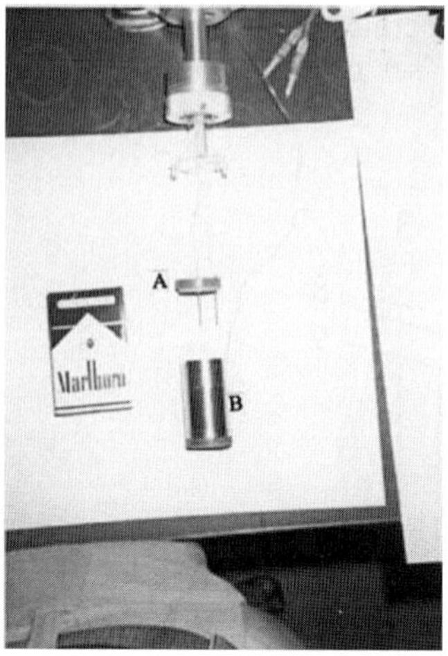

Figure 69. **A**. Upper pyrophyllite lid fitted with two alumina insulating sleeves; the latter sleeves are each cemented to the lid with an inorganic adhesive agent, and the thermocouples 1 and 2 are each inserted into the sleeves and are each supported and insulated by the sleeves; **B**. Aluminium cylinder; this is connected with the thermocouple 3 attached on the outside surface of the cylinder with silver paste for the cell-heating control and is covered with the lower pyrophyllite lid at the base.

In brief, every powdery specimen takes the form of a cylinder, 3 cm in diameter, 5 cm in length. Two stainless steel-sheathed CA thermocouples 1 and 2 are inserted vertically to the longitudinal center of the cylindrical powdery specimen at the axial center of the specimen and at a radius of 1.29 cm, respectively. It thus follows that the value of $r_{cylinder}$ takes a definite value of 1.29 cm in the case of this apparatus.

The thermocouples used are Philips stainless steel-sheathed CA thermocouples, 0.5 mm each in outside diameter, and are so selected that their thermoelectromotive forces may be almost the same as each other in the range of room temperature to 200 ℃.

(2) Experimental method to measure the values of ϕ and $(\Delta T_{rad})_{\lim}$ of a specimen of powdery AIBN in the non-steady state and in temperature differences of 1.25 K between the $T_{r\text{-}cylinder}$ and the T_0

A specimen of powdery AIBN is charged into the cell through a small hole, 8 mm in diameter, in the upper lid. The gas existing among particles of every powder charged in the cell is air in the case of this apparatus.

The holder for the cell containing the powdery specimen is next enclosed in the cylindrical furnace which is, at first, maintained at a constant starting temperature. After it has been ascertained that the value of ΔT_{rad} remains at a constant value of zero for 30～60 min since the holder has been enclosed in the furnace, the cell-heating is started at a very small value of ϕ.

The value of ϕ is recorded with the T pen on a two-pen strip chart recorder as the variation of the thermoelectromotive force of the thermocouple 2 with time;

on the other hand, the variation of the value of ΔT_{rad}, which is measured by means of a differential thermocouple composed of the two thermocouples 1 and 2, with time is recorded with the ΔT_{rad} pen on the recorder.

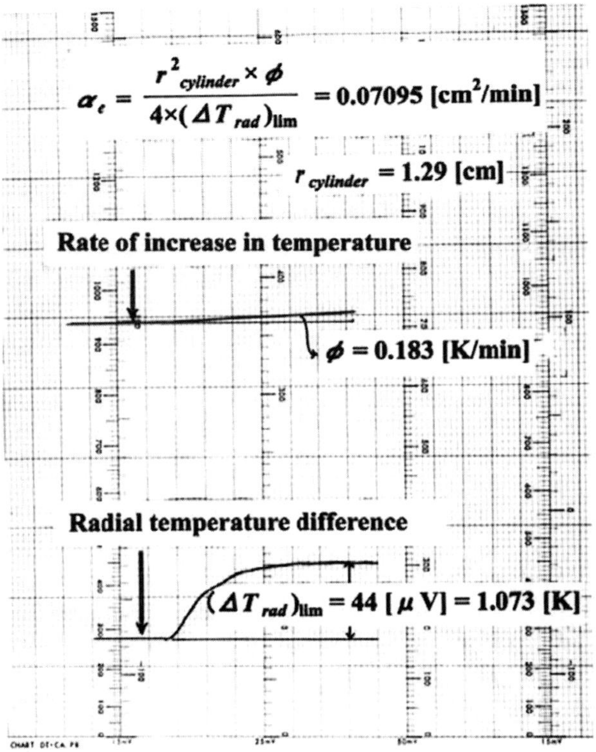

Figure 70. Curves drawn by the T pen and the ΔT_{rad} pen on the strip chart of the two-pen strip chart recorder by the time that a nearly constant value of $(\Delta T_{rad})_{lim}$ is effected, in the non-steady state and in temperature differences of 1.25 K between the $T_{r\text{-}cylinder}$ and the T_0, in the specimen of powdery AIBN charged in the cell heated at a value of ϕ of 0.183 K/min from a starting temperature near room temperature in the radial temperature difference measuring apparatus.

Curves drawn by the T pen and the ΔT_{rad} pen on the strip chart of the two-pen strip chart recorder are shown in Fig. 70.

In Fig. 70, "Rate of increase in temperature" and "Radial temperature difference" denote the variation of the thermoelectromotive force of the thermocouple 2, *i.e.*, the variation of the $T_{r\text{-}cylinder}$, with time and the variation of the value of ΔT_{rad} with time, respectively.

First, the value of ΔT_{rad} increases linearly with time, because only the $T_{r\text{-}cylinder}$ increases linearly, while the T_0 remains at the original value.

Soon, however, the ΔT_{rad} curve comes to decline, because the heat attains to the axial center from the periphery of the cell, so that the T_0 also begins to increase.

Ultimately, the ΔT_{rad} pen comes to run parallel with the time axis on the strip chart, because both the $T_{r\text{-}cylinder}$ and the T_0 come to increase at the same rate, so that a nearly constant value of $(\Delta T_{rad})_{\rm lim}$ is effected in the non-steady state between the $T_{r\text{-}cylinder}$ and the T_0.

It is clear in the procedure explained above that the temperature of the specimen as a whole continues to increase at a constant rate, ϕ, during the measurement of the value of $(\Delta T_{rad})_{\rm lim}$. Therefore, it has been made a rule in a series of measurements of this kind to regard the arithmetic mean of the thermoelectromotive force of the thermocouple 2 at the beginning of a run and that at the end as the measuring temperature of the run.

The specimen is exhausted from the lower end of the aluminium cylinder after each run.

It has been ascertained through a series of measurements performed by means of this apparatus that the values of ϕ of 8～12 and 18～20 K/h are optimum for organic powdery chemicals of the TD type and sawdusts, respectively.

The values of ϕ and $(\Delta T_{rad})_{\rm lim}$ of the nine powdery chemicals of the TD type, with the exception of MNTS,* tested herein were measured at a temperature near 50 ℃, respectively. The latter temperature was chosen as a temperature at which none of the nine powdery chemicals self-heats during the measurement. In this connection, it is also ascertained that the value of α_e calculated by substituting the values of ϕ and $(\Delta T_{rad})_{\rm lim}$ measured at a temperature near 50 ℃ into Eq. (85) and that calculated by substituting the values measured at a temperature near room temperature into the same equation were nearly equivalent to each other for every chemical.

(3) Concrete procedure to calculate the value of α_e of powdery AIBN

The value of α_e of powdery AIBN is calculated by substituting the values of ϕ and $(\Delta T_{rad})_{\rm lim}$ for the specimen of powdery AIBN, both of which are shown in Photo. 70, as well as the value of $r_{cylinder}$ of 1.29 cm into Eq. (85) in the following manner.

---

* Only MNTS, among the ten powdery chemicals of the TD type tested herein, is powdery at room temperature but self-heats as a liquid at temperatures higher than its melting point. It thus follows that it is the Semenov equation, not the F-K equation, that should be applied to calculate the T_c for an arbitrary volume of molten MNTS confined in an arbitrary closed container of the corresponding shape and size, and placed in the atmosphere under isothermal conditions. It is, therefore, useless to measure the value of α_e of a powdery specimen of MNTS at a temperature near room temperature.

$$\alpha_e = \frac{r_{cylinder}^2 \times \phi}{4 \times \left(\Delta T_{rad}\right)_{\lim}} = [(1.29)^2 \times 0.183] \div [4 \times 1.073]$$

$$= 0.07095.$$

The value of α_e thus calculated for powdery AIBN, 0.07095 cm^2/min, is finally rounded to 0.07 cm^2/min and is presented as such, together with the values of α_e calculated each for the eight powdery chemicals of the TD type, other than AIBN and MNTS, in the same manner as performed for powdery AIBN, in Table 15 in **Subsection 6.7.1**.

The variation of the value of T_c for a powdery chemical of the TD type with the value of α_e differs naturally from one powdery chemical to another. Generally speaking, however, a decrease of 0.01 cm^2/min in the value of α_e, the magnitude of which is the maximum error conceivable in the calculation of the value of α_e and corresponds to about 20 % of the value of α_e of an average organic powdery chemical of the TD type, causes a decrease of about 1 K in the value of T_c calculated by applying Eq. (79), keeping the values of the other variables in the equation constant. A fluctuation, of such an extent, of the value of T_c is, however, thought to be within the error range of the result of the isothermal storage test performed in order to measure the T_c for a powdery chemical of the TD type, having an arbitrary shape and an arbitrary size, confined in an arbitrary closed container of the corresponding shape and size.

6.5 Individual values of δ_c for the several specific shapes including the so-called class A geometries

The infinite slab, the infinite circular cylinder and the sphere were called the class A geometries by T. Boddington *et al.* As stated repeatedly above, the values of δ_c for the several specific shapes including the class A geometries have already been calculated by T. Boddington *et al.*, respectively. Table 13 is quoted from page 486 of their paper [58].

It thus follows that the heat transfer data required to calculate the T_c for a powdery chemical of the TD type, including every gas-permeable oxidatively-heating substance, having some one of the several specific shapes above referred to as well as an arbitrary value of r, placed in the atmosphere under isothermal conditions, is only the value of α_e of the chemical.

Table 13
Individual values of δ_c for the several specific shapes including the so-called class A geometries.

Geometry	Value of δ_c
infinite slab, width = $2r$	0.878
infinite circular cylinder, radius = r	2.00
infinite square rod, side = $2r$	1.70
sphere, radius = r	3.32
equicylinder, length = $2r$, radius = r	2.76
cube, side = $2r$	2.52

For instance, once the shape of a powdery chemical of the TD type is assumed to be an infinite slab, a value of δ_c of 0.878 is fixed at once for the chemical having an arbitrary halfvalue thickness. It then becomes possible to calculate the T_c for the imaginary infinite slab, having an arbitrary halfvalue thickness, placed in the atmosphere under isothermal conditions, provided the value of α_e of the chemical is known.

Similarly, once the shape of a powdery chemical of the TD type is approximated by an infinite cylinder, a value of δ_c of 2.0 is fixed automatically for the chemical having an arbitrary value of radius. It then becomes possible to calculate the T_c for the imaginary infinite cylinder, having an arbitrary value of radius, placed in the atmosphere under isothermal conditions, provided the value of α_e of the chemical is known; and so forth.

The variation of the value of T_c for a powdery chemical of the TD type with the value of δ_c is also of the same order of magnitude as that with the value of α_e. That is, a decrease of 0.25 in the value of δ_c, the magnitude of which is the maximum error conceivable in the assignment of the value of δ_c to the shape of the chemical and corresponds to about 10 % of the value of δ_c for the shape of an average fiber drum used to carry a powdery chemical of the TD type, causes a decrease of about 0.5 K in the value of T_c calculated by applying Eq. (79), keeping the values of the other variables in the equation constant.

6.6 Concrete procedure to calculate the T_c for a powdery chemical of the TD type, having some one of the several specific shapes including the class A geometries as well as an arbitrary size, confined in an arbitrary closed container of the corresponding shape and size, and placed in the atmosphere under isothermal conditions

It is of course possible to calculate the T_c for a powdery chemical of the TD type, having an arbitrary shape and an arbitrary size, confined in an arbitrary closed container of the corresponding shape and size, and placed in the atmosphere under isothermal conditions, by applying the reduced form of the F-K equation, *i.e.*, Eq. (79), provided the value of δ_c for the shape of the chemical is known. When, in particular, the powdery chemical has some one of the several specific shapes including the class A geometries as well as an arbitrary value of r, it is very simple to calculate the T_c.

In order to compare the values of T_c calculated each for the ten powdery chemicals of the TD type placed each in the atmosphere under isothermal conditions with one another, however, it is required to calculate the individual values of T_c, assuming that these chemicals are each placed under the same conditions of shape and size, apart from whether they are each charged in open containers at atmospheric pressure or they are each confined in closed containers.

A decision was thus made herein to calculate the individual values of T_c for the ten powdery chemicals of the TD type in the following two manners.

(1) The values of T_c for the nine powdery chemicals of the TD type, other than MNTS, are each calculated by applying Eq. (79), *i.e.*, the reduced form of the F-K equation, assuming that these chemicals are each confined in a fiber drum, 39.5 cm in inside diameter, 59.2 cm in inside length, and are each placed in the atmosphere under isothermal conditions. The calculation in this manner was performed, following an example that a fiber drum, 39.5 cm in inside diameter, 59.2 cm in inside length, about 72.5 L in net volume, is used by a blowing agent manufacturing company in Japan to deliver 50 kg of DPT to the users.

As an example, the concrete procedure to calculate the T_c for powdery AIBN confined in a fiber drum, 39.5 cm in inside diameter, 59.2 cm in inside length, and placed in the atmosphere under isothermal conditions is illustrated in **Subsection 6.6.1**. The values of T_c calculated each for the nine powdery chemicals of the TD type, including AIBN, but excluding MNTS, in the same manner as performed for powdery AIBN, are presented in Table 15 in **Subsection 6.7.1**.

(2) On the other hand, the values of T_c, in fact the values of the BAM test, for the ten powdery chemicals of the TD type, including MNTS, are each calculated by applying Eq. (72) derived in **Subsection 5.3.2**, *i.e.*, the reduced form of the Semenov equation, assuming that 400 cm^3 each of these chemicals are each subjected to the BAM heat-accumulation storage test, because, in order to compare the individual values of T_c for chemicals of the TD type, irrespective of powder or liquid, with one another, it is thought to be most appropriate to do so, assuming that 400 cm^3 each of these chemicals are each charged in the 500 cm^3 Dewar flask used in the BAM test and are each placed in the atmosphere under isothermal conditions.*

As an example, the concrete procedure to calculate the value of the BAM test for BSHA is illustrated in **Section 6.8**. The values of the BAM test calculated each for the ten powdery chemicals of the TD type, including MNTS, in the same manner as performed for BSHA, are presented in Table 16 in **Section 6.8**.

6.6.1 Concrete procedure to calculate the T_c for powdery AIBN confined in a fiber drum, 39.5 cm in inside diameter, 59.2 cm in inside length, and placed in the atmosphere under isothermal conditions

The heat generation data, *a* and *b*, of powdery AIBN were calculated in **Subsection 6.3.6** and are given in Table 15 in **Subsection 6.7.1**, respectively.

On the other hand, the value of α_e of powdery AIBN was calculated at 0.07 cm^2/min by applying the constant-heating-rate method in **(3)** of **Subsection 6.4.3**.

The value of δ_c for a solid cylinder, 39.5 cm in diameter, 59.2 cm in length, placed in the atmosphere under isothermal conditions was assumed to be 2.6 herein, taking into consideration the two data that the value of δ_c for the equicylinder** and that for the infinite cylinders are 2.76 and 2.0, respectively (see Table 13 in **Section 6.5**).

Further, the value of *r* of a cylinder, 39.5 cm in diameter, is of course 19.75 (= 39.5/2) cm.

The above three heat transfer data of powdery AIBN confined in a fiber drum, 39.5 cm in inside diameter, 59.2 cm in inside length, and placed in the atmosphere under isothermal conditions are also given in Table 15 in **Subsection 6.7.1**, respectively.

And, the value of ΔT is 1.25 K.

The value of the right-hand side of Eq. (79), *i.e.*,

* The Semenov model holds for a chemical of the TD type, irrespective of liquid or powder, charged in the Dewar flask used in the BAM test. For further details, refer to **Section 6.8**.

** A cylinder, the diameter of which is equal to the length, is called an equicylinder.

$$2\ln T_c + \frac{a}{T_c} = \ln\left[\frac{ar^2 \cdot \Delta T}{\alpha_e \cdot \delta_c}\right] - b, \qquad (79)$$

for powdery AIBN above referred to is thus calculated in the following manner.

$$\ln\left[\frac{ar^2 \cdot \Delta T}{\alpha_e \cdot \delta_c}\right] - b = \ln\{[21524.92 \times (39.5/2)^2 \times 1.25] \div [0.07 \times 2.6]\}$$

$$+ 58.7329$$

$$= 17.87016574 + 58.7329$$

$$= 76.60306574.$$

On the other hand, if the value of T_c for powdery AIBN above referred to is assumed to be 331.163617 K or 58.013617 ℃, the value of the left-hand side of Eq. (79) is calculated in the following manner.

$$2\ln T_c + \frac{a}{T_c} = 2\ln 331.163617 + 21524.92 \div 331.163617$$

$$= 11.60522513 + 64.99784063$$

$$= 76.60306576.$$

The difference between both sides is thus

$$76.60306576 - 76.60306574 \fallingdotseq 0.00000002.$$

The above whole calculation is performed actually by inputting the individual values of a, b, r, ΔT, α_e and δ_c to a computer program used to calculate the T_c for a chemical of the TD type, including every gas-permeable oxidatively-heating substance.

The value of T_c thus calculated for powdery AIBN above referred to, 58.013617 ℃, is finally rounded to 58.0 ℃ and is presented as such, together with the values of T_c calculated each for the eight powdery chemicals of the TD type, other than AIBN and MNTS, in the same manner as performed for powdery AIBN, in Table 15 in **Subsection 6.7.1**.

6.7 Results and discussion

6.7.1 The values of T_c calculated each for the nine powdery chemicals of the TD type, including AIBN, but excluding MNTS

The values of T_c were each calculated for the nine powdery chemicals of the TD type, including AIBN, but excluding MNTS, assuming that these chemicals are each confined in the fiber drum, 39.5 cm in inside diameter, 59.2 cm in inside length, and are each placed in the atmosphere under isothermal conditions.

The list of the ten powdery chemicals of the TD type tested herein is given in Table 14. These chemicals are of the industrial grade or of the reagent grade and were tested without further purification.

The adiabatic self-heating tests for the nine powdery chemicals of the TD type, other than AIBN, were also performed, in principle,* in the same manner as done for powdery AIBN, respectively.

The ten plots of $\ln \Delta t$ versus $1/T_s$ made each for the ten powdery chemicals of the TD type, including powdery AIBN, are presented in Fig. 71.

However, it should be noted here that the plot made based on the experimental data obtained with the closed cell in the adiabatic self-heating test is necessarily situated on the level of temperature higher than the plot made based on the data obtained with the open-cup cell in the test. Discussions relevant to this matter are made in **Subsection 4.6.3**.

* This adverb phrase means that some adiabatic self-heating tests for a few powdery chemicals of the TD type were performed herein with the open-cup cell, respectively.

Table 14
The ten powdery chemicals of the TD type tested herein.

Abbr.	CAS R. No.	Trivial Name and Purity
MNTS	80-11-5	98 % *N*-Methyl-*N*-nitroso-*p*-toluenesulfonamide (Diazald®).
NQC	3770-97-6	98 % 1,2-Naphthoquinone-2-diazido-5-sulfonyl chloride.
AIBN	78-67-1	98 % α, β-Azobis(isobutyronitrile).
BSHA	599-71-3	97 % Benzenesulfohydroxamic acid.
TCSH	6655-72-7	98 % 2,4,5-Trichlorobenzenesulfonyl hydrazide.
BPO	94-36-0	98 % Benzoyl peroxide.
OBSH	80-51-3	90 % 4,4'-Oxydibenzenesulfonyl hydrazide.
CHC	7778-54-3	Calcium hypochlorite (available chlorine *ca.* 70 %). (Another name; Chlorinated lime.)
1N2N	131-91-9	98 % 1-Nitroso-2-naphthol.
DPT	101-25-7	95 % *N*, *N'*-Dinitrosopentamethylenetetramine.

MNTS: A precursor to diazomethane, which is a useful reagent for the preparation of methyl esters of a wide range of biologically active compounds for GC analysis.
NQC: A chemical used as the raw material of a photosensitive substance, which is one of several components of a photoresist used in the manufacturing process of semiconductors or liquid crystal displays.
AIBN: A blowing agent or a radical polymerization initiator for vinyl monomers.
BSHA: A reagent included in a catalog handbook of fine chemicals.
TCSH: A reagent included in a catalog handbook of fine chemicals.
BPO: A radical polymerization initiator for vinyl monomers; besides, BPO is used as a curing agent for unsaturated polyester resins or a crosslinking agent for saturated polymers.
OBSH: A blowing agent for chloroprene rubber, polyethylene resin or polyvinyl chloride resin.
(Continued on the following page)

CHC: CHC is a powerful oxidizing agent but is used practically as a disinfectant or a bleaching agent and is the only inorganic chemical among powdery chemicals of the TD type tested herein.

1N2N: A reagent included in a catalog handbook of fine chemicals. This is said to be used as an analytical reagent for cobalt.

DPT: A blowing agent for rubber.

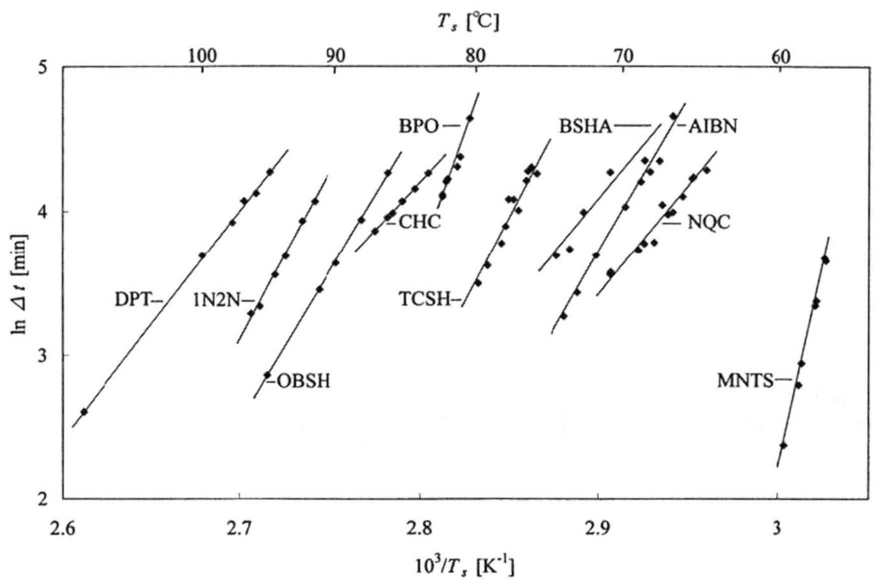

Figure 71. The ten plots of ln Δt versus $1/T_s$ made each for the ten powdery chemicals of the TD type.

The individual values of the two coefficients, a and b, of Eq. (44) holding for the individual self-heating processes, in the early stages, of 2 cm^3 each of the nine powdery chemicals of the TD type, other than powdery AIBN, confined each in the closed cell and subjected each to the adiabatic self-heating test were also calculated by applying the regression analysis to the individual combinations of the value of ln Δt with that of $1/T_s$ and are presented in Table 15.

It is possible to see roughly from Fig. 71 the relative liability of these powdery chemicals of the TD type to self-heating or ultimate thermal explosion. That is, we can tell that MNTS and NQC are relatively easy to explode thermally, but 1N2N and DPT are relatively hard to do so. In this regard, TCSH and BPO are medium in the liability to thermal explosion.

The values of T_c calculated each for the nine powdery chemicals of the TD type, including AIBN, but excluding MNTS, are summarized in Table 15 in the order of increasing value of T_c, together with some corresponding temperature values measured each in different ways by other researchers for some of the powdery chemicals of the TD type tested herein, for comparison [24].

As commented in a footnote in **(2)** of **Subsection 6.4.3**, only MNTS, in the ten powdery chemicals of the TD type tested herein, is powdery at room temperature but self-heats as a liquid at temperatures higher than its melting point. It is, therefore, required to calculate the T_c for MNTS by applying the Semenov equation. This calculation is performed in **Section 6.8** for the ten powdery chemicals of the TD type, including MNTS, assuming that 400 cm^3 each of these powdery chemicals of the TD type are each charged in the 500 cm^3 Dewar flask, which is used in the BAM test, and to which the Semenov model applies, and are each placed in the atmosphere under isothermal conditions.

In this connection, some corresponding temperature values measured each by other researchers for some of the powdery chemicals of the TD type tested herein are not necessarily fit to compare with some of the values of T_c calculated each herein, because principles, or methods, used each by other researchers to measure their temperature values are not necessarily the same as that adopted herein. The temperature values measured each by other researchers were, nevertheless, presented in Table 15 as precious reference data.

At all events, the values of T_c thus calculated each for the nine powdery chemicals of the TD type ranged from 51.3 ℃ for NQC to 80.8 ℃ for DPT.

These values of T_c calculated herein in general are in fair agreement with some corresponding temperature values measured each in different ways by other researchers for some of the powdery chemicals of the TD type tested herein, respectively.

However, it will be reasonable, in practice, to consider a temperature 20 K lower than the value of T_c calculated herein for a powdery chemical of the TD type confined in the fiber drum above referred to and placed in the atmosphere under isothermal conditions as the upper limit temperature for the safe handling of the chemical. For instance, 30 ℃ will be the upper limit temperature for the safe handling of NQC, 45 ℃ for TCSH, 55 ℃ for CHC, and so forth.

Table 15
Experimental parameters of the ten powdery chemicals of the TD type and comparison of the values of T_c calculated each for these chemicals, assuming that these chemicals are each confined in a fiber drum, 39.5 cm in inside diameter, 59.2 cm in inside length, and are each placed in the atmosphere under isothermal conditions, with, some corresponding temperature values measured each in different ways by other researchers for some of the powdery chemicals of the TD type tested herein. Unless otherwise noted in the superscripts, the heat generation data of these powdery chemicals were calculated based on the experimental data obtained with the closed cell, in principle, in the adiabatic self-heating test, respectively.

Powdery chemical of the TD type	Coefficients of Eq. (44)		Radius of the cylinder	Effective thermal diffusivity	The Frank-Kamenetskii number	The value of T_c calculated herein	The temp. values measured by other researchers
	a	b	r	α_e	δ_c		
			cm	cm^2/min		℃	℃
NQC	14453.46	-38.4811	19.75	0.06	2.6	51.3[a)]	-
MNTS	56611.14	-167.664	-	-	-	52.6[b)]	71.2[c)] [59]
BSHA	14653.50	-38.4433	19.75	0.06	2.6	56.2	-
AIBN	21524.92	-58.7329	19.75	0.07	2.6	58.0	53 [60], 64[d)] [61]
TCSH	25839.45	-69.6751	19.75	0.06	2.6	65.8	-
BPO	31564.00	-84.6620	19.75	0.05	2.6	71.6[e)]	69[f)] [62]
OBSH	20925.21	-53.9739	19.75	0.06	2.6	74.0[g)]	90 [60]
CHC	13725.85	-34.2354	19.75	0.13	2.6	75.9[h)]	76.3[i)] [63]
1N2N	23072.26	-59.1922	19.75	0.06	2.6	78.8	-
DPT	15744.86	-38.5099	19.75	0.06	2.6	80.8[g)]	79 [64]

Superscripts:
[a)] A value of T_c for NQC calculated by substituting the heat generation data, calculated based on the experimental data obtained with the open-cup cell in the adiabatic self-heating test, into Eq. (79) was 48.9 ℃.
[b)] The value of the BAM test for MNTS which is quoted from Table 16 in **Section 6.8**.

[c] A temperature at which a diethyl ether solution of MNTS was found to self-heat at a rate of 0.044 K/min in an ARC set.

[d] The so-called 10-h $t_{1/2}$ value for AIBN in toluene.

[e] A value of T_c for BPO calculated by substituting the heat generation data, calculated based on the experimental data obtained with the open-cup cell in the adiabatic self-heating test, into Eq. (79) was 67.9 ℃.

[f] A value of T_c for BPO calculated in accordance with the F-K equation, assuming that BPO is formed into an infinite cylinder, 26 cm in diameter, and is placed in the atmosphere under isothermal conditions.

[g] A value of T_c for OBSH, 74.0 ℃, and that for DPT, 80.8 ℃, were calculated by substituting the heat generation data, calculated based on the experimental data obtained with the open-cup cell in the adiabatic self-heating test, into Eq. (79), respectively. The heat generation data of these two chemicals were not calculated based on the experimental data obtained with the closed cell in the adiabatic self-heating test, because these are not volatile while tested.

[h] A value of T_c for CHC, 75.9 ℃, was calculated by substituting the heat generation data, calculated based on the experimental data obtained with the closed cell, covered with the tantalum small tube flange containing the thermocouple to measure the temperature of CHC, in the adiabatic self-heating test, into Eq. (79), because CHC decomposes to evolve corrosive and/or toxic gases such as HCl, Cl_2, *etc.* while tested. For relevant matters, refer to **Subsection 4.6.3**.

[i] A value of T_c for CHC determined by the extrapolation method in accordance with Eq. (86) in **Subsection 7.1.1**, assuming that CHC is confined in an infinite cylinder, 35.4 cm in diameter, and is placed in the atmosphere under isothermal conditions.

6.7.2 The plot of T_c versus r for a series of similar bodies of a powdery chemical of the TD type, having each a definite shape as well as an arbitrary value of r, confined each in a closed container of the corresponding shape and size, and placed each in the atmosphere under isothermal conditions

It is seen in Eq. (79) that, once the value of α_e, in addition to the heat generation data, a and b, is fixed for a powdery chemical of the TD type, having some one of the several specific shapes including the class A geometries as well as an arbitrary value of r, confined in a closed container of the corresponding shape and size, and placed in the atmosphere under isothermal conditions, only the value of r remains unfixed in the individual values of the variables, a, b, α_e, δ_c and r, apart from the constant, ΔT, in Eq. (79) which defines the T_c for the powdery chemical, because the shape of the chemical is specified, so that the value of δ_c is also fixed.*

That is, viewed at one angle on this subject, it follows that it is possible to make a plot of T_c versus r for a series of similar bodies of the powdery chemical of the TD type, having each a definite shape as well as an arbitrary value of r, confined each in a closed container of the corresponding shape and size, and placed each in the atmosphere under isothermal conditions.

Once the plot of T_c versus r is made beforehand for a series of similar bodies of a powdery chemical of the TD type, having each a definite shape as well as an arbitrary value of r, confined each in a closed container of the corresponding shape and size, and placed each in the atmosphere under isothermal conditions, it enables us to read approximately but readily the value of T_c for a similar body of the chemical, having the definite shape as well as an arbitrary value of r, confined in a closed container of the corresponding shape and size, and placed in the atmosphere under isothermal conditions, on the plot. Such a plot made for a series of similar cylinders of powdery AIBN, having each a definite shape as well as an arbitrary value of r, confined each in a fiber drum of the corresponding shape and size, and placed each in the atmosphere under isothermal conditions, is shown in Figs. 72 and 73 as an example.

* The same is true of a series of similar bodies of a gas-permeable oxidatively-heating substance, having each a definite shape as well as an arbitrary value of r, placed each in the atmosphere under isothermal conditions.

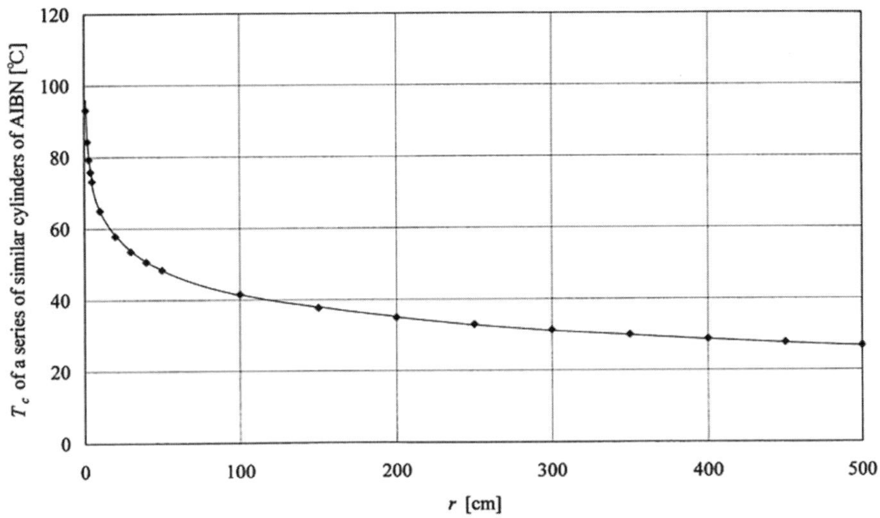

Figure 72. The plot of T_c versus r made for a series of similar cylinders of powdery AIBN, having each a definite shape as well as an arbitrary value of r, confined each in a fiber drum of the corresponding shape and size, and placed each in the atmosphere under isothermal conditions.

Now, it is shown in Figs. 72 and 73 that, as the value of r of the similar cylinder of powdery AIBN increases, the value of T_c decreases.

That is, viewed at the other angle on this subject, it follows that it is also possible to calculate, by applying Eq. (79), the critical (or the smallest) radius for the thermal explosion, r_c, below which the thermal explosion of a similar body of a powdery chemical of the TD type, including every gas-permeable oxidatively-heating substance, for which the individual values of the variables, a, b, α_e and δ_c, apart from the constant, ΔT, in Eq. (79) are fixed, placed in the atmosphere maintained at an arbitrary temperature, T_c, cannot occur absolutely.* For a concrete example, refer to **(2)** of **Subsection 8.4.4**.

* The same is true of the critical radius for the spontaneous ignition, r_c, of a similar body of a gas-permeable oxidatively-heating substance, having a definite shape, placed in the atmosphere maintained at an arbitrary temperature, T_c.

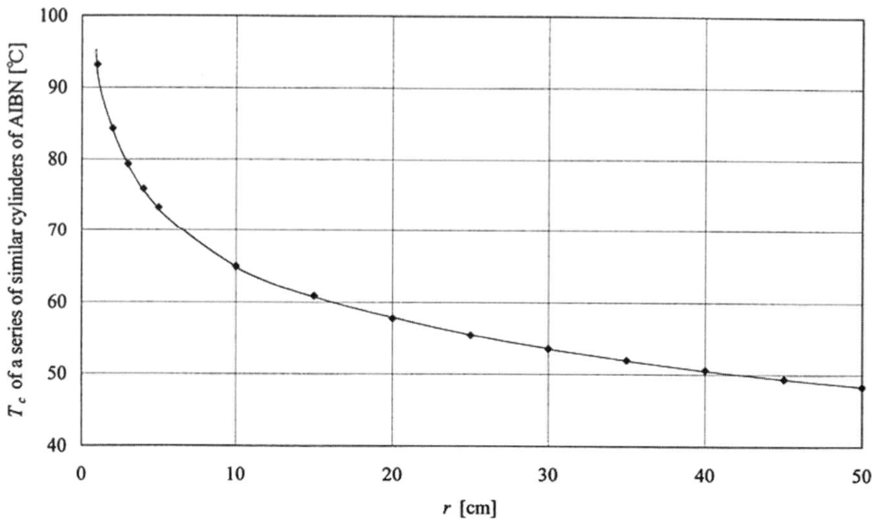

Figure 73. A partial magnification of Figure 47.

In this connection, it is seen in Fig. 72 that, when an extremely small, or large, value of r is substituted into Eq. (79), in which the individual values of the variables, a, b, α_e and δ_c are fixed, apart from the constant, ΔT, an extremely high, or low, value of T_c is calculated, respectively. At all events, however, it is certain that the best way for us is to avoid accumulating any self-heating chemical in bulk at all times.

6.8 Trial to calculate the value of the BAM test for an arbitrary powdery chemical of the TD type

As explained repeatedly above, the reduced form of the F-K equation, *i.e.*, Eq. (79), is exclusively used to calculate the T_c for a powdery chemical of the TD type, including every gas-permeable oxidatively-heating substance, having an arbitrary shape and an arbitrary size, placed in the atmosphere under isothermal conditions. On the other hand, the reduced form of the Semenov equation, *i.e.*, Eq. (72) derived in **Subsection 5.3.2**, is originally used to calculate the T_c for an arbitrary volume of a liquid charged in an arbitrary container and placed in the atmosphere under isothermal conditions.

If, however, the Semenov model holds for a powdery chemical of the TD type charged in one particular container, Eq. (72) is applicable to the calculation of the T_c for the powdery chemical as well.

According to the experimental measurements performed in a series of studies described herein, the values of c, ρ and α_e of average organic powdery chemicals of the TD type are of the order of 0.45~0.5 cal/(g·K), 0.7~0.9 g/cm^3 and 0.06 cm^2/min, respectively.* It thus follows that the individual values of λ of average organic powdery chemicals of the TD type are of the order of 3.8×10^{-4} cal/(cm·s·K).** On the other hand, the value of U of 400 cm^3 of a liquid charged in the 500 cm^3 Dewar flask used in the BAM heat-accumulation storage test is calculated at 3.5×10^{-5} cal/(cm^2·s·K) in **Section 5.8**. It follows, therefore, that the value of U of 400 cm^3 of a liquid charged in the 500 cm^3 Dewar flask is only about 9 % of the individual values of λ of average organic powdery chemicals of the TD type.

The result of the above calculation suggests that the condition, $U << \lambda$, may hold for 400 cm^3 each of average organic powdery chemicals of the TD type charged each in the 500 cm^3 Dewar flask used in the BAM test and placed each in the atmosphere under isothermal conditions as well; and therefore, the spatially uniform distribution of internal temperature may be effected in each of them in the early stages of the self-heating process, with the result that each of them may take the same values of q_2 and $(T_{liq} - T_{set\text{-}up})$ as 400 cm^3 of a liquid charged in the Dewar flask and placed in the atmosphere under isothermal conditions (For matters relevant to this subject, refer to **Subsection 5.5.1**).

If the above suggestion is reasonable, it follows that it is possible to calculate the individual values of the BAM test for organic powdery chemicals of the TD type after the example of the calculation performed in **Section 5.6**; and therefore, it is also possible to compare the values of T_c calculated each for organic chemicals of the TD type, irrespective of liquid or powder, with one another, assuming that these chemicals are each placed under the same conditions of shape and size, *i.e.*, under the definite conditions of the BAM test.

The values of the BAM test for the ten powdery chemicals of the TD type tested herein, in which CHC is the only inorganic powdery chemical of the TD

---

* For these data, refer to Table 8 in **Subsection 5.7.1**, Table 15 in **Subsection 6.7.1** and Table 16 in the present section.

** This calculation is performed in accordance with Eq. (77) presented in **Section 6.2**. Inversely speaking, the value of α_e of a powdery substance can also be calculated in accordance with Eq. (77), provided the individual values of c, ρ and λ of the substance are known. For instance, according to J. Isler, the values of λ, c and ρ of nitrocellulose powder are 0.16 W/(m·K), 1254 J/(K·kg) and 1300 kg/m^3, respectively [75]. The value of α_e of nitrocellulose powder is thus calculated at about 0.06 cm^2/min.

type,* were thus each calculated by applying Eq. (72), assuming that 400 cm^3 each of these chemicals are each charged in the 500 cm^3 Dewar flask used in the BAM test and are each placed in the atmosphere under isothermal conditions.

As an example, the concrete procedure to calculate the value of the BAM test for powdery BSHA is illustrated in the present section.

The heat generation data, a and b, of BSHA were calculated in **Subsection 6.7.1** and are given in Tables 15 and 16.

On the other hand, the values of q_2 and (T_{liq} - $T_{set\text{-}up}$) of 400 cm^3 of a liquid charged in the 500 cm^3 Dewar flask and placed in the atmosphere under isothermal conditions were measured in **Subsection 5.5.3** and are given in Tables 8 and 16.

The values of c^{**} and ρ of powdery BSHA are also given in Table 16, respectively.

Further, the value of V of 400 cm^3 of powdery BSHA is of course 400 cm^3.

And, the values of e and ΔT are 2.718281828 and 1.25 K, respectively.

The value of the right-hand side of Eq. (72), *i.e.*,

$$2\ln T_c + \frac{a}{T_c} = \ln\left[\frac{ac\rho V\mathrm{e}\cdot\Delta T\left(T_{liq} - T_{set-up}\right)}{q_2}\right] - b, \qquad (72)$$

for 400 cm^3 of powdery BSHA above referred to is thus calculated in the following manner.

---

* The value of λ of CHC is calculated at about 5.9×10^{-4} cal/(cm·s·K) in accordance with Eq. (77), using the data presented Tables 15 and 16. It follows, therefore, that the value of U of 400 cm^3 of a liquid charged in the 500 cm^3 Dewar flask amounts to about 6 % of the value of λ of CHC. It seems that, when charged each in the Dewar flask, the Semenov model holds better for inorganic powdery chemicals of the TD type than for organic ones. This tendency is thought to be effected by reason that the individual values of λ of inorganic powdery chemicals of the TD type in general are larger than those of organic ones.

** As stated above, the individual values of c of average organic powdery chemicals of the TD type are of the order of 0.45~0.5 cal/(g·K). As explained in **Subsection 5.5.4**, however, a decrease of 0.05 cal/(g·K) in the value of c, the magnitude of which is the maximum error conceivable in the measurement of the specific heat capacity and corresponds to about 10 % of the value of c of an average organic chemical, causes an increase of about 0.5 K in the value of the BAM test calculated by applying Eq. (72), keeping the values of the other variables in the equation constant. A fluctuation, of such an extent, of the value of the BAM test is, however, thought to be within the error range of the result of the BAM test performed actually for a liquid. The calculation in the present section was thus performed on the assumption that every organic powdery chemical of the TD type tested herein takes a definite value of c of 0.475 cal/(g·K).

$$\ln\left[\frac{ac\rho Ve \cdot \Delta T\left(T_{liq} - T_{set-up}\right)}{q_2}\right] - b$$

$$= \ln\{[14653.5 \times 0.475 \times 0.94 \times 400 \times 2.718281828 \times 1.25 \times 0.8853]$$

$$\div 0.560075\} + 38.4433$$

$$= 16.45858258 + 38.4433$$

$$= 54.90188258.$$

On the other hand, if the value of the BAM test for powdery BSHA is assumed to be 338.80097 K or 65.65097 ℃, the value of the left-hand side of Eq. (72) is calculated in the following manner.

$$2\ln T_c + \frac{a}{T_c} = 2\ln 338.80097 + 14653.5 \div 338.80097$$

$$= 11.65082565 + 43.25105681$$

$$= 54.90188246.$$

The difference between both sides is thus

$$54.90188258 - 54.90188246 \fallingdotseq 0.0000001.$$

The above whole calculation is performed actually by inputting the individual values of a, b, c, e, ΔT, V, ρ, q_2 and (T_{liq} - $T_{set\text{-}up}$) to a computer program used to calculate the T_c for a chemical of the TD type, including every gas-permeable oxidatively-heating substance.

The value of the BAM test thus calculated for powdery BSHA, 65.65097 ℃, is finally rounded to 65.7 ℃ and is presented as such, together with the values of the BAM test calculated each for the nine powdery chemicals of the TD type, including MNTS, but excluding BSHA, in the same manner as performed for powdery BSHA, in Table 16.

Table 16
Experimental parameters of the ten powdery chemicals of the TD type and comparison of the values of the BAM test calculated each for these chemicals, assuming that 400 cm^3 each of these chemicals are each charged in the 500 cm^3 Dewar flask used in the BAM test and are each placed in the atmosphere under isothermal conditions, with, the values of T_c calculated each for these chemicals in **Subsection 6.7.1**, assuming that these chemicals are each confined in a fiber drum, 39.5 cm in inside diameter, 59.2 cm in inside length, and are each placed in the atmosphere under isothermal conditions. The heat generation data used to calculate the values of the BAM test are quoted from Table 15 in **Subsection 6.7.1**, respectively.

Powdery chemical of the TD type	Coefficients of Eq. (44)		Specific heat capacity c[a)]	Specific gravity	q_2[b)]	$(T_{liq} - T_{set\text{-}up})$[b)]	The value of the BAM test calculated herein	The value of T_c calcd. in **Subsection 6.7.1**
	a	b		ρ				
			cal/(g·K)	g/cm^3	cal/min	K	℃	℃[c)]
MNTS	56611.14	-167.664	0.475	0.83	0.560075	0.8853	52.6	-
NQC	14453.46	-38.4811	0.475	0.89	0.560075	0.8853	61.1[d)]	51.3
AIBN	21524.92	-58.7329	0.475	0.67	0.560075	0.8853	65.4	58.0
BSHA	14653.50	-38.4433	0.475	0.94	0.560075	0.8853	65.7	56.2
BPO	31564.00	-84.6620	0.475	0.78	0.560075	0.8853	77.6[e)]	71.6
TCSH	25839.45	-69.6751	0.475	0.39	0.560075	0.8853	75.5	65.8
CHC	13725.85	-34.2354	0.16[f)]	1.70	0.560075	0.8853	84.5	75.9
OBSH	20925.21	-53.9739	0.475	0.72	0.560075	0.8853	82.9[g)]	74.0
1N2N	23072.26	-59.1922	0.475	0.83	0.560075	0.8853	86.2	78.8
DPT	15744.86	-38.5099	0.475	0.72	0.560075	0.8853	93.3[g)]	80.8

Superscripts:
[a)] The reason why the value of c of every organic powdery chemical of the TD type was assumed to be 0.475 cal/(g·K) is given in a footnote in **Section 6.8**.
[b)] These are needless to say the main heat transfer data of 400 cm^3 of a liquid chemical, or a powdery chemical, charged in the

Dewar flask, used in the BAM test, and placed in the atmosphere under isothermal conditions.

[c] These values of T_c are quoted from Table 15 in **Subsection 6.7.1**, respectively.

[d] The value of the BAM test for NQC calculated by substituting the heat generation data, calculated based on the experimental data obtained with the open-cup cell in the adiabatic self-heating test, into Eq. (72) was 59.2 ℃.

[e] The value of the BAM test for BPO calculated by substituting the heat generation data, calculated based on the experimental data obtained with the open-cup cell in the adiabatic self-heating test, into Eq. (72) was 74.6 ℃.

[f] The value of c of CHC was assumed to be 0.16, on referring to the value of c of $CaCl_2$, 0.16.

[g] The values of the BAM test for OBSH and DPT were calculated by substituting the heat generation data, calculated based on the experimental data obtained with the open-cup cell in the adiabatic self-heating test, into Eq. (72), respectively.

It is seen in Table 16 that the individual values of the BAM test for the ten powdery chemicals of the TD type are about 10 K higher than the corresponding values of T_c calculated in **Subsection 6.7.1**. It thus follows that, following the example of the consideration performed in **Subsection 5.7.1** regarding the upper limit temperature for the safe handling of each organic liquid peroxide, it is reasonable to consider a temperature 30 K lower than the value of the BAM test calculated herein for a powdery chemical of the TD type as the upper limit temperature for the safe handling of the chemical. For instance, 30 ℃ will be the upper limit temperature for the safe handling of NQC, 45 ℃ for TCSH, 55 ℃ for CHC, and so forth. The individual upper limit temperatures for the safe handling of the nine powdery chemicals of the TD type, other than MNTS, considered in the present section are then in perfect accord with the corresponding upper limit temperatures considered in **Subsection 6.7.1**.

At all events, an important and useful proposition obtained in the present section is that there is a prospect that it is possible to calculate the value of the BAM test for an arbitrary powdery chemical of the TD type as well as an arbitrary liquid; in other words, there is a prospect that it is possible to compare the individual values of T_c for various chemicals of the TD type, irrespective of liquid or powder, with one another under definite conditions of the BAM test, without performing actually the test.

References to Chapter 6

[24] T. Kotoyori, Critical Ignition Temperatures of Chemical Substances, J. Loss Prevention in the Process Industries, **2**, 16-21 (1989).
[43] D. A. Frank-Kamenetskii, Diffusion and Heat Transfer in Chemical Kinetics, 2nd Ed., translated from Russian by J. P. Appleton, Plenum Press, New York-London, 25 (1969).
[44] H. S. Carslaw and J. C. Jaeger, Conduction of Heat in Solids, 2nd Ed., Oxford University Press, Oxford, 201 (1959).
[45] M. Kosaka, T. Asahina and S. Ikuta, Measurement of Thermal Diffusivity by Applying the Constant-Heating-Rate Method (I), Application to Pyrophyllite and Stainless Steel (in Japanese), Research Reports of National Industrial Research Institute of Nagoya, **26**, 11-14 (1977).
[46] M. Kosaka, T. Asahina and S. Ikuta, Measurement of Thermal Diffusivity by Applying the Constant-Heating-Rate Method (II), Application to Carbon Steel and Titanium (in Japanese), Research Reports of National Industrial Research Institute of Nagoya, **27**, 107-110 (1978).
[47] M. Kosaka, T. Asahina and S. Ikuta, Measurement of Thermal Diffusivity by Applying the Constant-Heating-Rate Method (III), Application to Powdery Materials (in Japanese), Research Reports of National Industrial Research Institute of Nagoya, **28**, 73-78 (1979).
[48] Edited by R.P. Tye, Thermal Conductivity, II, Academic Press, London, 186 (1969).
[49] Edited by P. H. Egli, Thermoelectricity, John Wiley, New York, 320 (1960).
[50] J. A. Cape, G. W. Lehman and M. M. Nakata, Transient Thermal Diffusivity Technique for Refractory Solids, J. Appl. Phys., **34**, 3550-3555 (1963).
[51] K. Tajiri, H. Matsubara, T. Asahina and M. Kosaka, Thermal Conduction of Hydrogen Absorbing Alloy Powders (in Japanese), Sunshine Journal, **7**, No. 3, 16-20 (1986).
[52] K. Tajiri, H. Matsubara, T. Asahina and M. Kosaka, Thermal Conduction of Powders (I) - Some Metal Oxide Powders - (in Japanese), Energy & Resources, **7**, No. 5, 79-83 (1886).
[53] T. Tajiri, H. Matsubara, T. Asahina and M. Kosaka, Thermal Conduction of Powders (II) - Some Inorganic Salts Powders for Chemical Heat Pump - (in Japanese), Energy & Resources, **7**, No. 6, 89-93 (1986).
[54] Edited by Y. S. Touloukian, R. W. Powell, C. Y. Ho and M. C. Nicolaou, Thermophysical Properties of Matter, **10**, Thermal Diffusivity, IFI/Plenum, New York-Washington, 644 (1973).
[55] Edited by Y. S. Touloukian *et al.*, *ibid.*, 22.
[56] Edited by Y. S. Touloukian *et al.*, *ibid.*, 550.
[57] Edited by Y. S. Touloukian *et al.*, *ibid.*, 398.

[58] T. Boddington, P. Gray and D. I. Harvey, Thermal Theory of Spontaneous Ignition: Criticality in Bodies of Arbitrary Shape, Phil. Trans. Roy. London, **270**, 471 (1971).
[59] D.I. Townsend and J.C. Tou, Thermal Hazard Evaluation by an Accelerating Rate Calorimeter, Thermochimica Acta, **37**, 14 (1980).
[60] T. Yoshida, Safety of Reactive Chemicals, Elsevier, Amsterdam, 200 (1987).
[61] The Kirk-Othmer Encyclopedia of Chemical Technology, 4th Ed., **14**, 451 (1995).
[62] J. Nabeshima, M. Koshimizu, A. Miyake, T. Ogawa and I. Fukuyama, An Adiabatic Storage Test of Benzoyl Peroxide (in Japanese), Proceedings of the Annual Convention, the Industrial Explosives Society, Japan, Tokyo, 80 (1986).
[63] Y. Uehara, H. Uematsu and Y. Saito, Thermal Ignition of Calcium Hypochlorite, Combustion and Flame, **32**, 85-94 (1978).
[64] K. Okuse, A Technical Report (in Japanese), Unofficially Issued from Eiwa Chemical Industries Co. Ltd., Kyoto, Japan, 1980.
[75] J. Isler, Auto-Inflammation de la Nitrocellulose, Propellants, Explosives, Pyrotechnics, **9**, 130-134 (1984).

Chapter 7 Procedure to perform the adiabatic oxidatively-heating test in order to calculate ultimately the heat generation data of a gas-permeable oxidatively-heating substance

7.1 Equation to calculate the T_c for a heap of a gas-permeable oxidatively-heating substance, having some one of several specific shapes including the class A geometries as well as an arbitrary size, placed in the atmosphere under isothermal conditions

As stated in **Preface**, the oxidatively-heating behavior of a gas-permeable oxidatively-heating substance, such as sawdust, coal dust or oil-soaked lagging, is also of the TD type. Therefore, it is possible, in principle, to calculate the critical temperature for the spontaneous ignition or T_c for a heap of a gas-permeable oxidatively-heating substance such as sawdust of every wood species, having an arbitrary shape and an arbitrary size, placed in the atmosphere under isothermal conditions, by applying the reduced form of the F-K equation, *i.e.*, Eq. (79) derived in **Section 6.2**, provided the value of δ_c for the shape of the substance is known.

$$2\ln T_c + \frac{a}{T_c} = \ln\left[\frac{ar^2 \cdot \Delta T}{\alpha_e \cdot \delta_c}\right] - b. \qquad (79)$$

However, in the same manner as a powdery chemical of the TD type, if the heap of a gas-permeable oxidatively-heating substance, which is placed in the atmosphere under isothermal conditions, has some one of the several specific shapes including the class A geometries as well as an arbitrary size, *i.e.*, an arbitrary value of r, the calculation of the T_c for the heap becomes very simple, because the values of δ_c for these specific shapes have already been calculated by T. Boddington *et al.*, respectively [58], with the result that, as explained in **Section 6.2**, the heat transfer data required to calculate the T_c for such a heap as specified above is only the value of the effective thermal diffusivity, α_e, of the substance. For the values of δ_c calculated by T. Boddington *et al.*, refer to Table 13 in **Section 6.5**.

That is, for the purpose of calculating the T_c for a heap of a gas-permeable oxidatively-heating substance, having some one of the several specific shapes above referred to as well as an arbitrary value of r, placed in the atmosphere under isothermal conditions, we have only to perform, on the one hand, several adiabatic oxidatively-heating tests, which are started from each T_s with mutual intervals of 1～2 K, in order to calculate the heat generation data of the substance, for 2 cm^3 each of several samples of the substance charged each in the draft cell, into which air is supplied,* for the time, Δt, required for the temperature of each sample of the substance to increase by the definite value of ΔT of 1.25 K from the corresponding standard temperature, respectively, and, we have only to measure, on the other hand, in order to calculate the value of α_e of the substance, a heating rate, ϕ, and a limiting radial temperature difference, $(\Delta T_{rad})_{\lim}$, which is effected in the non-steady state in temperature differences of 1.25 K between the periphery and the axial center of a moderate-sized specimen of the substance, when the outside surface of a cylindrical cell containing the specimen is heated at the rate, ϕ.

As commented at the beginning of **Section 7.4**, however, there exist as a matter of fact four kinds of gas-permeable oxidatively-heating substances. It thus follows that there are four kinds of adiabatic oxidatively-heating tests in all, or rather four kinds of testing procedures, in all, corresponding each to the four kinds of gas-permeable oxidatively-heating substances. The four kinds of testing procedures are explained in detail in **Section 7.4**, respectively.

7.1.1 Equation and procedure used hitherto to determine the T_c for a heap of a gas-permeable oxidatively-heating substance, having a definite shape and an arbitrary value of r, placed in the atmosphere under isothermal conditions

The equation and the procedure used hitherto to determine the T_c for a heap of a gas-permeable oxidatively-heating substance, having a definite shape and an arbitrary value of r, placed in the atmosphere under isothermal conditions, are shortly introduced in the present subsection for convenience' sake [65].

(1) The values of T_c for several similar bodies of a gas-permeable oxidatively-heating substance, having each a definite shape and a relatively small value of r, placed each in the atmosphere under isothermal conditions, are determined actually by performing a series of isothermal storage tests, respectively.

(2) In the meantime, a suitable value of δ_c is assigned to the definite shape of a series of similar bodies.

(3) A plot of ln $[(\delta_c \cdot T_c^2)/r^2]$ versus $1/T_c$ is made on a graph in accordance with a re-arranged F-K equation shown below.

$$\ln\left[\frac{\delta_c \cdot T_c^2}{r^2}\right] = -\frac{E}{RT_c} + \ln\left[\frac{\Delta H \cdot A_0 E}{\lambda R}\right], \qquad (86)$$

---

* It is also of course possible to supply an arbitrary inert gas as well as an arbitrary oxidizing gas, other than air, into the draft cell.

where the second term of the right-hand side is treated merely as one of the two coefficients, *a* and *b*, of an empirical formula, ln $[(\delta_c \cdot T_c^2)/r^2] = - a/T_c + b$.

(4) The T_c, which corresponds to an arbitrary large value of *r*, for a heap is then determined on the graph by extrapolation in accordance with the empirical formula, ln $[(\delta_c \cdot T_c^2)/r^2] = - a/T_c + b$, established in **(3)**.

It is manifest that the above procedure is not a calculation method to the effect that the T_c for a heap of a gas-permeable oxidatively-heating substance, having a definite shape and an arbitrary value of *r*, placed in the atmosphere under isothermal conditions, is calculated by substituting various physical and chemical quantities concerned into an equation, but an extrapolation method to the effect that the T_c for the heap is determined by extrapolation on the graph in accordance with an empirical formula, ln $[(\delta_c \cdot T_c^2)/r^2] = - a/T_c + b$, which is determined by performing actually a series of isothermal storage tests for several small-scale similar bodies of the substance, respectively.

7.2 The cell assembly including some one of the three kinds of open cells, *i.e.*, the open-cup, the draft and the touch-flow cell

As stated in **Subsection 4.2.2**, the adiabatic jacket, which is set in the air bath of the adiabatic self-heating process recorder, is used to perform the adiabatic self-heating test, or the adiabatic oxidatively-heating test, for a chemical of the TD type, including every gas-permeable oxidatively-heating substance; in the meantime, the chemical is charged or confined in some one of the four kinds of cells, *i.e.*, the open-cup, the draft, the touch-flow and the closed cell, in accordance with the self-heating property of the chemical. The structure of the adiabatic jacket is shown in Fig. 74, in particular, in connection with the performance of the adiabatic oxidatively-heating test.

The draft cell and the touch-flow cell, in the four kinds of cells, are used exclusively in the adiabatic oxidatively-heating test. In this regard, the open-cup cell, one of the three kinds of open cells, is used only in the adiabatic self-heating test performed for a non-volatile liquid chemical, or powdery chemical, of the TD type at atmospheric pressure.

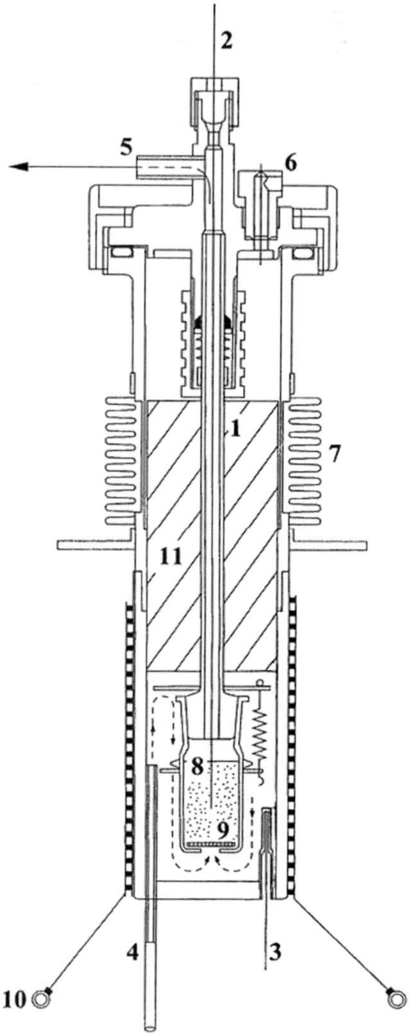

Figure 74. The structure of the adiabatic jacket into which the cell assembly including the draft cell is inserted in order to perform the adiabatic oxidatively-heating test.
1. Glass vent tube; **2**. Thermocouple to measure the T_{ref} or the temperature of an oxidatively-heating substance; **3**. Thermocouple to measure the T_{atm}; **4**. Gas inlet; **5**. Gas outlet; **6**. Safety valve; **7**. Bellows; **8**. Draft cell in which a reference material or a gas-permeable oxidatively-heating substance is charged; **9**. Thin gas-permeable silica fiber sheet; **10**. Heating wire; **11**. Glass wool.

Whenever some one of the three kinds of open cells is used, a glass vent tube having a ground glass joint at the lower end is used in place of the glass flange tube (Fig. 74). As to the cell assembly including some one of the three kinds of open cells, the stem serves us **(1)** as the suspender for the open cell, **(2)** as the vent tube through which the space in the cell leads to the atmosphere outside the air bath and **(3)** as the conduit pipe for the thermocouple to measure the T_{ref}, or the temperature of a chemical of the TD type in the adiabatic self-heating test, or that of a gas-permeable oxidatively-heating substance in the adiabatic oxidatively-heating test. The glass vent tube is taken together with an open-cup cell in a series of photographs exhibited in **Section 7.3**.

7.2.1 Gas supplying system for an oxidatively-heating substance charged in either of the two kinds of open cells, *i.e.*, the draft cell and the touch-flow cell

Whenever the adiabatic oxidatively-heating test is performed for an oxidatively-heating substance, which is charged in either of the two kinds of open cells, *i.e.*, the draft cell and the touch-flow cell, it is indispensable to supply it with some oxidizing or inert gas at atmospheric pressure. Such a gas is supplied into the adiabatic jacket, after having been preheated up to the air bath temperature, *i.e.*, the T_s of the run, in a thin copper pipe, 50 cm in length, which is set in the air bath. The gas then flows into the jacket and is heated up to the T_{atm}, which is kept always at the very slowly increasing temperature of the oxidatively-heating substance by the adiabatic control, by passing through a nickel pipe, 1 mm in outside diameter, which is welded on the inside wall of the jacket. The gas flows finally into the draft cell from a hole at the center of the base, or into the touch-flow cell from a hole in the side wall.

The heater is able to heat the atmosphere in the jacket at the maximum heating rate of 20 K/min in order that, even if some oxidizing gas is supplied into the jacket at the maximum flow rate of 20 cm^3/min, the condition, $\Delta T_{diff} = T - T_{atm} = 0$,* may hold while the adiabatic control is performed for the oxidatively-heating process, in the early stages, of the substance. The other points are the same as those described in **Subsection 4.2.2**.

7.2.2 Temperature measuring system for the three kinds of open cells

One thermocouple, which, as seen in a series of photographs exhibited in **Section 7.3**, is covered with a glass capillary tube, is inserted axially to the longitudinal center of 2 cm^3 of a reference material, or of 2 cm^3 of a chemical of the TD type, or of 2 cm^3 of an oxidatively-heating substance, charged in some

---

* For this condition, refer to **Subsections 4.5.4** and **4.5.7**.

one of the three kinds of open cells to measure the T_{ref}, or the temperature of the chemical of the TD type, or that of the oxidatively-heating substance. The other points are the same as those described in **Subsection 4.2.4**.

7.3 Procedure to prepare the cell assembly including some one of the three kinds of open cells

The primary purpose of the present section is to explain the procedure to prepare the cell assembly including either of the two kinds of open cells, *i.e.*, the draft cell and the touch-flow cell, used in the adiabatic oxidatively-heating test.*

The three kinds of open cells, *i.e.*, the open-cup, the draft and the touch-flow cell, are, however, the same to the effect that each has the ground-glass joint at the upper end. A difference in the three is only that the thin gas-permeable silica fiber sheet, which is used to support a reference material, or a gas-permeable oxidatively-heating substance, tested on the bottom of the draft cell, is not used in both the open-cup cell and the touch-flow cell.**, ***

The procedure to prepare the cell assembly including some one of the three kinds of open cells is, therefore, exhibited below by means of a series of photographs taken for the procedure to prepare the reference cell assembly including the open-cup cell, for convenience' sake. In this connection, every one of the three kinds of open cells used to prepare the sample cell assembly is, of course, of the same type and size as the one used to prepare the reference cell assembly.

Incidentally, as commented at the beginning of **Subsection 4.5.2**, and as explained in **Subsections 7.4.1**, **7.4.2** and **7.4.3**, it is not required, in principle, to determine the T_s of each run by inserting the reference cell assembly into the adiabatic jacket in the adiabatic self-heating process recorder, prior to the insertion of the sample cell assembly into the jacket, in the adiabatic oxidatively-heating test performed by means of the cell assembly including either of the two kinds of open cells, *i.e.*, the draft cell or the touch-flow cell, although it is indispensable to do so in the adiabatic oxidatively-heating test

---

* The touch-flow cell is, however, not fit to measure the heat generation data required to calculate the T_c for a gastight oxidatively-heating substance. For further details, refer to **Subsection 4.2.2**.

** Whenever the draft cell, which has a hole at the base, is used, it is required to place a thin gas-permeable silica fiber sheet on the bottom of the cell in order to support a reference material or a gas-permeable oxidatively-heating substance, before either of them is charged in the cell (refer to **Subsection 7.4.1**, *etc.*).

*** Whenever some one of open cells is used, a glass jig is used to provide a thin vertical hole at the center of the reference material, or of the oxidatively-heating substance, charged in the cell in order to facilitate the insertion of the thermocouple, which dangles from the glass vent tube (see Fig. 79), into the substance.

performed for a gas-permeable oxidatively-heating substance such as one dealt with in **Subsection 7.4.4**.

Figure 75. This photograph shows a general view of the reference cell assembly including the glass vent tube combined with the empty open-cup cell. The assembly is held in the vertical position by means of a clamp of a stand. It is possible to slide the stand horizontally on the laboratory desk. On the other hand, a laboratory jack, at the center of the upper plate of which a pedestal is stuck, is fixed on the desk. The position of the stand is then adjusted horizontally in order that the assembly may be aligned vertically with the pedestal. A pack of cigarettes is put on the laboratory jack, and by the side of the assembly, to show the relative size of the open-cup cell. The dimensions of the open-cup cell are almost the same as those of the closed cell, *i.e.*, 1.4 cm in outside diameter, about 3 cm in length, except the ground-glass joint at the upper end.

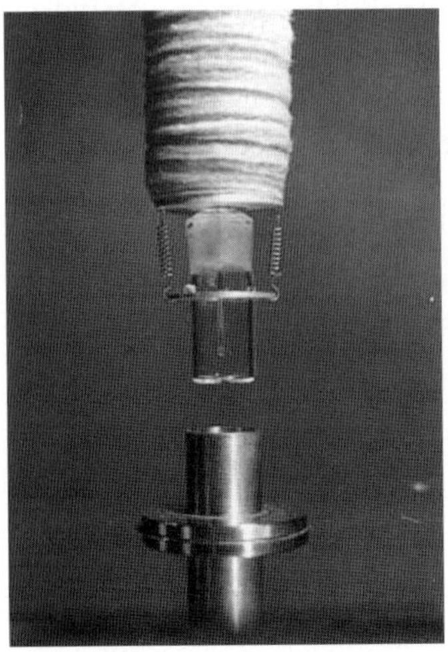

Figure 76. This is an enlarged view of the reference cell assembly including the empty open-cup cell and the pedestal. The cell is seen to be supported with a thin aluminium washer and two springs and is combined with the ground glass joint at the lower end of the glass vent tube.

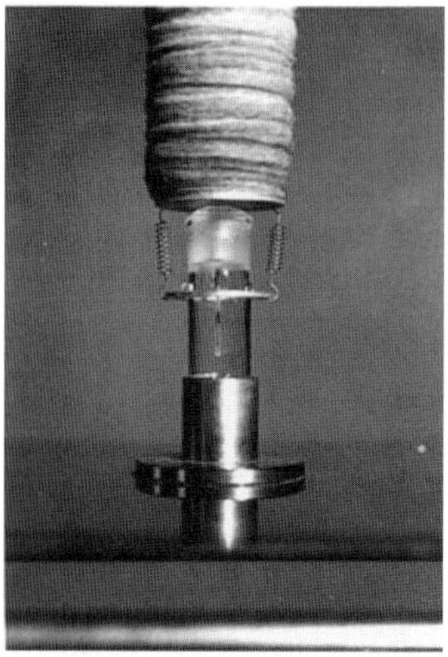

Figure 77. The empty reference cell assembly is set on the pedestal by raising the laboratory jack.

Figure 78. The empty reference cell assembly, which is set on the pedestal, is dismantled by detaching the thin aluminium washer and the two springs. The thermocouple covered with a glass capillary tube is seen to be inserted axially to the longitudinal center of the open-cup cell.

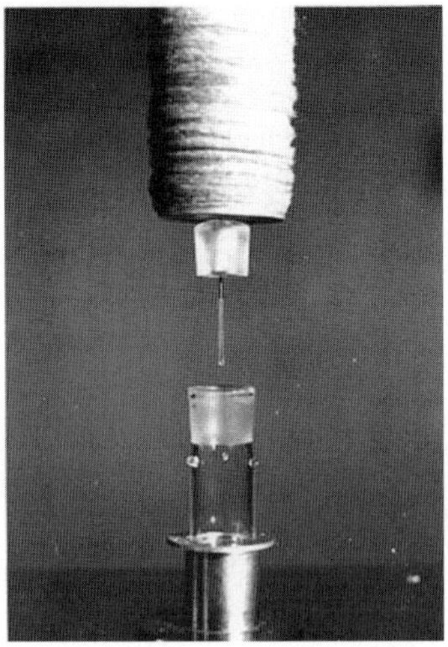

Figure 79. The empty open-cup cell is separated from the ground glass joint of the glass vent tube by lowering the laboratory jack.

Figure 80. About 2 cm^3 of silica of comparatively coarse particles is charged in an open-cup cell, *i.e.*, the cell with which the reference cell is prepared. Silica of comparatively coarse particles is used as the reference material in the adiabatic oxidatively-heating test. In this photograph, however, the cell is filled with milk in place of silica of coarse particles for the convenience of photography.

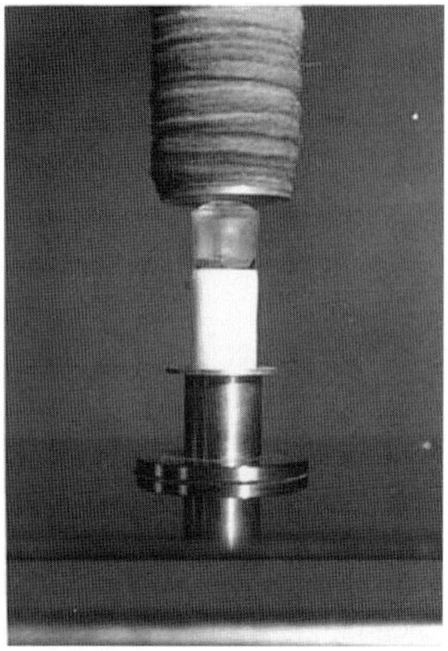

Figure 81. The reference cell thus prepared is then combined concentrically and softly with the ground glass joint of the glass vent tube by raising again the laboratory jack to construct the reference cell assembly; in the meantime, the CA thermocouple, covered with a glass capillary tube, to measure the T_{ref}, the temperature of an oxidatively-heating substance, or that of a non-volatile chemical of the TD type, is inserted automatically and axially to the longitudinal center of silica of coarse particles charged in the cell.

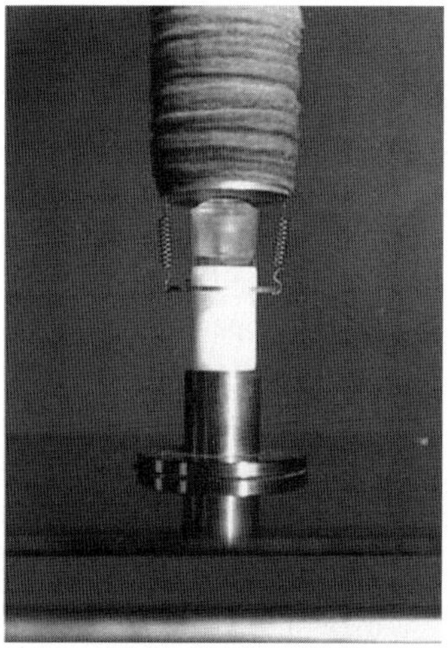

Figure 82. The reference cell combined with the ground glass joint of the glass vent tube is finally supported firmly with the thin aluminium washer and the two springs.

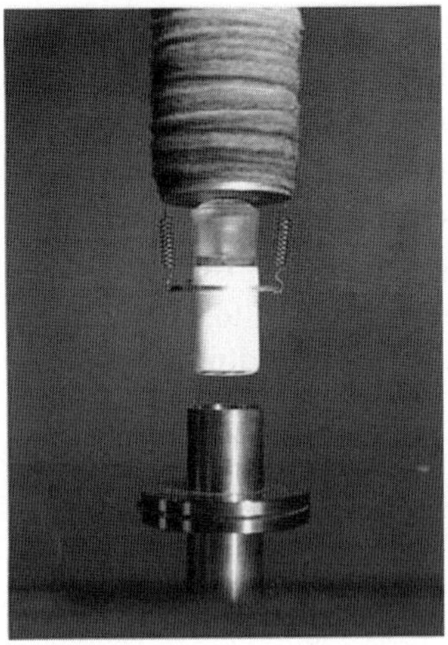

Figure 83. After having lowered again the laboratory jack a little, a fairly small vibrator is applied to the base of the open-cup cell in order that silica of coarse particles charged in the cell may come closely in contact with the glass capillary tube. The reference cell assembly is now ready for the adiabatic oxidatively-heating test.

Further explanations regarding the procedure to prepare the reference cell assembly including the glass vent tube combined with some one of the three kinds of open cells are the same as those given to Figs. 35, 36 and 37 exhibited in **Subsection 4.5.3**.

7.4 Four kinds, in all, of testing procedures corresponding each to the four kinds of gas-permeable oxidatively-heating substances

As commented in Section 7.1, there exist four kinds of gas-permeable oxidatively-heating substances; *i.e.*, **(1)** moisture-containing gas-permeable oxidatively-heating substances, **(2)** almost dry gas-permeable oxidatively-heating substances, **(3)** almost dry oxidatively-heating liquids and **(4)** gas-permeable oxidatively-heating substances, which are each almost dry but include some self-heating component such as hydroperoxide.

The four kinds of adiabatic oxidatively-heating tests, *i.e.*, the four kinds of testing procedures, corresponding each to the four kinds of gas-permeable oxidatively-heating substances above referred to, are thus explained in detail in numerical order cited above in the present section.

7.4.1 Procedure to perform several adiabatic oxidatively-heating tests, which are started from each T_s with mutual intervals of 1~2 K, in order to calculate the heat generation data of a moisture-containing gas-permeable oxidatively-heating substance, such as natural product, *e.g.*, sawdust or triiron tetraoxide, for 2 cm³ each of several samples of the substance charged each in the draft cell, into which air is supplied, for the time, Δt, required for the temperature of each sample of the substance to increase by the definite value of ΔT of 1.25 K from the corresponding standard temperature, respectively

In this connection, the whole procedure to perform the adiabatic oxidatively-heating test for a moisture-containing gas-permeable oxidatively-heating substance is explained in detail in **Subsection 8.4.1** by taking the procedure performed for 0.3 g of the sawdust of Port Orford cedar charged in the draft cell, into which air is supplied, as an example.

After a thin gas-permeable silica fiber sheet has been placed on the bottom of a draft cell, *i.e.*, the cell with which the sample cell is prepared, a definite quantity of a moisture-containing gas-permeable oxidatively-heating substance, the volume of which is about 2 cm^3, is charged in the cell. The glass jig mentioned in a footnote in **Section 7.3** is used at this time to provide a thin vertical hole at the center of the substance charged in the cell in order to facilitate the insertion of the thermocouple into the substance.

The sample cell thus prepared is then set on the pedestal which is stuck at the center of the upper plate of the laboratory jack, which in turn is fixed on the laboratory desk. The position of the stand, by means of which the stem including the glass vent tube is held in the vertical position, is next adjusted by sliding the stand horizontally on the desk in order that the glass vent tube may be aligned vertically with the sample cell set on the pedestal.

The sample cell is then combined concentrically and softly with the ground glass joint of the glass vent tube by raising the laboratory jack to construct the sample cell assembly; in the meantime, the CA thermocouple, covered with a glass capillary tube, to measure the temperature of the substance is inserted automatically and axially to the longitudinal center of the substance charged in the cell. The sample cell combined with the ground glass joint of the glass vent tube is finally supported firmly with a thin aluminium washer and two springs. After having lowered the laboratory jack a little, a fairly small vibrator is applied to the base of the draft cell in order that the substance charged in the cell may come closely in contact with the glass capillary tube.

For further details of the procedure to prepare the sample cell assembly including the draft cell, refer to **Section 7.3**.

The sample cell assembly thus prepared is inserted into the adiabatic jacket set in the air bath of the adiabatic self-heating process recorder, and nitrogen gas is supplied into the draft cell at a flow rate of 2 cm^3/min.

The temperature of the air bath is set at 110 ℃, at first, by means of the temperature dial on the air bath.

To begin with, the main power supply connected to the adiabatic self-heating process recorder is switched on.

The power supplies connected to the cold junction, the air bath, the digital D.C. microvoltmeter, the digital D.C. millivolt recorder and the two-pen strip chart recorder are then switched on, respectively. The ΔT_{diff} pen of the two-pen strip chart recorder is, however, left on the "short" position until the thermal equilibrium state is nearly attained again around the substance charged in the draft cell, into which nitrogen gas is supplied, and inserted into the adiabatic jacket maintained at a nominal T_s of the run, 1.5∼2 h after the reset of the temperature of the air bath. For the term, the ΔT_{diff} pen, refer to **Subsection 4.5.4**.

The sample cell assembly is then left for 270 min at 110 ℃ in nitrogen gas flow to remove all the moisture from the substance.

After the drying time above referred to has passed, the temperature of the air bath is reset at a proper value, *i.e.*, the nominal T_s of the run, by means of the temperature dial on the air bath on the basis of the oxidatively-heating property of the substance tested to give estimated rates of increase in temperature of 1.25 K/h in the adiabatic oxidatively-heating test.

As stated above, the thermal equilibrium state comes to be attained again around the substance charged in the cell, 1.5∼2 h after the reset of the temperature of the air bath. After the thermal equilibrium state has nearly been attained around the substance, the power supply to the analog D.C. microvoltmeter is switched on; in the meantime, the ΔT_{diff} pen of the two-pen strip chart recorder is also switched over from "short" to "on". It is then observed that the indicator of the analog D.C. microvoltmeter enters on to the scale span of the meter from the minus side, and, it comes to stay near the graduation line of zero at the center of the scale span of the meter; in the meantime, the ΔT_{diff} pen of the two-pen strip chart recorder also enters on to the strip chart of the two-pen strip chart recorder from the minus side. For the term, the minus side, refer to **Subsection 4.5.4**.

Curves drawn by the T pen and the ΔT_{diff} pen on the strip chart of the two-pen strip chart recorder, by the time that the thermal equilibrium state has been attained again around the substance charged in the draft cell and inserted into the adiabatic jacket maintained at the nominal T_s of the run, are similar to those illustrated in Fig. 38 in **Subsection 4.5.4**.

The digital output of the thermoelectromotive force of the CA thermocouple to measure the temperature of the substance is then noted down as the exact value of T_s of the run, and the zero-suppression procedure is performed. For the term, the zero-suppression procedure, refer to a footnote in **Subsection 4.5.5**.

Immediately after that, the supply of nitrogen gas into the draft cell is ceased, and the supply of air into the draft cell at a flow rate of 2 cm^3/min, the adiabatic control by means of the adiabatic self-heating process recorder and the record of the oxidatively-heating process, in the early stages, of 2 cm^3 of the substance charged in the draft cell by means of the digital D.C. millivolt recorder are started, respectively. This point of time corresponds to the point "**s**" in Fig. 15 presented in **Section 3.4**.

After the start of the adiabatic control, the T_{atm} is raised automatically by the adiabatic control in order that the condition, $\Delta T_{diff} = T - T_{atm} = 0$, may always hold, with the result that the heat generated in the oxidatively-heating substance is all accumulated in it, and, it continues to heat oxidatively at the rates depending on the value of T_s, and on the gradually increasing oxygen concentration in the atmosphere in the adiabatic jacket; in the meantime, the temperature of the space in the air bath, except that in the adiabatic jacket, is maintained at the T_s of the run throughout every run.

The oxidatively-heating process, in the early stages, of 2 cm^3 of the moisture-containing gas-permeable oxidatively-heating substance charged in the draft cell, into which air is supplied, and inserted into the adiabatic jacket kept always at the very slowly increasing temperature of the substance itself by the adiabatic control is recorded in the digital representation as the variation of the value, with time, of the thermoelectromotive force of the thermocouple to measure the temperature of the substance; to put it concretely, the numerical value of the thermoelectromotive force of the thermocouple is printed out every minute by means of the digital D.C. millivolt recorder, in such a manner as exemplified in Table 5 presented in **Section 4.7**, in order to utilize the record for the calculation of the values of the two coefficients, a and b, of Eq. (44), $\ln \Delta t = a/T_s + b$, holding for the oxidatively-heating process, in the early stages, of 2 cm^3 of the substance charged in the draft cell, into which air is supplied, and subjected to the adiabatic oxidatively-heating test.

On the other hand, however, the oxidatively-heating process, in the early stages, of 2 cm^3 of the substance charged in the draft cell and subjected to the adiabatic oxidatively-heating test is recorded, as an analog signal as well, with the T pen on the strip chart of the two-pen strip chart recorder to look about the process as a whole.

The time, Δt, required for the temperature of 2 cm^3 of the substance charged in the draft cell, into which air is supplied, and subjected to the adiabatic oxidatively-heating test started from a T_s below about 180 ℃ to increase by the definite value of ΔT of 1.25 K from the corresponding standard temperature is determined on the linearly-rising part of the oxidatively-heating process or curve of the substance.

That is, the test is interrupted as soon as the temperature of the substance in the cell increases by the definite value of ΔT of 1.25 K from the corresponding standard temperature.

The other combinations of the value of $\ln \Delta t$ with that of $1/T_s$, which are required to make the plot of $\ln \Delta t$ versus $1/T_s$ with regard to several oxidatively-heating processes, of 2 cm^3 each of several samples of the substance charged each in the draft cell, into which air is supplied, and subjected each to the adiabatic oxidatively-heating test started from each T_s with mutual intervals of 1 ~2 K, recorded each for the time, Δt, required for the temperature of each sample of the substance to increase by the definite value of ΔT of 1.25 K from the corresponding standard temperature, besides, which are required for the regression analysis to calculate the values of the two coefficients, a and b, of Eq. (44) holding for the oxidatively-heating process, in the early stages, of 2 cm^3 of the substance charged in the draft cell, into which air is supplied, and subjected to the adiabatic oxidatively-heating test, are also determined in the same manner as explained above.

For the procedure to calculate the heat generation data of a moisture-containing gas-permeable oxidatively-heating substance, *i.e.*, the values of the two coefficients, a and b, of Eq. (44), $\ln \Delta t = a/T_s + b$, holding for the oxidatively-heating process, in the early stages, of 2 cm^3 of the substance charged in the draft cell, into which air is supplied, and subjected to the adiabatic oxidatively-heating test, refer to **(5)** and **(6)** of **Subsection 8.4.1**.

For the procedure to calculate the value of α_e of a moisture-containing gas-permeable oxidatively-heating substance, refer to **Section 6.4**.

For the procedure to calculate the T_c for a heap of a moisture-containing gas-permeable oxidatively-heating substance, having some one of the several specific shapes including the class A geometries as well as an arbitrary value of r, placed in the atmosphere under isothermal conditions, refer to the concrete procedure, which is exhibited in **Subsection 8.4.3**, to calculate the T_c for a sawdust heap of Port Orford cedar formed into an infinite slab, 60.96 cm (2 feet) in thickness, and placed in the atmosphere under isothermal conditions.

7.4.2 Procedure to perform several adiabatic oxidatively-heating tests, which are started from each T_s with mutual intervals of 1~2 K, in order to calculate the heat generation data of an almost dry gas-permeable oxidatively-heating substance, such as organic powdery polymer, for 2 cm^3 each of several samples of the substance charged each in the draft cell, into which air is supplied, for the time, Δt, required for the temperature of each sample of the substance to increase by the definite value of ΔT of 1.25 K from the corresponding standard temperature, respectively

After a thin gas-permeable silica fiber sheet has been placed on the bottom of a draft cell, *i.e.*, the cell with which the sample cell is prepared, a definite quantity of an almost dry gas-permeable oxidatively-heating substance, the volume of which is about 2 cm^3, is charged in the cell. The glass jig mentioned in a footnote in **Section 7.3** is used at this time to provide a thin vertical hole at the center of the substance charged in the cell in order to facilitate the insertion of the thermocouple into the substance.

The sample cell thus prepared is then set on the pedestal which is stuck at the center of the upper plate of the laboratory jack, which in turn is fixed on the laboratory desk. The position of the stand, by means of which the stem including the glass vent tube is held in the vertical position, is next adjusted by sliding the stand horizontally on the desk in order that the glass vent tube may be aligned vertically with the sample cell set on the pedestal.

The sample cell is then combined concentrically and softly with the ground glass joint of the glass vent tube by raising the laboratory jack to construct the sample cell assembly; in the meantime, the CA thermocouple, covered with a glass capillary tube, to measure the temperature of the substance is inserted automatically and axially to the longitudinal center of the substance charged in the cell. The sample cell combined with the ground glass joint of the glass vent tube is finally supported firmly with a thin aluminium washer and two springs. After having lowered the laboratory jack a little, a fairly small vibrator is applied to the base of the draft cell in order that the substance charged in the cell may come closely in contact with the glass capillary tube.

For further details of the procedure to prepare the sample cell assembly including the draft cell, refer to **Section 7.3**.

The sample cell assembly thus prepared is inserted into the adiabatic jacket set in the air bath of the adiabatic self-heating process recorder, and nitrogen gas is supplied into the draft cell at a flow rate of 2 cm^3/min.

The temperature of the air bath is set at a proper value, *i.e.*, the nominal T_s of the run, by means of the temperature dial on the air bath on the basis of the oxidatively-heating property of the substance tested to give estimated rates of increase in temperature of 1.25 K/h in the adiabatic oxidatively-heating test.

To begin with, the main power supply connected to the adiabatic self-heating process recorder is switched on.

The power supplies connected to the cold junction, the air bath, the digital D.C. microvoltmeter, the digital D.C. millivolt recorder and the two-pen strip chart recorder are then switched on, respectively. The ΔT_{diff} pen of the two-pen strip chart recorder is, however, left on the "short" position until the thermal equilibrium state is nearly attained around the substance charged in the draft cell, into which nitrogen gas is supplied, and inserted into the adiabatic jacket maintained at the nominal T_s of the run, 2~3 h after the start of the air bath heating. For the term, the ΔT_{diff} pen, refer to **Subsection 4.5.4**.

By the time that the thermal equilibrium state is attained around the substance charged in the cell, 2~3 h after the start of the air bath heating, a trace quantity of moisture included in the substance finishes evaporating. After the thermal equilibrium state has nearly been attained around the substance, the power supply to the analog D.C. microvoltmeter is switched on; in the meantime, the ΔT_{diff} pen of the two-pen strip chart recorder is also switched over from "short" to “on”. It is then observed that the indicator of the analog D.C. microvoltmeter enters on to the scale span of the meter from the minus side, and, it comes to stay near the graduation line of zero at the center of the scale span of the meter; in the meantime, the ΔT_{diff} pen of the two-pen strip chart recorder also enters on to the strip chart of the two-pen strip chart recorder from the minus side. For the term, the minus side, refer to **Subsection 4.5.4**.

Curves drawn by the T pen and the ΔT_{diff} pen on the strip chart of the two-pen strip chart recorder, by the time that the thermal equilibrium state has been attained around the substance charged in the draft cell and inserted into the adiabatic jacket maintained at the nominal T_s of the run, are similar to those illustrated in Fig. 38 in **Subsection 4.5.4**.

The digital output of the thermoelectromotive force of the CA thermocouple to measure the temperature of the substance is then noted down as the exact value of T_s of the run, and the zero-suppression procedure is performed. For the term, the zero-suppression procedure, refer to a footnote in **Subsection 4.5.5**.

Immediately after that, the supply of nitrogen gas into the draft cell is ceased, and the supply of air into the draft cell at a flow rate of 2 cm^3/min, the adiabatic control by means of the adiabatic self-heating process recorder and the record of the oxidatively-heating process, in the early stages, of 2 cm^3 of the substance charged in the draft cell by means of the digital D.C. millivolt recorder are started, respectively. This point of time corresponds to the point “**s**” in Fig. 15 presented in **Section 3.4**.

After the start of the adiabatic control, the T_{atm} is raised automatically by the adiabatic control in order that the condition, $\Delta T_{diff} = T - T_{atm} = 0$, may always hold, with the result that the heat generated in the oxidatively-heating substance is all accumulated in it, and, it continues to heat oxidatively at the rates depending on the value of T_s, and on the gradually increasing oxygen concentration in the atmosphere in the adiabatic jacket; in the meantime, the temperature of the space in the air bath, except that in the adiabatic jacket, is maintained at the T_s of the run throughout every run.

The oxidatively-heating process, in the early stages, of 2 cm^3 of the almost dry gas-permeable oxidatively-heating substance charged in the draft cell, into which air is supplied, and inserted into the adiabatic jacket kept always at the very slowly increasing temperature of the substance itself by the adiabatic control is recorded in the digital representation as the variation of the value, with time, of the thermoelectromotive force of the thermocouple to measure the temperature of the substance; to put it concretely, the numerical value of the thermoelectromotive force of the thermocouple is printed out every minute by means of the digital D.C. millivolt recorder, in such a manner as exemplified in Table 5 presented in **Section 4.7**, in order to utilize the record for the calculation of the values of the two coefficients, a and b, of Eq. (44), $\ln \Delta t = a/T_s + b$, holding for the oxidatively-heating process, in the early stages, of 2 cm^3 of the substance charged in the draft cell, into which air is supplied, and subjected to the adiabatic oxidatively-heating test.

On the other hand, however, the oxidatively-heating process, in the early stages, of 2 cm^3 of the substance charged in the draft cell and subjected to the adiabatic oxidatively-heating test is recorded, as an analog signal as well, with the T pen on the strip chart of the two-pen strip chart recorder to look about the process as a whole.

The time, Δt, required for the temperature of 2 cm^3 of the substance charged in the draft cell, into which air is supplied, and subjected to the adiabatic oxidatively-heating test started from a T_s below about 180 ℃ to increase by the definite value of ΔT of 1.25 K from the corresponding standard temperature is determined on the linearly-rising part of the oxidatively-heating process or curve of the substance.

That is, the test is interrupted as soon as the temperature of the substance in the cell increases by the definite value of ΔT of 1.25 K from the corresponding standard temperature.

The other combinations of the value of $\ln \Delta t$ with that of $1/T_s$, which are required to make the plot of $\ln \Delta t$ versus $1/T_s$ with regard to several oxidatively-heating processes, of 2 cm^3 each of several samples of the substance charged each in the draft cell, into which air is supplied, and subjected each to the adiabatic oxidatively-heating test started from each T_s with mutual intervals of 1 ~2 K, recorded each for the time, Δt, required for the temperature of each sample of the substance to increase by the definite value of ΔT of 1.25 K from the corresponding standard temperature, besides, which are required for the regression analysis to calculate the values of the two coefficients, a and b, of Eq. (44) holding for the oxidatively-heating process, in the early stages, of 2 cm^3 of the substance charged in the draft cell, into which air is supplied, and subjected to the adiabatic oxidatively-heating test, are also determined in the same manner as explained above.

For the procedure to calculate the heat generation data of an almost dry gas-permeable oxidatively-heating substance, *i.e.*, the values of the two coefficients, a and b, of Eq. (44), $\ln \Delta t = a/T_s + b$, holding for the oxidatively-heating process, in the early stages, of 2 cm^3 of the substance charged in the draft cell, into which air is supplied, and subjected to the adiabatic oxidatively-heating test, refer to **(5)** and **(6)** of **Subsection 8.4.1**.

For the procedure to calculate the value of α_e of an almost dry gas-permeable oxidatively-heating substance, refer to **Section 6.4**.

For the procedure to calculate the T_c for a heap of an almost dry gas-permeable oxidatively-heating substance, having some one of the several specific shapes including the class A geometries and an arbitrary value of r, placed in the atmosphere under isothermal conditions, refer to the concrete procedure, which is exhibited in **Subsection 8.4.3**, to calculate the T_c for a sawdust heap of Port Orford cedar formed into an infinite slab, 60.96 cm (2 feet) in thickness, and placed in the atmosphere under isothermal conditions.

7.4.3 Procedure to perform several adiabatic oxidatively-heating tests, which are started from each T_s with mutual intervals of 1～2 K, in order to calculate the heat generation data of an oil-soaked adsorbent cotton, for 2 cm^3 each of several samples of the oil-soaked adsorbent cotton charged each in the draft cell, into which air is supplied, for the time, Δt, required for the temperature of each sample of the oil-soaked adsorbent cotton to increase by the definite value of ΔT of 1.25 K from the corresponding standard temperature, respectively

As stated in **Preface**, whenever the adiabatic oxidatively-heating test is performed for an oxidatively-heating liquid, such as unsaturated fatty acid, the liquid is tested, in principle, in the form of oil-soaked adsorbent cotton at relatively low temperatures, or in the form of oil-soaked glass wool at relatively high temperatures. And, the T_c for a heap of the oil-soaked adsorbent cotton, or that of the oil-soaked glass wool, having some one of the several specific shapes and an arbitrary size, placed in the atmosphere under isothermal conditions, is also calculated in the same manner as applied to the calculation of the T_c for a heap of a gas-permeable oxidatively-heating substance.

The liquid tested and adsorbent cotton or glass wool are kept in vacuum desiccators in the dark, respectively.

50 μL of an oxidatively-heating liquid is added, by means of a microsyringe, onto about 500 mg of ethyl ether placed in a small beaker. 50 mg of adsorbent cotton is next immersed in the ethyl ether solution to soak up the solution. The solution-soaked adsorbent cotton is allowed to stand at room temperature until ethyl ether has evaporated almost completely.

After a thin gas-permeable silica fiber sheet has been placed on the bottom of a draft cell, *i.e.*, the cell with which the sample cell is prepared, the sample of the oil-soaked adsorbent cotton prepared above, the volume of which is about 2 cm^3, is charged in the cell. The glass jig mentioned in a footnote in **Section 7.3** is used at this time to provide a thin vertical hole at the center of the oil-soaked adsorbent cotton charged in the cell in order to facilitate the insertion of the thermocouple into the cotton.

The sample cell thus prepared is then set on the pedestal which is stuck at the center of the upper plate of the laboratory jack, which in turn is fixed on the laboratory desk. The position of the stand, by means of which the stem including the glass vent tube is held in the vertical position, is next adjusted by sliding the stand horizontally on the desk in order that the glass vent tube may be aligned vertically with the sample cell set on the pedestal.

The sample cell is then combined concentrically and softly with the ground glass joint of the glass vent tube by raising the laboratory jack to construct the sample cell assembly; in the meantime, the CA thermocouple, covered with a glass capillary tube, to measure the temperature of the oil-soaked adsorbent cotton is inserted automatically and axially to the longitudinal center of the oil-soaked adsorbent cotton charged in the cell. The sample cell combined with the ground glass joint of the glass vent tube is finally supported firmly with a thin aluminium washer and two springs.

For further details of the procedure to prepare the sample cell assembly including the draft cell, refer to **Section 7.3**.

The sample cell assembly thus prepared is inserted into the adiabatic jacket set in the air bath of the adiabatic self-heating process recorder, and nitrogen gas is supplied into the draft cell at a flow rate of 2 cm^3/min.

The temperature of the air bath is set at a proper value, *i.e.*, the nominal T_s of the run, by means of the temperature dial on the air bath on the basis of the oxidatively-heating property of the oil-soaked adsorbent cotton tested to give estimated rates of increase in temperature of 1.25 K/h in the adiabatic oxidatively-heating test.

To begin with, the main power supply connected to the adiabatic self-heating process recorder is switched on.

The power supplies connected to the cold junction, the air bath, the digital D.C. microvoltmeter, the digital D.C. millivolt recorder and the two-pen strip chart recorder are then switched on, respectively. The ΔT_{diff} pen of the two-pen strip chart recorder is, however, left on the "short" position until the thermal equilibrium state is nearly attained around the oil-soaked adsorbent cotton charged in the draft cell, into which nitrogen gas is supplied, and inserted into the adiabatic jacket maintained at the nominal T_s of the run, 2～3 h after the start of the air bath heating. For the term, the ΔT_{diff} pen, refer to **Subsection 4.5.4**.

By the time that the thermal equilibrium state is attained around the oil-soaked adsorbent cotton charged in the cell, 2～3 h after the start of the air bath heating, a trace quantity of moisture included in the oil-soaked adsorbent cotton finishes evaporating. After the thermal equilibrium state has nearly been attained around the cotton, the power supply to the analog D.C. microvoltmeter is switched on; in the meantime, the ΔT_{diff} pen of the two-pen strip chart recorder is also switched over from "short" to "on". It is then observed that the indicator of the analog D.C. microvoltmeter enters on to the scale span of the meter from the minus side, and, it comes to stay near the graduation line of zero at the center of the scale span of the meter; in the meantime, the ΔT_{diff} pen of the two-pen strip chart recorder also enters on to the strip chart of the two-pen strip chart recorder from the minus side. For the term, the minus side, refer to **Subsection 4.5.4**.

Curves drawn by the T pen and the ΔT_{diff} pen on the strip chart of the two-pen strip chart recorder, by the time that the thermal equilibrium state has been attained around the oil-soaked adsorbent cotton charged in the draft cell and inserted into the adiabatic jacket maintained at the nominal T_s of the run, are similar to those illustrated in Fig. 38 in **Subsection 4.5.4**.

The digital output of the thermoelectromotive force of the CA thermocouple to measure the temperature of the oil-soaked adsorbent cotton is then noted down as the exact value of T_s of the run, and the zero-suppression procedure is performed. For the term, the zero-suppression procedure, refer to a footnote in **Subsection 4.5.5**.

Immediately after that, the supply of nitrogen gas into the draft cell is ceased, and the supply of air into the draft cell at a flow rate of 2 cm^3/min, the adiabatic control by means of the adiabatic self-heating process recorder and the record of the oxidatively-heating process, in the early stages, of 2 cm^3 of the oil-soaked adsorbent cotton charged in the draft cell by means of the digital D.C. millivolt recorder are started, respectively. This point of time corresponds to the point "**s**" in Fig. 15 presented in **Section 3.4**.

After the start of the adiabatic control, the T_{atm} is raised automatically by the adiabatic control in order that the condition, $\Delta T_{diff} = T - T_{atm} = 0$, may always hold, with the result that the heat generated in the oxidatively-heating oil-soaked adsorbent cotton is all accumulated in it, and, it continues to heat oxidatively at the rates depending on the value of T_s, and on the gradually increasing oxygen concentration in the atmosphere in the adiabatic jacket; in the meantime, the temperature of the space in the air bath, except that in the adiabatic jacket, is maintained at the T_s of the run throughout every run.

The oxidatively-heating process, in the early stages, of 2 cm^3 of the oil-soaked adsorbent cotton charged in the draft cell, into which air is supplied, and inserted into the adiabatic jacket kept always at the very slowly increasing temperature of the oil-soaked adsorbent cotton itself by the adiabatic control is recorded in the digital representation as the variation of the value, with time, of the thermoelectromotive force of the thermocouple to measure the temperature of the oil-soaked adsorbent cotton; to put it concretely, the numerical value of the thermoelectromotive force of the thermocouple is printed out every minute by means of the digital D.C. millivolt recorder, in such a manner as exemplified in Table 5 presented in **Section 4.7**, in order to utilize the record for the calculation of the values of the two coefficients, a and b, of Eq. (44), $\ln \Delta t = a/T_s + b$, holding for the oxidatively-heating process, in the early stages, of 2 cm^3 of the oil-soaked adsorbent cotton charged in the draft cell, into which air is supplied, and subjected to the adiabatic oxidatively-heating test.

On the other hand, however, the oxidatively-heating process, in the early stages, of 2 cm^3 of the oil-soaked adsorbent cotton charged in the draft cell and subjected to the adiabatic oxidatively-heating test is recorded, as an analog signal as well, with the T pen on the strip chart of the two-pen strip chart recorder to look about the process as a whole.

The time, Δt, required for the temperature of 2 cm^3 of the oil-soaked adsorbent cotton charged in the draft cell, into which air is supplied, and subjected to the adiabatic oxidatively-heating test started from a T_s below about 180 ℃ to increase by the definite value of ΔT of 1.25 K from the corresponding standard temperature is determined on the linearly-rising part of the oxidatively-heating process or curve of the substance.

That is, the test is interrupted as soon as the temperature of the oil-soaked adsorbent cotton in the cell increases by the definite value of ΔT of 1.25 K from the corresponding standard temperature.

The other combinations of the value of ln Δt with that of $1/T_s$, which are required to make the plot of ln Δt versus $1/T_s$ with regard to several oxidatively-heating processes, of 2 cm^3 each of several samples of the oil-soaked adsorbent cotton charged each in the draft cell, into which air is supplied, and subjected each to the adiabatic oxidatively-heating test started from each T_s with mutual intervals of 1 ~ 2 K, recorded each for the time, Δt, required for the temperature of each sample of the oil-soaked adsorbent cotton to increase by the definite value of ΔT of 1.25 K from the corresponding standard temperature, besides, which are required for the regression analysis to calculate the values of the two coefficients, *a* and *b*, of Eq. (44) holding for the oxidatively-heating process, in the early stages, of 2 cm^3 of the oil-soaked adsorbent cotton charged in the draft cell, into which air is supplied, and subjected to the adiabatic oxidatively-heating test, are also determined in the same manner as explained above.

For the procedure to calculate the heat generation data of an oil-soaked adsorbent cotton, *i.e.*, the values of the two coefficients, *a* and *b*, of Eq. (44), ln $\Delta t = a/T_s + b$, holding for the oxidatively-heating process, in the early stages, of 2 cm^3 of the oil-soaked adsorbent cotton charged in the draft cell, into which air is supplied, and subjected to the adiabatic oxidatively-heating test, refer to **(5)** and **(6)** of **Subsection 8.4.1**.

For the procedure to calculate the value of α_e of an oil-soaked adsorbent cotton, refer to **Section 6.4**.

For the procedure to calculate the T_c for a heap of an oil-soaked adsorbent cotton, having some one of the several specific shapes including the class A geometries and an arbitrary value of *r*, placed in the atmosphere under isothermal conditions, refer to the concrete procedure, which is exhibited in **Subsection 8.4.3**, to calculate the T_c for a sawdust heap of Port Orford cedar formed into an infinite slab, 60.96 cm (2 feet) in thickness, and placed in the atmosphere under isothermal conditions.

7.4.4 Procedure to perform several adiabatic oxidatively-heating tests, which are started from each T_s with mutual intervals of 1~2 K, in order to calculate the heat generation data of a gas-permeable oxidatively-heating substance, which is almost dry but includes some self-heating component such as hydroperoxide, for 2 cm^3 each of several samples of the substance charged each in the draft cell, into which air is supplied, for the time, Δt, required for the temperature of each sample of the substance to increase by the definite value of ΔT of 1.25 K from the corresponding T_s, respectively

As an example, the dry spray of some kind of paint including some unsaturated polyester resin as the main ingredient is one of substances such as specified in the above heading.*

The temperature of the air bath is set at a proper value, *i.e.*, the nominal T_s of the run, by means of the temperature dial on the air bath on the basis of the self-heating property of the substance tested to give estimated rates of increase in temperature of 1.25 K/h in the adiabatic oxidatively-heating test.

To begin with, the main power supply connected to the adiabatic self-heating process recorder is switched on.

The power supplies connected to the cold junction, the air bath, the digital D.C. microvoltmeter, the digital D.C. millivolt recorder and the two-pen strip chart recorder are then switched on, respectively. The ΔT_{diff} pen of the two-pen strip chart recorder is, however, left on the "short" position until the thermal equilibrium state is nearly attained around the reference material charged in the draft cell and inserted into the adiabatic jacket maintained at the nominal T_s of the run. For the term, the ΔT_{diff} pen, refer to **Subsection 4.5.4**.

After a thin gas-permeable silica fiber sheet has been placed on the bottom of a draft cell, *i.e.*, the cell with which the sample cell is prepared, about 2 cm^3 of some gas-permeable reference material, such as silica of relatively coarse particles or glass wool, is charged in the cell. The glass jig mentioned in a footnote in **Section 7.3** is used at this time to provide a thin vertical hole at the center of the reference material charged in the cell in order to facilitate the insertion of the thermocouple into the material.

The reference cell thus prepared is then set on the pedestal which is stuck at the center of the upper plate of the laboratory jack, which in turn is fixed on the laboratory desk. The position of the stand, by means of which the stem including the glass vent tube is held in the vertical position, is next adjusted by

* A substance of this kind has the property to heat oxidatively and the property to self-heat simultaneously. Accordingly, the noun clause of a gas-permeable oxidatively-heating substance which is almost dry but includes some self-heating component such as hydroperoxide is abridged, in the present subsection, to a simplified noun phrase of a gas-permeable self-heating and simultaneously slightly oxidatively-heating substance.

sliding the stand horizontally on the desk in order that the glass vent tube may be aligned vertically with the reference cell set on the pedestal.

The reference cell is then combined concentrically and softly with the ground glass joint of the glass vent tube by raising the laboratory jack to construct the reference cell assembly; in the meantime, the CA thermocouple, covered with a glass capillary tube, to measure the T_{ref} is inserted automatically and axially to the longitudinal center of the reference material charged in the cell. The reference cell combined with the ground glass joint of the glass vent tube is finally supported firmly with a thin aluminium washer and two springs. After having lowered the laboratory jack a little, a fairly small vibrator is applied to the base of the draft cell in order that the material charged in the cell may come closely in contact with the glass capillary tube.

For further details of the procedure to prepare the reference cell assembly including the draft cell, refer to **Section 7.3**.

The reference cell assembly thus prepared is inserted into the adiabatic jacket set in the preheated air bath of the adiabatic self-heating recorder, and air is supplied into the draft cell at a flow rate of 2 cm^3/min.

The thermal equilibrium state is attained around the reference material charged in the draft cell and inserted into the adiabatic jacket maintained at the nominal T_s of the run, 2～3 h after the insertion of the reference cell assembly into the jacket. After the thermal equilibrium state has nearly been attained around the reference material, the power supply to the analog D.C. microvoltmeter is switched on; in the meantime, the ΔT_{diff} pen of the two-pen strip chart recorder is also switched over from "short" to "on". It is then observed that the indicator of the analog D.C. microvoltmeter enters on to the scale span of the meter from the minus side, and, it comes to stay near the graduation line of zero at the center of the scale span of the meter; in the meantime, the ΔT_{diff} pen of the two-pen strip chart recorder also enters on to the strip chart of the two-pen strip chart recorder from the minus side. For the term, the minus side, refer to **Subsection 4.5.4**.

Curves drawn by the T pen and the ΔT_{diff} pen on the strip chart of the two-pen strip chart recorder, by the time that the thermal equilibrium state has been attained around the reference material charged in the draft cell and inserted into the adiabatic jacket maintained at the nominal T_s of the run, are similar to those illustrated in Fig. 38 in **Subsection 4.5.4**.

The digital output of the thermoelectromotive force of the CA thermocouple to measure the T_{ref} is then noted down as the exact value of T_s of the run, and the zero-suppression procedure is performed. For the term, the zero-suppression procedure, refer to a footnote in **Subsection 4.5.5**.

The power supply to the analog D.C. microvoltmeter is then switched off for a while; in the meantime, the ΔT_{diff} pen of the two-pen strip chart recorder is also switched over from "on" to "short" for a while.

The reference cell assembly is successively taken out of the jacket, and the sample cell assembly including a draft cell, in which a definite quantity of a gas-permeable self-heating and simultaneously slightly oxidatively-heating substance, the volume of which is about 2 cm^3, has been charged in the same manner as performed to prepare the reference cell assembly, is inserted into the adiabatic jacket; in the meantime, the supply of air into the draft cell is continued at the identical flow rate of 2 cm^3/min throughout every run.

Although the temperature of the substance begins to increase from a temperature near room temperature after the insertion of the sample cell assembly, the thermal equilibrium state comes to be attained again around the substance charged in the draft cell, into which air is supplied, and inserted into the adiabatic jacket maintained at the T_s of the run in the course of tens of minutes. After the thermal equilibrium state has nearly been attained around the substance, the power supply to the analog D.C. microvoltmeter is again switched on; in the meantime, the ΔT_{diff} pen of the two-pen strip chart recorder is also switched over again from "short" to "on". It is then observed that the indicator of the analog D.C. microvoltmeter enters again on to the scale span of the meter from the minus side; in the meantime, the ΔT_{diff} pen of the two-pen strip chart recorder also enters again on to the strip chart of the two-pen strip chart recorder from the minus side.

Once the indicator of the analog D.C. microvoltmeter reaches the graduation line of zero at the center of the scale span of the meter, the adiabatic control by means of the adiabatic self-heating process recorder and the record of the self-heating and simultaneously slightly oxidatively-heating process, in the early stages, of 2 cm^3 of the substance charged in the draft cell by means of the digital D.C. millivolt recorder are started, respectively. This point of time corresponds to the point "**s**" in Fig. 15 presented in **Section 3.4**.

At this time, the ΔT_{diff} pen also gets to the ΔT_{diff} base line on the strip chart of the two-pen strip chart recorder (see Fig. 39 in **Subsection 4.5.6**). However, the temperature of the substance indicated by the digital D.C. microvoltmeter in general takes a value slightly lower than that of the T_s at this time, because, while the T_{atm}, the temperature of the atmosphere around the substance, is still slightly lower than the T_s, the substance begins to self-heat in the cell, so that the temperature of the substance catches the T_{atm} up.

After the start of the adiabatic control, the T_{atm} is raised automatically by the adiabatic control in order that the condition, $\Delta T_{diff} = T - T_{atm} = 0$, may always hold, with the result that the heat generated in the gas-permeable self-heating and simultaneously slightly oxidatively-heating substance is all accumulated in it, and, it continues self-heating and simultaneously slightly oxidatively-heating at a very slow, but virtually constant, rate depending on the value of T_s; in the meantime, the temperature of the space in the air bath, except that in the adiabatic jacket, is maintained at the T_s of the run throughout every run.

The self-heating and simultaneously slightly oxidatively-heating process, in the early stages, of 2 cm^3 of the substance charged in the draft cell, into which air is supplied, and inserted into the adiabatic jacket kept always at the very slowly increasing temperature of the substance itself by the adiabatic control is recorded in the digital representation as the variation of the value, with time, of the thermoelectromotive force of the thermocouple to measure the temperature of the substance; to put it concretely, the numerical value of the thermoelectromotive force of the thermocouple is printed out every minute by means of the digital D.C. millivolt recorder, in such a manner as exemplified in Table 5 presented in **Section 4.7**, in order to utilize the record for the calculation of the values of the two coefficients, a and b, of Eq. (44), $\ln \Delta t = a/T_s + b$, holding for the self-heating and simultaneously slightly oxidatively-heating process, in the early stages, of 2 cm^3 of the substance charged in the draft cell, into which air is supplied, and subjected to the adiabatic oxidatively-heating test.

On the other hand, however, the self-heating and simultaneously slightly oxidatively-heating process, in the early stages, of 2 cm^3 of the substance charged in the draft cell and subjected to the adiabatic oxidatively-heating test is recorded, as an analog signal as well, with the T pen on the strip chart of the two-pen strip chart recorder to look about the process as a whole.

The test is interrupted as soon as the temperature of the substance in the cell increases by the definite value of ΔT of 1.25 K from the T_s.

The other combinations of the value of $\ln \Delta t$ with that of $1/T_s$, which are required to make the plot of $\ln \Delta t$ versus $1/T_s$ with regard to several self-heating and simultaneously slightly oxidatively-heating processes, of 2 cm^3 each of several samples of the substance charged each in the draft cell, into which air is supplied, and subjected each to the adiabatic oxidatively-heating test started from each T_s with mutual intervals of 1~2 K, recorded each for the time, Δt, required for the temperature of each sample of the substance to increase by the definite value of ΔT of 1.25 K from the corresponding T_s, besides, which are required for the regression analysis to calculate the values of the two coefficients, a and b, of Eq. (44), $\ln \Delta t = a/T_s + b$, holding for the self-heating and simultaneously slightly oxidatively-heating process, in the early stages, of 2 cm^3 of the substance charged in the draft cell, into which air is supplied, and subjected to the adiabatic oxidatively-heating test, are also determined in the same manner as explained above.

For the procedure to calculate the heat generation data of a gas-permeable self-heating and simultaneously slightly oxidatively-heating substance, *i.e.*, the values of the two coefficients, a and b, of Eq. (44), $\ln \Delta t = a/T_s + b$, holding for the self-heating and simultaneously slightly oxidatively-heating process, in the early stages, of 2 cm^3 of the substance charged in the draft cell, into which air is supplied, and subjected to the adiabatic oxidatively-heating test, refer to **(5)** and **(6)** of **Subsection 8.4.1**.

For the procedure to calculate the value of α_e of a gas-permeable self-heating and simultaneously slightly oxidatively-heating substance, refer to **Section 6.4**.

For the procedure to calculate the T_c for a heap of a gas-permeable self-heating and simultaneously slightly oxidatively-heating substance, having some one of the several specific shapes including the class A geometries as well as an arbitrary value of r, placed in the atmosphere under isothermal conditions, refer to the concrete procedure, which is exhibited in **Subsection 8.4.3**, to calculate the T_c for a sawdust heap of Port Orford cedar formed into an infinite slab, 60.96 cm (2 feet) in thickness, and placed in the atmosphere under isothermal conditions.

References to Chapter 7

[58] T. Boddington, P. Gray and D. I. Harvey, Thermal Theory of Spontaneous Ignition: Criticality in Bodies of Arbitrary Shape, Phil. Trans. Roy. London, **270**, 471 (1971).
[65] P. C. Bowes, Self-Heating: Evaluating and Controlling the Hazards, Elsevier Science Publishers B. V., Amsterdam, 196 (1984).

Chapter 8 Individual oxidatively-heating properties of the sawdusts of fifteen wood species; and, procedure to calculate the T_c for a sawdust heap, having some one of several specific shapes including the class A geometries as well as an arbitrary size, placed in the atmosphere under isothermal conditions

8.1 Introduction

Many research reports have appeared hitherto regarding various aspects of the thermal decomposition reaction or the combustion of woods or woody materials. However, instances in each of which the value of the critical temperature for the spontaneous ignition or T_c for a bulky sawdust heap was actually measured have been only a few so far. In this regard, the works performed by Gross *et al.* [66], Akita [67], Anthony *et al.* [68], John [69] and Schliemann [70] are thought to be quite precious.

The sawdust of every wood species is dealt with as a representative of gas-permeable oxidatively-heating substances herein. And, in the first half of the present chapter, are described the individual oxidatively-heating properties of the sawdusts of fifteen wood species, which are each measured, on the one hand, by TG-DTA performed in air* and, on the other hand, by the adiabatic oxidatively-heating test performed in air. In this connection, the oxidatively-heating property of the sawdust of a wood species discussed herein is not necessarily consistent with the combustibility of the wood. The former subject, the oxidatively-heating property of the sawdust of a wood species, is concerned predominantly with some characteristics of the sawdust, which are revealed by TG-DTA performed for the sawdust in air or by the adiabatic oxidatively-heating test performed for the sawdust in air at the T_s of 140 or 150 ℃; on the other hand, the latter subject, the combustibility of a wood, depends on the whole property regarding the combustion of the wood.

Now, as stated in **Preface** and in **Section 7.1**, the oxidatively-heating behavior of the sawdust of every wood species is also of the TD type. It is, therefore, possible to calculate the T_c for a sawdust heap, having an arbitrary shape and an arbitrary size, placed in the atmosphere under isothermal conditions, by applying the reduced form of the F-K equation, *i.e.*, Eq. (79) derived in **Section 6.2**, provided the value of δ_c for the shape of the heap is known.

---

* The two nouns, air and atmosphere, are used in the same sense in the present chapter. However, the noun, air, is used predominantly in the sense of one of several kinds of gases supplied, at atmospheric pressure, into a TG-DTA apparatus or into the adiabatic self-heating process recorder; on the other hand, the noun, atmosphere, is used, in connection with the T_c for a sawdust heap, in its original sense of the mixture of gases surrounding the earth.

However, in the same manner as a powdery chemical of the TD type, if the sawdust heap, which is placed in the atmosphere under isothermal conditions, has some one of several specific shapes including the class A geometries* as well as an arbitrary size, *i.e.*, an arbitrary value of r, the calculation of the T_c for the sawdust heap becomes very simple, because the values of δ_c for these specific shapes have already been calculated by T. Boddington *et al.*, respectively [58], with the result that, as explained in **Section 6.2**, the heat transfer data required to calculate the T_c for such a sawdust heap as specified above is only the effective thermal diffusivity,** α_e, of the sawdust. For the values of δ_c calculated by T. Boddington *et al.*, refer to Table 13 in **Section 6.5**.

That is, for the purpose of calculating the T_c for a sawdust heap, having some one of the several specific shapes above referred to as well as an arbitrary value of r, placed in the atmosphere under isothermal conditions, we have only to perform, on the one hand, several adiabatic oxidatively-heating tests, which are started from each T_s with mutual intervals of 2 K, in order to calculate the heat generation data of the sawdust, for 0.3 g each of several samples of the sawdust charged each in the draft cell, into which air is supplied, for the time, Δt, required for the temperature of each sample of the sawdust to increase by the definite value of ΔT of 1.25 K from the corresponding standard temperature, respectively, and, we have only to measure, on the other hand, in order to calculate the value of α_e of the sawdust, a heating rate, ϕ, and a limiting radial temperature difference, $(\Delta T_{rad})_{\lim}$, which is effected in the non-steady state in temperature differences of 1.25 K between the periphery and the axial center of a moderate-sized specimen of the sawdust, when the outside surface of a cylindrical cell containing the specimen is heated at the rate, ϕ.

The procedure to calculate, by applying Eq. (79), the T_c for a sawdust heap, having some one of the several specific shapes including the class A geometries as well as an arbitrary value of r, placed in the atmosphere under isothermal conditions, is thus introduced in **Section 8.4**, *i.e.*, in the latter half of the present chapter, by taking the procedure to calculate the T_c for a sawdust heap of Port Orford cedar, assuming that it is formed into an infinite slab, 60.96 cm (2 feet) in thickness, and is placed in the atmosphere under isothermal conditions, as an example.

The values of T_c thus calculated each for the sawdust heaps of fifteen wood species, including Port Orford cedar, ranged from 118 ℃ for the sawdust heap of zelkova to 142 ℃ for that of Sitka spruce.

These values of T_c calculated herein in general are in fair agreement with a few values of T_c measured each by other researchers for a few sawdust heaps, of wood species other than those tested herein, but similar to the heaps calculated herein in size, respectively.

---

* For the term, the class A geometries, refer to **Section 6.5**.

** For the term, the effective thermal diffusivity, α_e, refer to **Subsections 6.4.2** and **6.4.3**.

8.2 Experimental

8.2.1 Procedure to prepare the sawdust of each wood species

The list of the fifteen wood species tested herein is given in Table 17. The wood blocks of fifteen wood species tested are of the commercial grade and were tested without further purification, respectively.

Table 17
The fifteen wood species tested herein.

Wood species	The felling district
Zelkova	Japan
Red lauan	Southeast Asia
White lauan	Southeast Asia
Sawara cedar	Japan
Japanese cedar	Japan
Paulownia	Japan
Japanese red pine	Japan
Japanese cypress	Japan
Eli ayanskya	Siberia (Russia)
Western red cedar	U. S. A.
Douglas fir	U. S. A.
Port Orford cedar	U. S. A.
Alaska cedar	Alaska (U. S. A.)
Western hemlock	U. S. A.
Sitka spruce	Alaska (U. S. A.)

Wood strips, about 2.5 mm × about 2.5 mm × about 20 cm in length each, are first prepared by cutting out of a visually uniform part of a block of each wood species using a band saw. Strips are next cut into small pieces, about 2.5 mm × about 2.5 mm × about 2.5 mm each, with a nipper. The pieces are then pulverized by means of an ultra centrifugal mill. The sawdust of each wood species thus prepared is tested after having been size-graded to 35～60 mesh by sieving, because very fine sawdust is not appropriate for the adiabatic oxidatively-heating test performed by means of the adiabatic self-heating process recorder.*

8.2.2 Experimental conditions of TG-DTA and the adiabatic oxidatively-heating test performed each in Section 8.3 in order to measure the individual oxidatively-heating properties of the sawdusts of fifteen wood species

(1) Experimental conditions of TG-DTA

Sample quantity: 5 mg; Sample cell: an aluminium open-cup cell, 5 mm in diameter, 2.5 mm in depth; Atmosphere: air, nitrogen or oxygen gas; TG-DTA is, however, performed predominantly in air unless otherwise noted; Pressure: atmospheric pressure; Gas flow rate: 20 cm^3/min; Heating rate: 2.5 K/min.

(2) Experimental conditions of the adiabatic oxidatively-heating test

The quantity of the sawdust of every wood species tested: 0.3 g; Sample cell: a glass draft cell; Charging density: 0.12 ~ 0.14 g/cm^3; Atmosphere: air, nitrogen or oxygen gas; the test is, however, performed predominantly in air unless otherwise noted; Pressure: atmospheric pressure; Gas flow rate: 2 cm^3/min; T_s: 150 ℃ (the T_s for the sawdust of red lauan : 140 ℃). **

The procedure to start the adiabatic oxidatively-heating test for the sawdust of a wood species charged in the draft cell, into which air is supplied, from a proper value of T_s is explained in detail in **Subsection 8.4.1**. The difference between the procedure performed in **Section 8.3** and that done in **Subsection 8.4.1** is as follows:

In **Section 8.3**, after the sample cell assembly, which is inserted into the adiabatic jacket set in the air bath of the adiabatic self-heating process recorder, has been left for 270 min at 110 ℃ in nitrogen gas flow to remove all the moisture from the sawdust tested, the temperature of the air bath of the recorder is reset at the definite value of T_s of 150 ℃ (the T_s for the sawdust of red lauan : 140 ℃) in order to compare the rates of the oxidatively-heating reaction of the sawdusts of fifteen wood species with one another at the same temperature. On the other hand, in **Subsection 8.4.1**, after the sample cell assembly has been left for 270 min at 110 ℃ in nitrogen gas flow to remove all the moisture from the sawdust tested, the temperature of the air bath is reset at a proper value of T_s on

---

* It is hard for gases to pass through the layer of very fine sawdust charged in the draft cell.

** The rate of the oxidatively-heating reaction of the sawdust of red lauan at 150 ℃ is too fast to compare the individual effects of various additives on the rate with one another, so that 140 ℃ is chosen as the T_s for this sawdust in **Section 8.3**.

the basis of the oxidatively-heating property of the sawdust tested to give estimated rates of increase in temperature of 1.25 K/h in the adiabatic oxidatively-heating test, with the result that the T_s ranged from 158 ℃ for the sawdust of zelkova to 179 ℃ for the sawdust of Sitka spruce.

8.3 Experimental results regarding the individual oxidatively-heating properties of the sawdusts of fifteen wood species

8.3.1 The whole result of the TG-DTA measurements performed each in air at atmospheric pressure with the aluminium open-cup cell at the value of ϕ of 2.5 K/min for the sawdusts of fifteen wood species; and, characteristics of the oxidatively-heating process of the sawdust of an average wood species charged in the draft cell, into which air is supplied, and subjected to the adiabatic oxidatively-heating test started from a T_s below about 180 ℃

(1) The whole result of the TG-DTA measurements performed each in air at atmospheric pressure with the aluminium open-cup cell at the value of ϕ of 2.5 K/min for the sawdusts of fifteen wood species

To begin with, the TG-DTA measurements were performed in air at atmospheric pressure with the aluminium open-cup cell, 5 mm in diameter, 2.5 mm in depth, at the value of ϕ of 2.5 K/min for the sawdusts of fifteen wood species, to see the individual oxidatively-heating properties as a whole, respectively. The TG-DTA curve of the sawdust of an average wood species is presented in Fig. 84.

When heated at a slow rate, ϕ, in thermal analysis performed in air at atmospheric pressure, the oxidative decomposition reaction of the sawdust of every wood species proceeds in the following manner.

The dehydration process of the sawdust of every wood species, which contains 3～10 % of water, finishes by 90 ℃. It begins, thereafter, to heat oxidatively at 110～130 ℃.

The exothermic onset temperature or EOT of the sawdust of each wood species is determined by comparing the TG-DTA curve recorded in air with the curve recorded in nitrogen gas. The EOT of the sawdust of every wood species is, however, one of the data of poor reproducibility, so that it is rather difficult to determine distinctly the value by means of TG-DTA. As an example, when DTA is performed for the sawdust of Japanese cypress, which is one of wood species relatively hard to heat oxidatively, in air and in nitrogen gas, respectively, it is almost impossible to distinguish the enthalpy change of the sawdust recorded in air from the change recorded in nitrogen gas at temperatures below 193 ℃. On the other hand, the sawdust of Japanese cypress charged in the draft cell, into which air is supplied, and subjected to the adiabatic oxidatively-heating test started from the T_s of 150 ℃ is seen clearly to heat oxidatively; in the meantime, the sawdust of the same wood species, placed under the same conditions as the former, except that nitrogen gas is supplied, is not seen to heat at all. Nevertheless, however, it is certain that no sawdust has the EOT in excess of 120 ℃.

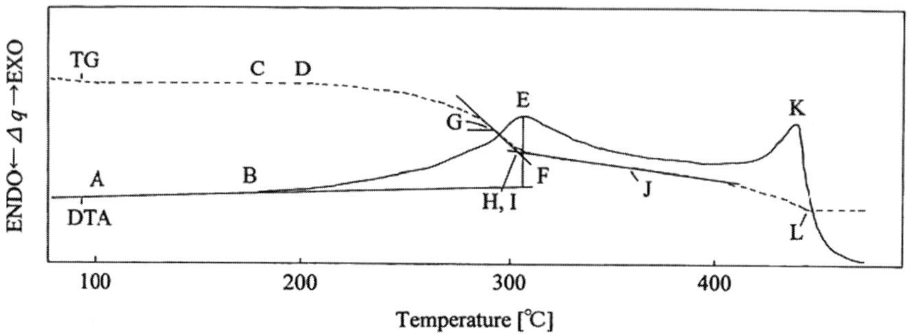

Figure 84. The TG-DTA curve of the sawdust of an average wood species.

Following the dehydration process, the very slow process of the reduction in weight, which is a different aspect of the very slow oxidative decomposition reaction or the very slow oxidatively-heating reaction, of the sawdust of every wood species continues. It is seen in the case of the sawdust of wood species relatively easy to heat oxidatively that the dehydration process of the sawdust does not separate decidedly from the oxidative decomposition reaction, so that the weight of the sawdust continues to reduce uninterruptedly and lazily until the sawdust is heated up to 160∼180 ℃. In any event, although the oxidative decomposition reaction, or the oxidatively-heating reaction, of the sawdust of every wood species proceeds at a slow, but virtually constant, rate up to about 180 ℃, it comes to accelerate gradually above the temperature just referred to. This fact coincides with the information obtained by the adiabatic oxidatively-heating test as well. For the matter relevant to this, refer to the explanation for Fig. 86 in **(2)** of **Subsection 8.3.1**. The rapid oxidatively-heating reaction of the sawdust of every wood species, then, begins immediately before the start of the rapid reduction in weight.

The active reduction in weight, which is caused by the active oxidative decomposition reaction, of the sawdust of every wood species is, thereafter, observed in the range of about 200 ℃ to about 300 ℃. That is, it is thought that the charring reaction of the sawdust of every wood species ceases by about 300 ℃. According to elemental analysis of some char, it is, however, known that a small amount of hydrogen and oxygen are still included in the char formed at this stage. In this connection, the maximum rate of reduction in weight of the sawdust of each wood species is thought to be the measure expressing the gasifying rate of the wood, *i.e.*, the size of flame per unit mass per unit time which the wood produces on burning.

In addition to the above, the noteworthy facts observed at temperatures near 300 ℃ are that the first exothermic peak temperature, *i.e.*, the finish temperature of the rapid oxidatively-heating reaction, agrees nearly with the finish temperature of the charring reaction, and, that the percentage of reduction in weight, caused by the oxidative decomposition reaction, to the quantity of the sawdust tested amounts to nearly 60 % by the time that the charring reaction finishes, *etc*.

In the range of 300 ℃ to 400 ℃ or more, the char of every wood species thus formed continues uninterruptedly to reduce in weight at a nearly constant rate on account of the oxidative decomposition reaction. In this connection, it is thought that the rate of reduction in weight of the char of a wood species may be the quantity proportional to the burning rate of the ember which arises from the wood. The oxidatively-heating reaction at this stage is, however, far milder than the reaction in the range of 200 ℃ to 300 ℃. A part* of the char, which has remained to the last, finally decomposes somewhat actively. The sawdust of every wood species is thus reduced to ashes by 450 ℃ in thermal analysis.

A list of the whole result of the TG-DTA measurements performed each in air with the aluminium open-cup cell at the value of ϕ of 2.5 K/min for the sawdusts of fifteen wood species is presented in Table 18 in the order of increasing hardness of the sawdust of each wood species to heat oxidatively.

The maximum rate of reduction in weight, which is expressed in terms of the angle from the temperature axis on the strip chart, of the sawdust of wood species relatively easy to heat oxidatively is 30～40° ; on the other hand, the maximum rate of reduction in weight of the sawdust of wood species relatively hard to heat oxidatively is approximately 50° , except that of Japanese cedar. In other words, it will be permitted to say that, when heated in thermal analysis performed in air, the sawdust of wood species relatively easy to heat oxidatively continues the oxidative decomposition reaction uninterruptedly but lazily from relatively low temperatures; on the other hand, although the sawdust of wood species relatively hard to heat oxidatively remains as it is up to relatively high temperatures, once the sawdust begins to decompose oxidatively in the course of time, the oxidative decomposition reaction proceeds more rapidly and actively than the former.

---

* This is supposed to be some tissue including condensed benzene rings derived very likely from lignin.

Table 18
A list of the whole result of the TG-DTA measurements performed each in air with the aluminium open-cup cell at the value of ϕ of 2.5 K/min for the sawdusts of fifteen wood species.[a), b)]

Wood species	W %	A ℃	B ℃	C ℃	D %	E ℃	F cm	G [°]	H ℃	I %	J[c)]	K ℃	L ℃
Zelkova	8	107	159	161	2.0	305	35	34	310	65	32	405	419
Red lauan	9	110	158	163	2.3	292	37	27	298	57	44	420	440
Western red cedar	5	112	159	167	3.9	310	26	45	309	59	25	421	453
Sawara cedar	10	113	164	173	2.2	314	27	39	315	61	25	441	453
Douglas fir	8	116	168	179	1.9	309	26	48	309	63	25	434	463
White lauan	8	123	168	172	1.1	306	27	50	305	64	26	427	447
Port Orford cedar	9	119	165	168	1.4	311	25	51	309	67	26	443	451
Japanese cedar	11	120	171	180	1.2	303	28	34	304	63	32	400	420
Paulownia	7	120	181	184	1.2	303	26	48	305	71	23	415	432
Japanese red pine	8	127	176	177	0.9	309	28	48	308	59	27	437	445
Eli ayanskya	8	125	161	163	1.0	311	27	49	310	65	26	429	443
Alaska cedar	7	127	171	174	1.2	311	25	50	309	66	25	431	440
Japanese cypress	8	131	167	172	1.9	314	26	49	316	24	428	430	434
Western hemlock	8	132	165	175	0.6	321	25	48	319	64	23	443	461
Sitka spruce	8	134	168	171	0.7	311	25	53	309	65	23	453	459

Superscripts:
[a)] With the exception of the symbol, W, the symbols used in this table correspond to those in Fig. 84, respectively.
[b)] Data including temperature values presented under the symbols, A, B, C and D, are measured separately at a value of ϕ of 0.625 K/min.
[c)] The unit of J : μg/min.

Symbols:
W. Percentage of the moisture content; A. Exothermic onset temperature; B. Onset temperature of the rapid oxidatively-heating reaction; C. Onset temperature of the reduction in weight; D. Percentage of the reduction in weight in the range of 90 ℃, by which the dehydration process of the sawdust of every wood species almost finishes, to 200 ℃ to the quantity of the sawdust tested; E. The first exothermic peak temperature; F. Exothermic peak height expressed in [cm] unit on the strip chart; G. The maximum rate of reduction in weight, which is expressed in terms of the angle from the temperature axis on the strip chart; H. Finish temperature of the charring reaction; I. Percentage of the reduction in weight up to the finish temperature of the charring reaction to the quantity of the sawdust tested; J. Rate of the reduction in weight of the char;[c)] K. The second exothermic peak temperature; L. Finish temperature of the process through which the sawdust of each wood species is reduced to ashes.

(2) Characteristics of the oxidatively-heating process of the sawdust of an average wood species charged in the draft cell, into which air is supplied, and subjected to the adiabatic oxidatively-heating test started from a T_s below about 180 ℃

Five oxidatively-heating processes, of 0.3 g each of five samples of the sawdust of Port Orford cedar charged each in the draft cell, into which air is supplied, and subjected each to the adiabatic oxidatively-heating test started from each T_s in the range of 164.8 to 173.3 ℃ with mutual intervals of 2 K, recorded each for the time, Δt, required for the temperature of each sample of the sawdust to increase by the definite value of ΔT of 1.25 K from the corresponding standard temperature, are presented in Fig. 85. The point marked with "**0**" on the time axis in Fig. 85 corresponds to the point of time "**s**" in Fig. 15 presented in **Section 3.4**.

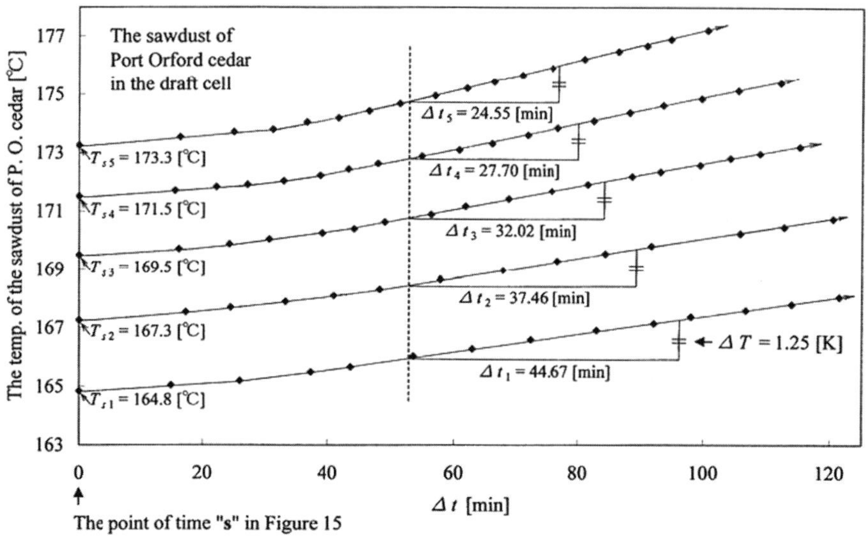

Figure 85. Five oxidatively-heating processes, of 0.3 g each of five samples of the sawdust of Port Orford cedar charged each in the draft cell, into which air is supplied, and subjected each to the adiabatic oxidatively-heating test started from each T_s in the range of 164.8 to 173.3 ℃ with mutual intervals of 2 K, recorded each for the time, Δt, required for the temperature of each sample of the sawdust to increase by the definite value of ΔT of 1.25 K from the corresponding standard temperature.

As shown in Fig. 85, as nitrogen gas in and around the sample cell is displaced by air for about 30 min after the start of the adiabatic oxidatively-heating test, the rate of the oxidatively-heating reaction of 2 cm^3 of a gas-permeable oxidatively-heating substance, including the sawdust of every wood species, charged in the draft cell, into which air is supplied, and subjected to the test started from a T_s is seen to accelerate gradually; but in due time, if the T_s is situated below about 180 ℃, the reaction comes to proceed at a virtually constant rate depending on the value of T_s.

This fact shows that the zeroth-order assumption holds for the rate of the oxidatively-heating reaction of the sawdust of every wood species at temperatures below about 180 ℃. At temperatures above about 180 ℃, however, the rate in general comes to accelerate gradually (Fig. 86).

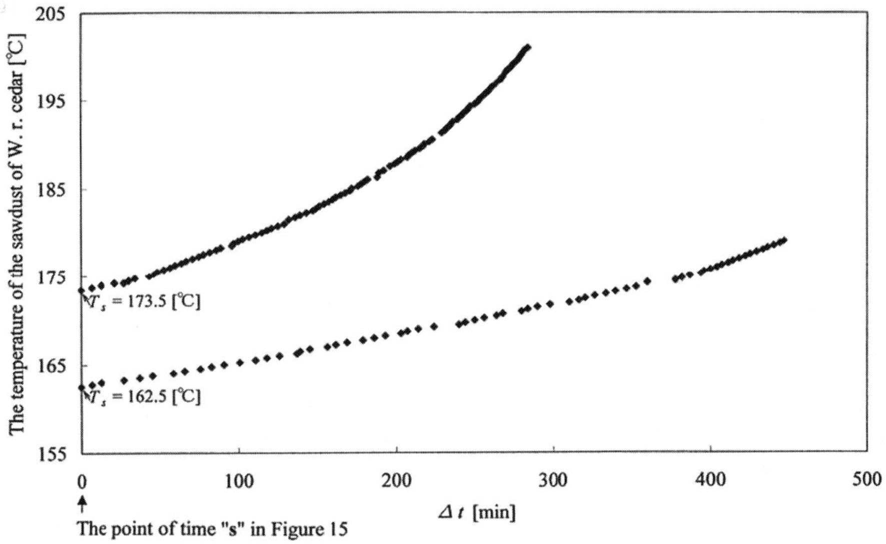

Figure 86. The difference between the oxidatively-heating process, of 0.3 g of the sawdust of Western red cedar charged in the draft cell, into which air is supplied, and subjected to the adiabatic oxidatively-heating test started from a T_s of 162.5 ℃, recorded until the temperature of the sawdust increases from 162.5 up to about 180 ℃, and, the process, of 0.3 g of the sawdust of the same kind charged in the draft cell, into which air is supplied, and subjected to the adiabatic oxidatively-heating test started from a T_s of 173.5 ℃, recorded until the temperature of the sawdust increases from 173.5 up to about 200 ℃.

The above findings are nearly in accord with Schliemann's report that the heterogeneous oxidatively-heating reaction of the zeroth order proceeds at temperatures below about 230 ℃, and, the heterogeneous oxidatively-heating reaction of the first order proceeds at temperatures ranging from about 230 to about 340 ℃ in the case of some wood [70]. Similar facts have been reported by Akita [67] and by Anthony *et al.* [68] as well.

An assumption has, therefore, been made herein that the gradient, dT/dt, of the linearly-rising part of the oxidatively-heating process or curve of 2 cm^3 of a gas-permeable oxidatively-heating substance, including the sawdust of every wood species, charged in the draft cell, into which air is supplied, and subjected to the adiabatic oxidatively-heating test started from a T_s below about 180 ℃ is proportional to the rate of the oxidatively-heating reaction of the substance at the T_s.

Thus, again as shown in Figure 85, it has been made an established rule in the case of a gas-permeable oxidatively-heating substance, including the sawdust of every wood species, that the time, Δt, required for the temperature of 2 cm^3 of the substance charged in the draft cell, into which air is supplied, and subjected to the adiabatic oxidatively-heating test started from a T_s below about 180 ℃ to increase by the definite value of ΔT of 1.25 K from the corresponding standard temperature is determined on the linearly-rising part of the oxidatively-heating process or curve of the substance.

In this connection, a symbol, such as **ϕ[a]**, which appears in Figures, ranging in Figure Number from 89 to 115, denotes the gradient of the linearly-rising part of the oxidatively-heating process or curve, of a sawdust "**a**", charged in the draft cell, into which air (oxygen gas in Fig. 89) is supplied, and subjected to the adiabatic oxidatively-heating test started from a T_s near 150 ℃ (140 ℃ for the sawdust of red lauan), recorded in temperature increments of 3 K from the corresponding standard temperature. However, a ratio, such as **ϕ[a]/ϕ[b]**, does not denote the strict ratio of a certain chemical property of the sawdust "**a**" to the property of the sawdust "**b**", but, does only the seeming and/or approximate ratio.

8.3.2 Effects of three kinds of gases on the individual oxidatively-heating properties of the sawdust of red lauan and that of Japanese cedar

(1) TG-DTA

Effects of three kinds of gases, *i.e.*, air, nitrogen gas and oxygen gas, on the individual DTA curves of the sawdust of red lauan and that of Japanese cedar are shown in Figs. 87 and 88, respectively. The figures attached to each curve denote the exothermic peak temperatures expressed each in ℃. The same is true of all the DTA curves presented herein. In this connection, the pattern of the TG curve of the sawdust of every wood species, including red lauan and Japanese cedar, does not depend remarkably on wood species, so that it is omitted herein, in principle, to present the TG curve of the sawdust of every wood species.

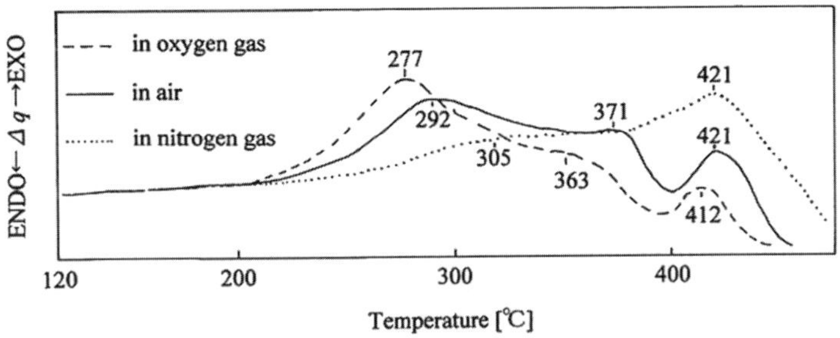

Figure 87. Effects of three kinds of gases on the DTA curve of the sawdust of red lauan.

The sawdust of red lauan has a remarkable feature that it affords three exothermic peaks in the three DTA curves recorded each in the three kinds of gases, respectively. It is clear in these three DTA curves that the value of the first exothermic peak temperature and that of the second exothermic peak temperature lower in the order of "in nitrogen gas", "in air" and "in oxygen gas", respectively. The third exothermic peaks in the three DTA curves, however, appear at temperatures near 420 ℃, irrespective of kind of gas, respectively. The latter fact may suggest that this peak does not arise on account of the surface oxidation reaction of the char, but on account of some heating reaction occurring in the interior of the char.

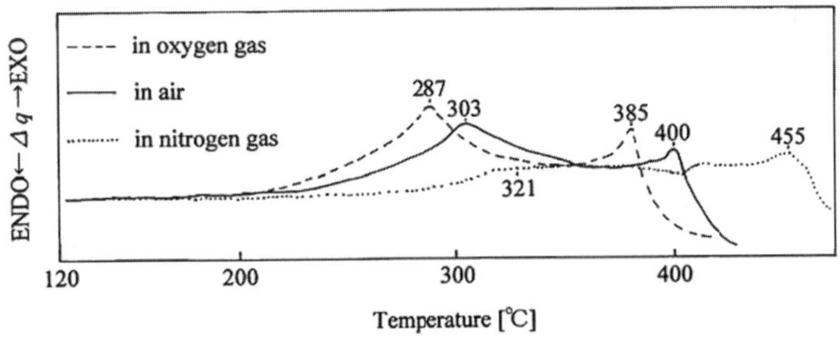

Figure 88. Effects of three kinds of gases on the DTA curve of the sawdust of Japanese cedar.

Judging from the oxidatively-heating property up to 200 ℃ and the size of the whole exothermic peak, both of which are seen in Fig. 88, Japanese cedar is thought to be one of wood species harder to heat oxidatively than red lauan. However, both the maximum rate of reduction in weight and the percentage of reduction in weight up to the finish temperature of the charring reaction to the quantity of the sawdust tested, of the sawdust of Japanese cedar, are larger than the corresponding those of the sawdust of red lauan. Synthesizing these informations, it may be possible to predict that the wood of red lauan is easier to oxidize or to heat oxidatively than that of Japanese cedar; but, once they catch fire, the wood of Japanese cedar will make probably bigger or stronger flames than that of red lauan, because the gasifying rate of the wood of Japanese cedar, *i.e.*, the size of flame per unit mass per unit time which it produces on burning, is larger than the rate of red lauan.

A noteworthy fact here is that the above two kinds of sawdusts decompose exothermically even in nitrogen gas at temperatures in excess of about 180 ℃, respectively. Akita reported that, when heated, some self-heating phenomena were observed in the interior of a wood block, *i.e.*, under the conditions of the absence of gaseous oxygen [67]. That is, he is understood to have described a different aspect of the same thing. Wood is regarded as a compact aggregate of polymers composed each of C, H and O,* so that, when heated up to temperatures near 200 ℃, it is thought to begin to decompose oxidatively, *i.e.*, exothermically, by means of its own oxygen atoms, even if gaseous oxygen is not present in the atmosphere. The oxidatively-heating properties of the two kinds of sawdusts, which are each shown in Figs. 87 and 88, are, therefore, thought to reflect not only the surface oxidation reaction of the sawdust or the char of either wood species but also the oxidative decomposition reaction occurring in the interior in parallel with the surface oxidation reaction.

Besides, although the onset temperature of rapid reduction in weight of the sawdust of either wood species in oxygen gas is certainly slightly lower than the temperature in nitrogen gas, there is little difference between the two temperatures in either case. Moreover, the percentage of reduction in weight up to the finish temperature of the charring reaction to the quantity of the sawdust tested takes almost the same value of nearly 40 %, irrespective of kind of gas.** Furthermore, it is shown that the rate of reduction in weight of the char of either wood species in oxygen gas is almost the same as that in air. That is, these facts are thought to suggest that the rate-determining step in the reaction sequence, by which the char of either wood species reduces in weight, is not the surface oxidation reaction but the oxidative decomposition reaction occurring in the

---

* There exists a paper in which the elemental composition of a wood is expressed as $C_{42}H_{60}O_{28}$ [71].

** According to elemental analysis of the char of some wood species, however, it is ascertained that the content of hydrogen and that of oxygen in the char formed in oxygen gas are slightly less than the corresponding those in the char formed in nitrogen gas, respectively.

interior of the char. In brief, the total information obtained above is thought to suggest that gaseous oxygen oxidizes only the thermal degradation products extruded out of the interior of the charring wood on and near the surface, without penetrating into the interior, in the oxidative decomposition reaction of every wood in the presence of gaseous oxygen.

(2) The adiabatic oxidatively-heating test

It is shown in Fig. 89 that the ratio of the gradient of the oxidatively-heating process or curve, of the sawdust of Japanese cedar charged in the draft cell, into which oxygen gas is supplied, and subjected to the adiabatic oxidatively-heating test started from a T_s near 150 ℃, recorded in temperature increments of 3 K from the corresponding standard temperature, to, the gradient of the curve of the sawdust of the same wood species placed under the same conditions as the former, except that air is supplied to the latter, is 4.2:1. This ratio is reasonably close to the ratio of the total pressure of pure oxygen gas at atmospheric pressure to the partial pressure of oxygen gas in air, *i.e.*, 100:21 (= 4.76:1).

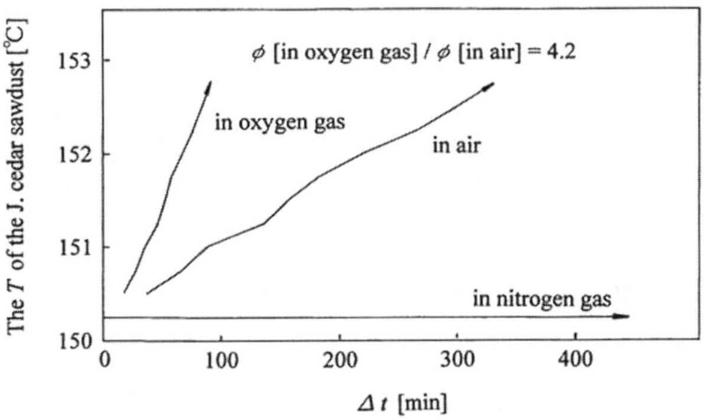

Figure 89. Ratio of the gradient of the oxidatively-heating curve, of the sawdust of Japanese cedar charged in the draft cell, into which oxygen gas is supplied, and subjected to the adiabatic oxidatively-heating test started from a T_s near 150 ℃, recorded in temperature increments of 3 K from the corresponding standard temperature, to, the gradient of the curve of the sawdust of the same wood species placed under the same conditions as the former, except that air is supplied to the latter.

8.3.3 Effect of the sawdust size on the individual oxidatively-heating properties of the three kinds of sawdusts

(1) TG-DTA

Effect of the sawdust size on the DTA curve of the sawdust of red lauan is shown in Fig. 90.

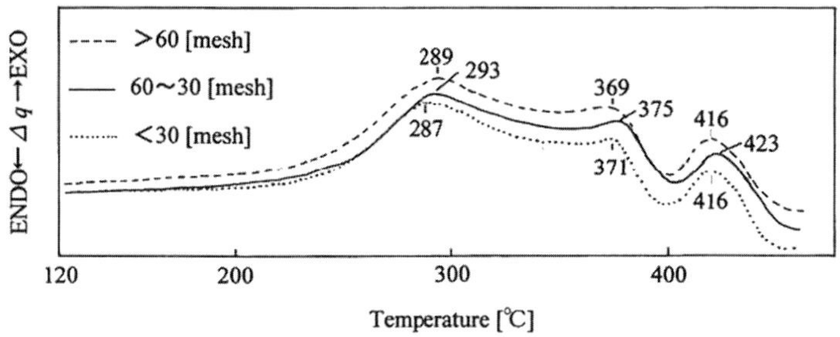

Figure 90. Effect of the sawdust size on the DTA curve of the sawdust of red lauan.

It is seen in Fig. 90 that the finer the sawdust, the larger becomes the exothermic peak effected in thermal analysis. This phenomenon reflects as a matter of course that the oxidatively-heating rate of a sawdust increases with increasing the surface area per unit mass of the sawdust.

(2) The adiabatic oxidatively-heating test

The effect of the sawdust size on the gradient of the oxidatively-heating curve, of the sawdust of Japanese cedar charged in the draft cell, into which air is supplied, and subjected to the adiabatic oxidatively-heating test started from a T_s near 150 ℃, recorded in temperature increments of 3 K from the corresponding standard temperature, and, the effect of the same kind on the gradient of the oxidatively-heating curve of the sawdust of Port Orford cedar placed under the same conditions as the former, are shown in Figs. 91 and 92, respectively.

It is significant here that the gradient of the oxidatively-heating curve of the sawdust of Japanese cedar finer than 60 mesh subjected to the adiabatic oxidatively-heating test started from a T_s near 150 ℃ is almost the same as that of the curve of the sawdust, of the same wood species, of 60～30 mesh placed under the same conditions as the former. On the other hand, it is certain in either case that the gradient of the oxidatively-heating curve of a sawdust coarser than 30 mesh subjected to the test started from a T_s near 150 ℃ is distinctly smaller than that of the curve of the sawdust, of the same wood species, finer than 30 mesh placed under the same conditions as the former.

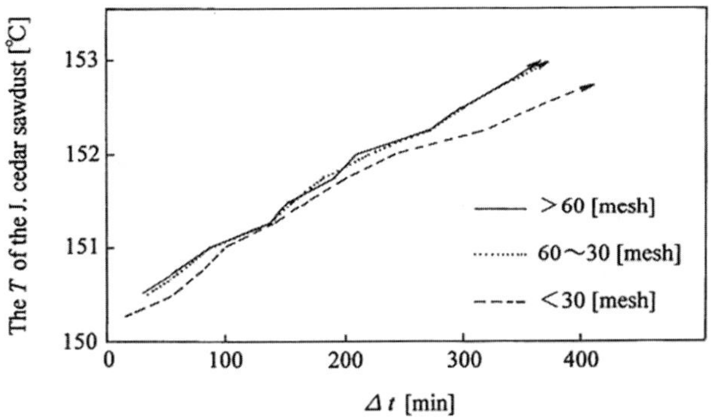

Figure 91. Effect of the sawdust size on the gradient of the oxidatively-heating curve, of the sawdust of Japanese cedar charged in the draft cell, into which air is supplied, and subjected to the adiabatic oxidatively-heating test started from a T_s near 150 ℃, recorded in temperature increments of 3 K from the corresponding standard temperature.

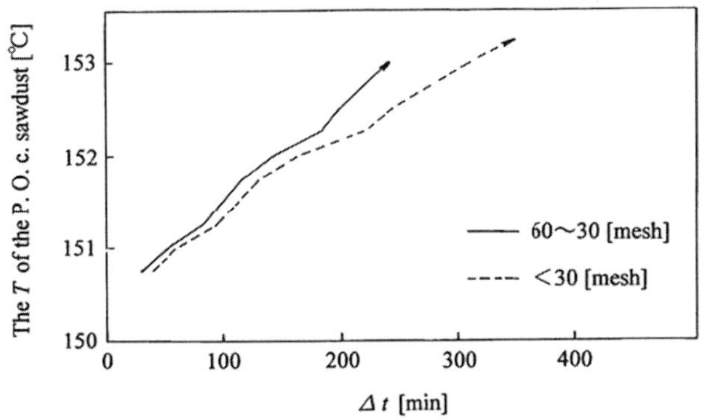

Figure 92. Effect of the sawdust size on the gradient of the oxidatively-heating curve, of the sawdust of Port Orford cedar charged in the draft cell, into which air is supplied, and subjected to the adiabatic oxidatively-heating test started from a T_s near 150 ℃, recorded in temperature increments of 3 K from the corresponding standard temperature.

8.3.4 Comparison of the oxidatively-heating property of the sawdust of a fresh lumber of Japanese cypress with that of the sawdust of an old lumber of the same wood species

(1) TG-DTA

Comparison of the DTA curve of the sawdust of a fresh lumber of Japanese cypress with that of the sawdust of an old lumber of the same wood species, which has been used as a pillar in a room for about 20 years, is given in Fig. 93.

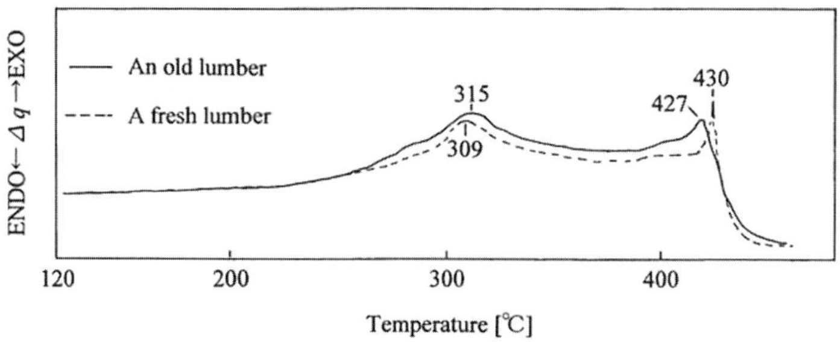

Figure 93. Comparison of the DTA curve of the sawdust of a fresh lumber of Japanese cypress with that of the sawdust of an old lumber of the same wood species.

As to Japanese cypress, it is seen that the calorific value of the sawdust of the old lumber is a little larger than that of the sawdust of the fresh lumber.

(2) The adiabatic oxidatively-heating test

Comparison of the oxidatively-heating curve, of the sawdust of a fresh lumber of Japanese cypress charged in the draft cell, into which air is supplied, and subjected to the adiabatic oxidatively-heating test started from a T_s near 150 ℃, recorded in temperature increments of 3 K from the corresponding standard temperature, with, the oxidatively-heating curve of the sawdust of an old lumber of the same wood species placed under the same conditions as the former, is given in Fig. 94.

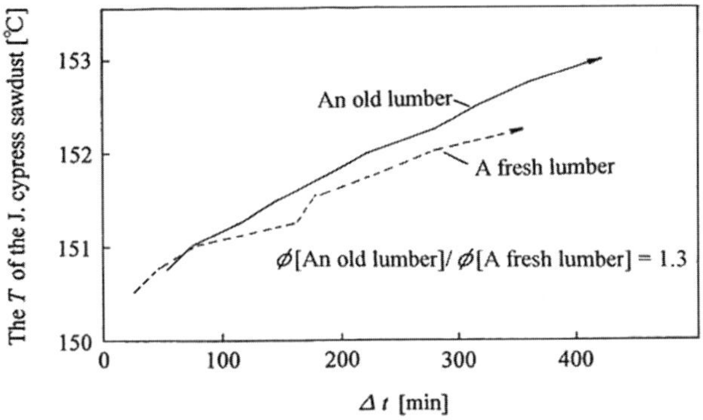

Figure 94. Comparison of the oxidatively-heating curve, of the sawdust of a fresh lumber of Japanese cypress charged in the draft cell, into which air is supplied, and subjected to the adiabatic oxidatively-heating test started from a T_s near 150 ℃, recorded in temperature increments of 3 K from the corresponding standard temperature, with, the oxidatively-heating curve of the sawdust of an old lumber of the same wood species placed under the same conditions as the former.

It is shown in Fig. 94 as well that the sawdust of the old lumber is a little more liable to heat oxidatively than that of the fresh one.

8.3.5 Comparison of the oxidatively-heating property of the sawdust of the bark made out of a tree of paulownia with that of the sawdust of the wood made out of the same tree, and, the comparison of the same kind regarding a tree of zelkova

(1) TG-DTA

Comparison of the DTA curve of the sawdust of the bark made out of a tree of paulownia with that of the sawdust of the wood made out of the same tree, and, the comparison of the same kind regarding a tree of zelkova are presented in Figs. 95 and 96, respectively.

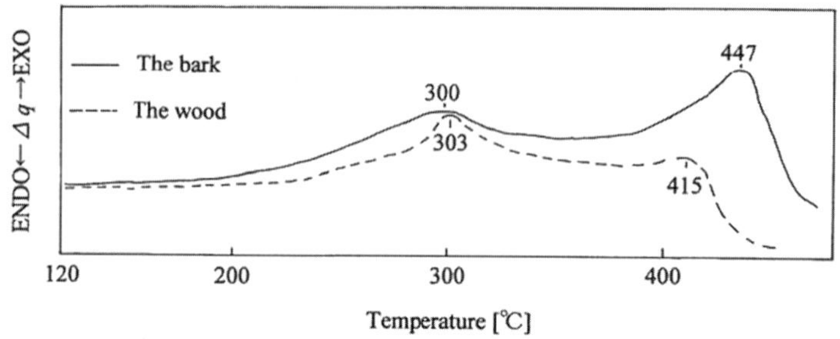

Figure 95. Comparison of the DTA curve of the sawdust of the bark made out of a tree of paulownia with that of the sawdust of the wood made out of the same tree.

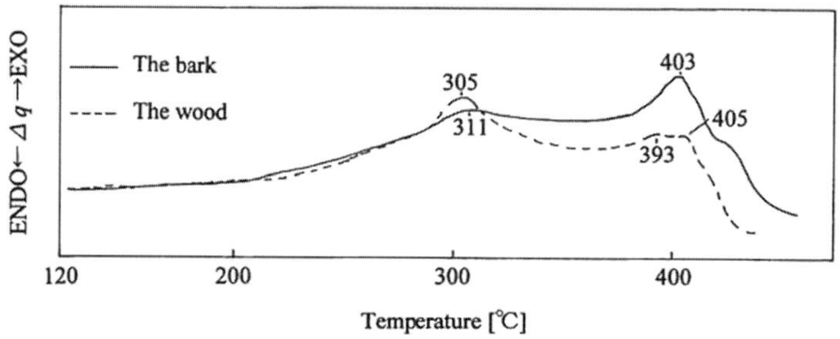

Figure 96. Comparison of the DTA curve of the sawdust of the bark made out of a tree of zelkova with that of the sawdust of the wood made out of the same tree.

It is seen in either case that the calorific value of the sawdust of the bark is larger than that of the sawdust of the wood made out of the same tree.

(2) The adiabatic oxidatively-heating test

Comparison of the oxidatively-heating curve, of the sawdust of the bark made out of a tree of paulownia and charged in the draft cell, into which air is supplied, and subjected to the adiabatic oxidatively-heating test started from a T_s near 150 ℃, recorded in temperature increments of 3 K from the corresponding standard temperature, with, the oxidatively-heating curve, of the sawdust of the wood made out of the same tree and placed under the same conditions as the former, and, the comparison of the same kind regarding a tree of zelkova are shown in Figs. 97 and 98, respectively.

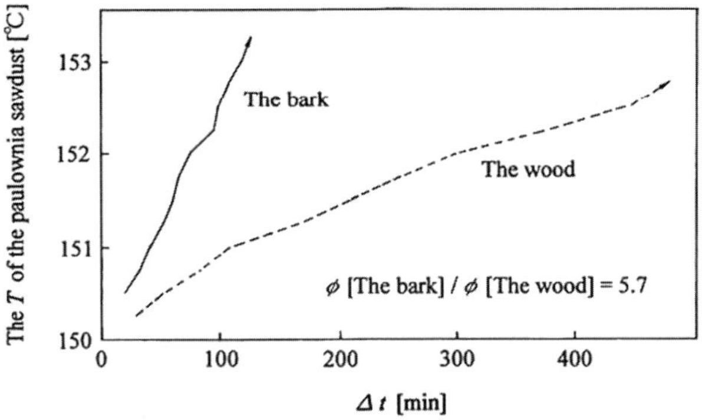

Figure 97. Comparison of the oxidatively-heating curve, of the sawdust of the bark made out of a tree of paulownia and charged in the draft cell, into which air is supplied, and subjected to the adiabatic oxidatively-heating test started from a T_s near 150 ℃, recorded in temperature increments of 3 K from the corresponding standard temperature, with, the oxidatively-heating curve, of the sawdust of the wood made out of the same tree and placed under the same conditions as the former.

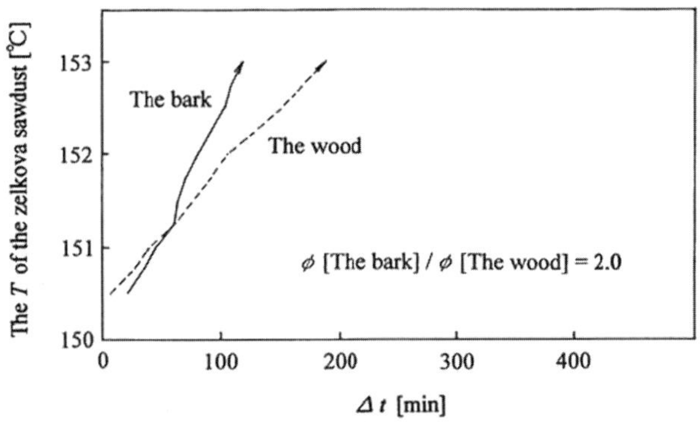

Figure 98. Comparison of the oxidatively-heating curve, of the sawdust of the bark made out of a tree of zelkova and charged in the draft cell, into which air is supplied, and subjected to the adiabatic oxidatively-heating test started from a T_s near 150 ℃, recorded in temperature increments of 3 K from the corresponding standard temperature, with, the oxidatively-heating curve, of the sawdust of the wood made out of the same tree and placed under the same conditions as the former.

It has been ascertained, in result, that the sawdust of the bark is far more liable to heat oxidatively than that of the wood of the same tree. Schliemann also reported the same fact regarding the sawdust of Kiefernholz (German pine) [70].

8.3.6 Difference, in the oxidatively-heating property, among the sawdust of the knot, that of the sapwood and that of the heartwood, made each out of an old lumber of Japanese cypress

(1) TG-DTA

The difference, in the DTA curve, among the sawdust of the knot, that of the sapwood and that of the heartwood, made each out of an old lumber of Japanese cypress, is presented in Fig. 99.

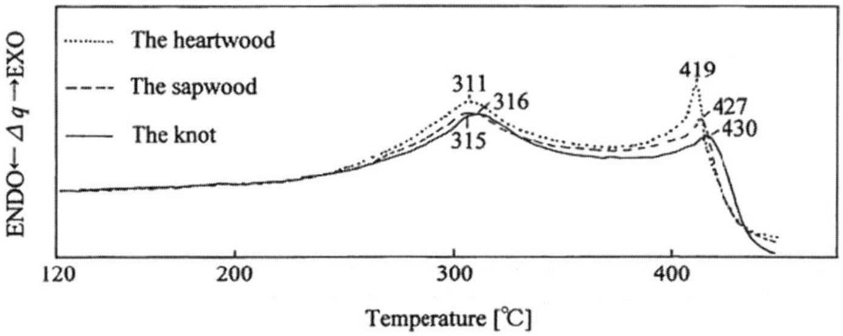

Figure 99. Difference, in the DTA curve, among the sawdust of the knot, that of the sapwood and that of the heartwood, made each out of an old lumber of Japanese cypress.

As to the old lumber of Japanese cypress, it is shown that the calorific value increases in the order of the sawdust of the knot, that of the sapwood and that of the heartwood.

(2) The adiabatic oxidatively-heating test

The difference, in the oxidatively-heating curve, among the sawdust of the knot, that of the sapwood and that of the heartwood, made each out of an old lumber of Japanese cypress and charged each in the draft cell, into which air is supplied, and subjected each to the adiabatic oxidatively-heating test started each from a T_s near 150 ℃, recorded each in temperature increments of 3 K from the corresponding standard temperature, is shown in Fig. 100.

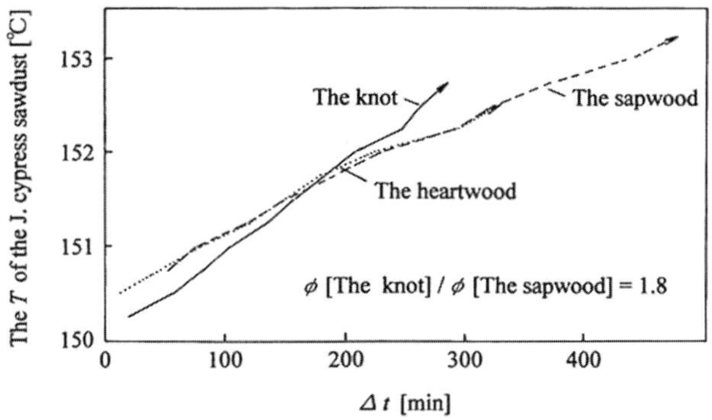

Figure 100. Difference, in the oxidatively-heating curve, among the sawdust of the knot, that of the sapwood and that of the heartwood, made each out of an old lumber of Japanese cypress and charged each in the draft cell, into which air is supplied, and subjected each to the adiabatic oxidatively-heating test started each from a T_s near 150 ℃, recorded each in temperature increments of 3 K from the corresponding standard temperature.

It has been clarified, in result, that, when maintained at a temperature near 150 ℃ in air, the sawdust of the knot heats oxidatively faster than the other two sawdusts, and, the latter two sawdusts heats oxidatively at almost the same rate.

Synthesizing the total information obtained above, it follows that three of the old lumber, the bark and the knot are appropriate for the kindlings, respectively; but, once some of them catches fire, the heartwood is fit to make the flame bigger or stronger.

8.3.7 Comparison of the oxidatively-heating property of the soot which arises from the incineration of the sawdust of Western hemlock and accumulates in the soot collector set up at the top of the incinerator, with, the oxidatively-heating property of the sawdust of Western hemlock

Most woodworking plants are each equipped with some incinerators or boilers to dispose of wood chips or sawdusts produced in the manufacturing processes. A soot collector is usually set up at the top of the incinerator or the boiler in order to trap the soot arising out of the incinerator from the viewpoint of the pollution control.

In general, the soot is known to be very inflammable. The oxidatively-heating property of the soot, which arises from the incineration of the sawdust of Western hemlock and accumulates in the soot collector set up at the top of the incinerator, has thus been compared with the oxidatively-heating property of the sawdust of Western hemlock.

(1) TG-DTA

Comparison of the DTA curve of the soot which arises from the incineration of the sawdust of Western hemlock and accumulates in the soot collector set up at the top of the incinerator, with, the DTA curve of the sawdust of Western hemlock is presented in Fig. 101.

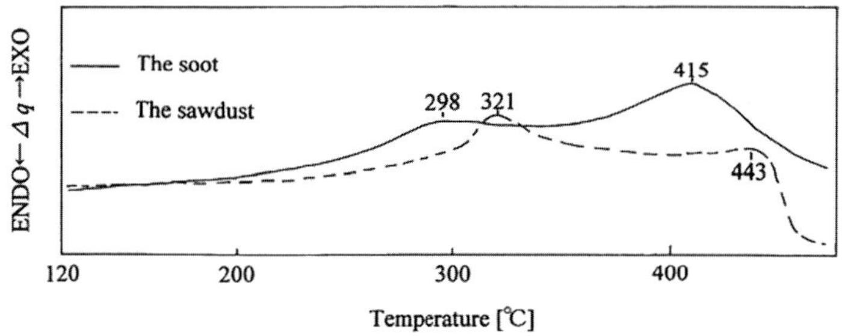

Figure 101. Comparison of the DTA curve of the soot which arises from the incineration of the sawdust of Western hemlock and accumulates in the soot collector set up at the top of the incinerator, with, the DTA curve of the sawdust of Western hemlock.

It is shown in Fig. 101 that the calorific value of the soot is far larger than that of the sawdust of Western hemlock.

(2) The adiabatic oxidatively-heating test

It is shown in Fig. 102 that the soot heats oxidatively about 4.4 times as fast as the sawdust of Western hemlock. That is, it has been proved that the soot is very inflammable. It thus follows that sufficient care should be taken to handle every soot.

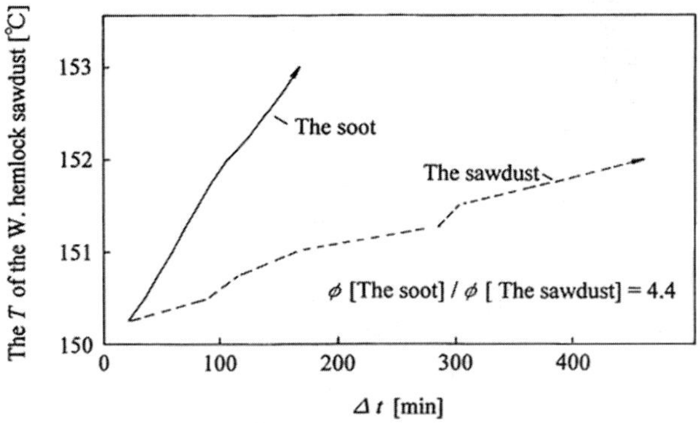

Figure 102. Comparison of the oxidatively-heating curve, of the soot, which arises from the incineration of the sawdust of Western hemlock and accumulates in the soot collector set up at the top of the incinerator and is charged in the draft cell, into which air is supplied, and is subjected to the adiabatic oxidatively-heating test started from a T_s near 150 ℃, recorded in temperature increments of 3 K from the corresponding standard temperature, with, the oxidatively-heating curve of the sawdust of Western hemlock placed under the same conditions as the former.

8.3.8 Effects of five kinds of metals or metal oxides on the individual oxidatively-heating properties of the sawdust of red lauan and that of Japanese cedar

The effects of five kinds of metals or metallic oxides, *i.e.*, copper (Cu), cupric oxide (CuO), iron (Fe), ferric oxide (Fe_2O_3) and platinum (Pt), on the individual oxidatively-heating properties of the sawdust of red lauan and that of Japanese cedar have been examined, on the one hand, by TG-DTA performed in air and, on the other hand, by the adiabatic oxidatively-heating test, which is performed for the sawdust of red lauan in air at a T_s near 140 ℃ and for the sawdust of Japanese cedar in air at a T_s near 150 ℃, respectively.

Cu, CuO, Fe and Fe_2O_3 are all powdery and of the A. C. S. reagent grade. The sample of Pt alone is, however, prepared by cutting out of a platinum strip, 0.1 mm in thickness, into fragments as small as possible with a nipper.

It has been ascertained, in result, that, as to the above five kinds of metals or metallic oxides, the effects on the individual oxidatively-heating properties of the two kinds of sawdusts do not depend noticeably on wood species, respectively.

(1) TG-DTA

The ratio of the sample quantity of the sawdust of either wood species to that of each metal, or metallic oxide, added to the sawdust is 5 mg to 5 mg, except that the sample quantity of Pt fragments is 33 mg.

a) Cu powder

The DTA curve of a mixture of the sawdust of red lauan and Cu powder, and, that of a mixture of the sawdust of Japanese cedar and Cu powder are shown in Figs. 103 and 104, respectively.

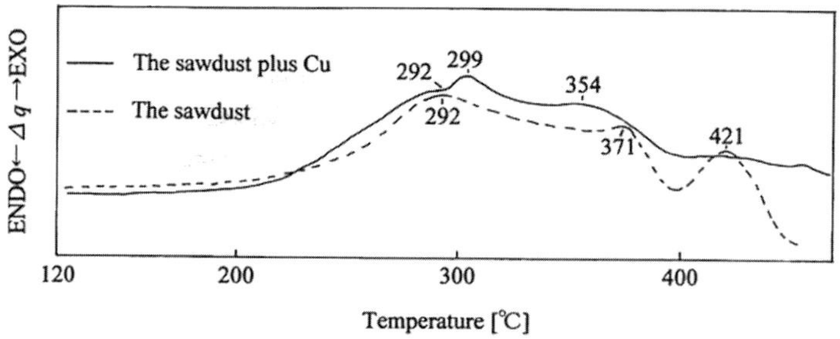

Figure 103. The DTA curve of a mixture of 5 mg of the sawdust of red lauan and 5 mg of Cu powder.

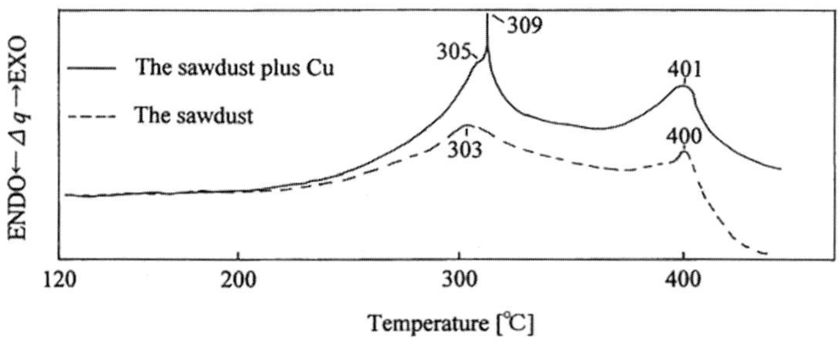

Figure 104. The DTA curve of a mixture of 5 mg of the sawdust of Japanese cedar and 5 mg of Cu powder.

It is seen that the oxidative decomposition reaction, or the oxidatively-heating reaction, of the sawdust of either wood species is promoted remarkably in the presence of Cu powder. In particular, the effect of Cu powder on the oxidatively-heating property of the sawdust of either wood species is characterized by a new exothermic peak appearing immediately after the first exothermic peak. For an experimental fact relevant to this, refer to a description, which is given in **(2)** of the present subsection, regarding the catalytic action of Cu powder on the oxidatively-heating reaction of the sawdust of either wood species. It is seen in the DTA curve of the mixture of the sawdust of red lauan and Cu powder that the sawdust is reduced to ashes by 390 ℃ and the third exothermic peak, which arises at about 420 ℃ in the absence of Cu powder, disappears nearly completely. In this connection, it is ascertained by the X-ray powder method that, when Cu powder is heated in air, Cu_2O is formed first on the surfaces of Cu particles at temperatures below 200 ℃, Cu_2O thus formed, then, changes gradually into CuO at temperatures above 300 ℃.

In any event, it is certain that, if brass or bronze powder as well as Cu powder is brought into contact with any sawdust, the oxidatively-heating reaction of the sawdust will be promoted remarkably.

b) CuO powder

The DTA curve of a mixture of the sawdust of red lauan and CuO powder, and, that of a mixture of the sawdust of Japanese cedar and CuO powder are shown in Figs. 105 and 106, respectively.

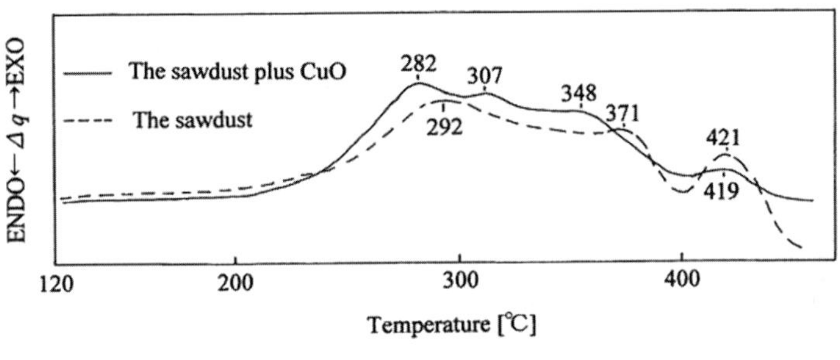

Figure 105. The DTA curve of a mixture of 5 mg of the sawdust of red lauan and 5 mg of CuO powder.

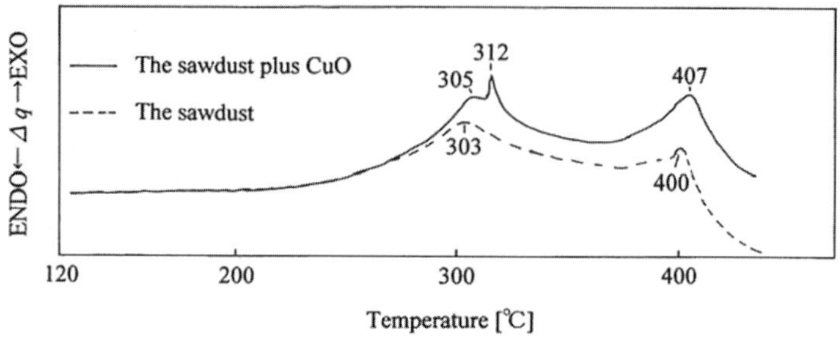

Figure 106. The DTA curve of a mixture of 5 mg of the sawdust of Japanese cedar and 5 mg of CuO powder.

It is known that CuO also catalyzes the oxidation reaction of organic substances by gaseous oxygen. According to the individual results of TG performed for the two kinds of mixtures above referred to, it is seen that the maximum rate of reduction in weight of each sawdust and the rate of reduction in weight of each char increases certainly in the presence of CuO powder; but, such effects cannot be seen noticeably at temperatures below 200 ℃. The similar tendency is observed in the adiabatic oxidatively-heating tests, performed each for the two kinds of mixtures above referred to, as well. Nevertheless, however, the action of CuO powder to catalyze the oxidatively-heating reaction of the sawdust of a wood species, such as Japanese cedar, which is relatively hard to heat oxidatively, seems to be more marked than the action to catalyze the oxidatively-heating reaction of the sawdust of a wood species, such as red lauan, which is relatively easy to heat oxidatively.

The catalytic action of CuO powder on the oxidatively-heating reaction of the sawdust of either wood species has thus been studied further by performing TG-DTA for a mixture of 5 mg of fragments of the Whatman filter paper, which is thought to include a very slight hemicellulose besides cellulose as the main component, and 5 mg of CuO (Fig. 107). The fragments of the Whatman filter paper were prepared by dieing a sheet of the Whatman filter paper to bits, 3 mm in diameter each.

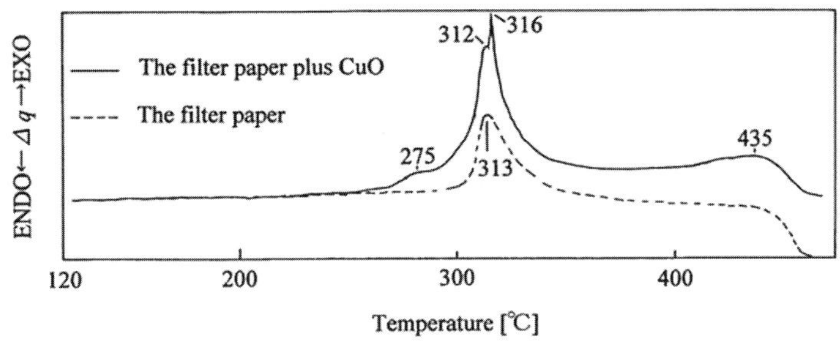

Figure 107. The DTA curve of a mixture of 5 mg of fragments of the Whatman filter paper and 5 mg of CuO powder.

It has been observed, in result, that a small exothermic peak, which appears at 275 ℃ and is thought to be afforded by the oxidatively-heating reaction of hemicellulose*, arises besides a large exothermic peak, which, no matter whether CuO powder exists or not, appears at 312-313 ℃ and is thought to be afforded by the charring reaction of cellulose. In this connection, it has been inferred from the TG curve that the exothermic peak appearing at 316 ℃ is afforded by the oxidatively-heating reaction of the char of cellulose.

It is thus inferred that, when CuO powder coexists with the sawdust of red lauan, which is considered to be one of wood species including hemicellulose rather in excess, hemicellulose in the sawdust of red lauan heats oxidatively at temperatures lower than cellulose, with the result that a large exothermic peak, which appears at about 290 ℃ in the absence of CuO powder, divides into two peaks; and in the first place, an exothermic peak afforded by the oxidatively-heating reaction of hemicellulose appears at about 280 ℃; in the meantime, cellulose remains as it is up to higher temperatures and then gives independently an exothermic peak afforded by its own oxidatively-heating reaction at about 310 ℃ (Fig. 105). Such being the case, it is expected that, even if CuO powder coexists with the sawdust of wood species relatively hard to heat oxidatively, the first exothermic peak, which appears at about 300 ℃ in the absence of CuO powder, does not shift to the low temperature side in the DTA curve, because the quantity of hemicellulose included in the sawdust is not so much (Fig. 106).

* Every wood is composed of three main components, *i.e.*, cellulose, hemicellulose and lignin. And, hemicellulose is thought to remain slightly in the Whatman filter paper.

c) Fe powder and Fe_2O_3 powder

The oxidatively-heating reaction of the sawdust of red lauan is not influenced appreciably in the presence of Fe and Fe_2O_3 powder over the whole temperature range of TG-DTA. The oxidatively-heating reaction of the sawdust of Japanese cedar is also not influenced in the presence of either substance. DTA curves concerned are presented in Figs. from 108 to 111, respectively.

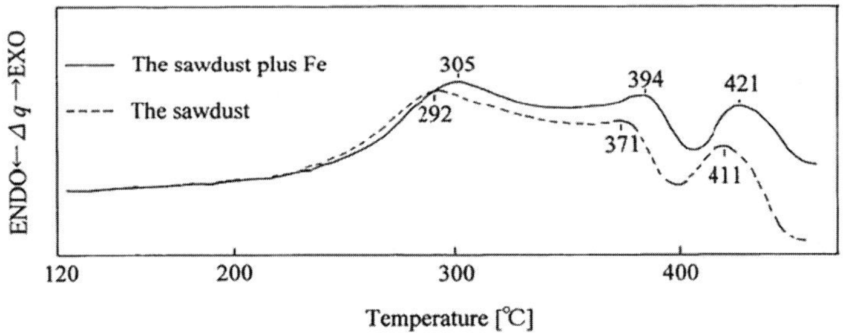

Figure 108. The DTA curve of a mixture of 5 mg of the sawdust of red lauan and 5 [mg] of Fe powder.

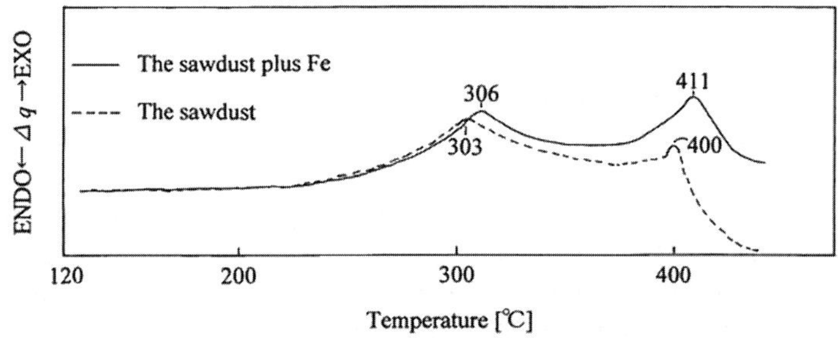

Figure 109. The DTA curve of a mixture of 5 mg of the sawdust of Japanese cedar and 5 mg of Fe powder.

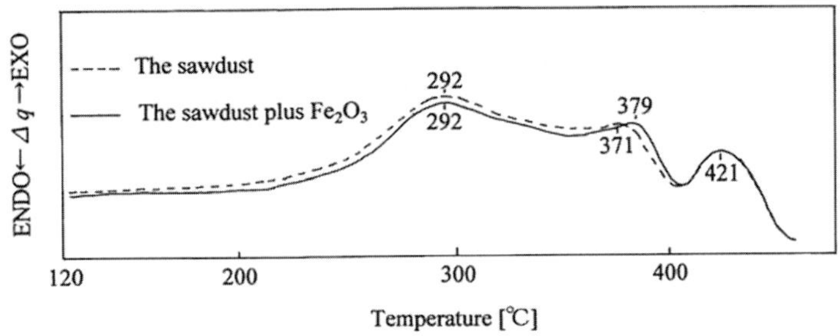

Figure 110. The DTA curve of a mixture of 5 mg of the sawdust of red lauan and 5 mg of Fe_2O_3 powder.

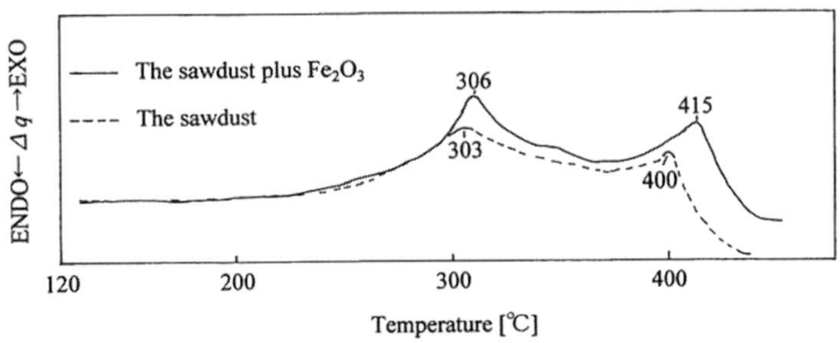

Figure 111. The DTA curve of a mixture of 5 mg of the sawdust of Japanese cedar and 5 mg of Fe_2O_3 powder.

It may thus be possible to predict that, even if iron powder or rusted iron arising from woodworking implements made of iron, such as sawing machines, is mixed into some one of the sawdusts above referred to, the liability of the sawdust to spontaneous ignition will not be promoted.

d) Pt fragments

The DTA curve of a mixture of the sawdust of red lauan and Pt fragments, and, that of a mixture of the sawdust of Japanese cedar and Pt fragments are shown in Figs. 112 and 113, respectively.

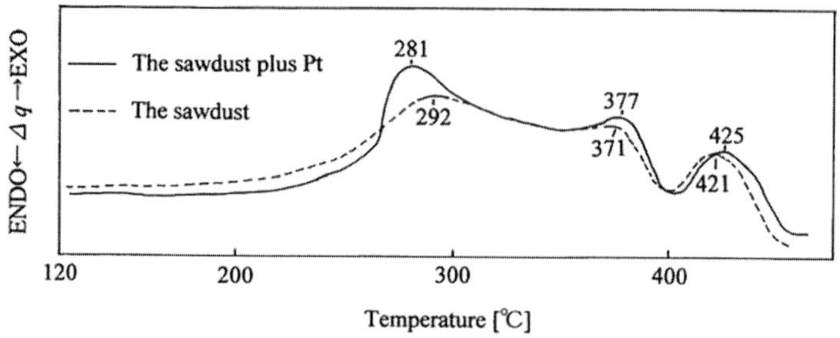

Figure 112. The DTA curve of a mixture of 5 mg of the sawdust of red lauan and 33 mg of Pt fragments.

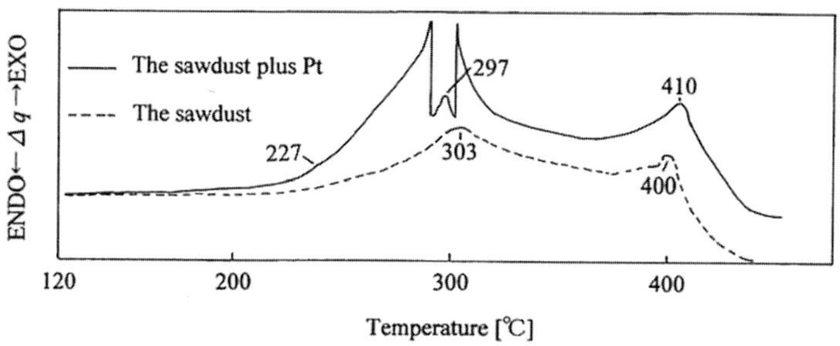

Figure 113. The DTA curve of a mixture of 5 mg of the sawdust of Japanese cedar and 33 mg of Pt fragments.

It is obvious in Figs. 112 and 113 that, once the rapid oxidatively-heating reaction of the sawdust of either wood species begins at temperatures above 200 ℃, Pt promotes the reaction remarkably; that is, the first exothermic peak shifts to the low temperature side and becomes larger besides.

(2) The adiabatic oxidatively-heating test

The individual effects of the five kinds of metals or metallic oxides, *i.e.*, Cu powder, CuO powder, Fe powder, Fe_2O_3 powder and Pt fragments, on the gradient of the oxidatively-heating curve, of the sawdust of red lauan charged in the draft cell, into which air is supplied, and subjected to the adiabatic oxidatively-heating test started from a T_s near 140 ℃, recorded in temperature increments of 3 K from the corresponding standard temperature, and, the individual effects of the same kind on the gradient of the oxidatively-heating curve of the sawdust of Japanese cedar placed under the same conditions as the former, except that the test for the latter is started from a T_s near 150 ℃, are shown in Figs. 114 and 115, respectively.

The ratio of the quantity of the sawdust of either wood species to that of each metal, or metallic oxide, added to the sawdust is 0.3 g to 0.1 g.

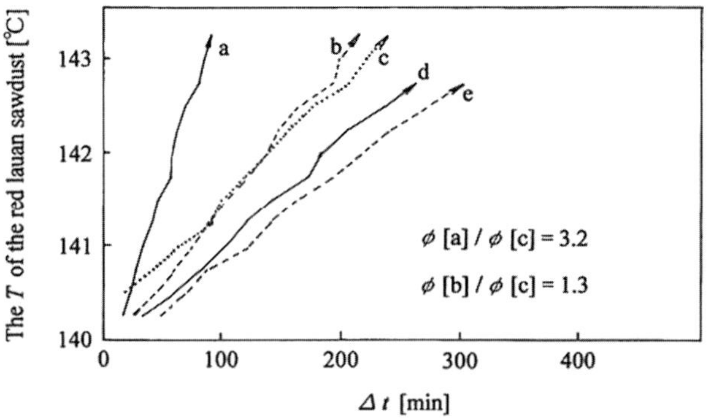

Figure 114. The individual effects of the five kinds of metals or metallic oxides, *i.e.*, Cu powder, CuO powder, Fe powder, Fe_2O_3 powder and Pt fragments, on the gradient of the oxidatively-heating curve, of the sawdust of red lauan charged in the draft cell, into which air is supplied, and subjected to the adiabatic oxidatively-heating test started from at a T_s near 140 ℃, recorded in temperature increments of 3 K from the corresponding standard temperature.

a. A mixture of the sawdust of red lauan and Cu powder; **b**. A mixture of the sawdust of red lauan and CuO powder; **c**. The sawdust of red lauan with no additive, and, a mixture of the sawdust of red lauan and Pt fragments; **d**. A mixture of the sawdust of red lauan and Fe powder; **e**. A mixture of the sawdust of red lauan and Fe_2O_3 powder.

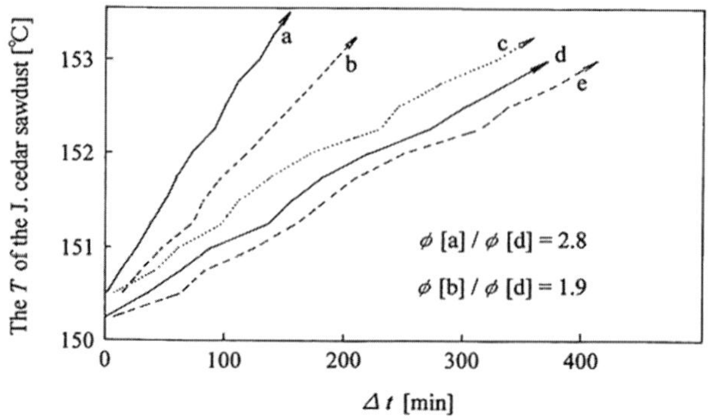

Figure 115. The individual effects of the five kinds of metals or metallic oxides, *i.e.*, Cu powder, CuO powder, Fe powder, Fe_2O_3 powder and Pt fragments, on the gradient of the oxidatively-heating curve, of the sawdust of Japanese cedar charged in the draft cell, into which air is supplied, and subjected to the adiabatic oxidatively-heating test started from a T_s near 150 ℃, recorded in temperature increments of 3 K from the corresponding standard temperature.
a. A mixture of the sawdust of Japanese cedar and Cu powder; **b**. A mixture of the sawdust of Japanese cedar and CuO powder; **c**. A mixture of the sawdust of Japanese cedar and Fe powder; **d**. The sawdust of Japanese cedar with no additive, and, a mixture of the sawdust of Japanese cedar and Pt fragments; **e**. A mixture of the sawdust of Japanese cedar and Fe_2O_3 powder.

It is noticeable in either case that the gradient of the oxidatively-heating curve of the sawdust of either wood species in the presence of Cu powder is about three times as large as that of the curve of the sawdust with no additive. Cu is thought to catalyze the oxidatively-heating reaction of the sawdust of either wood species at temperatures of 140∼150 ℃, because, while, although the rate of the oxidatively-heating reaction of Cu powder charged in the draft cell, into which air is supplied, and subjected to the adiabatic oxidatively-heating test started from a T_s near 140 ℃ is fairly high in the early stages, the oxidatively-heating reaction of Cu powder ceases after an increase in temperature of about 4 K from the T_s (Fig. 116),* a mixture of the sawdust of red lauan and Cu powder

* This phenomenon is thought to occur by reason that, once the surface of each copper particle, the aggregation of which constitutes the powder, is covered with the compact film made up of copper oxides, the film thus formed hinders gaseous oxygen from attaining to the surface of the unoxidized copper particle.

still continues to heat oxidatively even after the temperature of the mixture has increased by the same order of magnitude as that of Cu powder.

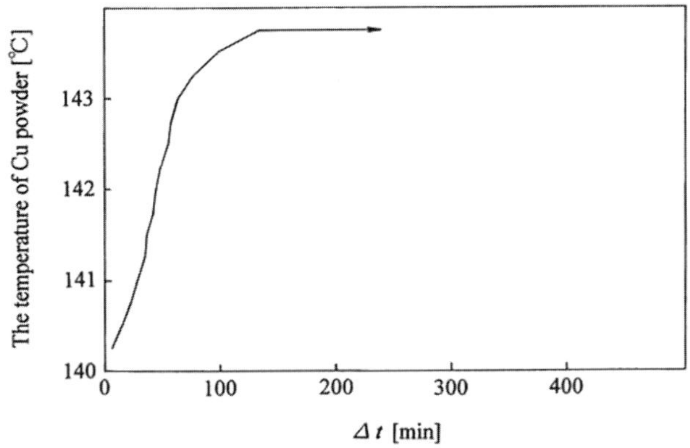

Figure 116. The oxidatively-heating curve, of Cu powder charged in the draft cell, into which air is supplied, and subjected to the adiabatic oxidatively-heating test started from a T_s near 140 ℃, recorded in temperature increments of 4 K from the corresponding standard temperature.

CuO catalyzes to a small extent the oxidatively-heating reaction, occurring at temperatures of 140～150 ℃, of the sawdust of either wood species. It seems that CuO catalyzes more markedly the oxidatively-heating reaction of the sawdust of wood species, such as Japanese cedar, which is relatively hard to heat oxidatively, than the reaction of the sawdust of wood species, such as red lauan, which is relatively easy to heat oxidatively, in the adiabatic oxidatively-heating test as well.

Pt fragments do not catalyze the oxidatively-heating reaction, occurring at temperatures of 140～150 ℃, of the sawdust of either wood species. From the results of both the TG-DTA measurements and the adiabatic oxidatively-heating tests performed each for the mixture of the sawdust of either wood species and Pt fragments, it may be possible to infer that, although Pt does not participate in the slow oxidatively-heating reaction, which occurs at temperatures below about 180 ℃ and is thought to be very likely a sort of dehydrogenation reaction, of organic polymers constituting wood, it catalyzes remarkably the rapid oxidatively-heating reactions, occurring at temperatures above 200 ℃, of the thermal decomposition products which are extruded out of the interior of wood and are of relatively low molecular weights.

On the other hand, Fe and Fe_2O_3 do not catalyze the oxidatively-heating reaction, occurring at temperatures of 140～150 ℃, of the sawdust of either wood species at all, or rather, these seem to hinder somewhat the sawdust of either wood species from decomposing oxidatively.

8.4 Procedure to calculate the T_c for a sawdust heap, having some one of the several specific shapes including the class A geometries as well as an arbitrary value of r, placed in the atmosphere under isothermal conditions

The procedure to calculate, by applying the reduced form of the F-K equation, *i.e.*, Eq. (79) derived in **Section 6.2**, the T_c for a sawdust heap, having some one of the several specific shapes including the class A geometries as well as an arbitrary value of r, placed in the atmosphere under isothermal conditions, is introduced in the present section by taking the procedure to calculate the T_c for a sawdust heap of Port Orford cedar, assuming that it is formed into an infinite slab, 60.96 cm in thickness, and is placed in the atmosphere under isothermal conditions, as an example.

$$2\ln T_c + \frac{a}{T_c} = \ln\left[\frac{ar^2 \cdot \Delta T}{\alpha_e \cdot \delta_c}\right] - b. \tag{79}$$

It is clear in Eq. (79) that the value of δ_c is the shape factor of a sawdust heap, and, the value of r is the size factor, or the quantity factor, of the heap.

In this connection, the value of α_e and the heat generation data, a and b, of a sawdust depend on the kind of the sawdust, but these do not depend on the shape and the size of the sawdust heap.

8.4.1 Procedure to perform several adiabatic oxidatively-heating tests, which are started from each T_s with mutual intervals of 2 K, in order to calculate the heat generation data of the sawdust of a wood species, for 0.3 g each of several samples of the sawdust charged each in the draft cell, into which air is supplied, for the time, Δt, required for the temperature of each sample of the sawdust to increase by the definite value of ΔT of 1.25 K from the corresponding standard temperature, respectively

The procedure described in the above heading is explained in detail in the present subsection by taking the procedure performed for 0.3 g of the sawdust of Port Orford cedar, the volume of which is about 2 cm^3, charged in the draft cell as an example.

(1) Procedure to prepare the sample cell assembly including the draft cell

After a thin gas-permeable silica fiber sheet has been placed on the bottom of a draft cell, *i.e.*, the cell with which the sample cell is prepared, 0.3 g of the sawdust of Port Orford cedar, which is of course a kind of the moisture-containing gas-permeable oxidatively-heating substance, is charged in the cell. The glass jig mentioned in a footnote in **Section 7.3** is used at this time to provide a thin vertical hole at the center of the sawdust charged in the cell in order to facilitate the insertion of the thermocouple into the sawdust. 0.3 g was chosen herein as the standard sample quantity in the adiabatic oxidatively-heating test performed for the sawdust of every wood species. For the procedure to prepare the sawdust of each wood species, refer to **Subsection 8.2.1**.

The sample cell thus prepared is then set on the pedestal which is stuck at the center of the upper plate of the laboratory jack, which in turn is fixed on the laboratory desk. The position of the stand, by means of which the stem including the glass vent tube is held in the vertical position, is next adjusted by sliding the stand horizontally on the desk in order that the glass vent tube may be aligned vertically with the sample cell set on the pedestal.

The sample cell is then combined concentrically and softly with the ground glass joint of the glass vent tube by raising the laboratory jack to construct the sample cell assembly; in the meantime, the CA thermocouple, covered with a glass capillary tube, to measure the temperature of the sawdust is inserted automatically and axially to the longitudinal center of the sawdust charged in the cell. The sample cell combined with the ground glass joint of the glass vent tube is finally supported firmly with a thin aluminium washer and two springs. After having lowered the laboratory jack a little, a fairly small vibrator is applied to the base of the draft cell in order that the sawdust charged in the cell may come closely in contact with the glass capillary tube.

For further details of the procedure to prepare the sample cell assembly including the draft cell, refer to **Section 7.3**.

(2) Insertion of the sample cell assembly into the adiabatic jacket set in the air bath of the adiabatic self-heating process recorder, the supply of nitrogen gas into the draft cell and the start of the air bath heating

The sample cell assembly thus prepared is inserted into the adiabatic jacket set in the air bath of the adiabatic self-heating process recorder, and nitrogen gas is supplied into the draft cell at a flow rate of 2 cm^3/min.

The temperature of the air bath is set at 110 ℃, at first, by means of the temperature dial on the air bath.

To begin with, the main power supply connected to the adiabatic self-heating process recorder is switched on.

The power supplies connected to the cold junction, the air bath, the digital D.C. microvoltmeter, the digital D.C. millivolt recorder and the two-pen strip chart recorder are then switched on, respectively. The ΔT_{diff} pen of the two-pen strip chart recorder is, however, left on the "short" position until the thermal equilibrium state is nearly attained again around the sawdust of Port Orford cedar charged in the draft cell, into which nitrogen gas is supplied, and inserted into the adiabatic jacket maintained at a nominal T_s of the run, 1.5~2 h after the reset of the temperature of the air bath. For the term, the ΔT_{diff} pen, refer to **Subsection 4.5.4**.

The sample cell assembly is then left for 270 min at 110 ℃ in nitrogen gas flow to remove all the moisture from the sawdust.

(3) Choice of the nominal T_s in the adiabatic oxidatively-heating test performed for 0.3 g of the sawdust of Port Orford cedar charged in the draft cell, into which nitrogen is supplied for the present, and the determination of the exact value of T_s of the run

After the drying time above referred to has passed, the temperature of the air bath is reset at a proper value, *i.e.*, the nominal T_s of the run, by means of the temperature dial on the air bath on the basis of the oxidatively-heating property of the sawdust tested to give estimated rates of increase in temperature of 1.25 K/h in the adiabatic oxidatively-heating test, with the result that the T_s ranged from 157.4 ℃ for the sawdust of red lauan to 178.6 ℃ for that of Sitka spruce in the case of the sawdusts tested herein. As to the sawdust of Port Orford cedar, the T_s ranged from 164.8 to 173.3 ℃.

As stated above, the thermal equilibrium state comes to be attained again around the sawdust charged in the cell, 1.5 ~ 2 h after the reset of the temperature of the air bath. After the thermal equilibrium state has nearly been attained around the sawdust, the power supply to the analog D.C. microvoltmeter is switched on; in the meantime, the ΔT_{diff} pen of the two-pen strip chart recorder is also switched over from "short" to "on". It is then observed that the indicator of the analog D.C. microvoltmeter enters on to the scale span of the meter from the minus side, and, it comes to stay near the graduation line of zero at the center of the scale span of the meter; in the meantime, the ΔT_{diff} pen of the two-pen strip chart recorder also enters on to the strip chart of the two-pen strip chart recorder from the minus side. For the term, the minus side, refer to **Subsection 4.5.4**.

Curves drawn by the T pen and the ΔT_{diff} pen on the strip chart of the two-pen strip chart recorder, by the time that the thermal equilibrium state has been attained again around the sawdust charged in the draft cell and inserted into the adiabatic jacket maintained at the nominal T_s of the run, are similar to those illustrated in Fig. 38 in **Subsection 4.5.4**.

The digital output of the thermoelectromotive force of the CA thermocouple to measure the temperature of the sawdust is then noted down as the exact value of T_s of the run, and the zero-suppression procedure is performed. For the term, the zero-suppression procedure, refer to a footnote in **Subsection 4.5.5**.

(4) Start of the adiabatic oxidatively-heating test for 0.3 g of the sawdust of Port Orford cedar charged in the draft cell, into which nitrogen has been supplied until the present, and inserted into the adiabatic jacket maintained at the T_s of the run

Immediately after that, the supply of nitrogen gas into the draft cell is ceased, and the supply of air into the draft cell at a flow rate of 2 cm^3/min, the adiabatic control by means of the adiabatic self-heating process recorder and the record of the oxidatively-heating process, in the early stages, of 0.3 g of the sawdust of Port Orford cedar charged in the draft cell by means of the digital D.C. millivolt recorder are started, respectively. This point of time corresponds to the point "**s**" in Fig. 15 presented in **Section 3.4**.

(5) Record of the oxidatively-heating process, in the early stages, of 0.3 g of the sawdust of Port Orford cedar charged in the draft cell, into which air is now supplied, and inserted into the adiabatic jacket kept always at the very slowly increasing temperature of the sawdust itself by the adiabatic control

After the start of the adiabatic control, the T_{atm} is raised automatically by the adiabatic control in order that the condition, $\Delta T_{diff} = T - T_{atm} = 0$, may always hold, with the result that the heat generated in the oxidatively-heating sawdust of Port Orford cedar is all accumulated in it, and, it continues to heat oxidatively at the rates depending on the value of T_s, and on the gradually increasing oxygen concentration in the atmosphere in the adiabatic jacket; in the meantime, the temperature of the space in the air bath, except that in the adiabatic jacket, is maintained at the T_s of the run throughout every run.

The oxidatively-heating process, in the early stages, of 0.3 g of the sawdust of Port Orford cedar charged in the draft cell, into which air is supplied, and inserted into the adiabatic jacket kept always at the very slowly increasing temperature of the sawdust of Port Orford cedar itself by the adiabatic control is recorded in the digital representation as the variation of the value, with time, of the thermoelectromotive force of the thermocouple to measure the temperature of the sawdust of Port Orford cedar; to put it concretely, the numerical value of the thermoelectromotive force of the thermocouple is printed out every minute by means of the digital D.C. millivolt recorder, in such a manner as exemplified in Table 5 presented in **Section 4.7**, in order to utilize the record for the calculation of the values of the two coefficients, a and b, of Eq. (44), $\ln \Delta t = a/T_s + b$, holding for the oxidatively-heating process, in the early stages, of 0.3 g of the sawdust of Port Orford cedar charged in the draft cell and subjected to the adiabatic oxidatively-heating test.

On the other hand, however, the oxidatively-heating process, in the early stages, of 0.3 g of the sawdust of Port Orford cedar charged in the draft cell and subjected to the adiabatic oxidatively-heating test is recorded, as an analog signal as well, with the T pen on the strip chart of the two-pen strip chart recorder to look about the process as a whole.

As stated in **(2)** of **Subsection 8.3.1**, the time, Δt, required for the temperature of 0.3 g of the sawdust of Port Orford cedar charged in the draft cell, into which air is supplied, and subjected to the adiabatic oxidatively-heating test started from a T_s below about 180 ℃ to increase by the definite value of ΔT of 1.25 K from the corresponding standard temperature is determined on the linearly-rising part of the oxidatively-heating process or curve of the sawdust of Port Orford cedar.

That is, the test is interrupted as soon as the temperature of the sawdust of Port Orford cedar in the cell increases by the definite value of ΔT of 1.25 K from the corresponding standard temperature.

The other combinations of the value of $\ln \Delta t$ with that of $1/T_s$, which are required to make the plot of $\ln \Delta t$ versus $1/T_s$ with regard to several oxidatively-heating processes, of 0.3 g each of several samples of the sawdust of Port Orford cedar charged each in the draft cell, into which air is supplied, and subjected each to the adiabatic oxidatively-heating test started from each T_s in the range of 164.8 to 173.3 ℃ with mutual intervals of 1~2 K, recorded each for the time, Δt, required for the temperature of each sample of the sawdust of Port Orford cedar to increase by the definite value of ΔT of 1.25 K from the corresponding standard temperature, besides, which are required for the regression analysis to calculate the values of the two coefficients, a and b, of Eq. (44) holding for the oxidatively-heating process, in the early stages, of 0.3 g of the sawdust of Port Orford cedar charged in the draft cell, into which air is supplied, and subjected to the adiabatic oxidatively-heating test, are also determined in the same manner as explained above.

Five oxidatively-heating processes, of 0.3 g each of five samples of the sawdust of Port Orford cedar charged each in the draft cell, into which air is supplied, and subjected each to the adiabatic oxidatively-heating test started from each T_s in the range of 164.8 to 173.3 ℃ with mutual intervals of 2 K, recorded each for the time, Δt, required for the temperature of each sample of the sawdust to increase by the definite value of ΔT of 1.25 K from the corresponding standard temperature, are presented in Fig. 85 in **(2)** of **Subsection 8.3.1**.

The plot of $\ln \Delta t$ versus $1/T_s$ made for 0.3 g each of five samples of the sawdust of Port Orford cedar is shown in Fig. 117.

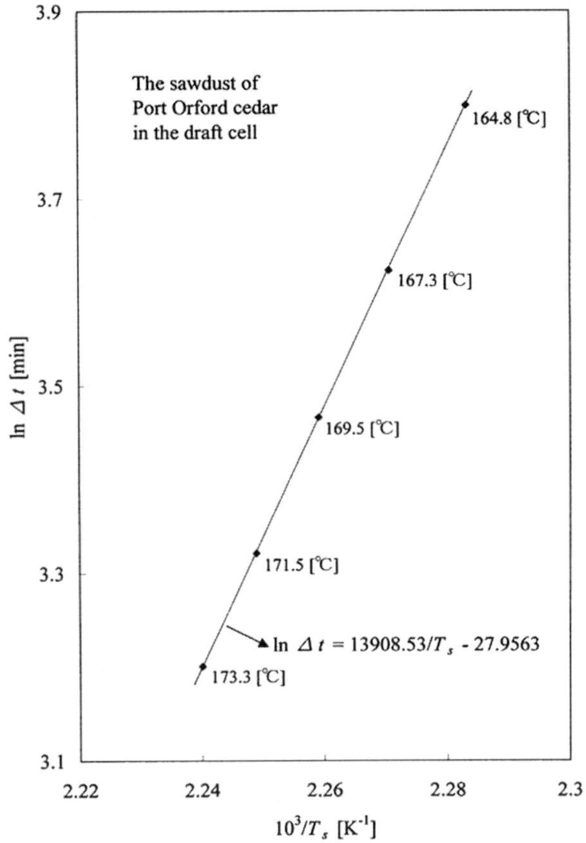

Figure 117. The plot of $\ln \Delta t$ versus $1/T_s$ made with five combinations of the value of $\ln \Delta t$ with that of $1/T_s$, which are each determined for five oxidatively-heating processes, which are presented in Fig. 85 in **(2)** of **Subsection 8.3.1**, of 0.3 g each of five samples of the sawdust of Port Orford cedar charged each in the draft cell, into which air is supplied, and subjected each to the adiabatic oxidatively-heating test started from each T_s in the range of 164.8 to 173.3 ℃ with mutual intervals of 2 K, recorded each for the time, Δt, required for the temperature of each sample of the sawdust of Port Orford cedar to increase by the definite value of ΔT of 1.25 K from the corresponding standard temperature.

It is obvious in Fig. 117 that the empirical formula, $\ln \Delta t = a/T_s + b$, *i.e.*, Eq. (44), presented in Fig. 15 in **Section 3.4** holds well between a T_s and the time, Δt, required for the temperature of 0.3 g of the sawdust of Port Orford cedar charged in the draft cell, into which air is supplied, and subjected to the adiabatic oxidatively-heating test started from the T_s to increase by the definite value of ΔT of 1.25 K from the corresponding standard temperature on the linearly-rising part of the oxidatively- heating process or curve of the sawdust.

For the value of a coefficient, 13908.53, of the equation, $\ln \Delta t = 13908.53/T_s - 27.9563$, *i.e.*, Eq. (44) holding for the oxidatively-heating process, in the early stages, of 0.3 g of the sawdust of Port Orford cedar charged in the draft cell, into which air is supplied, and subjected to the adiabatic oxidatively-heating test, refer to the explanation given under Table 19 in **(6)** of the present subsection.

(6) Calculation of the heat generation data of the sawdust of Port Orford cedar, *i.e.*, the values of the two coefficients, *a* and *b*, of Eq. (44), $\ln \Delta t = a/T_s + b$, holding for the oxidatively-heating process, in the early stages, of 0.3 g of the sawdust of Port Orford cedar charged in the draft cell, into which air is supplied, and subjected to the adiabatic oxidatively-heating test

The result of the regression analysis to calculate the heat generation data of the sawdust of Port Orford cedar is presented in Table 19.

Values of $\ln \Delta t$ and $1/T_s$ used in the regression analysis are in common with those presented in Fig. 85 and plotted in Fig. 117. The values of Δt and T_s presented in Figs. 85 and 117 are, however, all rounded. For an instance similar to this, refer to Tables 5 and 6 in **Section 4.7** and Figs. 45 and 46 in **Subsection 5.4.5**.

Based on the result, the value of a for the sawdust of Port Orford cedar is calculated by multiplying the value of A, which is presented in Table 19, by 1,000 in the same manner as performed for the value of A of TBPB in **Section 4.7**.

The values of the two coefficients, a and b, thus calculated, of Eq. (44), $\ln \Delta t = a/T_s + b$, holding for the oxidatively-heating process, in the early stages, of 0.3 g of the sawdust of Port Orford cedar charged in the draft cell, into which air is supplied, and subjected to the adiabatic oxidatively-heating test, 13908.53 and -27.9563, *i.e.*, the heat generation data of the sawdust of Port Orford cedar, are presented as such in Table 21 in **(1)** of **Subsection 8.4.4**.

Table 19

The result of the regression analysis applied, in order to calculate the heat generation data of the sawdust of Port Orford cedar, to five combinations of the value of ln Δt with that of $1/T_s$, which are each determined, based on five digital records obtained each from five adiabatic oxidatively-heating tests, which are started from each T_s in the range of 164.8 to 173.3 ℃ with mutual intervals of 2 K, performed each, for 0.3 g each of five samples of the sawdust of Port Orford cedar charged each in the draft cell, into which air is supplied, for the time, Δt, required for the temperature of each sample of the sawdust of Port Orford cedar to increase by the definite value of ΔT of 1.25 K from the corresponding standard temperature. Data used are in common with those presented in Fig. 85 and plotted in Fig. 117.

MATERIAL ... The sawdust of Port Orford cedar

DATA NUMBER	X	Y	A＊X+B
1	2.28313	3.79921	3.798678
2	2.27061	3.62325	3.624544
3	2.25912	3.46625	3.464735
4	2.24891	3.32134	3.322728
5	2.24009	3.20069	3.200055

COEFFICIENT OF Y = A＊TT + B A = 13.90853
COEFFICIENT OF Y = A＊TT + B B = -27.9563

DISTRIBUTION = 0.000002 STANDARD DEVIATION = 0.001481

8.4.2 Individual procedures to determine the two heat transfer data, *i.e.*, δ_c and α_e, of a sawdust heap, having an arbitrary shape and an arbitrary size, placed in the atmosphere under isothermal conditions

As stated in **Section 8.1**, when a sawdust heap, which is placed in the atmosphere under isothermal conditions, has some one of the several specific shapes including the class A geometries as well as an arbitrary value of r, the calculation of the T_c for the sawdust heap becomes very simple, because the values of δ_c for these specific shapes have already been calculated by T. Boddington *et al.*, respectively [58], with the result that the heat transfer data required to calculate the T_c for such a sawdust heap as specified above is only the value of α_e of the sawdust. For the values of δ_c calculated by T. Boddington *et al.*, refer to Table 13 in **Section 6.5**.

For instance, once the shape of a sawdust heap is assumed to be, or approximated by, an infinite slab, a value of δ_c of 0.878 is fixed at once for the heap having an arbitrary halfvalue thickness. It then becomes possible to calculate the T_c for the imaginary infinite slab, having an arbitrary halfvalue thickness, placed in the atmosphere under isothermal conditions, provided the value of α_e of the sawdust is known besides.

The variation of the value of T_c for a sawdust heap with the value of δ_c differs naturally from one sawdust heap to another. Generally speaking, however, a decrease of 0.1 in the value of δ_c, the magnitude of which is the maximum error conceivable in the determination of the value of δ_c and corresponds to about 10 % of the value of δ_c for a sawdust heap formed into an infinite slab having an arbitrary halfvalue thickness, causes a decrease of about 1.5 K in the value of T_c calculated by applying Eq. (79), keeping the values of the other variables in the equation constant. However, a fluctuation, of such an extent, in the value of T_c is thought to be within the error range of the result of an isothermal storage test performed in order to measure the T_c for a sawdust heap, formed into an infinite slab having an arbitrary halfvalue thichness.

For the equation and the procedure to calculate the value of α_e of the sawdust of a wood species by applying the constant-heating-rate method, refer to **Section 6.4**.

The individual values of ϕ and $(\Delta T_{rad})_{\lim}$ of the sawdusts of fifteen wood species tested herein were measured by means of a radial temperature difference measuring apparatus at two temperatures, *i.e.*, a temperature near 100 ℃ and a temperature near room temperature, respectively. The arithmetic mean of the value of α_e of the sawdust of a wood species calculated by substituting the values of ϕ and $(\Delta T_{rad})_{\lim}$ measured each at a temperature near 100 ℃ into Eq. (85) and that calculated by substituting the values measured each at a temperature near room temperature into the same equation is presented as the value of α_e of the sawdust of the wood species in Table 21 in **(1)** of **Subsection 8.4.4**, although the two values of α_e calculated each by substituting the individual values of ϕ and $(\Delta T_{rad})_{\lim}$ measured each at the two temperatures into Eq. (85) were nearly equivalent to each other for the sawdust of every wood species. Some values of α_e thus calculated each for the sawdusts of a few wood species are presented in Table 20.

Table 20
Some values of α_e calculated each herein for the sawdusts of a few wood species.

Sawdust	Value of α_e measured		Value of α_e in Table 21
	at room temp.	at 100 ℃	
The sawdust of Japanese red pine	0.1269	0.132	0.13
The sawdust of zelkova	0.1378	0.1412	0.14
The sawdust of Douglas fir	0.1368	0.1384	0.14
A value of α_e reported by Schliemann for the sawdust of Kiefernholz (German pine)			0.1∼0.2 [70]

The variation of the value of T_c for a sawdust heap with the value of α_e is also of the same order of magnitude as that with the value of δ_c. That is, a decrease of 0.02 cm^2/min in the value of α_e, the magnitude of which is the maximum error conceivable in the calculation of the value of α_e and corresponds to about 15 % of the value of α_e of the sawdust of an average wood species, causes a decrease of about 1.5 K in the value of T_c calculated by applying Eq. (79), keeping the values of the other variables in the equation constant.

8.4.3 Concrete procedure to calculate the T_c for a sawdust heap, having an arbitrary shape and an arbitrary size, placed in the atmosphere under isothermal conditions

In order to compare the values of T_c calculated each for the sawdust heaps of fifteen wood species placed each in the atmosphere under isothermal conditions with one another, it is required to calculate the individual values of T_c, assuming that these sawdust heaps are each placed under the same conditions of shape and size.

A decision was thus made herein to calculate the individual values of T_c for the sawdust heaps of fifteen wood species by applying Eq. (79), assuming that these sawdusts are each formed into an infinite slab, 60.96 cm (2 feet) in thickness, and are each placed in the atmosphere under isothermal conditions.

As an example, the concrete procedure to calculate the T_c for a sawdust heap of Port Orford cedar formed into an infinite slab, 60.96 cm (2 feet) in thickness, and placed in the atmosphere under isothermal conditions is illustrated in the present subsection.

The heat generation data, *a* and *b*, of the sawdust of Port Orford cedar were calculated in **(6)** of **Subsection 8.4.1** and are given in Table 21 in **(1)** of **Subsection 8.4.4**, respectively.

On the other hand, the value of α_e of the sawdust of Port Orford cedar was calculated at 0.17 cm^2/min by applying the constant-heating-rate method in **Subsection 8.4.2**.

The value of δ_c for every infinite slab is fixed at 0.878 (see Table 13 in **Section 6.5**).

Further, the value of *r* of an infinite slab, 60.96 cm in thickness, is of course 30.48 (= 60.96/2) cm.

The above three heat transfer data of the sawdust heap of Port Orford cedar, formed into an infinite slab, 60.96 cm in thickness, and placed in the atmosphere under isothermal conditions, are also given in Table 21 in **(1)** of **Subsection 8.4.4**, respectively.

And, the value of ΔT is 1.25 K.

The value of the right-hand side of Eq. (79), *i.e.*,

$$2\ln T_c + \frac{a}{T_c} = \ln\left[\frac{ar^2 \cdot \Delta T}{\alpha_e \cdot \delta_c}\right] - b, \tag{79}$$

for the sawdust heap of Port Orford cedar above referred to is thus calculated in the following manner.

$$\ln\left[\frac{ar^2 \cdot \Delta T}{\alpha_e \cdot \delta_c}\right] - b = \ln\{[13908.53 \times (60.96/2)^2 \times 1.25] \div [0.17 \times 0.878]\} + 27.9563$$

$$= 18.49960814 + 27.9563$$

$$= 46.45590814.$$

On the other hand, if the value of T_c for the sawdust heap of Port Orford cedar above referred to is assumed to be 403.67604 K or 130.52604 ℃, the value of the left-hand side of Eq. (79) is calculated in the following manner.

$$2\ln T_c + \frac{a}{T_c} = 2\ln 403.67604 + 13908.53 \div 403.67604$$

$$= 12.00122535 + 34.45468302$$

$$= 46.45590837.$$

The difference between both sides is thus

$$46.45590837 - 46.45590814 \fallingdotseq 0.0000002.$$

The above whole calculation is performed actually by inputting the individual values of a, b, r, ΔT, α_e and δ_c to a computer program used to calculate the T_c for a chemical of the TD type, including every gas-permeable oxidatively-heating substance.
The value of T_c thus calculated for the sawdust heap of Port Orford cedar above referred to, 130.52604 ℃, is finally rounded to 131 ℃ and is presented as such, together with the values of T_c calculated each for the sawdust heaps of fourteen wood species, other than Port Orford cedar, in the same manner as performed for the sawdust heap of Port Orford cedar, in Table 21 in **(1)** of **Subsection 8.4.4**.

8.4.4 Results and discussion

(1) The values of T_c calculated each for the sawdust heaps of fifteen wood species, including Port Orford cedar

The values of T_c were each calculated for the sawdust heaps of fifteen wood species, including Port Orford cedar, assuming that these sawdust heaps are each formed into an infinite slab, 60.96 cm in thickness, and are each placed in the atmosphere under isothermal conditions.
The list of the fifteen wood species tested herein is given in Table 17 in **Subsection 8.2.1**.
The adiabatic oxidatively-heating tests for the sawdusts of fourteen wood species, other than Port Orford cedar, were also performed in the same manner as done for the sawdust of Port Orford cedar, respectively.
The fifteen plots of $\ln \Delta t$ versus $1/T_s$ made each for the sawdusts of fifteen wood species, including Port Orford cedar, are presented in Fig. 118.

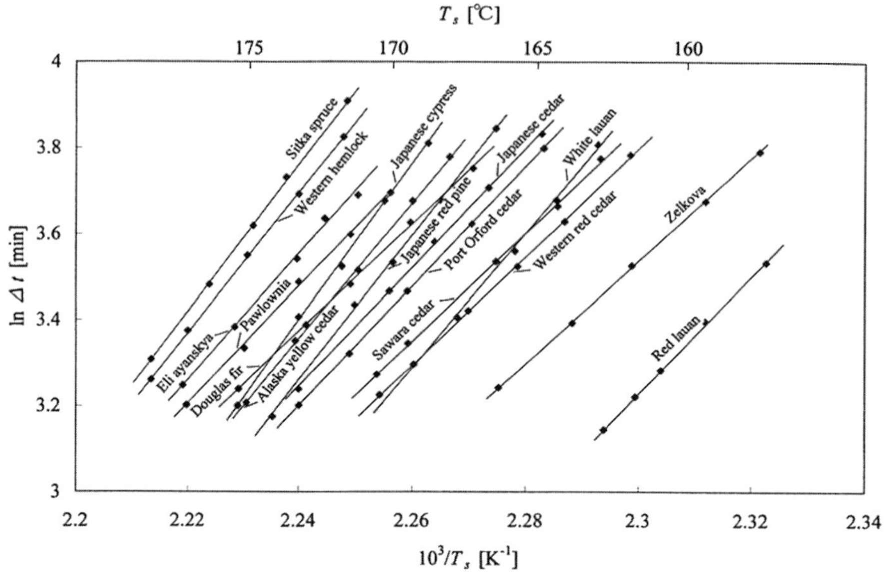

Figure 118. The fifteen plots of ln Δt versus $1/T_s$ made each for the sawdusts of fifteen wood species.

The individual values of the two coefficients, a and b, of Eq. (44) holding for the individual oxidatively-heating processes, in the early stages, of 0.3 g each of the sawdusts of fourteen wood species, other than Port Orford cedar, charged each in the draft cell and subjected each to the adiabatic oxidatively-heating test were also calculated by applying the regression analysis to the individual combinations of the value of ln Δt with that of $1/T_s$ and are presented in Table 21.

It is possible to see roughly from Fig. 118 the relative liability of these sawdusts to oxidatively-heating or ultimate spontaneous ignition. Although it is difficult, as stated in **(1)** of **Subsection 8.3.1**, to distinguish the relative liability of the sawdusts of various wood species to oxidatively-heating by means of thermal analysis, it is very easy to do so by means of the adiabatic oxidatively-heating test. That is, we can tell that the sawdust of zelkova and that of red lauan are relatively easy to heat oxidatively, but the sawdust of Western hemlock and that of Sitka spruce are relatively hard to do so. In this regard, the sawdust of Port Orford cedar and that of paulownia are medium in the liability to spontaneous ignition.

The values of T_c calculated each for the sawdust heaps of fifteen wood species, including Port Orford cedar, are summarized in Table 21 in the order of increasing value of T_c, together with a few values of T_c measured each by other researchers for a few sawdust heaps, of wood species other than those tested herein, but similar to the heaps calculated herein in size, for comparison [27].

The values of T_c thus calculated each for the sawdust heaps of fifteen wood species ranged from 118 ℃ for the sawdust heap of zelkova to 142 ℃ for that of Sitka spruce.

These values of T_c calculated herein in general are in fair agreement with a few values of T_c measured each by other researchers for a few sawdust heaps, of wood species other than those tested herein, but similar to the heaps calculated herein in size, respectively.

At all events, however, it will be reasonable, in practice, to consider a temperature 20 K lower than the value of T_c calculated herein for a sawdust heap, formed into the infinite slab above referred to and placed in the atmosphere under isothermal conditions, as the upper limit temperature for the safe handling of the sawdust. For instance, 100 ℃ will be the upper limit temperature for the safe handling of the sawdust of zelkova, 105 ℃ for that of Western red cedar, 110 ℃ for that of Douglas fir, and so forth.

Incidentally, the T_c for an infinite slab of the sawdust of every wood species increases naturally as the thickness of the slab decreases. In this regard, the order of increase in the value of T_c is not necessarily invariable among the sawdust heaps of the fifteen wood species, because the degree of increase in the value of T_c depends on factors inherent in the sawdust of each individual wood species, such as E, A_0, ΔH and α_e.

Thus, when the infinite slab is 20.32 cm (8 inch) in thickness, it follows that the values of T_c calculated each for the sawdust heaps of the fifteen wood species range from 147 ℃ for the sawdust heap of red lauan to 167 ℃ for that of Sitka spruce, although it is impossible to verify these values of T_c, because the corresponding measured values are not available at present, respectively.

Table 21
Experimental parameters of the sawdusts of fifteen wood species and comparison of the values of T_c calculated each for these sawdusts, assuming that these sawdusts are each formed into an infinite slab, 60.96 cm (2 feet) in thickness, and are each placed in the atmosphere under isothermal conditions, with, a few values of T_c measured each by other researchers for a few sawdust heaps, of wood species other than those tested herein, but similar to the heaps calculated herein in size. The heat generation data of these sawdusts were calculated based on the experimental data obtained with the draft cell in the adiabatic oxidatively-heating test, respectively.

Wood species	Coefficients of Eq. (44)		Half-thickness of the slab	Effective thermal diffusivity	The Frank-Kamenetskii number	Critical temperature for the spontaneous ignition calculated herein
	a	b	r cm	α_e cm^2/min	δ_c	T_c ℃
Zelkova	11901.28	-23.8369	30.48	0.14	0.878	118
Red lauan	13553.09	-27.9425	30.48	0.15	0.878	119
Western red cedar	12574.6	-25.1238	30.48	0.16	0.878	125
Sawara cedar	12542.79	-24.9954	30.48	0.16	0.878	125
Douglas fir	12489.87	-24.6042	30.48	0.14	0.878	127
White lauan	15723.73	-32.2512	30.48	0.15	0.878	130
Port Orford cedar	13908.53	-27.9563	30.48	0.17	0.878	131
Japanese cedar	13904.02	-27.9021	30.48	0.18	0.878	132
Paulownia	13607.92	-27.0064	30.48	0.17	0.878	133
Japanese red pine	16825.42	-34.4312	30.48	0.13	0.878	134
Eli ayanskya	14502.33	-28.9342	30.48	0.16	0.878	135
Alaska cedar	15882.93	-32.2211	30.48	0.17	0.878	136
Japanese cypress	18109.98	-37.1671	30.48	0.16	0.878	139
Western hemlock	16312.26	-32.8421	30.48	0.17	0.878	140
Sitka spruce	17289.89	-34.965	30.48	0.17	0.878	142

A few values of T_c measured each by other researchers for a few sawdust heaps, of wood species other than those tested herein, but similar to the heaps calculated herein in size:	
The sawdust, of mixed hardwood, formed into a sphere, 82 cm in diameter [68].	135
The sawdust, of Kiefernholz (German pine), formed into a sphere, 100 cm in diameter [69, 70].	130
The sawdust, of Kiefernholz, formed into a slab, 40 cm thick [69].	140

Now, if the sawdust of mixed hardwood is assumed to be in fact the sawdust of Western red cedar, the T_c for a sawdust heap of mixed hardwood, formed into a sphere, 82 cm in diameter, and placed in the atmosphere under isothermal conditions, which is cited in Table 21, is calculated at 134.8 ℃, because the values of the variables, a, b, r, α_e and δ_c, apart from the constant, ΔT, in Eq. (79), are fixed for the sphere at 12574.6, -25.1238, 41, 0.16 and 3.32, respectively. The value of T_c thus calculated is in fair agreement with the value of 135 ℃ measured actually by Anthony *et al.* for the sphere [68]. Similarly, if the sawdust of Kiefernholz (German pine) is assumed to be in fact the sawdust of Douglas fir, the T_c for a sawdust heap of Kiefernholz, formed into a sphere, 100 cm in diameter, and placed in the atmosphere under isothermal conditions, which is also cited in Table 21, is calculated at 131.8 ℃, because the values of the variables, a, b, r, α_e and δ_c, apart from the constant, ΔT, in Eq. (79), are fixed for the sphere at 12489.87, -24.6042, 50, 0.14 and 3.32, respectively. The value of T_c thus calculated is in fair agreement with the value of 130 ℃ measured actually by John for the sphere [69, 70]. Once again, if the sawdust of Kiefernholz is assumed to be in fact the sawdust of Douglas fir, the T_c for a sawdust heap of Kiefernholz, formed into an infinite slab, 40 cm in thickness, and placed in the atmosphere under isothermal conditions, which is also cited in Table 21, is calculated at 139.0 ℃, because the values of the variables, a, b, r, α_e and δ_c, apart from the constant, ΔT, in Eq. (79), are fixed for the infinite slab at 12489.87, -24.6042, 20, 0.14 and 0.878, respectively. The value of T_c thus calculated is in fair agreement with the value of 140 ℃ measured actually by John for the slab [69].

Judging from the whole information obtained in the present chapter, it seems that the probable heat loss, on account of air flow through the cell, from the sawdust of every wood species charged in the draft cell in the adiabatic oxidatively-heating test is covered almost perfectly by the adiabatic control; that is, it seems to be likely, at least, that the oxidatively-heating process of the sawdust of every wood species charged in the draft cell, into which air is supplied, and subjected to adiabatic oxidatively-heating test started from a T_s is recorded under almost perfectly adiabatic conditions in the range of 2～3 K immediately above the T_s.

(2) Critical radius for the spontaneous ignition, r_c, for a similar body of a gas-permeable oxidatively-heating substance, having some one of several specific shapes including the class A geometries, placed in the atmosphere under isothermal conditions

It is possible to calculate by applying Eq. (79), in the same manner as suggested for a similar body of a powdery chemical of the TD type in **Subsection 6.7.2**, the critical (or the smallest) radius for the spontaneous ignition, r_c, below which the spontaneous ignition of a similar body of a gas-permeable oxidatively-heating substance, for which the individual values of the variables, a, b, α_e and δ_c, apart from the constant, ΔT, in Eq. (79) are fixed, placed in the atmosphere maintained at an arbitrary temperature, T_c, cannot occur absolutely.

When a gas-permeable oxidatively-heating substance is heaped up, such a value of radius may be useful as the upper limit radius in heaping control to prevent the substance from igniting spontaneously from a viewpoint different from the temperature control to prevent the substance from igniting spontaneously.

The problem of calculating the r_c for a similar body of a gas-permeable oxidatively-heating substance thus reduces itself to one of determining the value of a variable, r, when the values of the variables, a, b, T_c, α_e and δ_c, apart from the constant, ΔT, in Eq. (79) are all fixed.

As an example, let us suppose that the sawdust of zelkova is formed into an infinite slab and is placed in the atmosphere maintained at 25 ℃. The critical thickness for the spontaneous ignition, *i.e.*, the value of $2r_c$, is then calculated at about 53.2 m, because the values of the variables, a, b, T_c, α_e and δ_c, apart from the constant, ΔT, in Eq. (79), are fixed for the infinite slab at 11901.28, -23.8369, 298.15, 0.14 and 0.878, respectively.

In this connection, Bergström reported an incident that a huge heap of wood chips, the volume of which was about 140,000 m^3, had ignited spontaneously at room temperature [72]. If it is supposed that the wood species of these chips was zelkova, and, the shape of the heap was a cube, the length of the side, *i.e.*, the value of $2r$, is calculated at about 52 m. Taking the difference in heaping conditions,[*] the difference in wood species, the difference in shape,[**] the difference in temperature, *etc.*, into consideration, it will be accidental that the length of the side of the imaginary cubic heap coincides fairly with the thickness of the infinite slab calculated above. This accidental coincidence, nevertheless, encourages us to develop the concept of the critical radius further.

---

[*] These wood chips are thought to have been heaped up outdoors, so that the spontaneous ignition of the heap may be ascribed to moisture, or to some biological effect, such as fermentation, as well.

[**] The dependence of the value of δ_c on the shape of the heap was ignored in the above calculation on account of the hugeness of the heap.

References to Chapter 8

[27] T. Kotoyori, Critical Ignition Temperatures of Wood Sawdusts, Proceedings of the 1st International Symposium on Fire Safety Science, Gaithersburg, Maryland, 1985, Hemisphere Publishing Corporation, Washington D.C., 463-471 (1985).

[58] T. Boddington, P. Gray and D. I. Harvey, Thermal Theory of Spontaneous Ignition: Criticality in Bodies of Arbitrary Shape, Phil. Trans. Roy. London, **270**, 471 (1971).

[66] D. Gross and A. F. Robertson, Self-Ignition Temperatures of Materials from Kinetic-Reaction Data, J. Research Natl. Bur. Standards, **61**, 413-417 (1958).

[67] K. Akita, Studies on the Ignition Mechanism of Wood (in Japanese), Research Report of National Institute of Fire Fighting of Japan, **9**, 1-106 (1959).

[68] J. E. Anthony and D. Greaney, The Safety of Hot Self-Heating Materials, Combust. Sci. and Technology, **21**, 79-85 (1979).

[69] R. John, Zur Selbstentzündung von Holz. Aufheizphase und Freiwerdender Wärmestrom. Brandentstehung und Brandausbreitung-Thema 1, Proceedings of the 4th International Brandschutz-Seminar, Zürich, Switzerland, 59-84 (1973).

[70] H. Schliemann, Die Anwendung der Differential-Thermoanalyse (DTA) zur Einschätzung des Selbstentzündungsverhaltens von Holz, Holzindustrie, **30**, 140-142 (1977).

[71] H. Kubler, Air Convection in Self-Heating Piles of Wood Chips, TAPPI, **65**-8, 79 (1982).

[72] H. Bergström, Proceedings of the 3rd International Conference on Bituminous Coal, 1097 (1932).

Chapter 9 Procedure to calculate the SADT for a high explosive of the true AC type, having an arbitrary shape and an arbitrary size, confined in an arbitrary closed container of the corresponding shape and size, and placed in the atmosphere under isothermal conditions

A series of studies described in the present chapter has been performed on the assumption that only high explosives are the chemicals of the true AC type. In this regard, however, it is very probable that there exist chemicals, other than high explosives, which decompose in accordance with the autocatalytic reaction mechanism. Besides, although it is quite certain that nitrate esters, such as nitroglycerine and nitrocellulose, decompose in accordance with the autocatalytic reaction mechanism, it is beyond the scope of the present document to discuss whether nucleus-substituted polynitro compounds, such as tetryl, TNT and picric acid, also decompose in accordance with the same mechanism or not. Some other possibilities are, therefore, also suggested herein for the decomposition reaction mechanisms of a few high explosives, respectively.

9.1 Introduction

A proposition is obtained in **Section 3.2** to the effect that it is possible, in principle,* to regard the SADT calculated in accordance with Eq. (59) holding for the induction period of the autocatalytic reaction, or of the quasi-autocatalytic reaction, of 2 cm^3 of a chemical of the AC type, including every powdery chemical of the quasi-AC type, confined in the closed cell and subjected to the isothermal storage test, as the SADT for the chemical, having an arbitrary shape and an arbitrary size, confined in an arbitrary closed container of the corresponding shape and size, and placed in the atmosphere under isothermal conditions.

$$\ln \Delta t = \frac{a}{T_t} + b. \tag{59}$$

That is, for the purpose of calculating the SADT for a high explosive of the true AC type, having an arbitrary shape and an arbitrary size, confined in an arbitrary closed container of the corresponding shape and size, and placed in the atmosphere under isothermal conditions, we have only to perform several

* Practically speaking, however, as commented in a footnote in **Section 3.2**, the larger the size of the chemical, the temperature of which has been maintained at room temperature until the placement, the longer becomes naturally the time required for the temperature of the chemical as a whole to increase from room temperature up to the T_t.

isothermal storage tests at each T_t with mutual intervals of 1~2 K, in order to calculate the values of the two coefficients, *a* and *b*, of Eq. (59) holding for the induction period of the autocatalytic reaction of 2 cm^3 of the high explosive confined in the closed cell and subjected to the isothermal storage test, for 2 cm^3 each of several samples of the high explosive confined each in the closed cell, for the time, Δt, from the insertion of each cell into the isothermal storage testing device till the start of the autocatalytic reaction of the high explosive at the corresponding T_t, *i.e.*, during the induction period of the autocatalytic reaction of the high explosive at the corresponding T_t, respectively.

Thus, the procedure to calculate the SADT for a high explosive of the true AC type, having an arbitrary shape and an arbitrary size, confined in an arbitrary closed container of the corresponding shape and size and placed in the atmosphere under isothermal conditions, by applying Eq. (59) holding for the induction period of the autocatalytic reaction of 2 cm^3 of the high explosive confined in the closed cell and subjected to the isothermal storage test, is introduced in the present chapter, by taking the procedure to calculate the SADT for collodion cotton (12.19 % N), having an arbitrary shape and an arbitrary size, confined in an arbitrary closed container of the corresponding shape and size and placed in the atmosphere under isothermal conditions, as an example.

The values of SADT thus calculated each for eight high explosives of the true AC type, including collodion cotton, ranged from 54.2 ℃ for nitroglycerin to 163 ℃ for TNT.

These values of SADT calculated herein in general are in fair agreement with some corresponding temperature values measured each in different ways by other researchers for some of the high explosives of the true AC type, tested herein, of relatively large quantities, respectively.

The procedure to calculate the SADT for a powdery chemical of the quasi-AC type, having an arbitrary shape and an arbitrary size, confined in an arbitrary closed container of the corresponding shape and size, and placed in the atmosphere under isothermal conditions, by applying Eq. (59) holding for the induction period of the quasi-autocatalytic reaction of 2 cm^3 of the powdery chemical confined in the closed cell and subjected to the isothermal storage test, in the same manner as performed for a high explosive of the true AC type, is introduced in **Chapter 10**. Principles and experimental procedures which are common to both high explosives of the true AC type and powdery chemicals of the quasi-AC type are, however, explained in the present chapter.

An isothermal storage testing device used to perform the isothermal storage test at a T_t, in order to calculate ultimately the SADT for a chemical of the AC type, including every powdery chemical of the quasi-AC type, having an arbitrary shape and an arbitrary size, confined in an arbitrary closed container of the corresponding shape and size, and placed in the atmosphere under isothermal conditions, for 2 cm^3 of the chemical confined in the closed cell, for the time, Δt, from the insertion of the cell into the isothermal storage testing device till the start of the autocatalytic reaction, or of the quasi-autocatalytic reaction, of the chemical at the T_t, *i.e.*, during the induction period of the autocatalytic reaction, or of the quasi-autocatalytic reaction, of the chemical at the T_t, is introduced in **Section 9.2**.

The procedure to perform several isothermal storage tests at each T_t with mutual intervals of 1 ~ 2 K, in order to calculate the values of the two coefficients, a and b, of Eq. (59) holding for the induction period of the autocatalytic reaction of 2 cm^3 of a high explosive of the true AC type confined in the closed cell and subjected to the isothermal storage test, for 2 cm^3 each of several samples of the high explosive confined each in the closed cell, for the time, Δt, from the insertion of each cell into the isothermal storage testing device till the start of the autocatalytic reaction of the high explosive at the corresponding T_t, respectively, is explained in detail in **Section 9.3**, by taking the procedure performed for 2 cm^3 of collodion cotton (12.19 % N) confined in the closed cell as an example.

The concrete procedure to calculate the SADT for a high explosive of the true AC type, having an arbitrary shape and an arbitrary size, confined in an arbitrary closed container of the corresponding shape and size, and placed in the atmosphere under isothermal conditions, is illustrated in **Section 9.4**, by taking the procedure to calculate the SADT for collodion cotton (12.19 % N), having an arbitrary shape and an arbitrary size, confined in an arbitrary closed container of the corresponding shape and size, and placed in the atmosphere under isothermal conditions, as an example.

9.2 An isothermal storage testing device used to perform the isothermal storage test at a T_t, in order to calculate ultimately the SADT for a chemical of the AC type, including every powdery chemical of the quasi-AC type, having an arbitrary shape and an arbitrary size, confined in an arbitrary closed container of the corresponding shape and size, and placed in the atmosphere under isothermal conditions, for 2 cm^3 of the chemical confined in the closed cell, for the time, Δt, from the insertion of the cell into the isothermal storage testing device till the start of the autocatalytic reaction, or of the quasi-autocatalytic reaction, of the chemical at the T_t, *i.e.*, during the induction period of the autocatalytic reaction, or of the quasi-autocatalytic reaction, of the chemical at the T_t

9.2.1 Structure and performance

The cross section of the device is shown in Fig. 119. The aluminium block bath measures 107 mm by 107 mm and 79.6 mm in height. The glass closed cell measures 1.4 cm in outside diameter and about 3 cm in length; in other words, it is about half the size of a thumb. The cell is of the same shape and size as that used in the adiabatic self-heating process recorder (compare Fig. 124 in **(14)** of **Subsection 9.3.2** with Fig. 20 in **Subsection 4.2.2**). The accuracy of the temperature control for the aluminium block bath is ±0.05 K.

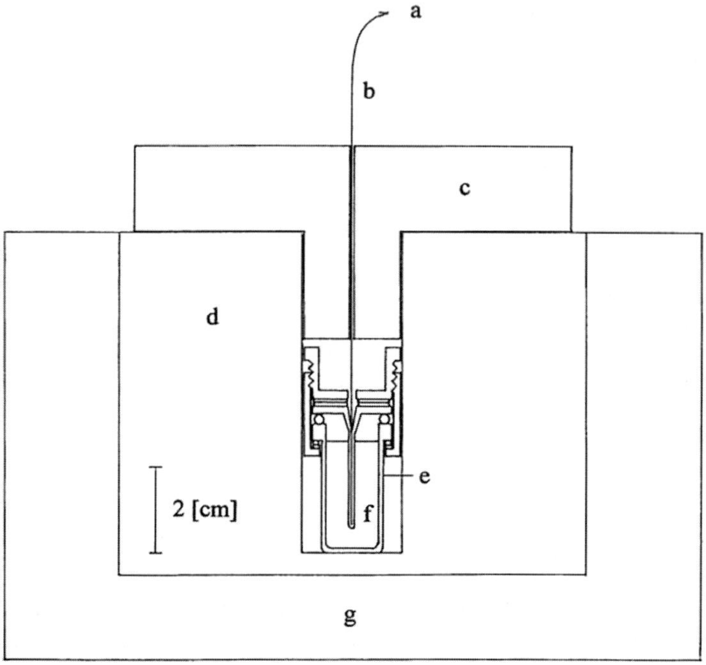

Figure 119. The cross section of the isothermal storage testing device.
a. To a temperature recorder; **b**. Thermocouple; **c**. Aluminium lid; **d**. Aluminium block bath; **e**. Glass closed cell; **f**. Sample; **g**. Heater.

It is indispensable in the isothermal storage test performed for a high explosive of the true AC type to confine the high explosive in any closed cell, because it is the prerequisite for the promotion of the autocatalytic reaction of a high explosive to confine the high explosive together with an autocatalyst such as NO_2 radical in a closed space.

The temperature of 2 cm^3 of a chemical of the AC type, including every powdery chemical of the quasi-AC type, confined in the closed cell and subjected to the isothermal storage test at a T_t is recorded by means of an analog/digital temperature recorder. The digital output of the recorder is read to 0.1 K and is printed out every 30 min; on the other hand, the analog signal of the recorder is recorded continuously with a T pen on the strip chart of the recorder to look about the induction period of the autocatalytic reaction, or of the quasi-autocatalytic reaction, of the chemical as a whole.

It is, however, evident that this device requires still considerable improvements. First of all, the temperature distribution in the aluminium block bath of this device is not necessarily uniform. In this regard, it may have been better to adopt a liquid bath rather than the aluminium block bath. Besides, it is also required to improve the thermal detection sensitivity of the temperature recorder. In this regard, it may be advisable to use the digital D.C. microvoltmeter, the digital output of which is read to 1 μV, in combination with the temperature recorder. How to use the digital D.C. microvoltmeter is described in **Section 4.7**. Moreover, if a more precisely operating thermoregulator is installed in the device, as long a time as 2 d will not be required to determine the exact value of T_t of each run [refer to **(6)** of **Subsection 9.3.3**]. Furthermore, if this device is equipped with a jack to lift and to hold the aluminium lid, it will become far easier and securer to insert the thermocouple into the reference cell assembly, or into the sample cell assembly [refer to **(4)** of **Subsection 9.3.3** and **(4)** of **Subsection 9.3.4**].

9.2.2 Dispensability of the adiabatic control

One may have some apprehensions for a fact that this device is lacking in the adiabatic control. In this connection, it is mentioned in **Section 4.1** that it is also possible, in principle, to perform the adiabatic self-heating test for a chemical of the AC type, including every powdery chemical of the quasi-AC type, confined in the closed cell by means of the adiabatic self-heating process recorder.

To perform the adiabatic self-heating test for a chemical of the AC type confined in the closed cell will be certainly more favorable than to perform the isothermal storage test for the chemical. It has, however, been thought herein that the adiabatic self-heating process recorder should be used only for the adiabatic self-heating test performed over a relatively short time, say, several hours, in order that every experimenter may be able to accompany the adiabatic self-heating process recorder throughout one run, by reason that, while the function of every adiabatic apparatus is elaborate, its structure in general is fragile, so that it is always under the necessity of being handled with care. A device such as the aluminium block bath, the structure and the function of which are tough and simple, is, therefore, necessary and optimum for the isothermal storage test which must be performed for a chemical of the AC type over a long time, say, several days.

At all events, however, once the concentration of an autocatalyst attains to the threshold value in a high explosive of the true AC type confined in the closed cell, the explosive starts the autocatalytic reaction, and thereafter, the reaction accelerates gradually, even if the test is performed under isothermal conditions. It is, therefore, possible also in the isothermal storage test to locate without much difficulty the exothermic onset point, *i.e.*, the point of time "**b**", such as indicated in Fig. 6 in **Section 3.1**, on the strip chart of the temperature recorder; in particular, it is possible and easy to do so, if the test is performed at a T_t, on the high temperature side, corresponding to a relatively small value of Δt in Eq. (59), $\ln \Delta t = a / T_t + b$, holding for the induction period of the autocatalytic reaction of 2 cm^3 of a high explosive of the true AC type confined in the closed cell and subjected to the isothermal storage test.

9.3 Procedure to perform several isothermal storage tests at each T_t with mutual intervals of 1～2 K, in order to calculate the values of the two coefficients, *a* and *b*, of Equation (59), $\ln \Delta t = a/T_t + b$, holding for the induction period of the autocatalytic reaction of 2 cm^3 of a high explosive of the true AC type confined in the closed cell and subjected to the isothermal storage test, for 2 cm^3 each of several samples of the high explosive confined each in the closed cell, for the time, Δt, from the insertion of each cell into the isothermal storage testing device till the start of the autocatalytic reaction of the high explosive at the corresponding T_t, respectively

The procedure described in the above heading is explained in detail in the present section by taking the procedure performed for 0.4 g of collodion cotton (12.19 % N), the volume of which is about 2 cm^3, confined in the closed cell as an example.

9.3.1 Preheating of the aluminium block bath of the isothermal storage testing device and the choice of a nominal T_t in the isothermal storage test performed for 0.4 g of collodion cotton confined in the closed cell

The isothermal storage testing device is placed in an air-conditioned room maintained at an almost constant (room) temperature throughout every run.

To begin with, the constant voltage power supply connected to the isothermal storage testing device is switched on.

The temperature of the aluminium block bath is set at a proper value, *i.e.*, the nominal T_t of the run, by means of the ten-key on the block bath on the basis of the self-heating property of the high explosive of the true AC type tested to give estimated values of Δt of 1～7 d in the isothermal storage test. It is usually a temperature 30～100 K lower than the EOT, which is measured by thermal analysis, such as DTA or DSC, of each high explosive in the case of high explosives of the true AC type tested herein, with the result that the T_t ranged from 55.04 ℃ for nitroglycerin to 179.9 ℃ for picric acid. As to collodion cotton (12.19 % N), the T_t ranged from 72.97 to 94.98 ℃.

The power supply connected to the block bath heater is then switched on.

9.3.2 Procedure to prepare the reference cell assembly including the closed cell

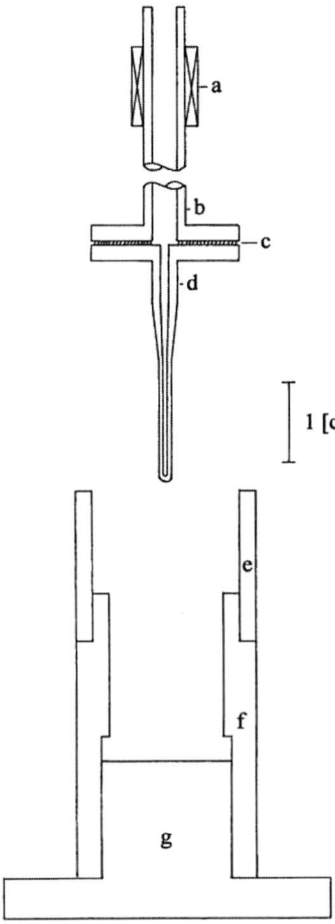

Figure 120. The temporary stem, the stainless steel jig Ⅰ and the pedestal.
a. Cramp of the stand; **b**. Glass flange tube, 106 mm in length; **c**. Fat clay; **d**. Glass capillary flange; **e**. Upper piece of the stainless steel jig Ⅰ; **f**. Lower piece of the stainless steel jig Ⅰ; **g**. Pedestal.

(1) A temporary stem, which is required to prepare the reference cell or the sample cell, is made by sticking the glass flange tube (Fig. 24 in **Section 4.3**) on the glass capillary flange (Fig. 25 in **Subsection 4.4.4**) with a bit of fat clay (refer to Fig. 120).*

(2) The stainless steel jig Ⅰ, which is composed of the upper piece and the lower piece, is set on the pedestal. The outside diameter of the pedestal and the inside diameter of the lower end of the lower piece are 16 mm and 16.1 mm, respectively. The pedestal is stuck at the center of the upper plate of the laboratory jack, which in turn is fixed on the laboratory desk. The position of the stand, by means of the cramp of which the temporary stem including the glass capillary flange is held in the vertical position, is next adjusted by sliding the stand horizontally on the laboratory desk in order that the glass capillary flange may be aligned vertically with the upper piece of the stainless steel jig Ⅰ set on the pedestal (Fig. 120). The outside diameter of the glass capillary flange and the inside diameter of the upper piece are 18 mm and 18.1 mm, respectively.

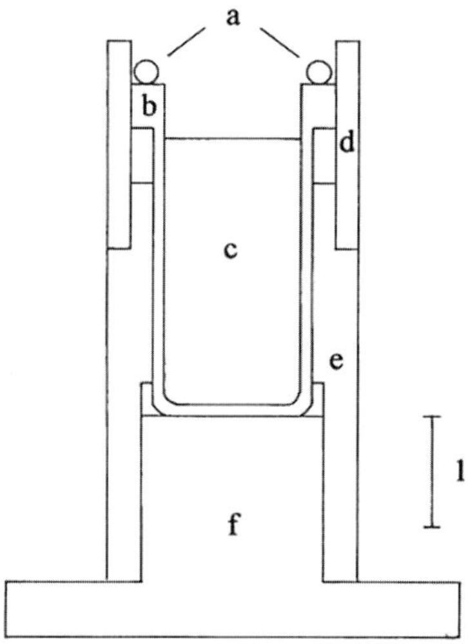

Figure 121. The stainless steel jig Ⅰ containing the closed cell, in which silica powder is charged.
a. O-ring; **b**. Closed cell; **c**. Silica powder; **d**. Upper piece of the stainless steel jig Ⅰ; **e**. Lower piece of the stainless steel jig Ⅰ; **f**. Pedestal.

* The glass flange tube is drawn, exclusive of a part of it, in Fig. 120.

(3) After having lowered the laboratory jack a little, the upper piece of the stainless steel jig Ⅰ is detached from the lower piece.

(4) 2.2 g of silica powder, the volume of which is about 2 cm^3, is charged in a closed cell, *i.e.*, the cell with which the reference cell is prepared.

(5) The closed cell, on the flange of which an O-ring is put concentrically, is set in the lower piece. The outside diameter of the flange of the closed cell and that of the upper end of the lower piece are 18 mm, respectively; in the meantime, the outside diameter of the cell body and the inside diameter of the upper end of the lower piece are 14 mm and 14.2 mm, respectively. The upper piece is then set on the lower piece. At this time, the surface of the upper end of the upper piece is higher than the upper side of the O-ring by 2 mm, which corresponds to the thickness of the flange of the glass capillary flange (Fig. 121).

(6) The stainless steel jig Ⅰ containing the closed cell, on the upper surface of the flange of which the O-ring is put concentrically, is pressed concentrically and softly up to the under surface of the glass capillary flange by raising the laboratory jack to construct the reference cell; in the meantime, the glass capillary tube projecting downward from the under surface of the glass capillary flange is inserted automatically into silica powder charged in the closed cell.

(7) After the temporary stem has been released by loosening the cramp of the stand, the stand is moved a little backward by sliding it on the desk.

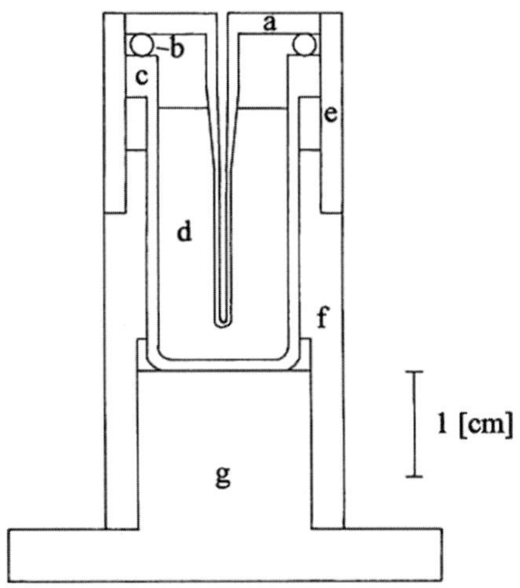

Figure 122. The reference cell constructed in the stainless steel jig Ⅰ.
a. Glass capillary flange; **b**. O-ring; **c**. Closed cell; **d**. Silica powder; **e**. Upper piece of the stainless steel jig Ⅰ; **f**. Lower piece of the stainless steel jig Ⅰ; **g**. Pedestal.

(8) The glass flange tube is detached from the glass capillary flange by sliding the former horizontally. This sliding is possible, because both the upper surface of the glass capillary flange and the surface of the upper end of the upper piece of the stainless steel jig Ⅰ are on the same horizontal plane. A bit of fat clay is then wiped fully off the upper surface of the glass capillary flange with acetone-soaked absorbent cotton (Fig. 122).

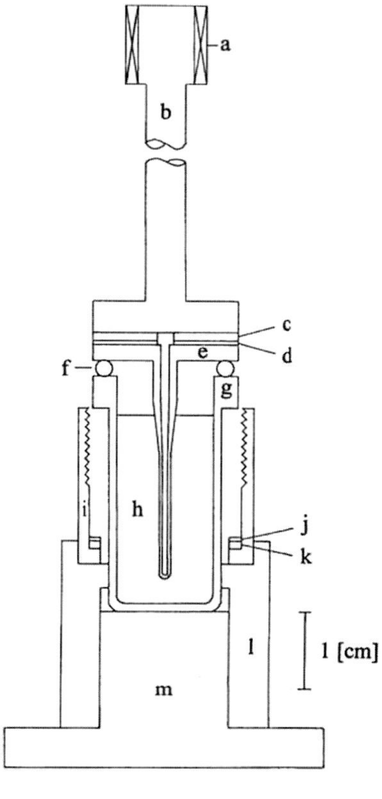

Figure 123. The state that the reference cell, on which two PTFE washers and a stainless steel washer are put, has been pressed concentrically and firmly up to the under surface of the stainless steel jig Ⅲ by raising the laboratory jack.
a. Cramp of the stand; **b**. Stainless steel jig Ⅲ, 75 mm in length; **c**. Stainless steel washer, 1 mm in thickness; **d**. Two PTFE washers, 0.3 mm each in thickness; **e**. Glass capillary flange; **f**. O-ring; **g**. Closed cell; **h**. Silica powder; **i**. Female cap nut; **j**. Two PTFE washers, 0.3 mm each in thickness; **k**. Stainless steel washer, 1 mm in thickness; **l**. Stainless steel jig Ⅱ; **m**. Pedestal.

(9) The upper piece is detached from the lower piece, into which the reference cell is now inserted. The reference cell is then taken down from the lower piece. Further, the lower piece is removed from the pedestal.

(10) The second stainless steel jig, the stainless steel jig Ⅱ, the inside diameter of the lower end of which is 16.1 mm, is set anew on the pedestal. The female cap nut, on the bottom of which a stainless steel washer and two PTFE washers are put in this order, is then set in the stainless steel jig Ⅱ. The outside diameter of the female cap nut is 22 mm, and, the inside diameter of the upper end and that of the flange of the stainless steel jig Ⅱ are 22.2 mm and 14.2 mm, respectively. Thereafter, the reference cell is inserted into the composite of the female cap nut and the stainless steel jig Ⅱ. Two PTFE washers and a stainless steel washer are then put concentrically in this order on the upper surface of the glass capillary flange (see **d** and **c** in Fig. 123).

(11) After the third stainless steel jig, the stainless steel jig Ⅲ, the diameter of the under flange of which is 18 mm, has been held in the vertical position by means of the cramp of the stand, the position of the stand is adjusted by sliding the stand horizontally on the laboratory desk in order that the under flange of the stainless steel jig Ⅲ may be aligned vertically with the reference cell (refer to Fig. 123).

(12) The reference cell, on the upper surface of the flange of which two PTFE washers and a stainless steel washer are put, is then pressed concentrically and firmly up to the under surface of the stainless steel jig Ⅲ by raising the laboratory jack (Fig. 123).*

(13) First the female cap nut is raised with the left hand. Then, pressing the female cap nut up to the under surface of the flange of the reference cell with the left hand, the laboratory jack is lowered. After the female cap nut, into which the reference cell is inserted, has been detached down from the stainless steel jig Ⅲ with the left hand, the male cap nut is screwed lightly into the female cap nut with the right hand.

(14) Holding the female cap nut with a pair of pliers in the left hand, the male cap nut, which is screwed lightly into the female cap nut, is tightened as fast as possible with the right hand. The male cap nut is then tightened further by about 30° using another pair of pliers in the right hand (Fig. 124). A fairly small vibrator is finally applied to the base of the closed cell in order that silica powder confined in the cell may come closely in contact with the glass capillary tube.

---

* The stainless steel jig Ⅲ is drawn, exclusive of a part of it, in Fig. 123.

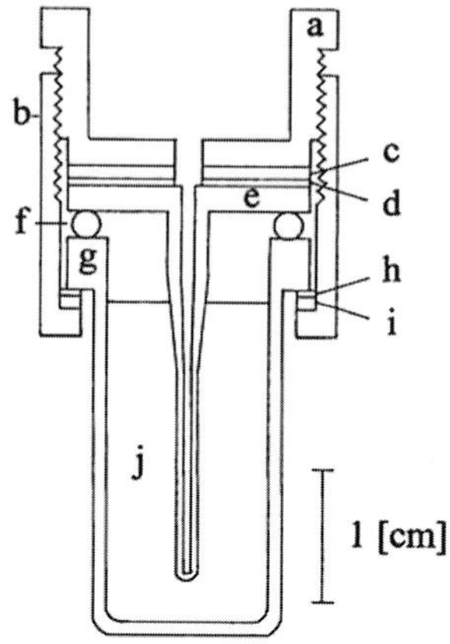

Figure 124. Completion of the reference cell assembly including the closed cell used in the isothermal storage test.
a. Male cap nut; **b**. Female cap nut; **c**. Stainless steel washer, 1 mm in thickness; **d**. Two PTFE washers, 0.3 mm each in thickness; **e**. Glass capillary flange; **f**. O-ring; **g**. Closed cell; **h**. Two PTFE washers, 0.3 mm each in thickness; **i**. Stainless steel washer, 1 mm in thickness; **j**. Silica powder.

9.3.3 Insertion of the reference cell assembly into the preheated aluminium block bath in the isothermal storage testing device and the determination of the exact value of T_t of the run

For a series of procedures performed in the present subsection, refer to Fig. 119.

(1) First the thermocouple is pulled out of the orifice at the center of the upper surface of the aluminium lid with the bare left hand; and, the thermocouple of about 30 cm from the tip is squeezed through between the thumb and the forefinger of the right hand to make the thermocouple straight. The thermocouple is then laid by the left side of the device.

(2) The aluminium lid is drawn out of the hole at the center of the upper surface of the preheated aluminium block bath with a handle* in the gloved hands, wearing a pair of working gloves in the isothermal storage test performed at a T_t up to about 80 ℃, and, wearing a pair of heat-proof gloves

* This handle is not drawn in Fig. 119, because it is demountable.

besides a pair of working gloves in the test performed at a T_t in excess of 80 ℃. Thereafter, the lid is laid by one side on the upper surface of the aluminium block bath.

(3) The reference cell assembly is raised with a pair of fairly large pincers and is inserted carefully down to the bottom of the hole, 23 mm in diameter, 75 mm in depth, bored vertically at the center of the upper surface of the preheated aluminium block bath which is set in the isothermal storage testing device; in the meantime, the temperature of the bath is maintained at the T_t K of the run throughout every run.

(4) The aluminium lid is raised with the handle in the gloved left hand. The thermocouple is then pierced through the orifice at the center of the upper surface of the lid. The diameter of the thermocouple and that of the orifice are 0.5 and 1 mm, respectively. After the thermocouple has been drawn by 20 cm or more out of the orifice at the center of the under surface of the lid, the aluminium lid is next brought from above little by little closer to the hole at the center of the upper surface of the aluminium block bath, in order that the tip of the thermocouple may be inserted into the orifice of the glass capillary tube at the center of the upper surface of the glass capillary flange of the reference cell assembly which is inserted down to the bottom of the hole in the aluminium block bath. After it has been confirmed that the tip of the thermocouple is inserted into the orifice of the glass capillary tube, the lid is inserted slowly and carefully into the hole while supported with the handle in the gloved left hand and the largish pincers in the gloved right hand.

(5) Thereafter, whether or not the thermocouple is inserted down to the bottom of the glass capillary tube is ascertained by holding the thermocouple above the lid with a few fingers of the naked right hand and then pushing it down to the bottom of the tube carefully once or twice.

(6) The exact value of T_t of the run is then determined as the arithmetic mean of a series of digital outputs of T_t recorded for 2 d prior to the insertion of the sample cell assembly into the aluminium block bath. Fluctuations of the values of T_t during this time are within ±0.05 K.

9.3.4 Insertion of the sample cell assembly into the aluminium block bath and the start of the isothermal storage test for 0.4 g of collodion cotton confined in the closed cell and inserted into the aluminium block bath maintained at the T_t

For a series of procedures performed in the present subsection, refer to Fig. 119.

(1) First the thermocouple is pulled out of the orifice at the center of the upper surface of the aluminium lid with the bare left hand; and, the thermocouple of about 30 cm from the tip is squeezed through between the thumb and the forefinger of the right hand to make the thermocouple straight. The thermocouple is then laid by the left side of the device.

(2) The aluminium lid is drawn out of the hole at the center of the upper surface of the preheated aluminium block bath with the handle in the gloved hands. Thereafter, the lid is laid by one side on the upper surface of the aluminium block bath.

(3) After the reference cell assembly has been taken out with a pair of fairly large pincers, the sample cell assembly, in which 0.4 g of collodion cotton has been confined in the same manner as performed to prepare the reference cell assembly in **Subsection 9.3.2**, is inserted carefully down to the bottom of the hole at the center of the upper surface of the aluminium block bath with the same pair of fairly large pincers.

The quantity of the high explosive of the true AC type tested depends naturally on its specific gravity, with the result that it ranged from 0.4 g for nitrocellulose, which is composed of gun cotton and collodion cotton, to 2.4 g for nitroglycerin in the case of high explosives of the true AC type tested herein.

Coarse crystals or particles should be tested after having been pulverized by means of an agate mortar.

When occasions demand, there are cases in each of which a fairly small vibrator is applied to the base of the closed cell in order that the high explosive confined in the cell may come closely in contact with the glass capillary tube.

(4) The aluminium lid is raised with the handle in the gloved left hand. The thermocouple is then pierced through the orifice at the center of the upper surface of the lid. After the thermocouple has been drawn by 20 cm or more out of the orifice at the center of the under surface of the lid, the aluminium lid is brought from above little by little closer to the hole at the center of the upper surface of the aluminium block bath, in order that the tip of the thermocouple may be inserted into the orifice of the glass capillary tube at the center of the upper surface of the glass capillary flange of the sample cell assembly which is inserted down to the bottom of the hole in the aluminium block bath. After it has been confirmed that the tip of the thermocouple is inserted into the orifice of the glass capillary tube, the lid is inserted slowly and carefully into the hole while supported with the handle in the gloved left hand and with the fairly large pincers in the gloved right hand.

(5) Thereafter, whether or not the thermocouple is inserted down to the bottom of the glass capillary tube is ascertained by holding the thermocouple above the lid with a few fingers of the naked right hand and then pushing it down to the bottom of the tube carefully once or twice.

(6) A point, on the T_t baseline* recorded on the strip chart of the analog/digital temperature recorder, where the T pen sprang suddenly away from the T_t baseline by reason that the thermocouple was pulled suddenly out of the orifice

* The linear locus drawn by the T_t pen on the strip chart of the analog/digital temperature recorder is called the T_t baseline.

at the center of the upper surface of the preheated aluminium lid in **(1)** of the present subsection, is regarded as the starting time of the isothermal storage test performed at the T_t for 0.4 g of collodion cotton confined in the closed cell. The record of the induction period of the autocatalytic reaction of 0.4 g of collodion cotton confined in the closed cell and subjected to the isothermal storage test by means of the analog/digital temperature recorder is then started. This point of time corresponds to the point, **Room temperature**, in Fig. 6 in **Section 3.1**.

(7) The exact value of T_t of the run, which was determined in **(6)** of **Subsection 9.3.3**, and the starting time of the isothermal storage test, which was determined in **(6)** of the present subsection, are noted down on a separate sheet.

9.3.5 Record of the induction period of the autocatalytic reaction of 0.4 g of collodion cotton confined in the closed cell and subjected to the isothermal storage test performed at the T_t

After the start of the isothermal storage test, as stated in **(6)** of **Subsection 9.3.4**, the induction period of the autocatalytic reaction of 0.4 g of collodion cotton confined in the closed cell and subjected to the isothermal storage test performed at the T_t, *i.e.*, the time, Δt, from the insertion of the cell into the isothermal storage testing device till the start of the autocatalytic reaction of collodion cotton at the T_t, is recorded by means of the analog/digital temperature recorder.

The test, including the heating of the aluminium block bath, is interrupted automatically as soon as the temperature of collodion cotton in the cell increases by 0.3 K (by 0.2 K, as to nitroglycerin) from the T_t in order to prevent the cell from exploding. As a matter of fact, however, the test is usually interrupted as soon as the temperature of the high explosive in the cell increases obviously in excess of the T_t.*

The other combinations of the value of $\ln \Delta t$ with that of $1/T_t$, which are required to make the plot of $\ln \Delta t$ versus $1/T_t$ with regard to several induction periods, of the autocatalytic reaction, of 0.4 g each of several samples of collodion cotton confined each in the closed cell and subjected each to the isothermal storage test performed at each T_t in the range of 72.97 to 94.98 ℃ with mutual intervals of 2～5 K, recorded each for the time, Δt, from the insertion of each cell into the isothermal storage testing device till the start of the autocatalytic reaction of collodion cotton at the corresponding T_t, besides, which are required for the regression analysis to calculate the values of the two coefficients, *a* and *b*, of Eq. (59) holding for the induction period of the autocatalytic reaction of 0.4 g of collodion cotton confined in the closed cell

* For the cleaning procedure performed for the sample cell assembly in which a chemical, which has solidified after the isothermal storage test, is confined, refer to a footnote in **Subsection 10.2.5**.

and subjected to the isothermal storage test, are also determined in the same manner as explained above.

Five induction periods, of the autocatalytic reaction, of 0.4 g each of five samples of collodion cotton confined each in the closed cell and subjected each to the isothermal storage test performed at each T_t in the range of 72.97 to 94.98 ℃ with mutual intervals of 2∼7 K, recorded each for the time, Δt, from the insertion of each cell into the isothermal storage testing device till the start of the autocatalytic reaction of collodion cotton at the corresponding T_t, are presented in Fig. 125. The time axis on the other side in Fig. 125 and that in Fig. 126 are graduated in d to meet the sense of long time, respectively. The points marked with "**b**" on the curves in Fig. 125 correspond to the point of time "**b**" in Fig. 6 in **Section 3.1**, respectively.

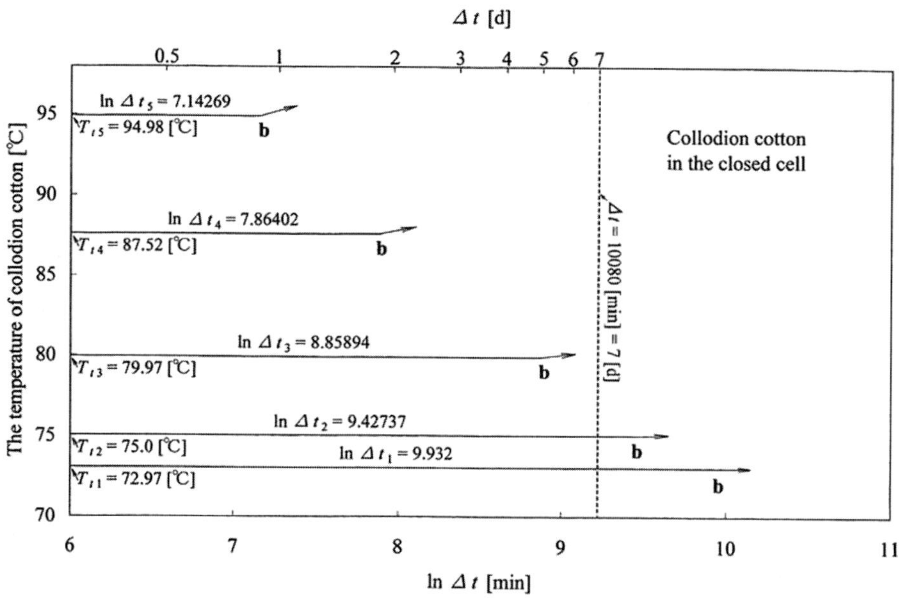

Figure 125. Five induction periods, of the autocatalytic reaction, of 0.4 g each of five samples of collodion cotton confined each in the closed cell and subjected each to the isothermal storage test performed at each T_t in the range of 72.97 to 94.98 ℃ with mutual intervals of 2∼7 K, recorded each for the time, Δt, from the insertion of each cell into the isothermal storage testing device till the start of the autocatalytic reaction of collodion cotton at the corresponding T_t.

The plot of $\ln \Delta t$ versus $1/T_t$ made for 0.4 g each of nine samples of collodion cotton is shown in Fig. 126.

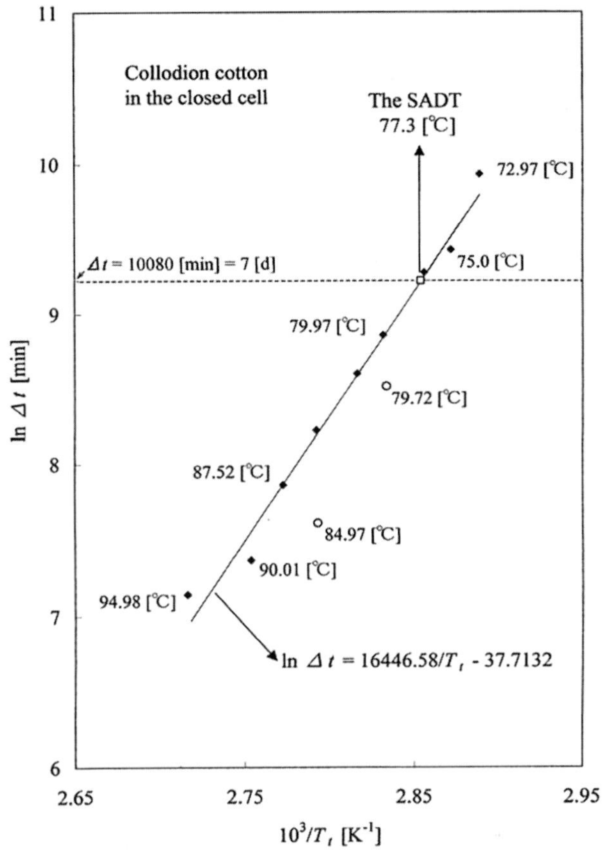

Figure 126. The plot of $\ln \Delta t$ versus $1/T_t$ made with nine combinations of the value of $\ln \Delta t$ with that of $1/T_t$, which are each determined for nine induction periods, five induction periods of which are presented in Fig. 125, of the autocatalytic reaction, of 0.4 g each of nine samples of collodion cotton confined each in the closed cell and subjected each to the isothermal storage test performed at each T_t in the range of 72.97 to 94.98 ℃ with mutual intervals of 2～5 K, recorded each for the time, Δt, from the insertion of each cell into the isothermal storage testing device till the start of the autocatalytic reaction of collodion cotton at the corresponding T_t.

The symbol "○" indicates a plot for wet collodion cotton.

It is obvious in Fig. 126 that the empirical formula, $\ln \Delta t = a/T_t + b$, *i.e.*, Eq. (59), presented in Fig. 6 in **Section 3.1** holds well between a T_t and the time, Δt, from the insertion of the closed cell, in which 0.4 g of collodion cotton is confined, into the isothermal storage testing device till the start of the autocatalytic reaction of collodion cotton at the T_t.

For the value of a coefficient, 16446.58, of the equation, $\ln \Delta t = 16446.58/T_t - 37.7132$, *i.e.*, Eq. (59) holding for the induction period of the autocatalytic reaction of 0.4 g of collodion cotton confined in the closed cell and subjected to the isothermal storage test, refer to the explanation given under Table 22 in the following subsection.

The broken line in Fig. 125 and that in Fig. 126 denote 7 d, respectively. The temperature coordinates, 77.3 ℃, of the intersection, which is indicated with the symbol "□" in Fig. 126, of the plot of $\ln \Delta t$ versus $1/T_t$ and the broken line must, therefore, be the SADT for collodion cotton tested herein, in accordance with the definition of the SADT.

It is seen in Figs. 125 and 126 that, when confined in the closed cell and subjected to the isothermal storage test performed at a T_t, the autocatalytic reaction of collodion cotton takes place even at temperatures below the SADT calculated herein. It thus follows that the thermal explosion of collodion cotton, having an arbitrary shape and an arbitrary size, confined in an arbitrary closed container of the corresponding shape and size, and placed in the atmosphere under isothermal conditions, is able to take place even at temperatures below the SADT calculated herein. Several induction periods, of the autocatalytic reaction, of 0.4 g each of several samples of collodion cotton confined each in the closed cell and subjected each to the isothermal storage test performed at each of several values of T_t below the SADT, were thus measured further.

When confined in the closed cell and subjected to the isothermal storage test performed at a T_t of 76.97 ℃, *i.e.*, a temperature a little lower than the SADT calculated herein, 0.4 g of collodion cotton started the autocatalytic reaction, though faintly, about 7.42 d after the start of the isothermal storage test. The sample was found to be yellow and gave off the odor of nitrogen dioxide after the test; the inside of the cell was found to be pressurized besides.

When confined in the closed cell and subjected to the isothermal storage test performed at a T_t of 75.0 ℃, 0.4 [g] of collodion cotton started the autocatalytic reaction, though faintly, about 8.63 d after the start of the isothermal storage test. The sample was found to be pale yellow and gave off the odor of nitrogen dioxide after the test.

When confined in the closed cell and subjected to the isothermal storage test performed at a T_t of 72.97 ℃, 0.4 g of collodion cotton started the autocatalytic reaction, though faintly, about 14.3 d after the start of the isothermal storage test. The sample gave off the odor of nitrogen dioxide but was not found to be colored after the test.

When confined in the closed cell and subjected to the isothermal storage test performed at a T_t of 69.29 ℃, 0.4 g of collodion cotton did not start the autocatalytic reaction within 23 d of the start of the isothermal storage test. It does not necessarily follow, however, that the autocatalytic reaction of collodion cotton that may leads to the thermal explosion does not occur absolutely at this temperature, 69.29 ℃, because, although the start of the autocatalytic reaction of collodion cotton was not observed clearly at this temperature, the center of the sample was found to be slightly yellow and the sample gave off a little the odor of nitrogen dioxide after the test.

It is, thus, clear that it is indispensable to assign a due safety margin to the value of SADT calculated for each high explosive of the true AC type tested herein. It is for this reason that it is stated at the final paragraph of **Section 9.5** that the upper limit temperature for the safe handling of a high explosive of the true AC type will be a temperature 30 K lower than the SADT calculated herein. Similarly, it is stated in **Chapter 10** as well that the upper limit temperature for the safe handling of a powdery chemical of the quasi-AC type will be a temperature 30 K lower than the SADT calculated herein.

In this connection, a case should also be mentioned here that an SADT of 69.1 ℃ was calculated for a certain lot of collodion cotton (11.75 % N), which was thought to be contaminated by trace amounts of metals which might have been derived from the nitration process (Fig. 127).

Even when confined in the closed cell and subjected to the isothermal storage test performed at a T_t of 65 ℃, 0.4 g of collodion cotton contaminated by metals, above referred to, started the autocatalytic reaction, though faintly, about 12.8 d after the start of the isothermal storage test. The sample was found to be yellow and gave off the odor of nitrogen dioxide after the test; the inside of the cell was found to be pressurized besides.

There are thus good reasons for considering 35 ℃ as the upper limit temperature for the safe handling of collodion cotton of the kind above referred to.

9.3.6 Calculation of the values of the two coefficients, *a* and *b*, of Equation (59), $\ln \Delta t = a/T_t + b$, holding for the induction period of the autocatalytic reaction of 0.4 g of collodion cotton confined in the closed cell and subjected to the isothermal storage test

The result of the regression analysis to calculate the values of the two coefficients, a and b, of Eq. (59), $\ln \Delta t = a/T_t + b$, holding for the induction period of the autocatalytic reaction of 0.4 g of collodion cotton confined in the closed cell and subjected to the isothermal storage test is presented in Table 22.

Values of $\ln \Delta t$ and $1/T_t$ used in the regression analysis are in common with those presented in part in Fig. 125 and plotted in Fig. 126. The values of T_t presented in Figs. 125 and 126 are, however, all rounded. For an instance similar to this, refer to Tables 5 and 6 in **Section 4.7** and Figs. 45 and 46 in **Subsection 5.4.5**.

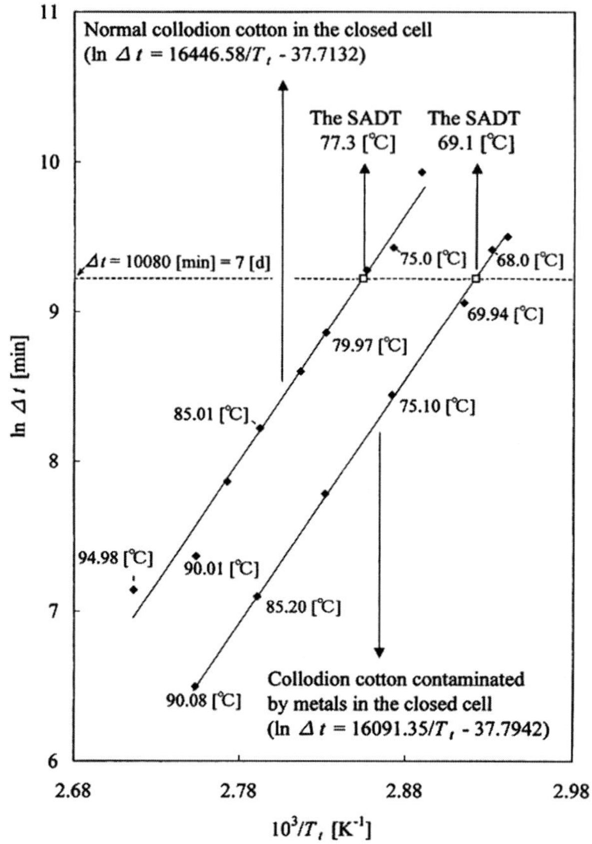

Figure 127. Comparison of the plot of ln Δt versus $1/T_t$ made with seven combinations of the value of ln Δt with that of $1/T_t$, which are each determined for seven induction periods, of the autocatalytic reaction, of 0.4 g each of seven samples of collodion cotton (11.75 % N), contaminated by metals, confined each in the closed cell and subjected each to the isothermal storage test performed at each T_t in the range of 66.95 to 90.08 ℃ with mutual intervals of 1∼5 K, recorded each for the time, Δt, from the insertion of each cell into the isothermal storage testing device till the start of the autocatalytic reaction of collodion cotton contaminated by metals at the corresponding T_t, with, the plot made for 0.4 g each of nine samples of normal collodion cotton (12.19 % N) placed each under the same conditions as the former. The latter plot is quoted from Fig. 126, for comparison.

Table 22
The result of the regression analysis applied, in order to calculate the values of the two coefficients, *a* and *b*, of Equation (59), $\ln \Delta t = a/T_t + b$, holding for the induction period of the autocatalytic reaction of 0.4 g of collodion cotton confined in the closed cell and subjected to the isothermal storage test, to nine combinations of the value of $\ln \Delta t$ with that of $1/T_t$, which are each determined, based on nine analog/digital records obtained each from nine isothermal storage tests performed each, at each T_t in the range of 72.97 to 94.98 ℃ with mutual intervals of 2∼5 K, for 0.4 g each of nine samples of collodion cotton confined each in the closed cell, for the time, Δt, from the insertion of each cell into the isothermal storage testing device till the start of the autocatalytic reaction of collodion cotton at the corresponding T_t. Data used are in common with those presented in part in Fig. 125 and plotted in Fig. 126.

MATERIAL ... Collodion cotton

DATA NUMBER	X	Y	A＊X+B
1	2.88913	9.93200	9.803077
2	2.87232	9.42737	9.526610
3	2.85620	9.27625	9.261491
4	2.83186	8.85894	8.861181
5	2.81649	8.60119	8.608397
6	2.79208	8.22191	8.206936
7	2.77262	7.86402	7.886886
8	2.75363	7.36703	7.574565
9	2.71640	7.14269	6.962259

COEFFICIENT OF Y = A＊TT + B A = 16.44658
COEFFICIENT OF Y = A＊TT + B B = -37.7132

DISTRIBUTION = 0.014731 STANDARD DEVIATION = 0.121372

Based on the result, the value of *a* for collodion cotton is calculated by multiplying the value of A, which is presented in Table 22, by 1,000 in the same manner as performed for the value of A of TBPB in **Section 4.7**.

The values of the two coefficients, *a* and *b*, thus calculated, of Eq. (59), $\ln \Delta t = a/T_t + b$, holding for the induction period of the autocatalytic reaction of 0.4

[g] of collodion cotton confined in the closed cell and subjected to the isothermal storage test, 16446.58 and -37.7132, are presented as such in Table 24 in **Section 9.5**.

9.4 Concrete procedure to calculate the SADT for a high explosive of the true AC type, having an arbitrary shape and an arbitrary size, confined in an arbitrary closed container of the corresponding shape and size, and placed in the atmosphere under isothermal conditions

According to the proposition obtained in **Section 3.2**, the SADT for a high explosive of the true AC type, having an arbitrary shape and an arbitrary size, confined in an arbitrary closed container of the corresponding shape and size, and placed in the atmosphere under isothermal conditions, is calculated, in accordance with the definition of the SADT, at a value of T_t corresponding to a value of Δt of 7 d, *i.e.*, 10,080 min, in Eq. (59) holding for the induction period of the autocatalytic reaction of 2 cm^3 of the high explosive confined in the closed cell and subjected to the isothermal storage test.

$$\ln \Delta t = \frac{a}{T_t} + b. \tag{59}$$

As an example, the concrete procedure to calculate the SADT for collodion cotton, having an arbitrary shape and an arbitrary size, confined in an arbitrary closed container of the corresponding shape and size, and placed in the atmosphere under isothermal conditions, is illustrated in the present section.

The values of the two coefficients, a and b, of Eq. (59) holding for the induction period of the autocatalytic reaction of 0.4 g of collodion cotton confined in the closed cell and subjected to the isothermal storage test were calculated in **Subsection 9.3.6** and are given in Table 24 in **Section 9.5**.

The value of SADT for collodion cotton, having an arbitrary shape and an arbitrary size, confined in an arbitrary closed container of the corresponding shape and size, and placed in the atmosphere under isothermal conditions, is thus calculated in the following manner.

$$T_t = \frac{a}{\ln \Delta t - b} \quad = 16446.58 \div (\ln 10080 + 37.7132)$$

$$= 16446.58 \div (9.21831 + 37.7132)$$

$$= 16446.58 \div 46.93151$$

$$= 350.4379 \text{ K} = 77.2879 \text{ °C}.$$

The value of SADT thus calculated for collodion cotton, having an arbitrary shape and an arbitrary size, confined in an arbitrary closed container of the corresponding shape and size, and placed in the atmosphere under isothermal conditions, 77.2879 ℃, is finally rounded to 77.3 ℃ and is presented as such, together with the values of SADT calculated each for the seven high explosives of the true AC type, other than collodion cotton, in the same manner as performed for collodion cotton, in Table 24 in **Section 9.5**.

Once the values of the two coefficients, *a* and *b*, of Eq. (59) holding for the induction period of the autocatalytic reaction of 2 cm^3 of a high explosive of the true AC type confined in the closed cell and subjected to the isothermal storage test are fixed, it becomes possible to calculate, for the high explosive, an arbitrary value of T_t, as well as the SADT, corresponding to an arbitrary value of Δt, *i.e.*, an arbitrary exposure time, such as 1 h, 1 d or 30 d. Such a value of temperature may be useful as the upper limit temperature in temperature control to prevent the high explosive from exploding thermally after the corresponding exposure time.

9.5 The values of SADT calculated each for the eight high explosives of the true AC type, including collodion cotton

The list of the eight high explosives of the true AC type tested is given in Table 23.

These high explosives of the true AC type, except nitroglycerin, are of the industrial grade or of the reagent grade and were tested without further purification. In this connection, each high explosive of the true AC type was tested, in principle, in the dry state. The dehydration was performed for the seven high explosives of the true AC type, except nitroglycerin, in a vacuum by means of a rotary pump at about 60 ℃ on a glycerin bath for 2～3 h, respectively.

The isothermal storage tests for the seven high explosives of the true AC type, other than collodion cotton, were also performed in the same manner as done for collodion cotton, respectively.

The eight plots of ln Δt versus $1/T_t$ made each for the eight high explosives of the true AC type, including collodion cotton, are presented in Fig. 128. For the whole plot for picric acid, refer to Fig. 140 in **Subsection 9.6.6**.

Table 23.
The eight high explosives of the true AC type tested herein.

High explosives	Composition, *etc.*	The maker
Nitroglycerin	1.598[a]	Nitroglycerin tested herein was synthesized at the N.I.I.S. on referring to directions given in a reference [79].
Guncotton	13.50 % N	NOF Co., Ltd.
Collodion cotton	12.19 % N	NOF Co., Ltd.
PETN used for percussion caps	98.90 % N	Asahi Chemical Industries Co., Ltd.
PETN used for medicine	>99.00 % N	Asahi Chemical Industries Co., Ltd.
Tetryl	b	Chugoku Kayaku Co., Ltd.
TNT	c	Chugoku Kayaku Co., Ltd.
Picric acid	d	Aldrich Chemical Co., Ltd.

[a]The specific gravity measured at 15 ℃.
[b]Result of elemental analysis for tetryl (theoretical values in parentheses): 24.82 (24.39) % N; 29.56 (29.3) % C; 1.77 (1.8) % H.
[c]Result of elemental analysis for TNT (theoretical values in parentheses): 18.65 (18.5) % N; 36.88 (37.0) % C; 2.207 (2.2) % H.
[d]Picric acid tested herein is of the A. C. S. reagent grade (98 % picric acid) and was got from Aldrich chemical Co., Inc. as moist picric acid containing 35 % water. The moist picric acid was dehydrated before testing in accordance with directions described under the heading of **Section 9.5**.

The individual values of the two coefficients, *a* and *b*, of Eq. (59) holding for the individual induction periods of the autocatalytic reaction of 2 cm^3 each of the seven high explosives of the true AC type,* other than collodion cotton, confined each in the closed cell and subjected each to the isothermal storage test were also calculated by applying the regression analysis to the individual

* As to nitroglycerin, the sample volume was 1.5 cm^3.

combinations of the value of ln Δt with that of $1/T_t$ and are presented in Table 24.

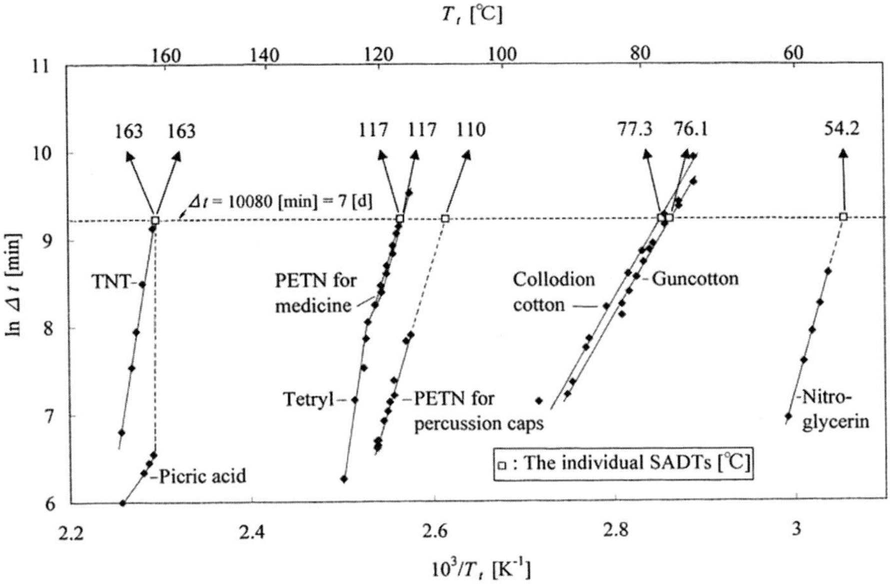

Figure 128. The eight plots of ln Δt versus $1/T_t$ made each for the eight high explosives of the true AC type.

It is possible to see roughly from Fig. 128 the relative liability of these high explosives of the true AC type to self-heating or ultimate thermal explosion. That is, we can tell that nitroglycerin and nitrocellulose are relatively easy to explode thermally, but TNT and picric acid are relatively hard to do so. In this regard, PETN and tetryl are medium in the liability to thermal explosion.

The values of SADT calculated each for the eight high explosives of the true AC type, including collodion cotton, are summarized in Table 24 in the order of increasing value of SADT, together with some corresponding temperature values measured each in different ways by other researchers for some of the high explosives of the true AC type, tested herein, of relatively large quantities as well as the conventional ignition temperatures of these high explosives, for comparison [73].

Table 24
Experimental parameters of the eight high explosives of the true AC type and comparison of the values of SADT calculated each for these high explosives, assuming that the SADT for a high explosive of the true AC type, having an arbitrary shape and an arbitrary size, confined in an arbitrary closed container of the corresponding shape and size, and placed in the atmosphere under isothermal conditions, is a value of T_t corresponding to a value of Δt of 10,080 min in Eq. (59) holding for the induction period of the autocatalytic reaction of 2 cm^3 of the high explosive confined in the closed cell and subjected to the isothermal storage test, with, some corresponding temperature values measured each in different ways by other researchers for some of the high explosives of the true AC type, tested herein, of relatively large quantities as well as the conventional ignition temperatures of these high explosives.

High explosive of the true AC type	Coefficients of Eq. (59) *a*	*b*	The SADT calculated herein ℃	The corresponding temp. value measured by other researchers ℃	Conventional ignition temperature [78] ℃
Nitroglycerin	36074.27	-100.971	54.2[a)]	50~60[b)] [74]	188
Guncotton	17059.36	-39.6227	76.1	145[c)] [75]	187
Collodion cotton	16446.58	-37.7132	77.3		
PETN for percussion caps	34593.34	-81.1463	110		205
Tetryl	36586.12	-84.6744	117	106[d)] [60] 136[e)] [76] 152[f)][40]	180
PETN for medicine	34583.67	-79.4851	117		
TNT	64132.49	-137.93	163	175[g)] [77]	240
Picric acid	-	-	163		

Superscripts:
a) The sample volume of nitroglycerin is 1.5 cm^3.
b) The temperature range in which nitroglycerin begins to decompose. This temperature range was quoted by T. L. Davis from a paper published by Snelling *et al.* [80].
c) A value of T_c for nitrocellulose powder (13.4 % N) formed into a cylinder, 1.1 cm in diameter, 1.3 in specific gravity, and placed in the atmosphere under isothermal conditions.

[d] This temperature value was quoted by T. Yoshida as the so-called SADT of tetryl from a paper published by M. Arai *et al.* [81].

[e] A value of T_c for molten tetryl charged in a cylindrical glass vessel, 4.94 cm in inner diameter, 14.82 (= 4.94 × 3) cm in length, and placed in the atmosphere under isothermal, but open, conditions.

[f] A value of T_c for molten tetryl charged in a cylindrical glass vessel, 4.90 cm in inside diameter, 14.7 (= 4.9 × 3) cm in length, and stirred vigorously and placed in the atmosphere under isothermal, but open, conditions.

[g] According to H. J. Pasman, when confined in the closed cell and subjected to the adiabatic self-heating test started from a T_s of 175 ℃, molten TNT exploded thermally about 50 h after the start of the test.

The values of SADT thus calculated each for the eight high explosives of the true AC type ranged from 54.2 ℃ for nitroglycerin to 163 ℃ for TNT.

These values of SADT calculated herein in general are in fair agreement with some corresponding temperature values measured each in different ways by other researchers for some of the high explosives of the true AC type, tested herein, of relatively large quantities, respectively.

It is pointed out in **Section 3.2** that the SADT, including an arbitrary value of T_t, for a chemical of the AC type, including every powdery chemical of the quasi-AC type, having an arbitrary shape and an arbitrary size, confined in an arbitrary closed container of the corresponding shape and size, and placed in the atmosphere under isothermal conditions, does not depend, in principle, on its size or quantity. This indication is substantiated in Table 24 by the fact that the values of SADT calculated each herein for 2 cm^3 each of the eight high explosives of the true AC type confined each in the closed cell are in fair agreement with some corresponding temperature values measured each in different ways by other researchers for some of the high explosives of the true AC type, tested herein, of relatively large quantities, respectively. The same is true of the individual values of SADT, which are presented in Table 27 in **Subsection 10.4.1**, calculated herein for 2 cm^3 each of five powdery chemicals of the quasi-AC type confined each in the closed cell.

At all events, however, it will be reasonable, in practice, to consider a temperature 30 K lower than the value of SADT calculated herein for a high explosive of the true AC type, having an arbitrary shape and an arbitrary size, confined in an arbitrary closed container of the corresponding shape and size, and placed in the atmosphere under isothermal conditions, as the upper limit temperature for the safe handling of the high explosive. For instance, 25 ℃ will be the upper limit temperature for the safe handling of nitroglycerin, 45 ℃ for nitrocellulose, but 35 ℃ for nitrocellulose contaminated by metals, 80 ℃ for PETN used for percussion caps, and so forth.

9.6 Particular high explosives of the true AC type

9.6.1 Nitroglycerin

Nitroglycerin tested herein was synthesized at the N.I.I.S. on referring to directions for synthesis which was given in a reference [79].

Nitroglycerin thus obtained was oily, heavy, transparent and colorless liquid. Its specific gravity was found to be 1.598 at 15 ℃.

A TG-DTA curve, which was recorded with a glass open-cup cell, 5 mm in diameter, 2.5 mm in depth, at a value of ϕ of 2.5 K/min in air at atmospheric pressure, of nitroglycerin is presented in Fig. 129.

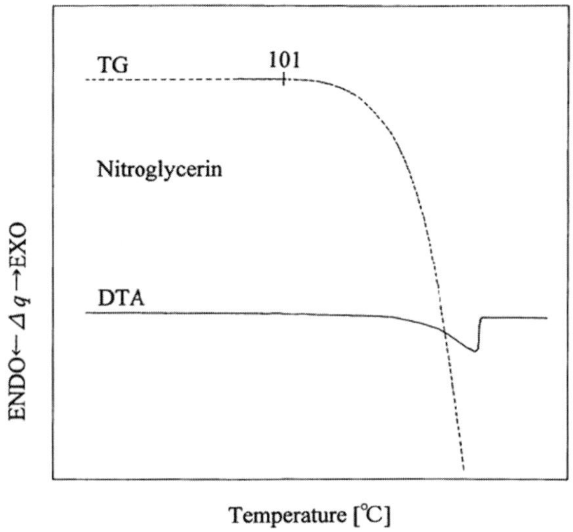

Figure 129. A TG-DTA curve of nitroglycerin.

It is seen in Fig. 129 that nitroglycerin begins to lose weight at about 100 ℃ but the autocatalytic reaction of nitroglycerin is covered with the endothermic effect caused by the vaporization of nitroglycerin itself.

When confined in the closed cell and subjected to the isothermal storage test performed at a T_t above 55 ℃, however, 1.5 cm^3 of nitroglycerin, the mass of which is about 2.4 g, behaves as a chemical of the AC type in such a manner as to start the autocatalytic reaction a long time after the start of the isothermal storage test in accordance with Eq. (59). This manner is the same as that shown in Fig. 6 presented in **Section 3.1**.

When confined in the closed cell and subjected to the isothermal storage test performed at a T_t of 61.11 ℃, 1.5 cm^3 of nitroglycerin started the autocatalytic reaction about 17.5 h after the start of the isothermal storage test. The sample was found to be pale yellow and gave off the odor of nitrogen dioxide after the test; the inside of the cell was found to be pressurized besides.

When confined in the closed cell and subjected to the isothermal storage test performed at a T_t of 58.07 ℃, 1.5 cm^3 of nitroglycerin started the autocatalytic reaction about 1.95 d after the start of the isothermal storage test. The sample was found to be pale yellow and gave off the odor of nitrogen dioxide after the test; the inside of the cell was found to be pressurized besides.

When confined in the closed cell and subjected to the isothermal storage test performed at a T_t of 57.08 ℃, 1.5 cm^3 of nitroglycerin started the autocatalytic reaction about 2.68 d after the start of the isothermal storage test. The sample was found to be pale yellow and gave off the odor of nitrogen dioxide after the test; the inside of the cell was found to be pressurized besides.

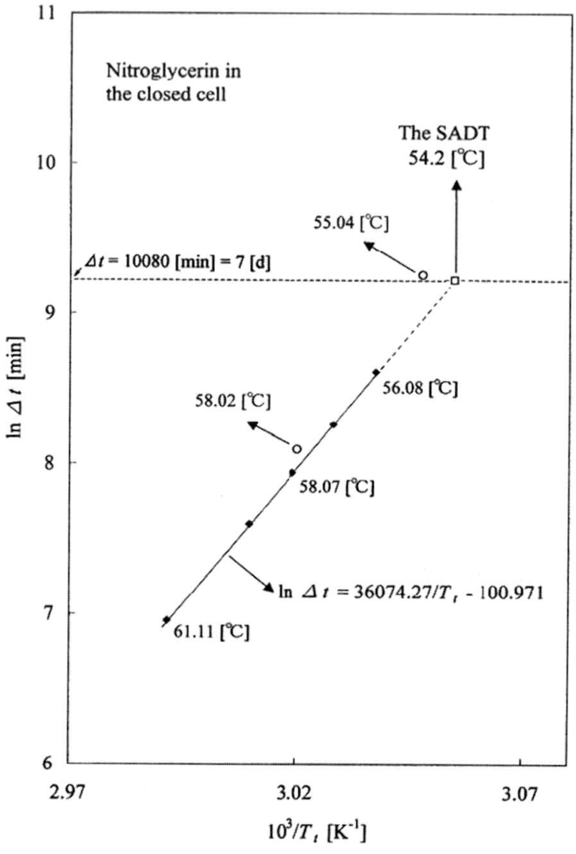

Figure 130. The plot of ln Δt versus $1/T_t$ made with five combinations of the value of ln Δt with that of $1/T_t$, which are each determined for five induction periods, of the autocatalytic reaction, of 1.5 cm^3 each of five samples of nitroglycerin confined each in the closed cell and subjected each to the isothermal storage test performed at each T_t in the range of 56.08 to 61.11 ℃ with mutual intervals of 1~2 K, recorded each for the time, Δt, from the insertion of each cell into the isothermal storage testing device till the start of the autocatalytic reaction of nitroglycerin at the corresponding T_t.

The symbol "○" indicates a plot for wet nitroglycerin.

When confined in the closed cell and subjected to the isothermal storage test performed at a T_t of 56.08 ℃, 1.5 cm^3 of nitroglycerin started the autocatalytic reaction about 3.81 d after the start of the isothermal storage test. The sample was found to be pale yellow and gave off the odor of nitrogen dioxide after the test; the inside of the cell was found to be pressurized besides.

The plot of $\ln \Delta t$ versus $1/T_t$ made for 1.5 cm^3 each of five samples of nitroglycerin is shown in Fig. 130.

The SADT for nitroglycerin is thus calculated, in accordance with the definition of the SADT, at 54.2345 ℃ as a value of T_t corresponding to a value of Δt of 10,080 min in the empirical formula, $\ln \Delta t = 36074.27/T_t - 100.971$, *i.e.*, Eq. (59) holding for the induction period of the autocatalytic reaction of 1.5 cm^3 of nitroglycerin confined in the closed cell and subjected to the isothermal storage test.

The value of SADT thus calculated for nitroglycerin, having an arbitrary shape and an arbitrary size, confined in an arbitrary closed container of the corresponding shape and size, and placed in the atmosphere under isothermal conditions, 54.2345 ℃, is finally rounded to 54.2 ℃ and is presented as such in Table 24 in **Section 9.5**.

9.6.2 Nitrocellulose

Two kinds of nitrocellulose, *i.e.*, guncotton (13.50 % N) and collodion cotton (12.19 % N), were tested herein.

A TG-DTA curve, which was recorded with the glass open-cup cell, 5 mm in diameter, 2.5 mm in depth, at the value of ϕ of 2.5 K/min in air at atmospheric pressure, of guncotton is presented in Fig. 131.

It is seen in Fig. 131 that guncotton begins to decompose exothermically at about 166 ℃ and then decomposes explosively at about 182 ℃. It appears, at first glance, that the TG-DTA curve of nitrocellulose, which is composed of collodion cotton and guncotton, shows that nitrocellulose is a typical and perfect powdery chemical of the TD type, because it begins to self-heat without melting and then decomposes explosively.

When confined in the closed cell and subjected to the isothermal storage test performed at a T_t of several tens of degrees C., however, 0.4 g of nitrocellulose, the volume of which is about 2 cm^3, behaves as a chemical of the AC type in such a manner as to start the autocatalytic reaction a long time after the start of the isothermal storage test in accordance with Eq. (59). This manner is the same as that shown in Fig. 6 in **Section 3.1**.

On the other hand, when charged in the open-cup cell and subjected to the isothermal storage test performed at a T_t below 100 ℃, nitrocellulose does not start the autocatalytic reaction. This result denotes that the confinement of a high explosive of the true AC type together with an autocatalyst such as NO_2

radical in a closed space is the prerequisite for the promotion of the autocatalytic reaction of the high explosive.

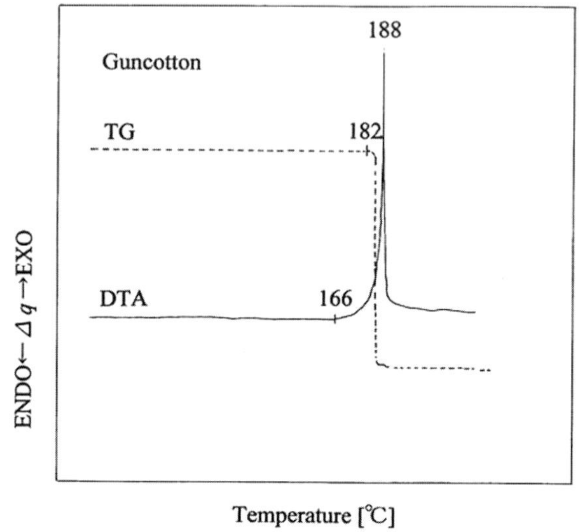

Figure 131. A TG-DTA curve of guncotton.

In this connection, as commented in a footnote given under Table 24 in **Section 9.5**, it has been reported by J. Isler that the critical temperature for the thermal explosion of nitrocellulose powder (13.4 % N) formed into a cylinder, 1.1 cm in diameter, 1.3 in specific gravity, and placed in the atmosphere under isothermal, but open, conditions, is 145 ℃ [75]. This temperature value, 145 ℃, is far higher than 76～77 ℃, *i.e.*, the value of SADT calculated herein for guncotton or collodion cotton, having an arbitrary shape and an arbitrary size, confined in an arbitrary closed container of the corresponding shape and size, and placed in the atmosphere under isothermal conditions (refer to the superscript, [c)], given in Table 24).

(1) Guncotton

The plot of $\ln \Delta t$ versus $1/T_t$ made for 0.4 g each of twelve samples of guncotton (13.50 % N) is shown in Fig. 132.

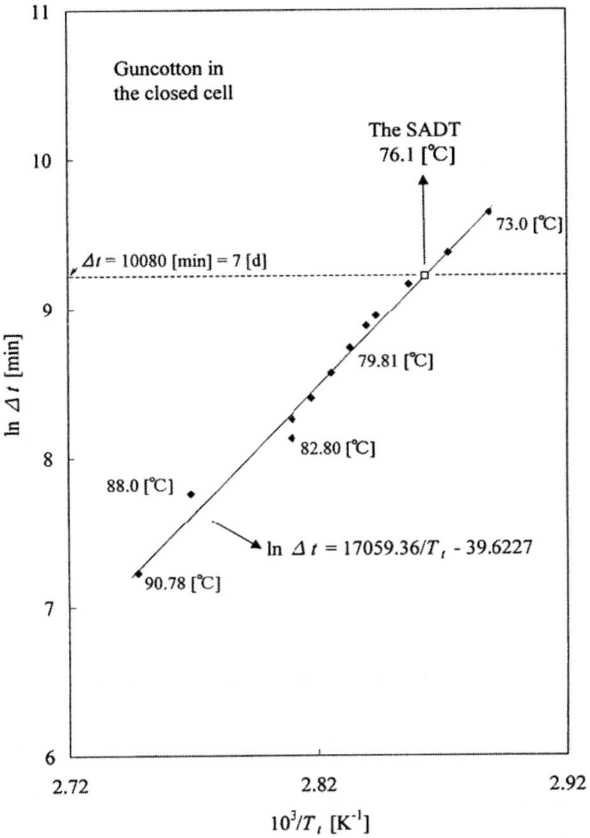

Figure 132. The plot of ln Δt versus $1/T_t$ made with twelve combinations of the value of ln Δt with that of $1/T_t$, which are each determined for twelve induction periods, of the autocatalytic reaction, of 0.4 g each of twelve samples of guncotton (13.50 % N) confined each in the closed cell and subjected each to the isothermal storage test performed at each T_t in the range of 73.0 to 90.78 ℃ with mutual intervals of 0.5~5 K, recorded each for the time, Δt, from the insertion of each cell into the isothermal storage testing device till the start of the autocatalytic reaction of guncotton at the corresponding T_t.

The SADT for guncotton is thus calculated, in accordance with the definition of the SADT, at 76.1335 ℃ as a value of T_t corresponding to a value of Δt of 10,080 min in the empirical formula, ln Δt = 17059.36/T_t - 39.6227, *i.e.*, Eq. (59) holding for the induction period of the autocatalytic reaction of 0.4 g of guncotton confined in the closed cell and subjected to the isothermal storage test.

The value of SADT thus calculated for guncotton, having an arbitrary shape and an arbitrary size, confined in an arbitrary closed container of the corresponding shape and size, and placed in the atmosphere under isothermal conditions, 76.1335 ℃, is finally rounded to 76.1 ℃ and is presented as such in Table 24 in **Section 9.5**.

As seen in Fig. 98, however, when confined in the closed cell and subjected to the isothermal storage test performed at a T_t of 74.97 ℃, 0.4 g of guncotton started the autocatalytic reaction clearly about 8.17 d after the start of the isothermal storage test. The sample was found to be bluish-yellow and gave off the odor of nitrogen dioxide after the test.

Besides, when confined in the closed cell and subjected to the isothermal storage test performed at a T_t of 73.0 ℃, 0.4 g of guncotton started the autocatalytic reaction, though faintly, about 10.7 d after the start of the isothermal storage test. The sample was found to be pale yellow and gave off the odor of nitrogen dioxide after the test.

It thus follows that the thermal explosion of guncotton, having an arbitrary shape and an arbitrary size, confined in an arbitrary closed container of the corresponding shape and size, and placed in the atmosphere under isothermal conditions, is able to take place even at temperatures below the SADT calculated herein.

In conclusion, it must also be added that, when confined in the closed cell and subjected to the isothermal storage test performed at a T_t in the range of 73.0 to 90.78 ℃, 0.4 g of guncotton continues to self-heat over the T_t, though slowly and faintly, in the same manner as a chemical of the TD type, prior to the start of the (active) autocatalytic reaction. It is thus probable that, when the adiabatic self-heating test is performed for guncotton, a value of T_c lower than the SADT calculated herein will be obtained.

(2) Collodion cotton

The characteristic of the self-heating process or behavior of collodion cotton has been described in detail in **Subsection 9.3.5**, so that only the difference, in the effect of humidity on the induction period of the autocatalytic reaction, between collodion cotton and nitroglycerin is described here.

The hydrolysis of a nitrate ester is needless to say promoted in the presence of water. In this connection, it has been ascertained that, when two samples of about 11 % water-containing collodion cotton, which had been each prepared by adding 0.05 cm^3 of water to 0.4 g of collodion cotton, were subjected to the isothermal storage test at a T_t of 79.72 ℃ and at a T_t of 84.97 ℃, respectively, they each started the autocatalytic reaction a little earlier than 0.4 g each of two samples of dry collodion cotton placed each under the same conditions as the corresponding wet collodion cotton (Fig. 126). Two samples of wet collodion cotton were each found to be uncolored after the test, although they each gave off the odor of nitric acid.

On the other hand, it has been ascertained that, when two samples of about 2 % water-containing nitroglycerin, which had been each prepared by adding 0.05 cm^3 of water to 1.5 cm^3 of nitroglycerin, were subjected to the isothermal storage test at a T_t of 55.04 ℃ and at a T_t of 58.07 ℃, respectively, they each started the autocatalytic reaction a little later than 1.5 cm^3 each of two samples of dry nitroglycerin placed each under the same conditions as the corresponding wet nitroglycerin (Fig. 130).

The reason why wet nitroglycerin starts the autocatalytic reaction later than dry nitroglycerin at the same temperature is not explainable herein. There may, however, exist some difference, in the mode of the decomposition reaction during the induction period of the autocatalytic reaction of nitrate esters, between the liquid water which may be present in wet nitroglycerin at temperatures near 55 ℃ and the aqueous vapor which may be present in wet collodion cotton at temperatures near 80 ℃.

9.6.3 PETN

Two kinds of PETN, *i.e.*, PETN used for percussion caps, which looks like refined sugar, and, PETN used for medicine, which looks like flour, were tested herein.

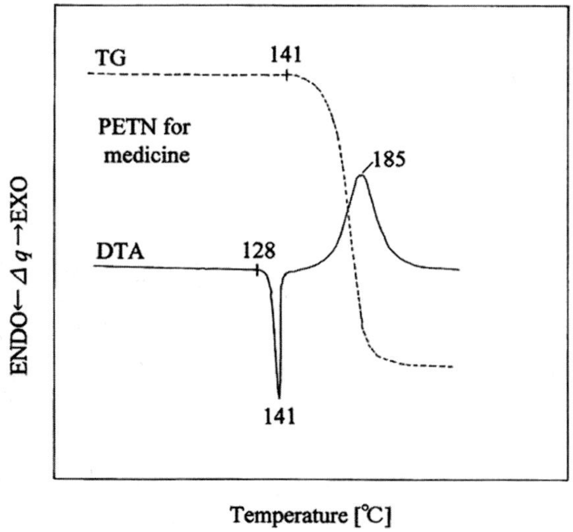

Figure 133. A TG-DTA curve of PETN used for medicine.

A TG-DTA curve, which was recorded with the glass open-cup cell, 5 mm in diameter, 2.5 mm in depth, at the value of ϕ of 2.5 K/min in air at atmospheric pressure, of PETN used for medicine is presented in Fig. 133.

It is seen in Fig. 133 that PETN melts at about 130 ℃ and then begins to lose weight at about 140 ℃. It appears, at first glance, that the TG-DTA curve of PETN shows that PETN is a typical powdery chemical of the quasi-AC type, because the DTA curve of PETN shifts successively from the endothermic peak caused by its melting to the exothermic peak caused by the exothermic decomposition reaction.

When confined in the closed cell and subjected to the isothermal storage test performed at a T_t, on the high temperature side, say, in the range of 125 to the melting point of PETN, *i.e.*, 130 ℃, 1.8 g of PETN used for percussion caps, the volume of which is about 2 cm^3, behaves certainly like a powdery chemical of the quasi-AC type in such a manner as to start the quasi-autocatalytic reaction simultaneously with the finish of its melting a very short time after the start of the isothermal storage test in accordance with Eq. (59). This manner is the same as that shown in Fig. 7 presented in **Section 3.3**.

When confined in the closed cell and subjected to the isothermal storage test performed at a T_t, on low temperature side, say, in the range of 115 to 121 ℃, however, 1.8 g of PETN used for percussion caps, or 1.2 g of PETN used for medicine, the volume of which is also about 2 cm^3, behaves as a powdery chemical of the true AC type in such a manner as to start the autocatalytic reaction a relatively long time after the start of the isothermal storage test in accordance with Eq. (59). This manner is the same as that shown in Fig. 6 presented in **Section 3.1**.

(1) PETN used for percussion caps

Results of elemental analysis for PETN used for percussion caps tested herein are as follows:

Calcd.	N, 17.7 %;	C, 19.0 %;	H, 2.55 %.
Found:	N, 17.50±0.25 %;	C, 19.48 %;	H, 2.57 %.

The purity of PETN in that used for percussion caps is 98.9 % on the basis of the percentage of nitrogen.

When confined in the closed cell and subjected to the isothermal storage test performed at a T_t of 120.9 ℃, 1.8 g of PETN used for percussion caps started the autocatalytic reaction about 12.4 h after the start of the isothermal storage test.

When confined in the closed cell and subjected to the isothermal storage test performed at a T_t of 119.7 ℃, 1.8 g of PETN used for percussion caps started the autocatalytic reaction about 16.9 h after the start of the isothermal storage test.

When confined in the closed cell and subjected to the isothermal storage test performed at a T_t of 118.0 ℃, 1.8 g of PETN used for percussion caps started the autocatalytic reaction about 1.1 d after the start of the isothermal storage test.

When confined in the closed cell and subjected to the isothermal storage test performed at a T_t of 115.1 ℃, 1.8 g of PETN used for percussion caps started the autocatalytic reaction, though faintly, about 1.88 d after the start of the isothermal storage test. The sample was found to be pale yellow and gave off the odor of nitrogen dioxide after the test.

Comparison of the plot of $\ln \Delta t$ versus $1/T_t$ made for 1.2 g each of five samples of PETN used for medicine with the plot made for 1.8 g each of eleven samples of PETN used for percussion caps is presented in Fig. 134.

The SADT for PETN used for percussion caps is thus calculated, in accordance with the definition of the SADT, at 109.670 ℃ as a value of T_t corresponding to a value of Δt of 10,080 min in the empirical formula, $\ln \Delta t = 34593.34/T_t - 81.1463$, *i.e.*, Eq. (59) holding for the induction period of the autocatalytic reaction of 1.8 g of PETN, used for percussion caps, confined in the closed cell and subjected to the isothermal storage test.

The value of SADT thus calculated for PETN used for percussion caps, having an arbitrary shape and an arbitrary size, confined in an arbitrary closed container of the corresponding shape and size, and placed in the atmosphere under isothermal conditions, 109.670 ℃, is finally rounded to 110 ℃ and is presented as such in Table 24 in **Section 9.5**.

It is, however, inferred that, as a matter of fact, PETN used for percussion caps will not start the exothermic decomposition reaction at temperatures below 115 ℃.*

(2) PETN used for medicine

PETN used for medicine is prepared by recrystallization from acetone solution of PETN used for percussion caps.

The purity of PETN in that used for medicine is >99.0 % on the basis of the percentage of nitrogen.

As seen in Fig. 134, the time, Δt, required for PETN used for medicine to start the autocatalytic reaction is much longer than that required for PETN used for percussion caps to do so. This may be regarded as an effect of the elimination, by recrystallization, of impurities contained in PETN used for percussion caps.

When confined in the closed cell and subjected to the isothermal storage test performed at a T_t of 121.1 ℃, 1.2 g of PETN used for medicine started the autocatalytic reaction about 2.64 d after the start of the isothermal storage test.

---

* For this inference, refer to the inference made for PETN used for medicine as well.

The sample was found to be pale yellow and gave off the odor of nitrogen dioxide after the test; the inside of the cell was found to be pressurized besides.

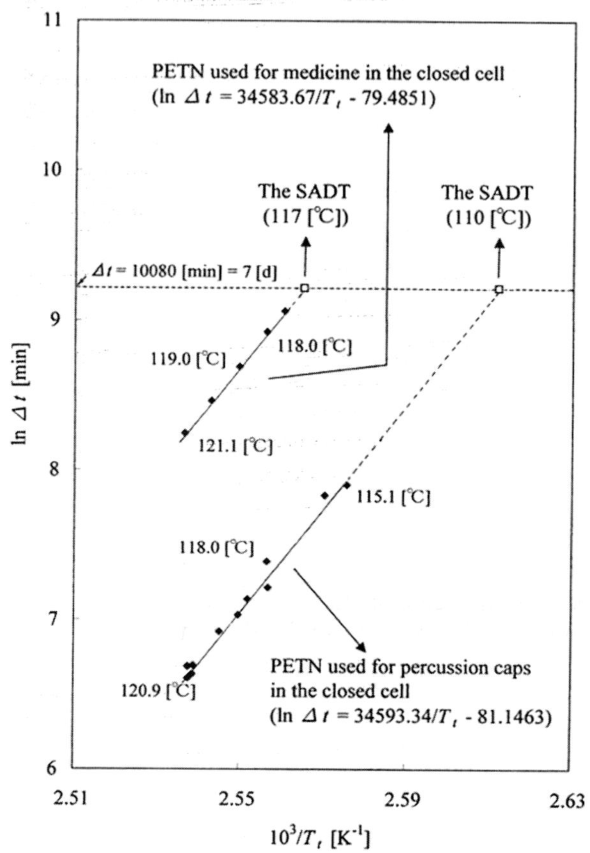

Figure 134. Comparison of the plot of $\ln \Delta t$ versus $1/T_t$ made with five combinations of the value of $\ln \Delta t$ with that of $1/T_t$, which are each determined for five induction periods, of the autocatalytic reaction, of 1.2 g each of five samples of PETN used for medicine, confined each in the closed cell and subjected each to the isothermal storage test performed at each T_t in the range of 115.1 to 120.9 ℃ with mutual intervals of 0.2 ～2 K, recorded each for the time, Δt, from the insertion of each cell into the isothermal storage testing device till the start of the autocatalytic reaction of PETN used for medicine at the corresponding T_t, with, the plot made for 1.8 g each of eleven samples of PETN used for percussion caps, placed each under the same conditions as the former.

When confined in the closed cell and subjected to the isothermal storage test performed at a T_t of 119.0 ℃, 1.2 g of PETN used for medicine started the autocatalytic reaction about 4.13 d after the start of the isothermal storage test. The sample was found to be pale yellow and gave off the odor of nitrogen dioxide after the test; the inside of the cell was found to be pressurized besides.

When confined in the closed cell and subjected to the isothermal storage test performed at a T_t of 118.0 ℃, 1.2 g of PETN used for medicine started the autocatalytic reaction, though faintly, about 5.22 d after the start of the isothermal storage test. The sample was found to be pale yellow and gave off the odor of nitrogen dioxide after the test; the inside of the cell was found to be pressurized besides.

When confined in the closed cell and subjected to the isothermal storage test performed at a T_t of 117.4 ℃, 1.2 g of PETN used for medicine started the autocatalytic reaction, though faintly, about 6.00 d after the start of the isothermal storage test. The sample was found to be pale yellow and gave off the odor of nitrogen dioxide after the test.

In any event, the SADT for PETN used for medicine is calculated, in accordance with the definition of the SADT, at 116.730 ℃ as a value of T_t corresponding to a value of Δt of 10,080 min in the empirical formula, $\ln \Delta t = 34583.67/T_t - 79.4851$, *i.e.*, Eq. (59) holding for the induction period of the autocatalytic reaction of 1.2 g of PETN used for medicine confined in the closed cell and subjected to the isothermal storage test.

The value of SADT thus calculated for PETN used for medicine, having an arbitrary shape and an arbitrary size, confined in an arbitrary closed container of the corresponding shape and size, and placed in the atmosphere under isothermal conditions, 116.730 ℃, is finally rounded to 117 ℃ and is presented as such in Table 24 in **Section 9.5**.

It is, however, inferred that, as a matter of fact, PETN used for medicine will also not start the exothermic decomposition reaction at temperatures below 115 ℃.

9.6.4 Tetryl

Results of elemental analysis for tetryl tested herein are as follows:

Calcd.	N, 24.39 %;	C, 29.3 %;	H, 1.8 %.
Found:	N, 24.82±0.19 %;	C, 29.56 %;	H, 1.77 %.

A TG-DTA curve, which was recorded with the glass open cell, 5 mm in diameter, 2.5 mm in depth, at the value of ϕ of 2.5 K/min in air at atmospheric pressure, of tetryl is presented in Fig. 135.

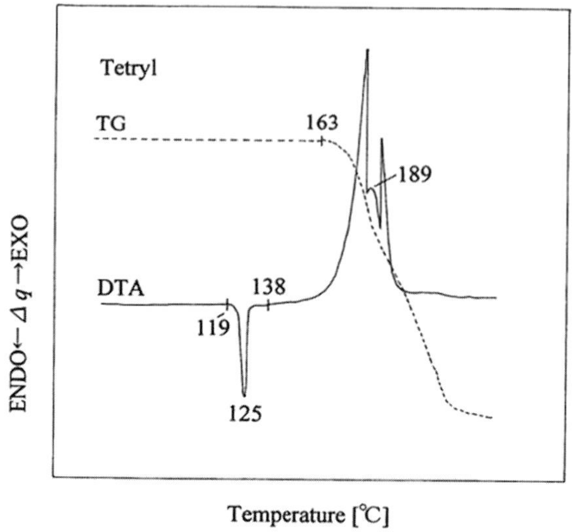

Figure 135. A TG-DTA curve of tetryl.

It is seen in Fig. 135 that tetryl melts at about 120 ℃ and begins to lose weight at about 163 ℃. It appears, at first glance, that the TG-DTA curve of tetryl shows that tetryl is a typical powdery chemical of the quasi-AC type, because the DTA curve of tetryl shifts successively from the endothermic peak caused by its melting to the exothermic peak caused by the exothermic decomposition reaction.

When confined in the closed cell and subjected to the isothermal storage test performed at a T_t, on the high temperature side, say, near 130 ℃, 2 g of tetryl, the volume of which is about 2 cm^3, behaves certainly like a powdery chemical of the quasi-AC type in such a manner as to start the quasi-autocatalytic reaction simultaneously with the finish of melting a very short time after the start of the isothermal storage test in accordance with Eq. (59). This manner is the same as that shown in Fig. 7 in **Section 3.3**.

And also when confined in the closed cell and subjected to the isothermal storage test performed at a T_t, on the low temperature side, say, in the range of 115 ℃ to the melting point of tetryl, *i.e.*, 120 ℃, 2 g of tetryl behaves like a chemical of the quasi-AC type in such a manner as to start the quasi-autocatalytic reaction simultaneously with the finish of melting a relatively long time after the start of the isothermal storage test in accordance with Eq. (59). This manner is the same as that shown in Fig. 16 in **Section 3.4**.*

Thus, when confined in the closed cell and subjected to the isothermal storage test performed at a T_t of 120.0 ℃, 2 g of tetryl started the quasi-autocatalytic reaction simultaneously with the finish of melting about 3.05 d after the start of the isothermal storage test. The inside of the cell was found to be pressurized after the test.

When confined in the closed cell and subjected to the isothermal storage test performed at a T_t of 118.0 ℃, 2 g of tetryl started the quasi-autocatalytic reaction simultaneously with the finish of melting about 4.77 d after the start of the isothermal storage test. The inside of the cell was found to be pressurized after the test.

When confined in the closed cell and subjected to the isothermal storage test performed at a T_t of 117.0 ℃, 2 g of tetryl started the quasi-autocatalytic reaction simultaneously with the finish of melting about 6.50 d after the start of the isothermal storage test.

The plot of $\ln \Delta t$ versus $1/T_t$ made for 2 g each of ten samples of tetryl is shown in Fig. 136.

It is seen that the plot bends at 120 ℃ which is the melting point of tetryl. The SADT for tetryl was, therefore, calculated herein, in accordance with the definition of the SADT, at 116.509 ℃ as a value of T_t corresponding to a value of Δt of 10,080 min in the empirical formula, $\ln \Delta t = 36586.12/T_t - 84.6744$, *i.e.*, Eq. (59) holding for the induction period of the quasi-autocatalytic reaction of 2 g of tetryl confined in the closed cell and subjected to the isothermal storage test performed at each T_t in the range of 115.2 to 120.0 ℃.

The value of SADT thus calculated for tetryl, having an arbitrary shape and an arbitrary size, confined in an arbitrary closed container of the corresponding shape and size, and placed in the atmosphere under isothermal conditions, 116.509 ℃, is finally rounded to 117 ℃ and is presented as such in Table 24 in **Section 9.5**.

When confined in the closed cell and subjected to the isothermal storage test performed at a T_t of 116.0 ℃, however, 2 g of tetryl started the quasi-autocatalytic reaction, though faintly, simultaneously with the finish of its melting about 7.83 d after the start of the isothermal storage test. The inside of the cell was found to be pressurized after the test.

Besides, as seen in Fig. 136, even when confined in the closed cell and subjected to the isothermal storage test performed at a T_t of 115.2 ℃, 2 g of tetryl started the quasi-autocatalytic reaction, though faintly, simultaneously

---

* It is beyond the scope of the present document to discuss whether tetryl decomposes in accordance with the autocatalytic reaction mechanism or not. It is, nevertheless, certain that the self-heating process of tetryl confined in the closed cell and subjected to the isothermal storage test is in accord with Eq. (59).

with the finish of its melting about 9.49 d after the start of the isothermal storage test. The inside of the cell was found to be pressurized after the test.

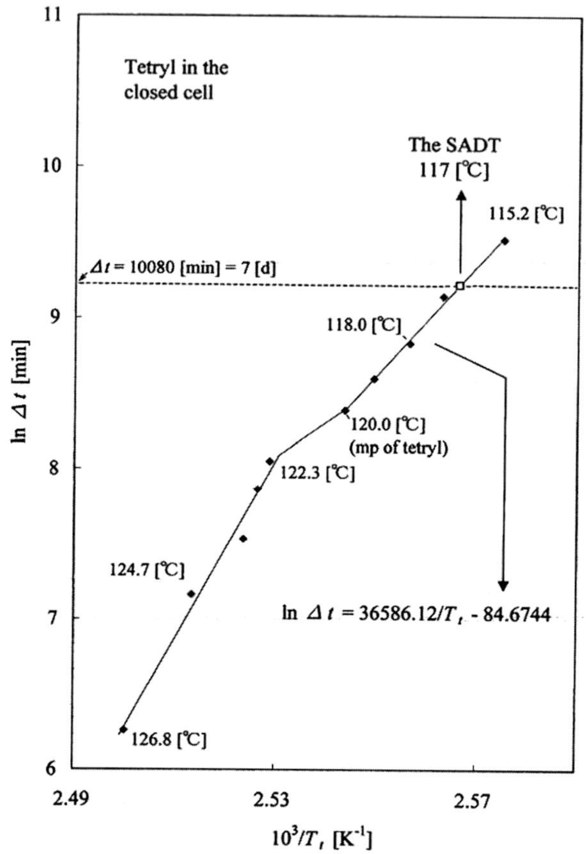

Figure 136. The plot of ln Δt versus $1/T_t$ made with ten combinations of the value of ln Δt with that of $1/T_t$, which are each determined for ten induction periods, of the quasi-autocatalytic reaction, of 2 g each of ten samples of tetryl confined each in the closed cell and subjected each to the isothermal storage test performed at each T_t in the range of 115.2 to 126.8 ℃ with mutual intervals of 0.4~2 K, recorded each for the time, Δt, from the insertion of each cell into the isothermal storage testing device till the start of the quasi-autocatalytic reaction of tetryl at the corresponding T_t.

It thus follows that the thermal explosion of tetryl, having an arbitrary shape and an arbitrary size, confined in an arbitrary closed container of the corresponding shape and size, and placed in the atmosphere under isothermal conditions, is able to take place even at temperatures below the SADT calculated herein.

Nevertheless, however, it is probable, based on the total information obtained above, that tetryl will not start the quasi-autocatalytic reaction at temperatures at which it does not melt.

Incidentally, Merzhanov *et al.* reported two values of T_c for molten tetryl: one value was 136 ℃, which was measured as a T_c for molten tetryl charged in a cylindrical glass vessel, 4.94 cm in inside diameter, 14.82 (= 4.94 × 3) cm in length, and placed in the atmosphere under isothermal, but open, conditions [76]; and, the other value was 152 ℃, which was measured as a T_c for molten tetryl charged in a cylindrical glass vessel, 4.90 cm in inside diameter, 14.7 (= 4.9 × 3) cm in length, and stirred vigorously and placed in the atmosphere under isothermal, but open, conditions [40]. These values of T_c, 136 and 152 ℃, are far higher than 117 ℃, the value of SADT calculated herein for tetryl, having an arbitrary shape and an arbitrary size, confined in an arbitrary closed container of the corresponding shape and size, and placed in the atmosphere under isothermal, but static, conditions. The reason why such high values of T_c for molten tetryl were obtained in a series of studies performed by Merzhanov *et al.* is thought to be that the experiment to cause the thermal explosion of molten tetryl was performed under isothermal, but open, conditions in the former case, and it was performed under isothermal, but open, besides vigorously stirred, conditions in the latter case.* For further details, refer to **Sections 5.2**, **5.5** and **5.8**.

9.6.5 TNT

Results of elemental analysis for TNT tested herein are as follows:

Calcd.	N, 18.5 %;	C, 37.0 %;	H, 2.2 %.
Found.	N, 18.65±0.02 %;	C, 36.88±0.04 %;	H, 2.207 %.

A TG-DTA curve, which was recorded with the glass open cell, 5 mm in diameter, 2.5 mm in depth, at the value of ϕ of 2.5 K/min in air at atmospheric pressure, of TNT is presented in Fig. 137.

---

* Merzhanov *et al.* stated in the latter case that the heat transfer in molten tetryl was performed by convection only, because molten tetryl was stirred vigorously by means of a piston stirrer, so that, while the temperature distribution in molten tetryl was uniform, the temperature gradient was present only in the vessel wall [40]. On the other hand, the balance between the rate of heat generation in a liquid and the rate of heat transfer from the liquid to the atmosphere at the critical state for the thermal explosion which exists at the end of the early stages of the self-heating process, is dealt with in the approach adopted herein with regard to the thermal explosion of the liquid. The latter orthodox approach to the thermal explosion of every liquid has thus no concern with any convective flow in liquids.

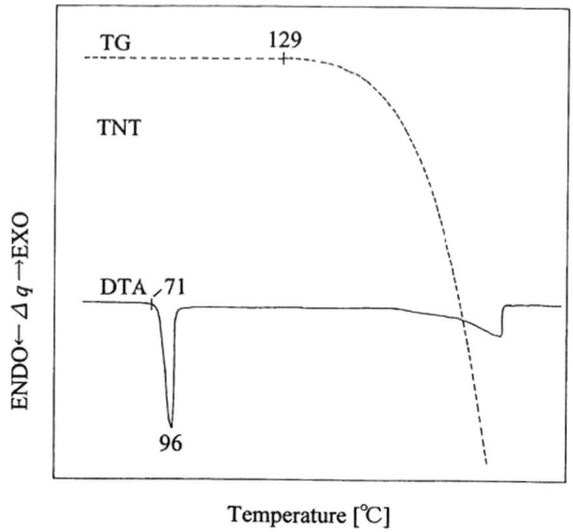

Figure 137. A TG-DTA curve of TNT.

It is seen in Fig. 137 that TNT begins to melt at about 70 ℃ and begins to lose weight at about 130 ℃ but the autocatalytic reaction of TNT is covered with the endothermic effect caused by the vaporization of TNT itself in the same manner as the reaction of nitroglycerin.

When confined in the closed cell and subjected to the isothermal storage test performed at a T_t in the range of 162.8 to 169.9 ℃, however, 1.6 g of TNT, the volume of which is about 2 cm^3, behaves as a chemical of the AC type in such a manner as to decompose first to form a fluid black tarry matter and then start the autocatalytic reaction as the tarry matter, though faintly, a relatively long time after the start of the isothermal storage test in accordance with Eq. (59). This manner is similar to that shown in Fig. 16 presented in **Section 3.4**.*

When confined in the closed cell and subjected to the isothermal storage test performed at a T_t of 169.9 ℃, 1.6 g of TNT started the autocatalytic reaction, though faintly, about 15.1 h after the start of the isothermal storage test. The inside of the cell was found to be pressurized after the test.

When confined in the closed cell and subjected to the isothermal storage test performed at a T_t of 167.6 ℃, 1.6 g of TNT started the autocatalytic reaction,

---

* It is beyond of the present document to discuss whether TNT decomposes in accordance with the autocatalytic reaction mechanism or not. It is, nevertheless, certain that the self-heating process of TNT confined in the closed cell and subjected to the isothermal storage test is in accord with Eq. (59).

though faintly, about 1.31 d after the start of the isothermal storage test. The inside of the cell was found to be pressurized after the test.

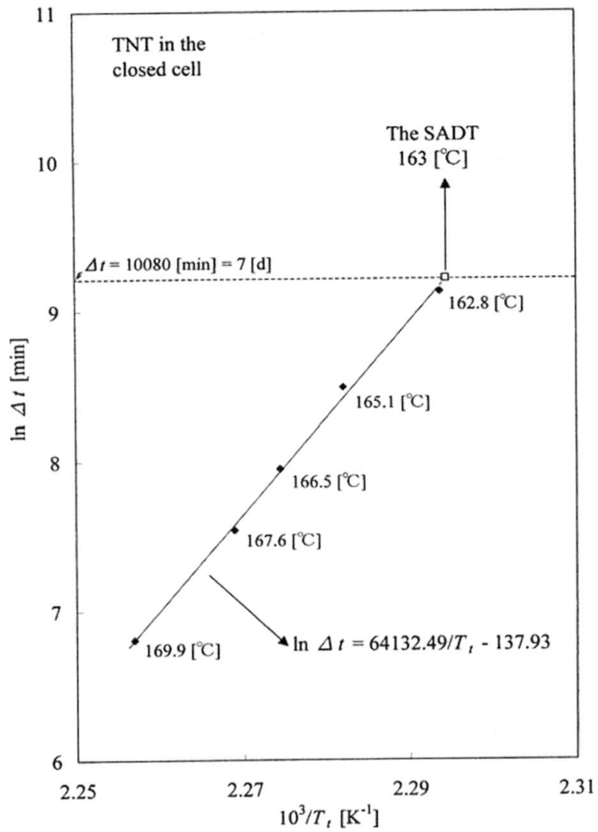

Figure 138. The plot of $\ln \Delta t$ versus $1/T_t$ made with five combinations of the value of $\ln \Delta t$ with that of $1/T_t$, which are each determined for five induction periods, of the autocatalytic reaction, of 1.6 g each of five samples of TNT confined each in the closed cell and subjected each to the isothermal storage test performed at each T_t in the range of 162.8 to 169.9 ℃ with mutual intervals of 1～2.5 K, recorded each for the time, Δt, from the insertion of each cell into the isothermal storage testing device till the start of the autocatalytic reaction of TNT at the corresponding T_t.

When confined in the closed cell and subjected to the isothermal storage test performed at a T_t of 165.1 ℃, 1.6 g of TNT started the autocatalytic reaction, though faintly, about 3.39 d after the start of the isothermal storage test. The inside of the cell was found to be pressurized after the test.

When confined in the closed cell and subjected to the isothermal storage test performed at a T_t of 162.8 ℃, 1.6 g of TNT started the autocatalytic reaction, though faintly, about 6.42 d after the start of the isothermal storage test. The inside of the cell was found to be pressurized after the test.

When confined in the closed cell and subjected to the isothermal storage test performed at a T_t near 140 ℃, however, 1.6 g of TNT did not start the autocatalytic reaction; in fact, it only blackened a little in the lapse of a long time.

When confined in the closed cell and subjected to the isothermal storage test performed at a T_t near 120 ℃, 1.6 g of TNT decomposed scarcely; in fact, it blackened scarcely in the lapse of a long time.

Taking the total information obtained above into account, The SADT for TNT was calculated herein, in accordance with the definition of the SADT, at 162.686 ℃ as a value of T_t corresponding to a value of Δt of 10,080 min in the empirical formula, $\ln \Delta t = 64132.49/T_t - 137.93$, *i.e.*, Eq. (59) holding for the induction period of the autocatalytic reaction of 1.6 g of TNT confined in the closed cell and subjected to the isothermal storage test performed at each T_t in the range of 162.8 to 169.9 ℃ (Fig. 138).

The value of SADT thus calculated for TNT, having an arbitrary shape and an arbitrary size, confined in an arbitrary closed container of the corresponding shape and size, and placed in the atmosphere under isothermal conditions, 162.686 ℃, is finally rounded to 163 ℃ and is presented as such in Table 24 in **Section 9.5**.

Incidentally, the self-heating processes, of 1.6 g each of several samples of TNT confined each in the closed cell and subjected each to the adiabatic self-heating test, were as follows:

When confined in the closed cell and subjected to the adiabatic self-heating test started from a T_s near 130 ℃, 1.6 g of TNT did not self-heat.

When confined in the closed cell and subjected to the adiabatic self-heating test started from a T_s near 148 ℃, 1.6 g of TNT self-heated by 10 μV in 100 min; that is, the temperature of TNT increased at a rate of about 0.0025 K/min.

When confined in the closed cell and subjected to the adiabatic self-heating test started from a T_s near 157 ℃, 1.6 g of TNT self-heated by 6 μV in 50 min; that is, the temperature of TNT increased at a rate of about 0.003 K/min.

When confined in the closed cell and subjected to the adiabatic self-heating test started from a T_s near 176 ℃, 1.6 g of TNT self-heated at a rate of about 0.007 K/min.

It is thus possible to predict that, if 1.6 g of TNT is confined in the closed cell and is kept under adiabatic conditions, its thermal explosion is able to take place even at temperatures below 150 ℃, which are temperatures lower than the SADT for TNT calculated herein.

Synthesizing the total information obtained above, it will be reasonable to consider 130 ℃ as the upper limit temperature for the safe handling of TNT.

9.6.6 Picric acid

Picric acid tested herein is of the A. C. S. reagent grade (98 % picric acid) and was got from Aldrich chemical Co., Inc. as moist picric acid containing 35 % water. The moist picric acid was dehydrated before testing in accordance with directions described under the heading of **Section 9.5**.

A TG-DTA curve, which was recorded with the glass open cell, 5 mm in diameter, 2.5 mm in depth, at the value of ϕ of 2.5 K/min in air at atmospheric pressure, of picric acid is presented in Fig. 139.

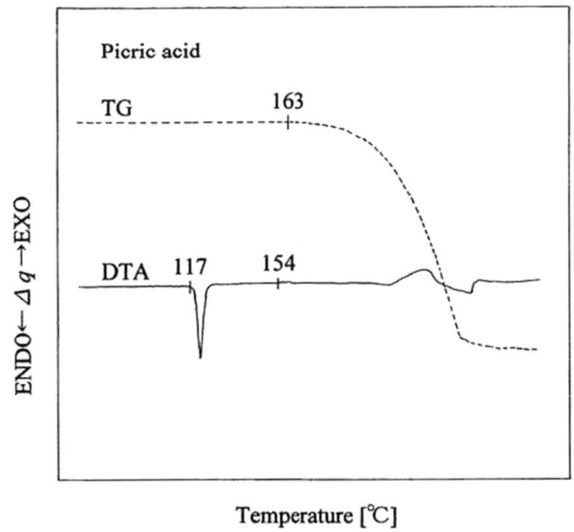

Figure 139. A TG-DTA curve of picric acid.

It is seen in Fig. 139 that picric acid begins to melt at about 117 ℃ and begins to lose weight at about 163 ℃ but the exothermic decomposition reaction of picric acid is covered with the endothermic effect caused by the vaporization of picric acid itself in the same manner as the reaction of nitroglycerin and that of TNT.

When confined in the closed cell and subjected to the isothermal storage test performed at a T_t above 163 ℃, however, 2 g of picric acid, the volume of which is about 2 cm^3, decomposes first to form a fluid black tarry matter then starts the exothermic decomposition reaction, though faintly, a relatively short time after the start of the isothermal storage test.

Thus, when confined in the closed cell and subjected to the isothermal storage test performed at a T_t of 179.9 ℃, 2 g of picric acid started the exothermic decomposition reaction, though faintly, about 5.38 h after the start of the isothermal storage test.

When confined in the closed cell and subjected to the isothermal storage test performed at a T_t of 170.1 ℃, 2 g of picric acid started the exothermic decomposition reaction, though faintly, about 6.66 h after the start of the isothermal storage test.

When confined in the closed cell and subjected to the isothermal storage test performed at a T_t of 165.2 ℃, 2 g of picric acid started the exothermic decomposition reaction, though faintly, about 9.42 h after the start of the isothermal storage test.

When confined in the closed cell and subjected to the isothermal storage test performed at a T_t of 163.0 ℃, 2 g of picric acid started the exothermic decomposition reaction, though faintly, about 11.6 h after the start of the isothermal storage test.

When confined in the closed cell and subjected to the isothermal storage test performed at a T_t of 162.6 ℃, however, 2 g of picric acid did not start the exothermic decomposition reaction within 5 d of the start of the isothermal storage test. Although the sample was found to have changed into a black tarry matter after the test, it was observed to burn vigorously.

When confined in the closed cell and subjected to the isothermal storage test performed at a T_t of 150.2 ℃, 2 g of picric acid did not start the exothermic decomposition reaction for 8 d after the start of the isothermal storage test. Although the sample was found to have changed into a black and transparent fluid after the test, the fluid was seen to burn vigorously.

When confined in the closed cell and subjected to the isothermal storage test performed at a T_t of 139.8 ℃, 2 g of picric acid remained uncolored for 6 d after the start of the isothermal storage test.

Synthesizing the total information obtained above, the plot of $\ln \Delta t$ versus $1/T_t$ for picric acid has been made herein in the manner described in the caption of Fig. 140.

The plot manifests a downward curvature. The reason why such a plot has been effected is thought to be that the reagent tested was not normal or that picric acid does not decompose in accordance with the autocatalytic reaction mechanism.*

At all events, it is certain that, when confined in the closed cell and subjected to the isothermal storage test performed at a T_t below 163 ℃, 2 g of picric acid tested herein does not start the exothermic decomposition reaction at all.

---

* In any event, it is beyond the scope of the present document to discuss whether picric acid decomposes in accordance with the autocatalytic reaction mechanism or not.

163 ℃ has, therefore, been considered herein as the value of SADT for picric acid, having an arbitrary shape and an arbitrary size, confined in an arbitrary closed container of the corresponding shape and size, and placed in the atmosphere under isothermal conditions, and is presented as such in Table 24 in **Section 9.5**.

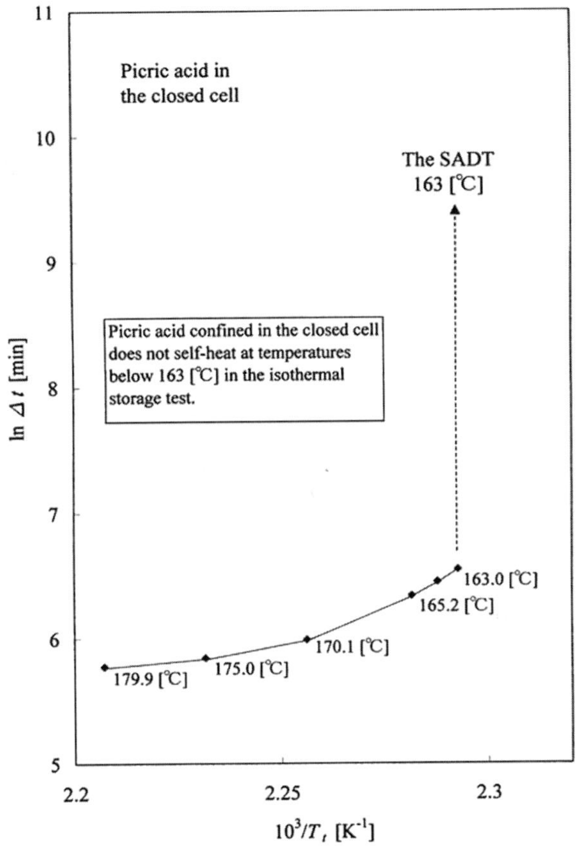

Figure 140. The plot of ln Δt versus $1/T_t$ made with six combinations of the value of ln Δt with that of $1/T_t$, which are each determined for six self-heating processes, of 2 g each of six samples of picric acid confined each in the closed cell and subjected each to the isothermal storage test performed at each T_t in the range of 163.0 to 179.9 ℃ with mutual intervals of 1～5 K, recorded each for the time, Δt, from the insertion of each cell into the isothermal storage testing device till the start of the exothermic decomposition reaction of picric acid at the corresponding T_t.

The tests described above were, of course, all performed with the closed cell. However, it has also been ascertained that, when charged in the open-cup cell and subjected to the isothermal storage test performed at a T_t of 162.1 ℃, 2 g of picric acid self-heats clearly. It is certain that this phenomenon is caused by the air oxidation of picric acid.

In conclusion

Every isothermal storage test has been performed, in principle, for a dry high explosive confined in the glass closed cell throughout a series of studies described in the present chapter. It is, however, very probable that, if the isothermal storage test is performed for a high explosive charged in the open-cup cell, or, if it is performed for a wet high explosive confined in the closed cell, a value of SADT, for the high explosive, different from that calculated herein will be obtained. Although a few tests have been performed herein for picric acid charged in the open-cup cell, or for wet nitroglycerin and nitrocellulose confined each in the closed cell, it is clear that the studies of this kind remain deficient herein.

In particular, it is quite certain that, if the isothermal storage test is performed for a mixture of a high explosive of the true AC type and a metal, a value of SADT, of the high explosive, considerably lower than that calculated herein will be obtained. However, this important subject also remains to be undertaken herein.

References to Chapter 9

[40] A. G. Merzhanov, V. V. Barzykin, V. G. Abramov and F. I. Dubovitskii, Thermal Explosion in the Liquid Phase with Heat Transfer by Convection Only, Russian J. Phys. Chem., **35**, 1024-1027 (1961).
[60] T. Yoshida, Safety of Reactive Chemicals, Elsevier, Amsterdam, 200 (1987).
[73] T. Kotoyori, Critical Temperatures for the Self-Heating of Eight High Explosives of the True Autocatalytic Decomposition Type, Proceedings of the 11th Symposium on Chemical Problems Connected with the Stability of Explosives, Båstad, Sweden, 1998, Sektionen för Detonik och Förbränning, Sundbyberg, Sweden, 221-239 (2000).
[74] T. L. Davis, The Chemistry of Powder and Explosives, John Wiley & Sons, Inc., New York, 204 (1943).
[75] J. Isler, Auto-Inflammation de la Nitrocellulose, Propellants, Explosives, Pyrotechnics, **9**, 130-134 (1984).
[76] A. G. Merzhanov, V. G. Abramov and F. I. Dubovitskii, Dokl. Akad. Nauk SSSR, **128**, 1238 (1959).
[77] J. Pasman, Adiabatic Experiments in Calorimetric Research, Proceedings of the 1st Symposium on Chemical Problem Connected with the Stability of Explosives, Stockholm, Sweden, 114 (1967).
[78] P. A. Davies, Accidental Initiation of Condensed Phase Explosives during Road and Rail Transport, J. Hazard. Mater., **38**, 75-88 (1994).
[79] T. L. Davis, *ibid.*, 202-204.
[80] Snelling and Storm, Bur. Mines Tech. Paper 12, The Behavior of Nitroglycerine When Heated, Washington, 1912.
[81] M. Arai, N. Mochizuki, M. Itoh, Y. Hara and T. Yoshida, Self-Accelerated Decomposition Temperature (SADT) of Explosive Substances (in Japanese), Kogyo Kayaku, **43**, 101 (1982).

10 Procedure to calculate the SADT for a powdery chemical of the quasi-AC type, having an arbitrary shape and an arbitrary size, confined in an arbitrary closed container of the corresponding shape and size, and placed in the atmosphere under isothermal conditions

10.1 Introduction

A proposition is obtained in **Section 3.2** to the effect that it is possible, in principle,* to regard the SADT calculated in accordance with Eq. (59) holding for the induction period of the autocatalytic reaction, or of the quasi-autocatalytic reaction, of 2 cm^3 of a chemical of the AC type, including every powdery chemical of the quasi-AC type, confined in the closed cell and subjected to the isothermal storage test, as the SADT for the chemical, having an arbitrary shape and an arbitrary size, confined in an arbitrary closed container of the corresponding shape and size, and placed in the atmosphere under isothermal conditions.

$$\ln \Delta t = \frac{a}{T_t} + b. \tag{59}$$

That is, for the purpose of calculating the SADT for a powdery chemical of the quasi-AC type, having an arbitrary shape and an arbitrary size, confined in an arbitrary closed container of the corresponding shape and size, and placed in the atmosphere under isothermal conditions, we have only to perform several isothermal storage tests at each T_t with mutual intervals of 1～2 K, in order to calculate the values of the two coefficients, a and b, of Eq. (59) holding for the induction period of the quasi-autocatalytic reaction of 2 cm^3 of the chemical confined in the closed cell and subjected to the isothermal storage test, for 2 cm^3 each of several samples of the chemical confined each in the closed cell, for the time, Δt, from the insertion of each cell into the isothermal storage testing device till the start of the quasi-autocatalytic reaction occurring simultaneously with the finish of melting of the chemical at the corresponding T_t, *i.e.*, during the induction period of the quasi-autocatalytic reaction of the chemical at the corresponding T_t, respectively.

Thus, the procedure to calculate the SADT for a powdery chemical of the quasi-AC type, having an arbitrary shape and an arbitrary size, confined in an

* Practically speaking, however, as commented in a footnote in **Section 3.2**, the larger the size of the chemical, the temperature of which has been maintained at room temperature until the placement, the longer becomes naturally the time required for the temperature of the chemical as a whole to increase from room temperature up to the T_t.

arbitrary closed container of the corresponding shape and size, and placed in the atmosphere under isothermal conditions, by applying Eq. (59) holding for the induction period of the quasi-autocatalytic reaction of 2 cm^3 of the chemical confined in the closed cell and subjected to the isothermal storage test, is introduced in the present chapter, by taking the procedure to calculate the SADT for LPO,* having an arbitrary shape and an arbitrary size, confined in an arbitrary closed container of the corresponding shape and size and placed in the atmosphere under isothermal conditions, as an example.

The values of SADT thus calculated each for five powdery chemicals of the quasi-AC type, including LPO, ranged from 28.4 ℃ for AMVN to 86.5 ℃ for ABCN.

These values of SADT calculated herein in general are in fair agreement with some corresponding temperature values measured each in different ways by other researchers for some of the powdery chemicals of the quasi-AC type, tested herein, of relatively large quantities, respectively.

The procedure to perform several isothermal storage tests at each T_t with mutual intervals of 1 ~ 2 K, in order to calculate the values of the two coefficients, a and b, of Eq. (59), $\ln \Delta t = a/T_t + b$, holding for the induction period of the quasi-autocatalytic reaction of 2 cm^3 of a powdery chemical of the quasi-AC type confined in the closed cell and subjected to the isothermal storage test, for 2 cm^3 each of several samples of the chemical confined each in the closed cell, for the time, Δt, from the insertion of each cell into the isothermal storage testing device till the start of the quasi-autocatalytic reaction occurring simultaneously with the finish of melting of the chemical at the corresponding T_t, respectively, is explained in detail in **Section 10.2**, by taking the procedure performed for 2 cm^3 of LPO confined in the closed cell as an example.

The concrete procedure to calculate the SADT for a powdery chemical of the quasi-AC type, having an arbitrary shape and an arbitrary size, confined in an arbitrary closed container of the corresponding shape and size, and placed in the atmosphere under isothermal conditions, is illustrated in **Section 10.3**, by taking the procedure to calculate the SADT for LPO, having an arbitrary shape and an arbitrary size, confined in an arbitrary closed container of the corresponding shape and size, and placed in the atmosphere under isothermal conditions, as an example.

---

* For the abbreviations of powdery chemicals of the quasi-AC type tested herein, refer to Table 26 in **Subsection 10.4.1**.

10.1.1 The reason why the adiabatic control is dispensable in the isothermal storage test performed for a powdery chemical of the quasi-AC type

It is indispensable also in the isothermal storage test performed for a powdery chemical of the quasi-AC type to confine the chemical in any closed cell, because, once a powdery chemical of the quasi-AC type finishes melting in the cell, the quasi-autocatalytic reaction of the chemical starts, accompanied with the vigorous evolution of some gases including the vaporized chemical itself.

Now, one may have some apprehensions for a fact that the isothermal storage testing device, which is used to perform the isothermal storage test at a T_t in order to calculate ultimately the SADT for a powdery chemical of the quasi-AC type, having an arbitrary shape and an arbitrary size, confined in an arbitrary closed container of the corresponding shape and size, and placed in the atmosphere under isothermal conditions, is lacking in the adiabatic control.

In this connection, it is mentioned in **Section 4.1** that it is also possible, in principle, to perform the adiabatic self-heating test for a powdery chemical of the quasi-AC type confined in the closed cell by means of the adiabatic self-heating process recorder. To perform the adiabatic self-heating test for a powdery chemical of the quasi-AC type confined in the closed cell will be certainly more favorable than to perform the isothermal storage test for the chemical. It has, however, been thought herein that the adiabatic self-heating process recorder should be used only for the adiabatic self-heating test performed over a relatively short time, say, several hours, in order that every experimenter may be able to accompany the adiabatic self-heating process recorder throughout one run, by reason that, while the function of every adiabatic apparatus is elaborate, its structure in general is fragile, so that it is always under the necessity of being handled with care. A device such as the aluminium block bath, the structure and the function of which are tough and simple, is, therefore, necessary and optimum for the isothermal storage test which must be performed for a powdery chemical of the quasi-AC type over a long time, say, several days.

At all events, however, once a powdery chemical of the quasi-AC type confined in the closed cell finishes melting, the chemical starts the quasi-autocatalytic reaction suddenly, even if the test is performed under isothermal conditions. It is, therefore, possible also in the isothermal storage test to locate without much difficulty the exothermic onset point, *i.e.*, the point of time "**b**", such as indicated in Fig. 7 in **Section 3.3**, on the strip chart of the temperature recorder; in particular, it is possible and easy to do so, if the test is performed at a T_t, on the high temperature side, corresponding to a relatively small value of Δt in Eq. (59), $\ln \Delta t = a / T_t + b$, holding for the induction period of the quasi-autocatalytic reaction of 2 cm^3 of a powdery chemical of the quasi-AC type confined in the closed cell and subjected to the isothermal storage test.

As to a powdery chemical of the quasi-AC type, there also exists the following fact. That is, as seen in Fig. 7 in **Section 3.3**, no heat loss occurs at all from the liquefied chemical of the quasi-AC type to the atmosphere at "**b**", *i.e.*, at the time when a powdery chemical of the quasi-AC type starts the quasi-autocatalytic reaction simultaneously with the finish of melting of the chemical, because the condition,

the T_t (the temperature of the aluminium block bath) > the temperature of the liquefied chemical of the quasi-AC type,

holds at "**b**". Under such circumstances, the thermocouple is able to detect sensitively the start of the quasi-autocatalytic reaction of the liquefied chemical.

In this connection, it is severe circumstances, compared with storage conditions in normal warehouses, for a powdery chemical of the quasi-AC type that 2 cm^3 of the chemical is confined in the glass closed cell and inserted into the hot aluminium block bath, because the rate of thermal conduction from aluminium to the chemical confined in the glass closed cell is far larger than that from air to the chemical confined in a polyethylene bag and packaged further in a fiber drum, so that the rate of heat flow into the chemical in the isothermal storage test by means of the aluminium block bath is far larger than the rate into the chemical under storage conditions in normal warehouses. It is thus certain that the melting process of the chemical will be much promoted in a simple isothermal storage testing device, such as introduced **Section 9.2**, with the result that a value of SADT on the low temperature side, or on the safety side, is necessarily obtained for every powdery chemical of the quasi-AC type.

10.2 Procedure to perform several isothermal storage tests at each T_t with mutual intervals of 1~2 K, in order to calculate the values of the two coefficients, *a* and *b*, of Equation (59), $\ln \Delta t = a/T_t + b$, holding for the induction period of the quasi-autocatalytic reaction of 2 [cm^3] of a powdery chemical of the quasi-AC type confined in the closed cell and subjected to the isothermal storage test, for 2 cm^3 each of several samples of the chemical confined each in the closed cell, for the time, Δt, from the insertion of each cell into the isothermal storage testing device till the start of the quasi-autocatalytic reaction occurring simultaneously with the finish of melting of the chemical at the corresponding T_t, respectively

The procedure described in the above heading is explained in detail in the present section by taking the procedure performed for 1.2 g of LPO, the volume of which is about 2 cm^3, confined in the closed cell as an example.

10.2.1 Preheating of the aluminium block bath of the isothermal storage testing device and the choice of a nominal T_t in the isothermal storage test performed for 1.2 g of LPO confined in the closed cell

The isothermal storage testing device is placed in an air-conditioned room maintained at an almost constant (room) temperature throughout every run.

To begin with, the constant voltage power supply connected to the isothermal storage testing device is switched on.

The temperature of the aluminium block bath is set at a proper value, *i.e.*, the nominal T_t of the run, by means of the ten-key on the block bath on the basis of the self-heating property of the powdery chemical of the quasi-AC type tested to give estimated values of Δt of 1~7 d in the isothermal storage test. It is usually a temperature 0~15 K lower than the endothermic peak temperature, which is measured by thermal analysis, such as DTA or DSC, of each chemical in the case of powdery chemicals of the quasi-AC type tested herein, with the result that the T_t ranged from 30.08 ℃ for AMVN to 94.0 ℃ for ABCN. As to LPO, the T_t ranged from 48.55 to 53.0 ℃.

The power supply connected to the block bath heater is then switched on.

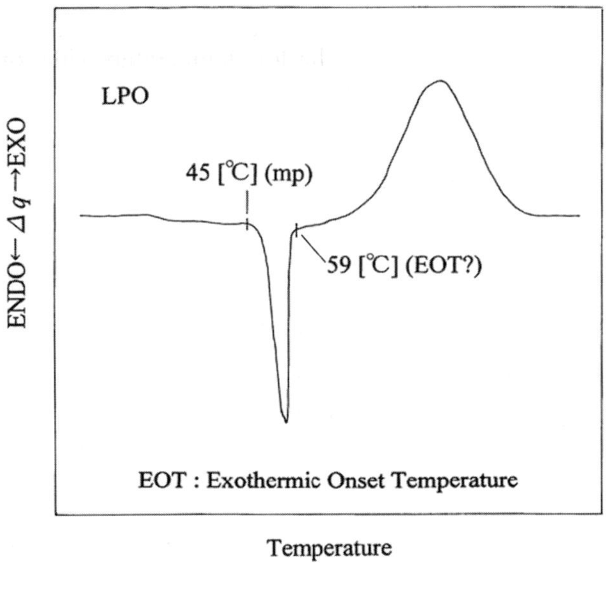

Figure 141. A DTA curve of LPO.

A DTA curve, which was recorded with a glass open-cup cell, 5 mm in diameter, 2.5 mm in depth, at the value of ϕ of 2.5 K/min in air at atmospheric pressure, of LPO is presented in Fig. 141.

It is seen in Fig. 141 that LPO begins to melt at about 45 ℃ and the EOT of LPO appears to be 59 ℃. The latter temperature is, however, too high and dangerous at which to perform the isothermal storage test for LPO. Thus, in practice, tests have to be performed at temperatures below the endothermic peak temperature, as illustrated for LPO in Fig. 142. As stated in **Sections 3.3** and **3.4**, this necessity arises from the fact that the exothermic decomposition reaction takes place in parallel with the endothermic melting in every powdery chemical of the quasi-AC type. Notes like '1 [d] at 51.6 [℃]' in Fig. 142, mean that, when confined in the closed cell and subjected to the isothermal storage test performed at a specified temperature, LPO starts the quasi-autocatalytic reaction simultaneously with the finish of melting after the lapse of the time corresponding to the temperature.

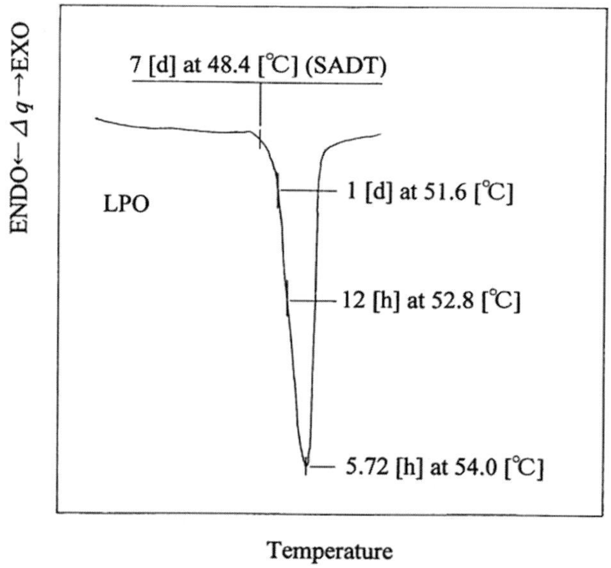

Figure 142. Positions, of several combinations of the value of Δt with that of T_t, determined each by the several isothermal storage tests performed for LPO and marked each on a DTA curve of LPO.

10.2.2 Procedure to prepare the reference cell assembly including the closed cell

Procedures performed in the present subsection are identical with those described in **Subsection 9.3.2**.

(1) A temporary stem, which is required to prepare the reference cell or the sample cell, is made by sticking the glass flange tube (Fig. 24 in **Section 4.3**) on the glass capillary flange (Fig. 25 in **Subsection 4.4.4**) with a bit of fat clay (refer to Fig. 120 in **(2)** of **Subsection 9.3.2**).

(2) The stainless steel jig Ⅰ, which is composed of the upper piece and the lower piece, is set on the pedestal. The outside diameter of the pedestal and the inside diameter of the lower end of the lower piece are 16 mm and 16.1 mm, respectively. The pedestal is stuck at the center of the upper plate of the laboratory jack, which in turn is fixed on the laboratory desk. The position of the stand, by means of the cramp of which the temporary stem including the glass capillary flange is held in the vertical position, is next adjusted by sliding the stand horizontally on the laboratory desk in order that the glass capillary flange may be aligned vertically with the upper piece of the stainless steel jig Ⅰ set on the pedestal (refer to Fig. 120). The outside diameter of the glass capillary flange and the inside diameter of the upper piece are 18 mm and 18.1 mm, respectively.

(3) After having lowered the laboratory jack a little, the upper piece of the stainless steel jig Ⅰ is detached from the lower piece.

(4) 2.2 g of silica powder, the volume of which is about 2 cm^3, is charged in a closed cell, *i.e.*, the cell with which the reference cell is prepared.

(5) The closed cell, on the flange of which an O-ring is put concentrically, is set in the lower piece. The outside diameter of the flange of the closed cell and that of the upper end of the lower piece are 18 mm, respectively; in the meantime, the outside diameter of the cell body and the inside diameter of the upper end of the lower piece are 14 mm and 14.2 mm, respectively. The upper piece is then set on the lower piece. At this time, the surface of the upper end of the upper piece is higher than the upper side of the O-ring by 2 mm, which corresponds to the thickness of the flange of the glass capillary flange (refer to Fig. 121 in **(5)** of **Subsection 9.3.2**).

(6) The stainless steel jig Ⅰ containing the closed cell, on the upper surface of the flange of which the O-ring is put concentrically, is pressed concentrically and softly up to the under surface of the glass capillary flange by raising the laboratory jack to construct the reference cell; in the meantime, the glass capillary tube projecting downward from the under surface of the glass capillary flange is inserted automatically into silica powder charged in the closed cell.

(7) After the temporary stem has been released by loosening the cramp of the stand, the stand is moved a little backward by sliding it on the desk.

(8) The glass flange tube is detached from the glass capillary flange by sliding the former horizontally. This sliding is possible, because both the upper surface of the glass capillary flange and the surface of the upper end of the upper piece of the stainless steel jig Ⅰ are on the same horizontal plane. A bit of fat clay is then wiped fully off the upper surface of the glass capillary flange with acetone-soaked adsorbent cotton (refer to Fig. 122 in **(8)** of **Subsection 9.3.2**).

(9) The upper piece is detached from the lower piece, into which the reference cell is now inserted. The reference cell is then taken down from the lower piece. Further, the lower piece is removed from the pedestal.

(10) The second stainless steel jig, the stainless steel jig Ⅱ, the inside diameter of the lower end of which is 16.1 mm, is set anew on the pedestal. The female cap nut, on the bottom of which a stainless steel washer and two PTFE washers are put in this order, is then set in the stainless steel jig Ⅱ. The outside diameter of the female cap nut is 22 mm, and, the inside diameter of the upper end and that of the flange of the stainless steel jig Ⅱ are 22.2 mm and 14.2 mm, respectively. Thereafter, the reference cell is inserted into the composite of the female cap nut and the stainless steel jig Ⅱ. Two PTFE washers and a stainless steel washer are then put concentrically in this order on the upper surface of the glass capillary flange (see **d** and **c** in Fig. 123 in **(12)** of **Subsection 9.3.2**).

(11) After the third stainless steel jig, the stainless steel jig Ⅲ, the diameter of the under flange of which is 18 mm, has been held in the vertical position by means of the cramp of the stand, the position of the stand is adjusted by sliding the stand horizontally on the laboratory desk in order that the under flange of the stainless steel jig Ⅲ may be aligned vertically with the reference cell (refer to Fig. 123).

(12) The reference cell, on the upper surface of the flange of which two PTFE washers and a stainless steel washer are put, is then pressed concentrically and firmly up to the under surface of the stainless steel jig Ⅲ by raising the laboratory jack (refer to Fig. 123).

(13) First the female cap nut is raised with the left hand. Then, pressing the female cap nut up to the under surface of the flange of the reference cell with the left hand, the laboratory jack is lowered. After the female cap nut, into which the reference cell is inserted, has been detached down from the stainless steel jig Ⅲ with the left hand, the male cap nut is screwed lightly into the female cap nut with the right hand.

(14) Holding the female cap nut with a pair of pliers in the left hand, the male cap nut, which is screwed lightly into the female cap nut, is tightened as fast as possible with the right hand. The male cap nut is then tightened further by about 30° using another pair of pliers in the right hand (refer to Fig. 124 in **(14)** of **Subsection 9.3.2**). A fairly small vibrator is finally applied to the base of the closed cell in order that silica powder confined in the cell may come closely in contact with the glass capillary tube.

10.2.3 Insertion of the reference cell assembly into the preheated aluminium block bath in the isothermal storage testing device and the determination of the exact value of T_t of the run

For a series of procedures, which are identical with those described in **Subsection 9.3.3**, performed in the present subsection, refer to Fig. 119 in **Subsection 9.2.1**.

(1) First the thermocouple is pulled out of the orifice at the center of the upper surface of the aluminium lid with the bare left hand; and, thermocouple of about 30 [cm] from the tip is squeezed through between the thumb and the forefinger of the right hand to make the thermocouple straight. The thermocouple is then laid by the left side of the device.

(2) The aluminium lid is drawn out of the hole at the center of the upper surface of the preheated aluminium block bath with a handle* in the gloved hands, wearing a pair of working gloves in the isothermal storage test performed at a T_t up to about 80 ℃, and, wearing a pair of heat-proof gloves besides a pair of working gloves in the test performed at a T_t in excess of 80 ℃. Thereafter, the lid is laid by one side on the upper surface of the aluminium block bath.

(3) The reference cell assembly is raised with a pair of fairly large pincers and is inserted carefully down to the bottom of the hole, 23 mm in diameter, 75 mm in depth, bored vertically at the center of the upper surface of the preheated aluminium block bath which is set in the isothermal storage testing device; in the meantime, the temperature of the bath is maintained at the T_t K of the run throughout every run.

(4) The aluminium lid is raised with the handle in the gloved left hand. The thermocouple is then pierced through the orifice at the center of the upper surface of the lid. The diameter of the thermocouple and that of the orifice are 0.5 and 1 mm, respectively. After the thermocouple has been drawn by 20 cm or more out of the orifice at the center of the under surface of the lid, the aluminium lid is brought from above little by little closer to the hole at the center of the upper surface of the aluminium block bath, in order that the tip of the thermocouple may be inserted into the orifice of the glass capillary tube at the center of the upper surface of the glass capillary flange of the reference cell assembly which is inserted down to the bottom of the hole in the aluminium block bath. After it has been confirmed that the tip of the thermocouple is inserted into the orifice of the glass capillary tube, the lid is inserted slowly and carefully into the hole while supported with the handle in the gloved left hand and the fairly large pincers in the gloved right hand.

---

* This handle is not drawn in Fig. 119, because it is demountable.

(5) Thereafter, whether or not the thermocouple is inserted down to the bottom of the glass capillary tube is ascertained by holding the thermocouple above the lid with a few fingers of the naked right hand and then pushing it down to the bottom of the tube carefully once or twice.

(6) The exact value of T_t of the run is then determined as the arithmetic mean of a series of digital outputs of T_t recorded for 2 d prior to the insertion of the sample cell assembly into the aluminium block bath. Fluctuations of the values of T_t during this time are within ± 0.05 K.

10.2.4 Insertion of the sample cell assembly into the aluminium block bath and the start of the isothermal storage test for 1.2 g of LPO confined in the closed cell and inserted into the aluminium block bath maintained at the T_t

For a series of procedures, which are almost the same as those described in **Subsection 9.3.4**, performed in the present subsection, refer to Fig. 119 in **Subsection 9.2.1**.

(1) First the thermocouple is pulled out of the orifice at the center of the upper surface of the aluminium lid with the bare left hand; and, the thermocouple of about 30 cm from the tip is squeezed through between the thumb and the forefinger of the right hand to make the thermocouple straight. The thermocouple is then laid by the left side of the device.

(2) The aluminium lid is drawn out of the hole at the center of the upper surface of the preheated aluminium block bath with a handle in the gloved hands. Thereafter, the lid is laid by one side on the upper surface of the aluminium block bath.

(3) After the reference cell assembly has been taken out with a pair of fairly large pincers, the sample cell assembly, in which 1.2 g of LPO has been confined in the same manner as performed to prepare the reference cell assembly in **Subsection 10.2.2**, is inserted carefully down to the bottom of the hole at the center of the upper surface of the aluminium block bath with the same pair of fairly large pincers.

The quantity of the powdery chemical of the quasi-AC type tested depends naturally on its specific gravity, with the result that it ranged from 0.9 g for ABCN to 1.25 g for TSH in the case of powdery chemicals of the quasi-AC type tested herein.

Coarse crystals or particles should be tested after having been pulverized by means of an agate mortar.

When occasions demand, there are cases in each of which a fairly small vibrator is applied to the base of the closed cell in order that the chemical confined in the cell may come closely in contact with the glass capillary tube.

(4) The aluminium lid is raised with the handle in the gloved left hand. The thermocouple is then pierced through the orifice at the center of the upper surface of the lid. After the thermocouple has been drawn by 20 cm or more out of the orifice at the center of the under surface of the lid, the aluminium lid is brought from above little by little closer to the hole at the center of the upper surface of the aluminium block bath, in order that the tip of the thermocouple may be inserted into the orifice of the glass capillary tube at the center of the upper surface of the glass capillary flange of the sample cell assembly which is inserted down to the bottom of the hole in the aluminium block bath. After it has been confirmed that the tip of the thermocouple is inserted into the orifice of the glass capillary tube, the lid is inserted slowly and carefully into the hole while supported with the handle in the gloved left hand and with the fairly large pincers in the gloved right hand.

(5) Thereafter, whether or not the thermocouple is inserted down to the bottom of the glass capillary tube is ascertained by holding the thermocouple above the lid with a few fingers of the naked right hand and then pushing it down to the bottom of the tube carefully once or twice.

(6) A point, on the T_t baseline* recorded on the strip chart of the analog/digital temperature recorder, where the T pen sprang suddenly away from the T_t baseline by reason that the thermocouple was pulled suddenly out of the orifice at the center of the upper surface of the preheated aluminium lid in **(1)** of the present subsection, is regarded as the starting time of the isothermal storage test performed at the T_t for 1.2 g of LPO confined in the closed cell. The record of the induction period of the quasi-autocatalytic reaction of 1.2 g of LPO confined in the closed cell and subjected to the isothermal storage test by means of the analog/digital temperature recorder is then started. This point of time corresponds to the point, **Room temperature**, in Fig. 7 in **Section 3.3** or that in Fig. 16 in **Section 3.4**.

(7) The exact value of T_t of the run, which was determined in **(6)** of **Subsection 10.2.3**, and the starting time of the isothermal storage test, which was determined in **(6)** of the present subsection, are noted down on a separate sheet.

10.2.5 Record of the induction period of the quasi-autocatalytic reaction of 1.2 g of LPO confined in the closed cell and subjected to the isothermal storage test performed at the T_t

After the start of the isothermal storage test, as stated in **(6)** of **Subsection 10.2.4**, the induction period of the quasi-autocatalytic reaction of 1.2 g of LPO confined in the closed cell and subjected to the isothermal storage test performed at the T_t, *i.e.*, the time, Δt, from the insertion of the cell into the isothermal storage testing device till the start of the quasi-autocatalytic reaction

* The linear locus drawn by the T_t pen on the strip chart of the analog/digital temperature recorder is called the T_t baseline.

occurring simultaneously with the finish of melting of LPO at the T_t, is recorded by means of the analog/digital temperature recorder.

The test, including the heating of the aluminium block bath, is interrupted automatically as soon as the temperature of LPO in the cell increases by 0.3 K from the T_t in order to prevent the cell from exploding. As a matter of fact, however, the test is usually interrupted as soon as the temperature of the chemical in the cell increases obviously in excess of the T_t.*

The other combinations of the value of $\ln \Delta t$ with that of $1/T_t$, which are required to make the plot of $\ln \Delta t$ versus $1/T_t$ with regard to several induction periods, of the quasi-autocatalytic reaction, of 1.2 g each of several samples of LPO confined each in the closed cell and subjected each to the isothermal storage test performed at each T_t in the range of 48.55 to 51.9 ℃ with mutual intervals of 0.4～1 K, recorded each for the time, Δt, from the insertion of each cell into the isothermal storage testing device till the start of the quasi-autocatalytic reaction occurring simultaneously with the finish of melting of LPO at the corresponding T_t, besides, which are required for the regression analysis to calculate the values of the two coefficients, *a* and *b*, of Eq. (59) holding for the induction period of the quasi-autocatalytic reaction of 1.2 g of LPO confined in the closed cell and subjected to the isothermal storage test, are also determined in the same manner as explained above.

Five induction periods, of the quasi-autocatalytic reaction, of 1.2 g each of five samples of LPO confined each in the closed cell and subjected each to the isothermal storage test performed at each T_t in the range of 48.55 to 51.9 ℃ with mutual intervals of 0.4～1 K, recorded each for the time, Δt, from the insertion of each cell into the isothermal storage testing device till the start of the quasi-autocatalytic reaction occurring simultaneously with the finish of melting of LPO at the corresponding T_t, are presented in Figure 143. The time axis on the other side in Fig. 143 and that in Fig. 144 are graduated in d to meet the sense of long time, respectively. The points marked with "**b**" on the curves in Fig. 143 correspond to the point of time "**b**" in Fig. 7 in **Section 3.3**, or in Fig. 16 in **Section 3.4**, respectively.

---

* After having been taken out of the hole in the hot aluminium block bath, the sample cell assembly should be dismantled as soon as possible in order to detach the glass capillary flange from the cell body before the liquefied chemical solidifies again in the cell. It is impossible, however, to loosen the cap nut while the vapor pressure in the cell is very high by reason that the chemical is completely liquefied at temperatures in excess of its melting point. Such being the case, the time when the chemical begins to solidify in the cell provides optimum opportunities for dismantling of the cell. In case that the chemical has solidified in the cell with the result that it is impossible to detach the glass capillary flange from the cell body, it becomes possible to dismantle the sample cell by inserting the cell once again into the aluminium block bath, after having loosened the cap nut a little, in order to melt again the chemical by heating it up to the original T_t, while the temperature of the chemical is watched with the thermocouple inserted into the glass capillary tube.

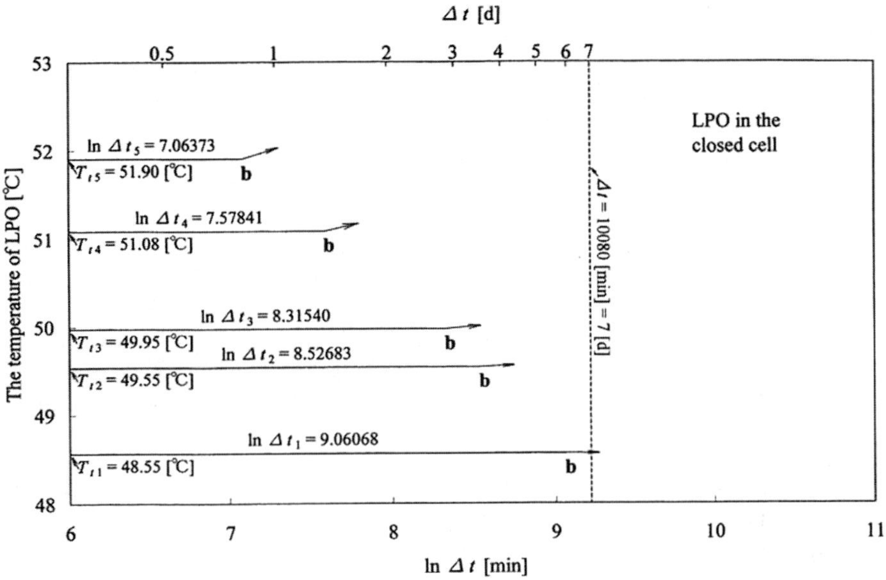

Figure 143. Five induction periods, of the quasi-autocatalytic reaction, of 1.2 g each of five samples of LPO confined each in the closed cell and subjected each to the isothermal storage test performed at each T_t in the range of 48.55 to 51.9 ℃ with mutual intervals of 0.4~1 K, recorded each for the time, Δt, from the insertion of each cell into the isothermal storage testing device till the start of the quasi-autocatalytic reaction occurring simultaneously with the finish of melting of LPO at the corresponding T_t.

The plot of $\ln \Delta t$ versus $1/T_t$ made for 1.2 g each of six samples of LPO is shown in Fig. 144.

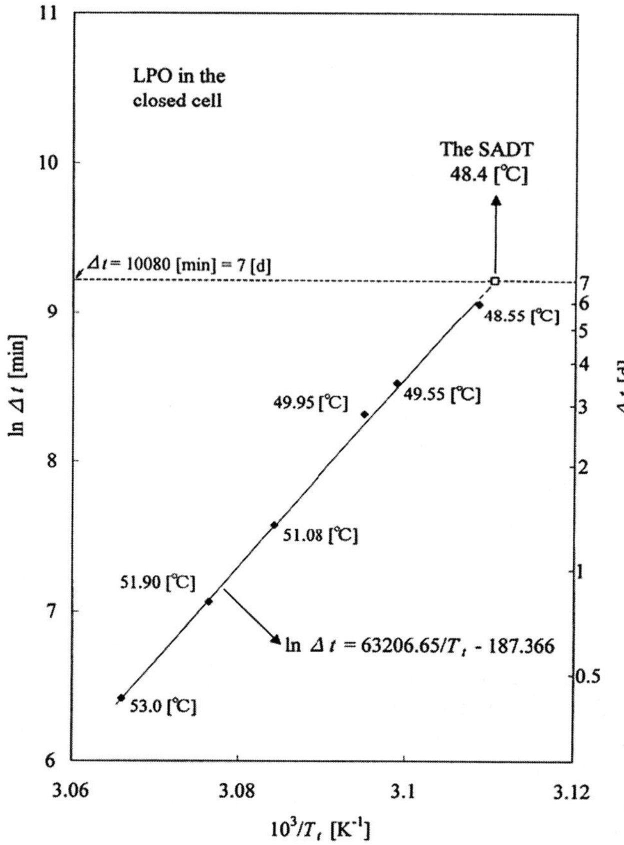

Figure 144. The plot of ln Δt versus $1/T_t$ made with six combinations of the value of ln Δt with that of $1/T_s$, which are each determined for six induction periods, five induction periods of which are presented in Fig. 143, of the quasi-autocatalytic reaction, of 1.2 g each of six samples of LPO confined each in the closed cell and subjected each to the isothermal storage test performed at each T_t in the range of 48.55 to 53.0 ℃ with mutual intervals of 0.4～1 K, recorded each for the time, Δt, from the insertion of each cell into the isothermal storage testing device till the start of the quasi-autocatalytic reaction occurring simultaneously with the finish of melting of LPO at the corresponding T_t.

It is obvious in Fig. 144 that the empirical formula, $\ln \Delta t = a/T_t + b$, *i.e.*, Eq. (59), presented in Fig. 7 in **Section 3.3**, or in Fig. 16 in **Section 3.4**, holds well between a T_t and the time, Δt, from the insertion of the closed cell, in which 1.2 g of LPO is confined, into the isothermal storage testing device till the start of the quasi-autocatalytic reaction occurring simultaneously with the finish of melting of LPO at the T_t.

For the value of a coefficient, 63206.65, of the equation, $\ln \Delta t = 63206.65/T_t - 187.366$, *i.e.*, Eq. (59) holding for the induction period of the quasi-autocatalytic reaction of 1.2 g of LPO confined in the closed cell and subjected to the isothermal storage test, refer to the explanation given under Table 25 in the following subsection.

The broken line in Fig. 143 and that in Fig. 144 denote 7 d, respectively. The temperature coordinates, 48.4 ℃, of the intersection, which is indicated by the symbol "□" in Fig. 144, of the plot of $\ln \Delta t$ versus $1/T_t$ and the broken line must, therefore, be the SADT for LPO tested herein, in accordance with the definition of the SADT.

10.2.6 Calculation of the values of the two coefficients, *a* and *b*, of Equation (59), $\ln \Delta t = a/T_t + b$, holding for the induction period of the quasi-autocatalytic reaction of 1.2 g of LPO confined in the closed cell and subjected to the isothermal storage test

The result of the regression analysis to calculate the values of the two coefficients, *a* and *b*, of Eq. (59), $\ln \Delta t = a/T_t + b$, holding for the induction period of the quasi-autocatalytic reaction of 1.2 g of LPO confined in the closed cell and subjected to the isothermal storage test is presented in Table 25.

Values of $\ln \Delta t$ and $1/T_t$ used in the regression analysis are in common with those presented in part in Fig. 143 and plotted in Fig. 144. The values of T_t presented in Figs. 143 and 144 are, however, all rounded. For an instance similar to this, refer to Tables 5 and 6 in **Section 4.7** and Figs. 45 and 46 in **Subsection 5.4.5**.

Table 25
The result of the regression analysis applied, in order to calculate the values of the two coefficients, a and b, of Equation (59), $\ln \Delta t = a/T_t + b$, holding for the induction period of the quasi-autocatalytic reaction of 1.2 g of LPO confined in the closed cell and subjected to the isothermal storage test, to six combinations of the value of $\ln \Delta t$ with that of $1/T_t$, which are each determined, based on six analog/digital records obtained each from six isothermal storage tests performed each, at each T_t in the range of 48.55 to 53.0 ℃ with mutual intervals of 0.4～1 K, for 1.2 g each of six samples of LPO confined each in the closed cell, for the time, Δt, from the insertion of each cell into the isothermal storage testing device till the start of the quasi-autocatalytic reaction occurring simultaneously with the finish of melting of LPO at the corresponding T_t. Data used are in common with those presented in part in Fig. 143 and plotted in Fig. 144.

MATERIAL ... LPO

DATA NUMBER	X	Y	A＊X+B
1	3.10849	9.06068	9.111676
2	3.09885	8.52683	8.502364
3	3.09502	8.31540	8.260282
4	3.08423	7.57841	7.578283
5	3.07645	7.06373	7.086535
6	3.06607	6.42454	6.430450

COEFFICIENT OF Y = A＊TT + B A = 63.20665
COEFFICIENT OF Y = A＊TT + B B = -187.366

DISTRIBUTION = 0.001698 STANDARD DEVIATION = 0.041207

Based on the result, the value of a for LPO is calculated by multiplying the value of A, which is presented in Table 25, by 1,000 in the same manner as performed for the value of A of TBPB in **Section 4.7**.

The values of the two coefficients, a and b, thus calculated, of Eq. (59), $\ln \Delta t = a/T_t + b$, holding for the induction period of the quasi-autocatalytic reaction of 1.2 g of LPO confined in the closed cell and subjected to the isothermal storage test, 63206.65 and -187.366, are presented as such in Table 27 in **Subsection 10.4.1**.

10.3 Concrete procedure to calculate the SADT for a powdery chemical of the quasi-AC type, having an arbitrary shape and an arbitrary size, confined in an arbitrary closed container of the corresponding shape and size, and placed in the atmosphere under isothermal conditions

According to the proposition obtained in **Section 3.2**, the SADT for a powdery chemical of the quasi-AC type, having an arbitrary shape and an arbitrary size, confined in an arbitrary closed container of the corresponding shape and size, and placed in the atmosphere under isothermal conditions, is calculated, in accordance with the definition of the SADT, at a value of T_t corresponding to a value of Δt of 7 d, *i.e.*, 10,080 min, in Eq. (59) holding for the induction period of the quasi-autocatalytic reaction of 2 cm^3 of the chemical confined in the closed cell and subjected to the isothermal storage test.

$$\ln \Delta t = \frac{a}{T_t} + b. \qquad (59)$$

As an example, the concrete procedure to calculate the SADT for LPO, having an arbitrary shape and an arbitrary size, confined in an arbitrary closed container of the corresponding shape and size, and placed in the atmosphere under isothermal conditions, is illustrated in the present section.

The values of the two coefficients, a and b, of Eq. (59) holding for the induction period of the quasi-autocatalytic reaction of 1.2 g of LPO confined in the closed cell and subjected to the isothermal storage test were calculated in **Subsection 10.2.6** and are given in Table 27 in **Subsection 10.4.1**.

The value of SADT for LPO, having an arbitrary shape and an arbitrary size, confined in an arbitrary closed container of the corresponding shape and size, and placed in the atmosphere under isothermal conditions, is thus calculated in the following manner.

$$T_t = \frac{a}{\ln \Delta t - b} = 63206.65 \div (\ln 10080 + 187.366)$$

$$= 63206.65 \div (9.21831 + 187.366)$$

$$= 63206.65 \div 196.58431$$

$$= 321.5244 \text{ K} = 48.3744 \text{ ℃}.$$

The value of SADT thus calculated for LPO, having an arbitrary shape and an arbitrary size, confined in an arbitrary closed container of the corresponding shape and size, and placed in the atmosphere under isothermal conditions, 48.3744 ℃, is finally rounded to 48.4 ℃ and is presented as such, together with the values of SADT calculated each for the four powdery chemicals of the quasi-AC type, other than LPO, in the same manner as performed for LPO, in Table 27 in **Subsection 10.4.1**.

Once the values of the two coefficients, *a* and *b*, of Eq. (59) holding for the induction period of the quasi-autocatalytic reaction of 2 cm^3 of a powdery chemical of the quasi-AC type confined in the closed cell and subjected to the isothermal storage test are fixed, it becomes possible to calculate, for the chemical, in the same manner as performed for a high explosive of the true AC type, an arbitrary value of T_t, as well as the SADT, corresponding to an arbitrary value of Δt, *i.e.*, an arbitrary exposure time, such as 1 h, 1 d or 30 d. Such a value of temperature may be useful as the upper limit temperature in temperature control to prevent the chemical from exploding thermally after the corresponding exposure time.

It is, however, not probable that a powdery chemical of the quasi-AC type melts completely at a low T_t corresponding to a very long exposure time such as 30 d. Or rather the appearance of melting of a powdery chemical of the quasi-AC type at a low T_t corresponding to a very long exposure time will result in such a degree that the surfaces of the particles of the chemical become slightly damp.

10.4 Results and discussion

10.4.1 The values of SADT calculated each for the five powdery chemicals of the quasi-AC type, including LPO

The list of the five powdery chemicals of the quasi-AC type tested is given in Table 26.

These powdery chemicals of the quasi-AC type are of the industrial grade or of the reagent grade and were tested without further purification.

The isothermal storage tests for the four powdery chemicals of the quasi-AC type, other than LPO, were also performed in the same manner as done for LPO, respectively.

Table 26
The five powdery chemicals of the quasi-AC type tested herein.

Abbr.	CAS R. No.	Trivial Name and Purity
AMVN	15545-97-8	95 % 2,2'-Azobis(4-methoxy-2,4-dimethylvaleronitrile).
LPO	105-74-8	99 % Lauroyl peroxide.
BSH	80-17-1	98 % Benzenesulfonyl hydrazide.
TSH	1576-35-8	97 % *p*-Toluenesulfonyl hydrazide.
ABCN	2094-98-6	98 % 1,1'-Azobis(cyclohexane-1-carbonitrile).

The five plots of ln Δt versus $1/T_t$ made each for the five powdery chemicals of the quasi-AC type, including LPO, are presented in Fig. 145.

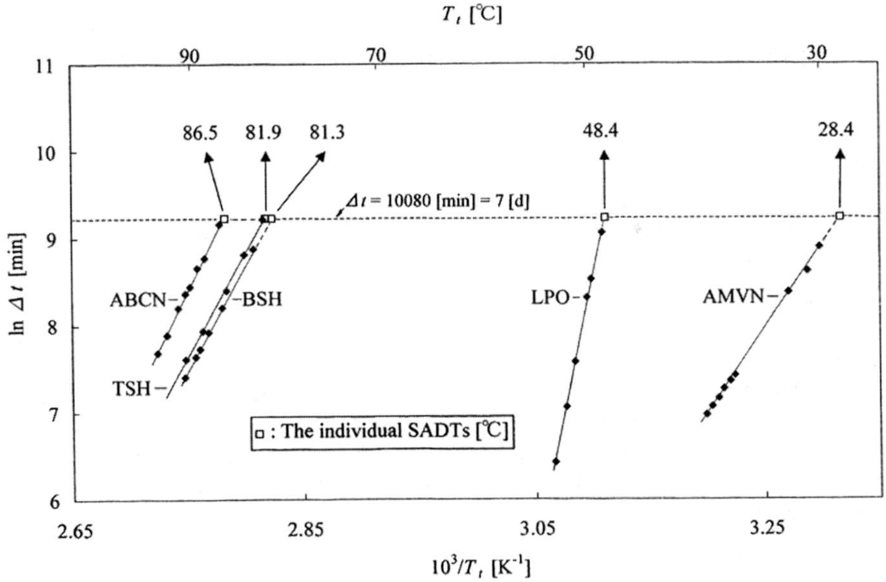

Figure 145. The five plots of ln Δt versus $1/T_t$ made each for the five powdery chemicals of the quasi-AC type.

The individual values of the two coefficients, a and b, of Eq. (59) holding for the individual induction periods of the quasi-autocatalytic reaction of 2 cm^3 each of the four powdery chemicals of the quasi-AC type, other than LPO, confined each in the closed cell and subjected each to the isothermal storage test were also calculated by applying the regression analysis to the individual combinations of the value of $\ln \Delta t$ with that of $1/T_t$ and are presented in Table 27.

It is possible to see roughly from Fig. 145 the relative liability of these powdery chemicals of the quasi-AC type to self-heating or ultimate thermal explosion. That is, we can tell that AMVN is relatively easy to explode thermally, but ABCN, TSH and BSH are relatively hard to do so. In this regard, LPO is medium in the liability to thermal explosion.

The values of SADT calculated each for the five powdery chemicals of the quasi-AC type, including LPO, are summarized in Table 27 in the order of increasing value of SADT, together with some corresponding temperature values measured each in different ways by other researchers for some of the powdery chemicals of the quasi-AC type, tested herein, of relatively large quantities as well as the other reference temperature values concerning these chemicals, for comparison [25].

The values of SADT thus calculated each for the five powdery chemicals of the quasi-AC type ranged from 28.4 ℃ for AMVN to 86.5 ℃ for ABCN.

These values of SADT calculated herein in general are in fair agreement with some corresponding temperature values measured each in different ways by other researchers for some of the powdery chemicals of the quasi-AC type, tested herein, of relatively large quantities, respectively.

It is pointed out in **Section 3.2** that the SADT, including an arbitrary value of T_t, for a chemical of the AC type, including every powdery chemical of the quasi-AC type, having an arbitrary shape and an arbitrary size, confined in an arbitrary closed container of the corresponding shape and size, and placed in the atmosphere under isothermal conditions, does not depend, in principle, on its size or quantity. This indication is substantiated in Table 27 by the fact that the values of SADT calculated each herein for 2 cm^3 each of the five powdery chemicals of the quasi-AC type confined each in the closed cell are in fair agreement with some corresponding temperature values measured each in different ways by other researchers for some of the powdery chemicals of the quasi-AC type, tested herein, of relatively large quantities, respectively. The same is true of the individual values of SADT, which are presented in Table 24 in **Section 9.5**, calculated herein for 2 cm^3 each of eight high explosives of the true AC type confined each in the closed cell.

Table 27
Experimental parameters of the five powdery chemicals of the quasi-AC type and comparison of the values of SADT calculated each for these chemicals, assuming that the SADT for a powdery chemical of the quasi-AC type, having an arbitrary shape and an arbitrary size, confined in an arbitrary closed container of the corresponding shape and size, and placed in the atmosphere under isothermal conditions, is a value of T_t corresponding to a value of Δt of 10,080 min in Eq. (59) holding for the induction period of the quasi-autocatalytic reaction of 2 cm^3 of the chemical confined in the closed cell and subjected to the isothermal storage test, with, some corresponding temperature values measured each in different ways by other researchers for some of the powdery chemicals of the quasi-AC type, tested herein, of relatively large quantities as well as the other reference temperature values concerning these chemicals.

Powdery chemical of the quasi-AC type	Coefficients of Eq. (59)		The SADT		Reference temperature	
	a	*b*	calcd. herein ℃	measured ℃	Catalog data[a)] ℃	The EOT by DSC [84] ℃
AMVN	19100.19	-54.123	28.4	33[b)] [61]	-	-
LPO	63206.65	-187.366	48.4	49 [82]	55(mp)	67
BSH	24427.45	-59.7056	81.3	-	101(mp)	113
TSH	23851.92	-57.9659	81.9	86[c)] [60]	108(dec.)	124
ABCN	26799.98	-65.303	86.5	80 [83], 88[d)] [61]	115(mp)	118

Superscripts:
a) To cite one example, Catalog Handbook of Fine Chemicals, Aldrich Chemical Co. Inc., Milwaukee (1992-93).
b) The so-called 10-h $t_{1/2}$ value for AMVN in toluene.
c) The SADT for TSH determined by the isothermal storage test.
d) The so-called 10-h $t_{1/2}$ value for ABCN in toluene.

At all events, however, it will be reasonable, in practice, to consider a temperature 30 K lower than the value of SADT calculated herein for a powdery chemical of the quasi-AC type, having an arbitrary shape and an arbitrary size, confined in an arbitrary closed container of the corresponding shape and size, and placed in the atmosphere under isothermal conditions, as the upper limit temperature for the safe handling of the chemical. For instance, 0 ℃ will be the upper limit temperature for the safe handling of AMVN, 20 ℃ for LPO, 50 ℃ for TSH, and so forth.

Incidentally, it is seen in Table 27 that the SADT for each powdery chemical of the quasi-AC type calculated herein is 10 ~ 30 K lower than the corresponding melting point, or the corresponding decomposition temperature, listed in some catalog handbook of fine chemicals and is 20~40 K lower than the corresponding EOT measured by DSC.

10.4.2 Powdery chemicals of the quasi-AC type exist in considerable numbers

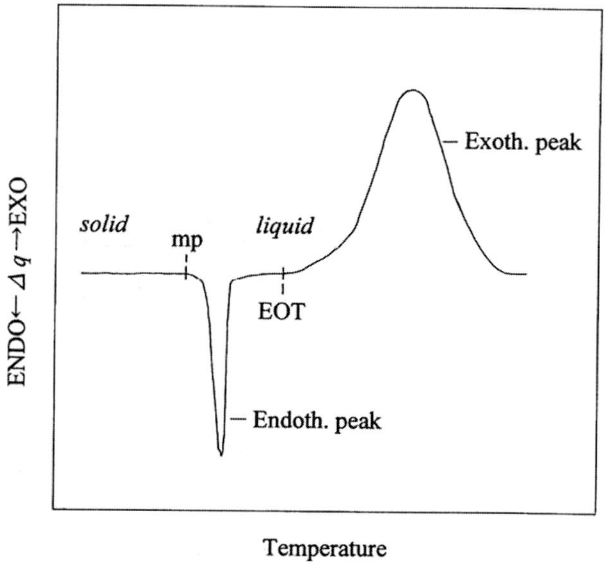

Figure 146. A typical DTA curve of a self-heating organic powdery chemical.

As shown in Fig. 146, the decomposition process of a self-heating organic powdery chemical that first melts and then decomposes exothermically is frequently seen in thermal analysis. And, it has been stated repeatedly herein that such a DTA curve as shown in Fig. 146 is nothing else but that of a powdery chemical of the quasi-AC type. It is, in this sense, possible to say that powdery chemicals of the quasi-AC type exist in considerable numbers.

As a matter of fact, however, there is a subtle difference between a liquid of the TD type and a powdery chemical of the quasi-AC type in terms of the interval between the endothermic peak and the exothermic peak in the DTA curve which each chemical affords (see Fig. 147).

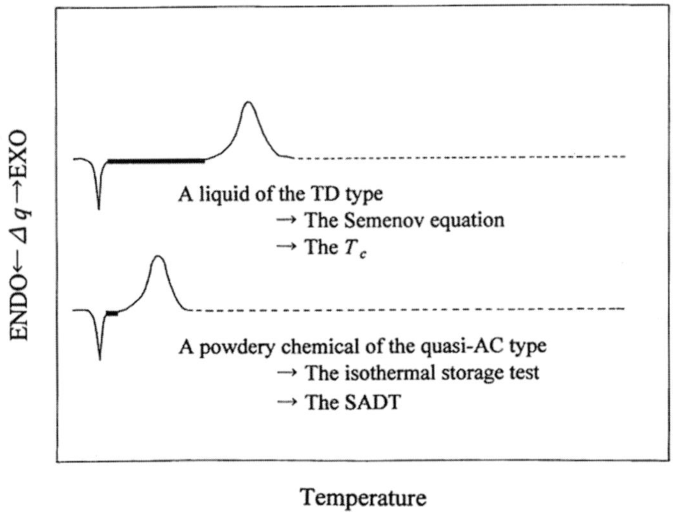

Figure 147. The subtle difference between the DTA curve of a liquid of the TD type and that of a powdery chemical of the quasi-AC type.

A chemical which is powdery at room temperature and shows a large interval between the two peaks of the DTA curve is, in principle, a liquid of the TD type. In case of a powdery chemical of this type, the melting is isolated, as a perfectly separate phase transition, from the exothermic decomposition reaction of the resultant liquid. In other words, the resultant liquid of this type decomposes exothermically, independent of the melting process, so that the Semenov equation is applied to calculate the T_c. For instance, the DTA curve of MNTS is a case in point (see Fig. 12 in **Section 3.3**).

On the other hand, a chemical which is powdery at room temperature but shows a very small interval between the two peaks of the DTA curve is a powdery chemical of the quasi-AC type, so that the isothermal storage test should be performed for it to calculate the SADT. For instance, the DTA curve of ABCN, or that of AMVN, is a case in point (see Fig. 9 in **Section 3.3**).

There is, however, also a powdery chemical having such an interval that the magnitude is so subtle that it is difficult for us to judge the chemical to be a liquid of the TD type or a powdery chemical of the quasi-AC type. For instance, the DTA curve of LPO, or that of TSH, is a case in point (see again Fig. 9 in **Section 3.3**). It is required, in such a case, to perform for the chemical concerned, separately, both the adiabatic self-heating test to calculate the T_c by applying the Semenov equation and the isothermal storage test to calculate the SADT. In result, in case that almost the same value of temperature is calculated in either case, it follows that the lower one of the two temperatures is used as the characteristic temperature to express the thermal instability of the chemical. There are, however, some cases in each of which an extremely low value of SADT, compared with that of T_c, is calculated as the result of the isothermal storage test. It is required, in such a case, to examine closely whether the value calculated is the one proper or not.

References to Chapter 10

[25] T. Kotoyori, The SADT of Solids of the Quasi-Autocatalytic Decomposition Type, J. Hazardous Materials, **A 64**, 1-19 (1999).
[60] T. Yoshida, Safety of Reactive Chemicals, Elsevier, Amsterdam, 200 (1987).
[61] The Kirk-Othmer Encyclopedia of Chemical Technology, 4th Ed., **14**, 451 (1995).
[82] M.W. Whitmore and J.K. Wilberforce, Use of the Accelerating Rate Calorimeter and the Thermal Activity Monitor to Estimate Stability Temperatures, J. Loss Prev. Process Ind., **6**-2, 95-101 (1993).
[83] Du Pont Company, E-64609: VAZO® Polymerization Initiators; Properties, Uses, Storage and Handling, Du Pont Company, Chemicals & Pigments Dept., Wilmington, DE 19898, 7/84.
[84] T. Ando, Y. Fujimoto and S. Morisaki, Analysis of Differential Scanning Calorimetric Data for Reactive Chemicals, J. Hazard. Mater., **28**, 251-280 (1991).

Index

B

C

D

L

M

N

O

T

U

V

W